Social Psychology

SECOND EDITION

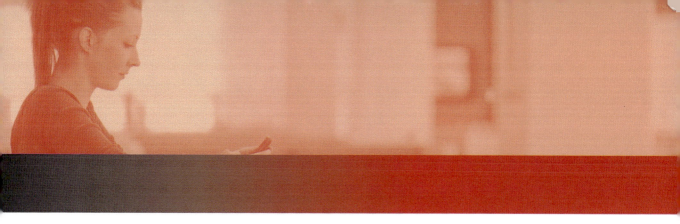

Social Psychology

SECOND EDITION

Wendy Stainton Rogers

Open University Press

Open University Press
McGraw-Hill Education
McGraw-Hill House
Shoppenhangers Road
Maidenhead
Berkshire
England
SL6 2QL

email: enquiries@openup.co.uk
world wide web: www.openup.co.uk

and Two Penn Plaza, New York, NY 10121-2289, USA

First published 2003
Reprinted 2007, 2008, 2009
First published in this second edition 2011

A catalogue record of this book is available from the British Library

ISBN-13: 978-0-33-524099-9
ISBN-10: 0-33-524099-2
eISBN: 978-0-33-524100-2

Library of Congress Cataloging-in-Publication Data
CIP data applied for

Typeset by Graphicraft Limited, Hong Kong
Printed in the UK by Ashford Colour Press, Gosport

Fictitious names of companies, products, people, characters and/or data that may be used
herein (in case studies or in examples) are not intended to represent any real individual,
company, product or event.

The McGraw·Hill Companies

This book is first dedicated, with my love, to my grandchildren: Katy, Tom, Bethany, Alex, Ruby, Tessa and Elizabeth

Contents

> In the seven years since this book was written, much water has flowed under the bridges of psychology.
>
> (Isaacs, 1928: v)

Not my words, but Susan Isaacs' preface to her fourth edition of *An Introduction to Social Psychology* written nearly a century ago. One of the things I love about my home is that we have a library. It is actually not much more than a wide corridor, but I enjoy living among my books. Some of them are pretty old, and I have a good few shelves of psychology textbooks that go back to the end of the nineteenth century. These become ever more precious as we move into a paperless world, though some cost only 5p in jumble sales and charity shops, and many were rescued when various people and Psychology Departments cleared their shelves. I tend to dip into them, now and again, rather than read them at great length. They mostly feel very alien, writing about a psychology we can hardly recognize as such today.

As I was writing this second edition of my textbook, I took to looking at prefaces, especially when there were several editions. Each told an interesting story in its own way, and this one by Susan Isaacs caught my eye in particular. She was not kidding when she wrote of water under the bridge. In the seven years since her first edition, she noted that quite a lot had been happening:

- Gestalt psychology had emerged, led by Köhler, Koffka and Wertheimer.
- Spearman and his co-workers had begun to develop intelligence tests and the statistics needed to analyse the data.
- Piaget got started on his theorizing about child development.
- Watson got involved in developing the theory of behaviourism.
- Melanie Klein applied psychoanalytic theory to young children using 'play technique' and Sigmund Freud got into studying group psychology.

You have to admire her time management. Social psychology had changed out of all recognition in those seven years, yet Susan Isaacs left the body of her text untouched and summarized all this in a three-page appendix!

Well, vast quantities of water have passed under a number of bridges over the past eight years, and I made the opposite choice. I have ended up writing virtually a whole new book, for a number of reasons.

First, social psychology has changed, it has grown and it has diversified. Previously I wrote about two 'camps' – experimental and critical. Now it is as though social psychology has spread across a whole landscape, certainly a pretty large field. Social psychology used to be a relatively small and coherent academic sub-discipline that was *applied* to subjects like health and community work. Over the past ten or so years, health psychology, in particular, has grown enormously in its scope and importance, drawing on social psychology's models and theories to consider how health-related behaviour can be changed. So, too, has community psychology, especially in the Spanish-speaking world. More generally barriers are breaking down between the human science disciplines, with an increasingly common interest in topics and a sharing of methods (especially in qualitative research).

Perhaps this is where the biggest change has happened in social psychology, which has seen a major rehabilitation of qualitative methods and the flourishing of critical social psychology, in Britain at least. As just one indication, in 2009 the British Psychological Society opened up a section on qualitative methods. Within months it became the largest section in the organization, with more than 1000 members. There is an expanding number of textbooks devoted to critical social psychology and critical psychology, including a second edition of the best-known, *Critical Psychology: An Introduction*, edited now by Stephanie Austin as well as Dennis Fox and Isaac Prilleltensky (2009). New editions of the standard textbooks have almost all, to some degree, added some extra sections on areas like discursive psychology, and some have gone further and realigned quite large chunks of text to make them more sensitive to issues of culture and more reflective of diversity in relation to age, ethnicity, gender, sexuality and disability. In part, this is because the subject of psychology is changing, in part, because of changes in its student audiences.

At the same time the growth of the Internet has changed everything. When I was writing the first edition of this textbook, I was heavily reliant on libraries as online access to journal articles was fairly rudimentary. Recent work was available, but much archive material was not. Writing a textbook today is utterly different. I can find and download original papers in a matter of moments. The point is, almost certainly, so can you, and that fundamentally changes, I think, what you need from a textbook.

The world changed too, and social life within it – *Facebook*, *YouTube*, *Second Life*, mobile phones with emails and apps, it is, truly, a new world.

All of these together meant that a second edition was not something I could fix with a three-page appendix! Nor, I soon found, was it something I could do by a little 'tweak' here and there, a systematic update of references and a few minor additions about new ideas and new work. Slowly, as the deadline got lost in the fuzzy memories of time past, I recognized that only a major rewrite would do. The good news is that one consequence of the move in social psychology towards a broader critical approach was having a publisher willing to support a major revision and expansion. And here it is.

I spell out the main changes in 'How to use this book', but I would like to add a bit more here about the overall 'feel' of the book, which has changed too. I do think textbooks are also changing in other ways. In a fascinating and insightful paper, Mary Smyth sharply criticizes standard psychology textbooks (although the books she scrutinized are a bit old by now – editions of standard books published in 1996 and 2000). The chapters she is talking about here were on social psychology:

> The chapters are not really about what people do and say in social situations, and why, but about what investigators did in their experiments, what they found and what it means. Given that particular questions are asked, they must be tackled via studies, possibly in laboratories. The conclusions are qualified accounts of what people do; in certain circumstances they conform, they obey, they help others, and in other circumstances they do not. The detail of the experiments and studies are the content matter for students.
>
> (Smyth 2001: 628)

When I found this article, it helped me to make sense of what was happening in my writing. As part of my preparation to get started I had read carefully several of the new editions of the social psychology textbooks most often used in British universities. Smyth put into words my own impressions – that (with a notable exception, the two texts published in 2007 by the team at the Open University for its course launched in 2007) these standard textbooks read more like an exhaustive and exhausting lexicon of what social psychologists have been able to find out in their studies. These days we get a lot of prettily coloured, nicely designed 'research highlight' boxes, and so on, to break up the density of the relentless study after study, theory after theory. There is so much of it that I, for one, find it utterly daunting.

For this and other reasons, this textbook is very far from big and glossy like those. I have done my best to keep it simple. One way is to make it more selective. Chapter by chapter I have picked out just one or two pieces of research or theorization under each heading in order to illustrate the points that I want you to really understand, at least in terms of basic principles. Often this means going into a lot of detail, so you can gain an in-depth understanding of what is at stake; in some ways, a bit 'narrow and deep', but this is to make it manageable. If you are keen or curious to know more, then you can follow up the ideas and research fields that interest you most, starting from recommendations for further reading and links to web resources that I have listed at the end of each chapter. There are the usual summary boxes at strategic points.

I have also done things with the language I use. I have done my best to keep to simple words when simple words will do – which, I think, is a lot more often than many social psychologists seem to think. There can be a bit of a game going on, when complex language is used to make text appear more 'intellectual'. And there may be times when you will need to play this game too – in which case you can easily find prose that you can use as a model for writing your essays and dissertations. But in a textbook, I maintain, it is better to use everyday language whenever you can, to make it more friendly, but mainly to make it more accessible. I have done this, rather brazenly, in many places when I am reporting other people's research and interpretation – sometimes, I suspect, in ways that will make the original authors wince. But my intention is a simple one – to make social psychology interesting and relevant to you and to do my best to make its ideas, knowledge and, indeed, its blunders easier to understand.

Wendy Stainton Rogers
Woburn Sands
March 2011

Acknowledgements

Acknowledgements for the first edition

As I have written this book I have become increasingly aware of the immense intellectual debt I owe to Rex, my husband, co-author, co-researcher and co-conspirator for 27 years until he died in 1999. It was a bitter-sweet experience, as I was so often reminded as I wrote of his vivacious and incredibly diverse and erudite scholarship. These memories go back to some amazing, giggly, rather well-lubricated conversations with Gun Semin about 'risky shift' and 'cognitive dissonance' when both of them were young (and incredibly handsome!) lecturers finishing their doctorates. And end with memories of, in the week before he died, painstakingly working with Rex on the manuscript of our last book together when we thought he was recovering. It is far, far too little to say I could never have written a book like this without all he taught me about social psychology. Rex was a brilliant and charismatic teacher, and I was his most privileged student in so many ways. Nor could I have written this book without the support and love of all those who have helped me in the last three years to come to terms with Rex's death. My heartfelt thanks to all of you.

More specifically I would like to give particular thanks to Paul Stenner, Marcia Worrell, Kerry Chamberlain, and two anonymous reviewers who helped me prepare the design and content of the book. Special thanks go to Robin Long who took the manuscript all over the world and gave me such valuable (and tactful) feedback on it. I would like to thank the reviewers who helped me improve it once I had drafted it. It is a much shorter and a lot better book because of their advice. My thanks too to Carole Wheeler, Patricia Kelly and Ian Lowe for their support and help in finishing the manuscript.

Acknowledgements for the second edition

It is interesting how these preliminary pieces to a book tell stories of how life changes for the author. I still remain enormously indebted to Rex who died more than ten years ago in 1999. This will always endure and I still consider myself his most privileged student. But now my more immediate debts are to Robin Long who became my husband in 2006, no longer travelling the world but retired and helping and supporting me in all sorts of ways from the domestic to the heroic (who else would plough through the References section of a dyslexic with such patience?). What is so lovely about Robin is that he does it all with such good humour, endless cups of tea and, it has to be admitted, rather too many Curly-Wurlies when the going gets tough!

This time I must add my thanks to Vicky Fowler and Venitia Williams from the Faculty's Information Technology (IT) Department, and Lynda Cambourne-Paynter for scraping me off the ceiling when a succession of laptops and a personal computer froze repeatedly as I was finishing the book.

But most of all I would like to thank all those who gave me inspiration and intellectual challenge from which this second edition benefited so much. In particular I will mention Zygmund

Bauman, Annemarie Mol, Angela McRobbie, Stephen Frosh and Robert Crawford. Mildred Blaxter died in the year I was writing this Second Edition, and here I can express my sincere gratitude for all she gave and taught me, as a scholar and as a much valued friend. I have relentlessly stolen the ideas they shared with me, and bravely followed the paths they opened up to me, both in their writings and their talk. There are many of them I will thank in person to keep this manageable, but I would like to express special gratitude here to Kerry Chamberlain, Suzanne Phibbs and Anne Scott in New Zealand, Catriona MacLeod in South Africa and Pedro Pinto in Portugal; and to Bridgette Rickett and all the rest of the Feminism and Health Research Group at Leeds Metropolitan University, Sally Johnson and Christine Horrocks at Bradford University, Marcia Worrell at Roehampton, John Cromby at Loughborough and Carla Willig at City. At the Open University, special thanks go to Richard Hester, Darren Langdridge, Margie Wetherell, the Feminist Reading Group and the Qualitative Research in Progress Group. And, of course, last but never least, Beryl Curt in all her manifest instantiations, the greatest inspiration of them all.

LEARNING OUTCOMES

When you have finished studying this chapter, you

1 Outline the main differences between experim
psychology.

2 Describe the three main 'metaphysical battles'

3 Trace the origins of social psychology through
William James, and the contributions made by
psychology.

4 Describe the two contrasting images of 'the pe

5 Identify the roots of and describe the historica
and critical social psychology.

6 Describe the main elements of Modernism and
to contemporary social psychology.

7 Explain how these two approaches are differen

Learning Outcomes

At the beginning of each chapter, these
objectives detail what you will be learning
and what progress you should make.
Try checking back later to see if
you have picked everything up.

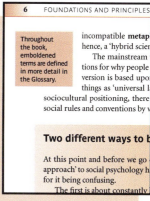

Margin Notes

These handy notes alongside the
text highlight key topics and direct
you to other areas of the book where
you can discover more. This will
give you another way of
learning about each subject.

how to dig underneath the plausible acco
they do.

Try it for yourself

Go back and look at the extract at the star
self how Bibb Latané and John Darley k
How did they find out what these people
windows? It is clear from the careful wor
leagues that the two psychologists did not
like those. So where did the powerful de
their windows at around 3 o'clock in th
think upon the need to question account

Above all, this book is intended to sho
that because there have been 'dozens of

'Try it for yourself' Boxes

We tend to learn a lot more when we
actively engage with the material we
are reading. These boxes offer
opportunities to do just that –
link it to your own experience,
or 'have a go' yourself.

gists, and not all sociological social psych
ing in and out of this simple dichotomy
approaches to social psychology that do
camps.

The ori' ins of social psycholo

- *Völkerpsychologie* and crowd psycholog
- From its beginnings, social psychology w
(arising from early psychology, and tak
social psychology (emerging from early
- The roots of experimental social psycho
be traced back to the work of William M
subject of external forces, lacking free v
- The roots of critical social psychology a
back to the work of William James, wh
agent with free will.

Summary Boxes

At the end of each section of learning these
boxes summarise the ground covered so far
in a few short bullet points. They will help
you see the main areas of understanding
worked on in each chapter and will be
helpful when you come to revise.

Resources

Outlines of what the website regards as
spring.org.uk/2007/11/10-piercing-insigh

A really good article from *The Psycholo*
periments have been misreported: http:
cfm?volumeID=21&editionID=164&Art

Further readin'

The history of psychology

Hollway, W. (2007) Social psycholog
H. Lucey and A. Phoenix (eds) (2007

Resources

These sections give web-links and details of online
materials helpful for your own studying and for
writing assignments. Includes a range of online
articles, databases and videos.

Further Reading

Do you want to know more?
Look for this section at the end
of each chapter which provides
a carefully-selected list of materials
including 'classics' in the field, more advanced or
specialised articles and books, and the occasional
'quirky read' for fun. Broadening your insight
and knowledge like this is the best way to
improve your marks on assignments and exams.

Further readin'

The history of psychology

Hollway, W. (2007) Social psycholog
H. Lucey and A. Phoenix (eds) (200
University Press.
This book forms part of the Open Univ
student-friendly and accessible. It is also so
and reflect on what you have read and co
from within psychology of its history than
you have learned here.

Experimental social psycholo

Myers, D., Abell, J., Kolstad, A. and Sa
Maidenhead: McGraw-Hill.

Africa took on the challenge of literally
for Africa among the otherwise Northern/V
in the context of the role played by psycl
the creation of the concept of aparthei
counterbalance to the standard US textb

Questions

1 'The different theories created by so
   Describe these two very different im
   into different approaches to social p
2 Is social psychology scientific? Shou

Questions

Coming to the end of the chapter proper, you will
find a few questions to answer which focus on a key
point of the chapter and will help to check your
understanding. Some questions provide a chance to
develop your own response to different theories and
concepts and these will be useful in preparing for
exams.

British Psychological Society guidelines for topics that should be included in courses on social psychology

Social perception	
Person perception	Chapter 7 Social cognition, social perception and attribution
Attitudes	Chapter 8 Attitudes and behaviour
Attribution	Chapter 7 Social cognition, social perception and attribution
Intergroup processes	
Prejudice	Chapter 13 The social psychology of prejudice
Intergroup conflict	Chapter 12 The social psychology of groups
Social identification	Chapter 10 Social selves and social identities
Small group processes	
Norms	Chapter 12 The social psychology of groups
Leadership	Chapter 12 The social psychology of groups
Decision making	Chapter 12 The social psychology of groups
Productivity	Chapter 12 The social psychology of groups
Social influence	
Conformity and obedience	Chapter 4 Quantitative research in social psychology
Majority and minority influence	Chapter 12 The social psychology of groups
The bystander effect	Chapter 1 What is social psychology?
	Chapter 4 Quantitative research in social psychology
	Chapter 11 The social psychology of relationships
Close relationships	
Interpersonal attraction	Chapter 11 The social psychology of relationships
Relationships	Chapter 11 The social psychology of relationships

With the expansion – perhaps better to say an explosion – of access to information on the Internet, textbooks are having to change. Historically the set book for a course provided students like you with your main source of detailed information, backing up the handouts provided by your tutors. Textbooks meant that they (your tutors) could avoid a lot of the donkey work involved in all that detail, and offered you (the student) a convenient resource for doing your assignments and for revision coming up to the examination.

I have written this book with this change in mind, recognizing that most of you will use it in combination with your own Internet searches (including suggestions from your tutor about good websites) and the electronic resources provided by your college library. As I wrote, I imagined my book as part of a paper/electronic hybrid, with my bit (the text on the page) being always used in conjunction with a whole range of other resources. I knew they would be a lot more colourful and exciting to look at but, at the same time, I reassured myself that my text, including the tables and figures as well as the odd picture, had one thing going for it – it is specifically designed for studying the subject of social psychology at an undergraduate level and is tailored to being used for learning about this subject. Thus, within the hybrid, it is the part that provides you with a systematic, step-by-step 'learning journey' (alongside your tutor's teaching, of course) where your initial steps provide the foundation for your broadening exploration of the whole range of topics in social psychology. In that sense this book has a stand-alone quality; it can be used on its own, and is a good way to get 'stuck in' in a concentrated, mindful way, without the constant distraction that the Internet can offer.

When to read what?

As the basis for your learning journey, this book is divided into five sections. The first two sections, **Foundations and principles** and **Methods and analytics**, are designed to provide you with a good grounding in the broad discipline of social psychology. The chapters in the first two sections are not just all groundwork, though. This part of the book is really crucial in helping you build up your skills as well as your knowledge. The historical elements in the various chapters, for example, are both fascinating in their own right, but also very helpful for gaining real understanding of what has happened afterwards. Going back to some of the fundamental philosophical and metaphysical issues not only helps you to get a clear understanding of the different approaches taken in social psychology; it also helps you introduce some impressively big words like 'epistemology' and 'ontology' into your vocabulary. This allows you to weave the 'illusion of excellence' that is so important in successful study. Using technical language like this (as long as it is with precision) in your assignments, presentations and discussions is how you demonstrate your competence and mastery of the subject.

The latter part of the book is made up of three key sections: **Social cognition and construction, Social identities and relationships** and **Communities, groups and intergroup processes**.

The eight chapters making up these three sections cover all of the different topics generally studied by social psychologists, and that form the basis of the social psychology curriculum recommended by the British Psychological Society (BPS) (see page xvii).

Section 1: Foundations and principles 'does what it says on the tin' – it introduces you to social psychology's main foundations, its history and the two different sets of principles on which it is based (Chapters 1 and 2). However, it also does something more. There is a substantial chapter (Chapter 3) introducing you to critical social psychology. Since the critical approach is the (relatively) 'new kid on the block', you are less likely to be familiar with it. This chapter 'brings you up to speed' so you can study the remaining eight, topic-based chapters (all of which include theory and research from both approaches) with confidence.

Section 2: Methods and analytics is also self-explanatory, in that it introduces you to the methods and analytics that social psychologists use to conduct research. I have followed the usual convention of dividing them up into quantitative and qualitative ones (Chapters 4 and 5).

Mainstream social psychology generally uses quantitative methods but, as you will see, this is nowhere near cut and dried. Increasingly qualitative elements are being introduced into today's experimental and survey studies, and, indeed, are often to be found within the classic experimental work upon which our current understanding of social psychological phenomena is based. If you go back and look at the original papers, you may be surprised by just how revealing are the debriefing interviews that contemporary social psychology's 'founding fathers' conducted (and yes, I use this term knowingly, almost all of them were men). You will find all this covered in Chapter 4.

The 'new' approach to social psychology that has been gradually established over the past 30 or so years (which in this book I have called 'critical', though it is a lot broader than that) has tended to use qualitative methods, often taken on from other disciplines. But, as you will see from Chapter 5, with this approach what makes for rigorous and convincing research is less about how the data are collected (notice the *are* here – data is a collective or plural term, like mice) and more about how these data are analysed. By the end of reading Chapter 5 you will be in no doubt about just how demanding and time-consuming that will be.

This is not a research methods book, but Chapters 4 and 5 should give you enough knowledge about how research is done in social psychology for you to really understand how and why the research studies covered in the rest of the book have been done.

All of these chapters include both experimental and critical theorization, analysis and interpretation, and give examples of research studies using both quantitative and qualitative methods. The overall purpose of this design is to give you a good understanding of the traditional, mainstream ideas, models and knowledge base of social psychology and what they are up to now, together with examples of critical developments and alternatives, and, in some cases, explicit critique.

Section 3: Social cognition and construction contains three chapters:

Chapter 6: Communication and language in social psychology

Chapter 7: Social cognition, social perception and attribution

Chapter 8: Attitudes and behaviour

All three relate to different social psychological theories about the way we use our thinking (cognitive) capacities to make sense of and understand the social worlds in which we all live and what goes on within them.

Chapter 6 is all about the representational capacities and strategies we use, mainly in the form of language but also in other ways like our gestures and through touch. Representation is an incredibly important part of cognition, as it is the means through which we know what things are and we communicate this 'knowing' with each other. Through representation we can both interpret the social world (such as *through* interpreting a 'look' as friendly or angry) and construct it (such as *through* calling someone a 'terrorist' or a 'freedom fighter').

Chapter 7 is about the way social cognition works, and some of the ways in which it is limited. Stereotyping is a good example. On the one hand, it is helpful to be able to make inferences, based on both what you have observed for yourself and have been told by others. Knowing that a priest or a mullah is someone likely to be unhappy with bad behaviour, for instance, gives you a good idea about how to act in their company without making a fool of yourself. On the other hand, stereotyping can have bad consequences. If you believe all priests or all mullahs are religious fanatics, then you are going to have real problems getting along with them.

Chapter 8 is about the interactions between our thoughts, our words and our deeds. It offers a good example of the ways that all of the chapters in Section 3 cover both mainstream experimental and critical approaches to social psychology's topics. I begin the chapter by identifying three of the best-known models developed by social psychologists who have adopted a social cognitive approach to the interplay between attitudes and behaviour: the theories of planned behaviour, of reasoned action and of stages of change. These are each discussed and explored in relation to criticisms about these models raised by critical psychologists, illustrating each to clarify the critiques being made.

Woven into this are some examples of the main alternative theories offered by critical health psychologists, which move away from the very idea of 'health behaviour' (such as 'condom use') as a singular 'thing' and, instead, look at specific instances of, for example, using or not using condoms in different contexts (such as on a first date, as described by 'agony aunts' and within a 'marriage-on-the-rocks').

Section 4: Social identities and relationships also contains three chapters:

Chapter 9: Values

Chapter 10: Social selves and social identities

Chapter 11: The social psychology of relationships

Chapter 9 is somewhat unusual in social psychology textbooks, with any consideration of human values often relegated to a few paragraphs at the end of a chapter on attitudes. Giving values a whole chapter reflects the nature of the approach I have taken, since considering how values differ between different groups and communities is a great way to open up social psychology to issues about culture and collectivity. Whereas attitudes are conventionally seen as located in individuals, values are recognized as bridges between individuals and their communities. Shared values are what holds particular communities together – a kind of sociocultural glue. I have included this chapter as a good place to start exploring the ways we, as individual selves, are also social selves and our identities are thus always socially and/or culturally situated.

Chapter 10 thus follows neatly after, taking up ideas about shared values from Chapter 9 and using these as a way into exploring questions about who we are, what makes us unique, and what binds us into the groups to which we belong and to whom we have loyalty. Building on earlier theories, much of this chapter is about the concept of social identity, which has come to dominate mainstream social psychology today, especially outside the USA. This is a particularly interesting development in that social identity theory was initiated in the 1980s by social psychologists who have now, mostly, moved into using the critical approach. This treats identity as something that is *inter*subjective (that is, framed by what is going on *between* people), where a person's individual biography is always deeply enmeshed within all sorts of social forces and processes (like those of gender, race, class and age).

Chapter 11 is specifically about the intersubjective – what goes on between people. It starts with an absence – first how we relate to utter strangers, and then about 'being single'. Then it explores a range of different kinds and levels of relationships, including between siblings and with grandparents, then how relationships work within communities.

Section 5: Communities, groups and intergroup processes contains two final chapters:

Chapter 12: The social psychology of groups

Chapter 13: The social psychology of prejudice

Traditionally social psychologists have tended to be wary of groups. Early psychologists showed great concern about the possibility of a 'herd instinct' that turned people in crowds into frenzied, uncivilized mobs, regressing back into brutish acts of violence and destruction. Even today psychological theories prevail that spell out the downsides of losing one's individuality. Chapter 12 sets out this work and the research evidence collected to support it. It then takes a fresh look at ways in which group membership can positively influence individual accomplishment and well-being, exploring cultural differences along the way.

The final chapter, 13, is about conflicts between groups and how this is manifested in the form of prejudice. It examines prejudice of different kinds – disablism, homophobia, racism and sexism, for example – and operating at different levels, for example, blatant prejudice, subtle prejudice and institutional prejudice.

Learning in the Internet age

Overall, you will soon find that I have adopted a much more selective approach than you will find in almost all other social psychology textbooks. The various chapters in those kinds of books are packed-full of detail about research study after study, theory after theory, intended to give students a thorough and comprehensive review of the field. Student feedback, however, says that many find all this detail very hard to digest. After a while your eyes glaze over and it all becomes a bit of a blur!

This is one of the main ways I have responded to the changed world of Internet access to information described earlier. In this book you will find that I have written the chapters around a small number of examples, carefully chosen to be interesting and relevant to you and your life. I have done my best to find intriguing and insight-provoking illustrations of particular instances of social psychology's work, approaches and concerns. Now that there are incredible amounts of information available to you through IT repositories and search engines, the detail is easily available to you from other sources. I have concentrated, instead, on helping you to get a good grasp of what is at stake, what researchers are 'getting at' when they study a topic in a particular way, and how and why certain theories and models have been developed.

A growing trend in relation to information is the move to the wiki-ization of knowledge; a shift from having a small number of authors sourcing text for large audiences to a more collaborative style, with more or less open-ended authorship. At the Open University, where I work, we are seeing rapid expansion of this kind, with our associate lecturers and students increasingly getting involved in developing elements of our course materials – such as glossaries, indexes and resources sections, alongside blogs and chat-room conversations that constantly expand the resources available to students. You may well find something like this growing up around your course – if not, maybe you will decide to get one started! I think it will be fascinating to come back in a couple of years and see what is happening. To get us started there are some links provided in the Resources section at the end of each chapter.

Studying and revising

A concept gaining real visibility as I write is that of 'mindfulness' (you will find some information about this in Chapters 7 and 8). It is that state of mind in which you concentrate on the 'now' and attend to it with as much awareness as you can bring to it. In therapy it is a means to manage anxiety, but in the context of learning it is crucial for memory. The rule is simple – the more mindful your engagement with particular information and explanations, the better you will understand it. And the better you understand it, the better you will remember it.

Using the summary boxes for revision

It is easy to give an example. You will see, throughout the chapters, that there is a summary at the end of each section (and, in some cases, subsection). These are really useful, especially when you are revising, because they help you to focus in on the broad basics. But their particular merit is that they give you 'triggers' to remembering a lot more. The bullet-point kinds of lists used in summaries can, if you revise them until you can remember them by rote, help you make sure your examination answer is comprehensive. You note them down and then use each one as a memory-trigger to remember more detail about each one. This is something you can practise easily – an excellent revision strategy, because doing it (that is, actually practising the art of remembering) is an *extremely* mindful task. It is also easy to do, in the sense that when you sit down to revise you have a very clear set of tasks:

1 Start by looking at the course outline. When you are familiar with it, go through each section and look at the relevant chapters in the book. Identify the exact sections in the chapter that relate to the curriculum you have been set. Find the summary. As you work through the book, mark these summaries (put a 'sticky note' on it if you do not want to mark your copy or if it is from the library).

2 Begin with an area you like most or simply find easy. Write down key words from the summary. Then, for each key word, brainstorm all you know about that idea, concept or whatever.

3 Note how long it takes you (when you are doing mindful activities time can go quickly – you may be surprised).

4   Go back to the section involved and check what you have managed to remember. Smile at how much you have remembered (or even reward yourself in some way). Write notes about any important bits you left out.

5   Now reflect a bit – think about how it went and what you learned, and how long it took you altogether (probably quite a long time on just this one section – but you will get faster).

6   Now you can begin to plan a revision timetable. Work out how many sections you can get done in a session no longer than 40 minutes (mindful engagement is hard work and you can not work much longer than this without taking at least a 5-minute break; and only two or three of these without taking a longer break).

7   The overall goal is to do each summary box at least once and, if you can (even in abbreviated form), twice.

8   You can further increase your memory power by making cards with the section titles on one side and, say, three to five key words on the other and using these to test yourself. Alternatively, design an electronic version.

However, a really, really good way of doing this memory training is not to use my summary boxes but, as you read each section, make ones for yourself. You need to check them out against mine to make sure you have not left anything out – but with a bit of effort I suspect you can do better than me. Do have a try.

Other ways of revising

'Learning outcomes' at the beginning of each chapter: it is easy to ignore these or just gloss over them. They are there in part to inform your tutors about what each chapter covers. But they can be used in a similar way to the summaries, as starting points for another form of mindfulness, in that they present tasks for you to do. Indeed, they can be a good starting point, as much of the initial work is done for you. You will need to do the selection first against the curriculum in your course outline but, once completed, all you need is a bit of planning into manageable sessions, each session consisting of responding to the tasks that you are expected to be competent to accomplish.

   'Questions' at the end of each chapter: these are provided, in part, to offer your tutor some ideas for assignments. But they are also a very useful resource you can use independently for your revision. This is a great task to do on your own, but even better to do as a group. If you can get together with others, then you should start by identifying some relevant questions relating to your course curriculum. Note that even the discussion you have while doing this is a mindful activity, and will help with your learning and remembering. Then you can work – alone or in pairs – on creating a marking scheme. This is another extremely mindful activity as it engages with the topic from a different perspective (that of the assessor rather than the student). Taking on this perspective is also useful in itself, since the insights gained gradually build up to a very high level of expertise in presenting your work for assessment. Being assessed is anxiety provoking, and it is tempting to just get it all over with as quickly as possible, just dumping out what you can manage to remember. But (and you probably already know this in your heart) this is not a good way to show what you know and how capable you are. The more you can put yourself in the position of the assessor, the easier it is to get a much calmer sense of distance, and to build up

more effective strategies for tackling your anxiety. Simple repetition is incredibly powerful in gaining academic skills, just as much as in sport, dancing and other physical forms of performance.

Once you have a marking scheme, then answer the questions in as close to examination conditions as you can, especially as regards timing. You may need to work up to this, but the goal must be to go into the examination with a solid record of questions answered right across the curriculum at a pace you will need in the examination itself.

If you are working independently, you will probably do best to leave a gap before marking your answers. It is a demanding task too (all the better for that, of course, because it is yet another bit of mindfulness). Check back against the book, your lecture notes and all the other sources you have consulted. Many course assessments offer extra credit for 'reading around' the topic, so this should be your aim wherever possible. Working with others you can mark and give feedback to each other. If you all want to be real 'stars' then you could make this a weekly get-together throughout the course. However good your tutor, they have to spread their effort across the whole class. A few students together can substantially increase the feedback each person gets, and build a mutually supportive group in the process (see Chapter 12).

In any revision strategy like this, be realistic and make an overall timetable, whether working alone or with others. Read and reflect on the questions, and choose the questions to work on for what you will learn rather than which seem easy (although this is not a bad way to get started). Make a practical estimate of how many you can do properly in the time you have available, this way you are far more likely to stick to it. If you can, find time in a task like this to reflect on your own learning. Identify what works for you, and practise to get better at it. And make time to include counting your achievements – do not just obsess about what you get wrong. The idea is to build your confidence alongside building your competence.

Further Reading

As described above, most assessment schemes offer extra credit for pieces of work that demonstrate that the candidate has gone beyond the standard teaching, and 'read around' the subject. However, going beyond the textbook is an important step, in itself, in becoming a scholar in a particular field. Social psychology is no exception, even if you are studying it as a route to expertise in another subject.

You will find that the Further reading sections at the end of the chapters offer guidance about a wide range of different kinds of resource, each useful for different purposes. These include:

1 *Chapters from standard textbooks* that offer the kind of detail that may be needed to demonstrate a sufficiently comprehensive and in-depth coverage of a particular approach, topic or field. I have mainly selected from non-US textbooks (or books modified to be more appropriate for students outside the USA) where the examples and illustrations given are more relevant to students who are using this as a main text. An example here is Myers et al.'s *Social Psychology: European Edition* (2010), selected for its Chapter 2 'What is social psychology?', in part because of its extra detail in some areas and in part as it is (in its own terms) more 'balanced' – that is, it follows the traditional, conventional line. As an alternative account of the topic, to mine, reading this will give you a better overall picture of how social psychologists approach this topic.

2 *Classic texts* that are essential reading for anybody who seeks to become an academic psychologist. One good example is Thomas Kuhn's *The Structure of Scientific Revolutions* (1970), made famous by his term 'paradigm shift'. This is a 'must read' for anybody who wants to be taken seriously as a social or natural scientist,

3 *Books that 'changed everything'* such as *Changing the Subject: Psychology, Social Regulation and Subjectivity*, by Henriques et al. (1984) recommended in Chapter 2. Like classic texts, they are essential reading if you aspire to being a critical psychologist.

4 More *specialized books that concentrate on a particular topic or approach*, such as Jill Reynolds's *The Single Woman* (2008) in Chapter 11. I chose this partly because the topic was one I thought you would find interesting enough to explore further, and in part because she has set out very clearly the theories, methods and analyses she used, and how she used them.

5 *Specific journal articles* that do something similar – help you broaden your knowledge and understanding through taking a particular issue or idea or approach further. Braun and Clarke's (2006) 'Using thematic analysis in psychology', recommended in Chapter 4, is a great example here. It has become the key text for anyone wanting to get started with this form of analysis.

6 *Specialized chapters* in books. In my recommendations these come in two kinds. First I have drawn extensively on the *Sage Handbook of Qualitative Research in Psychology* (Willig and Stainton Rogers 2009), and only in part because I was co-editor for it with Carla Willig in the lead role. The chapters have turned out to be excellent, often because of a strategy Carla instigated of getting career-young scholars to co-author chapters with the 'big names' in various fields. This produced chapters combining all the enthusiasm and vibrancy of the newcomer with the wisdom and experience of the old hand. In this way some very readable and enjoyable (as well as downright useful) chapters were written, covering different research methods, approaches and issues. One example is Frosh and Saville Young's chapter on 'Psychoanalytic Approaches'.

The other kind are specialized chapters in edited collections, such as *Critical Psychology* (Hook et al. 2004) produced and published in South Africa after the fall of apartheid. I chose Dennis Hook's chapter 'Fanon and the psychoanalysis of racism' for two reasons. First, it offers an analysis of racism situated in a particular time and place, providing valuable insights that come from experiences very different from my own – insights for which I have no authority, but that I found profoundly affecting and want to share with you. My other reading is that this chapter also offers analysis and forms of knowledge that will expand your understanding of how psychoanalysis can be applied to topics, such as racism, within social psychology.

Good luck!

So, that is it from me. I hope this small section is useful, and helps you to make best use of the book. I do hope you enjoy it – and your study of social psychology as a subject. It's one that has fascinated me since I was a student nearly 50 years ago, and it has been an amazing experience to watch the subject change in ways I could hardly have imagined. I can honestly say it is more exciting now than it has ever been, being pushed forward by a new generation of spirited young women and men of frighteningly powerful intellect and enormous passion. If this book can play even a tiny part in your journey to join them, then I will be a very happy woman.

SECTION 1

Foundations and principles

What is social psychology?

LEARNING OUTCOMES

When you have finished studying this chapter, you should be able to:

1 Outline the main differences between experimental and critical approaches to social psychology.

2 Describe the three main 'metaphysical battles' between them.

3 Trace the origins of social psychology through the work of William McDougall and William James, and the contributions made by *Völkerpsychologie* and crowd psychology.

4 Describe the two contrasting images of 'the person' in social psychology.

5 Identify the roots of and describe the historical development of both experimental and critical social psychology.

6 Describe the main elements of Modernism and Postmodernism, and how these relate to contemporary social psychology.

7 Explain how these two approaches are different, and why they cannot be integrated.

Introduction

On a March night in 1964, Kitty Genovese was attacked by a maniac as she came home from work at 3 A.M. Thirty-eight of her Kew Gardens neighbors came to their windows when she cried out in terror – but no one came to her assistance. Even though the attack, which resulted in her death, lasted more than half an hour, no one even so much as called the police. . . . The thirty-eight witnesses to Kitty

Genovese's murder did not merely look at the scene once and then ignore it. Instead they continued to stare out, fascinated, distressed, unwilling to act but unable to turn away: they were neither helpful nor heroic, but their behavior was not indifferent or apathetic either.

(Latané and Darley 1976: 309–10)

This is one of the most famous of social psychology's stories, told and re-told in social psychology textbooks ever since. The question of why nobody came to Kitty's aid was first raised in a report, just after the incident, in the *New York Times*, and from then on social psychologists have studied why and in what circumstances people sometimes show an unwillingness to help others in trouble. Kitty was raped too, and her story stimulated a massive programme of experimental social psychological research into the apparent paradox – that the more people who witness an event like this, the less likely it will be that any one of them will do anything about it. This came to be called the 'diffusion of responsibility' effect (about which you can learn more in Chapter 11).

You may be shocked to learn that this story as told by Latané and Darley (and numerous textbook writers who followed on after them) simply is not true. Historians of psychology (Manning et al. 2007) have, rather belatedly, looked at the court transcripts from the trial of Kitty's murderer. Of the 38 people who *could* have been aware of what was going on, it turns out that only a few were eyewitnesses with a clear sightline to the attack as it started. And one of them did shout out, causing the attacker to run away. Kitty then got up, clearly hurt, but able to get herself around to the back of the building to make her way towards her own apartment. Sadly her attacker followed her and caught her in the stairwell. It is there he raped and killed her, a place where nobody could directly see what was going on. So Kitty's case, however tragic, was not the outrageous incident portrayed in the press. This was not an example of horrific human callousness as they claimed.

At about the same time, but coming from a completely different direction, another psychologist, Frances Cherry (Cherry 2007), drawing upon feminist theory, argued that the sexist assumptions, prevalent in the 1960s, were a more likely explanation of what happened. In those days, she said, a lot of men's violence towards women was not really treated as a crime. The police in the USA and the UK usually treated attacks like this – even very violent ones – as 'domestic' incidents and hence private matters. Worse, common wisdom at that time assumed that any woman stupid or brazen enough to be out on the streets at 3 o'clock in the morning was to be regarded as 'fair game'. According to Cherry, this was not so much about 'bystander apathy' in general but, rather, a specific form of 'turning a blind eye' to something that is 'none of your business', a very different kind of explanation.

Going critical?

So why am I starting this book with this story, you may ask? My answer is that I wanted get you interested, to draw you in, right from the start, to thinking critically – cynically, even – about social psychology and what it does. The complex and fascinating *story of* the story of the rape and murder of Kitty Genovese opens up all sorts of cans of worms – which is what this book is all about.

Do not expect to find in this book any simple, factual account of 'what makes people tick' as discovered by social psychologists. You will, I hope, get a good, basic grounding in the key topics, methods and approaches that have been taken by mainstream social psychologists, predominantly by means of experimental studies used to test their theories of and explanations for a wider diversity of social psychological phenomena. At the same time this book is intended to take you somewhere else, well beyond simply 'soaking up' all the appropriate 'knowledge' of the discipline so you can regurgitate it in your assessments and examinations. It is designed to show you how to look behind the clever storytelling going on in textbooks and lectures and how to dig underneath the plausible accounts of why people behave and experience the world as they do.

Try it for yourself

Go back and look at the extract at the start of the chapter. Read it through again. Now ask yourself how Bibb Latané and John Darley knew what the witnesses did within their apartments. How did they find out what these people had been thinking as all 38 of them looked out of their windows? It is clear from the careful work on the court transcripts done by Manning and colleagues that the two psychologists did not get their insight into what happened from documents like those. So where did the powerful description of these dumbstruck watchers, standing by their windows at around 3 o'clock in the morning, come from? I leave you to speculate, and think upon the need to question accounts provided in textbooks that appear so plausible.

Above all, this book is intended to show you how to develop a healthy cynicism about claims that because there have been 'dozens of studies employing several thousand participants providing supportive evidence' (Latané 1997: 202, writing about the research that followed) this cannot offer any proof of fundamental laws of human nature. I will take up this argument in the next chapter – and, indeed, throughout the book. For now, just start with this motto: be constantly vigilant of people who tell you clever stories.

What is social psychology?

Early in the twenty-first century this is an increasingly difficult question to answer. But right from the start, social psychology was a rather fragmented and divided discipline, with its roots in sociology and anthropology in many ways more than in psychology itself. Social psychology has always been perched uncomfortably between the focus on social and cultural influences of these other disciplines, and mainstream psychology's preoccupation with explaining 'what makes people (in general) "tick"'. The tension is, indeed, a difficult one – between a curiosity to find out what makes people, as social groups or communities or as cultures or subcultures, *different* from each other, and a desire to discover the systematic and generalizable 'laws' that determine how people behave as they do, for instance, of the workings of processes like the attribution of responsibility and blame or how and why people's attitudes change and how this affects their behaviour.

The problem is not so much the lack of consensus – that is true for all academic disciplines. It goes deeper than that. In the 1990s, Rom Harré argued that psychology was 'working with two

Throughout the book, emboldened terms are defined in more detail in the Glossary.

incompatible **metaphysics** at one and the same time' (Harré 1997: 129), and was, hence, a 'hybrid science' (Harré 1997: 131).

The mainstream version of social psychology is bent on finding causal explanations for why people experience the world as they do and act within it. The dissident version is based upon an entirely contrasting metaphysics, where there are no such things as 'universal laws of human nature'. Instead, varying by time and place and sociocultural positioning, there is a rich and highly varied diversity of alternative systems of social rules and conventions by which people live their lives and realize their projects.

Two different ways to be 'critical'

At this point and before we go on, it is absolutely crucial to get something straight: a 'critical approach' to social psychology has two different (if partially overlapping) meanings. I apologize for it being confusing.

The first is about constantly keeping an open mind, and being willing to challenge what the mainstream does and what it is traditional for social psychology to do. In this sense, I believe, we should all strive to be 'critical' and most experimental social psychologists will agree with me.

The other is the use of 'critical' to refer to what, in sociology, is called 'critical theory', which is about a adopting an approach that has very different philosophical assumptions about, for example, what constitutes knowledge. The first five chapters of this book are devoted to helping you get a real understanding of this form of 'critical social psychology' and how it relates to and differs from the mainstream experimental approach; what each can and cannot do and, therefore, has to offer.

Different forms of critical social psychology

Harré listed three labels for this kind of social psychology: **ethogenics**, **Social Constructionism** (Nightingale and Cromby 1999) and **discursive psychology** (Edwards and Potter 1992). All three are approaches, he said, that 'take people to be active agents, whose conduct is to be seen as attempts to realize, together with others, plans, projects and intentions according to the rules and norms of the local society' (Harré 1997: 131). These days, 'ethogenics' has largely been dropped, but the other two are still commonly used.

There are a number of other approaches coming into the critical camp, including: **feminist psychology** (Henwood et al. 1998); **Marxist psychology** (Parker and Spears 1996); **postcolonial psychology** (Macleod and Bhatia 2009) and what is sometimes called **queer psychology** (Clarke and Peel 2007).

Another variant, always present in the field, if rather subdued, is having a renaissance. It is sometimes called 'psychosocial psychology' (see, for example, Hollway and Jefferson 2005). Confusingly, though, the same label has long been used to describe the hybrid approach that brings together psychology and sociology. So here I prefer the more descriptive term **psychoanalytic social psychology** (see Parker 1997a; Frosh and Young 2009). This approach to social psychology draws upon psychoanalytic theorizing about what Freud (1917) called the 'dream work' – 'the tricky, hard-to-observe ways in which unconscious material finds its way into consciousness' (Frosh and Young 2009: 109).

This then leaves us with **psychosocial psychology** as viewed, for instance, by Stenner and his colleagues as 'the study of the relationships between social processes (which always have a psychological dimension) and subjectivity (which is always socially, culturally and historically structured). . . . [The purpose is] to shed light upon the relations between forms of social regulation and governance on the one hand, and forms of subjectivity, selfhood, identity and experience on the other' (Stenner et al., Psychosocial Studies website, University of Brighton, 2010). What we can see here is critical psychology going **transdisciplinary**, psychosocial psychology being a good example, bringing together psychologists, sociologists and psychotherapists.

Problems with the label 'critical'

In this book I use the term 'critical social psychology' to cover all of these approaches, even though it is becoming an increasingly awkward umbrella under which to place such a motley crowd. It causes particular problems in translation. In Japan, for instance, critical psychology is as yet hardly known, and certainly not fully appreciated, even among the small number of Japanese psychologists adopting qualitative methods (Igarashi, 2006). Igarashi suggests this is mainly due to the word 'critical' translating in Japanese into an entirely negative form more like 'criticizing', with none of the sense of powerful and productive challenge it has in English.

Even with English-language speakers it carries negative connotations, which fails to convey its productive qualities. As Tuffin says, 'There is a certain emptiness with criticism that leads nowhere, criticism for its own sake' (2005: 4). But, like him, I would argue that, used properly, criticality is highly creative and purposive, and can (and should) act as a catalyst for change. The critical approach is not intended to destroy or rubbish psychology, but to reinvigorate and enrich it. So I think it is still the best generic term we have.

So the answer to the question 'What is social psychology?' will all depend on whom you ask – you will get a lot of different (and often contradictory) answers. But rather than being a 'problem', I would argue that perhaps it is more of a sign that the discipline of social psychology is alive, kicking and making trouble – which, after all, is what intellectuals are supposed to do!

The metaphysical battle

Harré's observation about the incompatible metaphysics of social psychology can be put another way – a battle between two camps. A sturdy Goliath (**experimental social psychology**) is fighting against a rather puny David (**critical social psychology**), with any number of skirmishes on the sidelines. Goliath is absolutely confident that social psychology is a **Science** (with a capital 'S'). His stronghold is the USA (with outposts all over the world) where most of the high prestige, high citation and high impact factor journals are published, and where there are enormous numbers of psychologists (both academic and in practice) and, therefore, psychology students. David, a nimble and plucky (but, many would argue, misguided) little fellow, is equally confident that it is not – or, at least, that it should not be, but is something else entirely.

There are a few bystanders sitting on the fence who think that David and Goliath should sit down, talk peace and work out a compromise (in academic terms, they should seek 'integration').

But the battle lines are firmly drawn, and social psychologists tend to identify themselves squarely in one camp or the other – with by far the largest group siding with Goliath.

There are three main disputes, over:

- whether or not social psychology should be pursued as a Science
- ideology – that is, over whether or not social psychology is an objective, value-free endeavour, or one that promotes a particular ideological position
- what constitutes the social world and the relationship between the individual and the social phenomena, events and processes in which they are involved.

The battle over Science

In this book, I use two different ways of writing the word 'science', to highlight two different interpretations. I use the uncapitalized term 'science' to refer to its general meaning: 'an effort to make accurate observations and valid causal inferences, and to assemble these observations and inferences in a compact and coherent way' (Brickman 1980: 10).

When I use the term 'Science', I am talking about what usually goes on in disciplines like physics, chemistry and biology (sometimes called the **natural sciences**). They seek to gain knowledge using Scientific method, the purest form of which is doing experiments. At the core of Scientific method are two key elements. The first is a search to discover universal laws, such as the laws of gravity in physics, or the principles underpinning genetic inheritance in biology. The second is the deductive **logic of inquiry**, where hypotheses are tested by systematically altering a specific variable (such as temperature), keeping other variables constant and measuring the effect – for example, the speed at which a chemical reaction takes place. This has been given the rather ugly but descriptive name **hypothetico-deductive method**.

Experimental social psychology is absolutely clear that this is what social psychology should do:

> Social psychology employs the scientific *method* to study social behaviour . . . Science is a method for studying nature, and it is the method, not the people who use it, the things they study, the facts they discover or the explanations they propose, that distinguishes science from other approaches to knowledge. . . . The alternative to science is dogma or rationalism, where understanding is based upon authority: something is true ultimately because authorities (e.g. the ancient philosophers, the religious scriptures, charismatic leaders) say it is so.
>
> (Hogg and Vaughan 2008: 7–8, emphasis in the original)

Hogg and Vaughan's assertion makes it clear that experimental social psychologists regard Science as the *only* valid way for social psychologists to go about gaining knowledge. Everything else is 'dogma'. I have adopted the term 'experimental social psychology' because it takes this position.

Critical social psychology argues that experimental method is not the only, or even the best, method that can be used to gain knowledge. It is unsuited to studying the social aspects of people's behaviour and experience, since these are so complex and fluid. There are alternatives other than 'dogma' that provide valid and useful ways of gaining knowledge. Critical social psychology adopts an alternative **logic of inquiry** to Science, and uses different (mainly qualitative) ways of going about research.

You will find out a lot more about logic of inquiry in Chapter 2.

The battle over ideology

Following on from its conviction that Scientific method is the only valid means to gain knowledge, experimental social psychology regards this knowledge as objective – unaffected by ideology and hence neutral in its values. Since Science, in its view, makes it possible to get at 'the facts' (and facts are facts, irrespective of politics, values, and so on), the Scientific basis of experimental social psychology places it outside of, and unaffected by, ideology.

Critical social psychology disputes this. It argues for '[a] social psychology which challenges social institutions and practices – including the discipline of psychology – that contribute to forms of inequality and oppression (Gough and McFadden 2001: 2–3). Informed by Marxist, feminist and Foucauldian theories about power and prejudice, critical psychology asserts that ideology permeates *all* attempts to gain knowledge. Critical social psychology is, therefore, profoundly committed to a social justice ideology that questions the neutrality claims of mainstream psychology, and seeks to overturn (or at least contain or curtail) it:

> Critical psychologists understand that overemphasizing values related to individualism and competitiveness disproportionately hurts members of relatively powerless groups. Equally damaging is the assumption that what's good for the Westernised world is best for everyone.
>
> (Fox et al. 2009: 8)

It is this ideological element of criticality that is the main reason why I have stuck with the term 'critical social psychology'. It makes plain its challenge to the way that experimental social psychology promotes the interests of the powerful (that is, the mainly white, Western, able-bodied, middle-class, male Establishment) and hence contributes to the exploitation and oppression of less powerful groups. It is this element of the battle, I believe, that means there is no 'fluffy bunny' solution. There can be no cosy compromise of 'integration'. Either you believe experimental social psychology is prejudiced or you do not.

The battle over the nature of the social world

This aspect of the battle is harder to understand, so I shall, here, just describe it in terms of analogies. I hope these are helpful in beginning to get a sense of the differences between the two positions. They will become clearer as you progress through the book.

Experimental social psychology has an image of people in the social world as something like creatures living in an ocean, immersed in but separate from the water that surrounds them. This way of being-in-the-world is one where our experiences, thoughts and feelings all go on 'inside' us, while interacting with and responding to the social forces going on 'outside' in the social world. Our social world, by this analogy, is fixed and consistent, as is its influence. The water may be warmer in some places than others, and currents rougher, but the ocean is all of a piece, a constant surrounding presence, largely unaffected by what the creatures do.

Critical social psychology has a different image altogether. Its social world is more like music-making. The social world is 'made' *by* people and only exists when and because people have made and are making it. All sorts of things may contribute to the music that is played and how it is performed – the instruments available, the skills of the players and singers, whether there is a conductor and, if so, their interpretation of the music. All of these will have an effect. Where and when, historically, the music is played will also make a difference. Sometimes there will be a need to please a paying audience. Sometimes there even may be political constraints on what can be performed. But it remains that without the players the musical instruments will be silent and there will be no music to hear.

I shall not push this analogy too far, but it does give a sense of the social world as something that is continually being created and re-created by people acting collectively together. It also carries the possibility of a diversity of social worlds if you think of different kinds of orchestras, musical bands and choirs throughout history and across the world, each making different kinds of music – from gamelan to rock, plainchant to jazz. Crucial to this image of the social world is that it is not a separate milieu on the 'outside'. It is something people do.

The battle

There are two competing approaches to social psychology.

Experimental social psychology
- asserts that the only valid way to gain knowledge about social phenomena, processes and events is by using Scientific method
- claims this knowledge is ideologically neutral
- views the social world as separate from the individual people acting within it.

Critical social psychology
- asserts that Scientific method is not the only way to gain knowledge and often not the best way to do it in social psychology
- regards all knowledge – including that of experimental social psychology – as inherently positioned ideologically
- views the social world as produced by people interacting with each other.

These alternative approaches to social psychology are antagonistic and cannot be integrated. But to gain a good grasp of social psychology, you need to have a grounding in both.

The origins of social psychology

The human sciences as we now know them began to be established during the late nineteenth and early twentieth centuries. The discipline boundaries were very fluid at this time, both between them and with philosophy (from which many of them had derived). Looking back there seems to have been a fair amount of jockeying for position and arguments over 'territorial' boundaries. Psychology was something of a 'late developer', having to fight hard to carve a place out for itself. This situation was rather quaintly described by one of its earliest historians like this: 'psychology was little more than a waif knocking now at the door of physiology, now at the door of ethics, now at the door of epistemology' (Murphy 1929: 172).

McDougall's social psychology

Social psychology's territory resulted from still harder – and later – infighting. According to William McDougall ([1908] 1919), a vigorous proponent for social psychology in its early days, its disciplinary field had to be reclaimed from sociology and anthropology. McDougall argued that social psychology should be recognized as the rightful domain in which to study 'the springs of human action, the impulses and motives that sustain mental and bodily activity and regulate conduct' (McDougall 1919: 3). He argued specifically that 'intellectual processes' (what we would now call cognitive processes) are 'but the servants, instruments or means' by which they are processed and stored. In this he was making a specific criticism of the psychology of the time, which, he said, was almost entirely preoccupied with cognition at the level of the individual. He attributed this to a misappropriation by other social sciences of much of the subject matter he considered to rightly be psychology's, forcing psychology to accept 'too narrow a view of its scope and methods and applications' (McDougall 1919: 6).

McDougall argued for a scientific approach to psychology and, crucially, for studying the impact of social processes, such as the process by which societies move from 'primitive' to 'civilized'. Central to McDougall's theorizing was the primacy of instinct. He viewed 'human nature' as the product of a set of instinctive tendencies – 'primitive urges' that, while they may be modified by the civilizing force of social and ethical mores, are nonetheless the primary basis of behaviour.

In this he was influenced by Darwinian evolutionary theory, which, at the time, was a dominant theme in sociology and anthropology. He specifically argued for an **evolutionary psychology** (McDougall 1919: 5). It is important to place this in historical context. At that time **Western** scholarship took a crude supremacist stance. When applying evolutionary theory to the social sciences, this was based on the belief that 'modern, civilized' (that is Western) societies had evolved from 'primitive, savage' societies through a process of civilization. All 'other' societies (that is, those studied in 'outlandish' places by anthropologists) were regarded as being at lower, less-developed stages of evolution. It is in this sense that McDougall was arguing for an 'evolutionary psychology', and it formed the basis of his theorizing.

> This racism that pervaded early psychology is explored in more detail in Chapter 13 on prejudice.

He took as his fundamental axiom that human action arises out of biologically pre-programmed instincts, but that this conduct is modulated through the influence of social regulations operating in the society to which a person belongs and, in civilized societies, by an individual's socially acquired self-control. It is basically, then, a three-stage process (see Figure 1.1).

What McDougall meant by an 'evolutionary psychology', then, is not what we understand it to mean today. He was promoting a social psychology that sought to understand the evolution of 'civilized man'; that is, the progressive stages that had led (in his view) to the pinnacle of human

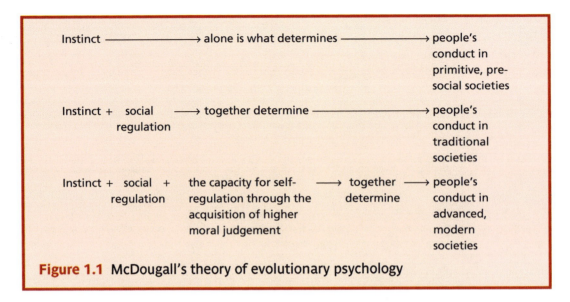

Figure 1.1 McDougall's theory of evolutionary psychology

civilization, a Western world in which a person's actions are determined by each individual's higher moral judgement. The racist supremacy of this worldview may be shocking to us, but was a commonly held stance among intellectuals in his day. You may think we have moved on, and certainly expressing this position is no longer acceptable. But as you move through this book you will see how this worldview still continues to influence mainstream social psychology, albeit in an undercover way.

William James's social psychology

William James's books – *The Principles of Psychology* (published in 1890) and *Psychology* (published in 1907) – were general rather than specifically social psychology texts. However, they included extensive theorization about social psychology and were highly influential in its establishment. In many ways James's ideas prefigured many aspects of critical social psychology.

James was critical (as was McDougall) of the **introspectionism** of early general psychology. However, this was not because he was concerned that it was 'unscientific' in its focus on subjective experience (as McDougall was), but because it failed to capture the connectedness of human thought. To describe this concept, James invented a term for which he has become famous: the **stream of consciousness**. In a person's stream of consciousness, James proposed, all manner of thoughts, emotions, states, feelings, images and ideas continually coexist at some level. At any one moment the vast majority of these are only immanent – outside of our full awareness and at the 'back of our minds'. James called this state **transitivity**. In human consciousness, James said that moment by moment we become aware of just some of these – we notice, we realize, we recognize, we become aware of something. James called this **substantivity**.

To explain what he meant, he used an analogy of a flock of birds whirling and weaving around in the air, never still, always moving, so that it is impossible to tell where they are. But every now and then each bird will come to rest – to sit on a post or fence or somewhere. At that moment we locate it – it moves from a transitive to a substantive state. James emphasizes that it is only in its substantive state that we can pin down what a thought, or whatever, 'is'. He wrote that to try to examine thoughts or feelings or impressions in their transitive states is like holding a snowflake in your hand. In doing so, it stops being itself and turns it into something else – a droplet of water. James applied these ideas, in particular, to the ways in which people know themselves as 'me' (that is the self-as-known) and how they know themselves as 'I' (that is the self-as-knower).

> These ideas are described more fully in Chapter 10, when we come to look at the social psychology of the self.

Two contrasting images of the person

In the late nineteenth- and early twentieth-century writings of McDougall and James, we can see the origins of two competing images of the person which persistently run through social psychological theorizing and research.

McDougall's image is of a person who is largely the product of their innate, biological instincts and drives, moulded by social and cultural forces into civilized members of society. This image portrays people as passive and lacking self-awareness. Even though they have, in civilized society, gained the ability to make moral judgements and thus behave ethically, this is through the internalization of civilized codes of conduct. Consequently, they lack free will.

James, in contrast, held an image of the person as a self-aware, self-conscious and self-determined being, who actively and purposively makes sense of the world in a connected manner and, crucially, has the capacity for free will:

> Of course we measure ourselves by many standards. Our strength and our intelligence, our wealth and even our good luck, are things that warm our heart and make us feel ourselves a match for life. But deeper than all such things, and able to suffice unto itself without them, is the sense of the amount of effort which we can put forth. Those are, after all, but effects, products and reflections of the outer world within. But the effort seems to belong to an altogether different realm, as if it were the substantive thing that we are, and those are but externals that we carry.
>
> (James 1907: 458)

At its heart, McDougall's social psychology sees people as pieces in a chess game between competing external forces (in his case, biological and social forces). Whether pawns or kings and queens, their destiny is in the control of these external forces. But in James's social psychology, people are the players. While other influences (whether biological, psychological, social or whatever) may set the rules within which people play the game of life, people may play well or badly, they may play to win or give up when the going gets tough, but it is they who play the game.

The difference between these two is that in McDougall's social psychology it is an easy and straightforward matter to determine universal, causal laws of human nature, since causes can be identified within external forces (external to the essential person, that is – even though they can be internal, psychological forces). In James's social psychology it is nowhere near as easy – if possible at all – to determine causal laws of human nature, since to do so involves getting to grips with the human will. This is ultimately a matter of metaphysics and ontology – about the nature of being-in-the-world – and therefore, James argues:

When, then, we talk of 'psychology as a natural science' we must not assume that that means a sort of psychology that stands at last on solid ground. It means just the reverse: it means a psychology particularly fragile, and into which the waters of metaphysical criticism leak at every joint, a psychology all of whose elementary assumptions and data must be reconsidered in wider connections and translated into other terms. . . . What we have is a string of raw facts; a little gossip and wrangle about opinions; a little classification and generalization on the mere descriptive level; a strong prejudice that we have states of mind, and that our brain conditions them: but not a single law in the sense that physics shows us laws, not a single proposition from which any consequence can causally be deduced. . . . This is no science, it is only the hope of a science.

(James 1907: 467–8)

This statement reads as highly prescient. It could almost have been written today, by a critical psychologist. In other words, the questions and issues raised by James's claim that 'This is no science, it is only the hope of a science' are as hotly debated today as they were when he wrote it – indeed, more so. In this chapter and those that follow, you will be tracing this argument through social psychology's history and development over the more than 100 years since James first raised it.

Early movements in social psychology

Social psychology was born out of aspirations to recapture certain aspects of 'the social' from sociology and 'the cultural' from anthropology. While there were earlier attempts to develop a 'psychology of society' (Lindner 1871), social psychology had its main roots in two movements in European psychology that predated the work of McDougall and James: German *Völkerpsychologie* and French and Italian work on 'crowd psychology'.

Völkerpsychologie

Völkerpsychologie is not an easy term to translate into English. 'Folk psychology', with its associated connotations in English of folklore and folk singing and dancing, is misleading, *Völk* does not mean 'folk' but 'people', so its literal translation is 'a psychology of the people', which is somewhat better – though 'a psychology of ordinary people' is possibly closer. It was developed as a specifically psychological discipline by proposing that people who belong to particular social groups tend to think in a collective rather than individual manner; to hold the same opinions and beliefs, and to share the same values. To put this into today's terms, consider, say, members of a religious sect or an issue-based political group (such as the Taliban or animal rights' activists). They can sometimes come across as though they have lost their capacity for independent judgement and that they 'think as one'.

Like most psychological movements, *Völkerpsychologie* was a product of the prevailing concerns of its time and place. When it was first developed in Germany, in the late nineteenth century, it was to try to understand what was going on as the nation state of Germany was being created from many small provinces and principalities. This was well before both world wars, remember. In this context *Völkerpsychologie*'s originators were mainly interested in discovering what it was that marked off a specifically German national character.

Murphy (1929) identifies Steinthal and Lazarus as its founders; they established its journal, *Zeitschrift für Völkerpsychologie und Sprachwissenschaft*, in 1900. But Wilhelm Wundt, the founder of modern experimental psychology, was its best-known proponent. Although he is generally most remembered as the 'father' of experimental psychology, according to Murphy, Wundt 'devoted some of his best energies' (Murphy 1929: 172) to the topic and completed five volumes of *Völkerpsychologie* between 1900 and 1920.

In some ways *Völkerpsychologie* was ahead of its time, in that its theories proposed a link between culture and language (see Chapter 6). Wundt, for instance, suggested that the vocabulary and grammar of a particular language profoundly affects the way people think and perceive the social world, and therefore argued that language can provide a unifying medium for group identity and membership.

Crowd psychology

Crowd psychology also arose from social and political concerns of the time in which it was originated – here the broader social upheavals that had occurred in Europe in the previous century, such as the French Revolution. In particular it was devised to seek to understand how and why, when large masses of people act together, they seem to function as an entity – a 'crowd' or a 'mob'– rather than as individuals. Its foremost proponent was the French theorist Gustave Le Bon, who brought these ideas together in a book, *Crowd Psychology* (published in 1896).

Its central idea was in many ways parallel to that of *Völkerpsychologie*; that of a '**group mind**'. Le Bon suggested that in certain situations, a 'mob' can best be seen as acting as a single, primitive entity, operating on a lower intellectual and moral plane than its average member would usually adopt (if you like science fiction, you will see resonances here with the Borg, half-machine, half-living-flesh, inhuman because each creature has lost its individuality and operates as a mindless member of a 'swarm'). Le Bon's writing was vivid, portraying 'the mob' as subject to collective madness and savagery. He drew upon the work of Charcot on hypnosis and suggestibility, arguing that mob leaders (or even the mob itself) exert psychic pressure that strips the mob's members of their individual wills and coerces them to act as one – for good or ill.

Another influential theorist in this field was Tarde. In his book, *The Laws of Imitation* (1903, first published in 1890), he also drew heavily on the concept of suggestibility, though his work was more comprehensive than Le Bon's. For example, Tarde speculated about the impact of cities upon outlying regions, with progress in popular opinion originating in cities and then diffusing out to the population as a whole. He also explored what happens when one nation is conquered by another, and how the values, opinions and practices of the conqueror tend to become adopted by the conquered. He suggested similar processes may occur between elite groups and the general population.

> These ideas have been taken up more recently in theorization about social representations (see Chapter 3).

The parting of the ways

In Western antiquity there were two main strands of philosophical thought about the relationship between the individual and society: Platonic – emphasizing the primacy of the state over the individual; and Aristotelian – emphasizing individual autonomy and freedom. Graumann (2001) calls these the individuo-centred and the socio-centred approaches.

- The **individuo-centred approach** focuses on the ways in which social grouping, social institutions and social forces are determined by the behaviour of individuals and the processes going on within individual minds. It is from this approach that psychology emerged as a discipline, focusing on what goes on within individual minds. Politically this approach is **liberal individualism**, which stresses individual autonomy and freedom.

- The **socio-centred approach** focuses on the ways in which the behaviour and experiences of individual people are strongly determined by their membership of social groups and social institutions. The underlying philosophy of this approach is found, for example, in the writings of Hegel (1770–1831), who viewed the state as the ultimate form of society and the basis of the social mind to which individuals belong. It is from this approach that sociology emerged, and social psychological work on the 'group mind' also followed from this tradition. Politically this approach is **liberal humanism**, stressing the responsibility of individuals to contribute to the good of society through collective effort.

These two philosophies and traditions underpin two different approaches to social psychology – usually called **psychological social psychology** and **sociological social psychology** (Stephan and Stephan 1990). These labels convey the different emphases of each and their different disciplinary origins. Each has its own history and its own pioneers and heroes, and, to a certain extent, their power-bases are located in different places. Speaking very broadly, the 'movers and shakers' of sociological social psychology have been and are European; whereas psychological social psychology almost entirely dominates the subject in the USA.

As you have probably worked out by now, these two approaches are, to a degree, the progenitors of experimental and critical social psychology. However, (sorry!) it is rather more complicated than that. What I am going to do next is trace the historical development of each of them and show how psychological social psychology gave rise to experimental social psychology and sociological social psychology gave rise to critical social psychology. Notice, though, that they are offshoots. Not all psychological social psychologists are experimental social psychologists, and not all sociological social psychology are critical social psychologists. Note that weaving in and out of this simple dichotomy there have always been some 'minor players' – other approaches to social psychology that do not fall neatly into either the experimental or critical camps.

The origins of social psychology

- *Völkerpsychologie* and crowd psychology were early progenitors of social psychology.
- From its beginnings, social psychology was a divided discipline: psychological social psychology (arising from early psychology, and taking an individuo-centred approach) and sociological social psychology (emerging from early sociology and taking a socio-centred approach).
- The roots of experimental social psychology are in psychological social psychology. They can be traced back to the work of William McDougall, whose image of the person was of a passive subject of external forces, lacking free will.
- The roots of critical social psychology are in sociological social psychology and can be traced back to the work of William James, whose image of the person was of an active, purposeful agent with free will.

The roots of experimental social psychology

Even before McDougall published his *An Introduction to Social Psychology* (McDougall [1908] 1919), a turn to experimentation had begun. Interestingly there seems to have grown up something of a myth about what was the first social psychological experiment, but it is usually attributed to Norman Triplett (1898).

Triplett's study of dynamogenic influence – the making of a myth

When he was studying the cycling records of the Racing Board of the League of American Wheelmen (a cycling organization) of 1897, Triplett noticed that the times recorded for cyclists racing against each other were faster than when they raced alone against the clock. This intrigued him, and he tried to work out why. He surmised that there must have been some kind of 'energizing force' – a sort of psychological dynamo – that arises from competition. From this he formed the general hypothesis that the presence of others has a 'dynamogenic' influence on an individual's behaviour; that is, it leads to an activation of performance. To test this hypothesis he carried out an experiment.

In the experiment Triplett gave fishing rods to forty 8- to 17-year-old boys and girls and asked them to wind them up as fast as they could. As in all good experiments (see Chapter 4) he had a control group (children winding on their own) and an experimental group (children winding with others). As the dependent variable he used the speed at which the children wound the reel, since it was something he could objectively measure. The trouble is, his results were not all that clear-cut. When in the presence of another, some children wound faster than when they were reeling on their own – but some were slower. Triplett attributed the faster reeling of the children who speeded up to 'the arousal of their competitive instincts and the idea of faster movement' and the slower reeling of the children who went less fast as them being over-stimulated by the task and 'going to pieces' (Triplett 1898: 526). There were not the statistical techniques we have today to sort out what was going on, so his results were inconclusive. This has not stopped people reporting that this 'experiment' clearly supported the hypothesis that the presence of others improves performance.

Hogg and Vaughan (1998) argue that Triplett's study is not a very good candidate for social psychology's first experiment, since it was not recognized as such at the time. They suggest that what is going on here is an 'origin myth'. As the story of Triplett's study has been told and retold, it has got reified as 'the first psychological experiment' (as reported, for example, by Allport 1954; Sears et al. 1991) and simplified to tell a good story (shades here of Kitty Genovese – and a surprising number of psychology's experiments). Smith and Mackie, for example, state categorically, '[s]ure enough, children's performance improved in the presence of others' (2000: 7).

It was certainly not the first study of **social influence**. In an earlier study by Ringleman (1913), a French agriculturalist, the results he obtained showed that when people work together to pull on a rope they tend to expend less effort than when pulling alone. Later work on social influence (as this area of social psychology is called) has shown that the situation is actually a highly complex one. But nonetheless Triplett seems to have found his place in history.

What is most important here, though, is that Triplett did adopt experimental method to provide evidence for developing his theory. Writing in 1929, Murphy commented: 'Probably the most striking event in contemporary social psychology is the introduction of experimental method' (1929: 298). To us today it may not seem at all a radical thing to do – but it was pretty enterprising at the time. In so doing Triplett was seeking to identify social psychology as a Science, acquiring for it the legitimacy of being based upon objective evidence. This was a very significant turning point, one that has led to a situation today where experimental social psychology has come to be the dominant approach in the field.

Behaviourism

While its origins were European, once experimental social psychology took root in the USA, it very much made its home there. From about 1890 to 1910, the USA became the centre for experimental research in psychology generally. In those 20 years, 31 universities in the USA set up experimental psychology faculties and departments (Ruckmick 1912). As an indication of just how dominant the position of the USA later became, it has been estimated that by the 1950s there were more social psychologists in the University of Michigan than in the whole of Western Europe (Smith and Harris Bond 1993)!

Where social psychology was studied at the turn of the twentieth century, this was very much within the approach to general experimental psychology that was dominant in the USA at the time – **behaviourism**. The shift in approach was dramatic. When read these days, McDougall's ([1908] 1919) *An Introduction to Social Psychology* is nothing like we would recognize as a social psychology textbook. It comes across as rambling, opinionated and highly speculative, constantly making unsubstantiated claims about 'human nature'. By contrast Floyd Allport's *Social Psychology* (1924) looks much more familiar, even though it was published back at the beginning of the twentieth century.

Allport proposed that social psychology needed to become an experimental science if it was to be taken seriously. The book set out this agenda, based on behaviourist principles. For example, in it Allport claimed that children develop language through conditioning. At its core, behaviourism assumes that all behaviours are stimulated by instinctive drives and learned though the contingencies with which those drives were either rewarded or punished. Allport argued that this applies just as much to social behaviour. He emphatically rejected the foreign notion of a 'group mind'. Groups cannot think or behave, he argued, only individuals can. Social influence, he said, is just one of the factors that shapes the motivations and perceptions of individuals. Allport conducted a number of experiments on this topic (see, for example, Allport 1920) and in his 1924 book he was the first to adopt the term '**social facilitation**' (Hollander 1971: 59). This interest in the influence of others led Allport to study **attitudes**, which he did very much from within the behaviourist tradition.

Social learning theory

A good illustration of how the behaviourist approach became modified into **social learning theory** in the 1950s is a description written by Hilgard:

> Social motives may be acquired in the course of social behaviour. . . . [S]ocial behaviour is learned, in the first instance, in the course of satisfying physiological drives in a cultural setting. Once social motives are acquired, they become the basis of further learning.
>
> (Hilgard 1953: 127)

Hilgard then went on to argue that this leads to the establishment of 'social drives' (such as a autonomy, achievement and aggression), which stimulate people to behave in certain ways and create the conditions for learning (that is, by the reinforcement of the behaviours that reduce the drive). He recognized that, unlike instinctive drives, social drives vary from one social group to another, seeing social learning as the means by which children become socialized according to the social drives of their social group.

Gestalt psychology

In the 1930s a significant number of social psychology's most distinguished thinkers fled from Europe to the USA. Many were Jews escaping from the Nazis. Indeed, so marked was this diaspora that one psychologist, Cartwright (1979), has claimed that the person who had the most impact on the development of social psychology in the USA was Adolf Hitler!

The European refugees had been trained in **gestalt psychology**, an approach that views context as a crucial driver for the way people perceive objects. Founded by Wertheimer in 1912 (Ellis 1938), gestalt psychology used **phenomenological methods** (where people are asked to report their experiences) to gain insight into what and how people perceive.

'Gestalt' is another German word that does not translate very well into English, but means something like 'configuration' where the whole is more than the sum of its parts. An example is the famous image that can be seen either as two faces or a candlestick (Figure 1.2). Whichever you 'see', it is only visible through the relationship between the figure and ground – in this case they are reversible.

Figure 1.2 The candlestick/faces image is a well-known example of a gestalt configuration, in which the figure constructs the ground and vice versa

When these refugees got to the USA and found social psychology dominated by behaviourism, there was something of a rebellion. Émigré social psychologists like Kurt Lewin and Mustafa Sherif refused to go along with behaviourism's demand that mental states must be excluded from study since they cannot be objectively observed.

The emergence of experimental social psychology

These émigrés developed the experimental social psychology that we know today. They did so by moving away from behaviourist concepts (such as 'drives') to concepts based on social influence.

Lewin is generally considered the 'founding father' of experimental social psychology. His particular interest was in the effects of social groups and **group dynamics** (Lewin 1947a, 1947b).

> You will look in more detail at Sherif's work on groups in Chapter 12.

Lewin developed **field theory** based on gestalt principles (Lewin 1951). In it he proposed that behaviour is influenced by the 'psychological field' or 'social climate' in the same way that the perceptual field influences what a person sees (Lewin et al. 1939). Sherif also developed a range of elegant experimental studies on social norms (Sherif 1936) and social judgement (Sherif and Hovland 1961).

The first book called *Experimental Social Psychology* was published by Murphy and Murphy (1931). By no means were all of the studies included in it experimental, but all were based upon hypothetico-deductive method. It is this that holds experimental social psychology together. Its status as a science is warranted by its use of scientific method:

> Social psychology is a science because it uses the scientific method to construct and test theories. Just as physics has concepts such as electrons, quarks and spin to explain physical phenomena, social psychology has concepts such as dissonance, attitude, categorisation, and identity to explain social psychological phenomena. The scientific method dictates that no theory is 'true' simply because it is logical and makes internal sense. On the contrary, a theory is valid on the basis of its correspondence with fact. Social psychologists construct theories from data and/or previous theories and then conduct empirical research in which data are collected to test the theory.
>
> (Hogg and Vaughan 2008: 4)

The roots of experimental social psychology

- A number of social psychological experiments were carried out in the late nineteenth century. Triplett's may not have been the first, but it is the best known. His experiment investigated what he called a 'dynamogenic' influence on the speed at which children wound fishing rods – what we would now call 'social influence'.

- Experimental social psychology soon became established in the USA, located, at the beginning, in behaviourism and later in social learning theory.

- However, experimental social psychology as we now know it, was originated by gestalt psychologists such as Lewin and Sherif, who emigrated to the USA in the 1940s. They expanded its scope to take in concepts like group dynamics and group norms, and introduced its main topics: **social perception**, social influence and **social interaction**.

The roots of critical social psychology

Sociological social psychology grew out of sociology, based upon the traditions set by Emile Durkheim (1858–1917). Durkheim (1898) believed that 'social facts' are largely independent and outside of individual consciousness, and that it is the **collective representations** shared between people that determine how people understand and make sense of the world rather than **individual representations**. This is, in psychology, what we now call **intersubjectivity**.

Both *Völkerpsychologie* and crowd psychology stimulated the development of sociological social psychology. Tarde's work, for example, was highly influential upon the sociologist Ross, who published his text, *Social Psychology*, in 1908. Ross saw the discipline as the study of the 'planes and currents that come into existence among men in consequence of their association' (Ross 1908: 1). Yet while Durkheim had called for a 'collective psychology' separate from individual psychology, there was actually very little activity in this field within psychology itself until the 1960s. It was sociologists like George Herbert Mead and Erving Goffman who pursued subjects like identity (Mead [1934a] 1977a, [1934b] 1977b; Goffman 1959) and behaviour in public (Goffman 1963).

> The theories of Mead and Goffman are described in Chapter 10.

Personal construct theory

George Kelly's personal construct theory (Kelly, 1966; Bannister and Fransella, 1986) has, in a sense, a foot in both camps. Like experimental social psychology, its theory and research assume that what mainly matters is what is going on *inside* people's individual minds. But there are no experiments, and it does assume that individuals 'make sense' of their lifeworld in an active way. Personal construct theory takes as its fundamental postulate that 'making sense of the world' is done on the basis of personal constructs achieved through active learning, and these are the basis of what it means to be a person, and underpins all of what constitutes human behaviour and experience.

> Personal construct theory and research is described in more detail in Chapter 5.

Social representations theory

The turning point came at the beginning of the 1960s, although its impact was limited until the 1970s when work done in France was translated into English. A major stimulus was provided by Serge Moscovici when he published his pioneering study on social representations of 'madness' (Moscovici [1961] 1976). He presented this as a study of social representations, which he saw as intermediate between collective and individual representations. He demonstrated these by showing how psychoanalytic terms (like 'complex') had come to be used by ordinary people in everyday conversations. His interest lay in looking at how the knowledge of experts – their ideas about, concepts of and explanations for madness – had seeped out of the domain of expert knowledge and into what 'everybody knows'.

Social representations research has had a long and chequered history, but it has become influential, for some as a stepping-point into critical psychology, for others in its own right (see, for example, Flick 1998). It is, in many ways, the contemporary site where sociological social psychology continues to operate – Flick calls it 'the psychology of the social'. Di Giacoma has defined social representations thus:

> Social representations theory and research is described in more detail in Chapter 3.

a socially determined 'universe of opinions . . . [and] beliefs' . . . about the material or social environment. A given group's social representations of an object are a complex product of available information about that object and attitudes towards it.

(Di Giacoma 1980: 330)

The role of cognitive psychology

Cognitive psychology is usually seen as instrumental in the creation of contemporary *experimental* social psychology, since its concepts and theories feature so strongly in research on attitudes, attribution, and so on. It is, therefore, seldom recognized that cognitive psychology has played a crucial role in the development of critical psychology. It had its origins in the highly prescient work of Frederick Bartlett (1932). Inspired by the game of 'Chinese whispers', he studied the distortions that people made when remembering stories and pictures. People's recall, he observed, reflected their attempts to make sense of what they had heard and seen. The stories got less fantastic, the pictures more familiar. Once they named a drawing (say, as a cat) the subsequent drawings made from memory became more and more cat-like. It was Ulric Neisser, though, in his book *Cognitive Psychology* (Neisser, 1966), who established cognitive psychology as a new and better paradigm (better, that is, than Behaviourism and Information Processing) for understanding the ways people's thinking affects their behaviour.

The cognitive paradigm moved away from modelling people as mindless, machine-like beings driven by instinct, conditioning and learning. Instead (like James) its models of perception and representation (in the form of memory and problem solving) portray people as purposive thinkers who strive to make sense of their social world and bring to this endeavour complex, sophisticated models-of-the-world which they use to interpret it and construct a social reality.

Absolutely central to all this was the way cognitive psychology was very much about meaning, and how, for humans, what mattered was what something meant and **signified**, as opposed to some kind of meaningless 'signal' or 'stimulus' (see, for example, Miller et al. 1960). For many of us (including me) cognitive psychology thus opened up the way into fields like semiotics and social constructionism, leading then into postmodernism and post-structuralism.

The branching off of critical social psychology

By the 1970s there was a distinct shift, with a number of social psychologists calling on their colleagues to 'put the social back into social psychology', including Rom Harré (see Harré 1979; Harré and Secord 1972) and Henri Tajfel (1972) in the UK and Ken Gergen in the USA (Gergen 1973; Gergen and Gergen 1984). This shift became a landslide by the 1980s (albeit a relatively small and local one). Again there were several influential people, including Henriques and his colleagues (Henriques et al. 1984) and Jonathan Potter and Margaret Wetherell (Potter and Wetherell 1987). By the end of the decade Ian Parker – another leading light of the new movement – was calling the shift 'the crisis in modern social psychology' (Parker 1989) and arguing that it needed to be resolved.

At this point I need to change my metaphor from geology to biology, as what was going on by now was not so much a shift as a branching off. What had started out as a social psychology with a socio-centred focus was becoming something else – or actually, more like a number of different something elses! For Reason and Rowan (1981) among others, it was turning into a 'new paradigm'. For Gergen it was turning into social constructionist social psychology. For Potter and Wetherell it was becoming a discursive psychology. And for Henriques et al. and Parker it was a revolutionary movement turning into critical psychology. New alignments were being made, allying this new species of social psychology variously with **symbolic interactionism**, **sociology of knowledge** and **semiotics**.

These aspects are described in Chapter 2 and further elaborated in Chapter 3.

The roots of critical social psychology

Sociological social psychology has its roots in sociology, and focuses on the ways in which people's thinking and actions are socially mediated and operate at a social level.

- Sociological social psychology has been heavily influenced by sociological theory, including those of Emile Durkheim, George Herbert Mead and Erving Goffman.
- Up until the 1970s, psychologists generally did not pursue sociological social psychology. It first gained momentum as a serious alternative to experimental social psychology through the work of Serge Moscovici on social representations.
- Cognitive psychology also played a role in the shift to critical psychology. It rejected information-processing and behaviourist models of learning, memory, perception and problem solving, replacing them with models based on meaning and meaning-making as active processes, essential to the way humans (as opposed to rats or machines) understand their lifeworlds and operate within them.
- In the 1970s and 1980s a number of psychologists such as Ken Gergen, Rom Harré, Jonathan Potter, Margaret Wetherell and Ian Parker began to draw new theories into social psychology – mainly social constructionism, postmodernism and discourse analysis. These provided the basis for what I have called in this book critical social psychology.

Modernism and postmodernism

In the previous section you have seen that experimental and critical social psychology developed from two different traditions. However, the division goes further than this. They draw on two fundamentally different philosophies – modernism and postmodernism. So, to understand where each of them are 'coming from', you need to start by understanding a bit about these two philosophies.

Modernism

Modernism is the name given to a set of theoretical and ethical beliefs and values, practices and endeavours that were developed in Europe and the USA during the historical period of the Enlightenment in the eighteenth century. Modernism is based on four main principles:

- *Democracy*: the rights of citizens to determine their own destiny.
- *Liberal individualism*: the rights of citizens to autonomy and freedom from state power.
- *Liberal humanism*: a commitment to human betterment.
- *Science*: an empirical approach to gain rational knowledge.

Democracy

Modernism gave birth to democracy. Key events in the founding of modernism were the French and American Revolutions, where the common people took up arms in order to challenge the authority of rulers (in France, the king and aristocracy, in the USA, the colonial power of England). They fought for the democratic rights of ordinary people to be treated as citizens rather than subjects.

Liberal individualism

They also fought to challenge the power of any state – whether democratic or not – to interfere in people's private lives, and for the rights of individuals to, among other things, freedom of religion and freedom of speech. This aspect of modernism champions the rights of the individual and seeks to limit the power of the state. Today we are seeing a hardening of these values in political terms, called **neo-liberalism**, which is especially associated with market-driven economics.

Liberal humanism

However, modernism was not just pursued through armed conflict. These revolutions were inspired by the great thinkers of the day. Modernism is sometimes called the post-Enlightenment project, since it was (and is) motivated by the conviction that people can – and, crucially, should – create a better world through their own efforts (rather than, say, relying upon the benevolence of God). This aspect of modernism is prepared to restrict some elements of individual freedom to maintain a well-ordered, well-functioning society (for example, to prevent crime). It therefore accepts that the state can have some power, so long as it uses it to serve human interests and protect human rights.

Science

At the very core of modernism is the conviction that only Science has the capacity to discover true knowledge. Modernism challenged the capacity of mysticism, superstition and religion to define what constitutes knowledge. It sought to replace irrationality and disorder with reason and rationality. It adopted **empiricism** in order to progress from knowledge based on subjective beliefs (those of religion, magic or the arcane) to knowledge gained by rational means, through scientific methods of empirical inquiry.

Epistemological evolution

Modernism is usually presented as the pinnacle of an evolution of **epistemology** (the theory of knowledge, covered in more detail in Chapter 2) (Douglas 1966). It is based on the assumptions shown in Figure 1.3.

This 'up the mountain' tale of epistemological progress (Rorty 1980) views Science as the supreme source of knowledge. It regards all other sources (such as magic, religion and traditional folklore) as not really knowledge at all, but merely 'beliefs' and 'myths'.

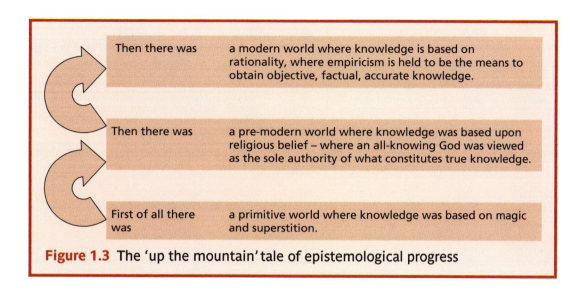

Figure 1.3 The 'up the mountain' tale of epistemological progress

Postmodernism

Postmodernism is a major influence on critical social psychology. The word reads as though it follows on from Modernism, a fourth stage in the progression set out above, but this is misleading. It is neither a historical period nor a stage following on from modernism – it is a reaction against and a challenge to it. Here we need to concentrate on its challenge to Science – the radically different position postmodernism takes on what knowledge is and how it can be gained. Postmodernism views knowledge as constructed rather than discovered, as multiple rather than singular, and as a means by which power is exercised.

Knowledge is constructed, not simply discovered

Modernism assumes that Science is capable of discovering the real things and real happenings that are 'out there' in the real world. Postmodernists do not deny the existence of a real, material world – a world of 'death and furniture' (Edwards et al. 1993). But they do deny that this real world can ever be simply 'dis-covered' – as if all that needs to be done is to gradually strip off the veils of human ignorance to reveal the facts about the-world-as-it-really-is. Postmodernism stresses that the knowledge obtained by Science is – like all other knowledge – a representation of the 'real-world', influenced by what scientists choose to observe, how they interpret what they find and, crucially, the stories they tell about what they have observed and found.

Donna Haraway describes Science as a storytelling craft. Scientists make their mark, she says, by telling clever and convincing stories about their data. And, she stresses, the 'story quality of the sciences . . . is not some pollutant that can be leached out by better methods, say, by finer measures and more careful standards of field experiment. . . . The struggle to construct good stories is a major part of the craft' (Haraway 1984: 79–80). Postmodern theory views Scientific knowledge – just like any other knowledge – as a product of human inventiveness, intuition, insight and creativity.

There is not just one true knowledge

Since, according to postmodern theory, there is no way to get direct knowledge about the real world, then there will never be one single reality (that is, one true knowledge). Rather people construct a variety of different knowledges. Each of these knowledges is made – and made real – by human meaning-making.

Postmodernists accept that some forms of knowledge may be more useful than others, according to the situation. Since Scientific method constructs knowledge in a rigorous and systematic way, Postmodernists acknowledge that it can be particularly functional in situations where it 'works' – where, for example, it tests different materials for their strength and durability and what they can do. All of the technology that makes modern life possible – from vacuum cleaners to jet planes, mobile phones to skyscrapers – have been developed using Scientific knowledge.

But postmodernists point out that there are circumstances where Scientific knowledge is not so useful. For instance, many of the disorders of modern life – stress, personality disorder, post-traumatic stress disorder – cannot be diagnosed through Scientific tests, because they are socially and culturally constructed, defined and experienced.

An example here is a disorder that is, in scientific terms, called 5α-reductase deficiency. This definition describes a genetic 'bug' that gives rise to a child being born who looks female, but is genetically male. The deficiency prevents the male foetus developing a penis and testicles. But, once the hormones of puberty 'kick in' they override the deficiency sufficiently for the boy's penis and testicles to develop – although they are small and the individual is infertile.

What the disorder means and signifies – both to the person concerned and the others around them – differs according to where it occurs. The condition is called *kwolu-aatowol* in Papua New Guinea, which means 'neither male nor female'. As it is a genetic condition that occurs quite frequently (though still quite rarely) in New Guinea, it is usually recognized at birth. The baby is accorded a 'third' gender – neither male nor female – and is brought up as neither a boy nor a girl. As such the individual is excluded from the usual rites of passage that mark transition into adulthood, and *kwolu-aatowol* tend to live on the margins of their community. But they have a recognized place in it.

The condition is also found in the Dominican Republic, where it is called *uevedoces* ('penis-at-twelve'), *machihembra* ('male-female') or *guevotes* ('penis-and-eggs'). The difference in this society is that the social rules allow such individuals to gain male status at puberty. Even though they are infertile they can become heads of households and they participate in male life. Today such individuals in the Dominican Republic sometimes opt for surgery, to 'reconstruct' them as women, travelling to the USA where it is available (see Lorber 1994, for a more detailed discussion).

Increasingly in the West this condition is one of many reasons for ascribing the label 'transgendered' to an individual, often in popular terminology shortened to 'tranny', often an affectionate way of describing another or oneself, but equally able to be used as an insult. This is similar to the way 'gay' now operates as an identifier in Western culture. We call these **polysemic** terms, because they can signify a very wide range of meanings – anything from abuse and offence to affection and pride.

In this example we can see that Scientific knowledge can tell us about the biological mechanisms at work. But it cannot tell us about the meaning of the embodiment, how it will be experienced, and how the affected person will be treated. For this, other forms of knowledge about human meaning-making are required.

Knowledge and power

Postmodernism offers an extensive and elaborate body of theorization about the relationship between knowledge and power. It regards scientific knowledge as a particularly powerful form of knowledge, since Science claims it has the authority of truth. Postmodernists argue that we need to be very wary of this claim and the power this gives to Science to tell us what is and what is not true. This is especially so when dealing with social actions and phenomena, since scientists are human and, therefore, will always have a stake in the stories they tell about human interests and concerns.

Social psychology, modernism and postmodernism

Historically, social psychology (and, indeed, psychology in general) is very much a product of modernism. In particular it has adopted two of the central principles of modernism:

- its principle that Science is the route to knowledge and, therefore, the view that social psychology should be a Science
- its liberal humanistic principle of human betterment and, therefore, the view that social psychology should seek to make the world a better place.

This section looks briefly at each of these two claims, in relation to the positions taken by experimental social psychology and critical social psychology.

Is social psychology a Science?

The answer to this question is – it all depends what you mean by science! I touched on this already at the beginning of the chapter. Social psychology is usually seen as a **human science** – one of a number of disciplines that study people. Human sciences are usually taken to include anthropology (people in culture), economics (people and money), geography (people and places), history (people over time) and sociology (people in society). However, in all these human sciences, there are different interpretations of the word 'science'.

Social psychologists differ in the position they take on whether social psychology is a 'science' (that is, based broadly on rigorous and empirical methods) or a 'Science' (that is, based solely on hypothetico-deductive method). Some social psychologists see it as a 'science' – as a rigorous, empirical form of inquiry, but not necessarily needing to use any particular method: 'contrary to what is sometimes asserted, science is a question of aim, not method' (Brickman 1980: 10). Others, however, stress the centrality of Scientific method: 'Social psychology is a science because it uses the scientific method to construct and test theories' (Hogg and Vaughan 2008: 4).

Experimental social psychologists generally adopt the second position – they regard social psychology as a Science, based on Scientific method. Critical social psychologists take the first position, viewing social psychology as a 'science' – a rigorous and systematic means of conducting research and developing theory. They deny that social psychology is a 'Science', because, they argue, hypothetico-deductive method is not the only or even the best way to be rigorous and systematic.

Just to give one example, semiotics was defined by de Saussure, its originator, as a 'science that studies the life of signs within a society' (de Saussure 1959: 16). In this contexts 'signs' are any form of representational system. Language is by far the most common sign system, but all sorts of other things are signs – mascots, brand images like Apple's apple-with-a-bite-taken-out or McDonald's golden arches, gestures, ring-tones, and so on. Semiotics is one of the main theoretical frameworks adopted by critical social psychologists to study human communication. It does not test hypotheses. Instead, it closely scrutinizes and interprets the signs and symbols through which meanings are made and managed. Semiotics is a good approach to use to understand the social and cultural aspects of 5α-reductase deficiency because it deals with

> Semiotics is explained in more detail in Chapter 6

symbols, meanings and significance. A semiotic analysis would consist of considering the different names given in different contexts – neither male nor female, penis-at-twelve, transsexual or tranny – interrogating what makes them so different and the consequences.

Should social psychology try to make the world a better place?

From its modernist beginnings, social psychology has had what Tiffin et al. (1940) termed a 'humaneering' mission:

> The value of learning more about ourselves and human nature is obvious. Our social, political and economic theories rest ultimately upon our understanding of human nature. Upon sound knowledge of human nature depends the possibility of directing social changes, so as to make social institutions and practices better suited to human needs. As citizens, then, we need to make our beliefs about human nature as sound and rational as possible. The nineteenth century was marked by great achievements in engineering. Advances in psychology, sociology, and physiology should lead to as striking advances in 'humaneering' during the twentieth century.
>
> (Tiffin et al. 1940: 23–4)

Most critical social psychologists have a strong commitment to social justice (Fox et al. 2009). Consequently, they would agree that social psychologists have a duty to 'make the world a better place'. However, they are often highly critical of institutionalized social psychology and its definition of 'better' – better for whom? Critical psychologists informed by Marxism, like Ian Parker, argue that we need to go further. We should use our study of the discipline as a form of political activism, specifically directed to challenge oppression:

> Social psychology should be about changes in the real world. It should also, though, be concerned with how people can collectively *change* the order of things for themselves. Unfortunately, social psychology as an academic institution is structured in such a way as to blot out that which is most interesting about social interaction (language, power and history) and to divert attention from efforts to de-construct its oppressive functions in a practical way.
>
> (Parker 1989: 1, emphasis in the original)

Much the same is argued by critical psychologists informed by **postcolonial theory** such as Catriona Macleod, who argue that 'at the very least, there should be an explicit focus on power-relations and undermining exclusionary and discriminatory practices' (Macleod 2004: 624–5). The *Critical Psychology* edited collection textbook written for the post-apartheid South Africa (Hook et al. 2004) is clear about the agenda – critical psychology must always be used to expose, oppose – and ultimately depose – elites who mistreat, marginalize and exploit others.

You will generally find that the topics studied by critical social psychologists are those concerned in some way with the abuse of power. Sometimes they specifically address issues of domination, exploitation and abuse. Examples include Wetherell and Potter's (1992) study of racism, and Kitzinger and Frith's (1999) study of how men exploit women's difficulties in rejecting unwanted sexual advances. In others, the topics may appear less overtly 'political'; an example here is Stenner's 1993 study of jealousy.

> These studies are described in Chapter 5.

However, the analysis applied always has a 'political' undercurrent. A term introduced by Michel Foucault – the **micropolitics of power** – is useful here. It neatly describes the main aim of much critical research: to tease out 'what is going on' in the small and local, everyday and often intimate processes by which power is exercised and resisted in people's relations with one another, as individuals and communities, within kinship, religious and social groups, institutions and organizations.

So, as you can see, again there is general agreement that social psychology should seek to 'make the world a better place'. However, there are significant differences in how this should be pursued, and what should be the targets for change.

Social psychology, modernism and postmodernism

- *Modernism* is based on the assumption that science is the only way to gain rational knowledge.

- *Postmodernism* is based on the assumption that knowledge is constructed rather than discovered, multiple rather than singular, and a means by which power is exercised.

- *Is social psychology 'scientific'?* It depends on your definition. Both approaches agree that it should be rigorous, empirical and systematic. But experimental social psychology views it as a Science, based on Scientific method. Critical social psychology regards Scientific method as just one possible means to gain knowledge, and often not the best one.

- Both experimental and critical social psychology have a commitment to '*making the world a better place*', but they have radically different ideas as to what this entails. Experimental social psychologists seek to promote liberal values, such as freedom, love and the pursuit of happiness. Critical social psychologists have a much more 'political' agenda – such as fighting oppression and exposing exploitation.

Resources

Outlines of what the website regards as the ten 'best' psychological experiments: http://www.spring.org.uk/2007/11/10-piercing-insights-into-human-nature.php

A really good article from *The Psychologist* on psychology's myths and the way famous experiments have been misreported: http://www.thepsychologist.org.uk/archive/archive_home.cfm?volumeID=21&editionID=164&ArticleID=1394

Further reading

The history of psychology

Hollway, W. (2007) Social psychology: past and present, Chapter 1 in W. Hollway, H. Lucey and A. Phoenix (eds) (2007) *Social Psychology Matters*. Maidenhead: Open University Press.

This book forms part of the Open University's Social Psychology Course, and, as such, is very student-friendly and accessible. It is also somewhat interactive, getting you now and again to pause and reflect on what you have read and consider implications. It provides a more detailed account from within psychology of its history than in this chapter, and is an excellent way to 'flesh out' what you have learned here.

Experimental social psychology

Myers, D., Abell, J., Kolstad, A. and Sani, F. (2010) *Social Psychology: European Edition*. Maidenhead: McGraw-Hill.

Chapter 1 'What is social psychology?' provides an alternative telling of the story I have told here and offers a complementary 'take' on the issues and ideas I have raised in this chapter, but coming primarily from an experimental social psychology position. It is a European version of an American textbook, that strives to give a more 'balanced' and nuanced account of social psychology.

Hewstone, M., Stroebe, W. and Jonas, K. (2007) Introduction to *Social Psychology: A European Perspective*, 4th edn. Oxford: Blackwell.

This is the fifth in a series of editions, by the leading social psychologists from the European Association of Social Psychology. It has a distinctly 'European' flavour, as its title suggests, and will give you a real insight into some of the differences in emphasis, both theoretical and empirical, from the more Anglo-Saxon version dominant in the English-speaking world. I suggest you read Chapter 1 at this point, as it gives an alternative history to the one I have told.

Critical social psychology

Gergen, K. (1973) Social psychology as history, *Journal of Personality and Social Psychology*, 26: 309–20.

This was a highly influential article at the beginnings of critical social psychology and still worth reading today.

Parker, I. (1989) *The Crisis of Modern Social Psychology – and How to End It.* **London: Routledge.**
Equally, this was incredibly influential at the time when it was written. If you plan to pursue critical social psychology, you certainly need to read this. It is, essentially, a manifesto for critical social psychology.

Gough, B. and McFadden, M. (2001) *Critical Social Psychology: An Introduction.* **Basingstoke: Palgrave.**
If this approach has 'grabbed' you already, this book should keep you contentedly busy for some time.

Sociological social psychology

Flick, U. (ed.) (1998) *The Psychology of the Social.* **Cambridge: Cambridge University Press.**
This is the best source if you want to find out where sociological social psychology is 'at' these days. Flick's introductory chapter sets this out cogently.

General critical psychology

Smyth, M.M. (2001) Fact making in psychology, *Theory and Psychology,* **11: 609–36.**
This paper is an analysis of what was written in psychology textbooks in the 1980s and 1990s. It gives you a really different 'take' on studying a textbook in this field. Only part of it is about social psychology, but it is fascinating and informative.

Fox, D., Prilleltensky, I. and Austin, S. (eds) (2009) *Critical Psychology: An Introduction,* **2nd edn. London: Sage.**
The first edition of this book was highly influential, especially as its editors were well known in the USA. This second edition is a major revision, with all the chapters at least rewritten, and several that are new. It does offer a particularly US version of the topic, but it is wide-ranging and, as separate chapters, a good book to dip in and out of. Chapter 6, by Frances Cherry, is specifically on critical social psychology.

Hook, D., Collins, A., Kiguwa, P. and Mkhize, N. (eds) (2004) *Critical Psychology.* **Cape Town: University of Cape Town Press.**
I have included this book as it is really fascinating to see how psychologists in post-apartheid South Africa took on the challenge of literally rewriting their subject to produce a discipline appropriate for Africa among the otherwise Northern/Western-dominated 'world' market. This is especially poignant in the context of the role played by psychologists, especially from the University of Stellenbosch, in the creation of the concept of apartheid, and the 'Scientific' justification for it. It is a wonderful counterbalance to the standard US textbook.

Questions

1 'The different theories created by social psychologists reflect different images of the person'. Describe these two very different images, and provide examples of how they are incorporated into different approaches to social psychology.

2 Is social psychology scientific? Should it be?

3 'Social psychology has always had a mission to "make the world a better place".' Compare and contrast the stance taken by experimental and critical social psychology in relation to this claim.

4 'Postmodernism is not a development from modernism, it is a reaction against it.' Do you agree? Illustrate your answer with examples from psychology.

5 What are the origins of the concept of 'group mind'? Say why you think this concept was rejected by experimental social psychology.

6 'Social psychological theories are the products of the times and places in which they are developed.' Discuss this statement, with illustrations from the early movements in social psychology, from experimental social psychology in the 1940s and from the emergence of critical social psychology in the 1970s and 1980s.

The foundations of experimental and critical social psychology

LEARNING OUTCOMES

When you have finished studying this chapter, you should be able to:

1 Outline the ontological and epistemological assumptions upon which experimental social psychology is based.

2 Describe the key elements of the inductive and deductive logics of inquiry, and define the difference between them.

3 List the main stages of the hypothetico-deductive method, illustrating this with reference to a study of the effects on problem solving of expressing the problem in abstract or meaningful terms.

4 Outline the ontological and epistemological assumptions of critical social psychology.

5 Describe the basic principles of social constructionism, and compare critical realist and critical relativist approaches to gaining knowledge.

6 Define *either* retroduction *or* abduction as a logic of inquiry. Whichever one you choose, describe how it can be the basis of discovery in Science and give an account of its strategic use in social constructionist research.

7 Summarize the main differences between the two paradigms of experimental and critical social psychology, in particular in relation to their approaches to gaining knowledge, how they deal with complexity and their position on objectivity.

Introduction

This chapter goes right back to the basic fundamentals on which the social psychology we know today has been built. It examines some elementary philosophical ideas about the social world in which we, as people, live; about who and what we are within it; and about *what* we can know about these things and *how* we can know them. Moving on from Chapter 1, it contrasts the very different assumptions made within the modernist and postmodern paradigms when applied to social psychology, and then spells them out in some detail.

This may be a chapter you are tempted to skip – wanting to move on straight away to the meatier and more practical chapters on research methods. But, take it from me, it is designed to make the rest of this book easier to understand. It provides a systematic working through of the basic philosophical ideas that underpin the two different approaches. At least try it and see.

Different philosophical foundations

To understand the differences between the experimental and critical approaches to social psychology you will need to understand two fundamental philosophical concepts – ontology and epistemology.

- **Ontology** is the branch of philosophy that addresses what things are and their being-in-the-world. In the context of this book it is about the assumptions social psychologists make about the social world – the everyday world of people's lived experience and actions. It is about what is going on in people's roles, relationships, attributions, attitudes, and so on, and the social influences upon them.
- **Epistemology** is the branch of philosophy that considers the nature of knowledge – what counts as valid knowledge, and how it can be gained. Here it is about the assumptions made by social psychologists about what constitutes well-founded knowledge about the social world (as opposed to beliefs or opinions) and how social psychologists should go about gaining it.

Different logics of inquiry

Next you need to understand how *different* epistemological and ontological assumptions lead to *different* research strategies that social psychologists can adopt. I will use the term **logic of inquiry** for this. I originally took this term from a very clever book by Blaikie (2000). I subsequently learned that it has much earlier origins, from the mainly philosophical work of Dewey, Mead and, most importantly, Charles Peirce (more about him later).

Blakie says there are four different logics of inquiry and each has a different aim and is based on a different set of assumptions about ontology and epistemology. Two are possibly familiar to you – **induction** and **deduction**, the logics of inquiry suitable for research carried out within a modernist paradigm. The other two – **retroduction** and **abduction** – are probably not! (This use of the word abduction has nothing to do with little green men!) Retroduction and abduction are suited to research carried out within the postmodern paradigm. The differences are clearer when seen in relation to each other, as in Table 2.1. This chapter moves through each in turn, so by the end of it, all should be clear.

Table 2.1 Four logics of inquiry

Dominant paradigm	Logic of inquiry	Research aim
Modernism	Induction	To develop universal laws of social behaviour and phenomena through systematically observing the social world and identifying systematic regularities in causes and effects
	Deduction	To develop universal laws of social behaviour and phenomena through deriving hypotheses from theory and testing them
Postmodernism	Retroduction	To gain insight into and understanding of how social realities are constructed and deployed through an analysis based on a particular theory or standpoint
	Abduction	To discover how and why different social realities are constructed and deployed through identifying puzzles and solving them.

These two underpinning themes – philosophical foundations and logics of inquiry – form the basis of this chapter. It begins with two sections, first looking at the philosophical foundations and logics of inquiry of experimental social psychology, second, looking at the philosophical foundations and logics of inquiry of critical social psychology. A section is then devoted to comparing and contrasting them. The aim is that by the end of the chapter you will have a clear and thorough understanding of the basic principles of each approach, why they are different, and what the implications are of these differences. It may feel quite hard work, but I promise it is worthwhile. If you can get these ideas firmly established in your mind, you will find it so much easier to really understand all that follows.

The foundations of experimental social psychology

Experimental social psychology is broadly based upon an epistemological position called **positivism**. At its purest and most simple, positivism holds that there is a straightforward one-to-one relationship between things and events in the outside world and people's knowledge of them. The goal of experimental social psychology is to get as close as possible to this ideal – to discover reliable, factual knowledge about the social-world-as-it-really-is.

Few Scientists today would claim that this is ever entirely possible. They accept that since human perception and understanding are fallible, people will always be somewhat selective and biased by their preconceptions (Chalmers 1999). However, most Scientists (including experimental social psychologists) take the position that by using Scientific method they can progressively pin down 'the facts' and get close enough to reality to develop working models of how processes and phenomena 'work' in systematic, lawful ways.

The goal of experimental social psychology is to unravel the lawful relationships between the different elements of the social world, and so to explain how they 'work'. To pursue this goal, experimental social psychologists seek to discover knowledge through Scientific method, that is, through the systematic collection and analysis of things that can be directly observed.

So let us now look at how Science goes about discovering knowledge and, in particular, how experimental social psychologists have worked within the Scientific paradigm to gain knowledge. In this section I shall refer to a range of studies to illustrate how Scientific method has been applied to experimental social psychological theorizing and research.

Hypothetico-deductivism

Contemporary Scientific method is based upon Popper's (1959) **hypothetico-deductivism** – put more simply, the process of making deductions from the testing of hypotheses. Underpinning this obscure language are some simple but powerful ideas. As an illustration I am going to begin by looking at a study of what happens when people try to solve logical problems.

Wason's selection task problem

If you want to know more about this field of research, see the Further reading section at the end of this chapter.

The study I have chosen was carried out by Cosmides (1989). In it she examined whether people find it easier to solve logical problems if the problem is expressed in a meaningful way that relates to their social knowledge about the world, compared with when the problem is expressed in abstract terms. To do this she used a problem-solving task called the **selection task problem**, originally devised by Peter Wason (1966, 1968). Cosmides was by no means the first person to explore the impact of meaningfulness on people's ability to solve the problem, but hers is one of the easiest to follow.

Peter Wason, a cognitive psychologist, was particularly interested in the errors people make in their reasoning. To investigate this he devised a number of highly creative problems of logic – problems that appear to be simple but are actually fiendishly difficult. Of these, the selection task problem, is probably his most famous. In his 1966 chapter, Wason describes how he got some of his students to try the problem. He placed before them four cards, as shown in Figure 2.1. Each card had a letter on one side and a number on the other. Comparing these allows a rule to be tested. The problem the person has to solve is to identify which cards must be turned over to see if the rule is true or not.

Try it for yourself

Wason commented that the problem 'proved to be particularly difficult' to solve (Wason 1966: 146). Try it for yourself and see how you get on. It really is worth experiencing the surprising difficulty of the task for yourself, so do not cheat by looking at the answers in the text. Spend a few minutes thinking about the rule and what is on the cards, and then write down your answers.

I wonder if, like almost all of Wason's students, you picked the A and the 2? The A is a right answer, but the 2 is wrong. You should have picked the A and the 1. Not convinced? Then take it slowly. You need to turn over the A because an odd number on the other side of the card would disprove the rule. But you do not need to turn over the 2 because it does not matter what is on the other side. The rule says: 'If there is a vowel on one side, there is an even number on the other.'

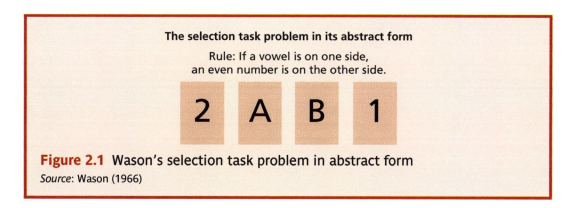

Figure 2.1 Wason's selection task problem in abstract form
Source: Wason (1966)

It says nothing about what kind of number may be on the other side of a consonant. So even if on the other side of the 2 there is a B, the rule is not disproved. Equally you do not need to turn over the B, since it does not matter what is on the other side. But you do need to turn over the 1, because if there is a vowel on the other side it disproves the rule.

Try it for yourself

Still not convinced? Then try Cosmides' meaningful version. This (in somewhat modified form) is shown in Figure 2.2.

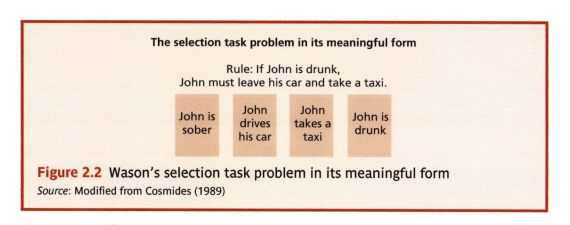

Figure 2.2 Wason's selection task problem in its meaningful form
Source: Modified from Cosmides (1989)

This version is very much easier to solve, as the alternatives are expressed meaningfully, so you can draw on your prior knowledge of laws about drink and driving. This tells you that you do not need to look at the cards about John being sober and John taking a taxi – they are 'obviously' (that is, meaningfully) irrelevant. All you need to know to test the rule is whether or not John, when he drove his car, was drunk or sober (the second card); and whether, when he was drunk, he took a taxi or drove his car (the last card). If you are still unconvinced about the abstract version, go back now and look at it again. It usually helps to have done the social knowledge question – it makes it easier to see what is at stake in the abstract one.

Stage 1: Constructing a hypothesis

A hypothesis is a specific, operational prediction about an outcome from a Scientific study, that you can test empirically. Devising a hypothesis consists of a series of stages. In Scientific method, in order to gain empirical knowledge, it must be possible to make logical and unequivocal predictions about cause and effect. To do this you need to have in mind one or more potential answers to your research question. What you have in mind will be guided by the theory you are working from.

The general prediction in this case is pretty obvious. Our theory claims that thinking works most efficiently when using meaning. So our general prediction in this study will be that when people solve the selection task problem, they will perform better if it is expressed in meaningful terms than if it is expressed in abstract terms. Notice what has gone on here. We started with a theory about the influence of meaning. From this we predicted what would happen, in a way that enables us to make an observation about whether the prediction 'works'. We moved from the abstract idea of problem solving being 'helped' by meaning to the practical prediction that people would 'perform better'.

Stage 2: Specifying an experimental hypothesis

Performance is something we can test empirically by observing and, crucially, measuring how people perform. We could, for example, measure the number of errors people make, or the speed at which they respond or even the degree of certainty they have about their answers. It is usual to go for the easiest and most unequivocal thing to measure. In this case it would be the number of errors they make – how many of the wrong cards they turned over and how many of the right cards they did not. So now we can specify an experimental hypothesis in the form of a formal statement, in which the prediction has been operationalized – described in terms of an outcome that can be measured. The hypothesis is:

> People will make fewer errors when solving a problem if it is expressed in meaningful terms than if it is expressed in abstract form.

Stage 3: Establishing significant difference and the null hypothesis

However, this is not yet exact enough – how many fewer is few enough to test the hypothesis? At this point we need to make recourse to statistics. You may already be familiar with the concept of **significant difference**. Basically, it is a matter of comparing the experimental hypothesis with the alternative – the **null hypothesis**. This states that there will be no difference that can be attributed to the problem being expressed meaningfully.

The basic idea behind 'significant difference' is that a difference will be found that is sufficiently large that it is extremely unlikely that the null hypothesis is true. The question is, how 'extremely unlikely' does it have to be? A small difference could be a matter of coincidence. Consider the situation where 10 people tried to solve the problem in each condition. Now, let us assume that only 2 of the 10 who tried the problem in its abstract form made no errors, but in the meaningful form 4 people made none. Is this just coincidence? Well, maybe. But let us say 100 people tried each condition, and with the abstract form two people made no errors but with the meaningful form 80 made none – they got it right. The difference here is much more convincing – the chance that this is just a fluke is much, much smaller.

Statistical procedures enable you to estimate the probability of this. For example, a 0.001 level of significance means that the difference has only one chance in 1000 of being a coincidence. The calculation takes account of the number of observations that are made of the hypothesis being tested – in this case this would be about how many people were asked to solve the problem. So here is the hypothesis in full:

> People will make significantly fewer errors when solving a problem expressed in meaningful terms than if it is expressed in abstract form.

Induction and deduction

This deals with the 'hypothetico-' bit of hypothetico-deductivism, but we are not there yet. We need to deal with the 'deductivism' part. It is here that Popper's work is most important. A philosopher of science, Popper (1959) argued that just because a prediction made in the hypothesis is supported by the observations made, this does not mean that the theory is proved. However many observations you make, and however convincing the significance level, there is always, logically, a small but nonetheless real possibility that the pattern of results is a matter of chance.

Induction

Induction is drawing inferences from observations, in order to make generalizations. It consists of four main stages:

1 You direct your attention to a particular event or phenomenon or activity, observe what is going on without any attempt to be selective, and then record careful and comprehensive notes on what you have observed.
2 You reflect on your observations, analyse, compare and classify them, and look for any regularity or pattern.
3 From this you seek to infer generalizations about the relationships between the things you have observed.
4 You test out these generalizations by further observation.

Wason's original experiment was like this. He devised the problem, made up the cards, gave them to his students, told them the rule, and then watched what they did. He had a hunch that they would find the problem difficult, and they did. He observed them making lots of errors, and speculated from this about why they kept turning over the even number card, even after they were told it was irrelevant.

As you will see in Chapter 3, some experimental social psychology research uses an inductive approach like this. Such studies are usually referred to as **descriptive research**. In them a situation is created or a naturally occurring event is observed, and the researcher seeks merely to record what happens in a dispassionate manner. When used by experimental social psychologists, this approach is usually intended to stimulate hypothetico-deductive research. By observing regularities in what happens – that, for example, people tend to make errors in the selection task problem – such studies offer a stimulus for generating hypotheses that can be tested. This is what Cosmides did. She speculated that the problem with the problem was that it was expressed in abstract form. So she set out to test it by an experiment in which she compared the abstract form with a meaningful form, using the hypothetico-deductive method we have followed in this section.

Induction is a common practice in everyday life. We make inferences such as 'the kids are always cranky around teatime' or 'I'm definitely not a morning person' all the time, and use them to organize the way we run our lives. As such, induction can be pretty much automatic.

Actually, I used Wason's selection task problem as my illustration deliberately. It gave you a chance to experience at first hand just how powerful a grip induction has on the way we think. When Wason's students made further attempts to solve the problem again they soon learned to look at the odd number card. But even when he gave them a careful explanation that they did not need to turn over the even number card, they still went on doing it. Wason commented that 'In spite of explicit instructions to the contrary, [it seems] they cannot inhibit a tendency to see whether the statement is "true"', and concluded that 'this implies that the need to establish the "truth" of the statement predominates over the instruction' (Wason 1966: 146–7).

Deduction

Popper argued specifically that induction can generate hypotheses but it cannot test them. To test a hypothesis it is necessary to use a deductive approach. Deduction, as shown in Wason's selection task problem, is based on **falsification** – putting a rule or a theory's predictions to the test in ways that allow for them to be disproved. This may still seem to you an odd thing to do. Was Popper really arguing that researchers should set out to deliberately prove that their theories are wrong? Not at all! Rather he was saying that studies must be designed in such a way that the hypothesis can be falsified.

Popper's view of deduction argument (as applied to social psychology) can be summarized as follows:

1 The social world operates in a lawful manner, and the aim is to discover these laws.
2 This is done by generating theories and testing hypotheses about cause and effect, in order to be able to explain why people think, feel and act as they do.
3 However, it is not possible to unequivocally establish these laws. All that can be done is to eliminate false theories, thereby moving gradually closer to the truth.
4 But we have no way of knowing for certain when we have arrived at a true theory, so even those theories that have survived testing must be regarded as provisional.

I have summarized the differences between induction and deduction in Table 2.2 to make the distinction between them clear.

Now we can begin to bring all the parts together for experimental social psychology – its overarching paradigm, its underpinning ontology and epistemology, its two logics of inquiry and its research aims. These are shown in Table 2.3.

Table 2.2 Comparison of inductive and deductive approaches to research

	How does it assume that knowledge can be gained?	What is the purpose of gaining evidence?	What is the evidence gathered intended to do?	How is progress to be made?
Inductive approach	Making inferences from observations	To look for regularities and patterns in the events observed	Establish generalizations	To use these generalizations to develop hypotheses that can be tested deductively
Deductive approach	Testing hypotheses	To put hypotheses to the test in ways that allow them to be falsified	To provisionally support the theory that the hypothesis was designed to test	To exclude theories that have been falsified, and develop and refine those that have not

Table 2.3 Foundations of experimental social psychology

Dominant paradigm	Ontology	Epistemology	Logic of inquiry	Research aim
Modernism	The social world exists 'out there' in nature, separate from human action. It consists of discrete and observable social events and phenomena that are lawfully related.	Positivism	Induction	To develop universal laws of social behaviour and phenomena through systematically observing the social world and identifying systematic regularities in causes and effects
		Rationalism	Deduction	To develop universal laws of social behaviour and phenomena through deriving hypotheses from theory and testing them

The foundations of experimental social psychology

- Experimental social psychology usually adopts an inductive or a deductive logic of inquiry.

- Its research aims are to discover, establish and refine universal laws of social behaviour.

- It is based on an ontology in which the social world is external to and separate from human action. It consists of discrete and observable social events and phenomena that are lawfully related.

- Its epistemology is that knowledge can be gained about the universal laws of social behaviour, phenomena and experience using the hypothetico-deductive method. Theory is used to generate an experimental hypothesis that can be tested by falsification (that is, deduction not induction).

- Where the predictions of a theory are falsified, the theory is abandoned. However, what generally happens is that research in experimental social psychology is used to gradually accumulate valid and reliable empirical evidence for theories that offer the best explanation for the causes of the social processes or social phenomena in question.

The foundations of critical social psychology

Critical social psychology is based on an ontology in which there is seen to be no social world 'out there' in nature – no naturally occurring social phenomena or social processes. The social world is not 'natural' at all (that is, not a product of laws of human nature). It is *constructed* – made, and made real through people's actions, through their efforts to make sense of it and navigate and negotiate their selves and lives within it. This approach is called **social constructionism**. It is a theoretical framework informed by postmodernism, but applied specifically to human sciences, most notably anthropology, social geography, sociology and critical psychology.

Social constructionism

Although, as usual, its roots go back much further, social constructionism arose from a theory called the sociology of knowledge. The key text was Berger and Luckmann's (1967) *The Social Construction of Reality*. In it they theorized that social reality is constructed through three 'moments': externalization, objectification and internalization.

- **Externalization** is about the way that cultures, societies and social groups of different kinds make sense of – and therefore 'make' – their social worlds, including a whole range of social institutions and constructs.
- **Objectification** is how those constructs and social institutions then get to be perceived as real. This is also referred to as **reification**. An uglier but in some ways more transparent term is '**thingification**' – the process whereby ideas get turned into socially real things.
- **Internalization** is where the objectified social world becomes known, understood and adopted by individuals through processes of socialization and enculturation.

Berger and Luckmann saw these three moments as in constant interplay, as shown in Figure 2.3.

Social constructionist social psychology

Social constructionism in psychology is part of a more general turn to an interpretative approach, which aims to gain insight into why people experience the world as they do, make sense of it and take actions by 'uncovering the largely tacit, mutual knowledge, the symbolic meanings, motives and rules, which provide the orientations for their actions' (Blaikie 2000: 115). This is knowledge that is only visible by looking at what people do with it, how they interact with each other, the ideas about what it means to be polite, what you wear to look right in particular situations, what to eat and how to eat it, where and with whom. It is the knowledge that 'everybody knows' but, because it is so familiar, nobody puts into words. This is what researchers need to uncover and then expose to scrutiny and ask 'what is going on'.

Social reality is the reality we all construct in what we think, say and do, alone in our own world sometimes but mainly when we do it collectively. It is powerfully constructed *for* us through institutions like religion, the law and schooling, all of which tell us versions of reality and make them real for us by drawing us into their rituals and practices. In our information-saturated, image-drenched world it is made real by what goes on in TV soaps and movies, on Facebook and YouTube and *Masterchef*, at church, the temple, at morning prayers, Brownie camp, school open days and

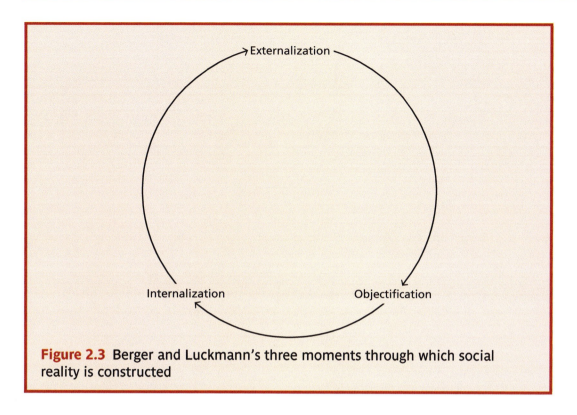

Figure 2.3 Berger and Luckmann's three moments through which social reality is constructed

village fêtes. It is created for us in the clubs and bars and the streets on a Saturday night, on the billboards, in the magazines and through the apps on our phones. Other realities are constructed in other locations with other regimes and other imperatives, other constraints and other opportunities, even within an ever globalized world. I have no doubt that reality looks rather different from within a monastery or a refugee camp to the comfortable life I lead in Milton Keynes.

Social constructionism is based on an ontology that regards social reality as constructed by way of human meaning-making, and operating by way of human meaning-interpretation and application. However, it is important to stress that this is not just about simply *describing* alternative social realities – different points of view or different worldviews. Social constructionism is about gaining insight into and understanding of the *means* by which 'realities' are constructed and the uses for which they are deployed. This is neatly described by Vivienne Burr in her book, *An Introduction to Social Constructionism*:

It is through the daily interactions between people in the course of social life that our versions of knowledge become fabricated. Therefore social interaction of all kinds, and particularly language, is of great interest to social constructionists. The goings-on between people in the course of their everyday lives are seen as the practices during which our shared versions of knowledge are constructed. Therefore what we regard as 'truth' (which of course varies historically and cross-culturally), i.e. our current accepted ways of understanding the world, is a product not of objective observation of the world, but of social processes and interactions in which people are constantly engaged with each other.

(Burr 1995: 4)

The aim of scholarship and research in critical social psychology is to gain insight into the *consequences* of social reality being constructed in particular ways and, most importantly, the impact this has upon how people can act and how they are treated. It asks different questions – not 'is this version of reality true?' but 'what actions does this version of social reality make possible? In what ways does it constrain what people can do? Who gets their own way? Who gets exploited? Crucially, from this epistemological standpoint, there is no independent 'benchmark' that can be used to establish which social reality is 'true'. Research does not seek to discover the 'facts' of social life, social processes or social phenomena, since it regards this as a wild goose chase leading nowhere. It simply is not possible to do so.

Post-structuralism

A key moment in the development of critical psychology was when psychologists, turned to **post-structuralism**, influenced particularly by the work of Michel Foucault. The book that changed everything (for some of us, at least) was *Changing the Subject* (Henriques et al. 1984), a play on words in that it was about changing psychology as a subject in the sense of a discipline like sociology or physics; *and* changing psychology's 'subjects', that is, those it studies:

> The use of Foucault's approach to histories of the production of knowledge is an important feature of out theoretical enterprise. . . . First, it permits the reconceptualisation of psychology as a body of knowledge. . . . Second, this alternative approach provides a strong starting point where the couple 'individual' and 'society' no longer constrains the question posed because from the outset it is prob-lematised; both are regarded as effects of a production to be specified, rather than pregiven objects of the human sciences. It is from this point of view that this new history feeds the task of retheorising the subject of psychology.
>
> (Henriques et al. 1984: 98)

Post-structuralism is defined by Wilbraham in a way I like:

> [a] specific philosophical stance within broader 'post-modernism', post-structuralists argue that there are only arbitrary and conventionalised relations between words and meanings; and it is within the critical disassembly of texts that the uncertainty of truth is explored. So post-structuralism destabil-ises language, social institutions and the self by opening up contradictions and power-relations.
>
> (2004: 498)

All right, this is not the easiest writing to get your head around! But it does give a sense of what is going on. Whereas structuralism is looking 'underneath' language for the structures through which meaning is made and deployed, post-structuralism is seeking to rock its foundations, or 'make trouble' (Curt 1994). Instead of trying to tie down explanations of what is going on, post-structuralism accepts that there is no 'benchmark of the truth' (Game 1991) and all that can be produced are undisciplined, messy, edgy and highly provisional explications and 'what if' speculations.

Post-structuralism is used by critical social psychologists to enable them to 'step beyond the consciousness of the individual "subject" and back from the personal meanings held by the members of a community' (Parker 1989: 52) and to look at the broader picture: to explore how language, for instance, 'works' at the intersubjective level rather than within some private subjectivity. Henriques et al. put it like this: instead of reducing meaning to 'a problem of the "influence" of the social environment on the unitary individual' (which is what social psychology has traditionally done), post-structural analysis operates 'by reference to differences of power and gender and different canalizations of desire' (1984: 149).

In other words, it moves beyond the study of *meaning-as-it-is-understood* by the individual subject, to the study of *meaning-as-it-is-made* by linking into broader theories, such as political theories about power, feminist theories about gender and psychosocial theories about desire. In this analysis meaning-making is not seen as an individual cognitive act of reactively 'making sense' that goes on inside a person's mind. Meaning-making is, instead, seen as going on *between* people, *inter*subjectively, constantly being made, remade and unmade in unremitting, shifting flux.

Try it for yourself

Let me borrow an example from the writings Beryl Curt (1994: 1). Read the following sentence and try to work out what it is – what meaning can you make of it? To set the scene, it is a dark and stormy night:

> Sister Mary Agnes coughed, spit up a gobbet of blood and tossed the severed goat's udder over the rim of the canyon.
>
> (Rice 1986: 3)

In fact 'It was a dark and stormy night' is a clue, and is also the title of Rice's book, which sets out the winning sentences from the Bulwer-Lytton Contest. This contest is where contestants vie with each other to create the most unbelievably clichéd and ridiculous first sentence for a novel. Once you know this, you can begin to make some sense of what is, on first reading, an extraordinary statement.

But to be able to do so you have to draw upon all sorts of other knowledge. You need to know what the words themselves 'mean' for a start. Each one is, on its own, pretty ordinary, it is just when you put them together it all gets a bit weird, even though the sentence is perfectly grammatical. On first reading most people find it rather puzzling. Beryl Curt (herself a puzzle, since she only exists is a postmodern sense of that word) used it as the first sentence of a textbook, and certainly in that context it looked decidedly odd. To get further you have to draw on your understanding about what a novel is, and what a competition is, and what is at stake in this one, and how this related to Snoopy and why it is amusing. You may be losing me at this point, as we are beginning to get into a particular set of culturally specific resonances and meanings, but that is the point.

Retroduction and abduction

In critical social psychology there are basically two alternative logics of inquiry: retroduction and abduction; and two corresponding alternative approaches to research: **critical realist** and **critical relativist**.

Charles Peirce brought the terms 'abduction' and 'retroduction' to our attention in his development of semiotic theory. But he was a man who has frustrated scholars enormously, since he left us almost nothing by the way of publications. We know his work only because others painstakingly sorted out a vast hoard of his notes. Charles Hartshorne working with Paul Weiss published six volumes of his works between 1931 and 1935. Arthur Burks added a further two volumes in the 1950s.

Because of the scrappiness of Peirce's notes there is confusion about whether Peirce saw retroduction and abduction as two dissimilar logics of inquiry, or just different names for the same thing. I agree with Sayer (1992) and Thompson (2006) that he thought they were different:

- *Retroduction* is a logic of inquiry which reasons 'backwards' (hence the 'retro') by using an already established theoretical or conceptual framework to interpret research findings, in order to work out 'what is going on'. This logic of inquiry is the basis for critical realism.

- *Abduction* is a logic of inquiry which generates hypotheses rather than testing them. The difference between this and retroduction is that with abduction, the researcher comes to the interpretation with an open mind about the appropriate theory or standpoint that will make most sense of 'what is going on'. This form of criticality is called critical relativism.

Critical realism and retroduction

Critical realist research is always done from a particular **standpoint** – it is research that adopts an ideological position such as Marxism (these days often called 'social justice'), feminism or postcolonialism. Marxist research draws on theories about the dynamics of exploitation by the powerful over the powerless. Feminist research draws on theories about patriarchal power to investigate topics like domestic violence and 'the glass ceiling'. Postcolonial theory is used to inform research on the impacts of geo-political events and systems such as colonialism, diasporas and migration, looking into what happened and is happening around the 'edgy' borderlines that locate individuals and communities by way of class and place and race. However, as MacLeod and Bhatia (2009: 577) make clear, this is not just a matter of theory: '[p]ostcolonial research . . . is inextricably linked to politics'. They argue that especially important for postcolonial research are the politics of location and of representation.

Critical realist epistemology brings such theorization to the task of challenging elite and dominant explanations of what is going on, that make them appear 'just natural' and, therefore, 'nothing to worry about' or even so taken-for-granted that they go unnoticed. A good example is, I think, the growth in opportunities for 'pampering' ourselves, presented as a reward for hard work, juggling complex demands and 'because we are worth it'. Think about it! (Or about any other marketing campaign for that matter.)

Critical realist research views social actions and phenomena as produced by social structures (such as structural inequality) and mechanisms (such as patriarchy). Starting from this framework, it uses a retroductive logic to identify systematic regularities in social action or social phenomena, in order to gain insight into and understanding of how these structures (and mechanisms that produce them) operate. In other words, researchers use retroduction to analyse how process like prejudice, exploitation and exclusion 'work'.

Consider how critical realist research could be conducted on the phenomenon of 'pampering'. How, for example, might Marxist or feminist theory be used as a framework for analysing, say, the websites advertising 'pampering' services? When I was in Japan I was fascinated to observe the very public services provided for men to be 'pampered', in a culture where a man looking for promotion will work very long hours, may well not take his holiday entitlement and is required to be meticulously subservient in his dealings with his bosses. I can see how either of these theories could be used to address that.

Critical realist researchers work from a 'backing' of ideology and prior theory for both positive and negative reasons. The positives are about having a starting-point from which to begin, and a ready-made framework for analysis, which certainly makes it easier to interpret data. The negatives arise from an anxiety about the relativism to be found in what is sometimes called the 'Postmodern carnival'. People can easily get beguiled into assuming that 'anything goes' since there are no foundational ethics by which we can judge 'right' and 'wrong'. Put colourfully by Smith, critical realism is seen as essential to 'bar the gate to the polis and keep the night, the jungle and the jackals at bay' (1988: 154). The fear is that research without a clear commitment to fight sexism, racism and other forms of oppression will be impotent at best and downright dangerous at worst.

Critical relativism and abduction

As I have argued elsewhere, critical relativists (of whom I am one) are perfectly aware of the dangers of a 'psychology without foundation' (Brown and Stenner 2009). Our fear is 'the claim that there ever is a single, foundationally proper "ideological position" from which any set of events must be read' (Stainton Rogers and Stainton Rogers 1997: 72). As Sawiki (1991) put it, so elegantly, it is not a position where 'anything goes' but one in which 'nothing goes'.

Peirce defines abduction as 'the process of forming an explanatory hypothesis' (Peirce [1940] 1955: 42). Instead of analysing data by reference to ideology and theory, abduction does so by identifying what does not fit – the unexpected, the contradictory, the puzzling. Finding an explanation to these puzzles – a hunch or a guess as to what is going on, based on the best available evidence – means that a hypothesis gets created.

According to Shank (1998), researchers can simply just look out for anomalies in their data when they happen to arise. But, he says, abductive research works best when it uses methods that specifically create opportunities to be surprised (more about this in Chapter 6). The political scientist, Steven Brown, has described this kind of research as

> a launch pad for an investigation, an entrée into a phenomenon, the scientist's best initial guess as to how a particular administrative situation, social consciousness, or whatever operates. The data gathered . . . may lead in quite different directions. . . . There is never any guarantee, in other words, that splash-down will occur in the same area as the point of departure.
>
> (1980: 39)

In my view, abduction is less about generating theories and more a means to achieve insight and to make discoveries. Critical relativists pursue abductory research in order to tease out 'what is going on' in ways that acknowledge that people generally do what they do for good reasons,

reasons that are meaningful to them. While not basing their analysis on theory, critical relativists usually want their research to challenge the explanations given by mainstream psychologists using a hypothetico-deductive logic of inquiry.

Abductive research involves either homing in on disjunctions and discrepancies – that which is surprising or intriguing because it does not fit into pre-existing frameworks – or creating conditions where researchers can be surprised. Just as Sherlock Holmes would always reach a point of identifying the crucial clue – such as 'the dog that did not bark' – abductory research looks for anomalies, inconsistencies and incongruities in what has been examined. And, just like Sherlock Holmes, the researcher now has to puzzle out what can possibly account for the anomaly.

One of the most persistent and powerful advocates of abductive research in psychology is Gary Shank (for example, Shank 1994, 1998). Shank argues that psychologists should give up on proliferating ever more detailed models and theories and, instead, concentrate on developing the craft tools to pursue research into meaning. And abduction, he says, is the way to go. To do this, he says, researchers do not need to wait to be surprised – though they should treasure serendipitous surprises when they come across them. Surprises can be made to happen, for instance, by juxtaposing things (such as areas of study) that, at first sight, appear to be entirely unconnected in any way. New paths to insight and discovery, he claims, can be gained by attempts to reconcile – to come up with a working hunch to explain – the dislocation that is highlighted by this kind of juxtaposition.

One of Shank's own uses of juxtaposition was to compare scientific research reports with medieval bestiaries. These are books where a whole mishmash of things – plants, animals, minerals – were described and classified, and moral and/or religious lessons drawn. For example, the nature of the hippopotamus was used to show the moral inferiority of sloth and laziness, while the nature of a lion was used to demonstrate the moral superiority of courage. In looking at the strengths and weaknesses as 'ways of knowing' of these two very different kinds of text, Shank was able to envision new and better ways of writing empirical reports.

As Shank himself acknowledges, such juxtapositioning of arbitrary and unusual ideas to gain insight is neither new nor uncommon. It is, for instance, frequently used in art – from movies to science fiction novels – and by market researchers to stimulate creative thinking. Rather, Shank makes the point that juxtaposition is an unusual research technique that has much to offer.

Blaikie uses the term 'abductive research' to describe the kind of interpretative approach Shank is promoting:

> Interpretativists argue that statistical patterns or correlations are not understandable on their own. It is necessary to find out what meanings (motives) people give to the actions that lead to such patterns. . . . For Interpretativism, the social world is the world interpreted and experienced by its members, from the 'inside'. Hence, the task of the Interpretative social scientist is to discover and describe this 'insider' view, not to impose an 'outsider' view on it. Interpretative social science seeks to discover why people do what they do by uncovering the largely tacit, mutual knowledge, the symbolic meanings, motives and rules, which provide the organization for their actions.
>
> (2000: 115)

Shank claims that 'we tend to see the world not in terms of truth, but in terms of significance. This means that we experience not a world of facts, but of signs' (Shank 1998: 856). And so, he argues, social psychologists should devise methods based upon semiotics – the study of signs, symbols and meaning. Shank recommends 'a semiotic strategy that uses an abductive focus' since this is 'general enough to address basic issues, while being sensitive enough to the complex and manifold issues of meaning' (Shank 1998: 853). The way critical social psychologists go about this is described and discussed in detail in Chapters 3 and 6.

Originally a branch of linguistics, **semiotics** was defined in that context as 'the science of the life of signs in society' (de Saussure 1974). As it is now utilized in fields like media studies (see Hodge and Kress 1988, for example), it has been adapted as an analytic – 'social semiotics'. It is used to gain insight into the ways in which meaning is produced, communicated and understood and, in particular, to scrutinize how meaning-making is deployed strategically.

Abduction in positivist research

What is interesting is that abduction is also present in the natural sciences. The scientific discoveries that really capture our attention are where a real breakthrough is made. Alexander Fleming's discovery of penicillin was just such a discovery. The story goes that he was preparing culture dishes of bacteria in order to be able to study the effects of various chemicals. One day he came into the laboratory, and noticed that one of them had gone mouldy. He was about to throw it away when he noticed something odd. Around the mould was a clear area. Strange, he thought, what is going on? He looked a little more carefully, and, sure enough, the mould seemed to be killing off the bacteria. The rest, as they say, is history – a history, for what its worth, in which countless lives have been saved by antibiotics.

Kuhn (1970) argued specifically that important scientific discoveries are not made through the incremental fine-tuning of knowledge through ever more meticulous hypothetico-deductive method, but through anomalies and surprises:

> Normal science . . . is a highly cumulative enterprise, eminently successful in its aim, the steady extension of the scope and precision of scientific knowledge. . . . Yet one standard product of the scientific enterprise is missing. Normal science does not aim for novelties of fact or theory and, when successful, finds none. New and unsuspected phenomena are, however, repeatedly uncovered by scientific research, and radical new theories have again and again been invented by scientists. History even suggests that the scientific enterprise has developed a uniquely powerful technique for producing surprises of this sort.
>
> (1970: 52–3)

What Kuhn is discussing here is a logic that is different from induction and deduction – abduction. Scientists use abduction in order to develop new theories. They look for the surprising and unusual, the data that do not fit, and they try to explain these anomalies. They develop hunches about why the anomalies have arisen, develop theories from those hunches, and then they use the hypothetico-deductive method to test out their theories. In Kuhn's terms, they 'learn to see nature in a different way' (Kuhn 1970: 53) and, thereby, they make progress in a way not possible by incremental 'normal' scientific method. In other words, the hypothetico-deductive method is only one part of the story. While necessary and useful, it is not necessarily the most interesting or even the most useful means to make major theoretical advances.

As you will see in Chapter 4, on quantitative research in social psychology, abduction goes on in social psychological experiments too. But that is a story for then, not now. It is, I think, a fascinating one.

We are now ready, at the end of this section, to put it all together and summarize the foundations of critical social psychology, in Table 2.4.

The foundations of critical social psychology

- Critical social psychology is based on an ontology in which there is seen to be no social world 'out there' in nature. It is socially constructed, through human meaning-making – through people's efforts to make sense of it and navigate and negotiate their selves and lives within it.

- Its epistemology is one where there are no 'facts' to be 'discovered', only socially constructed versions of reality, which are contingent on time, place and context.

- Social behaviour and phenomena like 'prejudice' are not real things. They are situated **social practices** which only make sense in the context of the time, the place and the circumstances in which they are acted out.

Critical Realist research:
- Views social actions and phenomena as produced by the prevailing social structures (such as structural inequality) and mechanisms (such as patriarchy) (even though it recognizes these labels are themselves socially constructed).

- Uses retroduction as the logic of inquiry most suited to identifying systematic regularities in social action or social phenomena, in order to gain insight and understanding of the structures and mechanisms that produce them.

Critical Relativist research:
- Considers there to be a multiplicity of dynamic and changing social realities.

- Specifically seeks to use abduction to pursue its research and theory development.

Abduction:
- Works by noticing or looking for surprises – inconsistencies, contradictions or anomalies – and then generating hypotheses to explain them.

- Provides a 'launch pad' for the generation of new theories.

- Is, according to Kuhn, an essential part of the scientific endeavour alongside the hypothetico-deductive method. It is how **paradigm shifts** are brought about.

Table 2.4 Foundations of critical social psychology

Dominant paradigm	Ontology	Epistemology	Logic of inquiry	Research aim
Postmodernism	The social world is socially constructed by human meaning-making, through people's efforts to make sense of it and navigate their selves and lives within it	Critical Realism	Retroduction	To gain insight into and understanding of how social realities are constructed and deployed through an analysis based on a particular theory
	Consistency and regularity arise from the rules and laws created by the culture/communities in which people live	Critical Relativism	Abduction	To discover how and why different social realities are constructed and deployed through identifying puzzles and solving them

Comparing and contrasting the two paradigms

As you have seen in this chapter, experimental and critical social psychology differ from each other in the two different underpinning paradigms and their ontological and epistemological foundations. Within each are different logics of inquiry reflecting different research aims. We can now bring together all four logics of inquiry into a single summary, as shown in Table 2.5.

Having looked at their foundations and principles, this last section is designed to help you gain a better understanding of the differences by addressing two key debates that are ongoing between experimental and critical social psychologists:

- Is it desirable – is it even possible – to be objective in the research social psychologists do?
- How should research in social psychology deal with complexity?

The ability to be and desirability of being objective

Experimental social psychology has one very important thing going for it – its agreement about what constitutes valid and reliable knowledge, and what kinds of research are appropriate for gaining it. Moreover, students doing a psychology degree are generally comprehensively trained in conducting hypothetico-deductive research. If you are one, then you will graduate with an understanding of, and skills in, quantitative methods in social psychology. You will feel confident that you know what you are doing and what is expected of you. Therefore, you are likely to succeed in a world where these standards are imposed as requirements for getting your conference paper accepted and your paper published.

Fundamentally all this works only if you are convinced that social psychology as a discipline and as a research endeavour *can* be objective. Indeed, it means signing up to the idea that objectivity

Table 2.5 The foundations of experimental and critical approaches to social psychology

Dominant paradigm	Ontology	Epistemology	Logic of inquiry	Research aim
Modernism	The social world exists 'out there' in nature, separate from human action. It consists of discrete and observable social events and phenomena that are lawfully related	Positivism	Induction	To develop universal laws of social behaviour and phenomena through systematically observing the social world and identifying systematic regularities in causes and effects
		Rationalism	Deduction	To develop universal laws of social behaviour and phenomena through deriving hypotheses from theory and testing them
Postmodernism	The social world is socially constructed by human meaning-making, through people's efforts to make sense of it and navigate their selves and lives within it. Consistency and regularity arise from the rules and laws created by the culture/communities in which people live	Critical Realism	Retroduction	To gain insight into and understanding of how social realities are constructed and deployed through an analysis based on a particular theory
		Critical Relativism	Abduction	To discover how and why different social realities are constructed and deployed through identifying puzzles and solving them

in social psychology is a 'good thing', an essential part of being a good social psychologist. For many students this works well, is no problem and is not really open to question.

Other students, however, are becoming more sceptical and suspicious. Student populations have changed a lot since the twentieth century (and were changing then), especially in those universities outside the elite, rich, exclusive and expensive few that tend to be populated by the better off and the better connected. Government policies have pushed for widening access to people who have not, traditionally, had opportunities for university education, including minority ethnic groups, students with disabilities, students coming from within the 'care' system and from families where nobody previously has gone to university.

Students like these – perhaps you are one of them – are much less likely to be convinced by claims that social psychology can be objective, or should even try to be. And that goes for students who are (or whose friends or parents or wider family members are) gay, lesbian, transsexual or transgender, or who have adopted an ideology or religion that does not favour the liberal humanistic values and principles of Modernism. A growing proportion of students, when they look at the traditional social psychological studies conducted in the twentieth century, find less and less they can identify with or that they can relate to their own feelings, lifeworlds and experiences. They do not feel very 'objective' at all, more like stories about other people's lives. Not surprisingly they (you?) turn to see what critical social psychology can offer.

Critical social psychologists have found sophisticated and clever ways to study meaning. But in denying the possibility of objectivity, critical social psychologists do make themselves vulnerable to the accusation that this approach is 'politics by other means' – highly subjective and biased, more hot polemic than cool, considered scholarship. Indeed, with the retroductive strategy, social psychological research is intentionally informed by an explicitly ideological standpoint – be that feminism, **queer theory** or **crip theory** or postcolonial theory or something else.

It remains the case that, however clever and convincing the analyses and interpretations of their data, they are still (and self-admittedly) anything but objective accounts. For a long time this led to critically informed research (mainly using qualitative methods) being either rejected or ignored by the social psychology establishment and its journals and funders. A telling example of this sort of response is an anonymous extract from a letter sent to Kerry Chamberlain, a critical health psychologist, in response to a request for advice about whether or not it was worth submitting a paper based on a qualitative study to a mainstream health psychology journal:

> Although I will not preclude you from submitting this article for review for possible publication in our journal, I must say that for several reasons I do not feel that its chances of acceptance after being sent to expert reviewers would be very good. First, although our readership is open to qualitative research methods, [journal name] is an empirical journal primarily interested in scientific issues relating to health and behavior. This in my view does not negate qualitative or other descriptive methods, but for this journal such methods should be in the interest of an empirical, scientific approach to problems. Secondly, although I realize that the methods you describe are often widely used in medical sociology and seldom (if at all) used in health psychology, this is for good reasons which have to do with the difference in methods, emphasis, and assumptions of these two disciplines.
>
> (Chamberlain 2000: 286)

Slowly this is changing (for a fuller account, see Stainton Rogers and Willig 2009). What matters now is that critical psychologists need to be clear that they are not bounded by the methodological requirements attached to research that claims to be objective. Rather researchers 'must be free to develop and apply methods that are appropriate for finding answers to the research questions under consideration, and they should not be constrained in a methodological straitjacket' (Chamberlain 2000: 289).

Potter and Wetherell (1987) described learning to do discourse analysis (see Chapter 5) as a bit like learning to ride a bicycle. It is hard to do, needs a lot of practice and, as it is difficult to explain, you get more out of doing it than following more than the barest of instructions. As you work through Chapter 5 on qualitative methods in social psychology you will begin to see why this is so. There are not the same hard and fast rules about what constitutes the 'proper' way to use a method, or even any automatic link between particular research topics and questions and a particular method. This is not to say there are no standards for making sure that critical research is of good quality – there are, as you will see. But once critical researchers face up to the inevitable lack of objectivity in their research, then life gets a lot more complicated. Research, especially its analytic stages, has to be reported by way of a clearly argued case for why *these* data can be meaningfully read in *this* way, to come up with *these* conclusions.

Dealing with complexity

Experimental and critical approaches to social psychology have very different goals in what they are seeking to achieve. But I also think it is interesting to observe that they deal with complexity in very different ways. Experimental social psychologists want to be able to **explain** the various social processes and phenomena that they study. Critical social psychologists have a more minimal agenda – they want to **explicate** 'what is going on' in relation to the topics and issues that they study. The difference is profound.

Smoothing it out

Experimental social psychology seeks to produce explanations about the general laws that govern psychological processes and phenomena, and to develop these through the gradual refinement of theory using the hypothetico-deductive method. Explanation provides a cause-and-effect account of how and why something happens. 'Explanation' originates from the Latin word for 'levelling out' and it is appropriate here. Complexity is dealt with by ironing it out – getting rid of everything extraneous and then working on just a limited, specified set of variables. That is just what experimental method does.

As you will see in Chapter 3, experimental method is all about taking a phenomenon – such as the incident where Kitty Genovese was attacked in front of witnesses, with which I began Chapter 1 – and using it to inspire experiments to explain why situations like this occur, why those witnesses did not get involved. As you will see as the story and its aftermath are gradually scrutinized in later chapters in this book, this incident led to a whole programme of experimental research into what its main instigators, John Darley and Bibb Latané (1968) called the 'bystander effect'. To design their experiments they stripped the incident of almost all of its highly complicated context (what happened in the early hours of the morning in New York, involving a white woman and a black man, and a whole series of events drawn out over time and in several locations). The experiments were conducted in small booths or rooms, with heavy control over contact between the subject and other people. They consisted of tightly scripted and controlled events and simple manipulation of small numbers and forms of interaction. There were precisely none, one or more other people in the room. Also varied in some of the more complex designs was the extent to which subjects were able to see/hear or be seen/heard by the other person/people. Almost all of the subjects were college students at universities in the USA. In other words, a great deal of smoothing out and simplifying went on, with the only data recorded *as data* being whether or not the subject responded to a staged 'emergency', and the time they took to respond.

This allowed Darley and Latané and their followers to arrive at very detailed and clear explanations of why the presence of other bystanders affects the likelihood of a person helping another in trouble, or reacting to a potential emergency.

Unfolding

Based on the assumption that knowledge is inevitably contingent, critical social psychology seeks to produce **idiographic** (that is specific to particular instances) explications. An explication does not seek to account for cause and effect. Rather it provides a teasing out. 'Explication' is also based on a Latin word, this time for unfolding, developing or laying open. The metaphor here is an origami of, say, a bird in flight. If you smoothed out the paper you would lose the very elements that make it what it is. To see 'what is going on' requires a gentler touch, a sequence of unfolding small bits, a peeking in and putting back, always maintaining the integrity of what you are looking at.

Explication teases out the particular social and cultural conventions that govern social interaction in particular circumstances, and that mediate the ways that people make and interpret meaning and significance in particular situations. In Chapter 11 you will be introduced to a critical social psychology reappraisal of the 'bystander effect' in general, and the Kitty Genovese story in particular, carried out by Frances Cherry. She based her explication on a close analysis of a variety of documents relating to what happened the night Kitty was murdered, including newspaper accounts and feminist critiques, and informed by the literature on violence by men towards women, rape in particular (Cherry 1995). Metaphorically we see, as her argument is unfurled, an unfolding, a teasing out, of what 'was going on'.

Methodologically critical social psychology deals with complexity in two main ways. The retroductive approach reduces complexity by framing interpretation from an already identified conceptual framework (such as feminist theory, as used by Cherry). The abductive approach reduces complexity by ignoring the expected and already understood, and focusing just on identifying and then explicating anomalies and surprises. An example here is the way Giles et al. (2007) used a **grounded theory** approach to 'unpick' the personal meanings that people's record collections have for them, and their music downloads. They recorded interviews with people into this sort of thing and from close analyses of these discovered that people's record collections have more 'symbolic' meanings, whereas downloading music was much more pragmatic. You will find out more about this and other explicatory studies in Chapter 5.

Which is best?

I am making no secret about my own position – I see myself and am known as a critical psychologist. I have no doubt my position is evident in the way I have written this book. But I also hope to convey my recognition that social psychology needs to be understood in terms of both experimental and critical approaches.

Deciding which approach is 'best' is in part about deciding what you think matters most – objectivity or the ability to deal with meaning. Crucially, it involves deciding whether you believe that objectivity is ever possible. This difference leads to a host of other ways in which these two paradigms are different. Instead of a summary box, I have summarized the main differences between the two paradigms in Table 2.6 at the end of this section.

However, I hope that this chapter has shown that at a more pragmatic level there are actually some important commonalties between the two. In particular the growing interest in abduction has the potential for more informed dialogue and debate between experimental and critical social psychologists. This is not going to lead to any resolution of the conflict over epistemology and ontology – the two positions are mutually exclusive. But maybe it will lead to an acknowledgement that we are engaged in the same enterprise, and debate can move away from mutual derision and name-calling to a more informed discussion.

Table 2.6 The main differences between experimental and critical social psychology

Experimental social psychology	Critical social psychology
Operates within modernism	Operates within postmodernism
Views the social world as 'out there' external to and separate from people	Views the social world as made *by* people
Asserts there is only one true, objective knowledge that transcends time and cultural location	Accepts that there are multiple knowledges, and that knowledge is highly contingent on time and cultural location
Views knowledge as based on facts that are 'out-there-in-the-world' waiting to be discovered	Views these knowledges as constructed through people's meaning-making
Asks of knowledge 'is it true?'	Asks of knowledge 'what does it do?', 'how can it be used – by whom, and to what ends?', 'whose interest does it serve?', 'what does it make possible?'
Seeks to gain knowledge through induction, but primarily through hypothetico-deductive testing of theory	Seeks to gain knowledge through retroductive interpretation and abduction
In research deals with complexity by 'smoothing it out' using experimental methods	In research deals with complexity by 'teasing it out' using a wide range of interpretative strategies
Seeks to provide cause-and-effect explanations	Seeks to provide explications that offer insight into specific social events and phenomena
Seeks to be and views itself as objective, dispassionate and apolitical	Is motivated by seeking to understand how power is being exercised and resisted, and often is explicitly political
Has a long tradition and established standards of what constitutes valid research	Is relatively new and as yet is only beginning to establish standards of what constitutes valid research

Resources

European Association of Social Psychology: http://www.easp.eu/

Access to materials from the Open University's social psychology course, with short videos on a range of definitions and a fair amount about ontology: http://www.sciencelive.org/component/option,com_mediadb/task,view/idstr,Open-podcast-feeds_dd307_social_psychology_rss2_xml/Itemid,98

This gives access to a free download of the critical psychology text: Ibáñez, T. and Íñiguez, L. (eds) (1997) *Critical Social Psychology*. London: Sage: http://www.ebook3000.com/Critical-Social-Psychology_49291.html

Further reading

Research strategies

Blaikie, N. (2010) *Designing Social Research: The Logic of Anticipation*, **2nd edn. Cambridge: Polity.**

This book is not (simply) a 'how to do it manual' – though it does offer detailed and relatively comprehensive (if a bit quirky) advice and information on all stages of the research processes used in social psychology. It is unusual in two ways. First, it covers both Scientific and social constructionist approaches to research. Second, it really tries to get to grips with the underlying philosophical issues. In relation to this chapter, his Chapter 4 'Strategies for answering research questions' is worth reading – but note that he takes a contentious line on abduction. In my view, Shank's (1998) article (see below) is both more accurate and easier to follow.

Classic texts

There are two classic texts that you should consult if you want to really get to grips with the basis of scientific method. These are:

Kuhn, T.S. (1970) *The Structure of Scientific Revolutions.* **Chicago, IL: University of Chicago Press.**
Popper, K. (1959) *The Logic of Scientific Discovery.* **New York: Basic Books.**

Experimental social psychology

Hogg, M.A. and Vaughan, G.M. (2007) *Social Psychology*, **5th edn. Hemel Hempstead: Prentice Hall.**

You will find Chapter 1 of this book particularly helpful if the basis of Scientific method as adopted by psychology is unfamiliar to you. It contains a comprehensive section on Scientific method on pages 7–16, which clearly explains its foundations, its goals and its various forms. Overall this first chapter is an excellent exposition of experimental social psychology, including a short critique of critical social psychological approaches.

Critical social psychology

Basic texts

Gough, B. and McFadden, M. (2001) *Critical Social Psychology: An Introduction.* **Basingstoke: Palgrave.**

Chapter 2 of this text presents a mixture of some of the history we covered in Chapter 1 and a critique of experimental social psychology that is more polemical and goes into a lot more detail than I can here.

Burr, V. (1995) *An Introduction to Social Constructionism.* **London: Routledge.**

This 'does what it says on the tin' – it introduces social constructionism in a very detailed and well-informed manner, yet it is also clear and readable, which is what you want when you get started.

Background texts

Henriques, J., Hollway, W., Urwin, C., Venn, C. and Walkerdine, V. (1984) *Changing the Subject: Psychology, Social Regulation and Subjectivity.* **London: Methuen.**

This is the book that changed everything and, as such, you will need to read sooner or later if you are planning to adopt a critical approach to psychology. As time passes it becomes more of a historical document, so to begin with you may want something more up to date (see above).

Curt, B. (1994) *Textuality and Tectonics: Troubling Social and Psychological Science.* **Buckingham: Open University Press.**

Not always easy to get hold of these days, and not an easy read, but generally seen as great fun. Beryl played a significant role in the creation of critical social psychology, and this book offers her own quirky take on it. I must own up to being a 'bit of Beryl' (indeed, I edited the book, comprised as it is of the writings of several amanuenses [look it up] who worked together to make Beryl's book possible). Seriously, this is not at all the first book I would suggest you get started on, but if you like the quirky, it is worth tracking down.

Abduction

Shank, G. (1998) The extraordinary ordinary powers of abductive reasoning, *Theory and Psychology,* **8(6): 841–60.**

This is the best entrée I have found into the use of abduction in social psychology. It is clearly written and, while the ideas expressed are complicated, you should be able to get a reasonably good understanding of what abduction is and its potential from this article.

Questions

1 What are the main ontological and epistemological assumptions on which scientific method is based? How do these differ from those on which critical social psychology is based?

2 Compare and contrast the approaches taken by experimental and critical social psychology to research.

3 What are the common assumptions about ontology shared by critical realism and critical relativism? How do they differ in their epistemological approaches?

4 Define induction, deduction, retroduction and abduction, and explain the main differences between them.

5 If Sherlock Holmes had been a social psychologist, what kind of social psychologist do you think he would have been? Explain the reasons for your answer. (Hint: Garry Shank's paper is very useful for answering this question.)

3

An introduction to critical social psychology

LEARNING OUTCOMES

When you have finished studying this chapter, you should be able to:

1 Outline the key features of *personal construct theory* and the *social representations approach*, and explain why they were staging-posts on the way to critical social psychology.

2 Explain why power is such an important an issue for critical social psychology, and how this is evident in the different approaches to this field taken in different parts of the world.

3 Define what is meant by the 'psy complex', the 'micro-politics of power', 'subject positioning' and 'resistance' and be able to give an example of each one.

4 List and explain five key goals of critical psychology.

5 Outline the key features of community psychology, its origins in both North and South America, and its main principles.

6 Explain what is meant by 'liberation psychology', 'social intervention' and 'quality of life' in the context of community psychology.

7 Set out the arguments for critical social psychology being based on certain ideological standpoints, as well as some of the risks this poses.

8   Explain how postcolonial theory contributes to critical social psychology, and the new strategies it brings to the subject.

9   Say why critical social psychology can be seen as 'adventurous' and why this should be so.

10   Briefly describe the approach taken by social psychoanalytic psychology, and how it differs from traditional social psychology.

Introduction

This chapter provides a broad introduction to critical psychology as a whole, within which critical *social* psychology has been developed alongside other branches – such as community psychology, critical developmental psychology and critical health psychology (all of which draw upon social psychology).

Right from the start you should know that critical psychology is not some systematically organized subdiscipline. Nor is it promoted or practised by a coherent group of people acting as a warm and cuddly collective of like-minded movers and shakers. As an approach, it is made up of a loose affiliation of ideas, challenges, and arguments. As a group, critical social psychologists share some common goals but have a vast range of different ways of being 'critical' about psychology. It is not possible to squeeze all this into a single chapter but what I can do is give you a partial summary and an overall sense of what it is all about. My aim is to provide an interesting and alluring 'taster' to get you started. As you move through the remainder of the book you will then be able to learn more, as the various topics of mainstream social psychology are first set out for you, and then exposed to various forms of criticality.

You have already had a broad introduction to critical psychology in Chapters 1 and 2, though much of this was in an abstract form. Here we get down to detail and, specifically, to examining how it 'works' and what it 'says' in relation to social psychology.

This chapter begins by considering two recent social psychological approaches – personal construct theory and social representations – that have been important staging posts towards critical social psychology. Indeed, the social representations approach is currently being modified and opened for use within a critical psychology approach (see Campbell and Jovchelovitch 2000, for a good example). Then there is a section on power, in my view an absolutely essential starting point for understanding where critical social psychology is coming from. This looks, in particular, at the unique role psychology has played, both as an academic discipline and as a series of practices, in exercising power – for example, to define what is 'normal' and what is 'deviant' (and hence in need of control or treatment). This has been most obvious in countries like Brazil and South Africa where psychologists have been at the front line of both engagement in oppressive uses of power and resistance against it. But, as you will see, psychologists (most notably Michel Foucault, to the extent he was a psychologist) have also been involved in creating critical theories about the way power is not some massive force, but a 'dense network' that is woven into our daily lives, our relationships, our hopes, desires and fears.

The final section is where things get rather brief, and selective. It is based on three of critical social psychology's main goals – to change the world for the better (looking particularly at community psychology); to promote social justice (looking particularly at postcolonial psychology); and to go places and do things other kinds of psychology cannot (looking particularly at social psychoanalytic psychology). Together with what you have learned from the previous chapter, this should give you a broad overview of the underpinning foundations of critical social psychology, an in-depth understanding of its overarching theory and knowledge-base, and a real sense of its aspirations an intentions.

Starting points for critical social psychology

This section mainly concentrates on two approaches that diverged from the dominant mainstream of experimental social psychology in the 1960s and 1970s – personal construct theory and the theory of social representations. You have already met both of these, briefly, in Chapter 1. What I want to show you here is that critical social psychology did not just get made because people like Ken Gergen, Ian Parker and Valerie Walkerdine went off and read a lot of philosophy and sociology and other work from outside the discipline (though their doing so was massively productive). It also got built on the achievements of social psychologists who also wanted to put a more human face on their discipline, and found ways to acknowledge issues of power and representation.

Personal construct theory

George Kelly's (1966) **personal construct theory** (PCT) portrays people as 'naïve scientists' who approach life by constructing a set of working hypotheses about what is going on and what is likely to happen, in order to plan how to proceed. These 'hypotheses' (hunches or 'working theories' are probably better terms, more true to Kelly's intentions) are continually being tested against what actually happens, and are then modified and refined. Operating in this manner allows people to live their lives in a functional, self-aware manner, having **agency** and being able to take action. In this way they can tackle the complex demands of living in society, making decisions, planning action and understanding their own actions and emotions, and the actions and emotions of others.

Transforming the subject

What is particularly important here is the shift in the image of the person – certainly a step on the road to criticality (see Chapter 1). Personal construct theory was devised to challenge the way people had come to be seen by psychologists in terms of the innate, biological instincts and drives that determine their behaviour, and the ways their behaviour is moulded by social and cultural forces. This image is of a person lacking in agency, a passive puppet without free will. Kelly (like William James before him) wanted to build a social psychology that treated people as self-aware, self-conscious and self-determined, who actively and purposively make sense of the world in a connected manner and, crucially, have the capacity for free will.

In using this image of person-as-scientist, Kelly was careful to say that this is just one aspect of many forms of what he called 'constructive alternativism' that, he claimed, occur within an individual's understanding of the social world. His followers (see, for example, Swift et al. 1983) have argued that Kelly's notion of 'scientist' has often been misinterpreted as an entirely rationalizing, unemotional image. Kelly, they argue, chose the term for its liberating properties – its ability to overcome the dehumanizing 'person-as-passive-organism' image.

In personal construct theory the uniqueness of each new event is made understandable by comparing it with the appropriate construct(s). Kelly and his followers have drawn up a list of descriptions as to what these are like, and how they operate, which they term **corollaries**:

- The commonality corollary states that people can and do experience the world in similar ways, to the extent that their construct systems are similar.
- The sociality corollary states that people have access to each other's construct systems, which enables them to 'inhabit each other's worlds' even where they are very different.
- The fragmentation corollary states that there are sometimes constructs that contradict one another.

These different aspects of personal constructs are held to be crucial to allow people to operate effectively within a social world. An individual's competence as a social being depends upon how predictive their constructs are, and how appropriately they are applied. Thus, while personal constructs have a lot in common with schemata from cognitive psychology, the theorization transcends some of the limitations of schema theory. It portrays people as more sophisticated, as sometimes confused and indecisive, as sharing common understandings and as able to empathize with and understand each other.

But only halfway there

If you recall from Chapter 1, the turn to criticality involves both a postmodern ontology (seeing the social world like music making, constructed through people actively creating it) and a postmodern epistemology (viewing knowledge also as a human product, socially constructed through people's meaning making). Look back at Table 2.4 in Chapter 2, which helps to put this in context.

Chiari and Nuzzo (1996) argue that Kelly's version of personal construct theory was based upon **epistemological constructivism**, that is, on a mix of modernist ontology (there is a real world out there separate from human endeavours) with postmodern epistemology. In other words, it was a hybrid with one foot in modernism and the other in postmodernism. Domenici (2008), taking a lead from Chiari and Nuzzo's later work, has more recently argued that personal construct theory can be converted to a hermeneutic constructivist approach:

> One of the basic assumptions of a hermeneutic constructivist framework is that experience emerges through an interdependence of subject and object that transcends both (Chiari & Nuzzo, 2000, 2004). In other words, reality is not something 'out there' that is separate from our experience and construction of it. Rather than detached construers of the world, we are embedded participants in the world, always in relationship with it.

> (Domenici 2008: 27)

Why personal construct theory is not fully 'critical'

I am not entirely convinced. I think personal construct theory is ultimately limited in three main ways. First, it is primarily a *personal* construct theory. Although its commonality corollary states that people can and do experience the world in similar ways, personal construct theory emphasizes the 'personal'. In stressing the uniqueness of each individual construct system, it actually has very little to say about the ways in which people may construct and negotiate meanings collectively, or how shared understandings operate within the medium of culture (as, say, semiotic theory does). Personal construct theory does not deal in any depth, for example, with social processes, such as the influence of social control and the construction of knowledge by powerful groups, which is then foisted upon the less powerful. Basically, it is an individualizing approach, which reifies the individual 'subject' (Henriques et al. 1984). If you recall from Chapter 1, psychological social psychology is inherently individuo-focused, and personal construct theory is an illustration of this.

Second, although Kelly himself argued that theories (including his own) should be treated as aids to understanding rather than as dogmatic assertions that they are (or ever can be) descriptions of what really is, his focus on construct bipolarity is highly specific and open to question. There are arguments for suggesting people's understanding of concepts cannot be understood just in terms of bipolar opposites. For instance, while 'good' makes sense as a concept because it is in opposition to 'bad', it also gains meaning in relation to concepts like 'fresh', 'virtuous' and 'valuable'. Terms like 'bad' and 'wicked' are even more slippery, as they can be applied in some contexts very positively – think of the term 'naughty but nice' to describe cream cakes! The constraints imposed by bipolarity are a serious problem for any theory that seeks to represent the full complexity and sophistication of human thinking.

Third, the assertion that people can only determine the accuracy of their constructs by acting upon them and thus testing them out can lead to some rather nonsensical implications. Wiggins et al. (1971) provide a telling illustration of the limitations of personal construct theory by considering how it would predict how parents deal with their children's crying. Personal construct theory predicts that when their child cries, parents would test out one of their constructs – say by giving the child sweets to see if that shuts them up. If the child was violently sick, they would need to try something else. But any parent will tell you this is not what they do. People do not simply choose between alternative constructs within their own cognitive system. Anybody who has ever cared for a sick child knows the enormous amount of effort you have to put into working out what the possible reasons for a child crying may be, and then deciding what to do about it. Dealing with a crying child is much more than an analytic search within individual thought. It is an active, insightful, search after meaning which will draw upon advice from others as well as one's own store of common-sense knowledge gained through a access to everything from 'supernanny' television programmes to Internet chat rooms, helpful leaflets from the hospital or what granny thinks best.

You will find work still being done using personal construct theory techniques, however. *The Journal of Constructivist Research*, where most of this work is now published, is still going strong, with much work done in applied areas like forensic psychology, counselling (Moradi et al. 2009) and sports psychology.

Personal construct theory

- Personal construct theory was devised by George Kelly.

- It portrays people as 'naïve scientists' who approach life by constructing a set of working hypotheses in order to decide what to do.

- The uniqueness of each new event is made understandable by personal constructs that are derived from one's own personal experience. It recognizes that people will share many constructs since they have been socialized in similar ways, and that people have access to (and can take account of) each other's constructs.

- Critics of personal construct theory point out that there are many other ways in which people learn about and make sense of the world, and do not rely just on their own experience.

- Some researchers continue to use personal construct theory techniques, mainly in applied areas.

Social representations

Again, you were briefly introduced to the **social representations** approach in Chapter 1. If you recall, it was devised by Serge Moscovici and it was his *La Psychanalyse, Son Image et Son Public* (Moscovici [1961] 1976) that first brought this approach to the attention of social psychologists. Interestingly it took until 2008 before an English translation of this text was published (Moscovici 2008). In this ground-breaking work Moscovici explored how psychoanalytic concepts (like 'complex'), which were once only known within the highly specialized world of psychoanalysts, were taken up by ordinary people in their everyday conversations – even cartoon characters, these days, can end up with a complex! These concepts then became, over time, 'what everybody knows'.

Origins and history

Ivana Marková, one of Moscovici's long-time friends and colleagues, argues that in order to understand the revolutionary nature of this new approach, it is necessary to know something of the history of that time (the 1950s and 1960s) and place (France):

> American social psychology had exported, more or less successfully, the experimental model prevalent in general psychology. It had also exported empirical, largely behaviouristic concepts dominant at the time. It followed the established Newtonian thinking of mechanistic physics: searching for universally valid laws of social behaviour, decomposing complex social phenomena into small elements in order to make them intelligible, looking for causal relationships between elements and postulating categories into which events and processes could be placed.
>
> (Marková 2008: 465)

In a social psychology dominated by this dogma, she comments, what amounted to a paradigm shift was not welcome. But slowly things changed. According to Marková, the optimism of the

1950s that had followed the end of the Second World War was replaced in the 1960s by pessimism and a sense of crisis. Founding fathers of experimental social psychology, like Festinger, were becoming highly disillusioned, complaining that social psychology 'instead of creating powerful and real conditions in the laboratory' had got itself sidetracked in dreaming up 'hypothetical situations [in] questionnaires' and turning 'to cognitive information processing' (Festinger 1980: 250). By the early 1970s theorists like Harré and Secord (1972) were in outright revolt, rejecting experimental social psychology's mechanistic models and logical-positivist methods. Instead they proposed that social psychologists should be inspired by the new physics, with ideas about agency, and should adopt a new image of personhood.

It is within this period that Moscovici developed his ideas about social representations theory. However, while his inspiration is usually attributed to Durkheim (see later), he himself tells a different story (Moscovici 2003). He says he was first inspired by reading Lenoble's essay on the philosophy of sciences, the *Essay on the Concept of Experience*, published in Paris in 1943. It provided him with the concept he was searching for to describe his own experience of social knowledge. Here is the relevant piece:

> There is no common sense, but as many common senses as there are civilizations. The common sense of the European, popularizing philosophy and the mechanical sciences, and Christian morality, is not that of the Asian or the Negro of Africa; the common sense of the French of the twentieth century differs deeply from that of the French from the eighteenth century. Carried by language, like language itself and all collective representations, it expresses the intermediate, the average: common sense wakes up thought in them who do not think; it overpowers thought in them who do think.
>
> (Lenoble 1943, cited in Moscovici 2003 trans. by Jodolet 2008)

Moscovici, reflecting upon how he responded to reading this, writes: 'You don't know how you know, but, in one instant, the generic image . . . knew its concept. "Collective representations" was only a term, but it was enough to direct my readings, my interpretation of research material and even the very idea that I had of social psychology' (Moscovici 2003, translated by Jodolet 2008: 212).

Jodolet (2008) suggests that social representations theory went through four distinct stages of development. The first ten years were, she says, its latency period, with some consolidation going on but with little impact in an environment hostile to its implications and wary of its focus on 'common sense'. This was regarded as too close for comfort to the perceived dogma and doctrine of what Jodolet calls 'theories of suspicion' such as Marxism and psychoanalysis. In the second phase, starting at the end of the 1960s, things got better, at least in France, with a higher take-up of social representations theory and, especially, interest in the concept of 'representation'. The third phase was marked by a conference in 1979, led by Moscovici and Farr from England and in 1984 the publication in English of the book, *Social Representations* (Farr and Moscovici 1984). During this period social representations theory and research were taken up by more and more social psychologists, especially in Europe and South America (probably because a high proportion of psychologists from South America study for their PhDs in Spain and Portugal).

Jodolet defines the fourth stage as the 'domain in expansion' for social representations research and theory, as it came into its own within social psychology: 'At a time of strong crisis in social psychology, the theory of social representation appeared as one of the major alternative trends to rethink the discipline together with ethogenic psychology, social constructionism, discursive social psychology, and critical psychology' (Jodolet 2008: 414).

Moscovici himself, writing with Marková, also looks back at that time as a period when social psychology was being opened up from within by those dissatisfied with the straitjacket imposed by experimental method, influenced by what was happening in the social and human sciences (such as anthropology and sociology) outside of the discipline: 'Although the experimental method seemed to work and the arguments in its favour were impeccable, it stood at variance with [the] shared epistemology of most social scientists and even psychologists. That is, they did not accept the view that one could study complex social phenomena in the laboratory. (Moscovici and Marková 2006: 258)

Is social representations work critical psychology?

Parker (1989) has criticized social representation theory as based on positivist and functionalist foundations.

> Because the 'representations' are imagined to operate inside the individual's head they are, effectively, 'individual'. So, for all the talk of finding a more 'social' interdisciplinary social psychology, Durkheim's original prescription for a division of labour between sociology and psychology are followed, and the social/individual dualism is reinforced.
>
> (Parker 1989: 98)

Potter and Wetherell (1987) have another more basic criticism, which is that Moscovici's writings were fragmented and contradictory, and his followers have interpreted them in different ways, so it is hard to say where Moscovici stands. Personally I think this does not matter. There are some who have adopted the language of social representations, but appropriated it back into hypothetico-deductive research. There are others who have moved, wholesale, into a critical social psychology approach where, often, research interplays elements of social representations and discursive theory and analysis.

Social representations as a form of critical social psychology

Either way the concept of social representation has had a very substantial impact upon social psychology. This has been, I believe, because of its usefulness as a concept rather than an articulated theory. It offers social psychologists a framework for sophisticated theorization about the social production and manipulation of knowledge, and how this may influence and be influenced by individual thinking. As such it provides a way to span the gap between traditional social psychology's preoccupation with subjectivity and critical psychology's interest in intersubjectivity.

Moscovici drew social psychologists' attention to the way that people make sense of the world as much within the 'unceasing babble and . . . permanent dialogue between individuals' (Moscovici 1985: 18) as within individual minds. Social representations theory is semiotic in all but name, stressing the importance of shared understandings, both as a medium for communication between people and a basis for social groups to share a social world. Moscovici has claimed that it is the sharing of common social representations among a number of people that *makes* them a cohesive social group rather than a collection of individuals. In this he was going a step beyond experimental social psychology's concepts like cohesiveness and social norms (see Chapter 8) and arguing that the boundaries between one social group and another can be identified by finding out where the influence of their different social representations begin and end.

Moscovici has speculated extensively about the ways that the knowledge and images that constitute the social representations of one group get to be taken up and incorporated into the social representations of another, and changed in the process. In particular, he has been interested in the ways that the common-sense representations of 'ordinary people' take into their discourse – and in so doing distort – expert knowledge (for example, scientific knowledge). Common themes with Bartlett's ideas (see Chapter 1) can be discerned, where the adoption of knowledge from one group by another consists of processes of oversimplification, of categorization and of rationalizing. In his own earliest work (Moscovici [1961] 1976) explored the way psychodynamic concepts (for example, 'complex') were taken from the domain of professional psychiatry into the discourse of everyday life. A later example of his work (Moscovici and Hewstone 1983) was about the way ideas of brain lateralization have been taken up and popularized. As a result they have now been recast as a full-blown theory about our 'intuitive' right side and 'analytic' left.

Social representations of health and illness

An example to help you get to grips with what is involved in social representations research is a classic and well-known study conducted by Claudine Herzlich on people's social representations of health and illness. It was published in French in the 1960s but translated into English only in the 1970s (Herzlich 1973). For her original study, Herzlich carried out a large number of interviews with predominantly middle-class Parisians (and a few country dwellers) which focused on health and illness. From the lengthy conversations she had with these people, she developed sophisticated descriptions of the social representations for health and illness that she saw as in use at that time in French society.

Influenced by Foucault's theories and Moscovici's work on social representations of mental illness being done concurrently (Moscovici [1961] 1976), she regarded these social representations as operating both subjectively and intersubjectively. That is, she saw them in use at both the level of individual thinking and at the level of discourses functioning at an intersubjective level, including conversations, medical consultations and treatment, in the mass media and in public education campaigns. Herzlich concluded that different understandings and explanations for health and illness are not polar opposites to each other, but quite discrete alternative conceptions. She demonstrated that individuals have access to multiple conceptions of what illness is, means and signifies, coexisting with formulations of different concepts of health.

Social representations of health

Herzlich identified these as health-in-a-vacuum, reserve of health and equilibrium:

- **Health-in-a-vacuum** was the term Herzlich used for the notion of health as the absence of illness, of a lack of awareness of the body, and/or simply not being bothered by it, essentially a state of 'bodily silence'.
- **Reserve of health** represents health as an asset or investment rather than a state. It has two main aspects: physical robustness or strength, and resistance to attacks, fatigue and illness. In

this social representation, health is something that you 'have' that enables you to perform your job, fulfil your social obligations, defend yourself against disease and recover from illness.

- **Equilibrium**. The people in the study described equilibrium as 'real health' or 'health in its highest sense'. It carried the notion of positive well-being in addition to a sense of balance and harmony. Herzlich commented that although her respondents used the term 'equilibrium' frequently in their conversations, they found it hard to pin down. Overall it seemed to carry a two-level meaning: a substratum of essential harmony and balance in bodily, psychological and spiritual life – that then provides the basis for a functional sense of self-confidence, alertness, freedom, energy and indefatigability. Thus, it had both a psychological reality concerned with self-perception and a bodily reality to do with physical capability and resilience.

Social representations of illness

Herzlich's respondents distinguished between four different classes of illness: serious illnesses which may be fatal; chronic conditions; everyday, trivial illnesses like colds and flu; and childhood ailments. They also referred frequently to intermediary states between 'real' illness and 'real' health: 'There are the little troubles, the little situations of discomfort which you have more or less all the year round, headaches, the after-effects of alcohol, digestive difficulties, fatigue' (Herzlich 1973: 54).

Herzlich identified three main metaphors for illness:

1 *Illness as destroyer*. The focus here is on the way illness can limit our ability to carry out our duties and responsibilities, and the loss of social position and subsequent social isolation we may suffer as a consequence.

2 *Illness as liberator*. This, in contrast, is a metaphor that stresses the capacity of illness to free us from our responsibilities or the pressures that life places upon us: 'When I'm very tired, I often wish I were ill . . . illness is a kind of rest, when you can be free from your everyday burdens. . . . For me, illness is breaking off from social life, from life outside and social obligations, it's being set free' (Herzlich 1973: 114).

3 *Illness as occupation*. This metaphor is based on the assumption that when you are ill, you should see illness as a challenge – as something that you must fight with all the powers you have. It stresses that an enormous amount of strength and willpower are needed to focus all your energies on recovery. You must not worry about your other responsibilities, but concentrate on getting better.

Social representations do not mark identity

Although these three descriptions tend to read as though people could be classified according to holding one or other perception, Herzlich was at pains to point out that only some individuals tended to utilize a single representation consistently. Most people drew upon two or all three at different times in their interviews, offering complex understandings and explanations woven out of them all. This is an important distinction between attitude theory and social representations theory. Attitude theory assumes that people have a single attitude – that, for example, they are strongly racist, full stop. Social representations can be used singly or in concert to, for example, make sense of illness and respond to it. But they also affect the way people see themselves and made sense of their own identity generally, even when they are well. They are, Herzlich concluded, particularly salient when people are in intermediate states between being ill and being well. Social representations thus act as resources that a person can use in different ways in different situations and in different bodily states.

Social representations of female orgasm

A more up-to-date example of recent social representations work which was carried out and interpreted within a critical social psychology perspective is a study conducted by Maya Lavie-Ajayi and Hélène Joffe on women's knowledge and beliefs about female orgasm.

In it they interviewed 50 women, and conducted a media analysis of representations in women's magazines. One of the dominant social representations they found was the assumption that 'orgasm is the goal-of-sex' – that to have sex but not reach orgasm is a failure. This 'common knowledge' was found particularly in media accounts, like this one from *Cosmopolitan*:

> Because our orgasm involves so much more than simply rubbing this or poking that. Sexual ecstasy for women is circular, lyrical and spherical. It's an expression of mind, body, heart, soul and spirit. It is a celebration of self . . . women demanding pleasure instead of faking it. Women masturbating to orgasm. Women taking charge of their sexuality. (Cosmopolitan, 1997)
>
> (As quoted in Lavie-Ajayi and Joffe 2009: 101)

As Lavie-Ajay and Joffe point out, orgasm is portrayed here as synonymous not just with stimulation and sensation (rubbing this or poking that) but of everything a woman can be (mind, body, heart, soul and spirit), as a right and a responsibility to herself. No pressure there, then! '"I sometimes think, when I listen to things on the radio or women's magazines, that there is a feeling of having to achieve an orgasm. It is a performance and you have got to do well" (Renee, 65, P)' (as quoted in Lavie-Ajayi and Joffe 2009: 102).

The paper goes on to explore the tension between orgasm as the goal-of sex and the several, subtle alternatives and, in particular, the way women challenge this and negotiate their way through its impact on them and their sexual partners. The end result is a sophisticated and informative analysis, based upon what they call a 'social representations *framework*' (my italics):

> The social representations framework allows systematic study of forces that shape women's conceptualization of a social object such as orgasm. A social representation is shared, though not necessarily consensually, by members of a social group . . . The framework concerns itself with how a shared 'common sense' evolves, what form it takes, and the consequences it has. People's social representations develop not so much by intrapsychic reasoning as by a process of communicating. . . . This includes communication of ideas that arise in the universe of the sciences to publics.
>
> The mass media do not impose ideas on publics. Rather, the individual and society are deemed to be in a dialectical relationship; the individual's thoughts and actions are a product of prevailing conventions, norms and values and individuals can effect changes in such entities. . . . Individuals bring ideas passed down through the generations to their readings of media material. A shared 'common sense' is steered by memory and traditional structures . . . rather than by contemporary messages alone. The social representational perspective . . . can enhance understanding of the social construction of sexual health 'problems'.
>
> (Lavie-Ajayi and Joffe 2009: 99)

Lavie-Ajayi and Joffe's account is fascinating and thought-provoking in its own right, and well worth reading in full if you have the time. However, I have highlighted this (rather long) quote about the way they see social representations as a framework for research because it shows how social representations work as done today. It is clearly informed by ideas about how knowledge is transmitted from one site to another and, especially, how it is transmitted from 'Science' into the everyday world, so important to social representation theory. But their paper also explicitly refers to social construction. As with personal construct theory we can see a hybrid being created, that shifts the approach *into* a form of critical psychology through a realignment with its ontological as well as its epistemological foundations.

Social representations

- Social representations theory was devised by Moscovici. It moves beyond not only 'attitudes' but also 'attributions', seeing them as interconnected and interwoven into broader social representations. Its main assumptions are:
  - In any social group, there will be a number of shared social representations in operation. Indeed, sharing common social representations is a lot of what makes a social group a social group.
  - The social representations that are available to a person enable them to make sense of their experiences and their lifeworld, and they use them to choose different courses of action in different situations. But, crucially, a person's social representations are not seen as locked in their individual mind. Rather they are culturally available and mediated resources, arising, for example, from the messages of the mass media, and in their interactions with experts (such as teachers or doctors).
- Herzlich's study of social representations of health and illness identified three main representations of health operating in French society in the 1960s: health-in-a-vacuum, reserve of health and equilibrium. It also identified three for illness: illness as destroyer, as liberator and as occupation.
- Lavie-Ajayi and Joffe's (2009) study of female orgasm is a good example of how social representations theory is being moulded to align it with critical psychology.

Psychology and power

In a ground-breaking book, one of several written to provide psychology textbooks suitable for the post-apartheid South Africa, Dennis Hook makes the following claim:

> The first and perhaps the most omnipresent theme within critical psychology is that of psychology and power itself. At its most basic, critical psychology is exactly an investigation of the relationship between power and psychology. It is an awareness that psychology itself is powerful – perhaps more powerful than we may first expect – and that psychology plays a part in maintaining and extending existing relations of power.

(2004: 13)

Critical psychology *matters* in South Africa in a way that is very different from how it matters in most other places. This is because it has been, in the raw times of the immediate post-apartheid era, a direct challenge to the psychology that had been used in South Africa to first create the concept of apartheid itself and then to justify and sustain it. Bulhan makes this argument very powerfully in his comparison between Franz Fanon and Hendrik Verwoerd:

> The two men . . . were psychologists who put into practice their profession in ways that made history and affected the lives of millions. . . . Verwoerd was a staunch white supremacist, a Nazi sympathizer, an avowed anti-Semite, and a leading architect of apartheid. . . . Fanon, in contrast, was a restless champion of social justice who, when barely 17 . . . volunteered for the forces attempting to liberate France from Nazi liberation.
>
> (Bulhan 1985: 3)

Verwoerd is often called the 'architect of apartheid', as he was prime minister at the time it was introduced. But it is less well known that he had been a Professor of Applied Psychology at Stellenbosch University from 1928, and that he played a key role, as an academic psychologist, in creating the *concept* of apartheid, providing evidence to support its contentions about white race 'superiority', and then turning it into something that could be put into law and government policy.

That is a chastening backcloth to psychology in South Africa – it is not necessary to convince students there that psychology is 'political'. I found much the same working in countries like Slovakia in the aftermath of the Velvet Revolutions in the late 1980s and into the 1990s. In the Slovak Academy of Science's Institute of Psychology there was a room with all the PhD theses in rows along several shelves, all in black bindings. And a big red book at the end. I asked if this was the PhD of some rather flamboyant student, and was sharply told that it was the reference book for quotations from Karl Marx, as every thesis had to have a solid number of such quotes to get it through the examination process.

We can see in these two instances what has come to be called **governmentality**, defined as 'those more or less rationalized programs, strategies, and tactics for the "conduct of conduct", for acting on the actions of others in order to achieve certain ends' (Rose 1998: 12). Psychology is, Rose argued, the discipline in the social sciences that engages most in governmentalism. The examples I have given are blatant instances of psychologists and psychiatrists colluding with – indeed actively engaged in (as were Verwoerd in South Africa and Radovan Karadžić in Bosnia) acts of 'ethnic cleansing' and the like, within repressive regimes and factions.

The psy complex

Nikolas Rose (a sociologist) introduced the term '**psy complex**' (Rose 1979) to describe the cluster of disciplines and praxes within and around psychology, psychiatry and psychotherapy that, he said, have become more and more powerful in their influence upon the lives of ordinary people going about their lives.

Goodley and Parker (2000: 4) define it as 'that dense network of theories and practices which make up the apparatus of psychology inside and outside colleges and clinics, including its power to define what people think about themselves and their own personal resources for change'.

Now more often shortened to just 'psy', Nikolas Rose has led the way in critically examining 'the historical development, transformation and proliferation of "psy"' and how it 'has been bound up with the transformation of rationalities for government, and in the technologies invented to govern conduct'. While recognizing that 'psy' is by no means the only player, he does argue for its dominant role – 'for it is psy that claims to understand the inner determinants of human conduct, and psy that thus asserts its ability to provide the appropriate underpinning, in knowledge, judgment, and technique, for the powers of experts to conduct whatever they are to be exercised'. He thus argues that we need to gain insight into 'the complex relations between problems of governability and the invention, stabilization and institutionalization of psy knowledges . . .' and the 'constitutive role' that psy has played in the 'practices of **subjectification** that are vital to the governability of liberal democracy' (Rose 1998: 13).

Foucault on power

It is impossible to mention power in this context without alluding to the work of Michel Foucault. His work fundamentally changed the way we understand power, and is tremendously important for psychology. He made his argument very vividly by beginning his book *Discipline and Punish* (Foucault 1975, translated into English in 1977) with a full-on description of the execution, in 1757, of Robert-François Damiens, for the attempted murder of King Louis XV (Figure 3.1). His was a death of actually being 'hung, drawn and quartered', a gruesome punishment for what was actually a symbolic act of protest.

Figure 3.1 'Hung, drawn and quartered'
Source: http://en.wikipedia.org/wiki/File_Robert_Francois_Damiens_before_the_judges.jpg

This extreme form of punishment for daring to even bring a knife into the presence of the king was, Foucault claimed, an obvious way in which people in power can exercise it. It was a brutal warning that any attempt to challenge the absolute authority of the sovereign would not be allowed.

However, Foucault argued, this is not how power is usually exercised in our everyday lives. That is much more subtle. He described in detail the 'dense networks of power' that permeate throughout our relationships with each other, at all levels from our personal, intimate dealings to the way we relate to – and are governed by – the institutions of the state, the church, medicine, and so on, including psychiatry and psychology. He wrote and theorized about the '**micro-politics of power**' going on in our interactions and relationships, even the most intimate. In particular he drew attention to the way that most of the control exercised to mould and shape who we are and what we do is done by *ourselves*.

Regulating the self

One of Foucault's most influential concepts is the '**technology of the self**' – his claim that we produce our selves through treating them, almost, as technological projects, entities that must be constructed and that need to be constantly tinkered with to maintain them. However, he did not see this as a self-indulgent kind of identity-DIY, where the person concerned can simply express their own creativity and originality. Crucially for Foucault, the technological work involved is both governed by society's institutions (for example, in the UK, you have to get planning permission to build a house) and some aspects are required by them (building regulations require you to construct it according to specific standards).

This is one half of the story – the technology of the self as directly and explicitly governed by institutional forces. The self we can build in this way is stringently constrained by the overt exercise of power. The concept that is important here is **subject positioning** – the way that regimes of social control impose restrictions on who a person can be. One example, detailed later in the chapter, is the choice for women being reduced to either being a 'madonna' or a 'whore'. Feminist theorists argue that a society or culture that offers only these two positions for a woman to occupy thereby exercises extreme levels of control over women. It denies them the possibility of occupying other positions, such as being a competent author of her own destiny, or somebody who can be taken seriously in, say, the work place or parliament.

Social control is often implicit and uncodified, but it can also be institutionalized. Laws against homosexuality are a good example here, and where homosexuality is made a crime (as it still is in many places in the world today) this exerts immense control over a person's freedom to construct themselves as a homosexual. But by 'institutional power' Foucault did not only mean the formal institutions like the law (that prohibited homosexual activity), religion (that teaches it is sinful) and medicine (that assumed that it is an illness that needs to be treated). He also included less formal elements, like pressures exerted by public opinion that stigmatized homosexuality and treated homosexuals as outcasts.

The other half of the story is self-regulation. To convey this idea Foucault adopted the metaphor of the **panopticon** (Figure 3.2). This is a design for a prison developed by Jeremy Bentham, in which there is a central guard room surrounded by a number of cells in a circle around it. Each cell has a window, allowing the guard to maintain constant surveillance over the prisoners

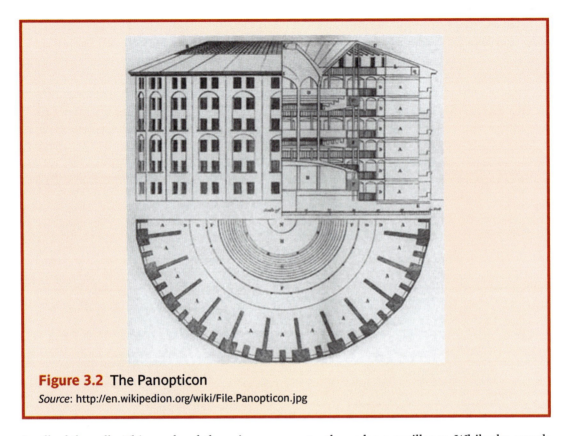

Figure 3.2 The Panopticon
Source: http://en.wikipedion.org/wiki/File.Panopticon.jpg

in all of the cells. This rendered the prisoners constantly under surveillance. While the guards could each look in only one direction at a time, the prisoners knew that they could be observed at any time. So if the prisoners acted in a way that the guard could punish, they did so in the knowledge that, at any time, they could be spotted. The effect is that prisoners become self-regulating. Constantly vigilant over their own behaviour, constantly aware that at any moment they could get caught out, the prisoners acted as though the guards were looking at them all the time, even though a lot of the time they were not.

Foucault claims that this self-regulation is the main way in which control is exercised. People come to act as if they are under constant scrutiny, even though most of the time they are not. In other words, institutions only need to directly and overtly exercise their governmental power occasionally and superficially. The mere fact that they have the power and can exercise it is enough to control what people do. Thus the selves that are produced through technologies of the self are highly governed and regulated.

Resistance

Foucault stressed over and over again in his writings that the exercise of power is never simple, nor is it usually unidirectional in its impact. While society's institutions may be very powerful indeed, people can and do resist. **Resistance** can also be exercised in a variety of ways. One example is where individuals collectively act together to encourage each other to reposition themselves. Child sexual abuse survivors' self-help groups are set up by survivors to specifically challenge the power of the 'helping professions' to position them as inevitably 'damaged goods' (however well-meaning the intentions) and to therefore justify intervening in their lives and requiring them to undergo therapy.

A psychologist who has specifically taken up the idea of resistance and studied it as a social psychologist is Steven Reicher. Publicly he is best known for his work with Alexander Haslam, on the making of the BBC television programme *The Experiment*, which reworked a version of Zimbardo's famous prison study (which we discuss in Chapter 4).

Reicher and Haslam did so in order to challenge the view that, under pressure when acting in groups, people tend to lose their individual identity and act badly. In particular they wanted to explore the potential for resistance:

> while members of certain groups may indeed use their power to act in discriminatory and oppressive ways, members of other groups may act more prosocially and use their power for constructive purposes . . . Moreover, even if some groups are tyrannical, group action is also the basis on which people gain the strength and confidence to resist, to challenge, and even to overthrow tyranny.
>
> (Reicher and Haslam 2006: 5)

The concept of resistance is one of the most potent and important of Foucault's ideas. It portrays people as capable of counteracting the deployment of social control if they see those mechanisms as harmful and exploitative. Moreover, it offers a positive perspective on how collective action (such as joining a trade union or a pressure group) can make resistance more effective.

Before we move on, it is important to recognize that – as Rose himself acknowledges – governmentality is not just about strategies and regimes that 'control, subdue, discipline and normalise or reform' individuals. It also encompasses action taken to 'make them more intelligent, wise, happy, virtuous, healthy, productive . . . enterprising, fulfilled, self-esteeming, empowered or whatever' (Rose 1998: 12). That is, governmentality is not simply a matter of elites crudely imposing evil and oppressive regimes solely for the purposes of exploitation. Governmentality may be equally well conceived as 'humaneering', an Enlightenment project where 'sound knowledge of human nature' is seen as the basis for 'directing social changes, so as to make social institutions and practices better suited to human needs' (Tiffin et al. 1940: 23).

Power and psychology

- In the modern world, psychology, as part of the 'psy complex', has become a major source of power through which people govern and are governed.

- Psychology's power can be used both for good and for bad. It has the potential to control and regulate (through, for example, its authority to define what is 'normal') and to emancipate and enable (through, for example, its capacity to show how to resist the misuse of power).

- Foucault has probably had the most influence on the way critical psychologists understand power, especially in his ideas about the 'micro-politics of power', 'technologies of the self', panoptical power and resistance.

The goals of critical psychology

There is no one critical psychology. Rather there are multiple forms, multiple critical perspectives on, and *uses of*, psychology which at best bear a family resemblance to one another. . . . [C]ritical psychology is more an *approach, a kind of orientation* towards psychological knowledge and practice – and to relations of power in general – than any one kind of theory, any one set of concepts. . . . [C]ritical psychology is by definition diverse and multiple . . . it cannot be localised to one form of theory, one type of critical practice, or single context. . . . Critical psychology as it is applied as a means of critiquing psychotherapy, for example, may look like a very different creature from the critical psychology that comes to play a proactive role in reformulating forms of community intervention.

(Hook et al. 2004: 11, emphases in the original)

As Parker (2009) points out, one reason for this variability is that critical psychology sounds and looks different, and works differently, from what he calls the 'imperialist heartlands' (by which he means, mostly, the USA, the UK, and their intellectual colonies such as Canada and Australia) compared with, say, South America. In this chapter I do my best to resist the tendency to stick with (what is to me) those familiar heartlands, but I cannot pretend to be other than an occasional 'tourist' anywhere else.

This section is a very brief overview of critical psychology in general, and its implications for social psychology in particular. You have already learned a fair amount about two aims of critical social psychology from Chapters 1 and 2, which are to do the following:

- challenge mainstream approaches, by spelling out what is wrong with them and their limitations
- develop theory, critique and research methods that 'work' for the epistemological and onto-logical basis of critical logics of inquiry.

This section looks at a further three aims for critical social psychology, which are:

1 To 'make a difference', both in the way psychology gets done and, crucially, in what it achieves.
2 To promote social justice and liberatory ideological and political goals and values.
3 To explore places, questions, phenomena and communication that mainstream psychology has misrepresented, avoided or ignored.

Each of these will be covered in turn, with a short, broad outline of what is at stake, illustrated in more detail with an example. The Resources and Further reading sections at the end of the chapter offer places to find out more if your interest is tickled or otherwise aroused! This way, I hope, you will get a broad, overall picture of what critical psychology is up to, and enough depth to get a meaningful sense of why it matters.

Critical social psychology and making a difference

Social psychologists are often – maybe even generally – motivated by wanting to make the world a better place for people to live in. Indeed, in an earlier book on critical social psychology (Stainton Rogers et al. 1995) I joined in with criticisms about the way mainstream social psychology tends to take on a bit of a 'warm and cuddly' do-gooding agenda, selling itself both as a way to claim the moral high ground and show how social psychology can be used to 'understand behaviour, thus also suggesting ways to improve it' (Myers et al. 2010: 420).

What makes critical social psychology different, I believe, is that it has been motivated by a more radical view of what 'making a difference' should be:

> The power of critical social psychology is in its challenge to prevailing frameworks of studying and understanding social life. . . . In social psychology we are constantly studying aspects of social life that engage deeply held values and moral positions with staggering consequences for the equality and inclusion of those on the margins of society.
>
> (Cherry 2009: 104)

Critical social psychology focuses its attention on inequality rather than seeking universal benefits for all. Its social justice agenda concentrates on social change to bring about a society that is fairer: it actively aspires to do something about the 'haves' and the 'have nots'. Most specifically its challenge is to prejudice, exploitation and oppression. This is not just about 'doing good' in a Lady Bountiful sort of way. It is about naming and shaming and doing something about those who, wittingly or unwittingly, seek to protect their own interests and those of big business and of powerful institutions (like ruling parties and religious institutions). Increasingly the target is named as '**neo-liberalism**', an ideology that has adopted the language of commerce – markets, efficiency, consumer choice – to shift risk from those in power (governments and multinationals) on to less powerful individuals and communities. Another way to see this is the creation of a 'blame the victim' culture, where the poor, the obese, the dispossessed and the pathetic losers, the homeless and the stateless are held responsible for their misfortunes, shifting responsibility away from those who otherwise might be held to account.

Probably the most vociferous voice in opposition to a neo-liberal world serving the interests of capitalism is Ian Parker, a self-defined (and proud) Marxist in days when most critical psychologists have found 'cooler' and less confrontational ways to describe themselves. He applauds critical psychologists' ambitions to transcend the conditions of early twenty-first-century capitalism to create a more just and fairer world, but makes it clear that history is against us:

> The stance we adopt should draw us beyond this ruinous economic order. Descriptive inconclusion, restorying of ourselves, the immersion in texts of our own creation, deconstruction and some way of letting go of the past which haunts us are positive utopian possibilities; they are ways of imagining a future without tying into the shapes of the present . . . The point, of course, is that we are not yet in this pleasure dome, and, if we imagine that we are, we have forgotten some fairly serious historical lessons about the role of practice in negotiating the contradictory reality of global capitalism.
>
> (Parker 2009: 84)

He may well be right. But rather than get too pessimistic too soon, let us look at what has been achieved by critical social psychologists in their ambition to put their theories and research into practice in a pursuit of social justice.

Possibly the greatest inspiration has been the writings of the Brazilian educationalist Paulo Freire. His concept of 'the pedagogy of the oppressed' (see Freire 1972; 1995) has been the inspiration for many critical psychologists, especially those operating in community psychology, which is what I will use as my illustration under this heading.

Community psychology

Community psychology arose out of the post-Second World War period of political change. It had at least two points of origin and development – in North and in South America. The contrasting political, economic and cultural contexts in which these two versions have been created have influenced the different kinds of approach we see today. But both have in common a specifically *political* agenda, arguing that psychologists should actively support not just social justice but economic and political justice too. Maritza Montero, describing community psychology in the twenty-first century, claims that:

> Both in Latin America, as in the United States, social transformations were put as the ultimate goal of its practice. . . . This conviction about the necessity to transform social conditions is political, in the sense of politics as the rightful occupation of public space in equal terms, by any citizen; and in such a way so they have the right and possibility to be heard, to express their ideas and opinions, and to receive answers to their demands, according to the law. This 'zeitgeist' has been present all along the American continent. And also is felt in other regions of the world where community psychology is trying to provide answers to social problems.
>
> (2009: 98)

Community psychology in North America

In North America, community psychology began in the1960s, at a time when humanistic psychology (and the hippie 'summer of love') held sway, California was the place to be, and radicals in the USA were embroiled in political action such as the anti-Vietnam War campaign and the civil rights movement, especially in relation to the racial segregation.

Against this backcloth, community psychology was established mainly as a more liberal and progressive way to work with people with mental health and other social and welfare problems than the highly positivist form of clinical psychology that was the main approach in the USA at that time. In its earliest days community psychology in the USA and Canada took a broadly ecological approach (Kelly 1966) concerned with improving people's lives in the context of the communities in which they lived. Kelly established four main principles for this approach to mental health:

1 *Working with the community rather than with the individual*, reflecting a shift from seeing 'problems' located in individuals' mental health, and relocating the cause in structural disadvantage (such as poverty) and social deprivation (such as prejudice).

2 *Reducing the use of community mental health services*, where mainly white middle-class professionals sought to intervene in the lives of poor, deprived, often Black and Hispanic (and hence socially excluded) people, in ways that were resented and rejected and, therefore, more than likely, ineffective.

3 *Strengthening community resources*, by building upon the strengths of communities, supporting them and working with community leaders to remove those conditions that exacerbate, if not cause, mental health problems.

4 *Planning for change*, including preventive work and promoting resilience in ways that improve both the material conditions of community members and what would now be called their 'social capital' – to do with trust, access to knowledge and advice, and social and economic leverage.

The focus of this work remains mainly on communities suffering hardship, deprivation and **social exclusion** (that is, being excluded from services or opportunities) through inequality, prejudice and marginalization. Community psychologists designed and delivered interventions to promote the health, well-being and life opportunities of these people.

Community psychology in South America

Maria Freitas (2010) gives a compelling description of the origins of community psychology in Brazil. It gives a real sense of the way that politics has influenced psychology, and is, I think, reasonably representative of how community psychology gained importance across South America.

Freitas begins with the 1950s where community-based welfare services were introduced, to support poor communities at a time of great change, moving from a dispersed agricultural base to one continually growing more industrialized and urbanized. Psychologists in these early days worked with government agencies in projects to improve housing, health, and so on. Inspired by the work of Paulo Freire, they developed programmes like 'De Pé no Chão Também se Aprende a Ler' (Barefoot People Can Learn How to Read) and other educational services for children and adults.

But then came the junta, in 1964, and with it totalitarian military control. At this time psychology became an official profession in Brazil, but was highly regulated, and its scope limited almost entirely to following European and, especially, North American models, where psychologists practised mainly as counsellors and clinicians, working almost exclusively for a small elite, able to pay for the services they provided. Only a very few psychologists were brave enough to try to continue to work with the poor and excluded, 'Some of them started to take part in ongoing community practices politically committed to social changes – despite the political persecution, the dangers of prison and, not least, the fear' that beset those times (Freitas 2010: 316). But, she says, in the 1970s the political situation gradually eased, and community psychology began to flourish:

> Psychologists were keen contributors to these interventions . . . and social movements as well as community associations became fields of action for the community practices developed by psychologists. . . . Work developed in the 1970s identified community psychology as a discipline politically committed to the reality of excluded populations and strongly advocated the belief that psychology could not be neutral, since it had a role to play in the construction of social change.
>
> (Freitas 2010: 317)

The 1980s was a time of expansion, and a time when psychologists made open and public commitments to a social psychology that would work actively to seek a liberatory social change, especially for the poor and excluded. They organized, for example, an important meeting on 'Social Psychology as Transforming Action'. It was an important milestone in the development of a critical and historical social psychology committed to the concrete reality of the population and to the theoretical development of this area. . . . [It] triggered various debates on issues related to the theoretical and methodological vagueness of community psychology practices. The expressions 'psychology in the community', 'psychology of the community' and 'community psychology' started to be used and heard everywhere, a development that expressed both concern with work on the community and a fertile debate about methodologies and concepts applied to the psychosocial problems under study.

(Freitas 2010: 317)

This is **liberation psychology**, a movement arising mainly in South America, based on the work of Ignacio Martín-Baró (1996), a Jesuit priest and psychologist who was assassinated by an elite army corps in El Salvador with five other activists at the University of Central America there. Currently the leading scholar of Liberation Psychology is Maritza Montero, a Venezuelan social psychologist (see Montero 2009). Most of the important work in this field is published in Portuguese and Spanish. It uses terms like *intervención psicosocial* (**social intervention**) and *calidad de vida* (**quality of life**) that are becoming incorporated into English but do lose something in the translation. *Calidad de vida* is not a way of measuring a person's evaluation of their bodily comfort and ability (as is usually the case in the English-speaking world). It is much more about life-quality as well-being and belonging, linked to cultural and community values.

Community psychology research

Community psychologists have in common an explicit social justice agenda, working mainly with excluded and marginalized communities and groups, in order to 'understand and promote shared values of empowerment and self-determination; collaboration and democratic participation; health, wellness and prevention; and social justice' (Hanlin et al. 2009: 527). Community psychologists see their work as directly contributing to the empowerment of the groups and communities with which they work, through two main means: by directly providing 'a means for marginalized people's voices and narratives to be heard'; and, more vicariously, through the researcher becoming 'the steward of stories, experiences and constructed knowledge of the respondents, rather than just a recipient of the data' (Hanlin et al. 2009: 526).

Granada provides an excellent checklist of requirements for good quality action research:

Knowledge must be acknowledged as socially and collectively constructed through complex processes. It is 'not found or taught. It is created by means of a dialectical interaction.'
    Both the researcher's and community's knowledges and the means by which they have been gained must be actively clarified; and
    must involve mutual education in which the community and the researcher(s) learn to produce 'expansion and democratization of knowledge'.

The research must be a participatory process:
    based on respect; and
    must acknowledge and tackle potential conflicts of interest
    which can develop interdisciplinary self-help.

Researchers must have appropriate skills and experience:
> must view the community as an active subject (rather than as a target group);
>
> must adapt how they communicate and discuss to be functional for and respectful of the communities with whom they work; and
>
> must negotiate with the participants in the study and their communities what constitutes well-being.

Projects must be centred on community development and improvement of quality of life.
> Certain political and social values will be overt and central.
>
> Projects should contribute more effectively to an interdisciplinary and multidisciplinary perspective.
>
> There should be a move to create projects that are increasingly organic, inter-institutional and interdisciplinary, with an effect on official policies.

(Based on Granada 1991: 176–7)

Granada based his article on action research work undertaken in Colombia, on child health interventions, interventions linked to substance abuse, and accidents. See Further reading.

Critical social psychology and making a difference

- Critical social psychology does not seek, in a general way, to 'make the world a better place' in the pursuit of human happiness. It specifically targets its energies on promoting social justice, through theory, research and action that challenge oppression, exploitation and inequality.

- Community psychology adopts this as its central goal. There are two main strands, one with its origins in the humanistic psychology of 1960s North America, the other in the political struggles in the 1970s and 1980s in South America.

- Community psychology strongly values the people and communities with whom they work, seeking their emancipation, inclusion, citizenship and self-determination.

- However, some (such as Ian Parker) are wary of the potential for this 'new' form of social action to become just another orthodoxy, promoting its own interests in the name of 'helping' and 'liberating' less powerful others.

Critical psychology: ideology and politics

Critical social psychologists are motivated by particular ideological or political standpoints. By ideology, I mean a general sense of morals, ethics and ideas about what 'ought' to be (such as feminism or Marxism). Politics, I think, implies a level of taking action and/or responding to political events and circumstances, such as revolutions and dictatorships and oppressive regimes like apartheid. It also includes political action taking place in more 'liberal' settings, such as the pressure group set up by critical psychologists to challenge the treatment of people who hear voices (see Parker 2009). I have chosen here as my illustration a movement very active in South Africa just now, in the period following the fall of apartheid – that is informed by postcolonial theory. There are others that have an equal claim – Marxism, feminism, queer and crip theory, to name but some. But I have been particularly inspired by a chapter on postcolonialism and psychology written by Catriona MacLeod and Sunil Bhatia (2009).

Postcolonial psychology

Postcolonial psychology is fundamentally about how power, not just in the 'now' but in terms of history, is deployed by the powerful against the weak(er), focusing directly on the effects of colonization and its aftermath. It offers a challenge to systems that 'create and sustain power relations of domination' (Foster 1993: 56). Don Foster was the first (or at least the best known) South African psychologist who, at considerable risk to himself, opposed the way psychology was been used to serve apartheid. Subsequent to its overthrow, many South African psychologists have adopted a critical perspective to their research.

Psychology in today's South Africa is explicitly concerned with racism. This is immediately evident when you look at the *Social Psychology* textbook (Ratele and Duncan 2003). It was brought home to me when I shared a platform as a keynote speaker at the Critical Methods Conference held in Rhodes University in 2008 with Norman Duncan, a professor of psychology at the University of the Witwatersrand. In his lecture he stated, baldly and with great passion, that it is impossible to conduct social psychological research in that country that does *not* in some way contend with the issue of race, since racism permeates the 'social' there in many and complex ways. And, he said, it would be wrong to do so, in a location where no social action, phenomenon or experience is anything but shot-through with the recent history of apartheid. It was a salutary experience.

Catriona MacLeod, head of the Psychology Department at Rhodes University, does not, as a respected feminist scholar, take quite the same line. Rather she argues, more generally, that 'at the very least, there should be an explicit focus on power-relations and undermining exclusionary and discriminatory practices' in the research undertaken by critical psychologists (MacLeod and Bhatia 2009: 524–5). Social psychological research, as far as she is concerned, must *always* be designed to expose, oppose – and, ultimately depose – elites that mistreat, marginalize and exploit others.

It is not surprising that postcolonial psychology has taken such a strong position. It explicitly condemns researchers (among them community psychologists, for example) who see themselves as the 'steward of stories, experiences and constructed knowledge of the respondents' (Hanlin et al. 2009). MacLeod and Bhatia (2009: 576) say this creates 'vantage points from which to colonize or objectify the subjects of research', and sometimes even 'seeks to impose First World' preoccupations on research in 'Third World' settings'. From a different continent, Linda Smith, a postcolonial theorist from Aotearoa, has pointed out that, among Maori, the word 'research' is 'probably one of the dirtiest words in the indigenous world's vocabulary' (Smith 1999: 1).

The criticality here is much sharper, much more cynical about what it sees as the naïve 'doing-goodism' of, say, community psychology as practised in the USA. It is especially sceptical about the superficial attempts to be reflexive. Gayatri Spivak has called this 'the banality of leftist intellectuals' lists of self-knowing' (1988: 70). She says it is a kind of ritual breast-beating that fails to understand – let alone recognize – that researching with deprived and oppressed people cannot help but 'capture' them 'via new technologies of inscription – such as tapes, surveys, interviews, word processing, videos and so forth' (Lal 1999: 117).

Thus a postcolonial take on social psychology is that there must be a fundamental *change* in what psychologists do, how they do it, and, most crucially, the nature of the relationships that psychologists create between themselves, for instance, as researchers and the people they 'do' research *upon*. This is not about getting better at representing what 'other people' say or mean or hold dear or are concerned about. Rather, MacLeod and Bhatia argue, we need new strategies altogether:

1 New aims, to identify and challenge the distortions of colonial and imperial imperatives (such as linguistic imperialism) and have liberatory goals (that is, goals designed to liberate).

2 New relationships, that are serious about sharing power in all aspects of the research process.

3 New topics, including the impacts of colonialism itself – such as economic exploitation, migration and civil war.

4 New locations, researching in the borderline spaces where class, gender, religious and 'racial' relationships and identities have been disrupted.

I describe this as 'getting into the dodgy and edgy', in locations that can be cultural more than geographical, and where colonization is extended to include the dominance, say, of **heteronormativity** (sorry about the mouthful! It means the way societies are based on the assumption that to be heterosexual is to be normal, but to be anything else is 'queer', or 'deviant' or 'sick'.) In a nice table-turning, the challenge to this is called **queer theory**, an out-and-proud transformation of meaning from a 'boo word' to a 'hurrah word' (that is, one that is celebratory rather than disapproving).

Critical social psychology: ideology and politics

- Critical social psychology is informed by particular critical ideologies and politics – those that challenge neo-liberalism and seek to empower and emancipate those who are oppressed, excluded and exploited. These include Marxism, feminism, postcolonialism, queer theory and crip theory.

- Postcolonial theory applied to social psychology is a good example. It offers a far tougher and suspicious challenge to researchers than community psychology, very wary of the potential for self-deluding 'do-goodism' by superficially well-meaning but patronizing outsiders.

- Postcolonial theory rejects any idea that others can legitimately 'give voice' to the excluded and oppressed.

- Instead it argues for research and theory that:

  o scrutinize the borderline spaces where class, gender, religious and 'racial' relationships and identities have been disrupted

  o identify the distortions produced by colonial and imperial power – such as economic exploitation, migration and civil war – and make them visible

  o seek ways to reverse and redress the oppressive and exclusionary impact of these events and phenomena

  o are designed to empower and liberate rather than 'help' those who have been denied full citizenship, and are serious about sharing power in all aspects of the research process.

Critical social psychology as a way to 'boldly go'

More than a few critical social psychologists enjoy science fiction – in part because it is a great way to explore 'what if' scenarios, and make the 'everyday' exceptional (and hence open it up for scrutiny). The late Rex Stainton Rogers (Stainton Rogers and Stainton Rogers 2001) wrote a decidedly quirky but illuminating chapter on using science fiction as a deconstructive device to play 'what if' games around sexuality and gender as portrayed in this genre. This is much the same experience as going somewhere 'exotic' (to you, not for the people who live there, of course) and being wrong footed over what you take for granted (for me this included finding out that eating with your fingers can be elegant if you have the skills, and that sitting on a table can be extremely offensive, particularly if a woman does it).

In much the same spirit, critical psychologists enjoy going to exotic locations in their thinking, theorizing and researching. Catriona MacLeod specifically encourages us to do so, in order to identify causes for concern and action we might otherwise overlook – such as how one's identity is affected by being a migrant or a pariah, or what life is like in shanty towns or on the street. In other words, critical social psychologists get a great deal out of 'getting out more' instead of sticking to the situations that are comfortably familiar. There is also a bit of a chicken-and-egg situation here. Once you devise all sorts of new methods and analytics, you can reach parts of the social world that standard experiments cannot reach – such as all the chatter and the twitter going on in the virtual world. Having ways to analyse discourse, narratives and experience opens doors to all sorts of things that simply were not around a very short time ago.

The logic of choice versus the logic of care

There is a counter-argument though – that if you want to study power, then go where it is being exercised. One version of this is to interrogate what goes on in professional encounters – a common encounter being between doctors and other medical staff and their patients. One that I like is part of a study carried on by Annemarie Mol on what she calls the 'logic of care' as opposed to the 'logic of choice' (she is a political philosopher, by the way, but critical psychologists can learn a lot from her work). It is worked around her observations of people with Type 1 diabetes, their family and carers, and the doctors and nurses who treat them. But she does other things too.

Health and market segmentation

Mol conducted a dense and wide-ranging analysis of an advertisement for a particular blood sugar monitor – EuroFlash. It features a group of young, fit, active people. There are three of them, climbing a hill, with mountains in the background, looking happy. The monitor is on the top of the picture, looking elegant and showing a reading of perfectly regulated blood sugar.

Mol writes to the manufacturer and asks if she can show the advertisement in her book. She gets permission and a visitor as well, 'a friendly young woman from the marketing department, involved in her work, concerned about her customers, eager to learn from my criticism' (Mol 2008: 20). The conversation they have is teased out, all about target groups. There are simple, practical monitors for people who are not very confident and cannot manage their diabetes too well, more sophisticated ones for others who do better, who want freedom:

They want to go abroad, visit cities, enjoy holidays, have novel experiences and indeed, walk in the mountains. These may be better-educated people, but this is not necessarily so. What is crucial is that they understand the intricacies of the disease and are willing to make an effort. 'People like you and me' she says. They form a separate target group. For them we have developed the *EuroFlash* and the advertisement of young people eagerly walking.

(Mol 2008: 20)

Try it for yourself

I wonder if you find this a bit disturbing? I do. Advertising that is targeted to different groups sounds so very reasonable and ordinary, even when it is healthcare that is being advertised. But these statements, obviously made in good faith, by someone from the marketing team, come across as neo-liberalism in action. There does not seem much concern about social justice here. It makes you think – or at least, I hope it does. Now would be a good time to reflect upon how power is being exercised in the design, manufacture and market targeting of technology like this.

Looking at how things are marketed is, in a sense, an exotic place to go – particularly for psychologists who traditionally worked in 'laboratories' (even if they were little more than cubicles along the corridor of the psychology department). Certainly critical social psychologists using qualitative methods are free to 'get out more', and this does offer the possibility of all sorts of adventures. However, I have chosen another 'exotic place' to go to illustrate this aspect of critical social psychology, though this is more of a rediscovery or rehabilitation of a devalued avenue than anywhere new to psychology: entering the labyrinth of the psyche.

Social psychoanalytic psychology

Here I am going to follow Helen Lucey's (2007) lead and use the term 'social psychoanalytic' to describe this approach. Many critical psychologists use the simpler term 'psychosocial', but this is confusing, as it also refers to social psychology when it is framed within a sociological perspective. This is where the argument against splitting 'individuals' from the 'social world' they inhabit is put into practice, on the disciplinary borderline between the psychological and the sociological. So, 'social psychoanalytic' is best here, I think.

Incorporating unconscious processes into theorizing

What makes this approach stand out is its specific interest in the unconscious processes that contribute to our subjectivity – to how we perceive, react to, make sense of and feel about the worlds in which we live and our experiences of them.

In part this is a reaction against the way some discursive approaches are preoccupied with talk and text, to the exclusion of feelings and emotions, and all those vague ideas and half-formed memories that bubble just under the surface of our stream-of-consciousness (as described by William James, see Chapter 1). In part it is a more pragmatic recognition that interpretation can be deeper and richer if we are willing to look beyond just the rational and simple-to-understand elements of our thinking (such as values and attitudes). By finding ways to observe and analyse 'gut feelings', irrational thoughts and free-wheeling emotion, adopting a psychoanalytic approach can take us to places that other approaches cannot reach.

Sigmund Freud (1917) talked about these as 'the tricky, hard-to-observe ways in which unconscious material finds its way into consciousness'. His interest in the unconscious came from observing that people, under hypnosis, recall all sorts of memories and feelings that they are not aware of or do not remember when they are fully conscious. Most famously, he became convinced that dreaming offers a pathway into our unconscious, allowing us to notice and consider why, for instance, we have strong feelings of anxiety we cannot rationally explain.

The influence of Lacan

However, the key theorist here is not Freud but Jacques Lacan. Freud's ideas about the internal battles going on between ego, id and superego portray a kind of 'wired in' unconscious that is insensitive to the socially constructed nature of the way we come to know our world and our place in it. Lacan took the position that the unconscious is structured like a language. It develops, he claims, through each person's engagement with their sense of self through interaction with what he called the **symbolic order** – the social and cultural structures that position us in terms of our gender, class, cultural heritage, and so on.

Feminist film theory, which draws extensively on Lacanian thinking, is a useful way into the kind of ideas involved. An example is Laura Mulvey's theorizing about the kinds of 'visual pleasure' we get through entering a darkened cinema, and losing ourselves in the film to such an extent that it becomes, for a while, an alternative reality in which we are totally absorbed. In that state the visual impact of what is being shown creates powerful emotions, and can lull us into making sense of what is happening in quite different ways than we would in 'normal life'.

As a feminist, she theorized particularly around gender. Her earliest and best-known piece was called 'Visual pleasure and narrative cinema' (Mulvey 1975). In it she drew attention to how, in classical Hollywood movies, the spectator is cast as inevitably male (and heterosexual – for which she has been strongly criticized). This is evident, she claims, especially in the way women actors are portrayed. To explain how and why, Mulvey drew on the psychoanalytic notion of **scopophilia** – the pleasure gained from looking at something attractive; in psychodynamic terms, the erotic pleasure of looking at someone or something sexually arousing. Mulvey described the heroines of these movies as coded with 'to-be-looked-at-ness' (an uglier but in some ways more accurate term is 'scopophilized') (Stainton Rogers 2006). According to Mulvey, from a heterosexual male point of view – called in feminist theory the 'male **gaze**' – women in films are presented as objects of either voyeurism (seeing them as whores) or of fetishism (seeing them as Madonnas).

Wendy Hollway, in particular, and the collective who produced *Changing the Subject* (Henriques et al. 1984), introduced psychoanalytic theorizing into critical social psychology, explicitly redefining the nature of 'the subject' (that is, the person) as shown in Table 3.1.

Social psychoanalysis as an analytic tool

In a more recent account, Stephen Frosh and Lisa Young describe how social psychoanalytic approaches have become incorporated into critical social psychology:

Table 3.1 Comparison of traditional social psychology and social psychoanalytic psychology

Traditional social psychology	Social psychoanalytic psychology
Assumes people can be understood as rational	Recognizes that people are also irrational
Sees a person as a fixed, single, coherent whole	Sees a person as a complex mix of different parts, that shift and shape all the time
Separates thinking from feeling	Says thinking and feeling cannot be separated from each other
Sees people as mainly the product of biological and/or social forces	Sees people as profoundly influenced by their personal histories
Sees people as individuals acting autonomously	Socially situates the individual, as always and ever experiencing and acting within the social

> The 'new' social psychology, with its roots in social constructionism, Foucauldian critique and methodologically scrupulous qualitative research . . . offers a grounded way in which to articulate the psychosocial bases around which personal and social accounts of experiences and beliefs are constructed.
>
> (2009: 110)

Frosh and Young give a number of reasons why a growing number of qualitative psychologists are becoming willing to introduce psychoanalytic ideas into the way they analyse their data and the interpretative techniques they deploy. Psychoanalysis offers them an interpretative language – for instance, about the role of emotional investment in subject positioning. More than that, it offers access to potentially new interpretative insights – that, for example, an account may be provided less as an explanation or mere 'telling it like it is' than as a form of defence. A good example is Burman's work on charity advertisements using depictions of children (Burman 1999).

> [P]sychoanalysis conceptualises discourse as a site where the internal world of psychic reality is expressed and revealed. . . . A psychoanalytic reading goes 'behind' the text as the positions that individuals construct through their talk are taken to be indicative of anxieties, defences and particular ways of relating.
>
> (Frosh and Young 2009: 110)

However, Frosh and Young stress that psychoanalytically informed narrative analytic research of the kind they do:

> is not analogous with 'psychoanalysing' . . . Rather it is the research relationship and the narrative produced within this research relationship that is under scrutiny. Therefore, throughout our analysis we attempt to anchor psychoanalytic ideas in the texture of the research relationship and a close reading of the text, processes that require commitment to reflexivity and systematic narrative analysis respectively.
>
> (Frosh and Young 2009: 124)

Critical social psychology as a way to 'boldly go'

- In its new and wide-ranging theorizing and research methods, critical social psychology is able to move into areas that traditional social psychology has tended to avoid or ignore.
- Examples include the social worlds opening up in virtual life, IT games and on the Internet, and places where products are marketed and targeted.
- Critical social psychologists seek out 'exotic' settings and circumstances in order to make the 'ordinary' (that is, all the things that are so familiar that we take them for granted) extraordinary.
- A major strand of critical social psychology is being developed using recent advances in psychoanalytic theory, often as intersecting with critical standpoints such as feminism, Marxism and postcolonialism.

Resources

This provides access to the Annual Review of Critical Psychology. True to its principles this is a free-access site, lacking the gloss and glitter of the high-end web material you can get in relation to the mainstream. But it is a great place to start exploring this field in a truly international manner: http://www.discourseunit.com/arcp.htm

This gives you access to short video clips from the Open University course, on critical social psychology: http://www.sciencelive.org/component/option,com_mediadb/task,view/idstr,Open-podcast-feeds_dd307_social_psychology_rss2_xml/Itemid,98

A free download of the edited text by Tomas Ibáñez and Lupicinio Íñiguez (see below): http://www.ebook3000.com/Critical-Social-Psychology_49291.html

This provides access to the journal *Subjectivity*, which is transdisciplinary but where many critical social psychologists publish their work. It offers access to free downloads of selected papers: http://www.palgrave-journals.com/sub/index.html

This website is from the BBC and enables you to view footage and find out more about the re-creation of the Zimbado Prison study: http://www.bbcprisonstudy.org/bbc-prison-study.php

Further reading

Progenitors

Personal construct theory

Bannister, D. and Fransella, F. (1986) *Inquiring Man: The Psychology of Personal Constructs*. London: Croom Helm.
This is the standard text if you want to begin to get to grips with personal construct theory.

Social representations

Farr, R.M. and Moscovici, S. (eds) (1984) *Social Representations.* **Cambridge: Cambridge University Press.**

This is the key text for gaining a thorough understanding of social representations theory, coming, as they say, from the horse's mouth.

Flick, U. (ed.) (1998) *The Psychology of the Social.* **Cambridge: Cambridge University Press.**

A collection of chapters, covering developments in both social representations theory and social representations research. It contains a chapter by Moscovici summarizing his current views.

Critical social psychology

These days there are many books to choose from. I have kept to books only on critical social psychology here, having suggested general books on critical psychology in earlier chapters.

Ibáñez, T. and Íñiguez, L. (eds) (1997) *Critical Social Psychology.* **London: Sage.**
Stainton Rogers, R., Stenner, P., Gleeson, K. and Stainton Rogers, W. (1995) *Social Psychology: A Critical Agenda.* **Cambridge: Polity.**

These are older books and I have to declare an interest in both, with two chapters in the first and as a co-author on the second. They are of more than historical interest, but probably more 'background' reading about what critical psychology was like when it was getting started.

Hollway, W., Lucey, H. and Phoenix, A. (2007) *Social Psychology Matters.* **Maidenhead: Open University Press.**
Langdridge, D. and Taylor, S. (2007) *Critical Readings in Social Psychology.* **Maidenhead: Open University Press.**

These two textbooks form the basis for the Open University's Level 3 Social Psychology course (together with web-based support and a range of learning resources and materials). The first is the general text covering a range of issues; the second contains some really useful annotated and augmented readings. I have drawn on both throughout writing my book. They both, explicitly, adopt a *critical* approach to social psychology (it is worth looking at the student feedback – this does seem to be a 'love it or hate it' course!) that makes no bones about its rejection of experimental social psychology. I would see these as mainly excellent resources, which will help you get your head around the critical approach.

Tuffin, K. (2005) *Understanding Critical Social Psychology.* **London: Sage.**

This book's first chapter offers a much more detailed critique of experimental approach to social psychology and is great to flesh out your understanding. But the book's main strength is its sustained and wide-ranging treatment of discursive psychology, covering topics including emotion and politics. It also has an excellent, entertaining and informative 'fly on the wall' tutorial to help you get to grips with criticality and what it means and why it matters.

Community psychology

Prilleltensky, I. and Nelson, G. (2009) Community psychology, in D. Fox, I. Prilleltensky and S. Austin (eds) *Critical Psychology: An Introduction,* **2nd edn. London: Sage.**

This offers a North American take on community psychology, but also a broad account of the underlying principles, issues and foundations for the approach. It has some very useful comparison tables and is informative about where community psychology is going.

Freitas, M.F.Q. (2010) Voices from the South: the construction of Brazilian community social psychology, *Journal of Community and Applied Social Psychology,* **10: 318–26.**
This is a readable and fascinating paper which, though its location is in Brazil, gives a clear overview of and 'feel' for the kind of community psychology operating in South America.

Postcolonial psychology

MacLeod, C. and Bhatia, S. (2009) Postcolonialism and psychology, in C. Willig and W. Stainton Rogers (eds) *The Sage Handbook of Qualitative Research in Psychology.* **London: Sage.**
This is stirring stuff! It is dense in places, but I believe it is the best place to start getting your head around the very challenging demands made by postcolonial theory about what social psychologists need to do to 'get out more' from their comfort zone and really begin to address the issues raised by colonialism.

Social psychoanalytic psychology

Hepburn, A. (2003) *An Introduction to Critical Social Psychology.* **London: Sage.**
Chapter 4 on psychoanalytic critics provides a detailed and highly readable account of this approach, including detailed sections on Lacan's theorizing and critiques of it from feminist, Foucauldian and other postmodern perspectives.

Frosh, S. and Young, L.S. (2009) Psychoanalytic approaches to qualitative psychology, in C. Willig and W. Stainton Rogers (eds) *The Sage Handbook of Qualitative Research in Psychology,* **London: Sage.**
This chapter focuses specifically on psychoanalytically informed research methods and techniques, and provides an ideal starting-point if you want to try this approach yourself.

Questions

1 Outline the key features of social representations theory. Illustrate your answer with examples about social representations of health and illness. How has social representations research been adapted for use as a critical social psychology approach?

2 The history of social psychology is the history of politics and ideology. Discuss this assertion giving at least three different examples of how psychologists have engaged with politics. What do you think this means for the future of psychology?

3 Critical social psychology is all about bringing about a better world. Is it? If so, what kind of a better world? Contrast its vision with that of neo-liberalism.

4 Why is power such an important issue for critical social psychologists?

5 Outline the key elements of postcolonial theory as applied to social psychology. In what ways does it differ from the community psychology approach?

6 Should social psychologists become more adventurous? Take a position and defend it. You are not expected to agree, a case against is fine. But do use specific examples to support your line of argument.

7 Outline the key elements of the social psychoanalytic approach to theory and research, illustrating your answer with specific examples.

SECTION 2

Methods and analytics

Chapter 4

Quantitative research in social psychology

LEARNING OUTCOMES

When you have finished studying this chapter, you should be able to:

1. Describe what is meant by 'descriptive research', giving two examples of it from the quantitative research in psychology.

2. Describe the main elements of:
   - survey research in psychology
   - social psychological experiments, both field and laboratory.

3. List and define the main terms used in experimental social psychology to designate the key elements to a well-conducted study.

4. Outline the main techniques for collecting data in experimental social psychological studies and the different kinds of measures that can be used.

5. Compare the usefulness of laboratory experiments, field experiments and surveys in relation to issues of control, realism and representativeness.

6. Outline at least two different ways in which qualitative methods and/or analyses may be included in a quantitative social psychological study.

7. Outline the key principles for carrying out quantitative research in social psychology, relevant to the location in which you are studying and, where relevant, where you plan to practise as a psychologist.

8. Explain how ethical principles vary from one location to another, illustrating your answer with examples of how this would work in practice.

Introduction

Social psychologists from both the experimental and critical paradigms gain their knowledge and refine and test their theories through research. Both gather and analyse data for research that is:

- *designed to answer research questions*. This can be a hypothesis to be tested or to gain insight into and understanding of a particular topic.
- *empirical*. Data are collected based on observations, measurements or records of what people do and/or say in particular circumstances.
- *directed*. Methods for collecting these data are selected as appropriate for the research question(s) to be addressed and the research paradigm adopted.
- *analytic*. The data gathered are analysed and interpreted in order to answer these questions.

There is often confusion between what is meant by the two words 'methods' and 'methodology' – even among researchers, who use them in different ways! In this book I use the word 'methodology' to mean a general, overall approach to carrying out research, and 'method' for a specific research technique. Research in social psychology is mainly divided into quantitative or qualitative methodologies. Within each there are a range of methods – such as observational, experimental and survey methods in quantitative research; ethnographic, narrative, discursive and phenomenological methods in qualitative research.

While there is not a perfect match, by and large research in experimental social psychology is quantitative, whereas most (but not all) research in critical social psychology is qualitative. This chapter is about quantitative research used in social psychology. Chapter 5 is about qualitative research.

Finally it is worth noting that if you plan a career as a research-active psychologist, mixed methods are becoming increasingly popular in applied fields such as health services, health care and health promotion; education, training, career development and management; and **market research** and other commercial applications used such as in personal selection. This is important since employers and grant funders are coming to expect psychologists to be competent in both spheres. For this reason alone psychology students need to know about both qualitative and quantitative research methods and analytics.

Types of quantitative research

There are two main kinds of quantitative research:

- descriptive research, which is based on an inductive logic of inquiry
- experimental method, which is based on a hypothetico-deductive logic of inquiry.

The chapter covers each of these in turn, then presents sections on qualitative research in quantitative studies, and ethics in quantitative research.

Descriptive research

Descriptive research is done to 'provide the researchers with an accurate description of the phenomenon in question' (Manstead and Semin 2001: 76). It is based on the inductive logic of inquiry where either a situation is set up or a naturally occurring situation or phenomenon can be observed. Inductive inferences are drawn from the particular patterns of behaviour observed.

> The inductive logic of inquiry is described in detail in Chapter 2.

Survey research

The most common form of descriptive research is based on conducting surveys to gather data which are then analysed through inferential statistical analysis. Numerical – or numerically coded – data are collected in relation to potentially relevant demographic variables in the population studied (such as each person's gender, age, social class, ethnic heritage, religion, sexuality, and so on) in order to link them with other variables – such as their voting intentions or behaviour. This sort of **survey research** will be familiar to you from what happens around elections. Newspapers and television stations (as well, of course, as political parties themselves) commission social research organizations to answer questions like 'who is most and least likely to vote for the Green Party?' or 'What are first-time voters going to do at this election?', and so on.

Similarly social psychologists use inferential statistical techniques to explore which values, attitudes and beliefs are associated with, for example, a person's personality or gender or age or religion.

Latino young people's values concerning sex

A good example is a study by Deardorff et al. (2008) in which they examined sexual beliefs and values among Latino young people. They were motivated by concern that young people from this group in the USA are at greater risk of sexually transmitted disease and early pregnancy. They wanted to find out how, as a specific group, Latino young people think about sex and the possible hurdles they may face in keeping themselves safe.

The sample they used was made up of 694 sexually active young people of Latino heritage (mostly Mexican American, but including 16 per cent as Salvadoran American, 9 per cent as Nicaraguan American and 20 per cent some combination of these three). Of these, 61 per cent were female, and ages ranged from 16 to 22. The majority completed the scales in English but 7 per cent did so in a version translated into Spanish. Half of the respondents completed the scales themselves, half by responding to the questions read out by one of the researchers over the phone. You can see some typical compromises have been made here. Probably the age range was limited by ethical and legal restrictions (for example, there are strong controls over conducting research about topics like sexual satisfaction with under-16s). It is usually easier to recruit women than men to take part in research of this kind.

This research was mainly carried out to produce and test questionnaires. However, they also used inferential statistics to look for demographic effects, and did discover gender differences. Young men's scores (levels of agreement) for 'Satisfaction of Sexual Needs', 'Female Virginity', 'Sexual Comfort' and 'Sexual Self-Acceptance' were all significantly more positive than they were for young women.

Political values and voting behaviour

Caprara et al.'s (2006) study on personality, values and political choices illustrates the way that social psychologists have explored the relationship between psychological attributes (such as personality) and somebody's political behaviour (such as the way they vote) as opposed to that person's claimed value system or beliefs. This study was carried out in Italy. In it a representative sample of people completed a personality trait scale (based on the 'Big 5' categorization of personality, see Chapter 12) and a questionnaire on values. They were also asked how they voted in the Italian national election of 2001. The analysis was based on data from the 3044 respondents who reported that they had voted for one of the two main coalitions (data were excluded if no response was given about voting, or if it had been for another party).

These data were subjected to a statistical analysis of correlation, which measures the extent to which one set of responses are systematically like or unlike another. In this case correlations were examined between voting behaviour (voting for the right-of-centre or the left-of-centre coalition) and both personality traits (such as energy, friendliness and openness) and values (such as achievement, security and tradition). Links were found with both. In terms of personality traits, the authors concluded:

> These results suggest that the emphasis of the center-left programs on solidarity and collective well-being and on education and tolerance for diversity made it more attractive to 'friendly' and 'open' people. Moreover, such people could better express and affirm their own personalities by voting for the center-left. The emphasis of the center-right programs on individual entrepreneurship and business freedom probably made that coalition more attractive for 'energetic, dominant' people and made voting for it more self-expressive.
>
> (Caprara et al. 2006: 21)

However, the links with values were even stronger:

> We based the hypotheses of relations between values and political preferences on the implications for value attainment of policy differences between the coalitions. The center-left coalition advocated social welfare, concern for social justice, equality, pluralism, and tolerance of diverse groups, even those that might disturb the conventional social order. Such a policy is most expressive of universalism values (emphasizing understanding, appreciation, tolerance, and protection for the welfare of all people) and also of benevolence values. This policy sharply opposes the self-enhancing goals of power and achievement values (status, dominance, personal success) and threatens the goal of preserving the social order central to security values. In contrast, the center-right coalition advocated the virtues of the market economy as a way to generate wealth and reward individual initiative and emphasized family and national security. This policy is congruent with the goals of power and security and achievement values.
>
> (Caprara et al. 2006: 21)

Induction and inferential statistics

These two studies are essentially descriptive, in that no variables were manipulated in an experimental sense. They are typical of a whole body of social psychology research that nonetheless set out with one or more hypotheses to be tested and, therefore, specific research questions to be answered. Inferential statistics are used to highlight regularities in the data, from which inductive logic can form the basis of the conclusions made. These can be of broadly two forms:

- demonstrating a **significant difference** between two or more conditions, categories or phenomena (such as the gender difference in the study of Latino youth's views about sexuality (Deardorff et al. 2008)
- demonstrating a **significant correlation** between two or more tests, traits and actions such as the study of voting, personality and values (Caprara et al. 2006).

Experimental demonstrations

A well-known example of descriptive research is the first of Stanley Milgram's studies of obedience to authority (Milgram 1963). In it he demonstrated that ordinary people can be persuaded to act extremely callously in a situation where there is strong pressure to obey.

Milgram was motivated to do this study, in part, by reports of the trials of Nazis who had been involved in the mistreatment and torture of people during the Second World War. When they appeared in these trials they gave every impression of being mild-mannered and courteous people. They said they had simply been 'following orders'. Milgram wanted to investigate how such apparently ordinary people came to act in such barbaric ways.

Milgram's original study of obedience

Milgram put advertisements in newspapers to recruit people to take part in a study that was ostensibly about the effects of punishment on learning. In fact it was an elaborate deception. The subjects of the study (40 men, aged between 20 and 50) were led to believe they were giving electric shocks to another person. In fact they were giving no shocks at all. The other person was a **stooge** – a member of the experimental team, briefed to act as if he were being hurt in predetermined ways throughout the study.

The recruited subjects came to the laboratory and met the second man whom, they were told, was another subject. They were informed that one of them would be the learner and the other the teacher in a study of memorizing paired words. The teacher would give electric shocks to the learner when he made mistakes, as a means to learning. Both then drew lots to decide who would be the 'learner' and who the 'teacher'. The lots were rigged so that the stooge always got the role of learner; the actual subject of the study always got the role of teacher.

The subject then saw the 'learner' being strapped to a chair and having electrodes attached to his arm with paste. They heard the experimenter explain that this paste was to prevent blistering and burning, and that while the shocks that would be administered might be painful, they would not cause any permanent damage. They also heard the learner telling the researcher he had a slight heart condition. The subjects were then taken into another room containing a dummy shock generator, which had a scale on it from 'slight shock' to 'XXX' – a point beyond 'Danger: severe shock'.

In this original study the subjects were not able to see the learner (who was in another room) but could hear his responses to the learning tasks and his (fake) reactions to the shock. They were told to administer progressively larger shocks to the learner each time he made a mistake. The study began and the learner gave some correct answers but also made mistakes. Soon the subject was apparently giving 'mild shocks' and could hear the learner grunting. At 120V the learner cried out that the shocks were becoming painful. At 150V he demanded to be released from the study and at 180V that he could not stand the pain any longer. The learner went on crying out in apparent pain, raising to an agonized scream at 250V. At 300V the learner fell silent, and the subject was told to take this as a mistake and continue giving ever-increasing shocks.

From the start of the study, subjects were agitated and soon began to tell the experimenter they wanted to stop. The researcher gave a predetermined response: 'Please continue.' As the subjects became more and more distressed at giving greater and greater shocks, the instructions to continue became increasingly stern – moving to 'It is absolutely essential that you continue' and then 'You have no other choice, you must go on.' Many subjects expressed concern about causing real harm to the learner, but were told: 'The responsibility is mine. Please continue.'

In this study Milgram found that more than 60 per cent of the subjects were prepared to go on giving what they believed were extremely severe shocks – 450V – to a plump middle-aged man. They did this even though they heard the man begging for the experiment to stop and screaming in pain, even though he had finally gone silent, and even though they had earlier heard him tell the experimenter he had a heart complaint.

Other descriptive studies

Another similar study by Philip Zimbardo and colleagues (Haney et al. 1973; Zimbardo et al. 1973) gave a similar demonstration that, given certain circumstances, ordinary men are capable of acting callously. Zimbardo and his colleagues set up a 'mock prison' and randomly assigned the subjects they had recruited to be either 'guards' or 'prisoners'. So aggressive and punitive did the 'guards' become that the study was ended less than halfway through its planned duration.

Neither study had a hypothesis as such. The data gathered in each case were descriptive. Therefore these descriptive studies did not – and could not – give any evidence to explain why the men in their studies behaved in the way they did. Writing from within the scientific paradigm, Manstead and Semin argue that for this reason 'social psychological research rarely stops at this point' (2001: 77).

Descriptive research

- Is based on observation and an inductive logic of inquiry.
- In principle there is no hypothesis – that is, no specific, theory-based predictions that are tested. Instead a phenomenon is observed or a situation is set up to 'see what happens'.
- In real life, though, descriptive research in social psychology usually does have a hypothesis, either explicitly or more covertly. Nonetheless, interpretation is based on the systematic patterns observed in the data, either of significant difference or significant correlation.

Experimental method

The purpose of an experiment in social psychology is to find an explanation for a social influence, social process or social phenomenon by identifying the cause(s) of particular effects. As you saw in Chapter 2, using Scientific method this is done by starting with a theory and devising a hypothesis from it. The hypothesis is then tested by systematically varying one or more specific elements and measuring their effects. From analysis of the effects, a causal explanation is generated.

Experimental settings

In the natural sciences, experiments are usually conducted in laboratories, although in some (such as in engineering) they are carried out 'in the field' – **field experiments**. Social psychologists also sometimes do field experiments if this is the best way to create the experimental conditions.

Field experiments

The **Capilano Bridge study** (Figure 4.1) is a good example, a field experiment on the attribution of emotion. In it Dutton and Aron (1974) tested the theory that arousal can be interpreted in different ways in different settings. They hypothesized that it can, in the right circumstances, be experienced as sexual attraction.

In order to test their hypothesis they had an 'attractive' woman interview young men when they were on a footbridge. When the interview was complete the woman gave the man a card with her phone number, saying he could call her to find out the results of the study if he wanted to. What the researchers actually counted, however, was how many of the men called her to ask for a date. That, by inference, was seen as a measure of whether the man experienced sexual arousal associated with the interview or not. This field experiment manipulated arousal by the

Figure 4.1

nature of the footbridge. In the 'low-arousal condition' the footbridge was just an ordinary one. In the 'high-arousal condition' it was the incredibly scary wooden suspension bridge at Capilano, where it spanned a deep crevasse, and scary because it sways alarmingly as you walk on it (I know, I tried it on a visit to Canada!) and the ground is a very, very long way down.

Another way of thinking about field experiments is that they are where researchers capitalize on situations in which relevant factors are being varied naturally. Instead of seeking to vary anxiety in the laboratory (for example, by giving subjects drugs that raise anxiety), Dutton and Aron capitalized on the different effects of walking on the two bridges. Such studies are therefore sometimes called **quasi-experiments**, since there is less ability to control the experimental conditions in them than in the laboratory.

A key principle of experimental design is that you must randomly allocate subjects to the different conditions to avoid the possibility that differences in the characteristics of the people in each group are what caused the effect, not your experimental manipulation. In the Capilano Bridge study the researchers had no control over which men walked on which bridge.

Try it for yourself

Think about how this may raise problems in this study. Spent a few moments considering alternative explanations for the finding that more men who had just walked over the scary bridge asked the interviewer for a date than those who were interviewed after coming off the non-threatening bridge.

Maybe it was that only men who liked taking risks went on the scary bridge, and risk-liking men are also more likely to ask women for dates. Maybe the interviewer gave unconscious signals, because she knew about the experimental hypothesis. Maybe you have come up with another possibility? You can see why controlling conditions is so important, both in terms of random allocation of subjects, and having a **double-blind experiment** where neither researcher nor subject knows what is being investigated.

Laboratory experiments

Laboratory experiments are conducted in much more controlled settings. In social psychology the 'laboratory' is often no more than an ordinary room, albeit one where people can be isolated from the outside world. But where, for instance, a subject's response times to different stimuli are measured, a social psychology experiment has all the trappings of what we generally think of as a 'laboratory'.

Increasingly researchers are using new technology to create virtual laboratories operating in what is called **immersive virtual environments** (IVEs). A good example is a study by Bailenson et al. (2001), examining the effects of eye gaze (you will come back to this in Chapter 6). In it participants in the study entered into the IVE and were asked to walk into a room in order to find out about the clothes that the avatars were wearing. In fact what was being studied was how they responded to eye contact. Avatars either had their eyes looking directly outwards, or downcast. You can see what they looked like in Figure 4.2.

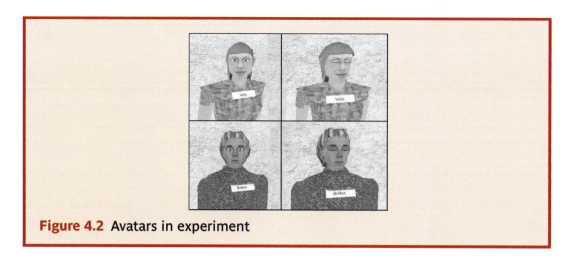

Figure 4.2 Avatars in experiment

Immersive virtual environments are being heralded as ideal laboratory conditions, since they allow for a greater degree of isolation from the social context than is ever possible in real life. Extraneous influences can be removed so that it is only the variables that are manipulated by the experiment that exert an influence.

Testing the hypothesis

Following his first descriptive study, Milgram went on to conduct a series of experiments to explore what was making his subjects obedient (Milgram 1965). In these studies he varied things like the gender of the subjects, the dress and demeanour of the experimenter, and whether the laboratory was sited in a university or in a scruffy downtown office. But for our purpose – to understand the basic format of an experiment – we will look at just one of these experiments: where Milgram deliberately set out to test the hypothesis that the closer the physical proximity between the subject and the learner, the less obedient the subject would be. In it Milgram tested four levels of proximity (see Table 4.1).

Table 4.1 The four levels of proximity used in Milgram's experiment

Level of proximity	Low	Moderate	High	Very high
Experimental condition	Subject cannot see or hear the learner	Subject can hear the learner but cannot see him	Subject can see and hear learner	Subject sits beside learner and holds his hand down on a metal plate for the shock to be delivered

As far as it was possible, all other conditions were kept the same, so that any differences between the behaviour of the subjects could be attributed to the differences in the level of proximity. The results from the study were as shown in Table 4.2.

Table 4.2 Percentage of subjects who went up to the 450V limit in relation to the four levels of proximity used in Milgram's experiment				
Level of proximity	**Low**	**Moderate**	**High**	**Very high**
Percentage of subjects who went up to the 450V limit	65	62.5	40	30

These data provide convincing evidence that proximity does affect participants' obedience. As you saw in Chapter 2, researchers apply statistical analysis at this stage of an experiment. This would turn the trend you can see here by just looking at the raw data into an estimate of the probability that such a pattern would arise by chance. This probability must be very low (in the order of one chance in 1000 or, better, one chance in 10,000) to be considered as evidence for an effect (though note it is not proof, as there is always that tiny probability it could happen by chance).

Milgram's later studies did use statistical analyses and were able to show that other factors exert an influence too: the behaviour and dress of the experimenter and the location of the experimental setting both had significant effects. However, what he found to be the most important influence was the presence of other 'teachers' (that is, additional stooges) and, in particular, their behaviour. If they refused to comply with instructions to go on giving shocks, then subjects almost always refused too. But if the others went on doing as they were told, then subjects generally did so as well.

Terminology

Milgram's (1965) experiment gives us the chance to get to grips with some important terminology used in relation to experiments. **Construct** is the term used to describe the abstract, theoretical concepts being studied – in the study we just looked at, these were obedience to authority and social proximity. **Operationalization** describes the way a construct is 'made operational' (that is, usable) in the form of variables that can be measured in a particular study. Hence the term **variable** describes the aspect of the construct that can be defined and/or measured. In this case, obedience to authority was measured by the point on the scale at which the subject refused to go on administering shocks, and proximity was measured by the level of proximity (low, moderate, high and very high) between the subject and the learner.

Variables come in one of two forms. The **independent variable** is varied by the researcher to test the hypothesis. In Milgram's experiment the independent variable was the level of proximity which he varied in four steps. The experiment therefore had four **conditions**. The **dependent variable** is used to assess the impact of the independent variable (that is, its magnitude depends upon the effect of the independent variable). In Milgram's experiment the dependent variable was the point on the scale at which the subject refused to go on administering shocks. The relationship between the constructs, variables and measurements in this experiment are shown in Table 4.3.

Data collection techniques

In experimental research there are three main ways in which measurable data can be collected (Table 4.4).

Table 4.3 Construct, variable and measurement in Milgram's experiment

Construct	Variable	Definition/measurement
Proximity	Independent	Low, moderate, high, very high
Obedience	Dependent	75V–450V

Table 4.4 Three data collection techniques

Measures	Definition	Examples
Observational	Recording actions directly relevant to the research question	Length of direct eye gaze; distance between people when they are interacting; categories of response such as wearing college sweatshirts
Self-report	Subjects' responses to questions	Questionnaire responses, responses in interviews
Implicit	Recording actions that imply an underlying effect	Response times to classifying items (for example, as belonging or not belonging to a category like 'attractive')

Observational measures

Observational measures are those taken from direct observation of the behaviour of subjects that is relevant to the research question. The behaviour can be in a form that is directly measured: for instance, the duration of eye gaze in seconds is frequently used as a measure of intimacy in relationships (Kleinke 1986). Or behaviours can be classified through a predetermined coding frame. Bales and Slater (1955), for instance, coded what people said in group discussions (for example, the number of requests for information, suggestions for action, and so on that a person made in a conversation) and used these frequency data to determine group members' roles in the group (for example, 'facilitator', 'leader').

Self-report measures

Many areas of social psychological research depend on **self-report measures**. Most research into people's attitudes, opinions and social cognition is done in this way. Reports may be in the form of answers to a scale or questionnaire, or in response to interview questions. In both cases the questions can be closed-ended (that is, where the question pre-specifies the responses that can be made) or open-ended (that is, where the question asks for an answer in the subject's own words). Closed-ended responses are coded through the instrument used. For example, many use a **Likert scale** with boxes to tick, ranging, say, from 'strongly agree' to 'strongly disagree'. In the Resources section links are provided for you to look at examples of Likert scales.

In experimental research, open-ended responses are pre-coded in relation to the hypothesis being tested. In the Bales and Slater study, for example, the coding frame was based on the hypothesis that facilitators and leaders would tend to make different contributions to the group discussion.

Kerb recycling – a study using observational and self-report measures

A study by Nigbur et al. (2010) on why people engage in kerb recycling schemes illustrates this approach. Here we will look at the first of two linked studies reported, carried out in Guildford in Surrey, UK, on two 'rounds' of a green-box recycling scheme where residents are offered the service of collecting recyclable waste as part of their weekly collection of refuse. It combined getting residents to complete a questionnaire with a measure of behaviour – whether a recycling box was placed out on a particular day or not. The questionnaire was delivered first, and then a few weeks later the researchers followed the refuse collection round in person and noted, for each address from which they had received a questionnaire return, whether or not a green box had been put out.

Table 4.5 Scale items for the Nigbur et al.'s kerb recycling study

Category	Number of items	Example items
Neighbourhood identification	10	Living in this street is an important aspect of who I am I would rather live elsewhere than in this street
Attitude towards recycling and perceived control over recycling	5	Participating in the green box scheme regularly is the right thing to do Participating regularly in green box recycling is entirely under my own control
Self-identity as a recycler and perceived social norms	5	To engage in household recycling is an important part of who I am My neighbours in this street would like to see others participate in kerbside recycling
Personal norm for recycling	5	I feel bad about putting recyclables into the bin
Intention to recycle	4	I will recycle my household waste wherever possible in the future

The questionnaire (see Table 4.5) combined a number of different categories of questions, each intended to tap a different attitudinal aspect that may influence recycling participation. The paper itself sets out details of the logic and research behind each category choice, the overall aim being to test out an expanded *theory of planned behaviour* explanation of how attitudes determine behaviour (this among other such theories is described in Chapter 8).

There were five categories, each with a number of items, with a five-point Likert scale used for responses in each case. Reliability and validity of the scale were tested using **factor analysis**, based on correlation. It showed, for instance, that attitudes towards recycling and social norms are, as predicted, systematically different attitudinal elements (in other words, that the scale did discriminate between them). As is common in experiments of this kind, statistical tests of 'fit' with the model worked well for predicting behavioural intention (what people said they planned to do) but was much less successful at predicting actual behaviour (what they actually did – that is, put out their green box). An interesting finding in this study was that self-identity as a recycler did, as hypothesized, improve the predictability. This suggests that at least some of what determines behaviour is due to acting out who you are – what I would call staking a claim to an identity. More of this in Chapter 10.

Implicit measures

Self-report measures rely on subjects giving accurate and honest answers to the questions they are posed. But they may not do so – for example, a subject may be unwilling to be seen as racist in reporting their opinions or attitudes. Social psychologists have therefore developed a range of **implicit measures**, from which a person's thinking (including their unconscious thinking) can be inferred indirectly. An example is a study of racial prejudice by Gaertner and McLaughlin (1983). They sat subjects in front of a computer screen, flashed up pairs of words (for example White-smart, Black-smart) and asked the subjects to press a button if they thought there was an association between the two words. In the UK we would probably have used the word 'clever' rather than 'smart' as the meanings of 'smart' are different. The implicit measure that Gaertner and McLaughlin used was the speed at which subjects responded. On average White subjects in the experiment responded significantly faster to the White-smart (White-clever) pairing than the Black-smart (Black-clever) one. From this the researchers inferred that these people were exhibiting racial prejudice.

A more recent study by Maas et al. (described in Maas and Cadinu 2003: 248) looked at the impact of stereotypical thinking on performance in a logic task by a group of men and women. They were either told it was a 'test of logical intelligence' or a 'test of social intelligence'. You may not be surprised to know that, on average, women got lower scores when they thought they were doing the 'logical intelligence' test, whereas the men got lower scores when they thought the task tested 'social intelligence'!

Triangulation

Interestingly, a later experiment by Cadinu et al. (2005) was able to give insight into what was going on through incorporating self-report measures (a thought-listing task) into the study. Not only did women in this study do worse when they were told that research showed 'gender differences' in test scores (compared with being told that men and women scored equally). They also reported fewer instances of negative thinking. This approach, where more than one kind of measure is used to get a better 'all-round picture' is called triangulation.

Experimental method

- Experimental method is based on the deductive logic of inquiry, where a hypothesis is generated and tested by keeping influences as constant as possible and manipulating just the experimental conditions.

- Any differences in the dependent variable can thus be attributed to the experimental manipulation – called the 'effect'.

- Statistical analysis is used to calculate the probability that the effect could have arisen by chance.

- Where this is very low (for instance, a probability of one in 10,000), then a conclusion can be made that the effect is probably a result of the experimental manipulation.

- A good example is Milgram's study of the effect of proximity on how long people will continue to administer ever stronger shocks to 'train' another person. He showed that the further the proximity, the more severe were the 'shocks' administered.

Quantitative research strategies

When experimental researchers plan social psychological studies they need to take three considerations into account:

- the representativeness of the data collected
- realism – how far the study can reflect real life
- the amount of control that can be exerted over the experimental conditions.

Representativeness

Representativeness involves trying to make sure that the people taking part in the study are representative of the people you want to find out about, or your theory is about. So, for instance, if your theory is about 'people in general', you need to make sure that the people taking part (in experiments they are called the **experimental subjects,** in surveys they are called respondents) are able to represent the population as a whole. Your sample should have, for instance, the same balance of males and females that occur in the general population, and representative proportions of different age groups.

Historically, social psychologists were very blinkered; the majority of studies were done with males only. Even today many (perhaps most) social psychological studies use students as experimental subjects, since they are, in effect, a 'captive market' (in many psychology departments, being a subject for the research of their tutors and their research colleagues is a course requirement). Cadinu et al. (2005) mentioned earlier did so. Making them take part is justified by the claim that they will gain from the experience.

This use of students to represent (in this case) 'women in general' is usually justified by the claim that psychology students are sufficiently representative in the qualities relevant to the study for it not to matter that they constitute a specific group (in terms of age, social class and level of education) and not representative of the population as a whole: '[T]here is often little reason to suppose that the processes underlying a phenomenon such as attitude change or stereotyping differs in some fundamental way between students and non-students' (Manstead 2009: 34). This is entirely logical. Experimental social psychology is based upon investigating what are assumed to be universal processes (like attitude change) that operate in essentially the same manner for all humankind. Thus, any convenient sample pool will do and, in this context, it is perfectly acceptable to use locally recruited students. Nonetheless, a range of other sampling strategies have been used – both Milgram and Zimbardo recruited their subjects through advertising, and other psychologists have targeted people waiting at airports.

In other settings, such as survey research, respondents are usually selectively sampled to be representative of the qualities held to matter in the study in question – for instance, in terms of social class, age and gender. In cases like the study of Latino youth's sexual attitudes, then the sample must be representative of the ethnic subgroups that make up 'Latino' as defined in the USA – as the Deardorff et al. (2008) study did.

Survey research is the best strategy when the research question is primarily a descriptive one and relates to public attitudes. **Opinion polls** (especially in the lead-up to elections) and market research are common examples, where what is wanted is to get an accurate description of trends and/or the differences between, say, different socio-economic groups. Studies of market segmentation, for instance, are used to identify different kinds of customers, particularly when a new product is launched and companies want to know where to direct their advertising. Where researchers want to find out about a specific subgroup, then they will seek to target just these people. Examples here are studies conducted by political parties, where they want to target just 'floating voters'. They use a questionnaire to identify such people and then invite just these to take part in **focus groups** about which policy initiatives 'go down well' with floating voters. Market researchers (a realistic job opportunity for social psychologists) use both qualitative and quantitative methods, according to the research questions they are paid to answer.

Realism

Realism has to do with the extent to which it matters that the setting in which your study is conducted and the design of the study itself are close to 'real life'. In the Zimbardo study the 'real life' being constructed was designed to be as close as possible to a real prison (Zimbardo et al. 1973). In this study the researchers saw realism as a crucial element in the variables they wanted to study. But in Wason's (1966, 1968) selection task study that you looked at in Chapter 2, the 'realism' of the setting was not seen as relevant. Increasingly, though, laboratory-like studies are being criticized for so decontextualizing the situation that the results obtained are not valid.

A good example here is the work that followed on from actual case of the rape and murder of Kitty Genovese, which was the first thing we looked at in Chapter 1: the laboratory study carried out to examine the bystander effect, investigating the difference between acting alone and acting in front of others (Latané and Darley 1968).

This and another study on the bystander effect are described in more detail in Chapter 11.

The experiment consisted of getting people to fill in questionnaires in a 'waiting room', and then having smoke coming into the room so that it gradually became more and more smoke-filled. The dependent variable was how long it took participants to report the smoke. The experimental results were clear-cut. Participants on their own were much more likely to report the smoke than those in groups of three, and did so significantly faster. The lowest response was where there were three people observing, with two of them stooges who played it very cool and did not respond. You can see parallels here with the Milgram experiment, where the subjects were most affected by what stooges did. This study by Latané and Darley used highly restricted conditions – participants were isolated in a small room, and the stooges were briefed precisely about what to do and say. The dependent variable was how long it took the subjects to respond to the 'emergency' – smoke filling the room.

Cherry (1995) criticized studies like this because they are a far cry from witnessing rape and murder. How, she asked, can an experiment like this tell us anything much about real attacks that are *always* observed in contexts that are far more realistic than taking part in a psychology experiment – where people are naturally suspicious about what is going on? We will come back to this point a bit later.

These criticisms are not a rejection of using experiments in social psychology. Rather they draw attention to their limitations, and the need to be cautious about what can be inferred from the data obtained. Over-claiming can be a real problem, but the solution is not to abandon experiments altogether. It is to take the question of realism much more seriously, and to acknowledge the limitations of how far findings can be generalized. There are signs this is happening, especially with the growing engagement with social psychology among a much more culturally diverse range of students and researchers.

Control

Control is crucial to the hypothetico-deductive method, in that the study itself can work only if the researcher can isolate extraneous variables, closely control the manipulation of the independent variable(s) and accurately measure the dependent variable(s). The more important it is for a study to follow the hypothetico-deductive method, the more crucial it is to have high levels of control. Thus control is relatively unimportant in descriptive research, but central to explanatory research.

Control can be a problem though. For example, the act of stripping away context and extracting **confounding variables** can end up in removing the very elements that are important for good performance. Experiments on 'social loafing' (the tendency for people to make less effort when in a group than when acting alone) show that the effect is highly sensitive to all manner of factors. These include the complexity of the task, its meaning and interest to the participants, whether they like working in groups or not, and so on. So, for example, to make the task that participants have to do very simple and bland usually leads to a high degree of social loafing. But if the task used is seen to be worthwhile, meaningful and relevant to members of the group, then they do the very opposite of loafing – they make a better job of it as a team than they would have done alone.

As with realism, this does not mean experiments are not useful or do not work or are invalid. It means that experimentalists must take real care that the steps they take to maximize control are appropriate for the research questions they are seeking to answer. It requires a high degree of reflexive insight to design how variables will be manipulated. We are now seeing a growth of more sophisticated studies that manipulate more, and more relevant, variables in conjunction with each other in a more sophisticated way.

Research design

When designing studies, researchers have to balance out these three factors. By and large greater realism means less control. The Capilano Bridge study is a good example (Dutton and Aron 1974). It was fairly realistic – in that anxiety varied naturally between the two experimental settings. But the researchers had no control over which men walked across which bridge. This meant they could not be sure that the two samples were comparable. Researchers also have to be pragmatic, since greater representativeness usually means that subjects must be selected more carefully, and this can be time-consuming, difficult and often costly.

Different research strategies are used according to the relative salience and importance of representativeness, realism and control. Broadly these are as shown in Table 4.6. From this it can be seen that where control is the most salient, laboratory experiments are best. Where realism is important, then field experiments are best. And where representativeness is crucial, then surveys are best. Of course, these are over-generalizations, but this is a broad rule of thumb that works most of the time.

Table 4.6 Suitability of different research strategies			
	Research settings		
	Laboratory experiments	**Field experiments**	**Surveys**
Control	High	Medium	Low
Realism	Low	High	Irrelevant
Representativeness	Varies	Low	High

Quantitative research strategies

- Measurement needs to be done to the best standard possible in terms of representativeness, realism and control.
- Different research strategies offer different options, each with their own benefits and limitations. Studies should select the most appropriate one for the research questions being addressed.
- Mixed methods *within* quantitative research can be a powerful strategy.

Qualitative research in quantitative studies

Mixing methods

There are some social psychologists who are experimental in their epistemological position but include qualitative methods in their research programmes. For example, they may begin a study with open-ended interviews or group discussions in order to gather a general sense of what people think and say about a topic, for instance, as part of the process of designing a questionnaire. Indeed, Manstead notes that 'it is common practice for social psychologists to use qualitative methods . . . in the early stages of their research (for example, to develop and refine the questions to be posed in a questionnaire)' (2008: 28). This is usually what is meant by the term **mixed method research**, where the ultimate goal is to arrive at hypothetico-deductive explanations for the ways people act and think.

Qualitative research as a development stage

The most common form of mixed methods is where they are expressly built into the study, usually seen as a preparatory or development stage. Here qualitative data collection methods and open-ended elements are included to, say, inform the selection of variables and/or to help design measurement instruments for the study proper.

The study described at the beginning of the chapter by Deardorff et al. (2008) is a good example. If you recall, the researchers wanted to find out about the sexual beliefs and values among

Latino young people. As little previous work had been done with this particular group, Deardorff and her colleagues started their project using qualitative methods and analyses. They called this the 'development phase'.

This phase consisted of conducting focus groups and interviews with relatively small numbers of participants – 55 in the focus groups, and 24 interviews. Both were semi-structured, using open-ended questioning and encouraging participants to move on to topics and areas not covered in the schedules. The transcripts were then subjected to thematic analysis (see Chapter 5) to identify key themes, which were then used to construct questionnaires for use in the quantitative (that is, 'main') phase of the study. These were intended as 'tools for assessment' of sexual beliefs and values among this specific population of Latino youth. The scale was administered to 694 sexually active Latino young people and statistical analysis allowed the validity and reliability of the scale to be tested and found satisfactory.

Qualitative research 'hidden' within quantitative studies

The role of qualitative research in quantitative studies is actually a lot more pervasive than just a preliminary stage to design an instrument for a quantitative study. Indeed, it is surprising that when you look closely at experimental studies, just how often the data obtained in debriefing interviews or even informal conversations at the end of experiments become part of the data-set used to inform the researcher's conclusions.

What is often overlooked is that there were other 'results' too that were reported in the Latané and Darley paper, when the researchers described what happened when the participants were debriefed. Before revealing what had been going on, the experimenter asked the subjects if they had had any problems with the experiment. All mentioned the smoke. But the people who had reported it gave very different responses from those who did not:

> Subjects who had reported the smoke were relatively consistent in later describing their reactions to it. They thought the smoke looked somewhat 'strange', they were not sure exactly what it was or whether it was dangerous, but they felt it was unusual enough to justify some examination. 'I wasn't sure whether it was a fire but it looked like something was wrong.' 'I thought it might be steam, but it seemed like a good idea to check it out.'
>
> Subjects who had not reported the smoke also were unsure about exactly what it was, but they uniformly said that they had rejected the idea that it was a fire. Instead, they hit upon an astonishing variety of alternative explanations, all sharing the common characteristic of interpreting the smoke as a non dangerous event. Many thought the smoke was either steam or air-conditioning vapors, several thought it was smog, purposely introduced to simulate an urban environment, and two (from different groups) actually suggested that the smoke was a 'truth gas' filtered into the room to induce them to answer the questionnaire accurately. (Surprisingly, they were not disturbed by this conviction.) Predictably, some decided that 'it must be some sort of experiment' and stoically endured the discomfort of the room rather than overreact.
>
> (Latané and Darley 1968: 219)

Something very interesting is going on here. These *qualitative* differences in the nature of the accounts of what participants experienced were, albeit implicitly and I suspect unreflexively, being categorized by the researchers into two 'themes' – one about justifying why they broke off the experiment to report the smoke, and the other justifying why they did *not*. This looks to me a clear example of abductive research (Chapter 2): the researchers observed something surprising (they themselves use the word 'astonishing') in their data, and then sought to explain it.

I could speculate just a bit further – which is that considerable insight was gained from, first, finding that all of their participants felt they had to account for what they did and, second, that their justifications were of a different nature. But, most importantly, it looks like these unexpected extra-experimental elements in the study contributed to the conclusions arrived at by Latané and Darley in this study.

In their other study, Darley and Latané (1968) led participants to think that the person they were talking to was having a fit. They found a similar distinction. Darley and Latané, writing about the difference between those who went to get help and those who did not, made the following observations:

> Subjects, whether or not they intervened, believed the fit to be genuine and serious. 'My God, he's having a fit,' many subjects said to themselves (and were overheard via their microphones) at the onset of the supposed fit. Others gasped or simply said 'Oh.' Several of the male subjects swore. One subject said to herself, 'It's just my kind of luck, something has to happen to me!' Several subjects spoke aloud of their confusion about what course of action to take, 'Oh God, what should I do?'
>
> When those subjects who intervened stepped out of their rooms, they found the experimental assistant down the hall. With some uncertainty, but without panic, they reported the situation. 'Hey, I think Number 1 is very sick. He's having a fit or something.' After ostensibly checking on the situation, the experimenter returned to report that 'everything is under control.' The subjects accepted these assurances with obvious relief.
>
> Subjects who failed to report the emergency showed few signs of the apathy and indifference thought to characterize 'unresponsive bystanders.' When the experimenter entered her room to terminate the situation, the subject often asked if the victim was 'all right.' 'Is he being taken care of?' 'He's all right isn't he?' Many of these subjects showed physical signs of nervousness; they often had trembling hands and sweating palms. If anything, they seemed more emotionally aroused than did the subjects who reported the emergency.
>
> (Darley and Latané 1968: 381)

Once again data are being reported here, but not acknowledged as data – and qualitative data at that:

> Why, then, didn't they respond? It is our impression that non intervening subjects had not decided not to respond. Rather they were still in a state of indecision and conflict concerning whether to respond or not. The emotional behavior of these non responding subjects was a sign of their continuing conflict, a conflict that other subjects resolved by responding.
>
> (Darley and Latané 1968: 381)

There is a lot more going on here between the two studies – which is picked up in Chapter 11. But the main point here is clear to you I hope, which is that what *appear* to be simple social psychological experiments are often not all that simple or even that experimental. Researchers either deliberately or serendipitously get other data than the bald numbers of the measures they have reported and, I suspect, often use this data to help them understand what is going on, either overtly or covertly.

What is interesting, though, is that this very important qualitative component and the abductive logic it stimulates are not so much covered up as ignored by social psychology textbooks. I consulted over 40 of these textbooks from different times and different places in my preparation for writing my book. As far as I can tell, all of them report the quantitative data from the two studies, none of them report this additional qualitative data (though my 'survey' has not been exhaustive – so, like Popper, I conclude that I think social psychology textbooks do not raise this issue, but I could be wrong). The consequence is that we are left with a sense that experimental work is all about the numbers, when, I suspect, it is seldom so clear-cut.

Qualitative research in quantitative studies

- Experimental social psychologists often deliberately use qualitative methods as a preparatory stage in an investigation – for instance, to devise or refine an instrument to measure or assess something like attitudes, opinions or beliefs.

- However, qualitative data can be found in quantitative research, but is not usually recognized as such.

- It is possible – even likely – that this qualitative data affects the conclusions derived, and possibly even the hypotheses claimed in some cases.

- It is always worth looking at the original paper if you want to understand what went on in a study and, thankfully, these days it is a lot easier to do that.

Ethics in quantitative research

Milgram's demonstration and the experiments that he went on to do (and, indeed, those that others did in replication) raised considerable concern about the ethics of convincing people that they were obliged to harm others. Interestingly, Milgram, aided by a psychiatrist, did follow-up surveys and interviews with more than a thousand of his experimental subjects, and reports that only 1.3 per cent reported they were 'sorry' or 'very sorry' they took part, with 83.7 per cent saying they were 'glad' or 'very glad' they did. I wonder if, like me, you think there may be a lot more to it than that?

These days the situation is very different. Many of the classic experiments you will read about in this book would, today, simply not be possible. Ethical approval would not be given. Without that you would be in trouble with your institution, because of their legal obligations to people involved in research with them, and a concern to avoid being sued. Journals also insist on ethical approval for all studies they publish. And professional organizations such as the British Psychological Society (BPS) also insist that psychology must be conducted ethically:

Thinking about ethics should pervade all professional activity. Ethics can be defined as the science of morals or rules of behaviour. Psychology can be defined as the scientific study of behaviour both internal (for example, cognition and feelings) and external (for example, language and actions). Thus whilst ethics and psychology are distinct, there is nevertheless an overlap as both are concerned with behaviour. Before embarking on professional work the ethical implications should be considered as part of the work context together with legal, professional and other frameworks.

(BPS 2009: 6)

The BPS code of practice is freely available online (see the Resources section at the end of this chapter). It is a clear and helpful document for anyone, and worth looking at. If you are studying elsewhere, do look for your local equivalent. This will give specific advice relevant to local circumstances. For example, the one for Aotearoa/New Zealand has a very well-designed section on 'Respect for the Dignity of Persons and Peoples'. It states explicitly the following ethical principles in ethical research and practice in relation to Maori:

- Psychologists practising in New Zealand recognise that the Treaty of Waitangi sets out the basis of respect between Maori and non-Maori in this country.
- Te Tiriti o Waitangi [the Maori version of the treaty] is given priority as the version that was offered to and signed by the majority of the Maori signatories.
- Psychologists, individually and collectively, seek to be informed about the meaning and implications of the Treaty of Waitangi for their work. This includes an understanding of the principles of protection, participation and partnership with Maori.
- Both non-Maori and Maori psychologists who work with Maori seek advice and undertake training in the appropriate way to show respect for the dignity and needs of Maori in their practice.

(Code of Ethics Review Group, NZ Psychological Society, NZ College of Clinical Psychologists and the NZ Psychologists Board 2002: 5)

This example demonstrates how ethics varies from one geo-political location to another. Ethics incorporates both the abstract ethical principles held by the people with the power to determine them, and the law as it operates in a location. In the case of Autearoa/New Zealand, the Treaty of Waitangi is centrally important in a way it is not anywhere else.

Having said that, most ethical codes used by psychologists have a strong commonality. Most, for example, include the following four key categories:

- respect
- competence
- responsibility
- integrity

Respect

This covers general respect about the way you treat the participants in your study and avoid any form of prejudice. It also includes respecting privacy and confidentiality, gaining properly informed consent, and making sure participants genuinely feel they have the right and the choice not to participate in any part of the research without having to give any reasons.

However, respect is not a simple principle to follow. It is all too easy to imagine we know how to be respectful to everyone and anyone on the basis of our own upbringing and under-standing of what is entailed. Linda Tuhiwai Smith, a postcolonial theorist, has pointed out: 'The word itself "research" is probably one of the dirtiest words in the indigenous world's vocabulary. When mentioned to many indigenous contexts it stirs up silence, it conjures up bad memories, it raises a smile that is knowing distrustful' (1999: 1). She goes on to explain: 'It galls us that Western researchers and intellectuals can assume to know all that it is possible to know of us, on the basis of their brief encounters with some of us' (Smith 1999: 1).

I use the term 'data vampirism' for this, something I frequently observed in the countries of Europe that, in the 1980s and 1990s, were undergoing dramatic political, social and economic change. Psychologists in these countries were very cheap to employ and were under pressure from their universities and institutes to form partnerships and alliances with psychologists from the 'West'. Many studies were done in which already established scales were simply translated from English, in a spate of cross-cultural research, with little recognition that words like 'democracy' meant very different things in different places.

Respect always involves knowing what it signifies and involves in the location in which par-ticipants live. This includes understanding the local rules operating about privacy, consent and self-determination. This means working *with* (and not simply employing or consulting) local people, in contexts of mutual respect. This issue will be addressed in more detail in the next chapter, since qualitative research, by its nature, involves more opportunities for disrespect and exploitation.

Competence

This is mainly, in the context of ethics, about the capacity to act ethically in research. It entails being well informed about the ethics of research in general and specific issues to do with particular kinds of research. For example, if you plan to use the Internet or other IT source for collecting data, you need to consider the specific ethical issues raised (see the Resources section for BPS guidance).

As you saw, what constitutes competence varies from location to location. In Aotearoa/New Zealand it requires knowledge of and training in the Treaty of Waitangi.

Responsibility

The primary principle is that your research should do no harm to your participants, though there are limits to this. For example, promising confidentiality can be problematic. Confidentiality needs to be negotiated against other ethical principles, such as protecting the vulnerable. Responsibility includes keeping participants informed, protecting them physically and in other ways, and debriefing them properly. It may involve seeking help or advice from others.

Integrity

Integrity is based upon honesty, accuracy, clarity and fairness in all your dealings with participants and others involved. It is not just about how you conduct your research, but how you report and disseminate your findings. It is also about avoiding conflicts of interest and any form of exploitation. This is especially important in relation to co-researchers and others involved in any aspect of the project, and includes limits to personal relationships.

Ethics

- Ethical research is important for its own sake, but also because you must be responsible to your institution, protect yourself and avoid harming or exploiting others.
- Pragmatically, you must gain official ethical approval for any research you undertake, and sometimes this will involve getting approval from more than one body (such as your university and the National Research Ethics Service, see Resources).
- Researching ethically is especially important when your participants may have different understandings from you – for example, what constitutes 'harm' and rules for showing respect.

Resources

Quantitative research in psychology

Research in psychology: http://www.socialpsychology.org/methods.htm

Using Twitter to conduct surveys: http://www.psychologytoday.com/blog/working-creativity/201003/the-tweetment-research

Ethics

BPS ethical guidelines: http://www.bps.org.uk/the-society/code-of-conduct/code-of-conduct_home.cfm

BPS ethical guidelines for Internet research: http://www.admin.ox.ac.uk/curec/internetresearch.pdf

National Research Ethics Service (NRES): http://www.nres.npsa.nhs.uk/applications/

American Psychological Association (APA) ethics guidance can be found at: http://www.apa.org/ethics/code/index.aspx

The Psychological Association of Ireland Code of Ethics: http://www.psihq.ie/2008Code%20of%20Ethics.pdf

Further reading

You are likely to find plenty of textbooks on experimental approaches to social psychology in your library and in academic bookshops. Here are some I think you will find particularly useful.

Manstead, A.S.R. (2009) Research methods in social psychology, in M. Hewstone, W. Stroebe, and K. Jonas (eds) *Introduction to Social Psychology: A European Perspective*, 4th edn. Oxford: Blackwell.

This chapter gives an excellently readable, detailed, comprehensive and up-to-date coverage of the research methods used in social psychology. It is mainly written from within the scientific paradigm, but it also offers a critique of some of the problems with experiments. It also does (albeit briefly) acknowledge that some social psychologists use qualitative methods to pursue research questions from the critical approach, and briefly outlines discourse analytic research. What marks this out compared with standard US textbooks is that it is considerably less ethnocentric, and highly inclusive of the broad range of research conducted by social psychologists in Europe and beyond. It sets out a clear rationale for research design and is a good source for planning your own research project.

Dunn, D.S. (2009) *Research Methods for Social Psychology*. Oxford: Blackwell/Wiley.

Although this is very much an US text, hence mainly about research as it is done in the USA, it is an extremely useful student text. It is very clearly and engagingly written, with lots of activities to help you develop the practical skills you need to carry out a project of your own. Billed in its publicity as 'teach[ing] students to think like an experimental social psychologist' and '[s]triking a balance between theoretical sophistication and hands-on activities and exercises', it is, as other books by the same author, thoroughly *practical*.

Clark-Carter, D. (2009) *Quantitative Psychological Research: The Complete Students Companion*. Hove: Psychology Press. Available as an e-book from Taylor & Francis.

This book is well written, up to date and thorough. As its title suggests, it is specifically designed to be student-friendly and accessible. Its focus in general remains the standard 'how-to-do' text for data collection techniques. It offers detailed and clear advice about designing and administering questionnaires and analysing and interpreting the data collected.

Mixed methods

Yardley, L. and Bishop, F. (2009) Mixing qualitative and quantitative methods, in C. Willig and W. Stainton Rogers (eds) *The Sage Handbook of Qualitative Research in Psychology*. London: Sage.

This is both a thorough analysis of the functions of, and approaches to, mixing methods, and a clear practical guide about how to do it well.

Questionnaire design

Oppenheim, N. (1992) *Questionnaire Design, Interviewing and Attitude Measurement*. London: Pinter.

This remains the standard 'how-to-do' text for these data collection techniques. It offers detailed and clear advice about designing and administering questionnaires and analysing and interpreting the data collected.

Questions

1 Using the knowledge you have gained from this chapter, go back to Triplett's study of 'dynamogenic influence' (described in Chapter 1) and illustrate how it follows the basic design and principles of an experiment.

2 Giving illustrations in each case, describe how laboratory experiments, field experiments and surveys differ in relation to their capacity to manage control, realism and representativeness in their design.

3 Describe what is meant by a 'mixed methods approach', illustrating your answer by reference to two studies that have used this approach.

4 By reference to a code of ethics that relates to the country where you are studying, outline the key principles of conducting ethical experimental research in psychology. Explain what particular issues you will need to address if you want to use Facebook (or something similar on the Internet) to recruit people to take part in a survey.

5 In what ways do you think new developments in IT *or* reality television will affect the way social psychologists conduct experiments?

Chapter 5

Qualitative research in social psychology

LEARNING OUTCOMES

When you have finished studying this chapter, you should be able to:

1 Explain what is meant by 'qualitative research' in social psychology, how it differs from quantitative methods, and the kinds of research questions it is most suited to addressing.

2 Outline two alternative forms of descriptive research using qualitative methods, and explain how they go beyond 'mere description' – and why this is so important.

3 List and briefly describe seven different *forms of data collection* that social psychologists use to carry out qualitative research.

4 List and briefly describe seven different *analytical approaches* that social psychologists use to carry out qualitative research.

5 Demonstrate insight into how and on what basis social psychologists select from these different methods and analytical approaches when planning their research.

6 Know where to look for more detailed information and guidance about these forms of data collection and analytic approaches.

7 Give reasons why ethical issues are often more difficult to identify and to tackle in qualitative research, and why it is more a matter of 'learning to be ethical'.

Introduction

The 1990s, Jonathan Smith, Rom Harré and Luk Van Langenhove declared, was 'an exciting time for psychology'. Their book, published in 1995 and entitled *Rethinking Methods in Psychology*, brought together a range of new, refurbished and realigned methods available to psychologists at a time of a 'changing discipline':

> A number of methodologies consonant with a shift to a post-positivist, non-experimental paradigm are now emerging and they are beginning to be used in a wide range of empirical studies. As these studies proliferate and are published, there will be a real chance of fundamentally changing the discipline of psychology, of radically redrawing its boundaries to include a whole new set of questions, asked and answered in new ways.
>
> (Smith et al. 1995: 1)

While being aware that qualitative research is nothing new in social psychology, the point being made here is well-founded. The shift to critical social psychology was as much a methodological shift as a theoretical one. If you stop trying to pin down universal laws of social behaviour, influence and experience and, instead, seek to understand the ways in which 'the social' operates, then you need to go about it in quite different ways. Put simply, it is a shift from exploring how people are the same to exploring how and why they are different, and this requires a different methodology.

Because it looks at the meaning-making people do, by and large, **qualitative research** involves investigating what they say, usually in language but sometimes in other forms, such as visually (for example, by taking photographs) or using other representational systems such as music and/or dance.

In this context, with qualitative research there is less of a connection between data collection and its interpretation. For instance, interviews and their transcripts (albeit coded somewhat differently) can form the basis of conversational, discourse, narrative and phenomenological analyses. So can accounts found in newspapers or the text on packaging (such as the box in which toothpaste is packed). For this reason I have separated them in this chapter. It begins by very briefly reviewing some of the methods of data collection, then has sections introducing some of the main ways of analysing data, starting (as did Chapter 4) with descriptive research and then moving on to research that is analytical.

This is a long chapter, because it covers a lot of ground – most of the approaches to analysis found in present-day critical social psychology. The good news is that the chapter is intended to be used differently from others – more as a chapter to dip in and out of, as the interest and need take you. My aim has been to give you enough information and advice to decide if you want to use a particular approach – for instance, in your dissertation. This, together with the suggestions in the Further reading section, should give you a good start. Otherwise, it is perfectly all right to read selectively, so you get a good overall 'feel' for the range of options available to you.

Data collection in qualitative psychology

There are a variety of ways by which qualitative researchers collect their data. We shall look only briefly at them here though, as in qualitative research, analysis is where most of the serious work is done. As the task is to seek understanding and insight rather than to explain in cause-and-effect terms, there is no need to turn constructs into variables, or work out how to measure some things, control others and exclude the rest. As there is no claim to objectivity, researchers are not particularly concerned about representativeness, realism or control.

Consequently, there is much greater diversity in means of data collection, and much more freedom for innovation. With the growth of networking and 'talk' through the Internet, and other developments such as gaming and Second Life, qualitative researchers are increasingly able to access social behaviour of all kinds from their laptops. There are, of course, ethical issues that need to be carefully worked out – this is dealt with later in the chapter. But we are seeing something of a revolution going on in qualitative research in social psychology, where some are even suggesting we should abandon the concept of methods altogether (Chamberlain 2000).

Quantitative researchers often see this as methodological sloppiness! But they are missing the crucial point: that different research questions are being asked and different kinds of answers sought, for which these methodological features are largely irrelevant. Do not get me wrong: qualitative research is not (or certainly should not be) sloppy. It always needs to be done with insight, with careful consideration of research ethics and it certainly needs to be done very meticulously. As you will see, the various methods of data collection all require good planning and organization. Many involve high-quality, high-technology equipment, painstaking transcription, and both transcribers and those who do the analysis (often the same person) need to develop high-grade skills in recording and interpreting what has gone on. All involve using subtle and theoretically sophisticated techniques to code data and then apply various interpretative strategies.

In our current situation of change in the way data is collected, there is no room for detailed accounts of all the possible ways to go about it. Instead I have summarized in Table 5.1 some of the main methods, and an example of each one you can follow up if you are particularly interested.

Table 5.1 Different ways of collecting data in qualitative research in social psychology

Source of data	Description	Example
Ethnography	Based on anthropological and sociological research, this is about 'hanging out' with people in places where what you want to study goes on. It produces records that can include written notes, photographs and sound recordings	Bengry-Howell (2005) used an ethnographical approach to the study of 'boy racers' and their constructions of masculinity
Autoethnography	This means, literally, to do an ethnographic study on oneself	Frentz (2009) reports his experiences of having a hip replacement, with an identity that shifts from 'trickster', through 'cyborg' to 'hybrid'
Interviews	These can be semi-structured or completely unstructured conversations between the researcher and a participant, with open opportunities for the participant to more or less express themselves in their own words about the topic set by the researcher	Rickett (2010) conducted semi-structured interviews with women who were nurses and door supervisors ('bouncers') to explore themes around risk and sacrifice

Table 5.1 *Continued*

Source of data	Description	Example
	Interviews can be conducted face to face, by phone and Skype, via the Internet and in virtual life	
Narrative interviews	Used for narrative analysis, the interview consists of an account, by the participant, of a series of life-events	Hanka's story in a study by Chrz et al. (2006) about how women cope with breast cancer
Biographical interviews	These explicitly ask participants to talk about the topic in question in relation to its time and place and significance within their life-story	Sheridan (2010) used a particular form of biographical interviewing to gain insight into what it takes for women to maintain their weight loss
Photo-elicitation	This is where participants take photographs, which are then used as the basis of interviews, either individual or group	Radley et al. (2005) used photographs taken by homeless people both as data in themselves and to stimulate talk about their lives and their places
Psychoanalytic interviewing	Specific forms of interviewing are used to open up the potential for psychoanalytic interpretation, such as free-association narrative interviews	Saville Young and Frosh (2009) studied an account of the relationship difficulties between the participant and his brother
Focus groups	In many ways a group interview, but able to use interaction between participants to enable more rhetorical data	Augostinos et al. (1999) used focus groups to explore racism in the conversations of Australian students
Group tasks	There are a variety of ways that talk can be generated beyond the standard interview or group discussion. These include getting participants to construct scripts or make group judgements in ways that they challenge each other to justify claims and interpretation	Stenner (1993) got small groups to work together to devise scenarios depicting 'jealousy' as one way to gain insight into popular understandings of it
Journals and diaries	Diaries are commonly used in quantitative work to gather data on actions like alcohol consumption. In qualitative work they can be elicited as biography; or analysis can be directed towards existing diaries, often used for phenomenological work	Butt and Langdridge (2003) gained access to the diaries of Kenneth Williams, to explore how the actor constructed his identity
Documents	Similarly 'found' documents of various kinds – newspapers, magazines and advertisements – can form part of the data set for analysis, often alongside other data, such as from focus groups	Bilic and Georgaca (2007) conducted a critical discourse analysis of the ways in which 'mental illness' is represented in Serbian newspapers
The Internet	Blogs, chat rooms, websites and online message boards all provide opportunities	Day and Keys (2008) looked at discussion and postings on pro-eating disorder (pro-anna) websites

Data collection in qualitative research

- As there is no hypothesis being tested and no assumptions that findings can be generalized. Most of the quality standards of quantitative research do not apply – the quality of qualitative research is mainly achieved through the quality of the interpretation.

- Usually studies involve only small numbers of participants, often chosen strategically to directly relate to the research question.

- There is a great and growing diversity of data-collection techniques, including:

    Ethnography
        Autoethnography
    Interviews
        Narrative interviews
        Biographical interviews
        Photo-elicitation
        Psychoanalytic interviewing
    Focus groups
    Group tasks

- Alternatively, text is taken from available sites – films, books, newspapers and magazines; advertising materials, websites and chat rooms; diaries, journals and recorded conversations such as counselling sessions.

- There is room to be inventive – to mix methods and to create tasks and situations tailored to achieving the data required.

Descriptive qualitative research

In critical psychology description is always – or certainly should be – a means to an end. To be considered research (rather than journalism or documentary making) its primary purpose is to gain insight into 'what is going on' in relation to the phenomenon or topic or issue being studied. Thus the description obtained (for example, through interviewing people or doing ethnography, including ethnography on the Internet) is then subjected to some form of interpretation.

Actually, as journalists gain greater access to academic work, it is sometimes hard to tell the difference between what they do and reports of qualitative social psychological research. However, as a student, it is important that your assignments and, especially, dissertations or theses show clear indications of academic scholarship, particularly if they are to be marked by tutors whose work is experimental – if you want to get good marks, that is! It is also important for your development as a researcher, and for getting the most out of the research you do. In the sections that follow, on specific research methods, you will find lots of practical advice about how to achieve good quality analysis, that goes beyond the mere descriptive into insightful interpretation.

'Giving voice'

The closest to simple descriptive work in qualitative psychology is where the research goal is to find out how the topic under study is understood by the account-giver. Underpinning this approach is usually a strong commitment to enabling those who belong to marginalized groups (such as those experiencing prejudice) or are service users (such as people in counselling) to be heard and their understandings and concerns used to inform training professionals or as the basis for developing services. Researchers using this form of analysis actively strive to avoid imposing their own ('expert') interpretation. Rather, they seek to 'give voice' to the views being expressed.

A good example is a study of gender differences carried out by Wendy Hollway (1989). She described her approach as **descriptive interviewing**, its purpose being to be able to present extracts which 'speak for themselves':

> The researcher's role has been to organize this material so that it conforms to an essentially descriptive theory. The value of the approach is typically that the researcher should not presume to question the truthfulness of the account and this position is usually coupled with the view that a person's own account is most relevant for research because it is meaningful to the teller. Once an account is given, it assumes the status of the expression of the person's experience in relation to a particular topic.
>
> (Hollway 1989: 40)

Descriptive phenomenological method

Descriptive phenomenological method is a growing trend among critical social psychologists. Originated by Giorgi (1985) and a number of colleagues, it focuses on gaining varied and detailed *descriptions* of 'the things themselves' drawing on the philosophical work of Husserl ([1900] 1970). In various ways participants give their accounts, concentrating on their experience of the phenomenon in question and avoiding any attempt to explain or interpret. An excellent introduction to this approach is provided by Darren Langridge (2007) who devotes a chapter of his book to describing this method and offering guidance on how to do it. You will come to his work later in the chapter, in the section on phenomenological analysis.

A study that impresses me is about gaining insight into the experience of 'life boredom' by Bargdill (2000). He interviewed six participants and found that 'emotional ambivalence' was a common element of their experience of boredom, including aspects of anger and frustration. He brought together the accounts to describe boredom as much like the freeze response of a rabbit caught in the headlights of a car – transfixed between conflicting emotions and fears, without a clear direction: 'They are in purgatory, waiting and dependent on other people's prayers. As if they have seen the Medusa, they stagnate, solidify. They are aware but paralysed. They are bored' (Bargdill 2000: 204).

Try it for yourself

Did this 'hang true' for you? I found it quite revealing, because my own experiences of boredom have always struck me as paradoxical. I do not get bored when I am happy and content, even when there is nothing much going on. Reading this interpretation made me realize that I get bored when I am under pressure with lots of conflicting commitments that make me feel frustrated. I got quite an 'aha' experience when I read Bargdill's paper, as it made me recognize that boredom is not about 'having nothing to do' but, rather, having too much to do! Maybe it does not work for you, but one of the features of phenomenological research is that the insight it provides can be quite striking.

As such, we can see this approach as good example of abductive research – where the researcher homes in on what in the data is counter-intuitive and surprising. Descriptive research, from this perspective, goes way beyond 'mere description'. Instead, it uses description as the 'raw data' for highly insightful interpretation.

Descriptive research in qualitative research

- Descriptive research studies must do more than merely describe (otherwise they are no more than journalism).
- Some descriptive research is done to 'give voice' to those otherwise unheard groups, such as users of services (such as those for mental health) or excluded groups. Analysis here involves identifying the contribution that can be made in relation to what has already been established.
- Descriptive phenomenological analysis uses descriptions of experience as a stimulus to gaining insight.

Analytics in qualitative research

This section introduces you to the five main forms of analysis used by social psychologists to conduct qualitative research:

- thematic analysis
- conversational analysis
- discourse analysis
- phenomenological analysis
- narrative analysis.

They have a fair amount in common, but have rather different histories and focus on different aspects of the way people 'make sense' of and operate within their social worlds.

Thematic analysis

This is where most psychology students start, in part because it is a relatively simple approach and in part because it does not necessarily imply particular epistemological and ontological assumptions. Indeed, in a really useful paper for anyone seeking to try out this approach, Virginia Braun and Victoria Clarke suggest it is 'the first qualitative method of analysis that researchers should learn, as it provides core skills that will be useful for conducting many other forms of qualitative analysis' (Braun and Clarke 2006: 78). They also point out that: 'thematic analysis is . . . compatible with both essentialist and constructionist paradigms within psychology. . . . Through its theoretical freedom, thematic analysis provides a flexible and useful research tool, which can potentially provide a rich and detailed, yet complex, account of data' (Braun and Clarke 2006: 78). It is an analytic approach suited to descriptive research and, importantly, can be applied across a wide range of theoretical and epistemological settings in psychology.

Usually thematic analysis consists of two phases: first, identifying, analysing and describing patterns or themes within the data; and, second, using these themes as a basis of further interpretation – making suggestions of 'what is going on' in relation to the topic. Braun and Clark offer systematic guidelines to conducting thematic analysis, keen to help students and researchers avoid falling into the trap of claiming that 'several themes emerged from the analysis' (as if they had somehow crawled, of their own volition, out of the data)! This kind of metaphor, Braun and Clarke argue, fails to recognize or account for the active role the researcher plays, and the very considerable work that has to be done in the process. Braun and Clarke identify six main stages of thematic analysis. These are summarized in Table 5.2.

Table 5.2 Six stages of thematic analysis

Stages		What you need to do
1	Familiarizing yourself with your data	Transcribe and translate your data, if necessary, and then 'immerse yourself' in it – repeatedly reading and re-reading it while carefully scrutinizing it and noting down your initial ideas
2	Generating initial codes	Code interesting features of the data in a systematic fashion across the entire data-set, then collate the data relevant to each code
3	Searching for themes	Collate codes into potential themes, then gather together all the data relevant to each potential theme
4	Reviewing themes	Check first (Level 1) if the themes work in relation to the coded extracts, and then second (Level 2) check against the entire data-set. Once this has been done, gradually distil and display a thematic 'map' of the analysis
5	Defining and naming themes	Continue the analysis to refine the specifics of each theme – keep doing this until each one is clear, coherent and convincing. This will enable you to generate an 'overall story' that your analysis tells. In the process you will need to identify and describe each theme, giving each one an appropriate name
6	Producing the report	This is the final opportunity for analysis. You should select vivid, compelling examples, and conduct a final analysis of selected extracts. Relate these back to a clear and careful analysis of the research question and the relevant literature. This last stage takes time and needs to be done carefully if you are to produce a good report demonstrating high-quality scholarship

Source: After Braun and Clarke (2006)

While they fully acknowledge that there are many variants on thematic analysis, Braun and Clark take a pragmatic approach, motivated by wanting to help students get started. Their paper provides a clear and detailed account of each of these stages, and lots more good advice and encouragement. Especially useful is a table setting out a 15-point checklist for doing thematic analysis properly – what you need to do to get it right, and make it of high quality. It offers an excellent guide to doing thematic analysis properly. This is set out in Table 5.3.

Table 5.3 A 15-point checklist of criteria for good thematic analysis

Process		Criteria for a properly conducted thematic analysis study
Transcription	1	Your data have been transcribed to an appropriate level of detail, and you have checked your transcripts against the tapes for 'accuracy'
Coding	2	You have given each data item equal attention in the coding process
	3	You have not generated your themes from a few vivid examples (an anecdotal approach). Rather your coding has been thorough, inclusive and comprehensive – good attention to detail, and carefully considered over time
	4	You have collated all relevant extracts for each theme
	5	You have made time to carefully and systematically check your themes against each other and back to the original data-set
	6	Your themes are internally coherent, consistent and distinctive
Analysis	7	Rather than just paraphrasing or describing, you have done the hard work needed to analyse, interpret and make sense of your data in a careful and insightful manner
	8	Your analysis and data correspond with and complement each other – the extracts you select each provide a convincing illustration of the particular analytic claim you make
	9	Your analysis yields a convincing, fluent and comprehensive story about the data and topic
	10	The space you allocate to your analytic narrative is balanced in relation to the illustrative extracts you use
Overall	11	You have spent enough time completing all stages of the analysis properly, without rushing any of them or just giving it a quick once-over
Written report	12	Given the flexibility of thematic analysis, you must be clear about what you have done with it. Your written report must contain a section setting out your assumptions about thematic analysis and explicating the specific approach you have taken towards it
	13	You must make sure there is a good fit between what you claim you do, and what you show you have done. The method you describe and the analysis you report must be consistent
	14	The language and concepts you use in your report must be consistent with the epistemological assumptions on which your analysis is based
	15	Themes never simply 'emerge'. They are the result of your active and purposeful effort at analysis. You, as the researcher, must make evident the active part you have played

Source: After Braun and Clarke (2006)

Actually, given that so much qualitative analysis is thematic, in one form or another, Table 5.3 provides a really good guide about how to do good qualitative research in general. It is a checklist, so it can come across as a bit too dictatorial (in a field where it is good to be creative and innovative, and tailor your method to the specific research questions you are addressing). But it is also a wonderful tool for making sure you have covered everything you need to. Possibly its strongest statement is the one about not simply basing your themes on a few vivid examples. It is so tempting, I know, to get a few juicy quotes that stand out and attract attention, and be beguiled by these into a far too rapid and superficial analysis. The checklist brings you down to earth and reminds you how important it is to stick at the lengthy and demanding process, which involves a thorough examination of *all* aspects of *all* of the transcripts. The point is, it shows in the depth and subtlety of your analysis, and gets you the 'brownie points' you need for your project work or thesis – and, one day, getting your work published!

Thematic analysis

- This is a good way to start doing analysis – it helps you develop the basic skills and insights you need.
- With modifications, thematic analysis can be used with both quantitative and qualitative designs.
- It consists of two main elements – identifying themes, and then interpreting them; and six main stages: familiarizing yourself with your data, generating initial codes, searching for themes, reviewing themes, defining and naming themes, and producing the report.
- Good thematic analysis takes time and hard work:
  - Transcription must be accurate.
  - Coding must be thorough, inclusive and comprehensive, with attention to detail and carefully considered over time.
  - Themes must be based on the data-set as a whole and not a few vivid examples; internally coherent, consistent and distinctive.
  - Analysis must be thorough and insightful, telling a convincing, fluent and comprehensive story about the data and topic.
  - The report must set out your assumptions and the specific approach you have taken towards it.

Conversational analysis

The origins of conversation analysis can be traced to the work of Harvey Sacks in the 1960s (see Sacks 1995) within the broader field of **ethnomethodology**. Conversation analysis uses very fine-grained classification and notation of interactive talk in order to examine what people are doing and seeking to achieve in the way they use language. It focuses on the units and forms of talk – such as conversational openings and closings and turn-taking. For example, it often examines in very fine detail the *timing* of talk – when people interrupt and speak over each other, or, alternatively, pause before they respond. Through this analysis researchers seek to determine how talk is being used and interpreted strategically.

Conversation analysis is the study of how people use talk in interaction, usually by scrutinizing naturally occurring talk – things like what goes on around the meal table, in parliamentary debate, in complaining to customer services, and so on. Examples include studies of the interactions between doctors and their patients (West 1984), and in judicial settings (Atkinson and Drew 1979). Conversation analysis is concerned with the 'natural organization' of talk (Psathas 1995) that arises from people tailoring their talk to the other person's and, especially to what the speaker wants to achieve. It looks at different kinds of conversational exchange – questions and answers, greetings, compliments, and so on – and how these may be responsive to different settings and used for different purposes.

Illustration of conversation analysis: just 'say no'

A study by Celia Kitzinger and Hannah Frith (1999) shows what this approach is seeking to do. In their study they examined what is going on when women refuse unwanted sexual advances. To make sense of their data you will need to know some of the conventions used in conversation analysis for annotating text. These notations allow paralinguistic information to be included in the analysis. Some examples are shown in Figure 5.1.

Conversation analysis: transcription notations

[	overlapping speech
:	sound is drawn out (the more :::, the longer the drawing out)
text	emphasis
(.)	pause of less than 0.2 seconds
(0.2)	pause measured in seconds
.hhh	in-breath (the more hhh, the longer the in-breath)
hhh	out-breath (the more hhh, the longer the out-breath)
=	no pause
,	slight rising intonation

Figure 5.1 A simple set of transcription rules for conversational analysis

First, Kitzinger and Frith (1999) made the point that refusing is harder in general than agreeing, starting off with examples of how an agreement tends to work:

Example 1
A: Why don't you come up and see me some[time
B: [I would like to.
(Atkinson and Drew 1979: 58)

Example 2
A: <u>We:</u>ll, will you help me [ou:t
B: [I certainly wi:ll.

(Davidson 1984: 116)

The overlapping speech, they point out, is typical of the immediate and direct way that people tend to talk when they are agreeing to a request (Heritage 1984: 266–7).

Next, Kitzinger and Frith (1999) contrast this with an example of an ordinary refusal:

Example 3
Mark: We were wondering if you wanted to come over Saturday, f'r dinner
(0.4 sec pause)
Jane: Well (.). hh it'd be great but we promised Carol already.

(Potter and Wetherell 1987: 86)

Far from being immediate and direct, this refusal is slow to be given and hedged around. There is a 0.4 second gap before Jane starts speaking, and another pause – indicated by (.) – after she uses 'Well' as a hedge. A **hedge** (sometimes called a **preface**) is a word or utterance like 'uh' at the start of speech, used to 'hedge around' difficulties to come. Then Jane uses a **palliative** – here an appreciation – to specifically ameliorate the potential rudeness of rejecting the invitation. Palliatives are conversational strategies used to temper the impact of what is being said. Appreciations are often used in rejections – 'That's awfully sweet of you, but', 'I would love to, but', and so on. Finally, Jane provides an **account** – here a justification for refusing. Accounts present culturally sanctioned reasons for acting (or not acting) in particular ways. In refusals, accounts convey the rationale that the person cannot (as opposed to will not or does not want to) agree to the request. Their purpose is to avoid the implication that the request is unreasonable or unattractive, and so avoid negative consequences for the relationship between the speakers.

Having used the fine-grained qualities of conversation analysis to make the point that refusals are generally problematic – and hence usually presented in ambiguous and hedged ways – Kitzinger and Frith (1999) turn their attention to the way people generally react to such refusals.

Example 4
A: hhhhh Uh will you call 'im tuhnight for me, =
B: = eYea:h
    (.)
A: Plea::se,

(Davidson 1984: 113)

In this example it is clear that the person asking the favour has recognized they are not getting the kind of definite, swift agreement that means that B has unequivocally agreed to make the phone call. So A responds by making a more powerful plea – Plea::se. Kitzinger and Frith provide a number of similar examples to show that people generally have no problem in recognizing refusals, even when they are tacit and vague and sometimes include hedged or even apparent agreement. They take action accordingly, for instance, by (as above) asking again more persuasively, seeking to reassure, or to counter the excuse being used.

Kitzinger and Frith then come to the main point of their article, which is to counter the explanations usually given for miscommunication in the context of sexual advances made by men towards women. It is generally attributed to women who 'lacked effective refusal skills' (Cairns 1993: 205), in a context in which 'often men interpret timidity as permission' (cited in Turner and Rubinson 1993: 605).

These attributions, Kitzinger and Frith argue, locate the problem in women's communication competence rather than in anything men do or do not do. Using their fine-grained analysis of refusals in ordinary settings, Kitzinger and Frith dispute this explanation, and maintain that the problem should be located in men's behaviour: 'Our analysis in this article supports the belief that the root of the problem is not that men do not understand sexual refusals, but they do not like them' (Kitzinger and Frith 1999: 310).

Kitzinger and Frith marshall a diversity of further evidence to support their case. One is the observation that when, in a university in Canada, posters were put up on the campus saying 'No means No', some men responded with posters of their own. The captions demonstrate incredible levels of hostility: 'No means kick her in the teeth', 'No means on your knees bitch', 'No means tie her up', 'No means more beer' and 'No means she's a dyke' (Mahood and Littlewood 1997).

Kitzinger and Frith's (1999) article demonstrates how conversation analysis can be used by social psychologists to examine how meaning is often interpreted not from the **semantic** qualities of language, but from the subtle paralinguistic ways in which it is deployed. The article also shows how, within a social constructionist paradigm, a number of different sources of data can be used together to address the way language is used strategically – for example, to warrant certain kinds of behaviour.

More recently Celia Kitzinger and Sue Wilkinson have produced a detailed and thorough guide to conversational analytic research in psychology (Wilkinson and Kitzinger, 2009): see the Further reading section.

Conversational analysis

- Conversation analysis is the study of how people talk in interactions, usually those that arise in actual conversations (such as counselling sessions or family discussion at meal times).

- The analysis is based on painstaking, systematic and formal transcription, working to a set of standard conventions and timing of overlaps and pauses.

- Analysis consists of a fine-grained classification and notation of interactive talk to examine what people are doing and seeking to achieve in the way they use language.

- It focuses on specific units and forms of talk, such as agreements and refusals, hedges and conversational openings.

- Conversational analysis offers a very powerful technique for understanding talk-in-action, talk as a wide set of social processes involving things like **self-presentation**, social manipulation and winning arguments.

Discourse analysis

Discourse is a term that was drawn originally from linguistics, where it is used to refer to a section of speech or writing. Within critical social psychology it is used to describe something more specific. Here a **discourse** is defined as the product of constructing and the means to construct meaning in a particular way.

Critical social psychologists have developed a number of different versions of **discourse analysis** but, at its simplest, we can divide them into two main strands: micro-discourse analysis, which is the form associated with discursive psychology; and macro-discourse analysis, these days usually termed **Foucauldian discourse analysis**.

I have thought long and hard about inventing my own labels, but here they are. I have chosen them because I think they make a clear distinction. There is a lot of confusion and, indeed, argument about what to call the two versions. These terms are at least simple and clear-cut, focusing on two analytic strategies at two rather different levels:

- **Micro-discourse analysis** looks in fine-focus at specific instances of **talk** and **text**, and seeks to understand what is going on in particular interactions. It can then generalize, identifying how particular discursive strategies can be deployed – for example, to defend oneself against accusations of, say, being racist. However, discourse in this approach is always being analysed in terms of activity – **discursive practices** – when people talk to each other, in speech and writing.

- **Macro-discourse analysis** is more concerned with identifying different discourses in play around a particular topic or phenomenon or social action. Remember how the rape and murder of Kitty Genovese (Chapter 1) can be read in very different ways – as an instance of 'society in tatters' (neo-liberal discourse), 'bystander apathy' ('psy' discourse) or 'sexist misogyny' (feminist discourse). Macro-discourse analysis starts from this kind of taxonomy, mapping out the discourses in play in rhetorical competition between competing ways of 'making sense'.

Some discourse analysts (Billig 1997; Wetherell 1998) see these two as differing only in emphasis or focus, while others (Parker 1997b; Potter 1996) regard them as distinct, having different theoretical frameworks, different historical roots and research traditions, and each designed to address different kinds of research questions.

Micro-discourse analysis

This approach to discourse analysis in psychology was initiated by Jonathan Potter and Margaret Wetherell in their classic book *Discourse and Social Psychology: Beyond Attitudes and Behaviour* (Potter and Wetherell 1987). The analytical method here has been defined by Carla Willig as 'discursive practices' discourse analysis, since it is 'primarily concerned with how people *use* discourse in order to achieve interpersonal objectives in social interaction' (Willig 2001: 91). However, Potter and Wetherell have made it clear that it is also concerned with **discursive resources**:

> Discourse analysis has a twin focus. It is concerned with what people *do* with their talk and writing (*discourse practices*) and also with the sorts of *resources* that people draw on in the course of those practices (the devices, category systems, narrative characters and interpretative repertoires which provide a machinery for social life).
>
> (Potter and Wetherell, 1995: 80–1, emphasis in the original)

To avoid this sort of confusion I have adopted the term micro-discourse analysis. It is based on the following assumptions:

- Language is the main symbolic system through which people construct their social realities. Discourse analysis thus always involves careful scrutiny of *content* – of what people are using words to say.
- People deploy language purposefully and strategically, to achieve particular outcomes or goals, using rhetorical devices.
- Language use is therefore always a discursive practice – 'discursive' in the sense of meaning-making, and a 'practice' in the sense that it is behaviour.

Discursive practices are deployed at many different levels: at the individual level (for example, when people have arguments); at the level of social groups and collectives (for example, when they develop their own slang); and at the level of culture and society (for example, where a particular worldview is so embedded in the language that it becomes taken for granted).

Try it for yourself – a micro-discourse analytic study of racism

Read the three extracts below, taken from an interview conducted as part of a study on racism. This was carried out in Aotearoa with participants who were from the pakeha ethnic group living there. The interviews were about these participants' views of 'Polynesian immigrants'. These three extracts are taken from a single person's interview:

Extract 1
I'm not anti them at all, you know, I, if they're willing to get on and be like us; but if they're just going to come here, just to be able to use our social welfares and stuff like that, then why don't they stay home?

Extract 2
What I would li . . . rather see is that, sure, bring them into New Zealand, right, try and train them in a skill, and encourage them to go back again.

Extract 3
I think that if we encouraged more Polynesians and Maoris to be skilled people, they would want to stay here, they're not, um, as, uh, nomadic as New Zealanders are [interviewer laughs] so I think that would be better.

What do you think is going on here? Do you think the person who said these things is being racist?

Micro-discourse analysis of these extracts identifies two main discursive practices in use:

- **Disclaiming**, where, at the beginning of the first extract, the participant says 'I'm not anti them at all, you know', using this disclaimer as a strategic practice to deny they are racist.

● **Extreme case formulation**, where the participant uses the most extreme situation – 'just going to come here, just to be able to use our social welfares'. The speaker is using another discursive practice here for another reason – exaggerating in order to justify a particular prescription for action (that they should 'stay home'). Expressing the worst-case scenario – that the immigrants have no motivation for 'coming here' other than to sponge off social welfare – enables the speaker to justify the claim that they should stay home.

These are two examples of discursive practices deployed to achieve particular outcomes. Much of this form of discourse analysis consists of identifying such strategies and practices and then seeking to 'best guess' the tactical purpose of each one.

I would suggest that this form of analysis adopts an abductive logic of inquiry, following two abductive strategies. First, the analysis homes in on those sections of text that stand out as 'needing to be explained'. Second, it then asks the question 'what is the speaker doing with it?' In this way, discursive researchers can begin to build up an understanding of the practices involved in people's use of discourse. Notice, too, that what is going on is what you observed Shank suggesting in Chapter 2 – researchers using their own 'effort after meaning' skills as a 'rich and complex tool of inquiry' (Shank 1998: 856).

However, you may also have noticed that the second two extracts contradict each other. Extract 2 says that immigrants should be encouraged to go back, Extract 3 is about it being better for them to stay once they have arrived. When contradictions can be spotted (that is, there are obvious surprises in the text – anomalies and dislocations), this offers a particularly valuable opportunity to use abductive reasoning. Just as with Shank's juxtaposition (described in Chapter 2), the contradictory sections of text can be compared to see how discourse is being deployed differently. To gain insight into what may be going on, researchers carefully scrutinize the different contexts in which each statement is made. Here are extended versions of Extracts 2 and 3 within the text as a whole. I have italicized the bits you have seen already:

Extract 2

Interviewer: [do] you think that, say, immigration from the Pacific Islands should be encouraged [ ] to a much larger extent than it is? It's fairly restricted at the moment.
Respondent: Yes. Um, I think that there's some problems in, in encouraging that too much, is that they come in uneducated about our ways, and I think it's important they understand what they're coming to. I, *what I would li . . . rather see is that, sure, bring them into New Zealand, right, try and train them in a skill, and encourage them to go back again* because their dependence upon us will be lesser: I mean [ ] while the people back there are dependent on the people being here earning money to send it back, I mean that's a very very negative way of looking at something. [ ] people really should be trying, they should be trying to help their own nation first.

Extract 3

Respondent: Polynesians, they are doing jobs now that white people wouldn't do. So in many sectors of the community or life, um, we would be very much at a loss without them, I think. Um, what I would like to see is more effort being made to train them into skills, skilled jobs, because we are without skilled people and a lot of our skilled people, white people, have left the country to go other places. *I think that if we encouraged more Polynesians and Maoris to be skilled people, they would want to stay here, they're not, um, as, uh, nomadic as New Zealanders are [interviewer laughs] so I think that would be better.*

Now the reason for the contradiction becomes clearer. In Extract 2 the participant is expressing concern about the outflow of money from the New Zealand economy. In Extract 3 they are expressing concern about the skills shortage in New Zealand, given so many skilled New Zealanders move away and the potential for immigrants to make up the shortfall. This kind of analysis shows, among other things, that when people speak, they shift from one concern to another, and therefore, in order to understand how they are using discourse, we need to look at how it is organized to achieve different functions. Mick Billig expresses this well: 'Instead of mining the discourse for the respondents' underlying "true" attitude or "real" view, discursive psychologists view respondents' comments as discursive acts that can only be understood in context' (1997: 44).

Textbook writing as a discursive practice

Before we move on, stop for a moment and think about my authorial discourse (that is, my discursive practice in the way I am writing this text for you). My plan was to give you an 'abductory moment', so I deliberately seeded a surprise for you – can you work out what it was? When I first began to describe the study, unless you knew the terms already you may have assumed that Aotearoa was some obscure country and pakeha some exotic group of people. But I suspect you soon worked out that Aotearoa is the original Maori name of New Zealand, and pakeha the Maori name for New Zealanders who are non-Maori.

By prioritizing the Maori terms, I was strategically deploying my language. Maybe you speculated about why I did so. You may have seen it as a form of 'politically correct' showing off. Maybe I wanted to impress my friends and colleagues in Aotearoa/New Zealand by demonstrating that I am aware of the argument that it is more respectful to Maori to use their words rather than the colonizing English words. Or maybe you saw it as a genuine attempt on my part to avoid being racist.

Now you can see that it was also a deliberate writerly, teacherly strategy. I hope you agree it is a good example of a 'surprise' that made you think. In making you wonder why I imported this terminology, I hope you began to ask questions about what I was 'getting at'. My purpose was to make you think about the preconceptions people often have about culture – that 'we' (whoever 'we' are) are 'ordinary people' outside of culture, whereas 'they' (whoever 'they' are) are 'exotic others' who have culture.

The term 'pakeha' is used by Maori – and, increasingly by pakeha – in Aotearoa to define people by what they are not (not Maori). What 'white' people often mean by the term 'black' is not so much to do with skin colour as with being not-white (that is, 'not like us'). If you are 'black' (including Maori) you do not need me to tell you what it feels like to be called a 'member of an ethnic group'. But if you are 'white' I hope being called a 'member of an ethnic group' (known as pakeha) was at least a little bit surprising, and maybe even disconcerting. That 'white' people are unused to this is a consequence, in part, of their lack of language skills. There are similar words in a number of languages (Rom and Japanese, for example) but most 'white' people do not understand them.

Discursive psychology

> Discursive psychology begins with psychology as it faces people living their lives. It studies how psychology is constructed, understood and displayed as people interact in everyday and more institutional situations. How does a speaker show they are not prejudiced, while developing a damning version of an entire ethnic group? How are actions coordinated in a counselling session to manage the blame of the different parties of the relationship breakdown? How is upset displayed, understood and receipted in a call to a child protection helpline? Questions of this kind require us to understand the kinds of things that are 'psychological' for people as the act and interact in particular settings – families, workplaces and schools. And this in turn encourages us to respecify the very object of psychology.
>
> (Wiggins and Potter, 2009: 73)

As the quote above makes clear, in the more than 20 years since then it has been developed into much more than a form of analysis – a whole theoretical realignment that was very much part of the creation of critical psychology, and one that remains influential within it. Here, however, we will stick to looking at the micro version of discourse analysis.

Wiggins and Potter (2009) stress that discursive psychology research today has moved on and diverged from the original discourse analysis promoted by Potter and Wetherell. One major difference is using 'naturalistic texts' rather than interview transcripts to situate the research in the 'messy' situations of everyday life. They outline a series of steps, as shown in Table 5.4. This is very much a summary to give you an overview of what is entailed. Wiggins and Potter's (2009) chapter provides a much more detailed – but still very clear – account of what it entails.

Macro-discourse analysis

Here the discourse analytic work draws extensively on French theory, especially the work of Foucault and his concern with the relationships between power and knowledge – therefore, it is also called Foucauldian analysis.

> From a Foucaultian point of view, discourses facilitate and limit, enable and constrain what can be said, by whom, where and when. . . . Foucaultian discourse analysts focus on the availability of discursive resources within a culture – something like a discursive economy – and its implications for those who live within it.
>
> (Willig 2001: 107)

This form of discourse analysis works at a different level. Instead of looking in fine-grained detail at the strategic use of discourse within a particular piece of text, it takes a broader-brush perspective. It examines how discourses work across situations and settings. Beryl Curt (1994) claims that this form of discourse analysis is concerned with:

1 the **textuality** of discourse – its functions, uses and ability to wield power
2 its sociocultural **tectonics** – the ways in which different discourse are produced, maintained and promoted, and how different discourses vie against and impinge upon, shape and mould each other.

Table 5.4 Steps in a micro-discourse analytic study

Step	What you need to do
1 Devising research questions	Begin by identifying what you want to understand better, such as how people talk about food during family meal times. Often the research question starts by being general, like this: 'What is going on here?' From this you can select the setting for the study (family meal times). The questions will get more precise and focused as the study progresses
2 Gaining ethical consent	These days gaining ethical consent is an essential starting point for any research project. It needs to be done soon enough to form a basis for negotiations to get access to settings, and with potential participants. Ethics in qualitative research is addressed at the end of the chapter
3 Getting access	Chapter 3 includes useful information about building respectful relationships with the communities and individuals that you wish to engage in your research
4 Data collection	You will need an accurate and clear record of the talk you plan to analyse. For face-to-face conversations this means good equipment and effective instruction where participants record themselves. If you use the Internet or other virtual sources, you have little control over quality, so you will need to select records that are technically good enough for analysis
5 Building a corpus	While you can analyse small sections of text, full discourse analysis requires a substantial corpus of records. The aim is to cover a wide range of discursive practice, probably by a mix of recording a range of participant/participant groups and a number of recordings from each. To conduct a good discourse analytic study, you must create a substantial corpus with many instances of particular discursive practices
6 Transcription	The task here is to create a transcript for analysis. In discourse analysis of this kind preparing the transcripts is very detailed and meticulous, and in this has become similar to conversation analysis. These days there are software packages to help you create a written and annotated transcription. It takes a long time – up to 20 hours for each hour of interaction. With digital data there are tools that can be used to copy, search and edit files which make the process easier and faster
7 Coding	Coding is based on a lengthy, iterative process of repeatedly listening to recordings alongside reading the transcript. It consists of sifting through the corpus as a whole, seeking out instances of a phenomenon. Wiggins and Potter give the example in their eating study of first identifying what they call 'gustatory mmms' used to convey approval of particular foods, and then searching the whole corpus for these 'mmms'
8 Analysis	Wiggins and Potter stress that this should not be formulaic, and can include a range of different approaches. The overall aim is to gain insight into *how* discursive practices are being made to work, and the functions for which they are being deployed. For more detail, see the worked example in Wiggins and Potter's chapter
9 Application	This is where links are made between the findings of the analysis and how these insights may be used. For example, learning about what goes on at family meal times can be useful in designing interventions with families wanting to change eating patterns

Source: After Wiggins and Potter (2009)

This approach is less concerned with what particular individuals say in particular settings than with the way discourse operates more generally and more globally as a social and cultural resource to be used in human activities and endeavours. Thus, data collection techniques are more varied and analysis is more taxonomic than micro-discourse analysis.

This form of analysis seeks to identify and describe, for a particular topic or issue, what are the main discourses in play, how they jockey with and exert power over each other, and how they vary and shift over time and from one discursive location to another. In Foucauldian discourse analysis the research questions are: what discourses operate in relation to this topic? Where do they come from? How and why were they constructed? How are they deployed and what can they be used to achieve?

Michael Arribas-Ayllon and Valerie Walkerdine in their chapter on Foucauldian discourse analysis (2009: 91) stress that in order to 'avoid the trap of formalizing an approach that clearly eschews formalization', they give no list of stages to follow. Instead, they discuss three dimensions of this version of discourse analysis:

- **Historical inquiry**, in Foucauldian terms, 'genealogy', that involves looking for the origins of a particular discourse and then tracing its 'life history' through different times and locations, to arrive at an overall understanding of its operations in the 'here and now'. One example they give is of Nicolas Rose's genealogy of the **psy complex**, as outlined in Chapter 3.

- An analysis of **power** that constantly operates in small ways far more than large, in small-scale personal and interpersonal relationships – Foucault sometimes called this the 'micro-politics of power'. It is also a power that operates through producing (rather than repressing). A good example is the production of 'docile bodies' – bodies that we are encouraged to hand over to others to pamper, depilate, corset; or that need to be kept young – all through the seductive idea that 'we are worth it'. Macro-discourse analysis examines 'what is going on' in this sort of setting, and asks difficult questions about consequences and motivations. Who stands to gain if people take-for-granted that women deserve facials, massages and manicures and their worth is measured by whether they get them?

- **Subjectification** specifically refers to the productive practices through which 'subjects' are made – subjects like psychology, and people-as-subjects (there is a lot of play on words going on here). Macro-discourse analysis seeks to identify which subjects are produced, how and why.

Try it for yourself – a macro-discourse analysis of jealousy

Using a variety of methods of data collection, Paul Stenner has conducted a macro-discourse analytic study into jealousy (Curt 1994; Stenner 1993). Read the four short extracts from his study (taken from Curt 1994: Ch. 7) given below, and think about what is similar between Extracts 1a and 1b, between Extracts 2a and 2b, and what is different between them. Paul Stenner is a member of the collective author, Beryl Curt.

Extract 1a

There was this young married couple called Scott . . . and Charlene . . . who went on holiday. While on holiday they became friends with a man called Steve . . . who was from the same town as them. Unfortunately after a couple of days Scott became ill so he couldn't go out or enjoy the holiday, but not wishing for his wife's holiday to be spoilt insisted that she go around with Steve to keep her company. So seeing what it meant to him that she was happy, she spent a lot of time with Steve sightseeing. But as the week went on and Scott saw so little of his wife, he became very bad tempered and resentful of Steve because he was seeing more of her than he was, and she was his wife!

Extract 1b

The man who has not been jealous, beaten his mistress, torn her clothes; he has yet to be in love.

Extract 2a

Jealous woman: I don't know why Fred [her boyfriend] wants me when he's had Wilma [his ex]. She's got a beautiful face, lovely skin, straight teeth and a perfect figure, I think he is just with me because he can't have her any more.

Friend: If Fred didn't want you he wouldn't be with you now, I don't know why you worry. You've got a lot to give.

Jealous woman: But if I was more pretty and had a better figure he might want me more than he wanted her.

Friend: I think you should just get on with living in the present and forget what's happened in the past.

Jealous woman: I'm not living in the past, it's just, I've always wanted good skin and I've put on weight and I'm not as tall as Wilma and I've always wanted longer legs. It's just so unfair that some people have got what I've always wanted.

Extract 2b

Jealousy is always the same no matter where you find it: (a) a neurotic need for approval, and (b) an intense feeling of inferiority. If you conquer those two conditions, nothing, not even having someone sleep with your partner, can make you jealous. In fact, you could have several people sleep with your partner on a regular basis and still not feel jealous if you did not have problems with inferiority feelings and a neurotic need for approval.

Stenner got the accounts of jealousy given in Extracts 1a and 2a by asking groups of students to work together to write a short scenario in which jealousy is played out. Using Q methodology (described later in this section) he identified them as describing two distinctly different discourses of jealousy. Extract 1a he identifies as an account of 'jealousy as natural'. This discourse, he says, usually relates to sexual (or, if you prefer, romantic) jealousy. In this discourse jealousy is seen as a sign of true love, and is thought of as a kind of 'emotional glue' which holds a loving relationship together. Extract 1b is another account of 'natural jealousy', taken from the historical writings of Lucian in 'Scenes of Courtesans' (quoted in Gonzalez-Crussi 1988). So Extracts 1a and 1b are similar in that they depict jealousy in the same way. But they are different in that Extract 1a is contemporary data gathered through getting people to write a scene, whereas Extract 1b is a historical account.

Stenner identifies Extract 2a as an account of 'jealousy as psychological immaturity'. This discourse, Stenner suggests, is much more recent in origin, arising from psychodynamic ideas. This discourse explains that a jealous type of person is insecure because of a lack of mother-love in childhood, and who was not trained properly as a young child to cope with jealousy – to deal, for example, with 'sibling rivalry'. Extract 2b is taken from a psychology text (Hauck 1981: 35). So Extracts 2a and 2b are once more similar because they articulate the same discourse of 'jealousy as psychological immaturity', and different because they are drawn from different kinds of sources.

In his detailed analysis of these two alternative discourses (Curt 1994; Stenner 1992, 1993), Stenner draws on a diversity of sources to 'build up a picture' of what each sees jealousy as being like and why it occurs. He explicates what each one can be used to achieve – that they justify taking different moral positions on whether jealousy is a good or bad thing, and they warrant different kinds of action – violence in one case and sexual infidelity in the other.

Discourse analysis

- Discourse analysis, like conversational analysis, is based on assumptions that:
  - language is the main way people make, communicate and understand meaning
  - people deploy language and other forms of representation *strategically*, to achieve particular outcomes
  - language-use is always a social practice – usually called discursive practice – that is situated in and part of the social setting in which it is used
  - however, in contrast to conversational analysis, the main focus is on the content of what is being said, rather than the technicalities of how it is spoken. Discourse analysis can be applied to a broader range of text including written documents such as diaries, novels, blogs and text messages.
- Discourse analysis comes in broadly two forms:
  - *micro-discourse analysis* looks in fine focus at what is going on in particular sections of particular interactions, observing how particular discursive strategies are deployed for particular functions
  - *macro-discourse analysis* is more concerned with identifying different discourses in play around a particular topic or phenomenon or social action. It is taxonomic, mapping out how competing discourses can be brought to play on a topic such as 'bystander apathy'.
- Broadly, micro-discourse analysis requires:
  - four *preparatory stages*: devising research questions; gaining ethical consent; getting access; data collection
  - five main *analytical stages*: building a corpus (by selecting text from a source like chat-room conversations); transcription; coding; analysis; application

- Macro-discourse analysis:
  - is a lot more varied and less formulaic
  - draws extensively on the analytical strategies of Foucault, including looking, for example, at the archeology of knowledge, the deployment of power and the production of subjectivity
  - is interested both in textuality (the content of discourse) and discursive tectonics (the way discourses mould and shape each other).

Phenomenological analysis

Becoming increasingly aware of the limitations of an exclusive focus on language and looking for ways in which embodiment and subjectivity may be studied, qualitative researchers have been exploring alternatives to and/or extensions of discourse analytic research. . . . A focus on the ways in which available discursive resources construct social and psychological realities has helped us make sense of much of what goes on in social life. However, there are dimensions of experience which people find difficult to put into words and which seem to involve their entire being, in a pre-reflective kind of way. These experiences seem to be about more than the use of language, even though data relating to them may take the form of written or spoken accounts. One way in which researchers have tried to get closer to capturing such experiences is by turning to phenomenology.

(Willig 2007: 209–10)

Phenomenology is the study of 'things themselves', of people's lived experience of them, within a conceptual frame that does not seek to separate these 'things' from people's subjective experience of them. Phenomenological research consists of eliciting 'rich descriptions' of concrete experiences, or narratives about them.

Phenomenology is very much an up-and-coming approach, even though some people are put off by the 'difficult' terminology! Mainly it arises because of translation problems. What has happened is that many English-speaking critical social psychologists have recently begun to take notice of a whole range of 'European' philosophers whose ideas are highly relevant to what critical social psychologists want to do. The list includes people like Edmund Husserl, Martin Heidegger, Jean-Paul Sartre, Simone de Beauvoir, Paul Ricoeur, and so on. A lot of the so-called 'jargon' around phenomenology arises because the terms they have used to describe their ideas do not easily translate into English! The message is, do not moan about the unfamiliar words, just 'deal with it'!

This section focuses mainly on the strategies and techniques that critical psychologists have developed for analysing and interpreting data collected in a wide variety of ways, but always focused on some aspect of lived experience and/or lifeworlds.

The best-known variant of phenomenological analysis is **Interpretative Phenomenological Analysis** (IPA). Here, however, I have decided to take a more general approach, drawing upon Darren Langdridge's (2007) book *Phenomenological Psychology: Theory, Research and Method*, which provides an excellent, clear introduction to this work.

Langdridge identifies three main approaches to phenomenological research in psychology:

1 descriptive phenomenology
2 interpretative phenomenology
3 critical narrative analysis.

Descriptive phenomenology

You have met this previously in the chapter, under descriptive research. First advocated by Giorgi (see Giorgi and Giorgi, 2009, for an up-to-date account), this approach has diversified into a number of forms, including work led by Peter Ashworth (2003) that shows real promise. It introduces a further stage of interrogative analysis around ideas of selfhood, embodiment, time and space, good for producing a highly systematic account of the phenomenon being studied. You have looked earlier at an example, of Bargdill's (2000) study of boredom.

Interpretative phenomenology

The currently highly popular form of this is IPA devised by Jonathan Smith. Eatough and Smith (2009) give a clear and detailed account. Langdridge also includes a number of other interpretative methods, including hermeneutic phenomenology and template analysis.

All are distinguished by their greater focus on interpretation (rather than description) and the hermeneutical aspects – that is, the study of meaning and the interpretation of texts. In some applications of this kind of analysis, links are made both with thematic and discourse analytic work in psychology, and even social cognitive approaches. Template analysis is currently being developed by Nigel King (1998) and also looks promising. A good example is a study by King et al. (2002), which uses template analysis to examine how people adjust to living with renal failure.

Critical narrative analysis

This is Langdridge's own approach, which applies phenomenological analysis to biographical or more generally narrative accounts, and it has six stages. Note that it is in the form of a circle, which shows the potential for iteration – going through the stages repeatedly and refining the interpretation as you go (Figure 5.2).

What marks out phenomenological analysis is a great deal of 'reflexive engagement', starting with Stage 1 'where the researcher thinks through their background and experience and the impact this might have on the questions being asked, the data that they have helped to produce and that will form the basis of the analysis' (Langdridge 2007: 134). He calls this stage 'a critique of the illusions of the subject'. What is going on here, compared with other **analytics**, is a more explicit engagement of the person doing the interpretation into the process itself. In this approach you do not start by looking at the data, but by looking – in depth – at yourself and your own preconceptions. This makes a benefit out of what quantitative researchers might see as bias, which is to see your own subjectivity as inevitably involved in the research you do, and both a resource for interpretation and something to be suspicious about.

This **reflexivity** gets more explicit still on reaching Stage 5, 'Destabilizing the narrative' which, Langdridge suggests, is made up of at least six potential **critical hermeneutics of suspicion**,

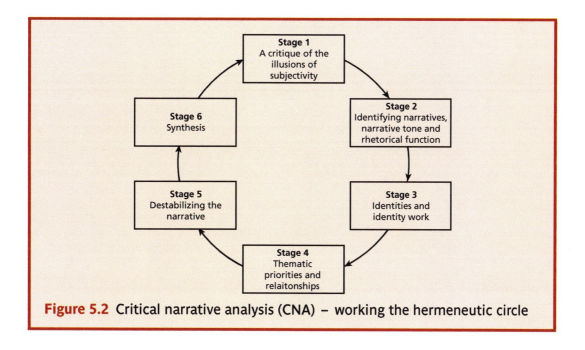

Figure 5.2 Critical narrative analysis (CNA) – working the hermeneutic circle

a concept drawn from the philosopher Ricoeur (1970). 'This is the mode of interpretation, employed by psychoanalysis for instance, that seeks to understand by peeling back the layers of meaning – digging beneath the surface of what is hidden – which may lead to suspicion over the initial account of meaning' (Langdridge 2007: 44).

This is a systematic and painstaking way of combining thematic analysis (as described above) with interrogation of the themes identified. Another good way of describing this is one used by Curt (1994): 'troubling the taken-for-granted'. The six of these he suggests are set out as a circle rather than a list, to make clear the cyclical nature of what needs doing, a repeated action of being suspicious, each one being suspicious through a different analytic frame: gender, class, race and ethnicity, queer theory, age and generation, and ability/disability (Figure 5.3).

Langdridge describes one of his own studies, on young gay men's expectations for parenthood, in his book (Langdridge 2007), using it to illustrate how to do critical narrative analysis. It is a very good read, and useful if you wish to adopt this approach in a study of your own.

Table 5.5 summarizes the overall stages involved in critical narrative analysis.

Phenomenological analysis

- Phenomenology is the study of 'things themselves', of people's lived experience of them, within a conceptual frame that does not seek to separate these 'things' from people's subjective experience of them.

- Phenomenological research consists of eliciting 'rich descriptions' of concrete experiences, or narratives about them.

- Langdridge identifies three main approaches to phenomenological research in psychology:

  1 **Descriptive phenomenology** – focuses on creating 'rich descriptions' of a particular experience (such as boredom), thereby gaining insight about what it is like.

  2 **Interpretative phenomenology** – focuses on analysis, often at several different levels and in different ways, to gain insight into the experiential aspects of, say, emotions (such as anger) or specific experiences (such as 'being sacked'). This may be applied in parallel with other analytic forms, such as discourse analysis.

  3 **Critical narrative analysis** – intensively analytic, incorporating critical hermeneutics of suspicion, peeling back layers of meaning to reappraise initial understandings. This also involves reflection on the researcher's own preconceptions.

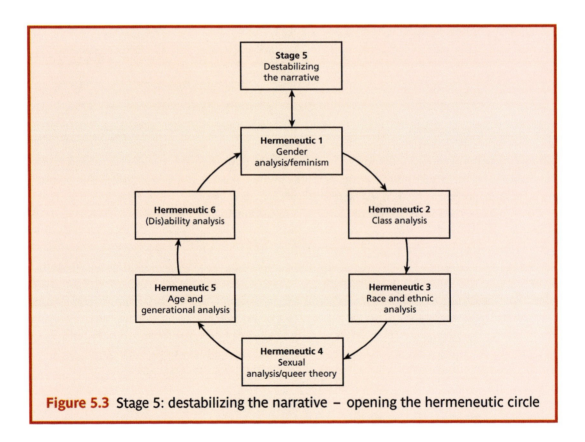

Figure 5.3 Stage 5: destabilizing the narrative – opening the hermeneutic circle

Narrative analysis

[N]arrative [is] a fundamental scheme for linking individual human actions and events into a contextualised and integrated whole. Narrative is essential to the meaning-making process, such that events and actions can be understood despite the fact that the 'reasons' for them are not fully known.

(Hiles and Čermák 2009: 149)

Table 5.5 Stages of critical narrative analysis

Stage		Actions
1	Critique of the illusions of the subject	Read through the transcript of the account and reflect upon its impact on how you understand the topic you are researching. Seek out things to read and observe that will help you gain deeper insight – for instance, into challenges that the account may pose for your own convictions
2	Identifying narratives, narrative tone and rhetorical function	This is fairly standard narrative analysis, but also looking at aspects like optimism/pessimism, and how and where arguments are being used – for instance, to justify access to services, being accorded rights or warranting love or empathy or respect
3	Identities and identity work	Seeing identity as something to which you have to stake a claim by what you do and say (as in 'doing girl' or 'doing gay'), identity work is all about how a person presents their actions, values and opinions in ways that define their identity. This stage focuses not only on how this is being done, but questions of why? And what for?
4	Thematic priorities and relationships	Thematic analysis here is derived from the narrative analysis in Stage 2
5	Destabilizing the narrative	As you have seen already, this stage is important, and needs to be thorough and sophisticated. The particular topic will determine the most important forms of 'suspicion work' that needs to be done (so, on gay parenthood, the obvious place to start is around queer and feminist theory). But it is also important to be exhaustive and also look at others to see if this promotes particular insights
6	Synthesis	This is where all the stages are brought together to generate an overall interpretation. Note the potential to go through the process again, refining the analysis further, until nothing new can be added

Source: After Langdridge (2007)

Narrative psychology focuses on how people make sense of the world through telling stories. Stories and storytelling were extensively studied by early psychologists (for example, Bartlett's 1932 experiential study of remembering stories, and Wundt's (1900–20) discussion of the role of myths and legends in his *Völkerpsychologie*) as ways of gaining insight into what we would now call **social cognition**. However, this approach was shunned from about the 1930s, mainly because storytelling is not very amenable to experimental research.

Narrative approaches began to return in the 1980s, marked by a book edited by Theodore Sarbin, based on a symposium he organized in 1983, entitled *Narrative Psychology: The Storied Nature of Human Conduct* (Sarbin 1986). This renewed interest was not only a matter of narrative interviewing and narrative forms of analysis. It was more fundamentally inspired by the broader shift towards social constructionism. Stories are powerful ways in which we gain understanding and create meaning out of chaos. We do not make sense of our lives and the things that happen within it as just 'one damned thing after another' (Gergen and Gergen 1984: 174). It is much more active than that. We *strive* to understand them as *related to* each other and as having *continuity* – in other words, in narrative form.

A good example is biography – telling a person's life story; or autobiography – telling one's own. Indeed, a whole research field has been built up called 'life history research' (Bornat 2002) and a specific method, biographical interviewing. Ricoeur calls this use of narrative organization 'emplotment' – the bringing together a string of incidents into a plot: 'to make up a plot is already to make the intelligible spring from the accidental, the universal from the singular, the necessary or probable from the accidental' (Ricoeur 1981: 123).

Narratives serve a **presencing function** (Heidegger 1971). That is, in postmodern theory, a narrative is seen as a special kind of discursive practice through which past or future events (imaginary or real) are 'presenced' – put into words in order to do something – recount, entertain, inform, influence, or suchlike. Moreover, these narratives powerfully inform the ways in which we live our lives. They tell us how to 'fall in love', how to 'do' jealousy, how to go on holiday, and so on.

Crucially, these stories in which we live are not figments of our individual imagination. They are profoundly semiotic and profoundly cultural – narrated through novels, plays and operas, both soap and serious. There is some commonality with cognitive psychology's term scripts here (Chapter 7). However, narrative psychology does not regard them as mere representations or encodings, but as powerful ways in which we make sense of our lives, its events, and of the world around us. They are not mere repertoires to follow, like a script. This is because they contain moral and prescriptive elements and, crucially, implications about fact and fiction.

Stories about the impeachment of the President of Brazil

A good example of the narrative approach is Jovchelovitch's (2002) study of narratives about the impeachment in 1993 of Fernando Collor de Mello, who in 1989 had been the first democratically elected President of Brazil in more than 30 years. Six months after the impeachment Jovchelovitch interviewed 11 members of parliament. All but one of them reported their views of the impeachment by telling it as a story. By a detailed examination of these narratives she was able to build up a 'map' of the conceptual framework through which the event was understood. It included aspects of political life – as self-sacrificing or corrupt; of the politicians' views about the voting population – as ignorant and credulous, 'expecting miracles'; of their values and ethics in relation to a new era of democracy. She comments on the complexity and the contradictory nature of these narratives, and how the narrative form of organization collapses time in order to impose a meaningful structure. From this analysis she is able to offer insight into the way in which the narratives they construct profoundly affect the ways in which people make sense of the world – and, crucially, act within it.

Narrative-orientated inquiry

Hiles and Čermák (2009) argue that while there are a variety of ways of doing narrative analysis, it is better to think in terms of narrative-orientated inquiry (NOI) that has a number of common elements.

First, it is not just another form of discourse analysis, but a method and a form of analysis in its own right. In particular, narrative analysis adopts a holistic stance on what is said, rather than separating out specific excerpts for scrutiny. Second, narrative analysis requires a particular kind of interviewing – the narrative interview (Mishler 1999). This is not an interrogation but a site for the 'co-construction of narratives' (Silverman 2001) – an open-ended invitation to tell a story or stories, led by the storyteller.

Table 5.6 Generic stages of narrative-orientated inquiry, as proposed by Hiles and Čermák (2009)

1	Research question	This needs to be identified and clarified, and oriented within a particular interpretative perspective (since this will determine how the narrative interview will be approached)
2	Identifying the narrative interview approach	Working from the research question, a guide is developed to frame the topics covered, questions asked, and approach taken
3	Narrative interview	Follows the guide, interviews recorded
4	Transcripts	The recording is transcribed in full – different formats are used
5	Iterative reading	The transcript is read through several times, as a whole, to build up an overall impression of the context and story as a whole. Where things are unclear, the recording is listened to again
6	Narrative analysis – segmenting phase	This is an initial breaking down of the text into segments, each one roughly covering a particular episode. Each one of these can itself be broken down into different units of analysis, depending on the analytic strategy being used
		Once completed, the text is arranged in separate 'chunks' down the left-hand side of the page, leaving plenty of room for notes and annotations to be made
7	Narrative analysis – interpretation and reintegration phase	This is done in a variety of different ways, depending on the focus adopted, and the interpretative perspective employed. However, all of these result in a reintegration of the holism so central to narrative analysis – the storied nature of accounts providing an integrated whole rather than a dividing up into different 'themes' or whatever

Mishler (1995: 89–90) offers a typology of different forms of narrative analysis, each of which focus on something different:

1 what is being *represented*, especially in relation to the passage of time and the order in which events are told
2 the *linguistic and narrative strategies* being deployed to achieve a meaningful structure and coherence
3 the *cultural, social and psychological contexts* in which the story is set.

Hiles and Čermák suggest a seven-stage approach to narrative inquiry, as set out in Table 5.6. As you can see, this has much in common with many of the other forms of analysis, but differs in the holistic stance adopted, where the storied nature of these accounts means that the various episodes and elements can only be fully understood as part of the story as a whole.

Ian Parker adopts a radically different approach, informed by his strong Marxist standpoint and, in harmony with that, his commitment to participatory research. His chapter on narrative (see the Further reading section) offers another approach, in which he recasts narrative inquiry as like a theatrical production (see Table 5.7).

If you plan to use narrative analysis, it will be worth consulting both of these sources to work out which one will work best for you.

Table 5.7 Narrative research, as proposed by Parker (2005)

1	Production schedule	Identify the research 'problem' and consider what you are going to focus on – what is going to give you insight into 'what is going on?' Make a plan and write it down
2	Auditions	Find the authors for your narratives – who you will treat as 'agents' able to discuss with you the impact of certain 'events'. Find co-researchers, actual or virtual (such as on the web)
3	Casting	Envisage the kind of preliminary interview that will benefit your research, and check out if these co-researchers will 'fit the bill'. Recruit them
4	Improvised scripting	Give stage to the authors and get them going. Make time to discuss with them the issues raised
5	Performance	Conduct the interview and transcribe it
6	Reviews	Interpret and write up your analysis, including a reflexive account of the various negotiations and the issues raised

Source: After Parker (2005: 81)

Narrative analysis

- Based on the recognition that people often make sense of their worlds, lives and what is happening to them through stories. Life-story research, with biographical interviewing, is a good example.

- It is generally agreed that a particular kind of interviewing is involved – *narrative interviewing* – that guides and encourages the participant in 'telling their story' rather than answering specific questions.

- Narrative analysis is holistic. Instead of dismembering what is said into 'themes' or 'discourses', it interprets episodes and elements of stories always in relation to the story as a whole.

- Different kinds of narrative inquiry focus on different aspects of stories – the content and sequence of events as they are told, or the linguistic strategies involved in the telling or the contexts (cultural, social, psychological) in which the story is set.

- Narrative research can be seen as a bit like a theatrical production, where researchers and storytellers both contribute to the performance.

Abductive methodologies

This section briefly explores two methodologies – that is, overall methodological approaches – that are both, in different ways, abductive. The first, grounded theory, has been taken from sociology. Its very basis is abduction – the production of hypotheses rather than the testing of them. This is its underlying philosophy. The second, Q methodology, was specifically designed by its inventor, William Stephenson, to be abductive.

Grounded theory

As its name implies, grounded theory is not so much a method as an approach to the way in which theory and method relate to each other. It argues that instead of using methods to test theories, it is more functional to use methods to generate them. You are already familiar with this argument, as it is the basis of abductory research. However, I have included brief mention of the methodological approach in this chapter, since you may well hear about it and wonder how it 'fits in' to social constructionist research.

Grounded theory as a method was devised by two sociologists Barney Glaser and Anslem Strauss (1967). Like discourse analysis, grounded theory starts with 'something to scrutinize' (most often interviews) and seeks to develop a theory about what is going on through detailed analysis. It is closest to Foucauldian discourse analysis in that it is less concerned with specific use of discourse analysis in specific pieces of text, and more interested in identifying common themes. Basically it comprises four key analytic strategies, as shown in Table 5.8.

Table 5.8 Four analytic strategies for grounded theory analysis

Analytic strategy	What is done
Coding	Coding is the process of identifying categories. It is done by researchers 'immersing' themselves in the data – transcribed talk, mostly – by listening to it and reading and rereading it, over and over again. By this process they gradually identify categories, refine them and reassign them, slowly building up a network of categories, with some superordinate over others. The aim is to develop new, context-specific, superordinate categories that do not fit in with existing theory. Hence they will allow new theoretical insights to be made
Constant comparative analysis	This is a process of refining categories. Having identified a new superordinate category, the researcher goes back to the transcripts and looks for instances they missed last time around. Comparing these with the ones already identified, it may be possible to identify meaningful subcategories. At this stage it is not unusual to go out and collect more data. Often researchers begin with just, say, three or four interviews. They then code and do comparison analysis on them, to give them inspiration about new questions they might ask, or different kinds of people they might include in their study
Theoretical sampling	This is the point at which the analysis moves from being descriptive to analytic. Theoretical sampling is a strategic and purposive scrutiny of the categorization achieved so far, and comparing it with the data overall, sampling incidents and extracts that may either challenge or elaborate it. It is concerned with refinement and rigour – of checking out in a systematic way that the categorization is as good as it can be. And it is not unusual at this stage to again collect more data, if the theoretical sampling throws up questions that the data collected so far do not allow to be fully explored
Theoretical saturation	Theoretical saturation is where, after numerous iterations of the three prior analytic strategies, the researcher reaches the point where no new categories are being identified. This is often more of an aspiration than something that is fully achieved. Most researchers stop at the point where they have a 'good enough' categorization to have been able to articulate a meaningful and useful theory

In some ways this may seem very similar to thematic analysis – and in practice it is. However, the big difference remains its purpose. Grounded theory research is not just about 'seeing what is going on' in relation to a particular topic. It is also, specifically, about generating insight, and from that developing theory – that is, theory grounded upon the outcome of the analysis and interpretation of the data obtained.

An up-to-date account of grounded theory in psychology is provided by Charmaz and Henwood (2009), which offers a history of this method and its adoption by psychologists, a review of differing approaches in psychology, and its use in mixed-methods design.

Collecting records and downloading

A good example of grounded theory research in psychology is a study by Giles et al. (2007) on the meaning of owning and making recorded music. From the interviews conducted three main themes emerged: recordings (records, CDs and downloads) as 'sacred objects'; as part of a person's identity; and listening to the music.

Records as sacred objects

Here the meaning is invested in particular records as having symbolic value – to own it is to bolster one's own sense of value and importance, rather like owning high-end branded goods like shoes, handbags and cars. The value lies in the social approval that such a thing confers:

> The significant feature of this aspect is that it relates to records as objects that are desirable to own in themselves; as works of art, both musically and visually. As artistic products they provide a link between the consumer (or owner) and the artists themselves. Like famous paintings, they make an explicit visual statement about the taste judgements of their owner, so it is important that they are on prominent display in the owner's home. In this way they allow the owner to absorb some of the glory of the artists' work.
>
> (Giles et al. 2007: 435)

Facets of the self

By contrast, here the meaning of the recording is as a personal possession, more as an extension of oneself as, for example, a memento of a particular time in your life, or a relationship. They are like the teddy bear treasured from childhood, or the stone you picked up from the beach on that amazing trip. They do not bring social approval, and may even be embarrassing – but they are yours:

> This aspect can be largely explained by . . . [the] concept of 'mere ownership' and also . . . [the] concept of 'self extension', whereby objects become incorporated into their owner's self-concept. This aspect, then, is concerned with the internal, private meanings held for specific recordings by the individual owner, rather than the external, artistic and aesthetic features of the recordings themselves.
>
> (Giles et al. 2007: 439)

Listening to the music

This meaning is pragmatic and simply about being a convenient means to listen to music, and expressed in relation to downloading music onto a computer or an iPod or the like:

[These] owned recordings are associated with high levels of aesthetic, or sensual, pleasure. This aspect incorporates three higher-order categories not associated with the first two: 'convenience', 'transience' and 'downloading as eclectic'. Convenience was mentioned as a positive feature of digital music players and downloading by all of the iPod owners in the sample. In many respects this category is the polar opposite of 'Commitment' in that the ease with which a digital music collection can be assembled does not seem to instil a sense of pride in its owner like a set of vinyl or CD recordings.

(Giles et al. 2007: 439)

It is worth noting that this study was published in the *Journal of Economic Psychology*, and has clear applications for enabling commercial concerns to gain insight into the market for recorded music. It demonstrates how this kind of qualitative research is becoming popular in commercial uses of psychological research.

Grounded theory

- Grounded theory is more of an approach than a specific method, with the purpose of building a theory about what is going on from close scrutiny of the data.
- It was developed in sociology, but has been adopted by psychology (among other disiplines).
- This theory involves four key analytic strategies:
  - **Coding** involves immersing oneself in the data to identify categories, deliberately looking for new, superordinate categories that do not fit with the existing theory, allowing theoretical insights to be made.
  - **Constant comparative analysis** involves refining categories, by looking for examples of the new superordinate category(s) that were missed first time around. More data may be collected at this stage.
  - **Theoretical sampling** is concerned with refinement and rigour. It is a strategic and purposeful scrutiny of the descriptions achieved, moving into a more analytical mode. Again more data may need to be collected to refine the analysis.
  - **Theoretical saturation** is where, after numerous iterations of the three strategies, nothing new is turning up. Sometimes more of an aspiration than achieved, researchers sometimes need to stop when their analysis is 'good enough'.

Q methodology

Q methodology is something of an oddball to include here. Although its popularity is slowly growing among critical social psychologists, it is still not very well known and often dismissed as a *quantitative* method since it uses numbers and statistics. But, when used properly, it does not set out to measure anything objectively. Certainly its inventor, Will Stephenson (Figure 5.4), was quite clear on this matter, even though he did not have the language to say so in a way we would easily recognize today. What he did say is very much to the point. Having rejected the idea that psychology needs to work with large data-sets – numerous cases, in his terminology –

Figure 5.4 William Stephenson

he moves on to say that its 'exaggerated regard for *measurement* is no less of a plague'. He goes on: 'It is widely believed that one must first measure a thing before it can be studied scientifically. Scales and tests of all kinds are therefore widely employed in psychology, although it is almost true to say that no one knows what he[sic] is measuring' (Stephenson 1953: 5).

William Stephenson created Q methodology explicitly as a means of gaining insight into the immensely diverse (and often contested) ways in which people – as individuals and as members of groups, communities and other collectivities – make sense of the lifeworlds they inhabit. Curt (1994) identified three main strands of Q methodological research, examining:

1 *alternative understandings or explanations of phenomena,* such as 'health and illness' (Stainton Rogers 1991) or 'hearing voices' (Jones et al. 2003).
2 *alternative representations of what things or people are like,* such as 'couple love' (Watts and Stenner 2005a).
3 *alternative opinions about what should be done,* such as views of social policy towards protecting children from abuse (Worrell 2001).

In this section I will be using the Jones et al. (2003) Q study that investigated alternative ways in which 'hearing voices' is understood – by 'voice hearers' themselves, by staff working in mental

Figure 5.5 Doing a Q sort

health services and by members of churches where 'voice hearing' is treated as a 'gift' from God. The Watts and Stenner (2005a) study on coupled love is described in more detail in Chapter 11.

As I said at the start of this section, Q is sometimes seen as a quantitative method (McKeown and Thomas 1988), mostly because it uses numbers. But the numbers are not used to *measure* anything; they are ordinal, arising from judgements about the relative value of items. For this reason Q method lies firmly within the range of qualitative methods. Q shares a common purpose with more easily recognizable qualitative approaches like those taken by narrative, discourse analytic and phenomenological research. Its goals and underpinning ontological and epistemological assumptions are qualitative in nature.

There are two distinctive elements in a Q study – the Q sort and Q factor analysis.

Q-sorting

This involves participants ranking items along a dimension like 'most strongly agree' to 'most strongly disagree', in the same way that judges rank contestants – winner, runner up, and so on. It becomes clearer when you look at what is going on in a Q sort, as shown in Figure 5.5. The participant is placing the items from 'most strongly agree' on the right, to 'most strongly disagree' on the left. Participants follow a grid, as shown in Figure 5.6. When completed, the item numbers are recorded in the spaces on the grid, as shown in Figure 5.7.

Examples of the sorts of items involved, taken from the Jones, Guy and Omrod 'hearing voices' study, are shown in Table 5.9.

Q factor analysis

Q factor analysis is a different way of doing factor analysis from the standard form of quantitative research most usually associated, in psychology, with studies of intelligence, personality and other individual differences like 'belief in a just world' and external/internal **locus of control**. Factor analysis is used more broadly in epidemiological studies seeking to pin down the causes

Table 5.9 Items from the 'hearing voices' study

Item number	Statement
2	People who hear voices are making contact with a different spiritual plane of reality
25	Hearing voices results from being mentally injured as a child
12	Untreated voice hearers are a risk to society
16	Voices can help a person take action that they have lacked the courage to perform

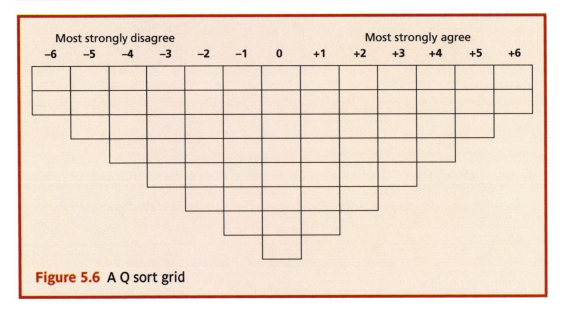

Figure 5.6 A Q sort grid

Most strongly disagree										Most strongly agree		
−6	−5	−4	−3	−2	−1	0	+1	+2	+3	+4	+5	+6
1	6	26	30	5	2	18	3	19	23	16	4	12
32	7	31	38	8	10	22	20	46	36	24	13	52
	9	37	44	15	11	28	25	48	39	27	47	
		51	45	41	14	34	29	50	42	33		
			55	49	17	35	43	56	53			
				58	21	40	60	59				
					62	54	61					
						57						

Figure 5.7 A Q grid completed

of obesity by gaining self-report or archived data from large samples, about a wide diversity of measured variables (such as of age and level of education) as well as categorized variables (such as gender, race and social class). Essentially this form of analysis is looking for systematic links between these measures and categories and measures of obesity, generally that of body mass index (BMI). From this conclusions are drawn – such as that children from families in which parents have attained higher levels of education tend to have lower BMIs than children from families where parents have less education.

With the Q version, the *complete sorting pattern* of each participant is compared with the sorting patterns of all the other participants. This 'inversion' from the norm allows for a **gestalt** approach – which works at a holistic level. It identifies different points of view about a topic or issue within a particular population. For example, the 'hearing voices' study identified six alternative understandings. One, a *positive spiritual* perspective, differed from the rest because it saw 'hearing voices' as something desirable – a 'gift'. By contrast, the *generic mental illness* perspective drew on the mainstream biomedical understanding of 'madness'.

Comparing conventional and Q factor analysis

In order to understand Q factor analysis, it is helpful to compare it directly with the usual way factor analysis is done.

Traditional **factor analysis** was developed for studies investigating 'traits' – such as whether intelligence is a single capacity of 'cleverness' or is made up of separate traits like 'cleverness with words' and 'mathematical ability', each independent of the other. If just one factor is identified, this indicates that intelligence is a single capacity. But if several different factors are found, this indicates that, say, verbal intelligence and mathematical intelligence are two, separate capabilities. In this approach, large numbers of people are given tests to do, each one designed to tap a different kind of ability. The data, when entered into the factor analysis program, would look like Table 5.10 although in real life there would be a lot more of it!

Factor analysis here begins with correlating the scores on the different tests and looking for clusters of tests that are highly correlated. Working systematically to parcel up the inter-correlating tests into clusters, factor analysis first identifies and extracts from the calculation the cluster that explains most of the **variance** in the data-set – Factor 1. The analysis then moves on to account for the variance that is left, again seeking the cluster of inter-correlation that explains the most variance within this depleted set – Factor 2. Although this process continues until all the variance is accounted for, researchers usually stop looking for factors once they become no longer informative.

Table 5.10 Conventional factor analysis

		Test scores			
		Verbal test 1	Verbal test 2	Maths test 1	Maths test 2
People	Shenaz	15	19	8	11
	Pete	3	8	9	5
	Akin	20	19	10	18

Table 5.11 Q factor analysis

		Q-sort placement of item		
		Prue's Q-sort	Dot's Q-sort	Evan's Q-sort
Q-sort items	1. Given the right circumstances, most of us would hear voices.	+1	−4	−1
	2. People who hear voices are making contact with a different spiritual plane of reality.	+4	−3	0
	3. People hear voices when the Devil or other evil spirit possesses them.	−2	0	−5
	4. Hearing voices is a lifelong condition	0	+2	−2

Q factor analysis works in the same way, but there is a crucial difference. The numbers indicating the placement of items in the Q sort are not keyed in as though they are the results of 'tests'. Instead, the placement is reversed, as shown in Table 5.11, though again, there would be a lot more data. Thus Q factor analysis uses a 'by sorting pattern'.

Studying subjectivity or intersubjectivity?

Studying subjectivity

Within the Q community, Q methodology is often referred to as a way of studying *subjectivity*. And certainly Q enables people to express their own point of view about a whole range of topics related to personal subjectivity like what it feels like to experience depression. Q methodology allows such subjective aspects to be mapped out in fine detail, providing researchers with a novel and powerful tool for interrogating subjective experience.

Q methodology is often used like this by clinical psychologists and psychotherapists to conduct fine-grained, case-study investigations of an individual's subjective experiences, self-perceptions, aspirations and the like, mapping out their client's subjectivity over time and across various aspects of their emotional and cognitive mental life. Here the **Q set** is drawn from statements made by the client in question in therapy sessions. Goldstein and Goldstein (2005) did so to investigate the subjective **self-esteem** of a client they call L. Having constructed a self-esteem Q set from her own conversations and writings, they had L carry out 12 Q sorts under different **conditions of instruction**, including 'the way I am as a parent', 'when I am riding a bike', 'how I am in my dreams' and 'when I was divorced'. Four different perceptions were found, and were then used in subsequent sessions with L, enabling her to become more self-aware and, hence, more able to resolve some of the issues for which she had sought therapy.

Q sorting makes people think about their own thoughts. It, almost literally, puts them 'on the line', where they must resolve a whole range of differing (sometimes conflicting) ideas, emotions and concerns. In so doing, the person becomes much more self-aware. A number of researchers have capitalized upon this to use Q sorting as an aid to reflexive practice, a means to gain personal insight into their own thoughts and emotional investments and apply these to improving their professional competence.

McKeown et al. (1999) used just such an approach to investigate the alternative ways mental health professionals thought risk should be managed in mental health services. As well as being a Q study in itself, the impact of doing the Q sort was also used as part of a training programme for managers working in the service. Doing the Q sort allowed these managers to grapple with the contradictions and ambiguities they faced when considering how the service should be run. Importantly, it also helped them to gain real insight into and empathy with alternative opinions and strategies, and be more willing to make compromises.

Studying intersubjectivity

Among researchers adopting a social constructionist stance, Q studies are primarily used to find out about 'what is going on' in the conversations and other forms of social interplay operating *between* people – including communicative processes like education, journalism, advertising, entertainment and, these days, increasingly through people's interactions on the Web and in the virtual worlds made possible by it. For us, Q research provides a powerful technique for studying *intersubjectivity*: how argument and truth claims are deployed within and between the competing positions taken by groups with different stakes to claim, statuses to defend, values to endorse and realities to construct.

Q methodology is an effective way to explore the dynamics operating in human meaning-making, in a whole range of contexts. It can survey and scrutinize how power is being exercised, for example, within the broad 'marketplace' of alternative standpoints and positions that are taken on a particular topic (such as mental health) and within a designated population, whether focused (such as between the different professions working in mental health for a particular local authority) or more broadly based (such as across the UK population as a whole).

In this approach, Q methodology is being used less as a means to interrogate individual subjectivities and more as a taxonomic tool. It thus has something in common with social representations research and macro-discourse analysis. Watts and Stenner (2005a) liken Q methodology to some features of narrative analysis, in that its analytic approach treats data in a gestalt manner rather than fragmenting it thematically (as does, say, much interpretative phenomenological analysis). Like narrative analysis, the interpretation of Q data allows us to observe how themes that are common across the sympatric alternatives can be articulated in quite different ways. Unlike narrative analysis, however, Q method produces data that offer a 'snapshot' view of what is going on (as opposed to a life-history or account, where timescale is an important analytical frame).

How to do a Q methodological study

Q methodology is done in discrete stages, which I can only summarize here (see Table 5.12). Watts and Stenner (2005a) and Stenner et al. (in Willig and Stainton Rogers 2009) provide much more detail (see the Further reading section) and if you plan to do a Q study I suggest you get hold of one or both of them.

Table 5.12 Stages in doing a Q study

Stage 1: Preparatory work

Formulating a research question	Two things matter here – being specific and focused about the topic or issue you want to study, and making sure it is not about generating a cause-and-effect explanation. Typical questions are about different perspectives on: 'what is going on in self-harm? or 'what does love mean' or 'what is a smoker like?'
Considering ethics	Getting ethical approval is never just a nuisance to be sorted just before you begin your fieldwork. Ethical concerns should be incorporated into your research at every stage, starting with formulating your research questions. In fact Q sorting as an activity has a lot going for it ethically. Participants can be anonymous by using online or postal/email delivery and response. They are not expected to divulge or discuss any personal or sensitive information about themselves. And they remain more in control throughout the task than is the case, say, with interviews and focus groups
Preparing consent form	It is never too soon to do this! Start now. Your consent form must conform to the requirements of your institution, the body from whom you are seeking ethical approval and, if relevant, your professional body
Estimating the concourse	The **concourse** is a term to describe all the things that can be thought or said about the issue or topic in question. Estimating it means going out and looking for it – from talking to people and observing them in conversation, watching soap operas, movies and posts on Facebook or YouTube, reading the academic literature but also newspapers, blogs and novels. Often Q researchers do other studies at this point, and mine the data for the Q study from them. You need to gather together a list of statements expressing a viewpoint or understanding. It is usual to aim for at least a hundred, all as different as possible from each other
Devising an initial draft of the Q set	A Q set needs to be manageable – usually somewhere between 30 and 60 items – which is about how many can be comfortably sorted in an hour or so (there is a lot of thinking involved). This means reducing the statements gathered very substantially. It is usually done through a process of repeatedly clustering items together, arriving at just one to capture the sense of several. It is helpful to share this task with others
Refining the Q set	This stage is part of standard good design for any instrument (like a questionnaire) where you make sure the items contain just one single idea or opinion and that the language is comprehensible to the people who will participate in the study (children can with simple enough language). Especially important in Q studies is to avoid items with similar meanings, and getting a roughly equal number at each end of the dimension to be sorted (agree/disagree; most like me/least like me). This may mean reversing some items, but it is essential to avoid double negatives. Think about how hard it is to be clear about what you are saying when you put 'Being a smoker is not about addiction' into a –5 slot. Many Q researchers aim for a balanced Q set by reference to a theoretically informed framework for selecting items
Designing the grid	This is a simple task of starting from the number of items and then considering the various ways in which they can be allocated within the inverted pyramid shape. The more items in the set, the more columns you will need – the usual range is from about +3 to –3 going up to +6 to –6. The extreme ends will need 1, 2 or 3 (seldom more) slots, and the rest is a matter of convenience. The best way to judge is to have a go at the Q sort yourself, and if you can get a few others to do so, or do it yourself several times playing different roles – right-wing rat-bag is always my favourite, stereotyped, of course, but helps me make sure that the sort will work for people with different views from mine!

Table 5.12 *Continued*

Preparing participant information form	It is a very useful strategy to provide participants with a response form. The data you collect needs careful thought, since you will not know what is important until you identify the factors. Obviously you will include categories identified for your framework. But to keep an open mind, a good approach is to ask participants to suggest, say, the three most important things that *they* think have influenced their views on the topic. This can add to the abductive nature of your study.
Preparing response materials	It is a helpful strategy to prepare an open-ended response sheet, listing all the items with a space beside each one. Ask participants to make comments beside all items that 'stand out' for them, such as ones they are in two minds about where to place – what is the dilemma? This helps interpretation no end

Stage 2: Q fieldwork

Selecting participants	Participants in a Q study are *strategically* selected and not intended to be a 'representative sample' of the population. The aim is to include people with opinions as diverse as possible, and hence this involves deliberately seeking widely for people likely to have different views from those already recruited. Often this is informed by the theoretically informed framework
Delivery and response	This can be face to face (linked with an interview or not), delivered by hand or by post or email. Increasingly researchers are administering the Q set online. Information on software for this is provided in the Resources section
Iterations	Wherever possible do a pilot study, analyse the data, look out for what you may have missed and reformulate the Q set, for instance, to give more opportunities for a viewpoint to be expressed. You can also analyse as you go along, and then recruit more participants to cover potential viewpoints you have missed

Stage 3: Q factor analysis

You may need more advice to tackle this. It is not difficult, but some of the software is, at present, rather clunky. Stenner et al. (2009) give clear instructions; so too do Watts and Stenner (2005a). Also use the Q website as a starting point for getting advice, listed in the Resources section at the end of the chapter

Stage 4: Q factor interpretation

Constructing factor summaries	For each factor, work from the 'ideal Q sort' that provides the best estimate for the viewpoint being expressed. Most people start with the items at the extreme ends, but as you gradually gain an understanding of what is being said, look also at the middle-ranking items. Use the 'identifying items' list provided by the software to home in on what makes each factor different from the others. Clear worked examples are given in Watts and Stenner (2005a) and Stenner et al. (2009)
Interpretation	This final stage is what brings quality to a Q study. It involves 'standing back' from the detail of the factor summaries, looking at what you have got, and relating this to theorization in the field in which you are working. The best way to do this is to read several Q studies in your field

Q methodology

- Invented by Wiliam Stephenson in the 1930s, Q methodology uses an inverted form of factor analysis to identify and gain insight into alternative:
  - representations of what a person or a thing is like
  - explanations for how something operates or is caused
  - viewpoints on what should be done about it.
- This is usually done by constructing a set of items (a Q set) which are sorted along a dimension (such as strongest agreement/strongest disagreement) in an inverted pyramid arrangement.
- Items are usually statements, but music clips, photographs and advertisements have also been used.
- The Q set of between 30–60 items is designed to provide a representative sample of all the things that can be thought and said about the topic in question (called its concourse).
- Q sorting can be done manually with statements on cards, or administered online with dedicated software.
- These days Q factor analysis is mainly done using other dedicated software, but can be done using generic statistical packages like SPSS together with some additional statistical calculations.
- Interpretation begins with devising an account of the representation, explanation or viewpoint associated with each factor identified. From these, researchers, by reference to theory and existing knowledge, gradually refine an account of 'what is going on'. Both of these processes use abduction.

Ethics in qualitative research

While much the same ethical issues apply here as do to quantitative psychology, even greater care needs to be taken in qualitative research. The nature of the methods used, the relationships between researchers and participants in the study and, especially, the intimacy of many of the topics – all of these can create much more ambiguous research settings, which can pose really acute ethical issues.

A good illustration came from a conversation I had with a psychologist who was, at that time, conducting two lines of research – one about gay men acting as sperm donors, the other about being a foster parent. As he pointed out, the nature of the 'rapport' he was able to establish (by being, himself, both a gay man and a foster carer) was very different in each case and carried different implications. The distinction between 'building rapport' with the participants in your study, and using your skills of persuasion and charm to inveigle somebody into disclosing something they later regret is a very difficult one to judge.

A new concern comes from the growing use of the Internet as a source of data, and the potential for harm in settings like these. Phillip Dyson, one of my doctoral students as I write this text, uses the terms 'lurker' and 'voyeur' for what he is doing when he downloads chat-room conversations and Facebook clips about 'self-harm'. Issues involve what is public, what is private, and how can you tell when people are 'whispering' on the Internet? Trouble needs to be taken to ensure anonymity when search engines have become so powerful they can pinpoint who wrote something from tiny samples of text.

Brinkmann and Kvale (2009) have specifically argued that qualitative research demands more than simply compliance with the requirements of ethical approval. Researchers must actively *learn* to become ethical:

> Good qualitative researchers master what has been called the art of thick description . . . [being] able to understand the contextual and relational features of the phenomena we are concerned with. . . . Similarly . . . in order to deal well with ethical issues, qualitative researchers should primarily cultivate their ability to perceive and judge 'thickly'. . . . As we 'thicken' event descriptions, we see more and more clearly what the moral implications of the event are.
>
> (Brinkmann and Kvale 2009: 276)

Their 2009 chapter in the *Handbook of Qualitative Research in Psychology* is a highly readable and very practical guide to 'learning to be ethical', and is recommended at the end of this chapter.

Ethics in qualitative research

- Ethical issues are often much trickier in qualitative research – because, for instance, there is much greater opportunity for exploitation given the close contact involved between researcher and participants.

- Research using 'found text' (such as on Facebook or in online blogs and chat rooms) poses particular ethical issues, especially about confidentiality and anonymity.

- Qualitative researchers must do more than just conform to the 'rules'. They must be a lot more reflexive than that! It is about learning to be ethical, and constantly engaging with ethics at every stage of the research process.

Resources

Ethical guidance

The British Psychological Society offers online guidelines for:

- assessing quality in qualitative research: http://www.bps.org.uk/publications/journals/joop/qualitativeguidelines.cfm
- ethics in research: http://www.bps.org.uk/the-society/code-of-conduct/code-of-conduct_home.cfm

- ethical research online: http://www.bps.org.uk/document-download-area/document-download$.cfm?file_uuid=2B3429B3-1143-DFD0-7E5A-4BE3FDD763CC&ext=pdf

Similar guidance is provided in most countries. For example, in New Zealand it is at: http://www.psychology.org.nz/cms_show_download.php?id=10

Methods

Discourse analysis: http://extra.shu.ac.uk/daol/about/

Template analysis: http://www.hud.ac.uk/hhs/research/template_analysis/index.htm

Q methodology: the official website of the Q community, http://www.qmethodology.net/, gives access to information, a chance to try Q sorting for yourself, and links to software to deliver Q sorts online and to analyse Q data.

FQ Factor analysis programs available include PQmethod which is downloadable free online (http://www.lrz.de/~schmolck/qmethod/index.htm) and PCQ for Windows (http://www.pcqsoft.com/) which has a licence fee. For up-to-date news, check the Q website.

Websites such as WebQ (http://www.lrzmuenchen.de/~schmolck/qmethod/webq/) and FlashQ (http://www.hackert.biz/flashq/home/) now provide Q researchers with an opportunity to administer Q sorts online. Both are available as free downloads.

Further reading

General texts

Parker, I. (2005) *Qualitative Psychology: Introducing Radical Research.* **Maidenhead: Open University Press.**
Ian Parker writes with great conviction, real flair and great authority. His work is politically informed and he makes no bones about saying what he thinks is wrong with mainstream approaches and telling you what to do to pull yourself out of its clutches and learn how to do research in a more honest, ethical and thoughtful manner. This book is both a good read and a great practical handbook. If you want to do research radically, this is where you should start.

Willig, C. (2008) *Introducing Qualitative Research in Psychology: Adventures in Theory and Method,* **2nd edn. Buckingham: Open University Press.**
Not only does this book give a thorough and clear exposition of social constructionist methods, it also includes a brilliant introduction to this paradigm and the rationale for it. It includes thought-provoking 'boxes' that discuss various methodological issues, and good examples of undergraduate projects.

Willig, C. and Stainton Rogers, W. (eds) (2009) *The Sage Handbook of Qualitative Research in Psychology.* **London: Sage.**
I am not just recommending this handbook because I co-edited it! It is much more in-depth than your standard research methods handbook, but its chapters do offer excellent overviews of a wide

range of qualitative methods, plus other useful topics such as computer packages for analysis, ethics and mixing qualitative and quantitative methods.

Stainton Rogers, W. (2009) Research methodology, in D. Fox, I. Prilleltensky and S. Austin (eds) *Critical Psychology: An Introduction*, 2nd edn. London: Sage.
I hope I can convince you this is not just another case of self-promotion, but this chapter does cover some important areas and ideas there was not room for in this chapter.

Ethics in qualitative research

Brinkmann, S. and Kvale, S. (2009) Ethics in qualitative psychological research, in C. Willig and W. Stainton Rogers (eds) *The Sage Handbook of Qualitative Research in Psychology*. London: Sage.

This chapter is a careful, thorough and very convincing account of 'how to become ethical' in your research.

Analytical approaches

Conversational analysis

Wilkinson, S. and Kitzinger, C. (2009) Conversation analysis, in C. Willig and W. Stainton Rogers (eds) *The Sage Handbook of Qualitative Research in Psychology*. London: Sage.

This chapter offers a detailed and up-to-date review of this approach, and excellent advice about how to do it.

Discourse analysis

Edwards, D. and Potter, J. (1992) *Discursive Psychology*. London: Sage.

Even though this is quite old now, I still think it is the best introduction to this field.

McKinlay, A. and McVittie, C. (2008) *Social Psychology and Discourse*. Chichester: Wiley-Blackwell.

This is a whole book taking a discursive approach to social psychology. It has lots of up-to-date examples of how discursive research informs social psychology's topics, issues and agendas.

Grounded theory

Charmaz, K. and Henwood, K. (2009) Grounded theory, in C. Willig and W. Stainton Rogers (eds) *The Sage Handbook of Qualitative Research in Psychology*. London: Sage.

This chapter brings together two of the foremost authorities on the use of grounded theory in psychology. As such, it provides a comprehensive and well-informed review of psychological research in this field, and guidance on how to apply it.

Narrative analysis

Emerson, P. and Frosh, S. (2004) *Critical Narrative Analysis in Psychology: A Guide to Practice*, London: Palgrave Macmillan.

Given the complexity of this approach, this offers a clear account of narrative analysis, especially as it is conducted from a psychoanalytic perspective.

Parker, I. (2005) Narrative, in I. Parker, *Qualitative Psychology: Introducing Radical Research*, Maidenhead: Open University Press.

I have already recommended this book, but I think you will find this chapter particularly useful if you plan to get into narrative analysis. It is a very particular take on it – Parker is known for his confrontational views. Read it and decide for yourself.

Hiles, D. and Čermák, I. (2009) Narrative psychology, in C. Willig and W. Stainton Rogers (eds) *The Sage Handbook of Qualitative Research in Psychology*. London: Sage.

What is clever here is that the authors take a single extract of text and show how it can be interpreted using six alternative analytic perspectives. If you are just starting out, I suspect this will be too fine-grained for you. But if you decide to get into this field, it is a very good place to start.

Phenomenological analysis

Langdridge, D. (2007) *Phenomenological Psychology: Theory, Research and Method*. Harlow: Pearson.

This is beautifully clearly written book, and makes a difficult set of ideas accessible and exciting. It offers detailed, helpful and practical advice about conducting different kinds of phenomenological studies, and is tailored precisely to psychology.

Q methodology

Stainton Rogers, R. (1995) Q methodology, in J. Smith, R. Harré and L. Langenhove (eds) *Rethinking Methods in Psychology*. London: Sage.

This was written by Rex some years before he died. It is a clear and relatively friendly entry point into doing Q methodological research.

Watts, S. and Stenner, P. (2005a) Doing Q methodology: theory, method and interpretation, *Qualitative Research in Psychology*, 2: 67–91.

This paper may well be more available to you, and is more up to date. It is strong on technical aspects of Q, and gives clear advice on how to approach the analysis.

Thematic analysis

Braun, V. and Clarke, V. (2006) Using thematic analysis in psychology, *Qualitative Research in Psychology*, 3: 77–101.

This paper is an excellent introduction to coding text of all kinds and from all different sources – interviews, focus groups, the Internet, and so on. It is not guided by a particular theory, but can form the basis of different kinds of interpretation. It is a good place to start doing social constructionist research in psychology.

Questions

1 Compare and contrast qualitative and quantitative research methods in social psychology. What are the main differences between them, and in what ways are they similar?

2 Descriptive research is conducted in both experimental and critical paradigms in social psychology. Using an example in each case published in the last three years, show in what ways they are similar and in what ways different. Say which approach you prefer, and explain why.

3 Select three different ways of collecting data for qualitative research in social psychology. Outline the key features of each one, illustrating this by reference to a recent study using it.

4 Trace the origins of discourse analysis research in social psychology. Using an example study from micro and macro versions of this approach, explain the key differences between them.

5 Select a social psychological topic of your choosing. Using an Internet search, identify two *different* studies of this topic that each use a *different* form of qualitative analysis (for example, thematic analysis and an interpretative phenomenological analysis; or a conversational analysis and a narrative approach). Outline the key elements of each study and the research question(s) in each case. Then compare and contrast the analytic approaches. Clearly identify the benefits and drawbacks/limitations of each approach to the study of your chosen topic.

6 What is meant by abductive research? Describe this approach, the ontological and epistemological assumptions on which it is based, and why it can be seen as a form of critical relativism.

7 Say what is special about either the narrative or the phenomenological approach to interpretation. Give at least three examples to illustrate your answer (you may well need to go and find papers of your own!).

SECTION 3

Social cognition and construction

6

Communication and language in social psychology

LEARNING OUTCOMES

When you have finished studying this chapter, you should be able to:

1 Speculate about some of the ways interpersonal communication has changed with the introduction of global forms of information technology, such as the Internet, Facebook and Wikipedia.

2 Outline the main features of communication theory, and list the ways in which human communication differs from the ways in which machines (such as telecommunication systems) communicate.

3 Drawing upon the experimental social psychology approach and literature, describe the different forms that non-verbal communication can take, their role in human communication, and how non-verbal behaviour can give cues that a person is telling lies.

4 Explain what is meant by the term 'knowing of the third kind', and its importance in critical approaches to non-verbal behaviour.

5 Explain the difference between seeing communication as a *form of behaviour* and as a *situated social practice*.

6 Define and explain linguistics, psycholinguistics and sociolinguistics, paralanguage and speech style, giving examples of each.

7 Challenge the idea that women's language is inferior to the language men use.

8 Outline the key assumptions and elements of semiotic theory, define 'sign', 'symbol' and 'sign system', and explain how it has been adopted as a means to understand the role of language in human communication.

9 Describe the role of the mass media when seen as a means of intersubjective communication.

Introduction

Social psychology is about the ways in which we influence each other; about our relationships with each other, as partners, families and communities; and about who we are, as mothers, friends, managers, citizens (or not), travellers and pensioners and all the other social roles we can (or cannot) adopt. And all of this is only possible because we communicate with each other in a multiplicity of different forms and, increasingly, through a range of technological tools and gizmos. This chapter explores the different ways that social psychology has theorized and conducted research into how people communicate with each other and the role that communication plays in social action and interaction. After a very brief review of general communication theory, and some issues to consider before getting into the main business of the chapter, I have divided it into three main sections.

The first focuses on the ways in which we communicate directly through our bodies – the looks we give, the gestures we make, the emotions we display by our smiles and our grimaces. Usually this is called non-verbal communication, and can be thought of as a 'simpler' form than language. It is often automatic and unconscious, some aspects are probably 'wired in' and innate and more like the way other animals communicate with each other.

The second section is about language, spoken and written, as well as other symbolic forms of communication that are representational, such as with signs telling what you can and cannot do in pictograms, or ways to signify membership of a specific group or class. In this section I concentrate on language as studied by social psychologists within the experimental paradigm.

The third section reviews the semiotic approach to language that is becoming popular in critical social psychology. This is informed by a number of critical theories and approaches including post-structuralism. Your study of Chapter 5 will have told you that language and other representational systems are incredibly important to critical social psychology, since its focus is on how we both construct meaning and have it constructed for us.

Communication in an information technology-saturated world

Before we move on, however, there is another overall issue that needs to be raised. As any *Star Trek* fan can tell you, communication is profoundly affected by the time and place in which it happens. The kind of social networking going on in Facebook is different from getting together with your friends over a meal. Both are very different from the ways I got together with my friends at college more than 40 years ago. Both the opportunities and rules, formal and informal, were different and it made our relationships different from how yours are now. One of these is just how small our circle was, limited because we had little access to phones, no personal computers let alone laptops, no Internet, no text or Twitter. Another big difference is how narrow our friendship networks were in terms of age, social class, ethnic heritage and even gender – the student body at my university was more than 90 per cent male and the very few black students were from rich families in Africa.

This is not just the rambling of a soon-to-be retired professor. It has a point, which is that most of the research conducted by psychologists into communication was carried out in the last half of the twentieth century from the 1960s through to the 1990s. Yet, over that time, technological progress was rapid and highly influential. Email got started in the 1970s, and personal computers in the 1980s. But it has only been in the twenty-first century that email and social networking have become something almost every young person in the UK does, and does electronically. Satellites, cheap SIM cards, phone-renting-by-the-call businesses are spreading this communication revolution globally in a way inconceivable even a few years ago.

Equally there have been massive technological changes in what used to be called broadcasting. A one-way system of a small number of people producing radio and television programmes for large audiences has been replaced by a densely interactive network of modes of communication where everyone with access to the technology is able to broadcast, podcast, webcast, or whatever, at a global level. A teenage girl can video herself dancing in her bedroom, and end up with a massive following of eager fans watching her in Japan. Equally, according to Beattie (2004), reality has brought the laboratory experiment onto our televisions and into our sitting rooms and our bedrooms, where we can watch people communicating for hours:

> Nearly all of the psychological research that has studied bodily communication in the past has been based on mere snapshots of behaviour. Small sets of individuals have been invited into a psychological laboratory, complete with one-way mirrors and hidden cameras. . . . No psychology experiment, with all the technology necessary to record the complexity of behaviour, ever had anyone actually living in the laboratory before. But *Big Brother*, of course, did just that.
>
> (Beattie 2004: 3)

Beattie tells of the conversations he would have with people about what was going on between inmates.

> People would stop me in the street and ask 'You're the Big Brother psychologist, what do you think is going on between Kate and Spencer?' I would stand there, not wishing to appear rude, rocking slightly, with embarrassment, trying to say something they had not heard before . . . I would offer up a comment and watch their reaction. 'Nah, you're wrong mate' they would say. 'Didn't you see that look Kate gave Spencer when he chatted to Adele?' We were all psychologists now, or so it seemed.
>
> (Beattie 2004: 4)

Your lifeworld (and mine) is a different one from that in which the classic studies of communication were carried out. Research in this field is not really keeping up with the way social life has shifted because of new technology, and the impact this is having on our modes of communication with each other. There is some, and it is growing, but most of it is too recent to hit the social psychology textbooks.

Figure 6.1 At first sight she is all on her own – but look again and you can see she is deeply involved in social communication

A good example is a recent study by Cinnirella and Green where they tried out a version of Asch's famous study of conformity (Chapter 12), examining the impact of culture but getting people doing the task on the Internet. Lots of other work had shown that people from collectivist cultures (like Japan and China) tend to be more conforming in their behavior in groups than people in individualistic cultures such as the dominant mainstream of the UK and the USA. But the researchers showed that this effect goes away when communication is by electronic means. This, they say, is important, in a world where email, texting and Twitter are coming to be the main way many people communicate. So they argue that 'cross-cultural (social) psychology needs to interface with the psychology of the Internet and computer-mediated communication, so that an understanding can be developed for the role of culture in CMC settings' (Cinnirella and Green 2007: 2023). So bear these points in mind as you read the chapter.

That having been said, there are real opportunities opened up by new technology. One that I find exciting is the potential to use avatars as part of experiments! In Chapter 4 you saw an example for yourself from the study by Bailenson and his colleagues researching into inter-personal space (proxemics): 'As we enter a new millennium, digital technology has raised opportunities as well as new issues for proxemics research. Digital representations of human beings are becoming common in communication media and entertainment, particularly in immersive virtual environments (IVEs)' (Bailenson et al. 2003: 819). We will come back to look at this study later in the chapter, but it does illustrate the way that psychology is rapidly changing in response to the potential offered by new social spaces.

Communication

Communication as a specific topic was first theorized and studied by the mathematician Shannon (1948). He wanted to find a way of measuring the transmission capacity of telephone and other similar communication systems by calculating the rate at which information could be conveyed. Shannon and Weaver (1949) constructed a basic model of communication, shown in Figure 6.2.

Communication theory has given us much of the basic terminology we use to understand human communication. It defines communication as involving six main elements: an information source, a transmitter or sender, a message, a communication channel, a receiver and a destination. Information transmission involves encoding and decoding, and is always subject to interference from noise.

Through the 1950s and 1960s, psychologists applied this theorization to human information processing and communication (see, for example, Miller 1953; Posner 1966). However, Shannon and Weaver's model was highly mechanistic and hence of limited value to understanding human communication.

Cognitive psychology

By the end of the 1960s the 'cognitive revolution' in psychology led to the recognition that people process and communicate information in a way that is very different from machines. Cognitive psychology had its origins in the work of Frederick Bartlett (1932) and Ulric Neisser (1966).

> The early work of Bartlett and Neisser were each described in Chapter 1.

Early cognitive models of communication stress that human communication:

- is not based (as are machines) upon the transmission of 'pure' information, but upon the transmission of meaning
- is a social activity, actively involving two or more people and influenced by the nature of the relationship between them

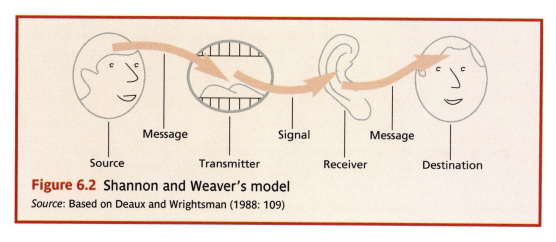

Figure 6.2 Shannon and Weaver's model
Source: Based on Deaux and Wrightsman (1988: 109)

- is ongoing and dynamic, working sequentially and building upon what went before
- usually works by multiple encoding, where, for example, a message is transmitted by both words and non-verbally (for example, in terms of gestures, or facial expressions or tone of voice).

Cognitive neuroscience

In human communication, voices and faces constitute the carrier signals for social signals conveyed via speech melody and facial expressions.

(Kreifelts et al. 2010: 980)

In Chapter 7 we will examine in depth the social cognition approach to social psychology. However, this work is also relevant to our understanding of the cognitive underpinnings of communication. Cognitive approaches to communication today increasingly use sophisticated cognitive neuroscience technology and techniques such as (magnetic resonance imaging, MRI) to study what they call 'the social brain'. Pelphrey and Carter (2008), for instance, have developed a research programme 'to identify and delineate the brain systems involved in social perception and to chart the development of those systems and their role as mechanisms supporting the development of social cognition in children, adolescents and adults with and without autism' (Pelphrey and Carter 2008: 1081). Kreifelts and his colleagues make the point that: 'The multimodal integration of social signals (verbal and nonverbal, e.g., facial expressions, speech melody, gestures) into a unitary perception is a basic part of successful social interaction. This perception then allows us to infer the intentions and emotional states of our counterparts' (Kreifelts et al. 2010: 980).

The outcome of this kind of research is identifying the specific areas of the brain associated with particular functions. Kreifelts and his colleagues were able to locate where integration of the different modalities (auditory from speech, visual from observing facial expression) gets done, and, by looking around at other functions located close by, speculate about links to other processes involved in social cognition.

It can be argued that this approach does little more than map brain function. However, where it comes into its own is when applied to the potentially social impacts of cognitive dysfunction. We will look at some of these studies as we progress through the chapter.

Cognitive approaches

- **Communication** involves six main elements: an information source, a transmitter or sender, a message, a communication channel, a receiver and a destination.
- **Human communication** is different from the mechanical forms of communication, such as telecommunication. It is active, meaningful, social and dynamic. It is also generally multiply encoded.
- **Cognitive neuroscience** uses techniques like MRI scanning to identify where particular processes – such as the perception of emotion – take place in the brain. It is particularly useful for understanding how problems in perception and understanding may contribute to disorders like learning disability, schizophrenia and autism.

Non-verbal communication

On the phone, even when the person we are talking to cannot see us, we tend to smile and frown and gesture. Accompanying our talk with body language is so 'natural' we are often unaware of what we are doing. We have even found ways to smile when we write :-)! Using tools like Skype and Elluminate, have you found it makes a difference to the ease and comfort of communication to be able to see each other? This is because **body language** complements and reinforces the talk, making effective communication easier to accomplish. In difficult negotiations with family and friends, for example, we can get cues about whether the other person is being honest by looking at their body language. Even when people control what they say and the way they speak so they sound as if they are being genuine, their gestures and stance can let them down (Argyle 1988).

Body language is usually given the generic term 'non-verbal communication' and it includes a range of behaviours and serves a number of functions:

- supplementing verbal communication – for example, by giving information about feelings and emotions, and hence motives and intentions

- replacing verbal communication – for example, using hand gestures to someone who cannot hear you

- expressing things more effectively – such as the intimacy conveyed by a kiss or the touch of a hand

- helping to manage verbal communication – for instance, by signalling when someone wants to speak.

Facial expression

Facial expression is important for expressing emotion. It is one of the things Charles Darwin studied in his development of the theory of evolution (1872), and early psychological work by Ekman, based on Darwin's, identified six basic facial expressions, much the same in every culture, for each of six fundamental emotions: happiness, surprise, sadness, fear, disgust and anger (Ekman 1973, 2003). In Ekman's original studies people were asked to look at photographs and say what emotion was being expressed. These basic emotional expressions are associated with distinctive facial muscle activity. Surprise, for example, involves raised eyebrows, dropped jaw, a wrinkled forehead and a widening of the eyes.

Such studies, of course, would be very difficult to do today, given the globalization of television, films and the Internet. There must be few places on earth now where people have not seen emotions played out on the faces of Hollywood and or Bollywood actors, or others from cultures very different from their own. Yet the idea that facial expressions are innate continues to fascinate evolutionary psychologists. Based in part on studies of continuity between humans and primates (Van Hooff 1972) and in part by the observation that people born deaf, blind and without hands still express basic emotions in much the same way as others, evolutionary psychologists argue that the ability to communicate emotion has an evolutionary advantage, and hence is 'wired in'.

However, this aspect is of less concern to most social psychologists. What interests them are the social and cultural conventions – called display rules – governing the way people communicate specific kinds of emotion to each other. For example, in northern Europe and Asia men, in particular, have been expected to 'damp down' emotional expression in general. Women are expected not to 'be emotional' in professional settings. In Japan both men and women learn to cover up the expression of certain negative emotions – for example, to use smiles to conceal anger or distress (Ekman 1973), the expression of which is culturally taboo in many settings. Smiling, on the other hand, is an emotional expression that people in many cultures learn to use for display purposes. For instance, in certain jobs – mainly those serving customers – staff are required to appear charming and cheerful, irrespective of what they may be feeling. Such work is called **emotional labour**, pointing to the effort involved in presenting a cheery face for hours on end, however obnoxiously the customers are behaving.

Recent cognitive research explores links between failure to 'read' facial expressions accurately and various disorders such as autism and schizophrenia (Gur et al. 2006) and even deviance (such as antisocial behaviour or conduct disorder). They have also looked at how well others can decode information about emotion from those with disorders like schizophrenia (Healey et al. 2004).

Gaze and eye contact

Gaze, in this context, refers to the time spent looking directly at another person (it has a totally different meaning in postmodern theory). Eye contact refers to mutual gaze, when people 'catch each other's eyes'. Gaze and eye contact are used in five main ways: as a means of communication in their own right, to signal status, to signal interest and sincerity, to manage conversations and to exert control.

We sometimes say things like 'his thunderous look spoke volumes' or talk about when 'our eyes met across a crowded room'. A 'knowing look' can be used to comment to a friend about something somebody else has said. Lovers use glancing eye contact to signal mutual but secret knowledge. Gaze and eye contact are powerful ways of communicating in their own right.

The use of gaze in conversation varies by cultural convention. For example, in some cultures people in subordinate positions are expected to keep their eyes lowered when speaking to a superior. But in other cultures a lot of eye contact goes on between both speakers. Argyle and Ingham (1972) estimated that when two white British people are conversing together they spend about 60 per cent of the time gazing, each gaze lasting about three seconds. Of this, eye contact occupies about 30 per cent of the time, and each one lasts less than a second.

Social rules and cultural conventions about eye contact not only differ between cultures, but also are very powerful. Transgressing them can lead to miscommunication and can therefore be highly disturbing. In white British culture, eye contact is more used to signal interest and sincerity than status. Consequently, someone who makes little eye contact will be regarded as 'shifty eyed', and the inference made that they are lying or 'up to no good'. In a culture where direct eye contact is used more to signal status, high levels of eye contact by a subordinate will be viewed as that person being 'uppity' and deliberately disrespectful. You can imagine how differences like this can lead to prejudice, where one person interprets the other's direct eye contact as insulting, impertinent or brazen or seductive, rather than 'interested' and 'open' as intended.

Most studies of gaze and eye contact have been conducted in cultures where they are regarded as signalling interest, openness and honesty. Not surprisingly, then, these studies have found that people tend to look more at those they like than at those they dislike, and for gaze and eye contact to be more frequent the more intimate the relationship (see Kleinke 1986, for a review). But even in such cultures, they are sensitive to status, though the pattern is different. Given that in such cultures gaze indicates interest, the person of lower status tends to gaze more, especially when listening to the person of higher status. Research done more than 30 years ago found that women tended to engage in gazing more than men do (Henley 1977). I wonder if this would be as true today. And note the heteronormative assumption here that takes no account of the mores among other groups and people of different ages.

Gaze and eye contact are also used to manage conversations, though again we need to read the research with caution. The main way people initiate a conversation is, in mainstream US culture, to make eye contact; and evading eye contact is the main way to avoid getting into conversation when you do not want to. Gaze is also used to manage turn-taking. African Americans in the USA were found to spend more time gazing when talking (LaFrance and Mayo 1976), whereas white people in Britain were more likely to spend more time gazing while listening (Argyle and Ingham 1972). Changing the pattern (whichever one it is) acts as a cue that you want to speak, or to stop speaking. The differences can make for difficulties when black and white people speak together, though in increasingly ethnically mixed communities people are learning to accommodate to them. Rather as people adjust their speech style to suit the person they are talking with, people can learn to adjust their gazing behaviour to improve communication.

Research where subjects enter into **immersive virtual environments** (IVEs) and interact with avatars (Bailenson et al. 2001) can be used to demonstrate these kinds of effects. In the Bailenson study you first met in Chapter 4, subjects were asked to walk into a virtual room in Second Life in order to find out about the clothes that the avatars were wearing. In fact what was being studied was how they responded to eye contact. Avatars either had their eyes looking directly outwards, or downcast (Figure 6.3).

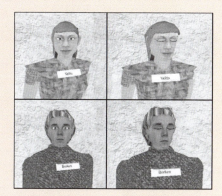

Figure 6.3 Pictures of the male and female virtual humans

Our results demonstrated that, proxemically, in some ways, participants treated virtual agents as if they were actual humans. Participants rarely violated a personal space bubble of 40 cm and, furthermore, approached more closely to the back compared to the front of virtual people. Moreover, we demonstrated compensation effects in IVEs – participants maintained a greater distance from virtual humans that maintained constant mutual gaze than from virtual humans that did not.

(Bailenson et al. 2003: 820)

Here what we are seeing is conventions being followed in virtual life, reflecting what is usual among both the experimenters and their subjects.

Finally, gaze can be used to exercise control, using what is called **visual dominance behaviour**. Being 'stared out' can be highly intimidating, making it hard to resist acting subserviently. But even a higher intensity of gazing can give the impression of authority. People who do so were seen as having greater leadership qualities than people who do not (Exline et al. 1975).

Postures and gesture

Postures are ways of positioning the body or certain parts of it, such as slouching in a chair or kneeling in prayer. Gestures are body movements such as bowing or pointing. Both postures and gestures are under more conscious control than facial expressions and more regulated by cultural norms and conventions. Most cultures have developed elaborate rules of etiquette about both the meaning and appropriate use of repertoires of behaviour – such as greeting people of different status. In Japan there are still formal rules about the degree to which one should bow, and in China people present their business cards in a specific manner according to status. Less formally, most cultures have more subtle rules about posture, often to do with status or intimacy (Mehrabian 1972).

In order to try to classify postures and gestures, they have been divided into illustrators and emblems. An **illustrator** is a posture or gesture that accompanies speech, generally reinforcing its message, such as using your hand to point directions. An **emblem** is a gesture that stands in for speech, such as a soldier's salute or a police officer's upheld hand signalling 'stop'. Some emblems are widely recognized across cultures. Others are culture specific. I remember well the difficulty I had talking with an Albanian once, for whom a nod meant 'no' and a sideways shake of the head meant 'yes', the exact opposite of the gestures I am used to. It felt very weird, even though both of us were fully aware of the conflicting conventions, and managed it with a lot of laughter! Just how much meaning can be packed into a gesture is shown by the observation that to represent suicide in the USA the gesture is usually a finger pointed to the temple with the hand clenched to represent a gun. In New Guinea it is more likely to be a hand clenched to the throat, pushing up to represent hanging. And in Japan it most likely to be plunging the fist to the stomach to represent hara-kiri or a finger across the neck to represent throat slitting.

Interpersonal distance

Interpersonal distance is about the distance people adopt when communicating with each other. Since the closer people are to each other, the more they can perceive non-verbal cues, so non-verbal communication may be made easier. Consequently, interpersonal distance can be used to signal and regulate privacy and intimacy.

This field is based on the work of Edward Hall (1966) which he called **proxemics**. He was interested in the way that people use physical space, and how this can influence their health and well-being.

Hall identified some systematic rules about the closeness/nature of the relationship between two people and how far they stand or sit from each other when interacting. From extensive observations, mainly in the USA, he identified four interpersonal zones:

- an intimate zone of about 40–50 cm that is limited to intimate relationships
- a personal zone going up to about two or three times that for friends and acquaintances
- a social zone of between 1–3 metres for formal interactions, such as doing business
- a public zone anywhere from 3 to 8 metres for public events – such as giving a lecture or making a presentation.

These are shown in Figure 6.4.

Hall did a lot of ethnographic work in various countries, through which he defined some as **contact cultures** (Southern European, Asian and Arab) because they tend to get closer up to each other and others as **non-contact cultures** (Northern European, North American) because people there tend to keep their distance. This general principle has had substantial empirical backing. Recent work by Beaulieu, for instance, demonstrated that:

> Anglo Saxons used the largest zone of personal space, followed by Asians, then Caucasians, and, as expected, Mediterraneans and Latinos used the shortest distance. Where Latinos adopt a face-to-face position, Caucasians tend to orient themselves to the side of the interviewer, which has an impact on interpersonal communication.

(2004: 794)

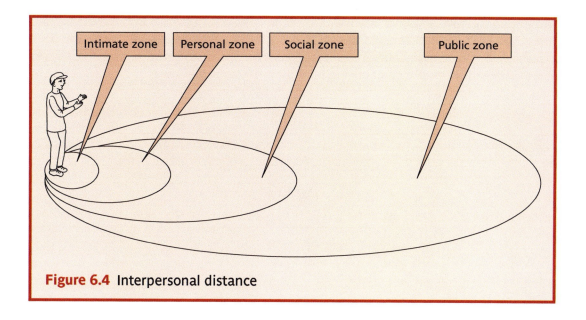

Figure 6.4 Interpersonal distance

Where different cultures have been compared, systematic differences are evident. A later study, also conducted in the USA, found that black and working-class children tend to stand closer when talking to each other than white and middle-class children (Aiello and Jones 1971). Interestingly, it seems that language acts as the cue to determine which norms are followed. In a study of bilingual French Canadians, Grujic and Libby (1978) found that when they were speaking French, subjects in the study sat closer at the beginning of the conversation and moved closer as it progressed than they did when speaking English.

More recent work confirms that in 'low-contact' cultures such as that dominant in the USA and the UK, people are more comfortable interacting further away from each other than in 'high-contact' cultures like Turkey (Ozdemir 2008). Ozdemir's study also showed the usual tendency for male/female couples to be closer to each other in interaction. But possibly most interesting is his finding that the built environment was influential in a surprising way – people tend to stand closer together when interacting in open spaces than cramped ones.

What does appear to be universal is that people are disconcerted when the local rules are broken. This is illustrated by one of what has to be social psychology's most professionally risky field experiments (Middlemist et al. 1976). In it a confederate of the researchers loitered outside an empty male urinal until a man went into it. When he did, the confederate took up a pre-determined position alongside the man, varying in distance from him. The results of the study showed that the closer the proximity, the longer the man took to start urinating and the faster he completed. One wonders what might have happened if the local police had been tipped off about what was going on! These results are taken to show the effects of over-close proximity. To me the study says more about the way that proximity is interpreted as meaning and cultural conventions, given that some nightclubs now provide female 'toilets for two'.

In the 1960s, Hall speculated that contact cultures would be more willing and able to tolerate crowded conditions because of their smaller zones of interpersonal space. However, this has not turned out to be the case. In a recent questionnaire study it was found that while people from contact and non-contact cultures report different perceptions of overcrowding 'all four ethnic groups suffer similar, negative psychological distress sequelae of high-density housing' (Evans et al. 2000: 204). What I like about this study is that it directly challenges what could be seen as a racist assumption. Just because some people get closer to each other when they talk, this does not mean they find it any easier to live in housing with insufficient space.

Touch

Like gestures and postures, touch can be illustrative (reinforce language) or emblematic (act in its stead). It is a powerful means of communication to do the following:

- show affection, reassurance, appreciation and nurturance
- communicate humour and playfulness
- express anger and aggression
- draw attention or gain compliance
- follow etiquette or perform rituals
- show or demonstrate action.

Most social psychology textbooks are rather coy about sexual touch. This is not really surprising, given the potential for embarrassment and the diversity of meanings that can be attached to it, from expressing love, compassion and comfort, through signalling dominance or submission, to expressing anger and aggression. However, most studies on touch make it clear that they are exclusively about who does what to whom in 'public spaces'. For this reason, and because sexual touch is rather a minefield of a topic, I have decided it is safest to 'go with the flow' and leave it at that, merely noting that it is an extremely potent means of communication (and therefore, I suspect, a fascinating area for research, but quite possibly one where no ethics committee would allow you to experiment).

The use of touch is, not surprisingly, highly culture and context sensitive. For a start there are wide variations in how much it is acceptable for people to touch each other at all. A classic study was conducted in the 1960s by Jourard (1966) who simply watched couples in cafés in different countries and counted how many times they touched each other. In a one-hour period Jourard observed not a single touch in London, 2 in Florida, 110 in Paris and 180 in Puerto Rico. Times have changed, and English-speaking cultures have become more 'touchy-feely' since then, but I suspect differences would still be found.

Most cultures, however, have prohibitions limiting touch between strangers, except in certain discount situations. For example, in Western biomedicine it is acceptable for medical professionals to touch patients, even parts of the body that would usually be regarded as off limits. Otherwise, touch is usually restricted to interactions between people who know each other (such as family members and close friends) and in social rather than professional situations, other than in exceptional circumstances. As with other non-verbal communication, culture-specific rules operate about who touches whom, varying in terms of intimacy, status, gender, sexuality and age.

Touch can have surprisingly strong effects, although which effects seem highly context specific. For example, Crusco and Wetzel (1984) found that waitresses who glancingly touched the hands of customers received higher tips than those who did not. This was true for both men and women customers. It looks like both men and women interpreted the touch positively in this situation. But in another study the results were different. Whitcher and Fisher (1979) varied whether nurses gave a brief and 'professional' touch to patients during an interview prior to their operation. When women patients were interviewed after the operation, those who had been previously touched reported less fear and anxiety and had lower blood pressure readings than those who had not been touched. However, men patients who had been previously touched reported more anxiety and had higher blood pressure. Here it looks as though the touches were interpreted differently by men and women – as having quite different meanings.

As I said earlier, sexual touch is rather a minefield of a topic, beyond the scope of a chapter like this. Also we are hampered by the fact that almost all work in this field – as in psychology generally – has been conducted in the English-speaking world, mainly in the USA. While culturally diverse, it has its own distinct mores shared, especially, among younger people. Hence the data to which we have access about gender differences are more a reflection of a specific set of cultural rules than universal laws about, for example, where it is acceptable and desirable for men to touch women and vice versa (Burgoon et al. 1989). The results are not at all surprising – areas around the breasts and genitals are very much taboo apart from different-sex intimates, but hands, arms and legs are much more available for touching across a broader range of relationships.

For me these data come across as too homogenous and obvious. Since the data represent averages, they obscure what I think must have been considerable variation. For a start a proportion of the people taking part in the study must have been gay and, presumably, would have expressed quite different preferences.

Smell

I am not sure if this is just another example of coyness, but while most textbooks include touch as a means of non-verbal communication, none, as far as I can tell, include smell. And yet evolutionary psychologists, in particular, regard smell as a critical means by which people communicate with each other – albeit usually unconsciously and instinctively. For example, smell is held to be a very powerful element in sexual attraction.

It is well known that many animals communicate in this way. Chemicals called **pheromones** are used to send olfactory signals – for example, to male dogs that a female is 'in season' and hence instinctively primed to be sexually available. The speculation about humans using pheromones as signals is based upon the identification of genetic material called the **major histocompatibility complex (MHC)**, which contains information that allows for the recognition of genetic similarity. It is the basis of the immune response, which allows an organism to detect bacteria, for example, as being alien and therefore needs to be destroyed. Humans are able to detect MHC from smelling the urine of mice, showing that they have the capacity to discriminate very subtle genetic differences through their sense of smell (Stoddart 1990).

Evolutionary psychologists have carried out studies to discover whether this ability could be used in the ways people select their sexual partners. The argument goes like this. One element of evolutionary theory proposes that people are instinctively primed to seek to have children that are as genetically dissimilar as possible, since genetic diversity is a positive evolutionary strategy. Hence, it is argued, women gain an evolutionary advantage if they can detect a potential father for their child who is genetically dissimilar from themselves.

Wedekind et al. (1995) tested this by getting men to wear T-shirts for 48 hours – long enough to become impregnated with the man's sweat and hence his pheromones. Young women were given the T-shirts to smell, and asked to choose which one they found most attractive. Generally they chose the T-shirts from men with the most different MHC from their own – except, that is, when the women were taking the contraceptive pill, when they chose the T-shirts of men whose MHC was most like their own. Since taking the pill mimics the physiological state of pregnancy, Wedekind et al. (1995) concluded that women choose men in ways that have an evolutionary advantage for them. If they are able to get pregnant, they choose men who are genetically dissimilar, since this is most likely to produce genetically diverse offspring. But if they are pregnant or unable to get pregnant, they choose men who are genetically similar to them, since this way they are more likely to get support and help from male kin.

Non-verbal cues to deception

As you have seen, while facial expression appears to be at least somewhat instinctive, much non-verbal communication is learned. As much as it may seem automatic and beyond conscious control, this is more a matter of well-learned habit. Otherwise actors would not manage to be so convincing. Therefore people have an ability to modify it, to a greater or lesser extent. Mostly, though, it is so well consolidated as a habit that they are unaware of it. As a consequence, a skilled observer can use non-verbal cues to work out whether, say, a person is being honest in what they say or seeking to deceive. Freud put this elegantly: 'He that has eyes to see and ears to hear may convince himself that no mortal can keep a secret. If his lips are silent he chatters with his fingertips; betrayal oozes out of him at every pore' (Freud 1905: 76). This phenomenon of non-verbal clues giving the lie to what a person says is called **leakage**.

Research studies (mainly US) suggest that when people are lying, their deception does tend to 'leak out' in their non-verbal behaviour. For example, they tend to touch their face more often (Ekman and Friesen 1974), and to fiddle more with their hands and things like glasses and necklaces (Knapp et al. 1974). The trouble is that people are not very effective at detecting deception. Even those people whose job it is to spot dishonesty – such as police and customs officers – are not that good at it (Kraut and Poe 1980). However, overall people seem slightly better able to recognize deception than to perpetrate it (Zuckerman et al. 1981).

Different standpoints, different explanations

Research by social psychologists into non-verbal behaviour tends to be conducted from one of two standpoints. The first assumes that the main driver is evolution, viewing most aspects of non-verbal behaviour as predominantly instinctive, linked, in particular to biological drives for 'survival of the fittest'. A good illustration of this is the report of studies on gender, age and touching by Willis and Dodds:

> In couples who were dating or newly married, the men were more likely to initiate touch; however, in couples married longer than 1 year, the women were more likely to initiate touch. The findings were consistent with sex differences in reproductive strategies: Early in a relationship, men initiate touch to obtain sex, whereas in an established relationship, women initiate touch in an effort to maintain resources and parental involvement.

(1998: 115)

The alternative standpoint views behaviours as arising from different local, social rules. An example here is a more recent study by Dibiase and Gunnoe (2004). In it they specifically challenged the evolutionary interpretation. They did systematic observations of young adult male/female pairs sitting at tables in 'dance clubs' in three locations – the USA, the Czech Republic and Italy. Their results showed complex differences between patterns of touching observed in the different countries with, for example, the Czech young men doing much more hand touching than the men in either of the other countries. Dibiase and Gunnoe linked this to the degree of gender imbalance in each location, testing the hypothesis that men would hand touch more in the culture most gender unequal. The results they gained supported this hypothesis. They concluded: 'One seemingly unambiguous finding is that male and female touching patterns are not universal and as such are unlikely to be the result of biological predispositions only. In fact quite different patterns of gender-related touch are evident in the three cultures that we examined' (Dibiase and Gunnoe 2004: 60). The standpoint here is still, however, that of mainstream social psychology – that behaviour, including non-verbal behaviour, is predominantly the product of social and cultural forces.

Critical social psychology and non-verbal behaviour

Critical social psychologists have a completely different 'take' on behaviours like making eye contact and touching. They see attempts to simply observe pre-categorized behaviours like a touch as clumsy and failing to attend to the sophistication and subtlety of the way people communicate through touch.

Try it for yourself

Imagine at least six different ways in which you could touch somebody with your hand. Think about different circumstances and different relationships – shaking hands when being introduced, squeezing your friend's hand to give them courage, holding hands with your partner, your Dad or your child. Think of when you might touch a stranger. Would you ever hit someone, or even just tap them in frustration? Would you use a flick of the hand to push somebody away who is bothering you? You are going to think at this point: 'it all depends on the circumstances'. And that is the point. How can you even begin to really understand what a touch means out of context – it is the context that gives the touch meaning.

Now think about all the different meanings these different touches have. Think too about how an observer might interpret them – and how far you think they can tell what you are thinking.

I hope you will agree that is highly context specific, both in the conventions governing what is acceptable and in terms of the meaning attached to a particular touch. A kiss – even a fleeting, tiny one – can mean everything or nothing. It can mean no more than a familiar greeting of no real significance, or such a kiss can signal a changing-point in a person's life, where nothing will ever be the same again. Even among experimental social psychologists this is recognized:

> A touch with the hand can as easily be tentative or placating as dominating, but a touch with some other body part can be quite controlling or dominating, especially if it has a relatively long duration, as non-hand touches tend to have. It is interesting that each sex has a distinctive way of holding onto the other: Males put their arm around the female; females put their arm through the male's arm. The difference in morphology may stem from average height differences or may reflect different connotations of the touches in terms of affiliation or dominance. In any case, without better data on the functions of specific touches, we believe one cannot argue that hand touches are deductively more dominating than other kinds.
>
> (Hall and Veccia 1990: 1161)

For critical psychologists, the whole idea of there being particular 'behaviours' that we can study is wrong-minded. It is meaningless and pointless to treat a 'hand touch' as a single 'communicative behaviour' that can be identified and classified out of context. Critical social psychologists think instead of **situated social practices** – such as going on a dinner date, celebrating a birthday, getting the family together for a meal, fasting and dieting. These are not just a set of 'eating behaviours', nor can we extract 'eating behaviour' from the complex situations in which they take place. You cannot just treat 'fasting' and 'dieting' as forms of 'food reduction' behaviour, given the fundamental differences between observing Ramadan or other religious or spiritual practices, and a diversity of practices intended for weight reduction.

Put non-verbal communication into this framework, and it too becomes a whole genre of situated social practices through which meaning is not just communicated but made and remade. Think back to the quote from the *Big Brother* psychologist, Geoffrey Beattie:

> People would stop me in the street and ask . . . 'what do you think is going on between Kate and Spencer?' . . . I would offer up a comment and watch their reaction. 'Nah, you're wrong mate' they would say. 'Didn't you see that look Kate gave Spencer when he chatted to Adele?'
>
> (2004: 4)

Actually it did not take reality television to make us all psychologists – in the sense of being highly skilled interpreters of the looks people give each other. In terms of non-verbal communication, most of us are brilliant at it much (but not all) of the time.

The big point here is that, as you will have observed from reading Chapter 3, the vast majority of critical social psychological research focuses almost entirely on *verbal* behaviour. Given the enormous capacity for a look, a touch, a smile and the way we use our faces to convey incredibly subtle messages, audio-transcripts lose a lot of what is going on.

However, there are exceptions. In critical psychology this topic has been extensively theorized and explored by John Shotter (1993b). He calls these kinds of gestures, touches, stances, postures, intonations, glances and so on a **'knowing of the third kind'**, a source of 'sensuous-practical moral knowledge' that provides us with an embodied sense of how an interaction is going. For instance, it is very much through this kind of 'knowing' that someone gets a sense of when, for the first time in a relationship, it might be OK to say 'I love you'. Here is an illustration he used to articulate in more detail the kind of thing he was getting at:

> They were walking very close now. Her hand brushed more than accidentally it seemed against his. He grasped it. She turned towards him, startled, eyebrows raised, a questioning look. He smiled and squeezed her hand more tightly in his. She turned away, head slightly bowed. He loosened his grip and silently her hand slipped away.
>
> (Shotter 1981: 165)

Shotter begins by suggesting that the man 'explains' his action in taking her hand by his smile – indicating that he does not intend her any harm and merely wants to indicate a move to greater intimacy. She, in turn, 'explains' how she is feeling about this in her look of surprise, signalled by the eyebrow flash and her failure to respond to his taking her hand. What she is communicating, Shotter surmises, is that there was no 'invitation' intended, or that she has changed her mind. He, at least has made his intentions clear, but is unlikely to take her hand again until he is more certain of its welcome.

Shotter's work will be taken up in more detail in Chapter 10, on attribution, since his analysis of what went on between the man and woman in this episode was directed specifically as a challenge to traditional attribution theory. For now, the point is made that critical social psychologists regard non-verbal communication as just as much forms of socially situated practice as other kinds of behaviour. As such we can only make sense of them by considering the contexts and circumstances in which they are enacted, the rituals and customs and 'ways of being' that frame and shape and script everything we think and do.

Non-verbal communication

- *Non-verbal communication* is a means of communication in its own right; but it also supplements, augments and helps to manage verbal communication. There are a number of modes of non-verbal communication: facial expression, gaze and eye contact, postures and gestures, interpersonal distance and touch.

- *Facial expression*: given that there is considerable cultural commonality in the facial expressions used to display basic emotions, it is likely these have an innate basis. The most likely explanation is that certain emotions trigger a reflex in the facial muscles. However, there are also culture-specific display rules governing, for example, whether people seek to cover up or display their feelings.

- *Gaze and eye contact* are used in five main ways: as a means of communication in their own right, to signal status, to signal interest and sincerity, to manage conversations and to exert control. They vary by cultural convention. In some cultures, for instance, people in subordinate positions are expected to keep their eyes lowered when speaking to a superior.

- *Postures and gestures* can either be illustrators to reinforce speech, or emblems that stand in for speech. Some emblems are widely recognized across cultures, others are culture specific. In some, for example, a nod of the head means 'yes' but in others it means 'no'.

- *Interpersonal distance* tends to reflect the closeness of the relationship and its context. Intimates get up close, friends less so, and strangers prefer to keep their distance. The rules are culturally mediated, but people are disconcerted when they are broken.

- *Touch* is a powerful means of communication. It can be used to show affection, reassurance or appreciation; to communicate humour and playfulness; to express anger and aggression; to draw attention or gain compliance; to follow etiquette or perform rituals; or to show or demonstrate action.

- *Smell* in the form of pheromones may influence certain instinctive elements of communication, such as sexual attraction.

- *Non-verbal behaviour* can act as a cue to deception – sometimes called leakage. Learning these cues can help spot when somebody is dissembling or lying.

- *Explanations* of what is going on vary, including:
  - evolutionary theory that stresses the biological basis of non-verbal behaviour
  - theories seeing non-verbal behaviour as the products of social and/or cultural forces
  - theories of 'knowing of a third kind' where communicating via gestures and body language are seen as situated social practices.

Language

Language 'lies at the very heart of social life' (Mead [1934b] 1977b). This is something both experimental and critical social psychologists can agree with, though what it means to them is very different.

Linguistics

Linguistics is a general term for the study of language itself. It begins by specifying the components of language. The basic, meaningless sounds are called **phonemes** – sounds like the 'th' at the beginning of 'think, or the 'oo' at the end of 'kangaroo'. The 'phonetic' qualities of language are to do with its sounds. Phonemes are connected together into morphemes. Generally these are words – basic units of meaning. **Morphemes** are then connected together through **syntactic rules** into sentences. So the syntactic qualities of language are to do with how words are fitted together:

Phonemes ⇐ Morphemes ⇐ Sentences

The meanings of words, sentences and utterances are determined by semantic rules. The semantic qualities of language are to do with its meanings. Semantic rules are highly complex and operate at different levels. For example, if you were sitting on a bench in a park with a friend and said 'It's getting cold', then the surface content of what you have said is purely descriptive – a comment on temperature. But it is quite likely that you intend this statement to convey depth content – that you are getting cold, and want to make a move (Chomsky 1957).

Psycholinguistics

Psycholinguistics is the study of the interrelationship between language and thought. One of its earliest and best-known theorists was Vygotsky, who claimed that language is the main medium in which people think: 'Thought is not merely expressed in words; it comes into existence through them. Every thought tends to connect to something else, to establish a relationship between things. Every thought moves, develops, fulfils a function, solves a problem' (1962: 125).

There are similarities here to William James's concepts of the transitive and the substantive (Chapter 1). Vygotsky argued that while we may have some thoughts that are vague and not verbalized, and we may sometimes say things automatically without conscious thought, most of our thinking consists of a kind of 'inner speech' that is interdependent with external speech. He depicted this diagrammatically, as shown in Figure 6.5.

Consequently, Vygotsky claimed, a person's capacity to think depends upon the linguistic resources they have available to them. This is a version of a theory proposed by Sapir and Whorf – the Sapir–Whorf theory of linguistic relativity (Whorf 1956). If you recall from Chapter 1, this was not a new idea. It had already been proposed by Wundt (1897) some 60 or more years earlier.

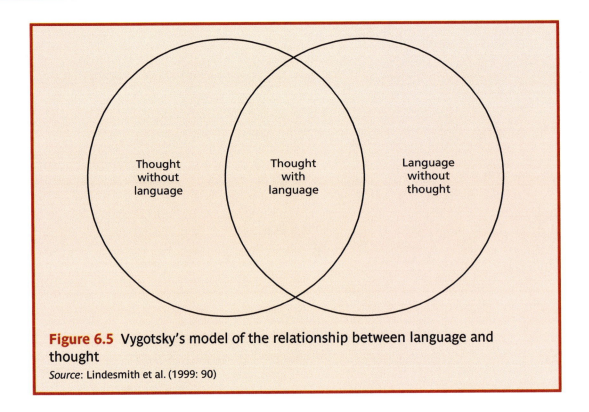

Figure 6.5 Vygotsky's model of the relationship between language and thought

Source: Lindesmith et al. (1999: 90)

Linguistic relativity

The theory of linguistic relativity claims that language determines thought – people cannot think about something for which they have no linguistic term. It is, literally, 'unthinkable'. The theory was built upon observations that different languages reflect different thought-worlds. For example, the language of Hopi Indians is very precise about, for example, how people travel, having different verbs for different kinds of travelling (going to and coming from, for example). But it does not differentiate between living and non-living flying things – all are called by the same name. English differentiates between birds, bats, aeroplanes, kites, and so on, because they are salient and meaningful in its thought-world.

The Sapir–Whorf theory is now regarded as too extreme. People are constantly developing language by constructing new words and phrases as the need arises to express new concepts – just think of wiki, twitter, and so on. We can also see this in the way that one language appropriates words from another. The French speak of 'le week-end' and the English speak of a 'raison d'être', since such phrases depict concepts more succinctly than they could be expressed in the original language. My favourite is 'kitsch' from German. These show that people can be inventive and can borrow words to express concepts they have no easy word for.

Nonetheless, as you will see as this section unfolds, it is equally clear that language powerfully moulds thought. Being given words to describe concepts is an important way of learning about a new topic. This is the main reason why this book (like most textbooks) gives you a lot of new words (or familiar ones used for new meanings) and defines them for you in a glossary.

It is one of the main ways you will get to know and understand the thinking behind social psychology's ideas and theories.

Sociolinguistics

Sociolinguistics focuses on how language is used in social situations: 'how speech (and other language in use) simultaneously influences social interaction and has its "meaning" constrained by its interactive context' (Grimshaw 1981: 241). Social psychologists studying language have, traditionally, been less concerned with what is said than how it is said – with paralanguage and speech style rather than speech content. For critical social psychologists, however, what is being said and how language is deployed as a situated social practice is absolutely central, as you will have observed from its data-collection methods and it analytics described in Chapter 5, and its theorizing in Chapter 3.

Paralanguage and speech styles

Paralanguage refers to the non-linguistic elements of speech – things like ums and ahs, grunts and sighs, speed, tone and pitch of voice, and so on. These are important aspects of how a message is imparted. Paralinguistic elements are especially important in conveying emotion. In English, low pitch typically communicates sadness or boredom, whereas high pitch communicates anger, fear or surprise (Frick 1985). Equally, people use a range of **speech styles** in different contexts. I know I use different speech styles when talking with my daughters, my grandchildren, my friends, my colleagues at work and my partner – and different styles with him when we are with my family, applying for a loan or when we are alone together.

Speech style has been extensively studied by experimental social psychologists (see Giles and Coupland 1991 for a review) since it is a sensitive marker of how people respond to social context. For example, Brown and Fraser (1979) mapped out a diverse range of influences on speech style, including both contextual (such as the setting, the activity the person is involved in and who else is present) and personal (the person's mood, their personality and interests).

In particular, cues are given by a person's speech style – their accent and/or the slang or jargon they use – about such things as social class, status and, of course, nationality. A person's accent usually says a lot about where they grew up, their peer group in childhood and adolescence and the social group to which they belong. Speech contains social markers that are usually highly recognizable. Consequently, it is an important influence on the way individuals are perceived and hence how others respond to them.

The impact of speech style has been studied using the **matched-guise technique** (Lambert et al. 1960). In it a series of speech extracts are recorded, all spoken by the same highly skilled actor but each one in a different accent or dialect. Subjects in the study give their impression of the speaker by responding to different evaluative dimensions. Lambert et al. (1960) for example, varied what they called status variables (for example, intelligence and competence) and solidarity variables (for example, warmth and friendliness). In their studies they found that subjects did indeed respond to the speech style cues. **Received pronunciation** was usually evaluated more favourably on status variables, whereas non-standard accents was usually evaluated more favourably on solidarity variables.

Speech style, social groups and social identity

Experimental social psychology has developed extensive theorization about relationships between social groups, group membership and **social identity**. Experimental social psychologists working in this field such as Giles et al. (1977; Giles and Johnson, 1981) adopted the term **ethnolinguistic groups** for groups defined by their ethnic commonality and their use of a common **patois**. A patois is a developed and inclusive way of talking that has not only a particular accent, but also its own grammar and terminology.

Social Identity is explored in detail in Chapter 10.

Rastafarian is a good example where, for example, the term 'I' is used differently from received pronunciation, as well as a strong accent and many specific words and phrases.

Speech style was identified as a highly effective marker of group membership and hence social identity. Throughout the last 30 or so years of the twentieth century a solid body of empirical research was created by experimental social psychologists seeking to understand the interplay between language, social identity and group membership. There was particularly prolific work on ethnicity and gender, in both cases seeking to understand the problems encountered in communication between groups – that is, between women and men when they spoke to each other, and between members of different ethnic groups.

A good example is the work of Lakoff. In her book, *Language and Woman's Place* (Lakoff 1975), she sets out her perception of 'women's language', how and why it is dysfunctional, and how women can be helped to change and thereby get taken more seriously. She described women's speech style as overly polite, overly grammatical, hesitant, ingratiating, full of empty adjectives and irritating 'tag' questions. Women, she claimed, cannot tell jokes and have no sense of humour. In fact, though, Lakoff had very little empirical evidence for her claims. Her approach was largely one of introspection (what we might now call autoethnography). Nevertheless, her work was enormously influential, well outside her own discipline (linguistics) including on social psychology. It led to a flurry of experimental studies, all seeking to confirm or reject the concept of a distinctly womanly speech style.

Feminist challenges

In a very clever chapter in a book on Feminist approaches to science, Donna Haraway (1984) describes how her discipline, **primatology** (the study of the social life of apes and monkeys), is 'politics by other means'. In it she argued that popularity of particular theories in a discipline is not a matter of how good they are. It is much more about who is doing the theorizing. Haraway observed that early theories explaining primate evolution were men's stories: they were all about dominance, hierarchy, territory and winning (what I have called 'shark-filled pool' story; Stainton Rogers 2011). These theories dominated primatology until women were no longer relegated to being lowly research assistants and allowed to become professors and theorists. Only then did theories become popular that were about the evolutionary advantages of communally shared care, nurture and cooperation (the 'all get stuck in' story, perhaps!).

Mary Crawford (1995) uses a neat term to describe the popular books that have been written around the idea that women and men talk different languages – '**bandwagon books**'. They include Deborah Tannen's (1990) *You Just Don't Understand*, and, perhaps the best known of the genre, John Gray's (1992) *Men Are from Mars, Women Are from Venus*. Popp and her colleagues (including Mary Crawford) sum up the general message well:

men are believed to have demanding voices; to be dominating, authoritarian, straight to the point, blunt, forceful, aggressive, boastful, militant; and to use swear words and slang. . . . Women are believed to use good grammar and enunciate clearly; to speak politely, gently, rapidly, and emotionally; to talk a lot; to talk about trivial topics; and to indulge in gossip and gibberish.

(Popp et al. 2003: 318)

Dale Spender said it rather more succinctly: 'In short, feminine talk is a lot of polite talk about silly things; whereas masculine talk is a little blunt talk about important things (Spender 1979: 41).

It is clear to see the sexism infused throughout these claims about 'sex differences' in language style. Mainstream psychology of the time did no better in its treatment of 'ethnic' speech styles. In both cases we can see, with hindsight, just how much these studies were based on a male/white-is-normal, female/ethnic-is-problem view of the world, with theories to match. We will come on to explore this further in the chapters that follow, especially in Chapter 13 on prejudice.

Language

- The experimental social psychological study of language is called sociolinguistics, which is based upon linguistics and psycholinguistics.
  - *Linguistics* is the study of language itself. It examines how language works as a means of communication, through the rules of syntax (how the different elements of language are structured) and the rules of semantics (how meaning is encoded into and decoded from language).
  - *Psycholinguistics* views language as the main medium for thought, and examines the ways in which language affects thinking. Its theory of linguistic relativity argues that each language makes some discriminations easier to make than others, and, therefore, makes some ideas easier to think about than others.
  - *Sociolinguistics* focuses on how language is used in social situations. Experimental social psychologists studying language have been less concerned with what is said than how it is said – with paralanguage and speech style rather than speech content.
- *Paralanguage* concerns the non-linguistic elements of speech – things like ums and ahs, interruptions and pauses, grunts and sighs, speed, tone and pitch of voice, and so on.
- *Speech style* is the manner in which people speak in different contexts (for example, talking to children or adults). Aspects like accent and vocabulary act as social markers, often indicative of a person's status, social identity (for example as a member of an ethnic group) and role.
- Language is not only a social marker, but also a key factor in *social identity*. It provides a sociocultural 'glue' which plays a significant role in sustaining social and cultural groups.
- However, challenges have been made about the sexism and ethnocentrism of the theories and studies in this field.

Semiotics and post-structuralism

This section moves us from the body of work on language primarily carried out by experimental social psychologists, to the very distinctive and different approach to language and other ways in which meanings are made, that is adopted by critical social psychologists. The origins of semiotic theory and that of post-structuralism are largely outside of psychology, but have very much become incorporated into the critical genre.

Semiotics

Ferdinand de Saussure (1959) described semiotics as about 'the organisation of shared meanings' (Parker 1989: 49) and how those shared meanings act as a kind of 'glue' that holds the social and cultural world together. You have already learned a bit about semiotics in relation to Charles Peirce and abduction, in Chapter 2. Semiotic theory is used by critical social psychologists to understand the systems by which meanings are organized, shared and communicated as well as made and unmade.

What makes it different from the approach taken by experimental social psychology is that in semiotics the systems for organizing meaning are not seen to be working solely within individual minds but externally as well, within what goes on between people. In this perspective, instead of culture merely being viewed as an influence *on* communication, culture is seen as the medium and the means, itself, *through which* communication works. Semiotic theory views culture as 'socially organised productions and flows of meaning and meaningful forms, related to likewise socially organised forms of power, material resources, time and space' (Fornäs 1995: 136). Meaning, by this definition, is not a subjective interpretation made by individuals, but is intersubjective; it operates between people.

Intersubjectivity

You may find it hard to grasp what is being claimed here. For people brought up in an culture focused on individual thought and action, semiotic theory is hard to understand, not because it is difficult, but because it is counter-intuitive. It is not how you may be used to thinking. An example should help. Ian Parker uses a study by Marsh et al. (1974) on the scarves worn on the terraces by football supporters. These scarves have enormous importance, not because it is somehow woven into the fabric of the scarf, but because of what the scarf symbolizes. Parker (1989) pointed out that football team scarves are only really significant to football fans, because only football fans know what they mean. But notice, this 'knowing what it means' is not some simple, isolated act of individual recognition. It works because recognizing the scarf is part of a whole system of knowing, that is, itself, part of being a football fan. And being a football fan is belonging to a community of football fans who share a common interest in and understanding of, not just of the game of football, but also of being a fan of football. Today, when football teams market football kit at great expense (I know, I am a grandmother!), being a football fan requires enormous investment – investment that seems perfectly justified to football fans because it is so much tied up in who they are (even if their grannies wince at the expense).

This is what is meant by saying that culture is the means and the medium of communication. Meanings are not individually made and sustained, they are collectively made and sustained. And the same applies to all sorts of other symbolic meanings, from Maori tattoos to Converse shoes, military uniforms to driving a BMW. Try this out for yourself. Ask around and get people to name their favourite brands, and notice how much these tell you about who they are, their values and what matters to them. Me, I'm an M&S, John Lewis and Frost's Garden Centre kind of person. People in Milton Keynes will know exactly what I mean!

Signs and sign systems

A sign has two elements: the **signifier** – the physical characteristics of the sign (such as the visual image of the tattoo) – and the **signified** – what it is intended to mean (what the person had to do and to be to earn the right to have it, and what says about their status in the eyes of other Maori). Thus clothes and cars and what we do to our bodies are all signifiers that communicate particular meanings (Barthes [1957] 1967).

Words, gestures and body language operate as signs too. They transmit meaning among those who can interpret them, operating as **sign systems** – systems of signifiers and signifieds whereby messages about meaning are communicated. The process of using signs is called **signification**. Perinbanayagam (1985) uses the term **signifying act** to describe when a person expresses a symbol by the articulation of a message. People, he argues, communicate and interact with one another through signifying acts, that work through the expression of signs and, thereby, their meanings.

de Saussure stressed that signs are arbitrary and specific. They are different in different cultures and subcultures, and each one is fully meaningful only to the people who belong to that particular culture or subculture. Being a football fan is one example. Another is what the gay community calls **gaydar** – a kind of cultural radar that allows gay people to recognize whether another person is gay or straight. Within gay communities, subtle signs are encoded into speech style, dress, demeanour and body language, which allow members of those gay communities to transmit and receive meanings that are not generally understood by straights.

Signs express value

Crucially, de Saussure pointed out, signs not only signify (tell us what something is), but also express value (tell us in what way it should be appreciated). Consider the word 'madam'. In French, madame is used in the way English would use Mrs and conveys little explicit value, either positive or negative. But in English 'madam' takes a number of differently valued and usually negative meanings. It can be used as a polite term – used, for example, for a customer in a snooty boutique ('Would madam like to try on the dress?') or at a meeting ('Madam chairman' Grrr!). But it can also refer to the woman who runs a brothel, or one who tells fortunes, and it can be applied to a girl child who is behaving precociously ('She was a right little madam'). The value attached to each use is quite different.

Signs, symbols and structuralism

Both signs and symbols represent meaning, but a sign is a particular instance whereas a symbol is a sign where its meaning is based upon a shared ideology or institution. It is not hard to think of some powerful symbols – national flags, religious symbols like the holy cross, clothes such as football insignia and uniforms. People can be symbols – a queen, a pope, a pop idol. What symbols signify transcends time and place. But symbols can be used as specific signs too, when used to signify something different according to context. A man who wears a uniform can be signalling that he is 'on duty'. But the band Queen sometimes wore sailors' uniforms to signal messages about being gay. In the first case the uniform was a symbol, in the second a sign.

Semiotics is the study of how sign systems are structured, and hence originated as a form of **structuralism**. Another way of putting this is that it is the study of the *architecture* of meaning – of what meanings can be constructed, by whom and how and why, and from what. It explores how particular meaning structures create particular meaning environments and how these shape the ways in which people experience their worlds in which they live and determine what they can and cannot do. This is what I meant earlier by saying that semiotics is the study of how meanings are organized. Geertz suggests that culture is made up of 'webs of significance' (1975: 5). The purpose of structuralism is to understand how the organization of meaning – the way its 'webs of significance' are structured – enables it to work as the medium of communication.

Post-structuralism

Parker (1989) nicely summarizes how, for critical psychology, this structuralist approach does not go far enough – it is still a 'search for the truth' of what things *really* mean. He refers back to the work on football fans:

> Researchers . . . gathered football supporters' explanations of their activities and produced an account which purported to represent the real meanings of the football-terrace community. In structuralist parlance, they captures the 'signifieds' held within the signs circulating in the social world studied, discovered the relations between them, and reconstructed the shared system of rules which made up the language of that world. Ethogenic texts, then, pretend to represent what their subjects really mean.
>
> (1989: 57)

A key moment in the development of critical psychology was when psychologists, unhappy with these 'truth claims', turned to **post-structuralism**, influenced particularly by the work of Michel Foucault. In what I earlier called 'the book that changed everything', *Changing the Subject* (Henriques et al. 1984), his importance is made clear:

> The use of Foucault's approach to histories of the production of knowledge is an important feature of out theoretical enterprise. . . . First, it permits the reconceptualisation of psychology as a body of knowledge. . . . Second, this alternative approach provides a strong starting point where the couple 'individual' and 'society' no longer constrains the question posed because from the outset it is problematised; both are regarded as effects of a production to be specified, rather than pregiven objects of the human sciences. It is from this point of view that this new history feeds the task of retheorising the subject of psychology.
>
> (Henriques et al. 1984: 98)

Post-structuralism had arrived. Wilbraham defines it thus:

> [a] specific philosophical stance within broader 'post-modernism', post-structuralists argue that there are only arbitrary and conventionalised relations between words and meanings; and it is within the critical disassembly of texts that the uncertainty of truth is explored. So post-structuralism destabilises language, social institutions and the self by opening up contradictions and power-relations.
>
> (Wilbraham 2004: 498)

All right, this is not the easiest writing to understand, but it does give a sense of what is going on. Whereas structuralism is looking 'underneath' language for the structures through which meaning is made and deployed, post-structuralism is seeking to rock its foundations, or 'make trouble' (Curt, 1994). Instead of trying to tie down explanations of what is going on, post-structuralism accepts that there is no 'benchmark' of the truth (Game 1991) and all that can be produced are undisciplined, messy, edgy and highly provisional explications and 'what if' speculations.

Post-structuralism is used by critical social psychologists to enable them to 'step beyond the consciousness of the individual "subject" and back from the personal meanings held by the members of a community' (Parker 1989: 52) and to look at the broader picture: to explore how sign systems 'work' at the intersubjective level rather than within some private subjectivity. Henriques et al. (1984) put it like this. Instead of reducing meaning to 'a problem of the "influence" of the social environment on the unitary individual', post-structural analysis 'interiorizes differences within the social process of signification, accounting for them by reference to differences of power and gender and different canalizations of desire' (Henriques et al. 1984: 149).

In other words, it opens up the analysis of meaning to move it beyond meaning-as-it-is-understood by the individual subject, to making links into broader theories, such as political theories about power, feminist theories about gender and psychosocial theories about desire. In other words, meaning-making is not seen as an individual cognitive act of reactively 'making sense' that goes on inside a person's mind. It is seen as a *collective* endeavour that is actively done for a purpose.

Mass media communication

An illustration of this kind of analysis is to look at the way that the **mass media** (that is, television, newspapers, and so on) construct meaning for us. Take television news broadcasts, that, typically, consist of a series of short 'news items'. These purport to be factual, a straightforward telling-it-like-it-is. But post-structural theorists claim they are anything but factual. Rather, they are made meaningful for viewers by being constructed as illustrated narratives – news stories. 'The message comes already interpreted; they overflow with meaning' (Lindesmith et al. 1999: 15).

To understand what is going on in the telling of 'news stories', you need to think what the mass media are trying to achieve. Are they simply seeking to inform us about what is going on in the world? Or do they have other motives? Smythe (1994), for example, claims that the mass media have four main goals; they seek to create **audiences** that:

- are motivated by 'possessive individualism' – the desire to acquire the goods and services that are provided by capitalism
- become and remain consumers of advertised products
- support the strategies and policies of the state that sustains capitalism
- are unaware they are being manipulated.

The mass media can be seen as an institutionalized sign system promoting a particular ideology (such as neo-liberalism) for a particular set of motives (creating politically passive but highly economically active consumers). You do not need to endorse this particular analysis to see that it at least provides a different understanding of human communication from that of experimental social psychology. If we accept the claim of semiotics that meaning 'works' through culture, and is not merely an individual, personal interpretation of culture, then it follows that those who have any control over the way that culture is constructed also have some control over the way meaning is interpreted and understood by individuals. They are powerful in that they have the capability to construct a person's social reality for them.

Go back once again to the example of football fans for a moment and think about this. Their subculture is not simply the product of what football fans say and do. It is powerfully constructed through the broadcasting of football games and news reports and programmes about football; through newspaper and magazine reports of not only football matches but also footballers' personalities, wives and girlfriends lives and lifestyles. It is also constructed through the aggressive marketing of consumer goods like football regalia; through the travel industry organizing trips to football competitions, and so on. There would be no football fans, as we currently understand this term, without the vast commercial and mass media infrastructures that create, support and sustain football fandom.

In this analysis, the 'trick' of the mass media – where it is really clever – is that it makes all this seem so very natural and real. In so doing it creates in people the sense that they are free and autonomous when, in truth, they are not. They are living in a world created for them in order that their behaviour serves the interests of those with the power and resources to create it. They think they are interpreting meaning when, in truth, they are consuming meaning that has already been pre-digested for them.

But ideas like this come not just from Marxist analysis. From the opposite side of the fence – management studies – Fenton-O'Creevy (2001: 7) makes the claim that the key quality of leadership is the ability to manage meaning: 'Studies of leadership have sought to understand leadership as a social process rather than as an attribute of the individual or even an interaction between individual and situation. Within this perspective the characteristic function of leadership is seen as "the management of meaning".'

> Leadership is examined in more detail in Chapter 12.

By this he means that leaders 'transform the needs, values, preferences and aspirations of followers' (Fenton-O'Creevy 2001: 9) and hence inspire them to abandon self-interest and serve the interests of the wider group. They provide vision and a sense of mission, instil pride and gain respect and trust. Leaders, he argues, give new meaning to people's lives and actions. His description fits both religious and political leaders, and this makes the point that meaning-making can be for both good and for ill. Contrast, for example, the leadership of Hendrik Verwoerd and that of Nelson Mandela. Both provided their followers with vision and a sense of mission, instilled pride in them and gained their respect and trust. The outcome of Verwoerd's leadership was the creation of a policy of apartheid and all of the consequences that followed. For Mandela the outcome was a (relatively) bloodless change of government with a policy of equity for all citizens. The ability to make meaning is, in human society, an incredibly effective way to wield power. While making things (like buildings, steam engines and computers) clearly plays a part in history, it is by making meaning that history's seismic shifts have been brought about.

A semiotic account of language

Language is the most complex and sophisticated – and hence the most powerful – sign system, a system of signification. Actually, as English speakers we are hampered here, since we have only one word for language. In French (the language in which de Saussure wrote) there are two words: *langue* (language as a system that operates in a speech community, such as English or French), and *parole* (language as it is used in communicating messages). We have to take the somewhat confusing option of arbitrarily imposing technical definitions. The convention in English is to use the term 'language' to mean *langue* – the abstract system of syntax and semantics that is 'virtual and outside of time' (Ricoeur 1955: 530) – and to use '**speech**' to mean *parole* – that which is particular to the use of language in a specific situation.

Semin illustrates the difference by reference to the sentence 'the sun is rising'. At the level of language, it is a comment about the sunrise. But as speech it can be used to say different things. For two lovers having an affair it could say 'we'd better get up, my spouse will be home soon', whereas to a farmer it could say 'we'd better get up and feed the animals' (Semin 1997: 296). Language and speech operate in **dialectical** relation to one another, by which is meant, they only achieve full meaning only through their reciprocal relationship to each other (Barthes [1957] 1967).

Language constructs reality

In signifying both meaning and value, social constructionist theory argues that language is the most powerful means by which reality is socially constructed. Each language (*langue*) constructs and conveys particular assumptions about the relative worth of the social groups that make up the speech community that uses it – about class, gender, sexuality, race, disability, and so on. We can see this, for instance, in the debate about 'political correctness'. It is a 'war of words' (Dunant 1994) where attempts are being made to change the way that language is used. Those who seek change do so in order to challenge the way that the conventions of language attach negative value to certain groups.

Within semiotics, language is a system of signs (words, phrases) connected together through a set of rules (syntax) that convey meaning and value. Language is such a powerful sign system because of these relational elements. It allows the signification of complexity, and not just knowing what something signifies but also being able to relate that signification to other more abstract significations. A cat or a dog can respond to the red glow of embers, avoiding it because they associate it with being burnt. But only a human can know it means heat, and that heat has to do with temperature, that heat and cold have a relationship to each other, and that this relationship can also be applied to a person's manner or character, because only humans have the sign system of language that allows them to do this.

Semiotics and post-structuralism

- *Semiotics* is the study of signs and sign systems. Its main concern is with the organization of shared meanings, and it is used by social constructionist social psychologists to find out how meaning 'works' and how it is structured.
- *Language* is the most complex, sophisticated and powerful sign system. As a social institution and a system of values that gives meaning to words, it is the main medium through which human social realities are constructed.

- Semiotics sees meaning not as individually but as collectively made and sustained. Thus meaning is *intersubjective* – it 'works' within culture, not within individual minds. Instead of culture merely being viewed as an influence on communication, culture is seen as the medium and the means by which and within which communication works.

- A *sign* has two elements: the signifier (the physical characteristics of the sign) and the signified (its meaning and significance). Signs transmit meaning within sign systems – systems of signifiers and signifieds that communicate meaning through a process of signification. Signs not only signify (tell us what something is), but also express value.

- A *symbol* is a sign where its meaning is based upon a shared ideology, institutional system or worldview. Symbols are very powerful signs that encapsulate meaning and convey it strikingly.

- *Structuralism* is the study of the architecture of meaning – of how it is organized in ways that shape the way people experience and make sense of the world.

- *Post-structuralism* aims to 'make trouble' around the certainties and truth-claims of structuralist approaches. It introduces ideological and political analyses of how power operates within different architectures of meaning, seeing these architectures not as fixed entities ('the way things are') but constructed in highly motivated ways – such as to promote neo-liberalism, liberal humanism, Christianity or Islam.

- The mass media, multinational companies and charismatic leaders use their power to construct meaning in ways that influence how people see the world and hence how they behave.

Resources

Social psychology and language

This link takes you to the main – and mainstream – journal in this field:
http://www.sagepub.com/journals/Journal200830

This is a link to the International Association of Language and Social Psychology:
http://www.ialsp.org/

Semiotics

This is a fairly good starting point if you want to know more about semiotics:
http://www.aber.ac.uk/media/Documents/S4B/

Further reading

Experimental social psychology

Most mainstream textbooks will give you lots of extra detail about the enormous amount of social psychological research and theorization that have been applied to communication, language and social interaction.

Hogg, M.A. and Vaughan, G.M. (2007) *Social Psychology*, **5th edn. Hemel Hempstead: Prentice Hall.**
This book has an excellent chapter on Language and Communication, mostly drawn from mainstream approaches but including a short account of discourse analytic work.

Giles, H. and Coupland, N. (1991) *Language: Contexts and Consequences.* **Buckingham: Open University Press.**
This book provides a very readable and comprehensive account of mainstream social psychological research into and theorization about language and its relationship with social processes and phenomena.

Beattie, G. (2008) *Visible Thought: The New Psychology of Body Language.* **Hove: Routledge.**
This is a fascinating book that builds on work Beattie did as the *Big Brother* psychologist. It does more than that and includes accounts of the experimental social psychological research that Beattie has done in this field, especially around hand gestures.

Critical social psychology

Lindesmith, A.R., Strauss, A.L. and Denzin, N.K. (1999) *Social Psychology*, **8th edn. London: Sage.**
This is a remarkable textbook, in that its general title gives no hint that it is, in fact, a very unusual one, based primarily on symbolic interactionism. It is the best source I have found for an introduction of semiotics as applied to social psychology.

Shotter, J. (1993) *Conversational Realities: Constructing Life Through Language.* **London: Sage.**
However, this offers stiff competition! John Shotter's work is especially helpful in getting your head around non-verbal as well as linguistic communication. This is a bit of a classic for critical social psychologists, and deservedly so.

Crawford, M. (1995) *Talking Difference: On Gender and Language.* **London: Sage.**
If you are seriously interested in finding out more about the myths around 'women's language' and 'men's language', this is a good place to start. She writes with clarity and style, in a powerful but not aggressive way, and makes her challenge to the 'bandwaggon books' very well.

Questions

1 What are the main elements of communication theory? Why was it abandoned by social psychologists as a theory to explain human communication?

2 'The touch of a hand can mean anything, nothing or everything.' Discuss this claim, describing three different ways in which social psychologists make sense of touch as a means of communication. Say which one you find most convincing and why.

3 What evidence is there for cultural differences in the way people communicate with each other?

4 How far is it true to say than men and women speak different languages?

5 Compare and contrast psycholinguistic and semiotic theories of language.

6 What is meant by the term post-structuralism? Define it, and explain how and why critical social psychologists have adopted it as a means to understand communication. Illustrate your answer with examples.

7 What does it mean to say communication is intersubjective? Illustrate your answer by reference to the role of the mass media.

Social cognition, social perception and attribution

When you have finished studying this chapter, you should be able to:

1 Outline the key features of the information processing approach and illustrate it by reference to a study of impression formation.

2 Describe how the social cognition approach is different from that of information processing.

3 Define and describe the main processes of social cognition, outline some of the ways in which social cognition is constrained by information processing limits, and describe how social cognition processes information strategically.

4 Define what is meant by the terms 'schema' and 'script' and describe their roles in social cognition.

5 Provide a brief historical account of the origins of attribution theory, outline its main elements, and define the main 'attribution errors' to which social cognition is prone.

6 Define what is meant by 'processing-depth models of social cognition', and explain the main reasons for their development.

Introduction

As you saw in Chapter 1, from the very earliest studies of social influence, social psychologists have been fascinated to discover how people acquire their knowledge of the social world, how they make sense of this knowledge and how they use it to guide their actions and interactions with others. They want to understand how different social contexts are perceived and recognized, and how they influence the way that people behave.

This chapter begins by examining the main theories that experimental social psychologists have devised to explain how people gain knowledge and understanding of the social world, and use how they use them to navigate their own behaviour within it. It looks briefly at information processing models and then moves on to social cognition. Next there follows a section on attribution theory – how people account for cause and effect, and ascribe responsibility and blame.

Information processing models

One of the main things we need to be able to make sense of the social world is to understand other people (indeed, we also need to understand ourselves, but we come on to that in Chapter 10). It is important to know who another person is in order to know how to treat them – think of the problems you would have if you talked to your boss or your tutor as if they were your younger sister. We need to have some idea about what kind of person somebody is – can we trust them, or do we need to be wary? We have to be able to predict how other people will react – will they take a smile as being friendly or a 'come on'?

Impression formation

A good example of an information processing approach to how people gain understanding of other people is Asch's classic work on **impression formation** – how people form first impressions of others (Asch 1946). Information processing models view people's thinking as limited in the amount of information that can be processed. Asch developed a configural model – a general theory that when people form their impressions of another person, they do so by 'homing in' to just the most significant qualities (he called these 'central traits') that overshadow all the rest. One example he used was warm/cold. If a person is described as 'warm', he argued, then this will have a disproportionate impact on how they are perceived, making them more likely to be seen in a favourable light. The opposite would happen if the person is described as 'cold'.

Asch's hypothesis was therefore that central traits (like warm/cold) will have more effect on impression formation than other less important traits (like polite or blunt – we would probably use the word 'rude' for the latter in the UK). To test his hypothesis Asch gave some of his students lists of seven trait descriptions (for example, intelligent, skilful, industrious, warm, determined, practical, cautious). He varied the trait descriptions included in the lists and asked the students to describe their impression of the individual described. Look at the four lists in Table 7.1 and you can see the kind of thing he did. As you can see, he used four experimental conditions – inserting into the list either the term warm, cold, polite or blunt. These are illustrated in Table 7.1.

Table 7.1 Lists used in Asch's experiment

List 1	List 2	List 3	List 4
Intelligent	Intelligent	Intelligent	Intelligent
Skilful	Skilful	Skilful	Skilful
Industrious	Industrious	Industrious	Industrious
Warm	**Cold**	**Polite**	**Blunt**
Determined	Determined	Determined	Determined
Practical	Practical	Practical	Practical
Cautious	Cautious	Cautious	Cautious

Table 7.2 The results Asch obtained in his study expressed in the percentage of students endorsing additional traits as a function of the trait included in the list

Additional traits	Traits inserted into the list			
	Warm	**Cold**	**Polite**	**Blunt**
Generous	91	8	56	58
Wise	65	25	30	50
Happy	90	34	75	65
Good-natured	94	17	87	56
Reliable	94	99	95	100

The students read the lists through. Then, in order to assess the impression they gained of the person being described they were given five more traits – generous, wise, happy, good-natured and reliable – and asked to say whether or not they thought the person had each of these qualities. The results Asch obtained are given in Table 7.2.

As you can see just by looking at the data, when the word 'warm' was in the list, the great majority of students endorsed the positive additional traits. When the word was 'cold' (except for 'reliable'), the great majority did not. The difference was most marked in relation to generous, happy and good-natured. By contrast, the differences between responses to polite/blunt were much less marked. Asch concluded that these results supported his hypothesis – central traits have a disproportionately large influence upon impression formation.

Later research by Rosenberg et al. (1968) led to viewing impression formation as more complex than this: that the centrality of a trait differs according to context. Rosenberg et al. (1968) therefore contested Asch's one-dimensional formulation and proposed, instead, that in different settings people use one of two alternative dimensions for evaluating character – either good/bad in social terms or good/bad in intellectual terms. Warm/cold, they argued, is clearly a social evaluation. Since Asch mainly used other social traits (like generous, wise, happy and good-natured) to assess the favourability of the impression, it is not surprising that varying warm/cold had more effect than varying polite/blunt.

Primacy and recency effects

Asch also found a **primacy effect**; that is, the earlier traits appear on a list, the greater the influence they have on the impression formed. If all the positive traits are at the beginning, the impression is more favourable compared with when all the negative traits are at the beginning. Later studies (for example, Jones and Goethals 1972) also found some evidence of a **recency effect**, where traits later in the list had more impact. This happened when subjects were distracted or tired. However, primacy effects are more common, suggesting that first impressions are most important.

Negative and positive bias

Experimental research has also produced empirical evidence to suggest that people tend to form positive impressions of others unless there is specific information to the contrary (Sears 1983). However, if people are told anything negative about the person at all, this tends to have a disproportionate effect. It immediately turns a good impression into a bad one (Fiske 1980). Moreover, once a negative impression is formed about someone, it tends to persist. Impression formation thus has a **negative bias** (see, for example, Hamilton and Zanna 1972).

The information processing approach

- Information processing models of how people understand the social world envisaged people as operating rather like a sophisticated computer. They stressed the limitations imposed by both 'hardware' and 'software' on the amount of information that can be processed.

- Asch's experiments on impression formation provided evidence that people cope with these limits by focusing on just some information – central traits.

- Later work showed that information processing limits have some effect. For example, people tend to take more notice of information they receive first.

- However, it gradually became recognized that context is important – processing is determined by the kinds of evaluation people are making, and for what purpose.

Social cognition

In Chapter 6, I described how a shift was made in the 1960s and 1970s from theories of communication based on information processing models to psycholinguistic theory. This was a general shift undergone by experimental social psychology at that time. Its greatest influence was in the subject area of this section, heralding a radically new paradigm for studying how people make sense of the social world – social cognition. The study of social cognition within social psychology arose from ideas and theories developed from general cognitive psychology. We look at this briefly first.

General cognitive theory

Ulric Neisser (1966) (whom you met already in Chapters 1 and 6) argued that information processing models took a far too mechanistic view of human thinking. They assumed that people play very little role in the making of the realities they experience, but simply take in the information they receive from their senses, process it in certain ways and then respond to it.

It was this mechanistic image of human thinking that Neisser's new cognitive psychology was designed to challenge. The shift was towards a theory of people's thinking that stressed their capacity to construct complex images and models of the world through effortful thought, and their capacity to process information strategically rather than automatically.

Neisser saw sensory data from the outside as both processed bottom-up and top-down. The world that people perceive, understand and with which they interact is a product of them both taking in information from the world and their own interpretation of this information through reference to the knowledge they have stored in their memory about it. Through **top-down processing**, sensory input always gets to be imbued with meaning, and it is this meaning that gets processed, not the sensory input itself. Vision, for example, should not be seen as working like a camera, where the eye simply records patterns of light that it sends as mental pictures to the brain. Rather, vision is a two-way process, with top-down and **bottom-up processing** in combination enabling people to make sense of what they see around them.

Social cognition

These principles were incorporated into the social cognition paradigm. It was a reaction against the machine-like models of the person in social learning theory and information processing approaches. Its intention was to reconstruct psychology's image of people. Instead of seeing them as the passive puppets of, say, social conditioning, social cognition views them as active, purposive thinkers who strive to make sense of their social world and bring to this endeavour complex, sophisticated models-of-the-world in order to interpret it. This was a very significant shift – from the image we can trace back to William McDougall to the one proposed by William James (you have had a brief look at all this already in Chapter 1).

Let us look at a specific example (Jenny) to see what this means. Jenny works in telesales, selling women's lingerie for a company that specializes in upmarket but somewhat racy lines – silk G-strings, basques and suspenders are their best-selling products. Last night Jenny had a row with her partner, and it is preying on her mind. They have got a date tonight, and she is worried that it could be the end of the relationship. And to make things worse, it is turning out to be a nightmare day. Just two weeks to go before Valentine's day, the day of all days when lovers send each other romantic or sexy presents. The phone lines are going mad!

Receiving information is a process of recognition

Jenny's job is to take calls from customers, answer their queries and take their orders. In terms of sensory inputs, she only has the words they say and the sound of the customers' voices to go on. But, as you saw in Chapter 6, these are enough for her to make a lot of inferences. By drawing on her prior knowledge she can recognize important cues about the caller. For example, she will pick up subtle voice cues and conversational content to distinguish between a man who is confident about ordering a gift for his girlfriend and one who is cautious and shy.

As she is on commission, Jenny wants to make as many sales as possible, and to do this she needs to 'read' the different kinds of customers and treat them differently. In cognitive terms, this is much more complex than just reading the cues about paralanguage and speech style that you met in Chapter 6. She will need to judge their motives in the context of what she is selling.

Lingerie is a somewhat unusual product, in that it carries with it an especially complex web of meanings and associations. For Jenny to be an effective salesperson she will need to have access to a lot of highly specific social knowledge to do so, so she can interpret what they are saying and not just how they are saying it. Once she has recognized what kind of customer she is dealing with and the context of their purchase, Jenny can shift into the right repertoire. For example, with a confident customer she will engage in extended repartee to try to sell extra products, but with a shy one she will act 'cool and efficient' and stress the confidentiality of the service her company provides.

Constraints on processing

However, human cognition is fallible. If you have done a job like Jenny's (maybe not in telesales, but in any job that involves dealing with large numbers of other people, such as working in a pub or a fast-food chain) you will know just how easy it is to make mistakes, especially when the pressure builds up. Jobs like these involve coping with all sorts of information coming at you from lots of different directions at once, and responding to each one correctly. And you will know that when the pace hots up beyond a certain point, your performance suffers.

It gets worse when there is a 'lot going on' in your head at the same time. Jenny's worries that the row with her partner is almost certain to undermine her performance. She will be prone to making mistakes – not always hearing accurately what her customers say and making a lot of keyboard errors, for instance. Numerous experimental social psychological studies have shown that when people are dealing with 'information overload', they make mistakes. Manstead and Semin (1980) attributed errors in task performance when in the presence of others to having to divide attention. Overload happens, in particular, when people have to deal with highly emotive inputs (see, for example, Lazarus 1991).

Social cognition continues to recognize that the human cognitive system has some fundamental limits on its capacities. Just like any other mechanism, limits are imposed by the material constraints of its 'hardware'. In the case of humans, these constraints arise from the biological make-up of the sensory organs, the nervous system and the brain. At its most basic this includes things like only being able to perceive certain bands of light and certain pitches of sound.

But 'software' sets limits too. In terms of social cognition some of the constraints are imposed by the particular ways in which knowledge is stored and processed in the human brain (as compared to a computer, for example). Nisbett and Ross (1980) introduced the term **cognitive miser** to describe how a person processes information. This rather negative view of the human cognitive system sees it as having a very limited capacity to deal with information and, therefore, of having to resort to all kinds of bodges, dodges and short-cuts to cope.

Telesales companies develop strict repertoires for their staff to follow, both in order to improve performance (in terms of accuracy and customer service) and to meet legal requirements. Workers are trained to use these and, as they become experienced, the repertoires become effectively automatic. Manstead and Semin (1980) found that automatic tasks are much easier to perform accurately in a situation where a person is distracted. What we can see here is a tactic being adopted specifically to cope with the limitations of human cognition. Learning her script 'by heart' – mainly by constant repetition until she is word perfect – allows Jenny to perform accurately, even when under stress. Despite her preoccupations, she is unlikely to make any serious errors in reproducing the repertoire she has learned.

However, Jenny's performance will probably become a lot more 'wooden' when she relies on her ability to process automatically. In doing so, she will miss out on the more subtle cues in the caller's voice and be less able to generate the subtlety of response that makes her come across as responding naturally. Her judgement will also be impaired, as she will fall back more heavily on stereotypical images and assumptions and so be less able to respond to unusual or distinctive information. Much of the skill in doing a job like Jenny's involves being able to use higher cognitive functions – like being intuitive and insightful, so she can make her well-rehearsed repertoire seem like a natural and lively conversation rather than a script. It is these capabilities that get compromised when she gets overloaded and shifts, strategically, into 'automatic' mode.

Processing strategically

This more flattering view of human cognition stresses that it is not so much limited as strategic (Showers and Cantor 1985). It is an image of the person as a **motivated tactician**: 'a fully engaged thinker who has multiple **cognitive strategies** available and chooses among them based on goals, motives and needs' (Fiske and Taylor 1991: 13). In many ways these two images of 'cognitive miser' and 'motivated tactician' are two sides of the same coin.

Compared to machines, people certainly do badly on long-running, repetitive tasks. They get bored, tired and all too easily distracted. They constantly take in a lot of information, but most of it decays before it ever gets recorded. Unlike a computer that can take in and store information at an incredible rate, humans rapidly get overloaded if expected to deal with too much information too fast.

But people are much more effective than computers at dealing with the complexities of human life, mainly because the information that does get retained is encoded much more efficiently – more efficiently, that is, in terms of being able to recall it and use it. This is because the information is encoded differently – human cognition operates with information that is encoded meaningfully. This allows the cognitive system to take short-cuts and work on hunches. The meaningfulness of the information means that gaps can be filled and errors rectified. This allows human cognition to be strategic – to home in on what really matters and cut out a lot of irrelevant and redundant work. In her work Jenny uses this capacity constantly. Within the cacophony of the call centre she concentrates on her own calls, filtering out all the spurious noise and action going on around her.

Try it for yourself

You can experience this for yourself by making a sound recording on your phone next time you go to a crowded place, such as when you are with a group of friends. Let it run for a good bit while you are chatting to your friends. Then listen to the recording once you get somewhere quiet. You are likely to find the recording pretty unintelligible – just a rumbling hubbub of noise with just the occasional catches of conversation coming through at random (this will vary according to the quality amd settings of the microphone). Then think back to what you experienced when you were sitting beside the recorder listening for yourself. You should be able to recall hearing the conversation with your immediate neighbours with clarity. This was because you were selectively attending to that particular conversation and filtering out most of the background noise.

You may not be too impressed by this demonstration as you have probably worked out for yourself that recording does not work well in busy situations. Students often find that they can get a good enough recording of a lecture for it to be useful, but soon give up on trying to record seminars when lots of people are talking. What may intrigue you more is to know that you were actually processing the background noise to a surprising degree.

Have you ever had the experience of chatting in a crowded place like that, and suddenly, out of the hubbub of noise around you, you hear your own name being mentioned? This is called (rather quaintly these days) the **cocktail party phenomenon**. In order to be able to pick up on your name, you must have been unconsciously processing the conversations going on in the background. The human cognitive system has the capability to detect words that are personally salient (such as one's own name) or other inputs that are distinctive or unexpected, even when they are not consciously attending to them (Broadbent 1958). People can strategically switch their attention, and this makes them much more efficient than any recording machine so far invented – though work continues to be done to design one that can fully match human capacities. When, say, a documentary maker wants to record a group conversation, they need a lot of equipment and, crucially, a sound technician to do the switching between inputs.

Selective attention is just one way in which human cognition operates strategically. As we go through the chapter you will see that the study of social cognition is very much the study of what these strategies are and how they function.

Basic processes in social cognition

Looking in depth at what Jenny's job entails brings home the amazing amount of knowledge and ability to encode and process it that is required to do even quite simple tasks. Cognition always involves making inferences from one's own knowledge of people and situations – that people, unlike machines, process meaning, not just 'bits' of information. Whereas machines like computers mainly gain processing efficiency because of the sheer magnitude of information that they can handle and the speed at which they operate, human cognition 'works' because:

- it draws upon an immense stock of social knowledge, stored in long-term memory, that has been built up through the life span

- of the complexity and subtlety of the way that this stored knowledge has been categorized and organized so that it is meaningful

- of the way that its component processes are fine-tuned to work with this meaning.

Things are changing, of course, and face recognition software in cameras, for example, is getting better and better. But it does so from being able to bring large amounts of information to deal with the task, and the immense capacity and speed information technology can achieve.

Categorization

The basic process by which input information is made meaningful is through **categorization**. A category is where similar things are classified together and treated as an entity. 'Lingerie', for example, is a category that covers items of women's underwear, its defining characteristics being underwear that is particularly feminine in style – frilly and lacy – and that has associations with being 'sexy'. If I gave you a list of items – boxer shorts, basques, handbags and vests – you should not find it too hard to recognize which of these is lingerie and which is not – depending, of course, if you are living in a context where 'lingerie' is meaningful to you.

But some items are easier to reject than others. The handbag is not even underwear, so that one is obvious. But what about the boxer shorts and the vest? Both are underwear, but are they lingerie? Given its characteristic of being 'feminine', the boxer shorts are out then – men do not (usually) wear female clothing, though sometimes women do wear more masculine stuff. So, what about the vest? Actually in some department stores their 'Lingerie Section' brings together all women's underwear. So it depends upon your definition and the situation. Yet the children's department would probably avoid calling a little girl's panties 'lingerie' even if they looked more 'grown up', because they would not want to be seen as sexualizing children. Categories are like that – they are influenced by context and can be fuzzy.

Stereotyping

However, categorization has its down-side. In allowing us to treat particular instances as a single class, it can lead to wrong inferences. Think about the assumptions you have made about Jenny. Conjure up an impression of her in your mind's eye. Maybe your image of her is a pretty feminine one; a bit 'sassy' possibly, given the job she's got, but rather 'girlie' nonetheless. Probably you picture her as young (most people who work in telesales are) and almost certainly you think it's her boyfriend she's worried about.

But what if I told you that Jenny was a lesbian, and in her fifties – that she got the job because she has a husky and rather sexy voice? Suddenly the image shifts dramatically. What was going on before is called **stereotyping**. Categorization is a process of 'going beyond the information given' (Bruner 1957), and quite often that information is wrong. Plenty of young, heterosexual women are anything but 'girlie', and there are certainly older, lesbian women who are!

Have you heard the joke about the Irish labourer who goes for a job on a building site and is given an interview by the foreman. 'Paddy,' the foreman asks 'what's the difference between a girder and a joist?' Paddy thinks for a minute and then says, 'Well, Mick, that's an easy question to answer. It's Goethe who wrote Faust, and it's Joyce who wrote Ulysses.' The joke is funny simply because it challenges the stereotype of the 'ignorant Irish labourer'. A psychological study by Haire and Grune (1950) found empirical evidence that demonstrated this kind of stereotyping in practice. When subjects in the study were asked to write sentences about a 'working man' in which they were told to incorporate stereotype-consistent descriptions (such as 'ignorant') they found this easy. It was much harder, they found, to incorporate stereotype-inconsistent ones (such as 'intelligent').

> Stereotyping like this is also examined in Chapter 13 on prejudice.

Associative networks

Categorization is a rather simple, essentially semantic operation. In cognitive social psychology it is recognized that the representation of meaning requires something considerably more sophisticated, whereby not only is information categorized but also, crucially, categories are associated with each other. Whatever the basis for category encoding, cognitive social psychologists agree that social knowledge is organized hierarchically. Taking our illustration of 'lingerie', its hierarchical organization is shown in Figure 7.1.

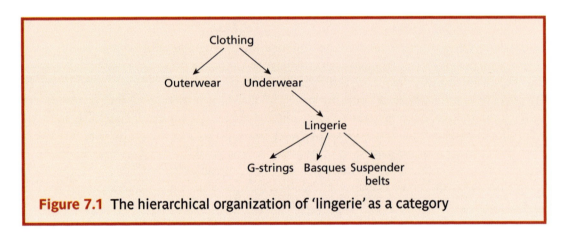

Figure 7.1 The hierarchical organization of 'lingerie' as a category

Formulations like these allow us to see how cognitive processes and structures influence behaviour. Their influence is not only to do with what is encoded, but also with how the interconnections between them are structured. General cognitive psychology has developed sophisticated models of these. Fiedler and Bless (2001) describe **associative networks**, where the connections between categories are organized semantically. An illustration is given in Figure 7.2.

Schema

However, a more radical model moves beyond semantic interconnections, and portrays social knowledge as represented by way of schema: 'a cognitive structure that represents knowledge about a concept . . . including its attributes and the relations among these attributes' (Fiske and Taylor 1991: 98).

The term **schema** was first developed in the 1930s by Bartlett (1932) to describe the conceptual frameworks through which people perceive and make sense of the world around them. If you recall, Bartlett was interested, particularly, in how memory works and conducted studies on

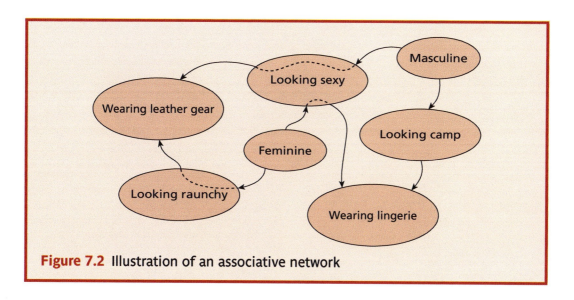

Figure 7.2 Illustration of an associative network

how people remember stories, pictures, and so on. He found that their account not only got shorter (a lot of detail got left out) but also aspects of the original story that were at all strange or unfamiliar got 'ironed out' – made more plausible according to the individual's own world-view and experience. Strictly, schema is the singular form and schemata the plural; in practice the terms 'schema' and 'schemas' have become the most widely used.

Bartlett saw this as providing evidence that when people take in information they interpret it through their existing knowledge, and store this interpreted version in their memory. He suggested that the way in which this is done is that remembered knowledge is organized into schemas, and that it is these schemas that enable us to make sense of what happens around and to us.

Schemas are thus more powerful than mere categories. They not only represent semantic information about what things 'are' but also schematic information about how concepts and ideas relate to each other and analytical information that acts as a basis for interpretation and reasoning. Thus schemas can 'guide information processing by structuring experiences, regulating behaviour, and providing bases for making inferences and interpretations' (Martin and Halverson 1981: 1120).

Jenny's line of work draws heavily on her gender schemas, for example. As Janoff-Bulman and Frieze have argued, 'our gender schemas represent deeply embedded assumptions that we hold about maleness and femaleness in our society, and that we use to evaluate ourselves as well as others' (1987: 169). To be any good at selling lingerie, Jenny needs to have a good understanding of the range of masculinities and femininities that may bring people to call up her company. She needs to be able to use this to infer what products she is likely to sell to what customers and in what circumstances.

In social contexts, schemas not only encode information about different sorts of people and groups of people, but also do so for different forms of social interaction. A specific term used here is **script** (see, for example, Abelson 1981). Hogg and Vaughan (2008) define scripts as 'schemas about events'. Examples here might include 'making a sale' and 'sending a Valentine gift'. Like other kinds of schemas, scripts provide conceptual linking frameworks that class a number of items into an entity. A script like 'going on a date', for instance, sets up a variety of expectations about the sequence of events, what each person should and shouldn't do, and so on. Further differentiation ('a first date', 'a Valentine date') specifies still further.

Schemas are thus very potent encoding devices because they carry so much information. Consequently, they are seen to play an important role in making cognition efficient. They make communication faster and more effective, since a lot can be conveyed in a single word or phrase. They aid problem solving by turning complexity into meaningful, manageable chunks that can then be processed more easily. They act as major organizing frameworks for perception and memory.

A highly oversimplified analogy is to see schemas as working a bit like the text-prediction function on a mobile phone. It can make text messaging a lot less onerous, and works well if the words you want to use are familiar ones. But it is not much use when the words you want to key in are out of the ordinary. Schemas work a bit like this. Once invoked they 'lock in' rapidly and save you the effort of having to think too hard about the immediate situation by filling in any gaps from your prior knowledge and preconceptions. Or, to put it more formally 'schemas facilitate top-down, conceptually driven or theory-driven processing, as opposed to bottom-up or data-driven processing' (Hogg and Vaughan 1998: 50). Schemas are therefore very useful, especially when you need to assess a situation and respond to it rapidly. But they do lead to stereotypical thinking, which can be a problem when dealing with situations that seem familiar but are not.

Social cognition

Cognitive psychology is a radically different paradigm from information processing for conceptualizing how people understand the world. Its basic principles are as follows:

- When taking in information from the outside, people do not just soak it up like a sponge, or passively record it like a computer. They actively seek to understand it through a process of recognition (that is, re-cognition), that encodes the information in terms of its meaning and salience.

- The design characteristics of the human cognitive system are such that it works best with meaningfully encoded information. This places limits on the speed, accuracy and efficiency with which information can be processed.

- However, encoding meaningfully brings enormous benefits. It enables people to be insightful and intuitive. In particular it allows people to be selective and therefore strategic – to direct cognitive effort to achieve particular goals.

- Social cognition draws on this theorization and applies it to cognition in relation to social situations, processes and phenomena.

- It acknowledges that there are processing limits on people's ability to deal with information, but sees them as adopting a range of active and purposeful cognitive strategies to do so in ways that help them achieve social goals.

- There are different views of the effects of this strategic processing. Some theorists see people as needing to be cognitive misers, others as motivated tacticians.

- It stresses that information is encoded in ways that make it meaningful – categorization; and in ways that link concepts and ideas together semantically – by way of associative networks, scripts and schema.

- However, while such encoding makes cognition more efficient, it can have its problems. For instance, stereotyping can lead to prejudice.

Attribution theory

Attribution theory became the favourite area for experimental research in social cognition in the 1960s and 1970s. Charles Antaki (1988) called it the 'jewel in the crown' of the social cognition approach. While it has its critics, it is still regarded by experimental social psychologists as an extremely important theoretical field, and of considerable value in applied settings. '[R]esearch on motivation, clinical psychology and close relationships demonstrates the continued vitality of attribution research, and the tremendous impact of attribution theory in advancing our understanding of applied problems' (Fincham and Hewstone 2001: 237).

Heider's theories of phenomenological causality

Attribution theorists acknowledge Fritz Heider (1953) as their 'founding father'. Apparently Heider devised his theory as a result of spending a very cold and hungry period just after the First World War writing up his doctoral thesis. This experience got him wondering why people become 'touchy and petulant' with one another (perhaps not the grandest basis for theory making, but certainly a reaction that many of us who have written doctorates can sympathize with very sincerely, as can the people around us when we were doing it).

Although the overall term Heider used for his theory was **phenomenological causality**, he carefully distinguished between attributions of causes and agency more generally, setting the scene for a continuing debate about the nature of how ordinary people understand cause and effect, and the errors they may make in doing so. Heider distinguished between specific and general explanations, explanations of what happened in the past and predictive explanations. Although he was primarily concerned with social perception (that is, the ways people explain their own actions and those of others) he also reviewed theories of the way people account for events and influences from the physical environment too.

A man 'ahead of his time'?

Even though Heider's work has been the basis for attribution theory, Heider himself was much broader in his theorizing, and much more philosophical in his approach. He regarded the process of explanation as something which both differs between people according to particular personal characteristics (such as personality) and something that is dynamic within the individual, changing according to circumstances (on mood, for example).

Heider was another psychologist 'ahead of his time' in that his formulations anticipated social constructionism in general and contemporary work in phenomenology in particular. He argued that the explanations that people use to explain the world are both products of the way they 'structure the world' and at the same time contribute to that structuring. Heider's theorization also anticipated discursive psychology. He suggested that a person's explanations of the world may be deployed for different purposes, for example that they may be used for self-justification.

Heider argued that explanation needed to be studied at a common-sense level. He stressed that people do not respond directly to how the world actually works but according to their perceptions of the workings of the world. The explanations that individuals use to structure their world are crucial to making sense of the strategies they adopt in responding to it. He argued that we can begin to develop psychological theories about the way people act only after we have gained access to the explanatory framework within which they operate.

Social psychology, Heider asserted, needed to study people as 'naïve physicists' who have developed theories to predict and to understand events in the physical world; as 'naïve psychologists' who have theories to predict and understand the behaviour and experience of others; as 'naïve sociologists' who have theories to predict and interpret social forces, and so on. It is easy to see how this kind of approach attracted those psychologists who wanted to adopt the cognitive approach.

Heider distinguished between two main kinds of attribution for an event: personal attribution (where a particular individual is seen as responsible, or to blame) and impersonal attribution (where nobody is blamed or held responsible). Impersonal attributions may be made towards naturally occurring events (for example, being struck by a branch falling from a tree), but could also arise from unintended actions (somebody accidentally knocking the branch off the tree). Personal attributions, however, always carry the implication of intended action (that is, somebody deliberately throwing the branch at you).

Drawing on gestalt psychology (see Chapter 1), Heider used a great deal of visual analogy, using metaphors from its theories of visual perception. He wrote, for example, that when Joan tries to understand why Mary did something, she tries to separate the 'figure' (Mary) from the 'ground' of the social situation in which Mary acted. Heider suggested that people have a tendency to misperceive actions, because they confuse figure and ground. They conceive the figure (that is the person acting) as dominating the conceptual ground (the social situation) in parallel fashion to the way figure can dominate ground in a gestalt analysis of visual perception. Thus people tend to be more willing than is justified to assume that actions are the deliberate intentions of the people involved, and less willing to attribute causes to what is going on in the social situation.

Attribution theory within social cognition

This propensity to blame the individual formed the major plank upon which attribution theory was built. Later theorists expanded upon it, and drew up a number of more detailed and complex formulations about the kinds of information people use to make inferences, and the ways in which they are calculated against one another.

Correspondence inference

The first moves were made by Jones and Davis (1965), who proposed the notion of **correspondent inference**. Basically, this concerns the degree to which the actor – the person whose behaviour is being judged – is seen as behaving according to a stable and enduring disposition. Examples are, anger expressed by a person who is usually grumpy and bad-tempered, and laughter from a person who has a well-developed sense of humour. People make correspondent inferences in these circumstances (that is inferences which correspond to the assumed disposition), attributing the cause of the action – the anger or the laughter – to the person, rather than the situation.

Jones and Davis (1965) theorized about the sorts of knowledge required for making correspondent inferences, and suggested that one element was to do with **role expectations**. Jones and Davis argued that when people act in-role, according to preconceived notions of what their role should be (for example, that nuns are devout, Australians brash and professors scholarly), their behaviour will be seen as role-driven, and thus less likely to be a product of personal qualities. When people act in ways that are counter to their assumed roles (for example, when a nun is brash, an Australian scholarly or a professor devout), their behaviour is much more likely to be accredited to something peculiar to them as individuals.

A number of experiments were carried out to test this hypothesis. A good example is the experiment conducted by Jones et al. (1961). When people in this study were asked to explain why job applicants in tape-recorded interviews pointedly acted counter to the job-description characteristics provided, they said it was to do with their personal characteristics. But they explained job applicants whose interviews conformed to the desired qualities as acting according to the demands of the interview situation.

Note that, unlike Heider's formulations, the concept of correspondent inference makes no claims about intentionality. All that is at issue here is whether attribution is about cause located in the person (intended or not) or in the situation. A good example is where people explain why somebody has a heart attack. If the person is seen as 'an ideal candidate' (they are overweight and take little exercise), then it is the overweight and laziness that will be seen to be the cause of the heart attack. But when a person who is a paragon of virtue health-wise is struck down, then the explanation given is that the individual must have had some specific susceptibility or have suffered some unexpected unique risk.

Kelley's 'naïve statistician' model

Harold (not George) Kelley (1967) devised an even more complex and sophisticated series of parameters to the attribution process. He suggested that people base an attribution about a particular action upon estimates of three main kinds of information:

- *distinctiveness*: the extent to which the person in question normally behaves in this kind of way
- *consistency*: the extent to which the person in question has, in the past, behaved like this before in similar situations
- *consensuality*: the extent to which other people normally behave like that.

Figure 7.3 Why did Marcia eat a lentilburger for lunch?
Source: Stainton Rogers (1991: 48)

Kelley theorized that people, when they make judgements about responsibility, act like 'naïve statisticians'. Kelley saw attributional judgement as a process of weighing the different sources of evidence available in relation to each other, and carrying out a technique rather like statistical analysis of variance. The different estimates of variability in the situation are computed together, and the attribution is then calculated. When asked, for example, why Marcia ate a lentilburger for lunch, the calculation might go a bit like the situation shown in Figure 7.3.

Attribution errors

The other set of well-known formulations were about the mistakes people make in their attributions; the ways in which 'naïve statisticians' (that is ordinary people) are not as clever as psychologists. Nisbett and Ross (1980) describe three kinds of errors:

- **Fundamental attribution error**: this is an enlargement of Heider's notion that people tend to overemphasize the personal, and underemphasize the situational causes of actions.
- **Actor–observer error**: this is when people (either as individuals, or as groups) assume their own behaviour to be more likely to be situationally determined, and the behaviour of others more likely to be a product of personal intentions.
- **False consensus effect**: this is where people tend to assume that others are more likely to behave like them than they actually do.

Basically, this set of principles construes people as imperfect logicians, unable to overcome their own prejudices when making judgements.

More recent attribution theorists (for example, Hewstone 1983) have suggested that in order to understand why this should be, we need to consider the functions – both social and psychological – of attributions. Hewstone suggests that there are three:

1 The need to assume control over the physical and social world by being able to explain and predict what will happen. This is particularly salient with regard to misfortune, where blaming it on a person's own actions offers the hope that you can avoid similar misfortune by not acting so stupidly. If you see yourself as to blame for a misfortune that has happened to you, then you can mend your ways. If you blame somebody else, then you can convince yourself that you would never do anything so stupid.

2 To promote self-esteem, by seeing yourself as competent, taking credit for your successes, and dismissing your failures as caused externally.

3 As a means of self-presentation in which the act of attribution is one of portraying yourself (to yourself, and to others) in a good light.

Attribution theory

- Contemporary attribution theory is based on the work of Heider, who first proposed a distinction between personal and impersonal (situational) attribution.

- Jones and Davis (1965) proposed that attribution is determined by correspondent inference – the inferences that people make as to whether people are behaving in relation to their social role or their personal disposition.

- Kelley (1967) offered a 'naïve statistician' model, where people compute distinctiveness, consistency and consensuality to work out how to attribute cause.

- Nisbett and Ross (1980) described three main kinds of attribution errors – predispositions to:

  o generally site cause in the person rather than the situation

  o but site cause in the situation rather than their own behaviour

  o believe others behave more like them than they actually do.

Processing-depth models

In Europe, at least, social cognition is undergoing a distinct shift. A new overarching theory is being developed that proposes that most forms of social cognition can operate in one of two distinctly and qualitatively different levels of processing:

- *automatically and largely mindlessly*, where cognition is heuristic – it works from 'rules of thumb' based, for example, on well-established stereotypes, schemata and scripts

- *consciously, actively and purposively*, where cognition is used in a thoughtful, strategic manner.

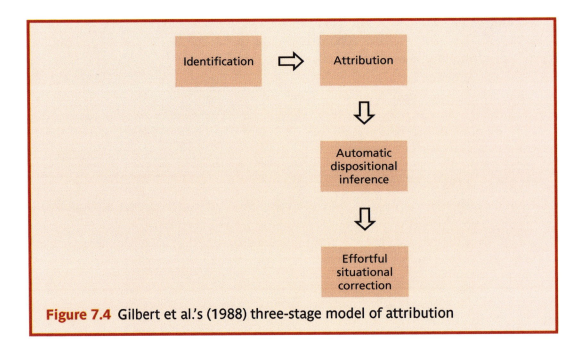

Figure 7.4 Gilbert et al.'s (1988) three-stage model of attribution

This has led to the development of a number of **processing-depth models** of social cognition. A good example is the one developed by Gilbert and his colleagues (Gilbert et al. 1988), based on reaction-time experiments on attribution. Subjects are presented with a stimulus on a computer screen and asked to attribute its cause – for example, whether or not a person is responsible for a particular outcome. The speed at which the subjects respond is seen as a measure of the 'depth' of processing needed to make the judgement. Using this technique, Smith and Miller (1983) found that decisions based on categorization of gender (that is, based on stereotypes) were fastest, and decisions based on attributing a situational cause (that is, requiring much more thought) were slowest. Gilbert et al. (1988) used these kinds of results as the basis of a three-stage model of attribution. This is shown in Figure 7.4.

In this model, identification is a necessary first processing step. A person has to identify what is happening and who is involved before they can begin to decide who or what is responsible. This is done automatically, through reference to categorical knowledge. Then, the model proposes, there are two sequential stages of attribution:

- The first attributional stage is **dispositional inference**. This is also a relatively automatic and mindless process. It requires little cognitive effort (see, for example, Uleman et al. 1996).
- The second attributional stage is making a **situational correction**. Making this kind of attribution is held to require much more cognitive effort – it needs more thinking to make a decision.

Gilbert et al. (1988) tested their model using a divided-attention technique. Subjects watched a video of a woman anxiously having a conversation with another person. Half were allowed to concentrate just on watching the video. The other half had to simultaneously carry out a distracting, attention-demanding task – they had to silently mutter lists of words to themselves while they were watching. These groups were subdivided, so that half of each subgroup were primed to view the woman's anxiety as arising from the topic she was discussing (situational attribution). The other half were primed to view her anxiety as arising from her anxious personality (dispositional inference). The results obtained are in Table 7.3 and show that, indeed, when distracted, subjects tend to fall back on stereotypical attribution.

Table 7.3 Results obtained by Gilbert et al. (1988)			
Distraction	**Subjects just watched the video**		**Subjects were distracted by an attention-demanding task**
Priming	Primed to see the woman as anxious	Primed to see the situation as anxiety provoking	Primed to see the woman as anxious	Primed to see the situation as anxiety provoking
Attribution	Attributed anxiety to the woman	Attributed anxiety to the situation	Attributed anxiety to the woman	Attributed anxiety to the woman

Drivers for change

Three main considerations have combined to give rise to these processing depth models of social cognition: a turn to language; a recognition that people generally go about their lives in a pretty mindless way; and a turn to researching social cognition in more realistic settings.

A turn to language in attribution theory

In Europe, at least, while most social psychologists retain a commitment to experimental method, there are a growing number who have taken on the message that a consideration of the semantic qualities of language needs to be drawn into theorizing and built into research.

Since the 1980s a group of mainly European experimental social psychologists have begun to argue for a 'turn to language' in attribution theory. They say that classical attribution theory takes insufficient account of the extent to which attribution is articulated through language. Semin and Fiedler (1988), for instance, propose that attribution research must take account of the categories that are built into the linguistic system and, particularly, the semantic qualities of the verbs people use to describe and explain their own actions and those of others. These studies stress the complexity and subtlety of language, and how particular words convey strong implications about the causal explanation of events. Others (such as Hilton 1990) emphasize the pragmatic and strategic qualities of speech, and he argues for a 'conversational approach' to attribution that has clear links to discursive psychology.

Most processing is mindless

Some experimental social psychologists, again, mainly from Europe, also criticize classical attribution theory for the way it portrays people as living in an experiential world constantly beset by ambiguity and confusion about what is going on, desperate to know the causes of each event and constantly needing to calculate alternatives and come up with answers. Semin and Manstead (1983) argued that this is nonsense. Most of the time, they say, people go through life experiencing it as a reasonably smoothly flowing series of events, that only need to be explained or justified when something unexpected comes along. To even ask the question 'Why did she do that?' changes things dramatically, since it implies that the action needs to be explained (that is, it was an unwarranted action, or one that broke the rules). Consequently, simply asking people to explain an action comes across as accusatory, and so invites particular kinds of response: justifications, denials of blame, excuses. If what you want to do is to study these kinds of explanation, fine. Asking the 'why' question would be legitimate. But, Semin and Manstead (1983) argue, what cannot be done is to assume that the answers given in this situation necessarily, or even probably, reflect the usual way in which people understand the reasons for things, when not called upon to explicitly explain them.

Langer (1978) had already raised similar concerns, suggesting that when people are involved in social situations in real life, they do not usually understand it through thoughtful attributional analyses of what is going on between people. Mostly they operate pretty 'mindlessly', often by following a script.

Alternatively, Försterling (1988) offers an evolutionary explanation for attribution, calling it the sexual attribution bias.

More realistic settings

Langer and her colleagues did a number of studies to demonstrate this, including a number of clever field experiments observing how secretaries dealt with memos sent to them and how they responded to requests to 'jump the queue' to use the photocopier (Langer et al. 1978). These were designed to examine social cognition in situations that are much more true to real life.

This is becoming a marked trend in attributional research. Fincham and Hewstone (2001), for example, review a range of studies in which people are asked to make attributional judgements in more realistic settings, such as when people are facing problems in their close relationships (see, for example, Fincham and Bradbury 1988). These yield much more sophisticated models of attribution, that take account of the state of the relationship itself (satisfactory or unsatisfactory), the attribution pattern (relationship-enhancing or distress-maintaining), and the behaviour in question of the partner (positive or negative). More recently Chiou (2007) examined how the different policies of different airlines affected customers' attribution of fault.

These models encompass, in particular, people's motivation to engage in in-depth cognition when making their attributions. Motivation is seen as a question of whether or not the attribution matters. When relationships are going well, for instance, the things your partner does are often not treated very seriously. Even when they do something irritating, this is passed off as relatively unimportant – as unintentional and therefore not blameworthy. But when the relationship is going badly, both positive and negative acts tend to be viewed negatively. When a partner in this situation does something good, then this is not seen as deliberate and receives no credit or praise. When they do a bad thing, this is seen as deliberate, as selfish and, therefore, as blameworthy.

This shift to more complex models that take account of meanings and salience moves closer to the kinds of model of, say, discursive psychology, that views cognition as motivated. The methodological approach used in discursive psychology is very different (as you saw in Chapter 5). The underlying theory base is also much more concerned with intersubjectivity. But even so, there is an agreement building up that modelling how people understand the world needs to take account of the subtlety and sophistication of human thinking that is intimately connected with language use.

Processing depth models of social cognition

- Some (mainly European) experimental social psychologists have begun to develop more sophisticated models of social cognition. These:
  o take much more account of the way language mediates social cognition
  o view it as operating through two kinds of processing: superficial and automatic, or in-depth and heuristic
  o recognize that social cognition is much more sophisticated and complex in real-life situations
  o view social cognition as motivated, and hence affected by what matters and is significant

Discursive approaches to attribution

Critical social psychologists have serious problems with attribution theory for two main reasons:

- It is articulated around a distinction between attributing cause to the person or to the social situation.
- It seriously underestimates the extent to which attributions are located within and articulated through the use of discursive practices and resources.

Challenging the person/situation distinction

Critical social psychologists argue that studies of social cognition 'treat linguistic materials (text, sentences and so on) as representations of the world and/or mind – of what happened, or of what somebody thinks happened – rather than as situated actions' (Edwards and Potter 1992: 77).

Edwards and Potter call for a relocation of attributional findings within a wider, discursive model (Edwards and Potter 1993: 37) and have suggested a discursive action model (DAM) to do just that. Edwards and Potter acknowledge that cognitive processes are involved in generating causal explanations, but propose that attribution is best understood as thought-in-action within a particular social context (situated social practices, in other words). They highlight the rhetorical aspects of making attributions, and the ways that attribution has to be accomplished.

An example is a study by Hanson-Easey and Augoustinos (2010) that uses a mix of discourse analytic techniques to gain insight into politicians' justifications for 'hard line' policy in immigrants to Australia from Sudan. Hanson-Easey and Augoustinos make a strong case for the Edwards and Potter position:

> This investigation has illustrated how language that employs causality functions as an action. In the political interview, the sketching of causal narratives to explicate a policy shift, and manoeuvre around issues of responsibility and blame, are not best understood as universal cognitive alignments, but as implicit inferences detailed in all descriptions of individuals, groups and events.
>
> (Hanson-Easey and Augoustinos 2010: 317)

Discursive psychology stresses that language is not simply a semantic representational system, it is a semiotic one – it is used to signify. And its semiotic qualities link any instance of talk into a whole network of cultural significations.

Go back and have another look at Marcia's lentilburger lunch (Figure 7.3). Answering the question 'Why did Marcia eat a lentilburger for lunch?' is not a matter of selecting just one of two, mutually exclusive alternatives – either it is to do with the kind of person Marcia is, or it is to do with the situation she is in. Ask a real person in a real situation that kind of question and their answer will be informed by a complex and rich set of ideas. In early twenty-first-century modern societies, one likely theme will be vegetarianism. This includes ethical concerns about the immorality of killing animals for food, both from an animal rights perspective and from ideas about the waste of resources of using animal protein as a food source. It is also likely to encompasses ideas about 'healthy eating' and the importance of eating high-fibre foods. Then there is the fact that lentils are less fatty than meat, and the pressures (particularly on young women) to strive for a slim body and thus eat low-fat meals. Then think of how lentils have become 'cool' things to eat.

Very soon the question of her lunch begins to take in all manner of subtle complexions, such as the marketing of 'health foods' and the effects of mass media advertising, of health education and of youth culture. Attributions in the real world (as opposed to the laboratory) are massively more complex than either classic attribution or even multiple-process models of attribution allow. Critical theorists stress that attributions are never purely matters of individual social cognition, but always the product of complex cultural and social forces providing discursive resources within and through which attributions are made.

Consequently, the 'cause' of any behaviour or event will seldom if ever be attributed unequivocally to a single site. We could ask whether it is Marcia's vegetarianism (or whatever) that led her to eat the lentilburger, or the qualities of the burger (that is, its vegetable and not meat base). Surely it is both. But the criticism goes further than this, for, as Rommetveit (see, for example, his 1980 article) has pointed out, when we try to make sense of any action, there are many stories we can tell, all of which may have validity. He used, as an illustration, explanations about why Mr Jones was mowing the lawn. Was it to get exercise, to avoid spending time with his wife, to beautify his garden or to annoy his neighbour? Maybe it was all of them!

Attribution is made within and through discourse

Discursive psychology stresses in particular that language is used to do things, not simply represent concepts, ideas and understandings. And the things people do are purposive, and the purposes are much more varied than attributional theory can accommodate.

Go back to the bit about Fincham's studies of relationships described in the previous section. While it accommodates things like whether a relationship is going well or badly, it assumed that this has a lawfully similar meaning and significance in all couple relationships. But these are not in any sense universal, but influenced by history and culture.

At different historical times and in different cultures, couple relationships are understood differently. It is very likely, for example, that where marriage is regarded as an institution rather than a source of personal fulfilment – where men and women live more separate lives, and where the roles of wives and husbands are highly gendered and specified – there will be much less agonizing over a partner's behaviour, whatever the state of the relationship. Cultures vary considerably in how they understand issues of duty and responsibility in relation to individuals as compared with social groups (such as families) and hence attributional conventions will also vary considerably across cultures (Smith et al. 2006).

Moreover today, in a virtually global sense, the mass media bombard people with messages about attribution in couple relationships – about 'men behaving badly', that 'men are from Mars and women are from Venus', and so on. Newspapers as well as women's magazines carry 'agony aunt' columns that minutely dissect who is and who is not to blame when relationships go wrong. Much fiction takes misattribution as its main narrative plot-line, from *Pride and Prejudice* to *Bridget Jones' Diary*. Discursive psychology thus locates attribution within discourse: 'The crucial point is that event description is not distinct from, nor prior to attributional work, but rather attributional work is *accomplished by* descriptions. Discursive psychology takes as a primary focus of concern, the study of talk and texts, for the situated reality-producing work that they do' (Edwards and Potter 1992: 91, emphasis in the original).

Discursive psychology redefines how attribution should be studied. If we are to understand attribution we need (according to Edwards and Potter) to see attribution as *work* – as something that is *done*. So we must attend much more closely to the nature and content of the conversation or other exchange in which attribution work is done, and the extent to which this work is constructive. We need to recognize that the things that people say do not reflect reality but construct particular versions of reality according to the purposes to which the conversation is put.

> A discursive psychology of attribution proposes an active, rhetorical process, which requires at least two participants. . . . Rather than viewing the entire process from the perspective of an inference making perceiver, who passively takes versions as given, we have to examine how versions are constructed and undermined within a discursive manipulation of fact and implication. Attribution is to be studied as a public and social process, done interactionally in talk and text, where fact and attributional inference are simultaneously and rhetorically addressed.
>
> (Edwards and Potter 1992: 94)

The power of discourse to 'make' the world

> When a cat wants to eat her kittens, she calls them mice.
>
> (Old Turkish proverb)

In Chapter 5 you looked at a study by Kitzinger and Frith (1999) that used conversational analysis to tease apart the rhetoric underlying 'Just say no' campaigns on US university campuses. In this analysis they identified an example of what the feminist philosopher Vickers has called the **reversal of agency**. Vickers proposes that this is 'the worst kind of context stripping . . . a grammatical, theoretical and methodological trick' (Vickers 1982: 39) that beguiles the language receiver (the reader or listener) into misattributing agency.

The conventional assumption is that it is women's lack of communication skills that is the site of the 'problem' (of, say, 'date rape'). Kitzinger and Frith, in effect, argue that this is an attribution error. But it is not one located in individual cognition. It is an attribution error woven into a particular social reality. From their explicitly Feminist standpoint this social reality is a patriarchal system in which '[m]en's self-interested capacity for "misunderstanding" will always outstrip women's earnest attempts to clarify and explain' (Kitzinger and Frith 1999: 311).

Feminist analysis of patriarchal social reality

It may seem a surprising place to go, but one of the main theories of how patriarchy constructs a particular social reality is a form of psychoanalytic theory developed by Jacques Lacan. He argued for a radical change in the way psychodynamic forces are seen to originate and operate (Lacan 1966). Rather than viewing them – as Freud had done – as biologically grounded and mediated, Lacan argued that they are grounded in and mediated by culture. He drew extensively on the work of de Saussure, particularly his ideas about the symbolic nature of language (see Chapter 6).

Subsequently a semiotic version of psychoanalytic theory has been generated by feminist theorists such as Julia Kristeva ([1974] 1984). She developed a complex theoretical framework in which social reality is seen to operate at different levels. For instance, she proposed that in the 'semiotic order' of meanings and meaning-making, social reality is consciously 'made sense of', but in the 'symbolic order' it is experienced at an unconscious level – as strong emotions and feelings that can profoundly affect behaviour.

To begin with, this new, semiotic version of psychoanalytic theory was most influential in areas like media studies. For example, Laura Mulvey suggested that 'sexual instincts and identification processes have a meaning within the symbolic order which articulates desire'. In Western culture, she suggests, the symbolic order is permeated by sexual difference, where 'women are simultaneously looked at and displayed, with their appearance being coded for strong visual and erotic impact' (Mulvey 1992: 25).

Both Kristeva and Mulvey were seeking to theorize about patriarchy, which they saw as a particularly powerful social reality in which the social world has been constructed by men and for men, to serve male interests – it is, literally, a man-made world of meanings. Mulvey, for instance, drew attention to the fact that films tend almost exclusively to be made by men and for men, and in them women are almost exclusively portrayed from a male perspective.

Playing tricks with agency

Now let us go back and see what Vickers is getting at in her claim that the patriarchal social world 'plays tricks' with agency. She illustrates her case with the following statement (cited by Daly) about suttee – the 'custom' or 'practice' in which widows are burnt on their husband's funeral pyres. It is taken from a textbook about Hinduism: 'At first, *suttee* was restricted to the wives of princes and warriors . . . but in the course of time the widows of weavers, masons, barbers and others of the lower caste adopted the practice' (Walker, cited in Daly 1978: 117, emphasis added by Daly). Vickers responded:

> Given the fact that widows were dragged from hiding places and heavily drugged before being flung on the pyre, often by their sons, this is like saying that although the practice of being burned in gas ovens was at first restricted to political dissidents, eventually millions of Jews adopted the practice.
>
> (Vickers 1982: 39, emphasis in the original)

Vickers is proposing here that language can be – and regularly is – used to 'play tricks' with meaning, especially meaning to do with agency. The way it is deployed primes a particular inter-pretation of what is going on (that is, it contends certain facts) and, in so doing, blames the victim rather than the perpetrator (that is, it promotes certain values). By calling *suttee* a 'practice' or a 'custom' that is 'adopted' by widows, responsibility for their deaths is located in the women themselves rather than in those who kill them. The sense is conveyed (by using the verb 'adopting' in the textbook sentence) that it is the widows who do the doing, rather than the sons who do the doing (Vickers uses three 'doing' verbs to make her point – 'dragging', 'drugging' and 'flinging').

In many ways discursive psychology as a whole is a study of attribution, in that it seeks to explicate the purposes to which talk and text are being put in the way they are deployed. A new term has been adopted for such work – the concept of agency. Work like that of Vickers (1982) provides a powerful framework for exploring the ways in which language is deployed to 'play tricks' with agency.

Vickers suggests that within a patriarchal social world, language is often used to obscure, deny and to reverse agency. One of her prime targets is academic text. She argues that it is, by convention, a style that is presented as academically 'pure' – objective and impersonal – in the pursuit of dispassionate and rational scholarly report and analysis. But often, in so doing, it at the very least obscures agency, often it denies it and, at worst, reverses it.

People as competent negotiators of reality

The concept of agency and the use of it as an analytic within discursive psychology shift social psychological research and theorizing about attribution into a new paradigm that takes a more radical stance on 'ordinary thinking' than attempts to apply it to 'realistic settings' like Fincham's.

Instead of concentrating on attribution errors and viewing the way people make sense of the world as flawed, discursive psychology regards people as 'competent negotiators of reality' (Potter and Wetherell 1987: 45) who can and do use language purposively to do 'attributional work' (Edwards and Potter 1992: 91). Like social cognition theory, this portrays the way that people understand the social world as an active and constructive process that enables them to operate effectively within it. However, where discursive psychology differs is that it does not regard this as a bumbling and bodging strategy to cope with the limitations of human cogni-tion. It does not portray people as 'naïve scientists' or 'naïve physicists' or naïve anyone. Instead it regards people as anything *but* naïve – as clever and often conniving and devious.

Try it for yourself

Putting it this way, in relation to Kitzinger and Frith's (1999) article, what do you think was going on when posters were put around a campus in response to 'No means no' signs that had been placed as part of a zero tolerance campaign?

These counter-offensive posters had captions reading 'No means kick her in the teeth', 'No means on your knees bitch', 'No means tie her up', 'No means more beer' and 'No means she's a dyke' (Mahood and Littlewood 1997).

Do you really think these were examples of attribution errors? That the men who made the posters were suffering from a lack of proper understanding of the situation? Or do you think the making and posting of the posters were a deliberate strategy intended to exercise power?

Discursive approaches to attribution

- Critical social psychologists suggest that attribution should be regarded as an integral part of discursive practice.
- They argue that attribution is a semiotic process, mediated by culture and used in all discourse to locate agency in ways that promote the power and interest of particular groups.
- Instead of seeing people as making attribution errors, they suggest that people should be seen as 'competent negotiators of reality', who use attribution strategically.

Resources

Attribution theory

This material offers a good introduction to attribution theory, looking specifically at its application to health: http://healthyinfluence.com/wordpress/steves-primer-of-practical-persuasion-3-0/thinking/attribution/

Another set of materials can be reached through a dedicated wiki site – psychwiki. As with all wikis, you need to constantly remind yourself that these are not necessarily authoritative. But if you bear that in mind, wikis can often be stimulating ways to get your head around a topic: http://www.psychwiki.com/wiki/Attribution_Theory

Further reading

Experimental social psychology

Parkinson, B. (2008) Social perception and attribution, in M. Hewstone, W. Stroebe and K. Jonas (eds) *Introduction to Social Psychology: A European Perspective*, 4th edn. Oxford: Blackwell.
This chapter is where to go for more detail. It offers a clear account of experimental social psychology theory and research in relation to social cognition and attribution theory. It includes a very short acknowledgement of the discursive account.

Critical social psychology

Edwards, D. and Potter, J. (1992) *Discursive Psychology*. London: Sage.
Chapters 5 and 6 in this book provide a clear (if, at times, dense) account of attribution as addressed by discursive psychology.

Langdridge, D. (2007) The fundamental attribution error, in D. Langdridge and S. Taylor, *Critical Readings in Social Psychology*. Maidenhead: Open University Press.
This consists of an abbreviated reading on the topic and then a detailed critique and commentary by Darren Langdridge and Trevor Butt, coming from a phenomenological perspective. It is quite hard work at times, but very instructive.

Questions

1 Explain what is meant by 'encoding' in social cognition, and give examples to illustrate the different forms it can take.

2 In terms of the way people deal with information overload, are they 'cognitive misers' or 'motivated tacticians'?

3 What kinds of errors do people make in social cognition and what causes them? Illustrate your answer with reference to both selective attention and attribution.

4 In the 1980s a shift was made away from traditional attribution theory to more sophisticated processing-depth models. Describe the theorizing behind this shift, and key studies that demonstrate how this new conception of attribution is different.

5 Explain the main challenges that critical social psychology makes to mainstream theory and research about attribution.

6 What is meant by 'playing tricks with agency'? What relevance has this to attribution?

Chapter 8

Attitudes and behaviour

LEARNING OUTCOMES

When you have finished studying this chapter, you should be able to:

1 Define 'attitudes', describe how they are formed and list their main psychological functions.

2 Outline the main conditions necessary for attitudes to predict behaviour.

3 Describe the *theory of reasoned action*, the *theory of planned behaviour* and the *stages of change* model.

4 Evaluate their usefulness for understanding behaviour change, and for being able to predict whether people will change their behaviour.

5 Describe the theory of cognitive dissonance, and list the conditions necessary for it to occur.

6 Describe two different ways in which persuasion can occur, and two processing-level models of persuasion.

7 Identify at least four criticisms of traditional attitude theory made by critical social psychologists, giving examples supporting each of these challenges.

8 Define 'social action' and 'social practices' and summarize the argument for using these concepts to understand why people act in the ways they do rather than attitude theory.

9 Suggest at least two ways in which social psychological research on behaviour change can be practically applied to 'real-world' situations. Choose one of them, and outline in more detail the impact that social psychologists can have.

Introduction

The study of attitudes has been a preoccupation of social psychology from its beginnings. Attitude is a key concept in experimental social psychology because attitudes are seen to operate at all levels of social influence:

- at an *individual level*, attitudes influence people's perception, thinking and behaviour
- at an *interpersonal level*, attitudes are a key element in how people get to know each other, and how to respond to each other; attitude change is a means by which people persuade others to act differently
- at the *intergroup level*, group members' attitudes towards their own group and other groups are at the core of cooperation and conflict between groups.

This chapter is divided into three sections. The first two – on attitudes and attitude change – are largely couched within the experimental social psychology paradigm. The final section brings together the critiques made by critical social psychologists of this mainstream work, and the alternative approaches and concepts they offer.

Attitudes

Gordon Allport defined an attitude in behaviourist terms as 'a mental and neural state of readiness, organized through experience, exerting a distinctive or dynamic influence upon the individual's response to all objects and situations with which it is related' (1935: 810). A more recent formulation is that an attitude is 'a psychological tendency that is expressed by evaluating a particular entity with some degree of favour or disfavour' (Eagly and Chaiken 1998: 269).

Most agree that the key elements are an **attitude object** and an evaluation towards it – attitudes are *about* something. Some kinds of attitudes are the subject of specific study by social psychologists and given particular labels. The study of negative attitudes to certain social groups is called the study of prejudice, and you will come on to this in Chapter 13 on prejudice. Attitudes towards oneself are usually studied in terms of self-evaluation, and often specifically as the study of self-esteem. This you will meet in Chapter 10 on selves and identities. The study of attitudes towards abstract concepts is generally called the study of values, which you cover in Chapter 9 on values.

Generally attitudes are seen as having three main components:

- *cognitive components*, made up of a person's understandings of and beliefs about the attitude object
- *emotional components*, made up of a person's feelings towards and emotional reactions to the attitude object
- *behavioural components*, made up of the person's past behaviour towards and their behavioural intentions to the attitudinal object.

A factor-analytic study by Breckler (1984), looking at students' attitudes towards snakes, showed that taking account of all three of these components was better at predicting overall attitudes than any single factor alone.

Attitude formation

It is almost too much of a truism to suggest that people form their attitudes by gaining information. It gets a lot less clichéd once we begin to consider where the information comes from.

Sources of information

Some information may be instinctive – such as feeling disgust about the smell and taste of putrefaction, which clearly has an evolutionary advantage. Evolutionary psychologists claim that people have inherent tendencies towards certain attitudes (Tesser 1993). One example given is the claim that men are instinctively geared to find women with waists about one-third narrower than their hips the most attractive (Singh 1993).

The emotional elements of attitudes are most obviously informed by direct experience – events where an attitude object is accompanied by a strong emotional response. One of my friends feels revolted by coffee, which he traces back to once drinking it with sour milk that made him violently sick. Since then he even avoids being in a room where coffee is being prepared or people are drinking it. Emotional information can predominate over cognitive information. Breckler and Wiggins (1989), for example, found that if people experience strongly negative emotional reactions to seeing blood, they are much less likely to donate blood, even when they know it to be a good thing to do.

Cognitive elements of attitudes are also influenced by direct experience. However, they are mainly the product of external sources of information – conversations with others, what people read in books and newspapers, see on television and so on (Fishbein and Ajzen 1975). External information often dominates over experiential information, especially that derived from hearsay (Millar and Millar 1996).

Behavioural elements arise from information about one's past behaviour. Fazio and Zanna (1981), for instance, showed that when people have regularly donated to a charity over a number of years, their approval of that charity is greater than if they have only recently donated. As we shall see, behavioural intention is also an important source of information.

Evaluating different sources of information

In many if not most cases, attitudes will be based on multiple sources of information (Breckler and Wiggins 1989). The question then arises – how is the information brought together? Theorization and research in this field have proposed two main strategies.

The first is by a kind of **cognitive algebra**, where all the relevant information is weighed according to its salience and value and then a calculation is made to end up with an overall evaluation of the attitude object. Fishbein (1967), for example, proposed a precise mathematical formula.

The alternative is a more **gestalt appraisal** where the 'whole' is more than just 'the sum of the parts'. Here information sources are interpreted via each other to gain a coherent, overall impression (Hamilton and Zanna 1974). For example, knowing that someone is a great artist, their outrageous rudeness might be interpreted as an aspect of 'artistic temperament' and, therefore, regarded as insignificant compared with their flamboyant character and genius.

Resolving ambiguity and inconsistency

These strategies would both work where attitudes towards a particular object are generally consistent. But often they are not – people can have ambivalent attitudes that evaluate an object both positively and negatively. This is well encapsulated in a slogan used for selling cream cakes: 'naughty but nice'. People often have ambivalent attitudes to their indulgences – food, alcohol, being lazy, and so on. They have cognitive information about the hazards they pose, but also emotional information about how pleasurable they are.

Experimental social psychology regards the need for consistency as a powerful force on cognition and has suggested three main psychological processes that enable people to resolve inconsistency in the information they have about a particular object.

- *Social judgements* can be made to prioritize particular information sources. For example, people tend to place greater reliance on information coming from more familiar (Zajonc 1968b), more attractive (Insko 1981) or more credible (Hovland and Weiss 1951) sources.

- *Priming* can increase the impact of subsequent information. Information tends to be interpreted in the context of prior information and affected by, for example, a mindset induced by a particular activity. For example, Tourangeau and Rasinski (1988) primed subjects in their study by asking them a series of pointed and biased questions before assessing their political attitudes. The attitudes expressed rejected the priming bias.

- *Increased depth of processing* can raise the salience of information. Depth of processing affects the extent to which information is attended to and understood. Information that is consciously and actively processed tends to have more effect than information processed automatically, and hence to influence its impact upon attitudinal evaluation (Hovland et al. 1953). For instance, people attend most to that information which is most personally relevant to them.

These processes have received most attention in studies of attitude change, and we will look at them in more detail later in the chapter.

The functions of attitudes

There has been considerable experimental social psychological research and theorization into the functions that attitudes serve (see, for example, Smith et al. 1956; Shavitt 1989). Drawing on a range of theoretical frameworks, four main kinds of function have been established, as follow.

Object appraisal function

Attitudes are seen to have an object-appraisal function (sometimes called a knowledge function) that simplifies information processing and orientates attention to particular aspects of the attitude object. For example, if you find even the idea of eating raw fish (attitude object) disgusting (evaluation), you know you hate not only sushi but also Mexican ceviche and Swedish gravlax, as raw fish is a common ingredient in all of them. Drawing on information processing theory,

Smith et al. (1956) saw attitudes as bringing together the different elements into a connected whole, making it easier to rapidly categorize – and hence be able to respond appropriately to – people, things, ideas and events. More recent theorizing based within the social cognition framework (see, for example, Judd and Kulik 1980) suggests that attitudes function as schemas (see Chapter 7).

Instrumental function

Attitudes are held to have an instrumental function (sometimes called a utilitarian function), that helps to steer behaviour in functional ways. Based originally on the principles of social learning theory, this views attitudes as allowing people to pursue rewarding outcomes and avoid unpleasant ones. If, for example, someone knows they hate going shopping, then this encourages them to act in ways to avoid shopping trips.

Social identity function

Since attitudes allow us to express values (Katz 1960), expressing attitudes enables a person to identify with and be identified by others sharing similar values. Social identity theory (see Chapters 10 and 11) stresses the role of identification with an ingroup in promoting a positive identity.

Self-esteem maintenance function

People can adopt particular attitudes as a means to distance themselves from those who threaten their self-image and to align themselves with those who enhance it. Drawing on the psycho-dynamic theory, Katz (1960) saw this as an **ego-defence** mechanism. From social identity theory, Cialdini et al. (1976) claimed that identification with a prestigious ingroup allows people to 'bask in reflected glory'. Hence, they theorized that positive attitudes to ingroups enable people to bolster their self-esteem and negative attitudes to outgroups allow them to distance themselves from groups who threaten their self-esteem.

Variations in the salience of functions

Shavitt (1989) recognized that attitudes will generally serve a number of functions simultaneously. Other work suggests that the salience of these functions differs between people. Snyder and DeBono (1987), for example, have gained support for their proposal that people differ in their degree of **self-monitoring**. Those who strongly monitor their behaviour to tailor it to different situations and circumstances tend to use attitudes for social identity purposes. By contrast those who engage in less self-monitoring, whose behaviour mainly reflects their own moods and disposition, tend to use their attitudes for value-expression.

Cultural differences

Evidence for cultural differences in attitudes is provided by a study comparing commercial advertisements used in the USA and in Korea (Han and Shavitt 1993). Advertising slogans in the USA stressed individualism – 'The art of being unique', 'You, only better', 'A leader among leaders'. The slogans used in Korean advertisements stressed harmonious relatedness – 'We have a way of bringing people together', 'Sharing is beautiful', 'We devote ourselves to our contractors'. Han and Shavitt showed that US and Korean subjects did indeed respond differently to the two kinds of slogan. The US subjects preferred slogans that stressed individual values and the Korean subjects preferred those that centred on harmonious relationships. These differences have also been found in a study of political advertisements (Tak et al. 1997).

Results like these pose a challenge to experimental social psychology's theorization about the functions of attitudes, in that it tends to overemphasize the importance of functions serving self-esteem, and underemphasize those serving group esteem. I would therefore argue that it is more useful to define attitudes as having the following four functions:

- an **organizational function**, where, by categorizing objects in the social world along evaluative dimensions, attitudes act as guides to help people – as individuals and collectively – attend to these objects, understand them and feel about them
- an **instrumental function**, where attitudes direct people to act within the social world in ways that enable them to pursue their goals, both individual and collective
- an **expressive function**, where attitudes allow individuals and collectives to communicate their beliefs, opinions and values, and, thereby, to identify with those individuals and groups who share them
- an **esteem function**, that enables individuals and collectives to achieve and maintain status, respect and honour.

Attitudes and behaviour

In the 1930s a sociologist, Richard LaPiere, took a Chinese couple on a three-month trip across the USA. They stopped at a total of 251 places like hotels, auto camps and restaurants on the trip, and only once did the staff refuse to serve them, even though people in the USA were generally hostile toward the Chinese people at the time. 'It appeared that a genial smile was the most effective password to acceptance. My Chinese friends were skilful smilers,' commented LaPiere, 'which may account in part for the fact that we received but one rebuff in our experiences' (1934: 232). Yet when he later wrote to all the establishments and asked if they would be willing to 'accept members of the Chinese race as guests', of the half who replied, only one said yes, all the rest (92 per cent) said they would not.

LaPiere's study is often held up to show that attitudes do not predict behaviour, though this is hardly fair. Given that the people answering the letters were not those who actually served the Chinese couple, it was hardly a study of any individual's attitudes. It remains, however, that initial experimental attempts to link attitudes with behaviour were not very successful. Reviewing what was, bluntly, a pretty awful catalogue of failure, Wicker (1969) was highly pessimistic about the possibility of ever demonstrating a simple and reliable connection between the attitudes that people express and what they actually do. In another review, 20 years later, McGuire called this the continuing 'scandal of social psychology' (1986: 91).

Others (see, for example, Zanna and Fazio 1982) have been much more optimistic, arguing that in order for attitudes to predict behaviour, more thorough and subtle research design is necessary. Five main principles have been established:

1 The behaviour must be at the same level of specificity as the attitude.
2 The attitude must be held with sufficient strength to influence the behaviour.
3 The behaviour tested must be salient to the attitude at the time of testing.
4 There must be sufficient opportunities for people to act in response to the attitude.
5 Social desirability effects need to be excluded.

Attitudinal specificity

Many of the unsuccessful studies had tried to predict specific behaviour from very general attitudinal concepts. Fishbein and Ajzen (1975) have proposed a principle of correspondence – that attitudes and behaviour should be measured at the same level of specificity. When there is a high level of specificity in the behaviour observed, prediction is much better. Weigel et al. (1976), for instance, assessed people's attitudes to general ideas (such as attitudes to 'protecting the environment') and to more specific ideas (such as support for the Sierra Club, a specific organization working to protect the environment). They then gave subjects the opportunity to do volunteer work for the Sierra Club. Subjects' attitudes to protecting the environment in general were not predictive of volunteering, but support for the Sierra Club was.

Attitudinal strength

In most situations a person's behaviour will be influenced by a number of different attitudes, motives and concerns. For instance, Insko and Schopler (1967) demonstrated that although an individual may express strongly positive attitudes to the American Civil Rights movement, they may well not give money to support it because of a stronger concern to spend money on the needs of their family. Approval of the movement was insufficiently important to persuade someone to donate to it.

The relative strength of an attitude depends on a wide variety of factors (discussed in more detail in the section on attitude change). These include its power to invoke strong emotions, the extent to which the individual holding it is directly involved, and the conviction with which it is held (depending, for instance, on the source of information from which it is derived).

Attitudinal salience

Shavitt and Fazio (1991) gained evidence for the importance of salience using a priming technique. They examined students' attitudes to two drinks – 7-Up and Perrier. They hypothesized that 7-Up would be more appealing in terms of its taste, but Perrier more attractive in terms of its 'cool' image. They thus began the experiment by asking the students to rate food items on a 20-point scale, either on their 'taste' or their 'image'. They then assessed the students' attitudes towards the two drinks and their intention to buy them. Intention to buy proved a more effective measure. As predicted, students primed to focus on image evinced a significantly stronger intention to buy Perrier than 7-Up, whereas students primed to focus on taste stated a greater intention to buy 7-Up.

Behavioural opportunities

Many of the unsuccessful studies observed only a single behavioural expression of the attitude assessed. Given that there are many things that may influence behaviour in a particular circumstance, it is difficult to sufficiently exclude these extraneous variables to obtain a clear-cut result. Increasing the number of measures taken leads to far better predictability. In another study, examining attitudes to protecting the environment, Weigel and Newman (1976) gave **respondents** 14 separate opportunities to take pro-environmental action. These included opportunities to sign a number of petitions, to recycle their rubbish over several weeks and to recruit friends to do so too. While there were only limited (though often significant) correlations between overall support for the environment and individual pro-environment actions, an aggregate of compliance with all 14 actions yielded a strong correlation.

Excluding social desirability effects

People are often unwilling to act out their attitudes because to do so would show them in an unflattering light. As the behaviour of the hotel and restaurant owners in LaPiere's study showed, people generally do not act in a prejudiced manner when presented with specific people in specific situations, especially when to do so would transgress social rules (such as those of courtesy). A large number of studies have demonstrated that people have a strong tendency to act in ways that make them look good, called the **social desirability effect** (Rosenburg 1969).

In order to study attitudes that may reflect badly on someone, it is necessary to use a more sophisticated approach. A good example is the study by Gaertner and McLaughlin (1983) you met in Chapter 4. They studied racist behaviour using an implicit measure (reaction times to making judgements) and inferred racist attitudes from subjects taking longer to give a positive response to a pairing of Black–smart compared with White–smart.

Attitudes

Attitudes
- Are evaluations of attitude objects and operate at personal, interpersonal and intergroup levels.
- Have cognitive, emotional and behavioural components.
- Are measured using attitude scales; the best known is the Likert scale.
- Can be seen to have four main functions: organizational (categorizing knowledge), instrumental (guiding behaviour and cognition), expressive (for communication), and esteem (both personal and collective).

Attitudes and behaviour
- Attempts to predict behaviour from general attitudes were not successful.
- Predictability can be improved by excluding social undesirability effects, and/or increasing specificity or strength of the attitude, salience of the behaviour, or behavioural opportunities.
- Predictability can be further improved by combining assessment of attitudes with assessment of other variables such as social norms and values.

Attitude change

If attitudes are a preoccupation in social psychology, attitude change is not far short of an obsession. This arises in large part from its humaneering mission (Chapter 1) to 'make the world a better place', but also because it is a field in which social psychology's expertise can be applied to practical issues and concerns (such as advertising and political campaigning).

Cognitive consistency

Cognitive consistency is regarded as one of the main reasons why people change their attitudes. Cognitive consistency theory is based on the assumption that people will tend to organize their attitudes in ways that maintain consistency and, where inconsistencies arise, will act to restore equilibrium – for example, between the attitudes they hold towards issues and their attitudes to people.

Balance theory

Heider (1946) proposed an early version of this that he called **balance theory**. In it he proposed that people seek balance in their attitudes. For example, if a man wanted to take his girlfriend – of whom he is very fond – on a trip to New York, but knew she hated the place, there would be an imbalance between his affection for her and his desire to go to New York. So, to regain balance, he could adjust his attitude to New York ('Actually, I never liked the place that much'). Or he could modify his feelings about his girlfriend ('She's getting to be a bit of a killjoy'). Or he could try to persuade her what a great place New York was really ('It has great museums – you love museums'). Any one would bring things back into balance again.

Various studies (for example, Jordan 1953; Zajonc 1968a) have shown that people find balanced attitudinal situations more comfortable than unbalanced ones. Zajonc and Burnstein (1965) have also shown that people find balanced situations easier to process and remember. Balance theory has been used to explain why people tend to like others better if they share similar attitudes (see, for example, Newcomb 1961).

Cognitive consistency theory

People sometimes behave in ways that contradict their attitudes. During the Korean War, for instance, US soldiers were interned in Chinese prisoner-of war camps. At the start of their captivity they were strongly opposed to communism. During their time there, these soldiers were exposed to considerable pressure to reconsider their attitudes. On their return home, many of them said that, while it might not work in the USA, communism 'is a good thing for Asia' (Segal 1954).

Cognitive dissonance theory was devised to account for attitude change in such situations. Its originator, Leon Festinger (1957) argued that when people realize that they have acted in ways that conflict with their attitudes, they experience anxiety and tension. They need to deal with this, but they cannot go back and undo what they did. So they change the only thing they can change – their attitudes.

Festinger and Carlsmith (1959) tested this by conducting an experiment where subjects were first asked to do an incredibly boring and repetitive series of tasks. Once they had finished, the experimenter asked some of them to take the place of an assistant who had failed to turn up, who was supposed to motivate subjects in the next experimental condition. Their task was to convince the next subject that the tasks they were about to do would be interesting. There were three conditions: some subjects were not asked to lie at all, some subjects were paid $1 to lie, and some were paid $10 to lie. The subjects then all rated the experiment according to how much they enjoyed doing it. Those who did not lie and those paid $10 to lie reported enjoying the experiment, on average, at about the same level (that is, not much!). Those, however, who lied and were only paid $1 rated the experiment as significantly more enjoyable.

Payment is not the only way to manipulate dissonance. Studies of **group initiation** have also shown cognitive dissonance effects. Aronson and Mills (1959), for instance, found that those women who experienced a **severe initiation** on joining a group discussion rated a taped discussion as significantly more interesting than either those who underwent no initiation or the mild initiation (who did not differ significantly from each other).

Since Festinger first proposed the theory, there has been extensive research into the process of cognitive dissonance. This has led to considerable clarification of the elements involved. The inconsistent act must:

- *Matter*: While some recent research suggests that inconsistency is enough in itself (for example, Johnson et al. 1995; Harmon-Jones et al. 1996), a much larger number show that the inconsistency needs to have negative consequences (see, for example, Scher and Cooper 1989). In particular, actions that damage self-esteem or self-worth have been found to have most impact on attitudes (see, for example, Steele 1988). We may surmise that in relational-self cultures, undermining of group worth or violation of group honour would have the strongest effects.

- *Be volitional*: When coerced or merely lavishly rewarded for acting inconsistently, there is no dissonance because the person can explain away their behaviour. Festinger and Carlsmith's (1959) study is a good example here.

- *Make the person anxious*: Croyle and Cooper (1983) tested this by attaching electrodes to subjects' fingers to measure their arousal while they were writing counter-attitudinal essays. They found that indeed, only in dissonance conditions (that is, where subjects believed they were freely choosing to write the essays) were levels of arousal raised.

- *Be seen as the cause of the anxiety*: This has been demonstrated in a number of studies. Pittman (1975), for example, tricked subjects into believing the anxiety they felt was due to having to wear prism goggles while writing the essay. In this situation there was no attitude change.

Social cognition models of behaviour change

Social psychologists working from the social cognition perspective have created a number of models of behaviour change (sometimes called **expectancy-value models**, though I call them 'cognitive algebra') and assume that people decide between alternative courses of action through estimating the probabilities for each possible action that it will bring about benefits and/or avoid negative consequences to themselves.

In other words, these models assume that people will act to optimize the consequences of their behaviour, based on their own views about which outcomes are most valuable. Here we will look at three of these models;

- the theory of reasoned action
- the theory of planned behaviour
- the stages of change model.

The theory of reasoned action

The best known of these theoretical models was developed by Ajzen and Fishbein (see, for example, Ajzen and Fishbein 1972; Fishbein and Ajzen 1975). In its initial formulation it was called the **theory of reasoned action**. The model differed in a number of ways from the assumption that attitudes simply trigger behaviour. First, it did not try to predict behaviour but rather the behavioural intentions that are assumed to mediate behaviour. Second, it acknowledged that attitudes are not the sole drivers determining behaviour. So the model includes a person's appraisal of what they think others will expect them to do (social norms) and their motivation to comply with these norms, and also takes account of a person's beliefs about the consequences of the behaviour and their evaluation of those consequences (values). The model is illustrated in Figure 8.1.

Figure 8.1 Schematic illustration of Ajzen and Fishbein's theory of reasoned action, applied to stopping smoking

Source: After Gergen and Gergen 1981

According to this model, an individual's intention to perform a given act can be worked out mathematically, by calculating the contributions to decision making from two main sources:

- Attitudes towards performing the act, calculated by multiplying measures of their beliefs about outcomes and of their evaluation of the benefits of outcomes
- **Subjective norms**, calculated by measures of what they think others expect them to do (normative beliefs) multiplied by measures of their motivation to comply.

The theory of reasoned action has been shown to be much better at predicting a variety of behavioural intentions and behaviour than a simple attitude scale on its own. Examples include studies on health-related behaviours (as illustrated above) and consumer choices.

The theory of planned behaviour

The theory of planned behaviour was developed in order to fine-tune predictability. Ajzen (1991) extended the scope of the model to include an additional element – perceived behavioural control. This was done to recognize that in some situations people have only a limited ability to control what they are able to do. This model is shown in Figure 8.2.

Ajzen tested this new model in a study examining US business students' behavioural intentions towards and actual achievement of gaining an A grade in an examination (Ajzen and

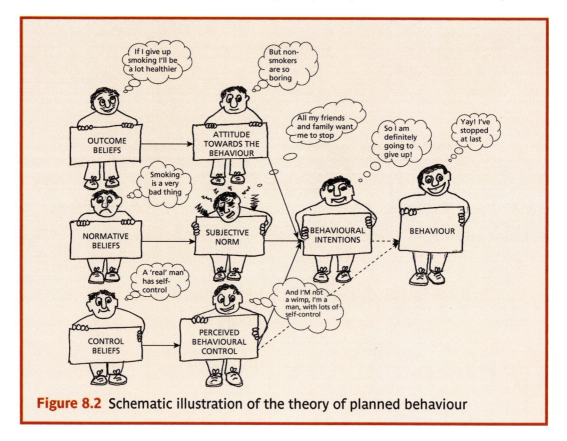

Figure 8.2 Schematic illustration of the theory of planned behaviour

Madden 1986). They hypothesized that estimates of behavioural control – whether or not they thought they could get an A – would improve predictability, and it did, both in terms of behavioural intention and behaviour. Further, they hypothesized that early in the semester the students would not be able to predict their level of behavioural control as well as they could closer to the examination. This, too, was confirmed in both cases. However, estimates of behavioural control are found to be less salient in situations where it is much easier to achieve the behaviour in question, such as attending a meeting (Kelly and Breinlinger 1995).

Stages of change model

This is model was devised by Prochaska and DiClemente in 1986. It is sometimes called the transtheoretical model as it brought together 15 different theoretical constructs (Sutton 2001) to provide a comprehensive framework for understanding how behaviour can be changed. Over time Prochaska and DiClemente modified and improved it, and by 1992, it had been turned into a model of stages of change, as shown in Figure 8.3.

This model has possibly become one of the best known, especially in applied settings where it is used to plan and deliver interventions to bring about behaviour change – such as helping people to overcome their addiction to drugs, alcohol and cigarettes.

Persuasion

Persuasion is where a deliberate attempt is made to change people's attitudes and is concerned with the cognitive processes involved in how that change is brought about. As with issues around the link between attitudes and behaviour, it is generally agreed among experimental social psychologists that persuasion works differently according to the level of processing involved in the change process (Petty and Cacioppo 1981).

Persuasion via automatic processing

While some attitudinal responses involve conscious judgements (Wilson and Hodges 1992), often attitudes are triggered unconsciously and automatically (Bargh et al. 1992). This kind of 'automatic' attitude change may affect other judgements without the person being aware of its influence. One interesting example is that people in the USA tend to like the letters in their own name better than other letters (Nuttin 1985). Such attitudes are called **implicit attitudes**. As you saw in Chapter 7 in relation to attribution, **automatic processing** is where people take in information and respond to it with little conscious awareness or cognitive effort.

Early theorists drew from learning theory to suggest that attitudes can be changed through the process of conditioning, where associative links are made between two otherwise unrelated things. Music, for example, can be very good at creating a 'feel-good' association, and has been shown to favourably influence approval ratings of products (Galzio and Hendrick 1972). Even quite trivial and fleeting associations can have an effect. Copper et al. (1993) demonstrated this by showing subjects simulated news broadcasts reporting on political candidates, where they varied whether or not the 'reporter' smiled when mentioning each candidate. While the subjects' evaluations of the candidates tended mainly to reflect their own political allegiances, the smiles also had a small but significant positive impact. Smiles associated with the opponent candidate led subjects to give a slightly better rating to him, and a slightly worse rating to their preferred candidate.

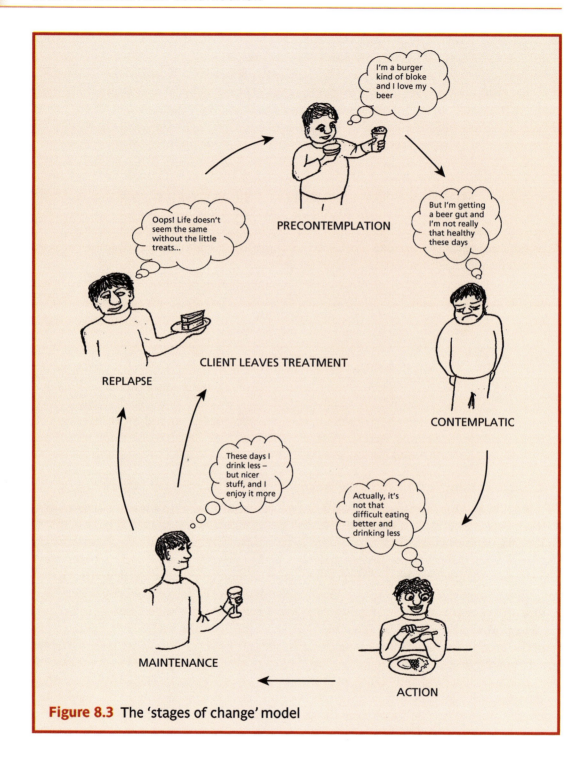

Figure 8.3 The 'stages of change' model

Operant conditioning is where people change their behaviour in response to either a regime of rewards (called reinforcement) or punishments (negative reinforcement). An early example is where Hildum and Brown (1956) interviewed students about their attitudes to university policies. In one condition they rewarded subjects for agreeing with the policies during the interview. Every time the student said anything good about the policies, the interviewer made approving noises ('Yes', 'Right' or just 'Mm-hmm'). In the other condition students were rewarded whenever they criticized university policies. Students' views on university policies were then evinced and, sure enough, those who had been rewarded for criticizing the policies in the interview reported less favourable attitudes to the policies than those students who had been rewarded for agreeing with them.

Beware experimenter effects!

Effects like those shown in the last two studies bring home how easy it is for a researcher to influence what participants in a study say and do – called **experimenter effects**. Even though an experimenter may not intend to 'give the game away', they can do so in all sorts of subtle ways. Survey interviewers are trained, for example, to give only neutral rejoinders to interviewees' responses, in order not to contaminate the results.

A final example of automatic processing is **heuristic processing**, where people are induced to change their attitudes through their tendency to resort to simple 'rules of thumb' to assess the quality of information they are given. Examples include 'What looks good is good', 'If I feel good, it must be good', 'I agree with people I like', 'I trust people who are credible' and 'The majority is usually right'.

Just as with the other examples of automatic processing, a person does not need to be aware of using heuristics and is frequently not. Heuristics are most generally used when someone has little motivation or opportunity to get bogged down in careful deliberation – they follow the 'principle of least cognitive effort' (Bohner et al. 1995). People often assume that 'what is beautiful is good', for example (Dion et al. 1972). Mere physical attractiveness in a person tends to lead to approval of that person in general – they are seen as more able, more confident and more trustworthy (Eagly et al. 1991 provide a review of the evidence). Advertisements often use popular celebrities – who, by definition, are chosen because they are attractive to particular consumer groups – to endorse their products, working on both the 'what is beautiful is good' and the 'I agree with people I like' heuristics. Empirical evidence for the effects of these heuristics on attitudes has been provided, for instance, by Chaiken (1987).

There have also been numerous studies demonstrating the effectiveness of the 'I trust people who are credible' heuristic in changing attitudes. An early study by Hovland and Weiss (1951) varied the credibility of the person communicating a message intended to influence attitudes, and found that people tend to be more swayed by the expertise of the message-giver rather than the arguments used.

Persuasion via depth-processing

Two models have been developed here, one building on the other. The first, a communication model, had its origins in information theory approaches. As this got refined, the focus moved to its cognitive elements. There was then a shift to a cognitive response model.

The communication model

The importance of in-depth processing for attitude change was first conceptualized as a matter of communication. Hovland and his colleagues (1953) identified three key aspects of communication that relate to persuasion: the source of the message (the communicator), the message and the audience (see Chapter 6) and argued that factors pertaining to each have the capacity to determine whether attitudes can be changed:

- The source – the *communicator* – can vary, for example, in terms of their expertise, trustworthiness, **attractiveness** and so on, and in how they deliver the message (how articulate they are or how clearly or quickly they speak).
- The *message* can differ, for example, in terms of the strength of its arguments, the order in which they are presented, its contents and whether, for instance, it simply promotes a single viewpoint or offers a balanced appraisal.
- The *audience* can vary, for instance, in terms of people's self-esteem, their self-interest or whether they feel they are being manipulated or not.

Hovland and his colleagues identified four stages in the persuasion process:

Attention → Comprehension → Acceptance → Retention

This research went on for more than 30 years, during which time they gradually documented how each of the three aspects affected the different processes (see Petty and Cacioppo 1981 for a review). Some of their findings have proved robust – for example, that expert communicators tend to gain message acceptance better than non-experts (Hovland and Weiss 1951) and that attractive communicators are more effective than unattractive ones (Kiesler and Kiesler 1969). But other findings have proven less so. Janis (1954) claimed to show that people with low self-esteem were easier to persuade than people with high self-esteem. However, subsequent work (Baumeister and Covington 1985) has suggested that this is not so. Their claim is that people with high self-esteem are persuaded, but they are less prepared to admit it.

What has endured is an acceptance within experimental social psychology that persuasion works in stages, where a series of steps need to follow one from the other to bring about attitude change. There are disagreements about what are the most crucial stages and how they work, but there is a fair consensus that the audience needs to pay attention to the message, understand its contents and actively consider what it signifies for them (Eagly and Chaiken 1984).

The cognitive response model

The approach that focuses on this latter stage – the active consideration of what the message signifies – shifted theorization about attitudes into the social cognition paradigm, where it has been developed as a cognitive response model of persuasion (see, for example, Greenwald 1968). Its assumptions are as follows:

- People actively relate the content of the message to their prior knowledge about the attitude object and their current attitude towards it. In so doing they make cognitive responses – new ideas or thoughts about the attitude object.
- It is these cognitive responses that mediate attitude change.
- The degree and direction of the change are determined by the overall number and direction of the cognitive responses. If, on balance, there are more that are favourable to the new argument than unfavourable, then attitude change will happen.

Processing level models of persuasion

As with attribution theory, since the 1980s most research in this field has been based on a re-cognition that persuasion generally involves two kinds of processing: superficial processing and in-depth processing. In the attitude field, two alternative, processing level models have been devised: an elaboration likelihood model and a heuristic–semantic model.

The elaboration likelihood model

This model proposes that persuasion works via two routes: a central route that involves active, purposive, in-depth processing, and a peripheral route that operates via mindless processing such as conditioning or the use of heuristics. The two are seen as antagonistic to each other (Petty and Cacioppo 1986). According to this model, generally the peripheral route wins out, since people mostly go about their lives more or less on 'automatic', filtering out the messages with which they are bombarded. Only in exceptional situations do they stop to really think about a message they receive – situations where they are motivated and able to pay attention to it.

Motivation and opportunity thus create the conditions that encourage people to elaborate. However, when they do, the impact on their attitudes is stronger and more durable. An example is where a communicator is somebody important to you, and they express an unexpected opinion at variance to your own. The research studies conducted to develop this theory were complex and subtle, and beyond the scope of this chapter. Bohner (2001) provides a detailed review of them.

The heuristic–systematic model

This model claims that when people have to evaluate something they strive for sufficient confidence to make an informed decision:

- When they feel confident of their attitudes, people are not motivated to process in-depth, and rely on heuristic processing (that is, habitual 'rules of thumb') as long as they have a heuristic cue to act as a trigger.
- When they are ambivalent or uncertain, people are more likely to turn to in-depth **systematic processing** as long as the arguments in the message are strong and unambiguous.

In this model the threshold at which uncertainty 'kicks in' is seen to differ according to circumstances. When the judgement is important or personally very relevant, then the threshold will be low and hence systematic processing more likely. When buying a house or a car, for example, people usually devote considerable effort to making their choice. But when the judgement is trivial – such as choosing which flavour of ice cream to have for supper – then heuristics are more likely to carry the day. That is, unless it is somebody important coming for supper and you need to impress them! Again, the studies conducted to develop this model have been subtle and detailed, and Bohner's review is the place to go if you want to know more.

Attitude change

- Cognitive consistency is where people change their attitude in line with unwarranted counter-attitudinal behaviour – for example, lie without sufficient justification.
- For it to work, the inconsistent act must matter, must be chosen, must make the person anxious, and must be explicitly associated with the anxiety.
- Models of behaviour changed include the *theory of reasoned action*, the *theory of planned behaviour* and the *stages of change model*.
- Persuasion is where attempts are deliberately made to change behaviour through changing attitudes. Recent theorization suggests that persuasion can work in one of two ways, through:
  - Automatic attitude processes where, for example, associations are made between the attitude object and 'feel good' music; or where heuristics (such as 'what is beautiful is good') are triggered. These are relatively easy to achieve, but tend to have a superficial effect.
  - In-depth attitude processes where, for example, conditions are arranged so that people attend to persuasive messages. These are harder to achieve, but tend to have a stronger and more enduring effect.
- Different mechanisms have been suggested to explain what it is that determines whether processing is automatic or in-depth.

Critical approaches to attitudes and attitude change

You will not be surprised to hear that critical psychologists in general and discursive psychologists in particular have been very critical of the work conducted by experimental social psychologists into attitudes and attitude change. This final section begins by summarizing these criticisms, and then illustrates the alternative ways of understanding how and why people may change their behaviour. In particular, critical social psychologists challenge the idea that attitudes work mechanically – like turning a key as you do with a clockwork toy to make it work.

Discursive psychology's criticisms

Jonathan Potter and Margaret Wetherell gave their ground-breaking 1987 book on discourse analysis the subtitle *Beyond Attitudes and Behaviour*. In it they argued for a new way to understand attitudes and their relationship to behaviour.

Social cognition models consider attitudes to be internal cognitive entities within individual minds, that perform like levers to 'turn on' and 'turn off' behaviour. Discursive approaches think about this quite differently – behaviour is seen as a complex of social practices – particular actions done in particular circumstances and settings.

More recently Potter (1996) has criticized attitude research and theorization under four main headings:

- atomism
- individualism
- variability with context
- ignoring the question of what attitudes are for.

Atomism

Potter argues that 'attitudes are often assumed to be scattered around in people's heads, rather like currants in a fruitcake' (Potter 1996: 135). Discursive psychologists then ask the question – why? Their answer is that this is pragmatic rather than theoretical. The requirements of experimental method mean it is a lot easier to *study* processes and phenomena in fragmented, atomistic ways. But that does not mean that attitudes actually *work* in isolation, merely that the experimental work on attitudes treated them as discrete.

Potter is especially critical about the social cognition models. He says they do not work and argues that they cannot work. Even when extended to include extra elements (such as values, social norms and expectations) as well as attitudes, they are still not really able to predict behaviour, he says. You can make richer fruitcakes (containing cherries and nuts as well as currants) but they still consist of isolated 'things' working independently from each other. By contrast, discursive psychology views all the various ideas and motivations as interconnected and interrelating with each other in meaningful and systematic ways. More on this later.

Individualism

Potter also challenges the individualism of attitude research and theory. By assuming that attitudes are, at base, held in individual minds and merely 'influenced' by factors such as social norms and expectations, he points out that attitude researchers have studied them almost exclusively at an individual level. Yet, as you saw in Chapter 6, meaning operates intersubjectively – in the ways people converse with one another, and our attitudes are informed by advertising, argument and persuasion.

Variability with context

Potter's strongest criticism, however, is that attitude research and theory cannot deal with variability. To see what he is getting at, let us look once more at the extract from Potter and Wetherell's (1987) discourse analytic study of racism that you met in Chapter 5.

Extract 2

What I would li . . . rather see is that, sure, bring them into New Zealand, right, try and train them in a skill, and encourage them to go back again.

Extract 3

I think that if we encouraged more Polynesians and Maoris to be skilled people they would want to stay here, they're not, um, as, uh, nomadic as New Zealanders are [interviewer laughs] so I think that would be better.

The two extracts are taken from subsequent pages of a person's interview transcript. Potter and Wetherell (1987) comment that examples like this display not so much 'variability' but stark contradiction. They then go on to argue:

> The variability in people's discourse cannot be explained merely as a product of a more complex, multi-faceted attitudinal structure which a more complex scale can assess, because the views expressed vary so radically from occasion to occasion. It is impossible to argue that the claim Polynesian immigration is desirable, and the claim that it is undesirable, are merely facets of one complex attitude. The notion of enduring attitudes, even multidimensional ones, simply cannot deal with this.
>
> (Potter and Wetherell 1987: 53)

Ignoring the question of what attitudes are for

Potter concludes his argument by pointing to one final 'blind spot' in traditional attitude work – which is what people use their attitudinal evaluations for. Early theorizing proposed a whole range of different functions of attitudes – seen as organizational (enabling the categorization of knowledge), as instrumental (guiding behaviour and cognition and helping people to pursue their goals) as expressive (for communicating with oneself and others) and useful for esteem purposes, both personal and collective.

Yet attitude researchers today, he says, have come to virtually ignore these other functions. They have become completely preoccupied with just two things – working out how and when attitudes can be predictive, and working out how attitudes can be changed. They seem to have almost entirely lost sight of questions about what people do when they express attitudes – and what they want to achieve.

The discursive practices approach reconnects with this question. It is not at all interested in whether attitudes predict behaviour. Its concern is with, for example, the way that expressing an attitude can enable someone to justify a particular behaviour, course of action or policy. Kitzinger and Frith's (1999) conversation analysis study you met in Chapter 5 was crucially concerned with the ways in which certain behaviours can be warranted by a particular discursive strategy. In their analysis, when a man refuses to acknowledge a hedged refusal to his sexual advances *as* a refusal, he is doing so for a purpose – to justify pursuing his advances.

Behaviour as social action and social practice

Even from the beginning, critics from within mainstream psychology have complained about the social cognition models of behaviour change, pointing out that they are actually not at all effective at predicting behaviour change. In the 1980s, McGuire, for example, called it 'a scandal of social psychology' (McGuire 1986). I myself was part of this movement, though newly recruited into the 'critical camp'.

> It is hardly surprising that you can predict fairly accurately what somebody will do if you ask them just before they do it whether they think it is a good idea, if they think other people will approve and whether they care what people think. It is even less surprising that you can improve predictability by introducing mathematical variables (i.e. weightings) to do just that. But getting consistent answers does not mean that you understand very much about their thinking except at a very trivial level.
>
> (Stainton Rogers 1991: 53)

Ogden (2003) makes a similar point, giving as an example of what is going on the wording from questions asked about snacking. Participants had to answer a question to assess perceived behavioural control and another on their behavioural intentions, listed within other questions:

Perceived behavioural control question   'How easy or difficult will it be for you to avoid between-meal intake of sugared snacks and drinks in the future?'

Behavioural intention question   'How likely or unlikely is it that you will avoid between-meal intake of sugared snacks and drinks in the future?'

Try it for yourself

Imagine if you were asked questions like this. How likely would you be to give the same answer? Indeed, are they not the same question just written in a slightly different form?

Reflect a bit on the way these have been taken out of context. You maybe thought to yourself, 'it all depends'.

What is so shocking is that this kind of research persists today and shows no sign of abating – take a look in the high-end social psychology journals and you will still find plenty of papers that are tinkering around with these models.

In a paper specifically criticizing social cognition models of health behaviour as used in health psychology, Mielewczyk and Willig (2007) weave a clever story about how these psychologists cling on to their 'old clothes' instead of going for a radical makeover, which, they say, is what is really needed. The authors get a lot of fun out of using this metaphor, talking about baubles and beads, crinolines and corsets. But they also get down to being serious about what is wrong.

> the overwhelming majority of the investigations conducted ... have adopted a single theoretical framework and, as a result, a single methodological approach: the literature in this area is dominated by applications of models in which social cognitions such as attitudes and control beliefs are combined and assessed according to specific algorithms aimed at maximizing the proportions of variance explainable (by means of multiple regression analyses) in the performance of target health behaviours.
>
> (Mielewczyk and Willig 2007: 812)

Earlier Ingham (1993) had described this as being like an adult who has to go through all manner of contortions to continue wearing the clothes they first bought as teenagers. Mielewczyk and Willig take up this metaphor with glee:

> social cognition researchers have been reluctant to abandon the old clothes, preferring instead to make repeated adjustments to their darts and waistbands (i.e. to the definition and measurement of their component variables) and to dress them up with a variety of beads, baubles and bangles (in the form of supplementary variables) in the ongoing struggle to improve both their fit and their appearance.
>
> (Mielewczyk and Willig 2007: 812)

Mielewczyk and Willig then go on to spell out what is wrong with this modelling and offer a critical psychological alternative. But, before we look at that, it is worth noting that the social cognition camp is itself far from consensual. Vociferous infighting goes on in the journals, as proponents of the different models (or even different versions of the same model!) vie for credibility and dominance. As just one example, the *stages of change model* (Prochaska and DiClemente 1983) has been targeted for attack, with a stream of papers given titles like 'Breakthrough or bandwagon?' (Ashworth 1997); 'When popularity outstrips the evidence' (Herzog 2005); 'Back to the drawing board' (Sutton 2001) and 'Another nail in the coffin of the transtheoretical model?' (Sutton 2005).

Not behaviour but social practice

Critical psychologists argue that the reason why the social cognition models have such trouble predicting 'health behaviour' is because 'health behaviour' is a fabrication – a made-up phenomenon. Health behaviours are theorized and written about as if they are 'easily identifiable, unitary entities whose meaning does not change across the diverse contexts and settings within which they may be carried out' (Mielewczyk and Willig 2007: 824).

But they are not. Take 'condom use', a so-called 'health-related behaviour' that experimental social psychologists have invented by totally cutting it off from the time, place and occasion in which it is done, and lacking in any salience and meaning. Now compare this with research that looks at how people use or do not use condoms in very specific settings.

A condom can be 'a moment killer' (Williamson et al. 2009) that gets avoided because using one ruins the experience: 'And then all the magazines that tell you they can become a fun part of foreplay. Lies! Lies! They're the worst things. I've been having sex since I was 14 years old and I still can't put one on somebody properly' ('Kathy', quoted in Williamson et al. 2009: 564). This is a very different setting from why someone avoids even raising the possibility of using a condom, because in a long-lasting, committed relationship to do so can scream 'I don't trust you': 'Because it's a very tricky thing, there's pride and there's suspicion and there's jealousy and there's all these terrible things, all mixed up together, and these are the things that kill a marriage, and therefore it's very delicate ground that you are treading on' (cited in Willig 1995: 81).

Just these two examples say it all, for me at least. But there are many other possibilities, including women's concerns that carrying condoms can make them 'look like a slag'; men's anxiety about how putting them on can make them lose their erection; and finding they cause allergic reactions. All of these come over as perfectly understandable reasons, none of which have much at all to do with attitudes about 'safe sex' being a sensible way of protecting your own health and that of your partner.

As Mielewczyk and Willig point out, 'health-related behaviours acquire their meaning and significance on the basis of their relationship to the particular social practice of which they form a part and that, therefore, what appears to be the "same" behaviour can take on radically different meanings within different contexts' (2007: 829). The core idea promoted in their paper is that instead of trying to predict health-related actions in an experiment that smoothes out all of the context and meaning, it is better to examine the social practices within which actions like using/not using condoms take place.

What we are seeing now is a proliferation of critical social psychological research that takes 'social action' and/or 'social practice' as its core concepts.

discursive social psychology has replaced the traditional attitude construct by identifying discursive practices and resources that are drawn upon in everyday talk when people express opinions, argue and debate. . . . From this perspective, talk and discourse are viewed as *social practices* and are analysed with the aim of showing how various linguistic resources and rhetorical devices constitute particular constructions of reality.

(Auguostinos et al. 2006: 142, emphasis in the original)

Sarah Riley and her colleagues' (2006) work on men's attitudes to gender inequality illustrates this new approach well. In it she interviewed professional men about gender and inequality in the workplace. She found two main discourses in play – one about 'equality' that argued that everyone should be treated the same, completely ignoring who they are; and another about 'individual merit', saying that promotion should be given to those whose performance shows they deserve it. Riley pointed out that they both operate in abstract terms, stripped of context or any recognition that there might be hidden advantages that benefit only some groups and not others. This is manifested in antagonism towards any suggestion that there should be any positive action to help women overcome historical disadvantages. Riley's study shows how the expression of opinions can be understood within the social practices going on within the workplace, where particular discursive resources are used to pursue particular arguments in order to achieve particular outcomes – in this case to resist all forms of positive discrimination.

Critical approaches to attitudes and attitude change

- Critical approaches see attitude theory is failing because it:
  - sees attitudes as located in people's individual minds, operating as one of a number of social cognitive processes
  - views different attitudes as operating independently from each other, and separate from any social setting and circumstances
  - cannot account for what goes on when a person is ambivalent in their attitudes, or even faces conflict between them.
- Critical social psychologists do not see attitudes as manifested by categories of behaviour (such as snacking or using a condom). Rather they look at them as specific forms of social action that take place within broader social practices.
- This means that the same overt act (such as using or not using a condom) can only be understood in terms of the context within which it takes place, and that it can have very different meanings and significance within different social practices.
- Critical social psychologists criticize the mainstream for being preoccupied with studying attitude change and attitude-behaviour links and ignoring more important questions about the functions that attitudes serve.

Resources

Attitudes

You have to register to use this website but it is free. It offers you access to the British Social Attitudes survey data, and interesting and useful information about questionnaires used: http://www.britsocat.com/Body.aspx?control=HomePage

Further reading

Experimental social psychology

Hogg, M.A. and Vaughan, G.M. (2008) *Social Psychology*, **5th edn. Harlow: Pearson/Prentice Hall.**
This provides in Chapter 5 'Attitudes' the standard, highly detailed and conventional account of attitudes from the experimental perspective. It is an up-to-date and a readable source for gaining an in-depth understanding of the mainstream approach. The same goes for Chapter 6, 'Persuasion and attitude change'. However, there are a number of aspects not covered, so if you want to get a fully comprehensive understanding of mainstream thinking here, you would also need to consult the book below.

Haddock, G. and Maio, G.R. (2001) Attitude: content, structure and functions, and Stroebe, W. (2001) Strategies of attitude and behaviour change, both in M. Hewstone, W. Stroebe and K. Jonas (eds) *Introduction to Social Psychology: A European Perspective*, **4th edn. Oxford: Blackwell.**
These two chapters have been remodelled from the previous edition and, written by leading European social psychologists, give a much better account of recent work in Europe.

Myers, D., Abell, J., Kolstad, A. and Sani, F. (2010) *Social Psychology: European Edition.* **London: McGraw-Hill.**
This European version of a US textbook takes a rather different approach to attitudes and behaviour change from more standard textbooks like the two above. Chapter 5, 'Attitudes and behaviour', takes a negative view of models that claim attitudes can predict behaviour, and opens up discussion on how behaviour can influence attitudes. It also briefly covers the 'social action' approach, mainly based on Potter and Wetherell's approach.

Critical social psychology

Potter, J. and Wetherell, M. (1987) *Discourse and Social Psychology: Beyond Attitudes and Behaviour.* **London: Sage.**
This is where it all began, the book that challenged the dominance of attitude theory and theories of behaviour changed linked with attitudes in psychology, and offered up not only critique but a whole new way of addressing these issues.

Potter, J. (1996) Attitudes, social representations and discursive psychology, in M. Wetherell (ed.) *Identities, Groups and Social Issues*. London: Sage.
This more recent and much shorter account of the arguments against the mainstream approach is a lot easier to get your head around.

Mielewczyk, M. and Willig, C. (2007) Old clothes and an older look: the case for a radical makeover in health, *Theory Psychology*, 17: 811–37.
This paper is surprisingly easy to read. The authors have worked hard to make some difficult ideas clear and understandable, mainly through good use of examples from research studies.

Questions

1 Outline the origins of attitude theory, including a description of what attitudes are, how they are formed and their functions.

2 Under what circumstances can attitudes predict behaviour?

3 Describe what is meant by cognitive consistency and how it is a useful concept for understanding how and why people change their behaviour.

4 If you wanted to plan an advertising campaign for a new product, how could different-process models of attitude change help?

5 Outline the main criticisms of attitude theory raised by critical social psychologists. Illustrate your answer with specific examples.

6 Describe three social cognition models of behaviour change. Based on an Internet search, write your own critique of this approach. You can choose to endorse the approach, or to challenge it. Either way you will be assessed on the power of your argument.

7 Identify a recent journal article that reports a study of attitude change. Briefly outline what was done and its findings, and then give your own evaluation of its strengths and weaknesses.

8 Identify a recent journal article that reports a study of health-related action (of any kind) approached as social action, within one or more situated social practice(s). Briefly outline what was done and its findings, and then give your own evaluation of its strengths and weaknesses.

9 'Social psychologists – like all academics – just sit in their little rooms in their ivory towers, writing stuff nobody wants to read and really nobody cares about.' What would you say to challenge somebody who held a view like this?

SECTION 4

Social identities and relationships

Chapter 9

Values

LEARNING OUTCOMES

When you have finished studying this chapter, you should be able to:

1 Outline Rokeach's formulations about values as an object for social psychological study, including how they differ from attitudes, their functions and their different kinds.

2 Summarize Rokeach's research into the links between values and political affiliation and action.

3 Describe cross-cultural studies of values conducted by Hofstede, the Chinese Culture Connection and Schwartz.

4 Explain in detail the differences between individualistic and collectivist cultures, and some of the implications for social psychological theory and research.

5 Define 'intellectual imperialism', give examples and say why social psychologists need to be careful not to fall into this trap.

6 Outline the main issues raised by two key cultural dimensions – traditional/secular and survival/self-expression – and make a critical appraisal of these concepts.

7 Specify the different approach taken by critical social psychologists, illustrating this by reference to a study on the way values influence 'grandmothering' as a social practice.

Values/attitudes

What do you think would be the difference between the two claims in the cartoon? Using this as a starting point, think about what marks out one from the other. Then ask yourself whether it is attitudes or values that are most important in determining how we behave.

Now have a look at the differences by the psychologist, Milton Rokeach, set out in Table 9.1. How did his analysis compare with yours? You probably also found some differences, and agree with Rokeach that values are much more deep-seated than attitudes, more fundamental.

Introduction

Do you, like me, find all this a bit strange? The study of attitudes covered in the previous chapter has been a key area of research and theory in experimental social psychology since Allport began working on them in the 1930s. It remains a massively important topic in social psychology. Values are hardly mentioned and social psychology students are seldom taught about values. And yet it is generally acknowledged among attitude theorists that attitudes have their *foundation* in

Table 9.1 Rokeach's differentiation between attitudes and values

Attitudes	Values
A person has thousands of attitudes	A person has only a few dozen values at most
Attitudes are the organization of several beliefs around a specific object	Each value consists of a single, specific belief
Attitudes are composed of many different kinds of beliefs	Values tell us what to do and what not to do – they implicate action
Attitudes are ephemeral – they can vary quite a lot according to context, circumstance and even mood	Values have 'a transcendental quality' – they operate consistently across objects and across situations
Attitudes can be changed relatively easily, and often quickly – sometimes in a few seconds or minutes	Values seldom undergo change, and when they do, the change usually takes much longer – weeks or months
Attitudes are specific	Values are broad in their scope – they are general standards against which attitudes are judged
Attitudes are superficial	Values are foundational and perform a central organizing role in cognition
Attitudes are reflexive and responsive – they tend to react to situations	Values are dynamic, playing a central role in motivation and hence in directing behaviour
Attitudes only serve tangential functions in relation to identity and esteem	Values serve central and highly influential functions in relation to identity and esteem

Source: Based on Rokeach (1976)

values. Values are 'the consistent, personal assumptions we make which underpin our attitudes' (Hayes 1993: 93). These days the study of values has mainly been diverted off into applied fields such as political and cross-cultural psychology and market research.

I think part of the problem is that the study of attitudes fits neatly with the focus on what goes on within each individual's cognitive system, as you saw in the previous chapter. It's all about models of internal mental processes (I call them cognitive algebra models; Stainton Rogers 1991: 52). The study of values, by contrast, is about what goes on *collectively*, a matter of **intersubjectivity**, within families, religious, political and ideological communities, and cultures big and small. A person's values are instilled into them by their upbringing, their education, their peer group, the systems that govern them, both institutional (such as the law) and commercial (such as the market). Values reflect:

- time – in terms of the historical period in which people live
- place – their location in terms of its geography, its economy, its politics, its resources
- identity – how they are positioned in terms of things like gender, sexuality, class and inclusion/exclusion, majority/minority status.

Milton Rokeach bucked this trend. To understand why he did, it helps to know that he studied for his doctorate at Berkeley at the time (the 1960s) and the place (California, USA) when a new, post-Second World War generation were getting into 'flower power', civil rights and 'make love not war'. He was a member of a group studying the authoritarian personality (see Chapter 10). This was clearly influential on his choice of values as his main area of study. His doctorate was on rigidity in thinking and its links to prejudice, and his work on values was an attempt to pursue this broad agenda, but in ways that were more comprehensive than a specific focus on deviant and dysfunctional thinking.

Led by his example, this chapter is devoted to looking at values, starting from Rokeach's work and then looking at more recent theory and research examining the ways that values vary from one culture to another. As you will discover in Chapter 10, this has a substantial impact on the way people make sense of their identity. It also informs our understanding of prejudice, covered in Chapter 13. I hope by the time you have finished reading this chapter you will agree that it is an important topic you need to know about and understand to be able to get to grips with the chapters that follow.

Rokeach's theory and study of values

Rokeach formally defined a **value** as 'an enduring belief that a specific mode of conduct or end-state of existence is personally or socially preferable to [its] . . . opposite or converse mode'. He defined a **value system** as an 'enduring organization of beliefs concerning preferable modes of conduct or end-states of existence along a continuum of relative importance' (Rokeach 1976: 345). However, he pointed out that 'enduring' has to be seen as relative: '[i]f values were completely stable, individual and social change would be impossible. If values were completely unstable, continuity of human personality and society would be impossible' (Rokeach 1976: 345).

In so doing, Rokeach is making it clear that values are not simply the possessions of individuals, but also operate at a much broader social and cultural level.

> Values are the cognitive representation not only of individual needs but also of societal and institutional demands. They are the joint results of sociological as well as psychological forces acting upon the individual – sociological because society and its institutions socialize the individual for the common good to internalize shared conceptions of the desirable; psychological because individual motivations require cognitive expression, justification and, indeed, exhortation in socially desirable terms.
>
> (Rokeach 1976: 257)

Functions of values

Rokeach listed a number of different ways in which values guide our thinking and conduct. I have modified his list, relating it directly to issues of concern to contemporary social psychology and expanding it to include collectively held as well as individually held values.

Whether as individuals or collectively, values provide:

- a basis for social judgement – about our own or our group's behaviour and that of others/ other groups, and for apportioning praise and blame

- a means to generate, maintain and defend our individual or group esteem, in part, by enabling us to justify our beliefs and actions, even if they are deviant or unpopular, and, in part, by stirring us into action to pursue our goals

- guides to our or our group's opinions – the positions we should take on moral and social issues

- guides to the attitudes we should adopt, and how to reconcile conflicting attitudes and opinions within ourselves or among the group

- principles of behaviour – how to act, and how to present ourselves/our group to others

- a source of motivation – guiding us to act in ways that are instrumental in achieving our goals

- guides to **affiliation** – about who does and who does not share our/our group's beliefs, and with which political or religious ideology we should align

- guides to social influence – telling us what beliefs, attitudes, values and behaviours of others are worth challenging, protesting or seeking to change.

Classification of values

Rokeach defined two main kinds of values: instrumental (concerning modes of conduct) and terminal (concerning end-states). He then subdivided these into two kinds of instrumental values (moral and competence values) and two kinds of terminal values (personal and social). His classification is shown in Table 9.2.

Rokeach assumed that the two kinds of values – instrumental and terminal – 'represent two separate yet functionally interconnected systems, wherein all the values concerning modes of behavior are instrumental to the attainment of all of the values concerning end states' (Rokeach 1968: 351). However, it would be wrong, he argued, to see them as simple in their influence on behaviour. He recognized that particular values will conflict in different ways. For instance a person may have to choose between behaving morally or lovingly, between pursuing a logical or an imaginative solution to a problem, between acting politely or offering intellectual criticism. He noted that different people and different societies have different priorities in their values – for instance, some people and groups prioritize personal end-states (for example, seeking salvation in a religious sense) whereas others may prioritize social end-states (for example, seeking 'world peace').

Table 9.2 Rokeach's classification of values

Instrumental values concern modes of conduct	Moral values	Values that, if transgressed, lead to feelings of guilt or wrongdoing, such as 'honesty' or 'love'
	Competence values	Values that relate to competence, such as 'intelligence', 'logical' or 'imaginative'
Terminal values concern end-states – goals or aspirations	Personal end-states	Values relating to one's own goals, such as 'salvation' or 'peace of mind'
	Social end-states	Values relating to the goals of your community, country, or even humankind in general, such as 'brotherhood' or 'world peace'

Rokeach suggested that the main way in which competing values are reconciled is through individual values being organized into value systems – 'a learned, organization of principles and rules to help one choose between alternatives, resolve conflicts and make decisions' (Rokeach 1976: 352).

Rokeach's research into values and political positioning

In order to explore systematically how and why people's values differ, Rokeach and his colleagues devised a list of 18 terminal and 18 instrumental values. These are shown in Table 9.3.

As you will see later in the chapter, the values selected reflect Rokeach's particular worldview, as a white, male citizen of the USA. Later work in this field has modified and expanded the list of values used for research, to better reflect a worldwide diversity.

Rokeach himself used his value-lists to conduct a large number of studies into the ways in which people's values vary according to their personality, beliefs and attitudes, which he published as a book, *The Nature of Human Values* (Rokeach 1973). In order to do this, the values in Table 9.3 were each typed onto movable labels. People were asked to work on each list separately, and to 'arrange them in order of importance to YOU, as guiding principles of YOUR life'

Table 9.3 Rokeach's list of values

Terminal values	Instrumental values
A comfortable life (a prosperous life)	Ambitious (hard-working, aspiring)
An exciting life (a stimulating, active life)	Broadmindedness (open-minded)
A sense of accomplishment (lasting contribution)	Capable (competent, effective)
A world at peace (free of war and conflict)	Cheerful (lighthearted, joyful)
A world of beauty (beauty of nature and the arts)	Clean (neat, tidy)
Equality (brotherhood, equal opportunity for all)	Courageous (standing up for your beliefs)
Family security (taking care of loved ones)	Forgiving (willing to pardon others)
Freedom (independence, free choice)	Helpful (working for the welfare of others)
Happiness (contentedness)	Honest (sincere, truthful)
Inner harmony (freedom from inner conflict)	Imaginative (daring, creative)
Mature love (sexual and spiritual intimacy)	Independent (self-reliant, self-sufficient)
National security (protection from attack)	Intellectual (intelligent, reflective)
Pleasure (an enjoyable, leisurely life)	Logical (consistent, rational)
Salvation (saved, eternal life)	Loving (affectionate, tender)
Self-respect (self-esteem)	Obedient (dutiful, respectful)
Social recognition (respect, admiration)	Polite (courteous, well-mannered)
True friendship (close companionship)	Responsible (dependable, reliable)
Wisdom (a mature understanding of life)	Self-controlled (restrained, self-disciplined)

(Rokeach 1973: 27). They were instructed to start from the value most important to them and gradually construct a rank-ordered list by transferring the labels onto a grid. The labels could be moved, and subjects were told to work slowly and carefully, and move labels where necessary.

Rokeach and associates carried out a large number of studies looking at, for example, how values relate to people's politics. They found few differences in terms of affiliation to political parties. It is worth recognizing here that party politics in the USA is and has been, relatively one-dimensional, in comparison to, say, politics in countries like France and Brazil where there are far greater differences between, say, right-wing and left-wing factions. In other countries there are long-standing and very powerful antagonisms in political affiliations to do with conflicts between radically opposed political groups – such as in Northern Ireland, Pakistan and Burma. These sorts of political differences are considered later in the chapter.

Nevertheless, in Rokeach's studies that looked directly at political attitudes there were highly significant and consistent differences between what was called in the USA at that time 'conservatives' (broadly Republicans) and 'liberals' (broadly Democrats). This is not surprising given that when this research was done, the USA was experiencing political turmoil. First, the issue of race was highly volatile, and there was an active civil rights movement fighting for the emancipation of what were then called 'Blacks' and would now be called African Americans. Second, there was a great deal of civil protest against the involvement of the USA in the war in Vietnam.

The value that distinguished most strongly between conservative and liberal standpoints was 'equality'. In a series of studies, questionnaires were used to identify attitudes to (among other things) the assassination of Martin Luther King, race, the poor, student protest, US involvement in the Vietnam War and whether the church should get involved in social and political issues. The differences in the rating of 'equality' between these two positions is highly consistent, as summarized in Table 9.4. You should note that I prepared this in a highly selective manner, drawing these data from a vast catalogue accumulated by Rokeach and his associates, in which there were very many more complex trends observed.

Table 9.4 Ranking of 'equality' according to whether people express liberal or conservative attitudes (1 = highest, 18 = lowest)

Liberal attitudes	Average rank given to equality	Conservative attitudes	Average rank given to equality
Reacted with anger to the assassination of Martin Luther King	5	Felt he brought the assassination on himself	13
Antiracist	4	Racist	14
Pro-social support for the poor	5	Think poverty is the fault of the poor	13
Strongly in support of student protest	4	Strongly against student protest	12
Think the USA should withdraw from the Vietnam War	5	Think the USA should escalate the war in Vietnam	12
Think the church should get involved in social and political issues	4	Think the church should stay out of social and political issues	12

Freedom	Equality
is valued more by	is valued more by
• conservatives	• liberals
• right-wing political parties	• left-wing political parties
• Republicans	• Democrats
is associated with	is associated with
• Capitalism	• Socialism
• Liberal individualism	• Liberal humanism

Figure 9.1 The freedom/equality dichotomy

Importantly, similar patterns were found for links between self-reported behaviour (such as taking part in civil rights demonstrations) and the ranking of 'equality'. People who said they had taken political actions like these were, similarly, significantly more likely to value 'equality' highly than those who did not. The other marker of political opinion was 'freedom'. This value was much more likely to be ranked highly by conservatives. Rokeach himself rejected the liberal/conservative dichotomy, arguing that it is not useful for a number of reasons. Instead, he spent much of the book developing a two-value model of ideology, which located political opinions along these two dimensions – high/low equality and high/low freedom.

It is certainly a dichotomy that is robust – it stands up to changes in context and time. However, equally clearly we can see how political affiliations and ideological positions map on to this value dichotomy, as shown in Figure 9.1.

You should be able to identify the political parties or movements that are relevant to where you are, though the freedom/equality dimension may well be less important if your lifeworld is outside of the Western world. We will come back to this later in the chapter.

While Rokeach was working in the USA, his values were at the same time extensively used by Feather in Australia to study links between values and attitudes, personality and behaviour (see, for example, Feather 1971). Subsequently Feather went on to contribute to the development of expectancy value models (Feather 1982). Feather has sustained this research ever since, continuing to study how values relate to attitudes, attributions and personality, and also influence behaviour. He has shown, for example, that assessing values can predict people's attitudes to 'a just world' (Feather 1991).

Rokeach's study of values

- Rokeach established the social psychological study of values in California, USA, in the 1970s.
- He asserted that values are more important 'guides to how to live your life' than attitudes. However, because priorities differ from one situation and context to another, it is harder to link values to particular behaviour.

- Rokeach saw values as having a wide range of functions, including informing social judgement, guiding opinions and attitudes, and acting as the basis for affiliation.

- He constructed a scale listing two main kinds of values – instrumental and terminal – and covering a wide range of values salient to his own (US white, male, middle-class) concerns and experiences.

- Together with various colleagues, Rokeach conducted a large number of studies to explore systematic differences between different groups, and relationships between values and political viewpoints.

- He established a key value dichotomy between ideologies and standpoints that place a higher value on 'equality' than 'freedom' (broadly liberal humanism) and those that place a higher value on 'freedom' than 'equality' (broadly liberal individualism or neo-liberalism).

Cross-cultural studies of values

Rokeach carried out some cross-cultural work of his own between the USA and Canada, and brought together studies conducted by Feather (1970) in Australia and Rim (1970) in Israel. He saw the results as promising, since they indicated some systematic differences. However, he recognized that 'a systematic cross cultural approach is still some years away' (Rokeach 1973: 89). This section reviews the key studies in that development.

Hofstede's studies

In an intriguing study based on a survey conducted by a multinational company, Hofstede (1980) used its data to explore cultural differences in value systems. In the survey, staff from the 40 countries in which this company had offices were asked to complete a questionnaire. This was administered in 1967 and then again in 1973, and asked employees a wide range of questions – about disagreements with bosses, how long they planned to work for the company, how much they valued high earnings compared with recognition, and so on. Hofstede took average scores on each item for each of the countries and used a variety of statistical techniques to look for systematic patterns. He identified four main dimensions on which they varied:

- *Power distance*, relating to the amount of respect and deference expected between staff in superior positions and their subordinates.

- *Uncertainty avoidance*, relating to the degree to which staff sought to plan their future and how much they valued stability.

- *Individualism/collectivism*, relating to whether a person's identity is defined by personal choices and achievements, or by the aspirations and success of the group to which the person belongs.

- *Masculinity/femininity*, relating to whether a person places more value on achievement or interpersonal harmony.

Hofstede (1983) subsequently enlarged the sample to cover a total of 50 countries plus three regions (East and West Africa and the Arab region) in order to try to get as comprehensive a picture as possible. The coverage was good, but it did exclude most of Africa and the communist countries such as the then Soviet Union and satellite states like Hungary, Czechoslovakia, China and Cuba. In his analysis of data from the 53 countries/regions he identified two main cultural clusters:

- a cluster where, on average, the values expressed were *high on individualism and low on power distance*. In other words, the value system was one in which people have an individualistic focus together with low levels of deference to superiors. The countries where these values predominated were from Western Europe, North America, Australia and New Zealand. Of the 53 measures, the top five countries ranked on individualism were the USA, Australia, Great Britain, Canada and the Netherlands. The lowest five on power distance were Australia, Israel, Denmark, New Zealand and Ireland.

- a cluster where, on average, the values expressed were *low on individualism and high on power distance*. In other words, the value system was one in which people have a collective focus together with high levels of deference to superiors. The countries where these values predominated were from Latin America and Asia. The lowest ranking countries on individualism were Guatemala, Ecuador, Panama, Venezuela and Colombia. The highest on power distance were Malaysia, Panama, Guatemala, the Philippines and Venezuela.

It is important to stress that these are averages, and so the data do not indicate that all Australians, for example, are brash individualists who are irreverent in their dealings with their bosses, or that all Guatemalans are obsequious to their bosses and care more about others than themselves. Rather, the data give us some insight into the value-systems that are dominant in two different sorts of culture. Hofstede's work is useful to the extent that it provides empirical support to a broad divide between two opposed worldviews – one in which there is an individualistic concept of the self, and the other in which the concept of the self is relational. These two perspectives – an individual and a relational self – are examined in more detail in Chapter 10.

Hofstede's data were somewhat limited – not really surprising, given that he piggybacked his research onto a survey conducted for another, commercial purpose. First, all of the people who took part in the survey were employed by a company that is known to have a specific set of cultural values of its own. Second, they were drawn only from the company's 'white-collar workers' in their marketing and services departments. So they were hardly a representative sample of the general populations of the countries in question. What is striking is that he found such marked cultural differences, even despite these limitations.

The Chinese Culture Connection's study

Another study was conducted by an international group working at the Chinese University in Hong Kong, who called themselves the Chinese Culture Connection (Chinese Culture Connection, 1987). This study was specifically carried out to counter the ethnocentric bias of most survey instruments designed to elicit values, and to begin to remedy this by including values important within Chinese culture.

The group began their work by asking Chinese people to list values that were fundamentally important to them. These responses were then used to construct an expanded value scale. It was then administered to university students and teachers in 23 different national cultures. The same statistical techniques as used by Hofstede were applied to the data that the group obtained.

This survey, expanded to include Chinese values, when analysed also came up with four main dimensions. When a subset of the data was compared to Hofstede's, it was found that three had fairly close equivalence to his dimensions, but one was completely new:

- **Integration**, which takes a relational view of the self and is broadly equivalent to Hofstede's individualism/collectivism. This seems to be the most culturally universal value dimension.

- **Human-heartedness**, which shares some of the elements of Hofstede's femininity (since it favours values of kindness, compassion and emotional nurturance, for example) as opposed to masculinity (endorsing values of conscientiousness, perseverance and thrift in order to achieve goals).

- **Moral discipline**, relating to respect for superiors and the value of diligence and hard work. This had a fair degree of equivalence to Hofstede's high power distance and uncertainty avoidance.

- **Confucian work dynamism** that strongly endorses values of interpersonal harmony and cooperation among groups who work together, and views time as elastic and expendable rather than needing to be 'saved'.

The last of these – the Confucian work dynamism dimension – did not show any correlations with Hostede's data. The Chinese Culture Connection claimed that this set of values arises from the Chinese roots of its value configuration. The countries rated as strongest on this dimension were Taiwan, Hong Kong, Japan, South Korea and Singapore.

Values and behaviour

Hofstede looked at relationships between his data and a measure of wealth (gross national product – GNP) and found that the countries high on individualism and low on power distance tended to be the richest (remember, this was in the late twentieth century). The Chinese Culture Connection did the same, but they found that Confucian work dynamism was most strongly positively correlated with GNP (that is, values relevant in what came to be called the 'Tiger Economies').

Comparing these two sets of findings provides some evidence, at a cultural level, that values influence behaviour. The rapid economic growth at the time these studies were conducted in countries like Japan, Taiwan, Hong Kong and Singapore has been attributed to the Confucian work ethic (Segall et al. 1990). What we can see in today's global economic landscape opens up all sorts of questions about the links between values and political systems, and their influence on economic prosperity. From a time when the USA held a dominant position in terms of economic prosperity in the twentieth century, we are seeing, in the twenty-first century, a shift where the economies of China and India are gaining ground and (as I write) soon likely to overtake Western economies.

Certainly much has changed in our information-rich, globalized world. You might think, therefore, that social scientists must be much more aware that the values that underpin Western culture are by no means universal. Economists, certainly, cannot afford to be blinkered about the far wider range of value systems driving productivity and hence economic performance. Yet, as you will see in the section on the World Values Survey, it appears that some still do adopt something of a head-in-the-sand approach to studying values.

Schwartz's studies

For some time now, Salom Schwartz has been working together with social psychologists in 25 countries to examine values across cultures. He defines values as:

> conceptions of the desirable that guide the way social actors (e.g. organisational leaders, policy-makers, individual persons) select actions, evaluate people and events, and explain their actions and evaluations . . . values are trans-situational criteria or goals (e.g. security, hedonism), ordered by importance as guiding principles in life.

> (Schwartz 1999: 23)

His studies and analyses (based on a very large amount of questionnaire data) are particularly interesting because they have covered a large geopolitical range. They have included many that have experienced major social changes, including the transition from communism in many European countries (Schwartz et al. 2000).

Producing a value map

In early work in the 1990s, Schwartz and his confederates used the findings of earlier studies (including those of Hofstede and the Chinese Culture Connection) to identify 56 values operating across both Eastern and Western cultures (Schwartz 1994).

What they wanted to do, initially, was get a sense of how, when people prioritize their values, these different values relate to one another. But rather than looking for a small number of clusters (as Hofstede and the Chinese Cultural Connection had done) their aim was to generate a more topological model – a map of how different values are broadly associated with one another. To do this they constructed a questionnaire asking respondents to rate them in terms of how much each one was 'a guiding principle in my life'. The data were factor analysed (Chapter 5), identifying how, statistically, the different items relate to each other. Separate analyses were done for each of the 60 population samples included in the survey (in most countries data were collected from two groups – students and teachers). This analysis was used to 'map out' how values tend to cluster in ways that relate to different, distinct, positions, as shown in Figure 9.2.

As you can see, Schwartz's analysis identifies seven clusters of what he calls 'cultural value orientations'. At the top are egalitarianism, harmony and embeddedness, different versions of collectivism. At the bottom are intellectual autonomy, effective autonomy, mastery and heirarchy, different facets of individualism.

Schwartz and his colleagues then mapped on the different patterns observable from looking at data-sets from different geopolitical locations, in terms of where these values are most highly endorsed. Some interesting patterns emerge. Table 9.5 sets out the groups and countries that scored highest on the broad value domains.

Different variants of individualism

These patterns suggest that individualism is by no means a simple, unitary, value system. It is much more complex than that. Whereas the USA is usually regarded as the most highly individualistic country in terms of its values, this is to do with a very particular aspect of individualism: mastery. According to this analysis, the dominant value-system in the USA is one

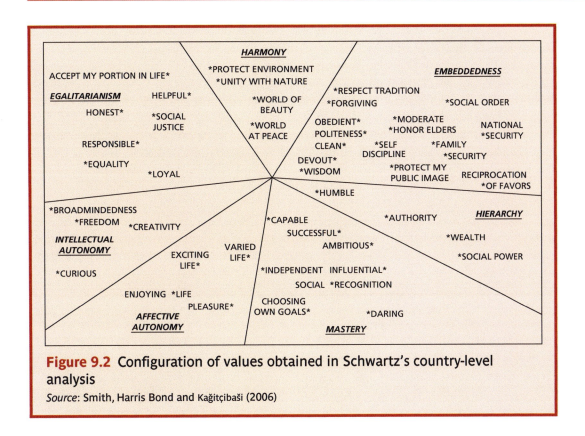

Figure 9.2 Configuration of values obtained in Schwartz's country-level analysis

Source: Smith, Harris Bond and Kağitçibaši (2006)

Table 9.5 Nations most strongly expressing cultural value orientations

Core cultural value orientation	Specific cultural value orientations	Highest scoring samples derived from:
Collectivist	Egalitarianism	Italian, Spanish, Swedish, Norwegian, Finnish
	Harmony	Slovenians, Chilians, Estonians
	Embeddedness	Filipinos, Indonesians, Malaysians, Nigerians
Individualist	Intellectual autonomy	Switzerland, Germany, Austria, Denmark, France, French Canadians, Netherlands
	Effective autonomy	British, New Zealanders, Australians, British Canadians
	Mastery	North Americans, Israelis, Japanese, South Koreans
	Hierarchy	Thais, Indians, Chinese, Zimbabweans

Source: Smith, Harris Bond and Kağitçibaši (2006: 44)

that stresses independence, self-directedness, daring, capability, ambition and success. At the same time the dominant cultural values in the USA are, in Hofstede's terms, relatively hierarchical in terms of power relations, with clear deference to authority, for example. Interestingly, Schwartz also found high correlations between mastery values with responses from Japan and South Korea, which, I believe can best be understood by reference to the histories of those two nations following World War II.

By contrast these data identify a 'British' variant of individualism (Australia, Britain, British Canada and New Zealand) which values excitement, hedonism and diversity, and a more 'European' intellectual individualism in which the most important values are curiosity, creativity and broadmindedness. Heirarchy is also included here, though notice it is bordering onto embeddedness. So as far as values are concerned, it sits close to overall collectivism.

Remember, the data from which these analyses were based were gathered from very restricted samples – mainly students and teachers – so are hardly representative of national samples at all! I suspect, like me, you will take the conclusions with some caution. But I find that the patterns identified also 'ring true' to me to some degree. I think they have some 'face validity' in that they reflect our general impressions of cultural differences between students coming from places where individualism is the dominant worldview. I think we can use these data to identify three main categories, as shown in Table 9.6.

Collectivism

Collectivism, according to this analysis, is also a complex and multifaceted value system that goes a lot further than prioritizing relatedness. It includes three main orientations: egalitarianism, harmony and embeddedness. We will look at this in more detail later in the section.

Intellectual imperialism

At this point I want to raise some words of caution in interpreting these data. Not only were they collected from unrepresentative samples, but they only tell us about dominant value-systems, not about individuals. However, I hope you will agree they are fascinating and, crucially for the purpose of this book, tell us something worth knowing about the particularity of the dominant

Table 9.6 Cultural differences in individualistic values

My label	Schwartz's label	Values	Culture where these values reflect the 'majority' worldview
Ambitious, achieving individualism	Mastery + hierarchy	Ambitious, independent, choosing own goals, successful, influential, social power, wealth, authority	North American
Thrill-seeking individualism	Affective individualism	Enjoyable, exciting and varied life, pleasure	British (includes Australia, Britain and New Zealand)
Curious, creative individualism	Intellectual individualism	Broadminded, curious, creative	Northern Europe

culture in universities in the USA (since this is where most of our baseline data about social psychology has, historically, come from).

But the point is, it is impossible to escape from our own prejudices and preconceptions. Let me give you just one example of mine. In the 1980s, on a trip to a 'liberal arts college' in the USA, I stayed in an apartment on the campus with my late husband Rex Stainton Rogers. As was our usual habit, we shopped a bit before moving in, and bought several bottles of wine. Later in the week we invited some students over one evening, and were completely shocked when they refused to share the wine with us. All were over 18 and several over 21 (the legal age for drinking alcohol in that state at that time). Their refusal, they said, was because the college had a strict honour code. It required them to report on each other if the rules were broken. If one of them found out another student had broken the rules, they were supposed to tell the person concerned they knew about the infraction and they had 24 hours to 'own up'. And if the student did not 'own up', then they had to report them.

The honour code puzzled us – it felt completely alien, more like a boarding school than a university. But what shocked us was that students followed it. To my mind, at that time, this was asking students to tell tales on each other, in a very dishonourable manner. Which, looking back on it now, only goes to show the limitations of my own experience and my ignorance of communities and countries where honour codes like this are not only perfectly common, but also conform to local value systems. Now I know better, having learned a lot more about strict rules over alcohol in certain religions and communities, and that 'honour' means very different things in cultures different from my own.

There is, though, an equally important point, and this is that we all, inevitably, are ignorant about cultures other than our own. Being a psychologist does not make you immune to prejudiced preconceptions. In fields like the study of values, psychologists need to tread very carefully. Just because you get your scale translated does not mean you can study cross-cultural effects with it. But the same is true for most social psychological investigations.

Schwartz and his colleagues' data show very vividly just how culturally particular and specific value systems are in the context of a diversity of value systems across the world. Smith et al. (2006) argue that this is the reason why many studies conducted in the USA fail to be replicated elsewhere, even in other 'individualistic' cultures. For instance, social psychology's old chestnut – social inhibition/facilitation – appears to work very differently in different cultures. So, too, does social conformity (as you will see in Chapter 12). The point Smith et al. make is that what US social psychologists (who are the vast majority of experimental social psychologists) assume to be universal laws of human behaviour are, in practice, the manifestation of local norms and conventions based upon a local value-system that stresses mastery and a local conception of the individual self as autonomous, ambitious and striving for success.

Schwartz's theory of basic human values

Schwartz, working with a number of colleagues and drawing on work from a number of theorists, has used his extensive questionnaire studies to develop a *theory of basic human values* (Schwartz 1992). He begins by making the following claims about values:

- Values are beliefs. But they are beliefs tied inextricably to emotion, not objective, cold ideas.
- Values are motivational – they indicate the desirable goals that people strive to attain.

- Values transcend specific actions and situations. They are abstract goals. The abstract nature of values distinguishes them from concepts like norms and attitudes, which usually refer to specific actions, objects, or situations.
- Values guide the selection or evaluation of actions, policies, people, and events. That is, values serve as standards or criteria for judgement and for action at both individual and collective levels.
- People's values are systematically connected – ordered into a system of value priorities that reflect back upon identity, both personal and social.
- This hierarchical feature of values also distinguishes them from norms and attitudes.
- Value systems vary in relation to the different belief systems associated with cultural, political and ideological standpoints.

> (based on Schwartz, http://segr-did2.fmag.unict.it/Allegati/convegno%207-8-10-05/
> Schwartzpaper.pdf)

You will get a better understanding here if you look at the way Schwartz sets it out on his website – follow the link to look at it. Drawing on his large amount of survey data, Schwartz identifies ten distinct *types* of values that, he says, are recognizable both within and across cultures:

Power	Social status and prestige, control or dominance over people and resources (authority, social power, wealth, preserving my public image)
Achievement	Personal success through demonstrating competence according to social standards (ambitious, successful, capable, influential)
Hedonism	Pleasure or sensuous gratification for oneself (pleasure, enjoying life, self-indulgent)
Stimulation	Excitement, novelty, and challenge in life (daring, a varied life, an exciting life)
Self-direction	Independent thought and action – choosing, creating, exploring (creativity, freedom, independent, choosing own goals, curious)
Universalism	Understanding, appreciation, tolerance and protection for the welfare of all people and for nature (equality, social justice, wisdom, broadminded, protecting the environment, unity with nature, a world of beauty)
Benevolence	Preservation and enhancement of the welfare of people with whom one is in frequent personal contact (helpful, honest, forgiving, loyal, responsible)
Tradition	Respect, commitment, and acceptance of the customs and ideas that traditional culture or religion provide (devout, respect for tradition, humble, moderate)
Conformity	Restraint of actions, inclinations, and impulses likely to upset or harm others and violate social expectations or norms (self-discipline, politeness, honouring parents and elders, obedience)
Security	Safety, harmony, and stability of society, of relationships, and of self (family security, national security, social order, clean, reciprocation of favours)

These values are presented in Schwartz's model in a circle, representing a continuum of interconnected value positions. This depicts the ten types of values as similar to those next to them, and different from those opposite. Have a look via the link to his website. You will see that stimulation, for example, is associated most closely with hedonism and self-direction, and most opposed to security. Power links with security and achievement, and is opposite to universalism. See how it applies to you – where does your value system lie? Does this organization work for you?

The theory recognizes a degree of flexibility – that circumstances will play a part in which values are salient to (and activated by) specific situations. Links can be drawn here with theorization in social identity theory, where a person's sense of who they are, and hence how to act, is situated in relation to the social group most relevant at the time. In other words, when home with our parents in a family context, we are likely to act differently than, say, when we are with our peer group. Different values are activated.

Schwartz claims that 'actions expressive of any value have practical, psychological, and social consequences that may conflict or be compatible with the pursuit of other values' (Schwartz and Boehnke 2004: 231). Some support for values influencing behaviour has been gleaned from the factor analysis of questionnaire data (Bardi and Schwartz 2003). But the main problem here, according to experimental social psychologists, is that no behavioural data have been collected (that is, the theory has not been tested experimentally) (Hogg and Vaughn 2008).

The World Values Survey

The social scientists in charge of the World Values Survey are certainly confident that their work is important: 'For the first time in human history, the World Values Surveys have measured the values of people throughout the entire world (covering 85% of its population). These surveys provide unprecedented insight into how human values vary and how and why they are changing' (Inglehart 2005: 3). I will admit to being rather wary of claims like this in the light of the argument I have just made. At the same time, this is a powerful and well-known initiative that is genuinely global in its scope, and takes a very open policy on sharing its data and making its questionnaires available for scrutiny and for use. Indeed, before you go further I suggest you have a look at its website (see the Resources section at the end of the chapter) and make up your own mind about the design of the questionnaires, the items used and the aspects of values that are covered.

This line of research started as a European Survey in the 1970s, carried out by an informal group of social science academics (though I cannot find evidence of any psychologists) calling themselves the European Value Systems Study Group (EVSSG). This organization continues to function as a foundation: European Values Study (EVS). As its name implies, its focus was, at first, very much on what was the European Union, asking questions like:

- Do Europeans share common values?
- Are values changing in Europe and, if so, in what directions?
- What are the implications for European unity?

Looking at it from the twenty-first century, it was very **Eurocentric** – that is, based on a set of culturally specific assumptions, preconceptions and priorities that reflect a European view of the world. For instance, in its early form it concentrated on Christian values rather than those of other religions, and is still, today, preoccupied with concerns most relevant to the more affluent nations of the world.

The first survey was carried out in 1981, based on interviews conducted in ten European countries (interestingly including Northern Ireland which was investigated separately from the rest of the UK). The interest aroused in other countries led to agreements for use of the questionnaire and interview schedule, and the exchange of data so that comparisons could be made across cultures and locations. This led to an expansion of the survey into 26 nations. Further surveys were conducted in 1990 (surveying in, it is claimed, all European countries, including those from the former Communist bloc, and the USA and Canada); 1999 (that was not able to include all European countries) and in 2008 (surveying 46 European countries 'from Iceland to Azerbaijan and from Portugal to Norway'). One of the main aims of these approximately ten-yearly surveys was to explore the ways in which political, economic and social changes are associated with changes in values.

We can see that very rapidly the impetus shifted from a focus on Europe to one that is more 'global', particularly once scholars from the USA got involved. Its website is extensive and is the best way to easily access papers and information (see Resources). There are large numbers of papers, both general and specific reports of the data collected. In general they identify two key dimensions, as shown in Figure 9.3. These, they claim, together with socio-economic differences, can explain the broad variations in worldview across the world.

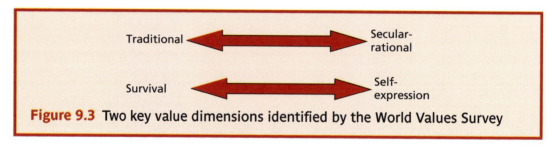

Figure 9.3 Two key value dimensions identified by the World Values Survey

Broadly the analysis suggests that cultures who strongly endorse values of tradition (versus secular-rationalism) and survival (versus self-expression) tend to be the poorest. The richest tend to endorse secular rationalism and self-expression.

The papers on specific issues and analyses cover a wide range of topics, such as findings indicating a general increase in happiness, subjective well-being and life satisfaction (Inglehart et al. 2008), but no evidence for a simple relationship between improvements in living standards being linked with a rise in secularism (Li and Harris Bond 2010).

What is really good about this work is its openness and the efforts taken to recruit a truly international community of scholars to contribute to the studies conducted. However, it is clear that the ethos underpinning all the research and theorization is positivist, and based on both inductive and hypothetico-deductive logics of inquiry. For instance, great care is taken to recruit representative samples of participants in each national location, and to translate in ways intended to reflect a common meaning of words and phrases across languages.

Coming from a critical standpoint, some of this troubles me, especially the assumption that recruiting scholars internationally to conduct surveys under the management of an executive committee is the best (or even a good) way to gain insight into and understanding of values in a wide variety of different cultures. Nonetheless, there is much of interest here. Inglehart's report on the values embedded in Islamic cultures (Inglehart 2005) can, as I have noted above, read as rather self-congratulatory. It is, at times, a bit clumsy by equating 'economic development' with 'progress' in a way that hints at a value judgement. But it is an insightful attempt to tease out how the values underpinning democracy (for example, around gender equality and tolerance of diversity in relation to sexuality) may not, in fact, be at all necessary when placing a high value on democracy.

What it does offer to social psychology is a good illustration of how demographic data (such as income levels and rates of literacy) can help us to understand how life experiences and circumstances can affect the way people understand the world, and inform how they behave.

Cross-cultural studies of values

- Studies of values by Hofstede identified two main value clusters:
  - an individualistic focus together with low levels of deference to superiors
  - a collectivist focus, with high levels of deference to superiors.
- The Chinese Culture Connection identified four main dimensions on which values vary from one culture to another:
  - in terms of integration (individualistic or collective)
  - human-heartedness (rational or emotional)
  - moral discipline (hedonistic or diligent)
  - Confucian work dynamism (time- and task-pressured or transcendental).
- Schwartz and his colleagues have produced detailed 'value maps' showing, for example, that while people in Europe and the USA both have an individualistic focus to their values, these are of different kinds.
- The World Values Survey is the most sustained and comprehensive, with waves of surveys going back to the 1980s. It identified two key value dimensions:
  - traditional versus secular-rational
  - survival versus self-expression.

It ties these to economic development, the richest countries valuing secularism and self-expression, and the poorest values favouring tradition and survival.

Critical approaches to the study of values

You have now looked at two ways of studying values – smallish-scale studies where people rank order a set of values provided by the researcher(s), and larger-scale surveys using Likert scales where, again, researchers provide a series of carefully selected questions about values for participants to rate in terms of the degree of their agreement/disagreement.

Critical work in this field looks at values in a different way. I am sure, by now, that you are not at all surprised to find them understood less as isolated cognitive entities (albeit more diffuse and deeply embedded ones than attitudes), but more as intertwined into social and cultural practices – such as how we pursue our goals, treat our neighbours and our workmates, bring up our children, who we look after and care for and how we do it.

There appears not yet to be much qualitative research conducted by critical social psychologists into values explicitly. Rather values appear as elements of interest within studies of the contexts within which values are played out – such as in relation to professional roles, to public policy and in education. There does seem to be a start being made, though, within research about relationships. An example is a recent study of grandmothering. Looking at how different values can affect expectations about the role a grandmother plays in a child's life, what she considers her responsibilities to be, and the range and limits of her authority.

Values and grandmothering

Work on grandparenting styles suggests that they vary considerably – being very involved, rather remote, or acting like companions, for example (Cherlin and Furstenbberg 1986). However, in a study conducted by Donna Nagata, Wendy Yang and Amy Tsai-Chae (2010) the focus was on the influence of values, and Chinese values in particular. The authors interviewed 17 grandmothers who had emigrated as adults to the USA from China, Taiwan and Hong Kong, to live with or be close to their American-Chinese sons or daughters and grandchildren. The authors were especially interested to explore ways in which two important Chinese values may affect the way these women perform the role of grandmother: filial piety and respect for elders.

- *Filial piety* is a value focused on the relationship between children and their parents, that brings together ideas of particular respect towards and gratitude for one's parents for their upbringing and strong obligations to protect and promote the good character of the family name.
- *Respect for elders* is a broader-based Confucian value of deference towards elders in general for the wisdom they have gained over their long life. It is enacted by all manner of social actions – greeting them first in any group encounter, everyone waiting until they start eating before beginning their own meal, and making a big fuss of them on their birthday.

Together these values create, within the Chinese home culture, a situation where it is usual for women to look forward to being grandmothers. They are brought up to believe that this will accord them not only all sorts of special treatment, but also more power than before, in roles of mother and wife. Grandmothers, in this worldview, are entitled to specify how things should be done in the rearing of their grandchildren, and expect their opinions to take precedence over those of the child's parents.

Nagata and her colleagues looked at how moving to the USA and grandmothering in an alien culture can alter these expectations and the relationships that grandmothers had with their grandchildren and the parents. They found, first of all, that these grandmothers did not fit comfortably into any of the categories identified by Cherlin and Furstenbberg (1986). Even though they had a lot of contact with the children, they said they did not feel they knew them very well. Asked about how good the relationship was, their answers portrayed rather different criteria from those usual in the dominant culture of the USA, drawing more on Chinese values. For instance, this is how one grandmother described how she got on with her grandchildren: 'Pretty well, they always say "hello" to me after they wake up in the morning. They have to have the basic courtesy principles by saying "hello" to me. Their parents taught them those. And while we have our meal, I have to begin before they can begin eating. These are basic aspects of courtesy' (Chinese grandmother, as cited in Nagata et al. 2010: 155).

This emphasis on the importance of children learning and following ethical values, and their own important role in guiding their grandchildren was found in many of the interviews. For instance:

> I tell them that they should recognise four (Chinese) characters, 'Li' (propriety), 'Yi' (righteousness), 'Lien' (integrity/humility) as in not indulging in worldly pleasures, and 'Chi' (a sense of shame). I told them as long as they understand the essence of the four characters and do what is right for themselves, they will be able to stand out in society.
>
> (Chinese grandmother, as cited in Nagata et al. 2010: 155)

Consequently the grandmothers would correct their grandchildren, in terms of posture, for example, or the right way to eat. They would also strongly stress the importance of academic success.

However, like other grandparents the USA, these Chinese grandmothers adopted a strategy of non-interference, and were concerned about maintaining harmony and good relations with the child's parents. It is clear, as the authors of the study recognize, that in migrating to the USA to join their families, these women were placed in a subservient position, usually dependent on their sons and daughters for a home and for help in navigating an alien culture, especially if they did not speak the local language fluently. This dependency disrupts the social mores of the homeland, and, however strongly held the values of these grandmothers, they had to act warily and hold themselves back. As they got older, the children themselves also played a part in challenging what they saw as 'old-fashioned' ideas that did not transplant. The grandmothers were well aware of where they stood, and the position they were expected to take: 'The mother and the father should take responsibility and grandmother should try her best not to take charge of too many things. Not taking charge will make everybody happy. We should give opinions to the parents but not directly to the grandchild since that would cause resentment to us (grandmothers)' (Chinese grandmother, as cited in Nagata et al. 2010: 157).

Critical studies of values

- Critical social psychology sees values – like attitudes – as intertwined with and manifested by social action, very much a product of the context in which they are enacted and the meanings given and constructed in that context.

- Research into grandmothering provides a good example. Migrant grandmothers to the USA approach the role differently from the dominant ideal there of a companionate role. Instead they see their role as guardians of Chinese traditional values, who should make sure their grandchildren know them and apply them to their lives. However, in the migrant situation, grandmothers downplay their traditional grandmotherly role in order to maintain harmony, in a culture where grandmothers are expected not to interfere.

- From this example, values can be seen as strongly influential in determining how people act, but modulated by other concerns and pressures.

Resources

European Values Survey: http://www.europeanvaluesstudy.eu/

Schwartz's theory of values: this is, at the time of writing, the best website account of his work and ideas. Do see if you can find better. http://changingminds.org/explanations/values/schwartz_inventory.htm

World Values Survey: their website is http://www.worldvaluessurvey.org/ and provides open and easy access to their data and the instruments they used in their research. To get started, though, you will get a better impression of the organization and its values and cultural positioning by looking first at its brochure: http://www.worldvaluessurvey.org/wvs/articles/folder_published/article_base_110/files/WVSbrochure4.pdf

Further reading

Rokeach, M. (1973) *The Nature of Human Values*. New York: Free Press.
Not always easy to get hold of, this is, of course, the classic book on this subject. It is a user-friendly read, and a fascinating glimpse, along the way, of what the world was like in the USA in the 1960s.

Smith, B., Harris Bond, M. and Kağitçibaši, C. (2006) *Understanding Social Psychology across Cultures: Living and Working in a Changing World*. London: Sage.
If you want to know more about the surveys of values carried out by Hofstede, the Chinese Culture Connection and Schwartz, they are described in a lot more detail here. The book also provides an excellent review of cross-cultural psychology generally.

Questions

1 Should social psychologists take the study of values more seriously than they currently do?

2 What contribution has Rokeach made to our understanding of values and their relationship with social psychology. What do you think he got wrong?

3 What can social psychology learn from cross-cultural studies of values?

4 Link to the World Value Survey website http://www.worldvaluessurvey.org/ and download the first and the most recent questionnaires that have been/are being used. Carefully review their design and contents, considering, especially, the degree to which they reflect the diversity of value systems worldwide. Do this first in a general way, looking at both versions. Then focus specifically on the changes that have been made over time, and how successful these have been in making the research more culture-fair.

5 Why is it hard to gain evidence that our values have a strong influence upon our behaviour?

6 Find and download two codes of ethics for psychological research (see Chapters 4 and 5), one from your own country, and one from another as different as possible from your own. Both are likely to have a section spelling out values. Compare and contrast them, in ways that allow you to reflect upon why they are similar and why they are different. Use this to identify at least three different kinds of influence on the values we adopt personally, and as psychologists.

Chapter 10

Social selves and social identities

LEARNING OUTCOMES

When you have finished studying this chapter, you should be able to:

1 Outline the contributions made to our understanding of the self by James, Mead and Goffman.

2 Explain the difference between an 'individual' and a 'relational' concept of the self, and describe how these are prioritized in different ways in different cultures.

3 Through examples, outline social psychological theories about the ways in which the self is determined by social forces and influences.

4 Explain what is meant by an 'intersubjective self', and outline the key elements in this theorization.

5 Summarize what is meant by 'presencing practice', 'technologies of the self' and 'subject positioning', and explain their functions in the construction of the intersubjective self.

Introduction

Tell someone you are a psychologist and often enough they will flash you a look, act slightly nervous, and ask you if you are analysing them. This is not too bothersome, you just have to point out the difference between a psychologist and a psychiatrist or psychoanalyst. But the suspicion can linger on, and they will still feel in some way you are classifying them or judging them. Not a good reputation to inherit! The trouble is, psychologists have a long history of judging and testing people – intelligence tests, personality tests, tests of skill and performance. So no wonder the stereotype persists.

You may be relieved to know that this is not what this chapter is about, as indicated by its title. There is nothing here about personality, nor about evolutionary explanations of innate character and intelligence. Rather, as is fitting for a social psychology textbook, it is about our social selves and social identities.

But do not be too relieved! There is a lot to cover. Margaret Wetherell expresses just how wide the net is spread around the study of identity, right across the social sciences and beyond:

> In the most basic sense, the study of identity is about what Avtar Brah (1996) calls 'names and looks', and what is done with these. But even this simple initial focus opens up a wide range of topics – orderings of 'us' versus 'them', inward-outward movements of subjectivity, narrative and memory, and political acts of intense solidarity and sometimes great violence.
>
> (2010: 3)

In this book and for the purpose it serves (to introduce you to social psychology), it is only possible to touch on some of these incredibly fascinating topics. This chapter locates the study of social selves and identities within our discipline and will tell a little of how social psychologists have grappled to make sense of the interplay between 'the self' and 'the social'.

To do this the chapter is divided into four sections. It begins with the historical origins of studying selves and identities, woven around the work of its three main 'founding fathers': William James, George Herbert Mead and Irving Goffman. The next section raises and begins to address a key issue in this field – the contrast between images and understandings of the self in terms of each person's individuality and that of their connections and relatedness to others – a divide explored in Chapter 9 on values. This leads into what has now become the dominant framework within the social psychology of the self – social identity theory. To end is one more section on intersubjective selves, including ideas around performavity and more generally the growing move into psychoanalytic theory to understand the self.

Who am I?

Each of us experiences ourselves as being a 'self'. We are aware of being someone with a past, a present and a future, all of which affect who we are. We are also aware of the distinctive facets of our temperament that seem to have been constant since childhood, and make us the individual and unique person that we are. But as a 'self' we are not only aware of inhabiting a distinctive personal world, but also distinct social and cultural worlds. We are who we are because of our relationships to others – because we are a mother or a son, a husband or a friend, a student or a teacher. We are also who we are through belonging to different communities and our membership of other groups that reflect, construct and sustain our identity – as, for example, a social worker, someone who is deaf, a political dissident, a football fan, a biker, a vegetarian, or whatever.

Try it for yourself

Before starting the chapter in any detail, stop for a few minutes and do the following task. Write down 20 statements to answer the question, 'Who am I?' It is very important that you do write *at least 20 answers*. Just a few will not do. When answering this question in each case, do it as if you are giving the answer to yourself, not another to person. The order does not matter. Do not try to be systematic or logical, or think about importance. Just write down the first 20 answers that come into your head. Keep this list – it is important. We will come back to it later.

Historical origins of psychology's concept of 'self'

More, perhaps, than with any other subject in social psychology, ideas about the self – what it means to be a person, what a person should be, what makes us who and what we are – have a long and varied history going back far beyond the time when there was no psychology. These questions have been incorporated into all religions, traditional belief systems and folklore, as well as in the various philosophies of the world. Here we concentrate on a relatively recent history, the origins of how social psychology, from its beginnings in the late nineteenth century, began to conceptualize the self.

William James's theories of 'I' and 'me'

You met William James's work in Chapter 1. Now we are going to look in greater detail at his theorization about the self. James distinguished between two aspects of the self: the 'me' which he saw as 'the self as known', and the 'I' which is, he said was 'the self as knower'. He then went on to look at different aspects of each one.

The me – the self-as-known

James divided up the self-as-known into three main elements: the material, social and spiritual.

The material me

In this James included not just the body, but also a person's clothes, home, wealth, possessions, and works (such as his or her writings).

The social me

James saw this as about the recognition one gets from others. James said that people are, by nature, social and gregarious and it would be impossible to have a meaningful sense of one's self without the respect and concern of others.

> No more fiendish punishment could be devised . . . than one should be turned loose in society and remain absolutely unnoticed by others. If no one turned around when we entered, answered when we spoke, or minded what we did, but if every person we met 'cut us dead' and acted as if we were nonexisting things, a kind of rage and impotent despair would ere long well up in us, from which the cruellest bodily tortures would be a relief.
>
> (James 1907: 179)

James recognized that there are multiple social selves, whereby people show different sides of themselves to different people – different selves that they show to their parents, their teachers, their friends, their customers, to those who work for them. He suggested that a man's fame or honour were crucial parts of his social self, and important influences on his behaviour. Whereas others, for example, may flee from a city infected with cholera, a priest or doctor would consider this incompatible with his honour and stay.

The spiritual me

James defined this as the 'entire collection of my states of consciousness, my psychic faculties and dispositions taken concretely', and saw it as '[t]he very core and nucleus of ourself, as we know it, the very sanctuary of our life, the sense of activity which certain inner states possess' (James 1907: 181). In other words, while James recognized what we would now regard as 'the spiritual' (in terms of, say, religious faith) he was in many ways referring here to what we would now call our experiential self.

From these three aspects of the self-as-known, James said, follow a range of psychological elements such as self-appreciation, self-interest and the pursuit of self-betterment and self-respect.

The I – the self-as-knower

James notes that this is a more difficult concept: '[I]t is that which at any given moment is conscious, whereas the Me is only one of the things which it is conscious of' (James 1907: 195). The difficulty is in defining what 'it' is – the soul, the transcendent ego, the spirit?

James saw a person's conscious awareness in terms of a 'stream of consciousness', in which thoughts, emotions, states, feelings, images, and ideas continually coexist together immanently – outside of our awareness and at the 'back of our minds' in a state that James called transitivity. The transitivity of consciousness, James claimed, provides the basis for an enduring, ongoing, unitary self – a self that stays the same. But at any moment some part or parts of it become substantive. We experience and act out our 'I', our self-as-knower, substantive moment by substantive moment.

> It is this trick, which the nascent thought has of immediately taking up the expiring thought and 'adopting' it, which leads to most of the remoter constituents of the self. . . . The identity which we recognize as we survey the long progression can only be the identity of a slow shifting in which there is always some common ingredient retained. . . . Thus the identity found by the *I* in its *Me* is only a loosely constructed thing: an identity 'on the whole'.
>
> (James 1907: 205, emphases in the original)

Implications for social psychology

Experimental social psychology has studied James's concept of 'Me' – the self-as-known – since it is what can be known about the self from the kinds of self-reports that can be used as dependent variables. However, it makes no attempt to study James's concept of 'I' – the self-as-knower, since this element is not amenable to experimental method. It is this aspect of the self that is the focus of study for experiential psychology (see, for example, Stevens 1996). It is also the main focus for many critical social psychologists, including social constructionists and those working with a social representations approach. Most recently the study of oneself has been developed as autoethnography (see Chapter 5).

George Herbert Mead's theory of a social self

George Herbert Mead was a philosopher, like James (in that he worked as a professor of philosophy), but can also be considered an influential sociological social psychologist. An American, he did postgraduate training in Germany from 1889 to 1891. His doctoral thesis (though he never finished it) was on the relationship between vision and touch, supervised by the gestalt psychologist Wilhelm Dilthey. Mead gave a lecture series on social psychology at the University of Chicago from 1900 to 1931. However, these lectures were mostly attended by sociology students, not psychologists, and Mead's influence was greatest on the development of sociology. Mead is often regarded as the originator of **symbolic interactionism**, but this is not so. The term was invented by Herbert Blumer, who took over Mead's lecture series after Mead died in 1931 (Farr 1996). Joas argues that Mead's theorization was based not on symbolic interactionism, but on the concept of 'symbolically mediated interaction' (Joas 1985: 228). Largely ignored by psychologists until relatively recently, Mead's work is receiving renewed attention with the emergence of critical social psychology, mainly because it is semiotic in its approach (see Chapter 6).

Farr notes that it is difficult to pin down Mead's theoretical work, since he did not write it up in any systematic way and lectured without notes. The books published in his name (for example, Mead [1934a] 1977a, [1934b] 1977b) were not written by him, but prepared from drafts he worked on but did not complete, from notes taken by his students and from transcripts prepared by a stenographer whom they smuggled into Mead's 1927 lecture course!

Mead spent a lifetime trying to resolve the tension between the individual mind and society. Influenced both by Darwinism and by the *Völkerpsychologie* he learned in Germany and reviewed when he returned to the USA, he tried to work out how the 'self' can be understood in relation to three main determinants – human evolution, each individual's own development, and social forces and processes. He saw language as central to the way these three contributed to the construction of the 'self', and symbolically mediated interaction as the means by which it operates. Mead's theorization about language differed fundamentally from that of behaviourists. Behaviourists like Watson (who was Mead's student) believed that language is produced by the minds of individuals. Mead believed that each individual's mind is the product of language. Like Vygotsky (Chapter 6) Mead saw language as the basic medium through which thought operates, and, given the inherently social character of language, he emphasized the importance of intersubjectivity.

Thus the 'self', according to Mead, is intersubjective, constituted through social interaction in which people have to assume the role of the other in order to gain an understanding of themselves. Thus, Mead argued, human consciousness is an awareness of self in relation to others, and therefore human consciousness is a fundamentally social consciousness. Like language, Mead saw this social self as producing – not produced by – human consciousness. Mead's theorization described a **reflexive self** – a self that is able to observe, plan and respond to one's own behaviour. This image is nicely conceptualized in Cooley's ([1902] 1922) term 'the looking-glass self'.

Mead took James's conceptions of a separated but coexisting 'I' and 'me' and recast them as two facets of the self that are in constant dialectical relation to each other (that is, in dialogue with each other). The 'I', Mead claimed, is the part of the self that responds directly and impulsively to the outside world. The 'me' is the socialized self, the self-reflective, conventional aspect of the self that incorporates society's values, norms, ideals, and expectations. The 'me' is the self that has internalized the standpoints and group standards embedded in a person's culture.

Implications for social psychology

As I have mentioned, Mead's professional life was conducted outside of psychology, and largely dismissed by the behaviourists who took over the discipline in the USA. They saw him as engrossed in metaphysics that had nothing to offer to a 'science of mental life'. Alongside that of Charles Peirce, since the early 1980s Mead's work has been reappraised by social psychologists taking a dialectical view of human being (Marková, 1987) and a semiotic approach to language (including, most notably, discursive psychologists like Potter and Wetherell 1987). More generally Mead's work has informed social constructionism, and we shall come back to it when we examine the socially constructed self at the end of the chapter.

Irving Goffman's dramaturgical model

Irving Goffman took up Mead's ideas about social interaction and stressed that everyday life takes place in an essentially interactional world. He portrayed this world as akin to a theatre in which people are actors in the 'drama of life'. Goffman (1959) constructed a dramaturgical theory of the self in which the self arises out of acting a particular kind of role – not so much a hero or heroine, but the kind of character who is morally and socially competent and insightful.

A key concept in this theory is that of **face** – 'the positive social value a person effectively claims for himself by the line others assume he has taken during a particular contact' (Goffman 1967: 5).

Note that this use of 'face' is rather different from its meaning in cultures where 'face' is about maintaining one's honour and credibility. It is a Westernized version, if you like.

Goffman claimed that in social interaction, people have a mutual commitment to keep each other 'in face' by what he called '**face work**' (Goffman 1955). These are ritualized strategies, such as face-saving devices that serve a 'repair function' whenever the smooth flow of interaction is under threat. This kind of device enables someone who commits a social gaffe (who breaks the social rules) to deal with the potential embarrassment it poses, and thus to maintain the impression of being an authentically competent person. 'Each person takes on the responsibility of standing guard over the flow of expressive events. . . . He must ensure that a particular expressive order is maintained – an order which regulates the flow of events, large or small, so that anything that appears to be expressed by them will be consistent with his face' (Goffman 1967: 9).

Maintaining 'face', Goffman claimed, is not so much the goal of interaction as the very basis for it to happen and the means by which it does happen. During social interaction, according to Goffman, people act out 'lines' (as do actors in a drama) that are provided through their knowledge of social norms and rules. Goffman (alongside other ethnomethodological sociologists such as Garfinkel 1967) stressed the role of this 'interactional self' in maintaining the small-scale social order of everyday life.

Implications for social psychology

Goffman's image of the 'self ' has been particularly influential on social psychologists such as Rom Harré (1977) who have adopted an ethnomethodological approach. Critical social psychologist have something of a problem with Goffman's preoccupation with interaction in rather formal settings that tend to rely on 'scripts', and hence his work fails to capture the whole range of situations in which people interact. However, his ideas have been generally influential, mainly because of its stress on the purposive nature of self-presentation.

Historical origins of the self in psychology

- James distinguished between the 'me' – the self-as-known, made up of material, social and spiritual elements; and the 'I' – the self-as-knower, produced in the 'flow of consciousness'.
- Mead saw the 'I' and the 'me' as in a dialectical relationship with each other, and saw the self as reflexive – able to observe, plan and respond to its own thoughts and behaviour.
- Goffman proposed a dramaturgical model of the self, in which interaction consists of 'face work' as people strive to maintain their own 'face' and protect that of others.

What kind of self?

Clearly lots of different things add up and interact together to make us who we are. There are many different ways of carving these up, but for present purposes I suggest we start by thinking of three different aspects of 'self', somewhat loosely based on James's three aspects of 'me':

- a **personal self** – the self that is self-aware of being 'me' and conscious of one's own thoughts and feelings (as well as, possibly, aware of having some unconscious ones). This is a person's enduring self that has developed from childhood into adulthood but is still the same 'me'. It is an individual self, that, while it has been shaped by social and interpersonal influences, has a sense of individuality in relation to having particular values, attitudes and beliefs and so on.
- a **social self** – or, perhaps, a collection of social selves that are different in different social situations. These are the selves that are defined by the social context – who a person is in private and in public, in formal situations and informal ones, and so on. This includes the self as defined by your occupation.
- a **relational self** – the self that comes from a person's interconnected relationships with others – family, friends, community, the country where they were born, and so on. This is the self defined in terms of the expectations a person has of others and they have of them, the self that exists within an interconnected network of duties, obligations and responsibilities.

This section is devoted to a brief outline of the social psychology theory and research about each of these in turn.

The personal self

Experimental social psychology, with its individualistic focus, understands the self very much in this manner. In social cognitive terms, for example, it talks of **self-schemas** (Markus and Wurf, 1987) by which people create a self-image of themselves, based on their various qualities – such as being sporty, being ambitious, being clumsy.

Experiments where people have to rate themselves against qualities like this show that they respond faster to qualities most like or most unlike them, indicating that people tend to be self-referential in the way they see their world. You may recall the 'cocktail party phenomenon' from

Chapter 7 – where, even in a crowded room with a great hubbub of voices, we will 'hear' our own name if it is spoken in a way we do not consciously recognize anyone else.

> The self-reference effect illustrates a basic fact of life, especially in the Western world: the sense of self is at the centre of everybody's world. In an individualistic culture people tend to see themselves at centre stage, overestimating the extent to which they are noticed by others. Similarly they overestimate how much other's behaviour is aimed at them.
>
> (Myers et al. 2010: 62)

Try it for yourself

When you come home after a social event, and you run what happened through your mind, what or who is the focus of your reflections? Do you kind of do an 'action replay'? If so, who is the centre of your attention?

If you said 'me' then that is what people often do. I remember when I was younger I would come home from a night out with my friends and agonize over all the embarrassing things I said and did, feeling rather sick and quite distressed about how foolish I must have looked. That is until the thought struck me just how little, in these late-night reveries, I thought about anyone else's behaviour. It was an enormous relief when I talked to my closest friend, and found out that, like me, his after-the-party musings were all about how stupid, how embarrassing *he* had been. I asked more friends and they said the same. It allowed me to gradually learn not to be so self-conscious and, indeed, so self-obsessed.

Within a modern Western worldview there is great concern about problems to do with having negative evaluations of our selves – poor self-esteem, poor self-image, self-evaluations of low self-efficacy, and so on. Coming in part from social learning theory, in part from traditional psychoanalytic theory ideas around the *ego* and *ego*-strength in particular, having a low sense of one's own self-worth and capabilities is seen as highly problematic, especially in children.

Research studies link low self-esteem to increased risks of depression, delinquency and substance abuse; to poor school performance, poor parenting skills, and so on. Even success can be anxiety provoking to those with low self-esteem (Wood et al. 2005). By contrast high self-esteem is linked to having initiative and resilience – to getting ahead, succeeding and overcoming hard times. Indeed whole industries of books and magazine articles, workshops and counselling services have been built on the idea that improving self-esteem is the route to happiness and success.

However, there is something of a 'Goldilocks' effect. Overgrown self-esteem – egotism – can be a problem too, potentially leading to a tendency to be more aggressive (Heatherton and Vohs 2000). One of the most prolific researchers in this field, Baumeister, has come to the conclusion that people with high self-esteem are more likely to be obnoxious, to interrupt and to talk at people rather than with them: 'After all these years, I'm sorry to say, my recommendation is this: Forget about self-esteem and concentrate more on self-control and self-discipline. Recent work suggests this would be good for the individual and good for society' (Baumeister, 2005, as cited in Myers et al. 2010: 79).

In another article Baumeister and his colleagues (Baumeister et al. 2003) systematically challenge the claims made in the self-esteem literature. They point out that many of the studies were based on self-reports and argued that it is hardly surprising if people with high self-esteem report themselves to be more popular and more capable than their more modest peers. Baumeister and his colleagues then go on to review experimental studies that show far less conclusive results in favour of self-esteem than those based on correlation.

What does seem to be the case is that emotion-provoking assaults on self-esteem, such a public rejection and humiliation, do affect people's confidence and their ability to cope with difficult tasks and hard times. This leads us into the next section.

The social self

As in other fields, early experimental social psychology work on the social self was located within behaviourism generally and social learning theory in particular. One of the best known is Daryl Bem's (1972) **self-perception theory** in which he suggested that we know who we are by observing our own behaviour: 'Individuals come to "know" their own attitudes, emotions and other internal states partially by inferring them from observations of their own overt behaviour and/or the circumstances in which this occurs' (1972: 5). For example, a person who attends church regularly will conclude they are religious; someone who enjoys social events and is always the 'life and soul of the party' will see themself as an **extrovert** (Salancik and Conway 1975; Rhodewalt and Augustsdottir 1986).

Learned helplessness

Social learning theory assumed that people learn to tackle their lives according to the rewards and punishment they have received, particularly in childhood. One well-known example is the theory of **learned helplessness** (Seligman 1975 is the standard text) devised from observations of rats in the laboratory. The rats were exposed at first to a regime where they were repeatedly punished without being able to do anything to prevent it. When, later, the regime was altered (so that they could now avoid the punishment) instead of changing their behaviour, the rats remained passive. They seemed to have lost the capacity to do anything to save themselves. They had 'learned to be helpless'.

Analogies were drawn by Seligman and his followers, to suggest that people may react to parallel situations in similar ways. People who grew up in environments where, whatever they did, they were treated badly, become, according to this theory 'eternal victims'. Either they become completely passive, seeing themselves as totally incapable to gaining life's rewards. Or they blame themselves whenever harmed by misfortune, beset by feelings of recrimination and guilt. This theory of learned helplessness has been used, for example, to seek to explain symptoms of depressive illness (for example, Seligman et al. 1979).

Locus of control

Another, similar example is Rotter's locus of control construct (see Rotter 1966). According to this formulation, the way adults explain the things that happen to them is a product of their learning experiences as children. Those with early experiences of good behaviour being consistently rewarded, and bad behaviour being consistently punished, come to see themselves as 'in control'. Their successes are construed as just rewards for hard work and diligence; failure is that which they must expect if they are lazy, or do not try hard enough. Thus they learn to site control within themselves, and within their own actions. These people are termed 'internals'. In contrast, those who have had inconsistent experiences as children – who were rewarded and punished indiscriminately, irrespective of their behaviour, come, as adults, to see the things that happen to them as the consequence of chance. Their own behaviour is, from this standpoint, irrelevant – success is a matter of 'good luck', failure a matter of 'bad luck'. They site control in the vicissitudes of the outside world, and are labelled 'externals'.

Try it for yourself again

Go back and look at the list of 20 statements about yourself that you wrote at the beginning of the chapter. Underneath your list, write down the three categories just mentioned: personal self, social self, relational self.

Then do your best to work out in which category each of your statements falls, and put a tick against that category. If some statements do not fit neatly into any of them, do not worry. Count them as falling into two categories if need be, or just leave them out if they really do not fit anywhere. Now look at which category gets the most ticks. The aim is to see whether you see yourself most in terms of your personal self, your social self or your related self.

The Twenty Statements test (as this task you have been doing is called) was used by Cousins (1989) to examine how concepts of the self may vary between cultures. He tested university students in Japan and the USA, and coded their responses into several categories, three of which were broadly similar to the ones you have just used. Cousins found a substantial difference between the responses to the test in the two countries. Table 10.1 sets out the differences, recast in the terminology I have used.

Cousins's results provide evidence that US students tend to have a more individualistic sense of self, whereas Japanese students have a more relational sense of self. Mansur Lalljee

Table 10.1 Responses to the 20 statements task given by US and Japanese students

	Average % of 'personal self' answers	Average % of 'social self' answers	Average % of 'relational self' answers
US students	58	9	9
Japanese students	19	9	27

Source: After Cousins (1989)

argues that this reflects a systematic difference in the concept of the self in different societies and cultures:

> In the West, the person is thought of as an autonomous unit, consisting of a set of core attributes, that are carried with the person through time and context . . . In Japan, India and most parts of the world other than 'the West', people are seen in terms of their roles and relationships, in terms of their activities and interests, because of the interconnected networks in those societies. For people living in such societies, the self integrally includes social relationships and social context.
>
> (2000: 13)

Lalljee backs up this assertion with evidence from an ingenious field study by Semin and Rubini (1990). It was carried out in Italy, and compared the forms of insults used in the north and the south of the country. The basis of the study was that Northern Italy has a more individualistic culture than Southern Italy. They predicted that insults would tend to be more personal in the north – calling people stupid, fat, or comparing them with animals like pigs. In the south, they argued, insults would be more likely to be about relationships – your mother is a *****! (you know the kind of thing) and cursing family members. The results were not entirely clear-cut, but some support for the hypothesis was obtained.

These days, especially outside the USA, the main approach to the social self is **social identity theory**. This is such a large field now that there is an entire section on it later in the chapter.

Try it for yourself, one more time

Now go back and look at what balance you found in your response to the 20 statements test. Did you have more 'personal self' or 'relational self' items in your list? How far do you think your answers reflect the customs and values of your family, your heritage and the community to which you now feel you most belong?

Relational selves

In Chapter 9 on values you have already learned about the differences between individualistic and collectivist world views. These take very different perspectives on self and identity. Hamaguchi (1985) for instance, points out that in Japan, a highly collectivist culture, the word for self, *'jibun'*, means 'one's portion of the shared space'. For someone like me brought up in the West, it is a shockingly powerful marker of the very different 'self' – the relational self – that predominates elsewhere.

Wetherell and Maybin (2000) provide a lovely illustration of what this means in practical terms in everyday life. It comes from an anthropological study carried out by Kondo (1990), an ethnically Japanese woman born and raised in the USA. She did the research when she was later studying, working and living in Japan. Here is what Kondo wrote about a conversation with her landlady, following a phone call from a man she had been consulting about making contacts for her research. In it he created a situation where she felt obliged to take on a task – teaching English to a student of his – she knew would be very time-consuming and intrusive.

> I was in a foul mood the entire evening. I complained bitterly to my landlady, who sympathetically agreed the sensei should have been more mindful of the fact that I was so pressed, but she confirmed that I had no choice but to comply. She explained that the sensei had been happy to give of his time to help me, and by the same token he considered it natural to make requests of others, who should be equally giving of themselves, their 'inner' feelings notwithstanding. '*Nihonjin wa ne*' she mused, '*jibun o taisetu ni shinai no, ne.*' [The Japanese don't treat themselves as important do they? That is, they spend time doing things for the sake of maintaining good relationships, regardless of their 'inner' feelings.] I gazed at her in amazement, for her statement struck me with incredible force. Not only did it perfectly capture my own feelings of being bound by social obligation, living my life for others, it also indicated to me a profoundly different way of thinking about relationships between selves and the social world. Persons seemed to be constituted in and through social relations and obligations to others. Selves and societies did not seem to be separate entities: rather the boundaries were blurred.
>
> (Kondo 1990, cited in Wetherell and Maybin 2000: 272)

Experimental social psychology has tended to farm out consideration of alternative understandings of the self to 'cultural psychology' or even 'indigenous psychology' in a move that reflects its ethnocentrism. Anything other than good old Western individualism is treated as exotic and alien, to be hived off away from the 'proper' study of 'the individual in the social world'.

Critical social psychology fares somewhat better, in part because it is practised and pursued by psychologists from a broader range of geopolitical locations. For instance, in the post-apartheid world of South Africa its psychologists have actively produced textbooks that portray an African-based psychology (see, for example, two chapters by Mkhize in *Critical Psychology* Mkhize 2004a, 2004b). They argue for a critical, emancipatory psychology, one that is at pains to 'take into account indigenous people's languages, philosophies and worldviews . . . [since] it is through these worldviews and philosophies that people make sense of themselves and the world' (Mkhize 2004a: 25).

In these texts a clear distinction is made between individual and relational selves:

> Traditional Western cultures regard the self as a bounded entity. People are defined in terms of internal attributes such as thoughts and emotions. This view of selfhood is also known as self-contained individualism . . . or the independent view of the self . . . On the other hand, indigenous cultures define the self in terms of one's relationships with others, such as family, community and status or position within the group. Children are socialised to harmonise their interests with those of their family and the community.
>
> (Mkhize 2004a: 36)

Mkhize draws on the work of Vygotsky (see Chapter 6) and particularly Bakhtin (1981) and Shotter (1993a) to propose that a relational self is dialogic – constructed through dialogue with others, and an 'inner dialogue'. In this way ideas about personhood are taken from the external world of parents and teachers, television and storytelling, and internalized, which Shotter views as an ethical-moral transformation of the self: 'In learning how to *be* a responsible member of a certain social group, one must learn to *do* things in the right kind of way: how to perceive, think, talk, act and to experience one's own surroundings in ways that make sense to the others around one in ways considered legitimate' (Shotter 1993a: 73, emphases in the original).

A dialogic relationship is one that can only be fully understood in the context of the relationship between oneself and the other. Selves are made and lives are lived, from this perspective, in an ethical and responsible relationship with one's family, tribe and community. Mkhize explicitly claims that we can see this in the way that Rolihlahla Nelson Mandela and Bantu Steve Biko lived their lives in order to 'establish a democratic society in which people live together in harmony and as equals' (Mkhize 2004b: 61). He refers to the **horizon of understanding** (Gadamer 1975) within which we are able to make sense of our worlds – the social and cultural taken-for-granted knowledge against which we make sense of who people are and the actions they take. This has strong resonances with gestalt psychology, where the focus of our attention (figure) only makes sense in terms of the background (ground) against which we see it.

Gestalt psychology is described in more detail in Chapter 1.

To illustrate how this works, Mkhize opens up the phrase *umunto ngumuntu ngabuntu*, which is usually translated into English as 'a human being is a human being because of other human beings'. This translation, he says, does not fully capture the full dialogic implications, since underneath the simple words are strong associations with ideas about participation in a community. This is better conveyed by the Tshivenda equivalent, *muthu ubebelwa manwe*, which translates as 'a person is [already] born for the other'. We can see strong similarities with the Japanese word for self – '*jibun*' – translated as 'one's portion of the shared space':

> The saying '*umunto ngumuntu ngabuntu*' is a call for us to enrich our own self-understanding through contact with, and recognition of the Other who is different from us. This requires that we come to terms with the Other's points of views, or lenses through which he or she makes sense of the world. . . . To deny others the right to mean (voice) is to deny them individuality. Recognising others' views is also important because it is through them that we come to be conscious of who we are.
>
> (Mkhize 2004b: 76–7)

Personal, social and relational selves

We can think in terms of three different aspects of the self – a personal self, social selves and relational selves. Cultures differ in terms of whether people see themselves as individual, personal selves, or in terms of their relationships with others.

- An *individual view of the self* regards people as autonomous, self-contained and self-reliant, with their own concerns, motives, aspirations and desires. It is preoccupied with the 'well-being' of the self – self-esteem and self-efficacy.
- The *social self* is the one favoured by experimental social psychology, which views the self as moulded by social processes (such as socialization and identification with particular social groups) and by social influences (such as the kind of upbringing a person is given).
  - Social learning theory claims that people acquire their personal capabilities and failings through the child-rearing regimes to which they are exposed.

○ The theory of learned helplessness proposes that children exposed to chaotic forms of child-rearing, where they are rewarded and punished indiscriminately, become, as adults, eternal victims – lacking the capacity to help themselves.

○ Locus of control suggests that chaotic child-rearing regimes produce adults who locate control of their lives in the external world – chance, luck and fate. By contrast, child-rearing regimes where good behaviour is rewarded and bad behaviour punished produce adults who locate control over their lives in their own actions, and are more likely to be self-motivated and self-disciplined.

● A *relational self views identity* as inexorably integrated with others, in terms of mutual duties and obligations, deference and authority. Another way to see it is as a dialogic self – a self constructed through dialogue with others, and in terms of one's responsibilities to one's family, collectivity and community.

Social identity theory

In social identity theory we can see a bringing together of the social and the relational self. This approach has transformed social psychology's understanding of the self and identity. According to Reicher et al., it does so in three main ways:

> First, social identity is a relational term, defining who we are as a function of our similarities and differences with others. Second, social identity is shared with others and provides a basis for shared social action. Third, the meanings associated with any social identity are products of our collective history and present. Social identity is therefore something that links us to the social world. It provides the pivot between the individual and society.

(2010: 45)

While its origins are in the social cognition paradigm, social identity theorists have increasingly incorporated critical thinking and ideas around the relational self. Social identity today is framed around identity as something we actively, collectively and dialogically *co-construct*, rather than something we 'fit into', 'providing a link between social identities and social realities' (Reicher et al. 2010: 59). It is particularly articulated around ideas about defining who we are through our relationships with others, including our sense of where we 'belong' and who 'speaks for' us. What matters are our allegiances to, aspirations to and antagonism towards particular groups. These reference groups are crucial in constructing our identities.

Social identity theory assumes that there is not one 'personal self' but a more complex and flexible self that works in different ways. If you again refer back to your 20 statements, you can undoubtedly see this kind of variation. For instance, if you put down 'mother', 'daughter', 'student' and 'football player', then you can see how you would act differently in the different roles. The woman you are that your mother knows is different from the woman your teammates or your friends know. The man you are that your teacher knows is different from the man your grandfather knows (if these do not work for you, invent your own contrast). We will look later at specific theories about multiple and flexible selves viewed through discursive terms.

Social identity theory was constituted as a direct challenge to the view that people's behaviour is primarily a product of internal, individual psychological heritability (as in having a neurotic personality), learning (as in learned helplessness) or pathology (as having a 'sick mind'). Identity is instead seen as moulded and shaped by and through our relationships with others, the roles we play and our identification with various social groups.

I hope you will agree that Mkhize's work is really useful here, for he makes people like me take relationality more seriously and think of a 'bigger picture' that draws in concepts like ethics, respect, honour and social responsibility alongside the 'warm and cuddly' images that the English word 'relational' implies.

By identifying with a particular social group we define ourselves as having the characteristics of that social group. To belong to the Muslim faith, one does what Muslims do, thinks like a Muslim does, understands the social world and what goes on within it through a Muslim world-view. Alternatively, to belong to a community of feminists, one acts and thinks as a feminist, and understands the social world by way of feminist theory and ideology. This identification and its consequences can be in relation to large-scale, socially recognizable groups (such as being Palestinian or Israeli, Catholic or Protestant), to professional demarcations (being a nurse or doctor; casual staff or on the payroll) or to a group defined by the football team you support, what music you listen to, going on a gap-year as a traveller or a tourist.

However, old identity-markers are, in some places, losing their power. And global capitalism is having an impact, especially in affluent countries. Nowadays, if you live in a politically stable and prosperous location, you are less likely to define yourself by your nationality, your family, your neighbourhood, your social class or your politics. Your reference groups are more likely to be your peer group and what they consider desirable and authentic. Increasingly, it is claimed, those who thrive in market-led societies identify and constantly reinvent ourselves through consumption. They (we?) know who they are more by the brands they buy than anything else.

The sociologist Zigmunt Bauman proposes that in what he calls the 'liquid life' of modern society, old ways and tradition are spurned in the quest for being 'in the loop', at home with the latest technology and gizmos, decked out in the latest fashion, with the hairstyle and body-form to match. More disturbingly, he argues that many are forced into a liquid identity in what he calls 'a sinister version of musical chairs' (Bauman 2005: 3). Jobs have become more casualized – more part-time, fixed contract, demanding 'flexibility', offering little security or continuity and little chance to build your identity on 'what you do' professionally.

Try it yourself

Go back and look at your 20-statements list – how many of your answers relate to your membership of a particular group? How far is your identity bound up in your nationality, your family heritage, your ancestors, your religion? How far is 'being a student' part of your identity? How far do you know who your friends are by who is signed up as your friend on Facebook? Do you have any statements like 'love to shop at Harvey Nics', 'wouldn't be seen dead in Crocks', 'in love with my iPad' or 'Hate reality TV'?

The origins of social identity theory

You have already seen that Mead's early work included theorization about the social self (Mead [1934b] 1977b). However the 'founding father' of social identity theory was Henri Tajfel (see Tajfel 1978; Tajfel and Turner 1986). It is hardly surprising Tajfel was so interested in identity. Born a Polish Jew in 1919, he was studying in France when he was called up into the French army to fight in the Second World War. He was captured but, because he managed to hide the fact that he was a Jew, he was sent to a prisoner-of-war rather than a concentration camp. All this time he had to pass himself off as somebody he was not or face almost certain death. At the end of the war he discovered that none of his boyhood friends or immediate family had survived the Holocaust. After his release, Tajfel spent time working with war refugees and orphans across Europe, but then moved to London where he trained as a psychologist. His early work was done at the University of Oxford. He took up a professorial appointment at Bristol University in 1967.

Tajfel thus had much personal experience of prejudice and intergroup conflict, and soon set up a research group at Bristol to develop theory and conduct research into social identity and its role in conflicts between groups, in a field now known as the social identity theory of intergroup relationships. Tajfel et al. (1971) conducted a series of experiments on whether just being designated as a member of a group can get someone to favour those in their group over those in another group. Surprisingly it works. Children allocate more 'pretend' money to members of the group that they have been told that they belong to, even when they have never met them and do not even know who they are. These are called **minimal group experiments**, since they were designed to discover the minimal conditions that would lead members of one group to discriminate in favour of the group to which they belonged – called their '**ingroup**' – and against another group – called the '**outgroup**'.

We will look in more detail at these minimal group studies in Chapter 12. Here it is important to note that these studies, while important, were done at a time when the pressures to adopt experimental approaches were very powerful. Tajfel himself was always clear that context and salience are very important, and only limited understanding can be gained in studies that exclude them. Many who worked with him moved away from this field and went on to develop discursive approaches to identity and became critical social psychologists in the process. Most notable of these are Mick Billig, Steven Reicher and Margie Wetherell. It was John Turner, though, who did most to develop social identity theory in itself, working it around the idea of self-categorization.

Self-categorization theory

Turner (1982) argued that when people identify with their group, they undergo a degree of de-personalization – they abandon some of their uniqueness and engage in a process of **self-stereotyping**. Turner suggested that in order to strengthen their identification, people are motivated to take on and define themselves in terms of stereotypical characteristics of the group. An example would be when a young man who had seen himself as 'a bit of a lad' changes his ways, gets into sport in a serious way and adopts a new style of dress and attitude to being fit. Another would be a young woman who was brought up as non-religious adopts the veil and the devout demeanour when she identifies herself as Muslim. In both cases, the people involved cease to see how to dress and how to behave as matters of personal choice, but rather by reference to the group with which they identify.

However, Turner (1991) makes clear that such self-stereotyping can be very fluid, and shift according to the reference group. For example, yet another woman might identify herself as belonging to a reference group of 'professional women' at work, yet as a 'babe' when she goes out socializing on a 'girlie night out', and adjust her dress and demeanour accordingly. In each case she is conforming to a stereotype, but the stereotypes are different. In other words, it is important to recognize that social identity can be activated in different ways – ranging from a consistent and enduring identity to a range of dynamic and situation-specific identities.

Turner's work marked the beginnings of **social categorization theory**, a more broadly based formulation 'to account for the interplay between the personal and the social than social identity theory' (Simon and Trötschel 2008: 105). Turner and his colleagues set out this theory in detail, asserting that both personal and social identity are based upon a person's self-categorizations, defined as 'cognitive groupings of oneself and some class of stimuli as the same' (Turner et al. 1987: 44).

In social categorization theory a person's identity is seen as:

- constructed at different levels
- based on comparison against 'others'
- a product of the range and salience of the groups to which they 'belong'.

Social categorization theory views identity as constructed at different levels

This is about levels of abstraction but also distance between the personal and the social self. Think of the biggest category that you can apply to yourself – something like being 'human' or a 'person'. Now work out a lower level. You might go for gender (male or female) or for sexuality (straight or gay) or geopolitical location (Asian, European, African). Or something else entirely, you get the general idea. As can be seen from Figure 10.1, the broader the category, the less exclusive the membership.

Every person in the world is a human being, fewer of those would identify themselves as African, only some of those as Kenyan and yet smaller numbers Kikuyu. The broader the category, in this sense, the more 'social' and the less 'personal' the identity. Telling you she is a human being is almost no information at all, but once you know my friend Wanjiku is Kikuyu, then you already know a lot about who she is as a person, and so does she.

Social categorization theory views identity as based on comparison

Identity is defined by and constructed through comparison groups. At the level of nationality, to work out what being a Kenyan means can be understood through comparing being Kenyan with being Ethiopian or Ghanaian (but not Japanese or French). It is the next level up (here African) in the level that determines the nature of the comparison. African people often rightly complain that Europeans treat the category 'African' as if it were a single country – just as Europeans like me complain that Americans do the same to us. In our self-categorization we are acutely aware of our differences from others within our own comparison category.

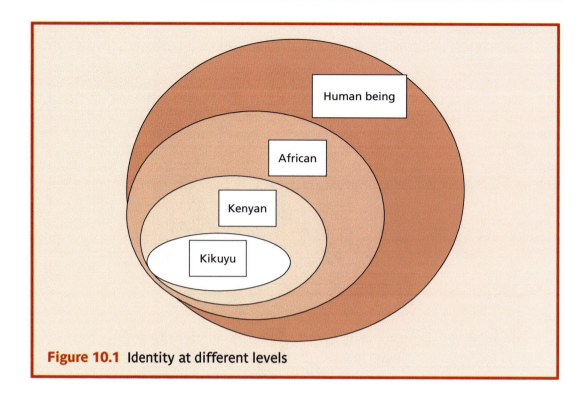

Figure 10.1 Identity at different levels

In social categorization theory identity is a product of the range and salience of group memberships

Most people categorize themselves in relation to a number of social groups reflecting different aspects of their lifeworld (such as at home, at work, in the community). For some there are many and possibly conflicting public and private selves, for others like members of closed religious groups or isolated communities like the Amish in the USA, there are fewer groups to which they belong. Crucially, group membership can vary enormously in salience. To be a Protestant or a Catholic in Birmingham matters much less than it does in Belfast. To be 'a coloured' has meaning in South Africa that it does not have in Britain.

Try it for yourself

An amusing game to play with your friends shows the power and subtlety of social categorization. There are several versions. One is for you to write down names of other people to describe – it is better if these are topical, and everyone in the group must know who they are. Write each name on a scrap of paper, and hand one out to each person. Then, in turn, each person has to describe their target according to the following categories:

What kind of fruit are they? Animal? Car? Plant? Building? Brand name?

The game is to guess the person from the description. Marks are awarded for the first person to identify who it is. Another way to do this is just use the names of the people taking part in the game. What makes it funny is just how well people can do on this limited and somewhat odd information. Think of who you know – who is a peach, a prickly pear, a cherry? Who is a mouse, a cat or a dog?

Social identity theory

- Social identity theory, originated by Tajfel, proposes that one's identity is relational – it comes through belonging to some social groups and distancing oneself from others.
- You identify with your ingroup, and distance yourself from your outgroup(s). Experimental support for this came from studies of 'minimal groups'.
- *Social categorization theory*, developed mainly by John Turner, views identity as flexible, multiple and contextual, combining individual and collective elements arising from categorizing oneself in relation to different levels, kinds and numbers of social groups.
- In social categorization theory a person's identity is seen as:
  - o constructed at different levels
  - o based on comparison against 'others'
  - o a product of the range and salience of the groups to which they 'belong'.

The intersubjective self

Intersubjectivity is a concept used in a number of ways in different approaches to identity, including phenomenology and social psychoanalysis. I also include what has come to be called 'the performative self', based around the work of Judith Butler, and linked to Bakhtin, Shotter and the kind of relational self that Mkhize sees as more relevant to identity in postcolonial and indigenous settings.

Changing the subject

Changing the Subject (Henriques et al. 1984) argued for a radical overhaul of psychology's view of the self. Its explicit agenda was, literally, to change our conception of both 'the subject' *of* psychology and 'the subject' *in* psychology – 'to demonstrate that the individual is not a fixed or given entity, but rather a particular product of historically specific practices of social regulation (Henriques et al. 1984: 12). It was written in reaction to what its authors saw as the ethnocentrism and prejudice built into experimental social psychological theories of the self. It argued that the self is not a subjective, personal, self-contained, individual entity, but a reflexive, connected, situated-in-the-world, intentional and constantly presenced intersubjective self.

All that is a bit of a mouthful! Bear with me, and we will take each of these different elements of the intersubjective self in turn and gradually build up a picture of what is meant by 'the inter-subjective self'.

The reflexivity of the self

First, intersubjectivity takes a particular stance on the role our own subjectivity plays in the way we constitute our selves. If you recall, Mead's image of the person was as a reflexive self, stressing people's ability to observe, plan and respond to their own behaviour – to know themselves and to be self-directed. Mead also placed James's self-as-known and self-as-knower in a dialogical relationship with each other, in constant conversation. To be reflexive is to be aware and insightful, to be able, for example, to be ironic and make a joke against yourself. It is a portrayal of the self that is much more shrewd and intuitive, for example, than Goffman's face-saver.

The connectedness of the self

The second element of intersubjectivity is about how we construct and know who we are through our connected subjectivity with others – through our relationships and shared under-standings with the people and the other things and abstract concepts (like religious faith) that give significance and meaning to our lives. These are as diverse as opera to soap opera, parents to pop idols, from the groups to which we belong as well as those from which we want to dis-tance ourselves. Our **connected self** is constructed both for us (for example, through the duties and obligations others expect us to fulfil) and by us (through, for instance, emotional feelings towards another person or a pet, belief in God, or a sense of national pride).

From an intersubjective perspective, connectedness is not just a quality of 'exotic others', though it undoubtedly has more salience in some value systems than others. It is central to all people, even those who live in a world that prioritizes the individual. To reiterate James, we could not be the selves we are 'If no one turned around when we entered, answered when we spoke, or minded what we did, but if every person we met "cut us dead" and acted as if we were nonexisting things' (James 1907: 179).

This element also has a lot in common with the idea of social identity, but the connected self is not just a matter of alliance to and identification with ingroups and hostility to outgroups. It is about a far denser and wider network of connections – to our 'significant others' and all those other others with whom we have specific relationships, including, for example, our ancestors and people who matter to us but have died or with whom we no longer have contact.

The being-in-the-world of the self

The third element of intersubjectivity is what the philosopher Heidegger ([1928] 1962) called our **being-in-the-world**. As you saw in Chapter 2, experimental social psychology assumes there is a separation between two entities – the person and the social world – the situation or context in which that person operates. Persons are seen as individual, self-contained beings. They can be influenced by internal forces (whether instinct, values, attitudes or social cognitions) and by external forces (the situation, social context, the group). But in this viewpoint the person is still thought of as preformed and fully present, and the situation is similarly seen as a kind of independent, objective 'frame' which exerts an independent causal effect on the person.

An intersubjective view of the self challenges this separation, arguing as follows:

1   A person is never *not* in a situation that is not subject to 'social influence'. Therefore separating them creates an artificial partition, dividing up that which is inseparable. As long as they are conscious, a person is always in a state of being-in-the-world or, as James might have put it, they are always immersed in a flow of consciousness about the world, a flow of consciousness on which the world (either/both immediately present or imagined) always-ever impinges.

2   A situation is never simply an objectively present set of environmental conditions. It always-ever influences people's thoughts, experiences and actions through its significance to and meaningfulness for them. In simpler words, people are always-ever – but only ever – influenced by the situation through the way that they construe that situation. This is a similar idea to 'horizon of understanding' (Gadamer 1975) you met earlier.

3   A person is never simply just 'there' as a timeless entity, but is constantly constructed, moment by moment, through the immanent possibilities presented by the situations that they are 'in', which are continually transformed and negotiated by the person.

Stainton Rogers et al. put it like this:

> people are inexorably part of, involved with, and inseparable from the circumstances that make up their world. To conceive of our selves (or whatever is denoted by the words 'I' and 'Me') as the 'inside' and the world as the 'outside' (a collection of stimuli) is to fail to recognize the extent to which we exist alongside-and-within the world. It is through and against our everyday involvements and engagements with the circumstances of our worlds (especially including other people) that we come to know ourselves.
>
> (1995: 55)

As I mentioned at the beginning of the section, experimental social psychology treats people as self-contained individuals who respond mechanistically to external and internal stimuli. Its theories of the 'self' therefore treat issues of concern, significance and involvement as things that 'get in the way' of being able to predict how people will behave. An intersubjective view of the self takes the opposite position. It says that if you want to know why a person is acting in a particular way, you cannot do so unless you also know what they are interested and involved in, what their concerns are, what the situation means to them:

> Here I am following the convention of referring to myself (as I was part of the et al.) as just a disinterested other because I played only a small contribution in writing these words.

> In short, to unproblematically separate personality from situation is to be already stepping blithely along an intellectual path which renounces our fundamental worldliness in favour of a radical objectification and subjection of all that is (i.e. either everything is subjective or everything is objective). What we mean by 'the world' here is not some external objectivity that we, as primarily detached subjectivities, strive to get to know. To us the world comprises the meaningful constitutive circumstances which are the source and target of our ongoing concerns and interests. The world is that which we are already involved with, and hence that which is significant for us: *our* world.
>
> (Stainton Rogers et al. 1995: 56, emphasis in the original)

The intentionality of the self

The fourth element of intersubjectivity is a perception of the person as purposive and strategic – as acting intentionally – an intentional self. In Chapter 1, I drew attention to James's understanding of the self that stressed his vision of people as intentional, and thus having free will.

Of course we measure ourselves by many standards. Our strength and our intelligence, our wealth and even our good luck, are things that warm our heart and make us feel ourselves a match for life. But deeper than all such things, and able to suffice unto itself without them, is the sense of the amount of effort which we can put forth. Those are, after all, but effects, products and reflections of the outer world within. But the effort seems to belong to an altogether different realm, as if it were the substantive thing that we are, and those are but externals that we carry.

(James 1907: 458)

In this perspective the situations and circumstances and social influences, both those that directly impinge from the outside and those that are 'in our heads' and exert influence from the inside, are not what ultimately determine our actions. They are not causes. They do not produce a passive puppet that cannot move unless these external and internal forces pull the strings. Rather they provide a stage in which a range of possible actions can be acted out – but acted out intentionally through, for want of a better word, our will. Our actions are wilful, intended actions – or, at least, they can be, and (usually) are when it matters.

Here we can draw parallels with what is happening in theorization in experimental social psychology. As you saw in Chapters 7 and 8, their perception of attribution and attitudes is moving to a position where it is recognized that a lot of what we do in the ordinary, mundane, everyday living of our life is pretty mindless. We go along a lot of the time running on autopilot, in a largely pre-programmed manner. We are barely conscious of the things we say and do, and act them out virtually automatically. In such circumstances we are somewhat like robots – very efficient, but also servile to the vicissitudes of our programming that is encoded highly stereotypically and heuristically, and hence open to thinking and acting in mindless ways that can lead to mindless stupidity.

To claim that people have the capacity to be intentional is not to claim that they always act with great deliberation and intention, or even that they do so most of the time. It is to claim that they *can* be intentional, and usually are when it matters to them to be so. In other words, stressing intentionality directs our attention to the ways in which people are strategic in what they do – including constructing themselves.

When a woman says, for example, 'I am a lesbian', she is not somehow looking within herself and reporting what she has discovered there. She is actively and intentionally staking a claim, on the basis of what matters to her in her life and on what matters in the 'now' of the conversation she is having. The person she is speaking to might make a counterclaim, such as, 'Well, you don't look like one and you don't act like one, and I think you are just playing at it because you think it's trendy. You're not a real lesbian, you're just a lipstick lesbian'. This person is staking a counterclaim, based on what matters to them in their life and on what matters in the 'now' of the conversation they are having.

Situations like this, where people contest or confirm their own or each other's definitions of their selves, are the norm when saying something about your self. There are formal situations – such as filling in a form to get a passport or to apply for a job. In neither case do you merely look inside your self to tell who you are. The circumstance sets up an agenda, telling you what kind of claim you need to stake. There are intimate situations – sending your lover a text message that says 'You are my earth, moon and stars' or being told by your irate friend 'Who do you think you are – my mother?' These circumstances also set their own agendas. They have what is sometimes rather clumsily called '**issuance**' – there is an issue at stake, around which one or more stakes are claimed and often counterclaimed.

To send a text to your lover saying 'You are my earth, moon and stars' is not some kind of pallid conveying of a description, it is sent for a purpose (I am sure you can think of all sorts of possible reasons, from the sweetly romantic to the cynical). Whenever a self (or an aspect of a self) is defined, it is done for a reason, to stake some kind of a claim, in order to achieve some sort of end. Even done mindlessly, the habitual nature of such a claim arises from a purpose, albeit, in this case, a purpose that, itself, has become habitual. Sociologically speaking, the term here is 'habitus' (Bordieu 1993).

The self as constituted through presencing practices

Staking a claim is always provisional and contingent. An intersubjective perspective of the self denies the assumption that 'personality' or 'character' is a static and consistent quality of being-a-person. It sees instead a self as constituted through **presencing practices**, a self that is always-ever in a state of being re-produced, both through the 'flow of consciousness' and through being-in-the-world. The analogy I have used is music-making, where the music exists only through being played. It helps, I hope, to understand what is being said here. This is probably the most difficult claim for most people to accept, because it is seen to imply that the self is entirely fragmentary, with nothing holding it together – a chameleon that is in a constant state of transformation.

To get a handle on it, you need to take all the other aspects of intersubjectivity into your frame of reference. Crucially you need to transcend the person/situation division that, in a modern worldview, at least, is so deeply sedimented it feels natural and incontrovertible. If you can accept that the self is in a constant state of being presenced – the self not as a thing but as a product of presencing practices – then you are more than halfway there.

An example may help here. In Shakespeare's time homosexuality was not seen as an identity but as a practice, conceptualized as something that some people sometimes *did*, rather than something some people enduringly *were*. Taking an intersubjective stance on the self is to re-connect the person and the situation into an interconnected presencing practice (that is, action) rather than regarding them as two separate entities in interaction. The person/situation distinction is seen, in this theoretical frame, as reifying (thingifying, if you like, see Chapter 6) the self. Let us take our example of homosexuality, and tease apart what is signified by 'reification'. Here is a clear illustration of what I mean, drawn from an account of homosexuality written in the 1960s, when it was classified as an illness:

> The homosexual has been a stumbling block to many clinical theorists – especially in that he fails to respond to treatment – and he has been described as obstinate, uncooperative, etc. The profile places him actually as an anxiety neurotic, perhaps as a result of undischargeable ergic tensions, but also with a peculiar emphasis on extraversion and radicalism. Thus unlike the introverted neurotic he is compelled to 'act out' his difficulty, and to do so without conservative inhibitions.
>
> (Cattell 1966: 331)

Because this is written in the homophobic language of the 1960s and uses the terminology of Eysenck's extraversion/introversion theory, it is relatively easy to 'see through' what is going on – Cattell is staking a claim. It is that 'the homosexual' (that is, a particular category of person) is 'an anxiety neurotic' (that is, has particular innate psychologically dysfunctional qualities) and therefore that he is 'compelled to act out' (that is, that he is unable to help himself behaving in a dysfunctional way). Put this all together and you have constructed homosexuality as a thing – a category of person with psychologically dysfunctional qualities that impel him to act in a dysfunctional way.

All the presencing practices that could still today add up to being given this identity of homosexual-as-mentally-ill – acting in a 'camp manner', going to gay bars, marching in Gay Pride processions (I could go on, but you get the picture) – would be merely seen, through that identity, as forms of dysfunctional 'acting out' of a 'difficulty'. But for a gay man today, certainly in places like San Francisco or Sydney, they are something else entirely – the presence being practised is not an 'acting out of neurosis' but a celebration of a gay identity.

The point is, either way, presencing practices like these do not inevitably make a person into a homosexual. A gay man might celebrate his gay identity with pride, and through identifying with a gay community that both provides opportunity for and approval of these presencing practices. But that does not make his identity a 'real thing'. Now all we need to do is close a loop. Throughout the book you have been exposed to the claim that, from a discursive psychology point of view, people construct their social realities through discursive practices – by purposively and strategically doing things whenever they use language. Discursive practices are one form of presencing practice. Staking a claim is a discursive practice that is also a presencing practice. Claiming an identity is to reproduce it through discursive practices, within situations of other presencing practices (like going to gay pubs, marching in Gay Pride rallies). It is in this sense that a self is seen to be not an identity (who you are) but a practice (what you do, in relation to what your deeds mean).

The performative self

The performative self is, in many ways, just a different way of saying self as constituted through presencing practice. They both draw on similar philosophical foundations, and are also linked to the kind of 'relational self' Mkhize is drawing upon in his quest for a more appropriate form of self for indigenous people. However, the concept of 'performativity' is both a crucial one for critical psychologists, and a very misunderstood one. It sounds more like a continuation of the work of Goffman with which this chapter began. But it is nothing like that. It is important, therefore, to spend a bit of time sorting it out, which is not easy, because it is a tricky idea to understand.

This approach is generally associated with Judith Butler, a feminist philosopher, whose books *Gender Trouble* (1990) and *Bodies that Matter* (1993) shifted feminist theory, particularly, away from a focus on identities to ideas about the performativity of the self. Butler strove very actively to separate her theories from any notion of theatre or an actor, as a real person, playacting a fiction: 'There is no "I" who stands *behind* discourse and executes its volition or will *through* discourse. On the contrary, the "I" only comes into being through being called, named, interpolated, . . . and this discursive construction takes place prior to the "I"; it is the transitive invocation of the "I"' (2003: 109).

As Chinn (2010) points out, at the time Butler was developing her ideas, this strong position set her up against others working in the fields of gender and sexuality who were interested in overt forms of performance – the ways that people were acting out characters like 'queen', 'dyke', 'butch', 'femme' and 'tranny' in a variety of marginal and private spaces. For some the fight was between academic and activist positions, in a situation where many of these theorists were fighting against discrimination and prejudice. But Chinn rejects this as too simplistic, and argues that Butler's concept of 'performativity' provided a way out from arguments about whether gender and sexuality are either 'built into our DNA' or no more than a 'lifestyle choice'.

Chinn traces the idea of performativity back to another philosopher, Austin (1962) who divided language into two different kinds:

- **constitutive language**, that simply describes – as in 'the grass is green';
- **performative language**, that makes things happen – as in a minister saying 'I pronounce you man and wife'.

A performative statement is not the end of the matter, obviously. Declaring a marriage needs to be backed up with a valid, signed marriage licence or other such formal record. And it can only work within institutions like law, and conventions about what marriage signifies and means.

Indeed, it is these taken-for-granted understandings that make the language capable of doing things, which is what Butler means by 'the transitive invocation of the "I"'. The pre-figured conventions that tell us about what being an 'I' means and signifies, and what being a 'psychologist' means and signifies are what make the claim 'I am a psychologist' performative. I can claim to be a Jedi, but I can only be a Jedi in a world where the Jedi are real and not fictional. But Jedi become real through claims made about being one (as some people do when asked their religion on census forms and the like).

Another example might work better. Worrell (2001) studied the way in which women, who, when they were children, had been sexually assaulted by adults, repositioned themselves from 'victims' to 'survivors'. This they did through taking part in self-help group meetings, that featured members making quite formal, public statements like 'I am Nema, and I am an incest survivor.'

In this performative speech act they did not simply lay claim to a particular identity but, in so doing, contributed to creating and sustaining this identity as one that is meaningful, available and demands that a person be treated in a particular way. The very concept of 'incest survivor' is a relatively new one, made and made real within the local and contingent set of circumstances in the 1980s and 1990s, in the USA and the UK particularly, where 'child sexual abuse' became a major preoccupation (some would say moral panic) in child welfare policy and practice. The naming of the identity of a 'survivor' was very much a conscious ideological act, specifically created and intended to change the way people think about those who have experienced sexual assaults in childhood (and note that I, in my words, am taking a very particular ideological position). And in changing the way they are thought about, the aim is to change the way they are treated. The perception being challenged was (and is) that of the 'harmed victim' who, according to much of the professional literature of the time, is inevitably so damaged by the experience that they have no hope at all of ever functioning as a 'healthy' and 'normal' person ever again (see O'Dell 1997). Victims like this are harmed, and hence doomed to being pathetic and pitied. Survivors have been wronged, and hence have pride in their own resilience and demand respect.

Foucault's work is important here, especially his work on sexualities. Foucault viewed sexualities not as natural or inevitable, but rather the products of complex networks of power that construct subjectivity. In order to be a 'subject', in this sense, you have to 'have' or 'be' a specific sexuality (even if that is 'celibate'). You have to somehow parcel up all your situated sexual practices, sexual desires and sexual feelings towards people with whom you have relationships and turn them from things you feel and think and do into a sexual *identity*. And you do not have a free hand in this, you cannot pick and choose. Only some feelings, some practices, some relationships count, and they have to be ordered in a particular way to make something recognizable as a sexuality. *This* is what is meant by sexuality being performative. Having or being or owning to a certain sexuality makes some things happen and prevents others, just as being a 'survivor' prevents some things from being done and thereby creates the space for other things to be done: ' "performance" is not a singular "act" or event, but a ritualized production, a ritual reiterated under and through constraint, under and through the force of prohibition and taboo, with the threat of ostracism and even death controlling and compelling the shape of the production' (Butler 1993: 95).

The psychoanalytic self

According to Lucey (2007), the social psychoanalytic approach:

- emphasizes the dynamic, relational and *inseparable* nature of social and psychological life to look at how subjectivity emerges in the social domain
- theorizes and analyses *unconscious* as well as conscious processes
- maintains that anxiety and the strategies developed to defend against the difficult feelings that anxiety provokes play an important part in the construction of individual, social, cultural and institutional lives
- is theoretically plural in that it brings concepts together that can take account of the *interior* processes of the human mind (individual and group emotions) with those that relate to arenas of the social world (structure and power) (Lucey 2007: 80–1).

Examining the unconscious, such as unconscious **defence mechanisms**, allows psychologists to explore features of our 'inner world' of emotions, desires and motives. Considering anxiety allows us to gain insight into the conflicts that a person may face – between desire and duty, for example – and the strategies or tactics a person may use to tackle this conflict. One tactic is 'projection', where a person is made so anxious by their feelings – of weakness or shame, for instance – that they find it impossible to 'own' as their own. They deal with this conflict by projecting it onto something or someone else, such as a person ('my sister') or an outgroup (Islamists).

The authoritarian personality

A good example of this kind of approach is work done by Adorno and his colleagues on the authoritarian personality (Adorno et al. 1950). They undertook one of the earliest studies of personality, shortly after the end of the Second World War, with the specific purpose of seeking to understand the anti-Semitism that had been such a central part of Nazisim. Their explicit objective was to discover what it is that leads some people to become prejudiced, in order to be able to ensure that the horrors of the Nazi regime would not be repeated.

Adorno and his colleagues found that people expressing authoritarian personality traits (racist attitudes, antagonism to homosexuals, very rigid ideas about what men and women should be like) tended to have had very harsh, traditional upbringings. Their parents adopted rigidly traditional gender roles, imposed strict and inflexible rules of conduct, and applied harsh punishments for rule-breaking. Adorno and his colleagues developed their ideas from psychodynamic theories about the impact of child-rearing practices and events in childhood upon adult personality. They concluded that authoritarianism was the product of repressed aggression which got projected onto others. Children brought up in this manner, they argued, experience feelings of hostility towards their parents because of their harsh treatment. But, because of their parents' repressive control, when they were children they were unable to express this anger. As a consequence, Adorno and his colleagues argued that the anger became displaced onto less 'dangerous' (from a psychodynamic point of view) targets, such as members of other races or homosexuals.

Subject positioning as an investment

Unconscious anxiety is seen in psychoanalytic theory as not just normal and inevitable, but functional in the production of a healthy adult 'self'. Properly managed, conflicts between internally engendered wishes and desires, on the one hand, and the internalized norms and codes of 'proper conduct' from the outside, on the other, result in a 'self' that is capable of navigating successfully through life and achieving relevant goals. 'Identity is, crucially and centrally, a developmental achievement of the ego, and one that is necessary for the wellbeing of each subject', claims Stephen Frosh, one of the foremost social psychoanalytic theorists (2010: 31). He cites Erikson, the post-Freudian psychoanalytic theorists who has had perhaps most influence on social psychology: 'I have been using the term *ego identity* to denote certain comprehensive gains which the individual, at the end of adolescence, must have derived from all of his pre-adult experiences in order to be ready for the tasks of adulthood' (Erikson 1956: 56, emphasis in the original).

This stance regards psychodynamic processes as 'work to be done' in order for children – and especially adolescents – to develop. Rex Stainton Rogers (Stainton Rogers and Stainton Rogers 1992) had a neat way to describe this theory of child development – the 'Jack the Dragonslayer' tale in which the child, like Jack, is sent out on a series of quests where, in order to gain the hand in marriage of the Princess, he must face and conquer a series of dragons and other threatening creatures. According to this story, dealing with our psychodynamic monsters is how we, as people, are able to come into ourselves as fully matured, functioning adult members of society.

Think back to the ideas of Bakhtin and Shotter on internalization, and Butler on performativity. Both theorize about how the 'outside' – the norms and rules and values of society and culture – gets incorporated into our inner worlds through dialogue between them. Intersubjectivity as a whole is about the way 'inner' and 'outer' implicate each other and cannot be treated as separate. 'In psychoanalytic versions of intersubjectivity, each person is made up, psychologically speaking, of introjected (unconsciously internalized) parts of others that flow dynamically between people' (Hollway 2007: 128).

Psychoanalytic theory does two things in this. First, it provides a language and a set of concepts (like ego, repression, complex, projection) to theorize what is entailed in the 'work to be done' not only of psychic development but our ongoing navigation through our lives and in our relationships. Second, it adds to the somewhat cold and rational accounts of the processes involved a recognition of what Shotter has otherwise called the 'knowing of the third kind' – the pre-conscious and unconscious feelings and emotions involved, the muddled, troubled quandaries, ambivalences and uncertainties that pervade our attempts to make any sense of who we are and what we want, and what we ought to be doing.

At times the language used can feel awkward and unrealistic. I do, for example, find it hard to take on Melanie Klein's description of the 'paranoid schizoid' position adopted when children see the world and objects within it as either entirely good or entirely bad, to be followed, in reaching emotional maturity, by the 'depressive position' when the child recognizes that people (including themselves) can be partially good and partially bad. It is hard to accept statements like 'The depressive position enables the self to be more integrated' (Hollway 2007: 129). I do feel sometimes that psychoanalytic theorists are being deliberately obstructive and making their ideas difficult to understand. But I would also say that, uncomfortable as it may be, this approach to intersubjectivity is important. Without it we are definitely 'missing something'.

The social psychoanalytic approach provides an important resource for investigating the socially and culturally situated self, and the dynamic processes and changes involved in the formation, maintenance and defence of our identities. It widens the scope of our understanding of how people make meaning out of experiences, and how they incorporate what they have learned into who they are. While there has been no room here for any real coverage of this aspect, it has also become a significant resource for studying the embodiment of the self, and the role of emotions.

The intersubjective self

- The intersubjective self is seen as reflexive, connected, situated-in-the-world, intentional and the product of presencing practices.

- This approach is pursued in different ways – including discourse and narrative analysis, phenomenology, social psychoanalysis and by attending to performativity.

- In all cases there is a rejection of dualisms – self/other, inside/outside, thinking/feeling. Instead the focus is on interplays and interconnections – on how these 'talk to' each other and are mutually constitutive of the self.

Resources

The UK's Economic and Social Research Council (ESRC) funded a five-year project investigating identities and social action. There were 25 projects on a diversity of aspect of identity. Find out more about these here: http://www.esrcsocietytoday.ac.uk/ESRCInfoCentre/research/research_programmes/identities_social_action.aspx

Further reading

Wetherell, M. and Mohanty, C.T. (eds) (2010) *The Sage Handbook of Identities.* London: Sage. This handbook is one of the outcomes from the ESRC identities project, and offers a wealth of well-written, contemporary and inspirational chapters about identity on a massive scale. Like most handbooks, it is expensive and more of a reference book, but well worth consulting to find chapters in fields of special interest to you. It is not a 'social psychology' book, but it is surprising just how many chapters are relevant.

Experimental social psychology

Myers, D., Abell, J., Kolstad, A. and Sani, F. (2010*) Social Psychology: European Edition***. London: McGraw-Hill.**
Chapter 3 on 'The Self' is, in my view, the best source for all the traditional work carried out within the experimental paradigm on this subject, It covers locus of control, learned helplessness and self-esteem in much more depth than in this chapter.

Critical social psychology

Hollway, W. (2007) Self, in W. Hollway, H. Lucey and A. Phoenix *Social Psychology Matters*. **Maidenhead: Open University Press.**
Lucey, H. (2007) Families, in W. Hollway, H. Lucey and A. Phoenix *Social Psychology Matters*. **Maidenhead: Open University Press.**
These two chapters together provide an excellent account of the self from a critical perspective, and are especially good for learning more about the phenomenological and social psychoanalytic approach, much of it based on Hollway's and Lucey's own work in this field, both as theorists and a researchers.

Blackman, L. and Walkerdine, V. (2001) *Mass Hysteria: Critical Psychology and Media Studies.* **Basingstoke: Palgrave.**
This book provides a much deeper and broader analysis of intersubjective identity than I have been able to give here. Chapter 10 – 'Post-identities: sexuality and the colonial subject' – is particularly useful. There is a great deal to get your head round in this book, but it is a sustained project of linking critical (social) psychology and media studies and, as such, set to become an influential text. You might like to begin with Chapter 10 on Princess Diana and practices of subjectification (another way of putting subject positioning), which is a gripping read.

Reicher, S., Spears, R. and Haslam, S.A. (2010) The social identity approach in social psychology, in M. Wetherell and C.T. Mohanty (eds) *The Sage Handbook of Identities***. London: Sage.**
This chapter is an excellent introduction to social identity theory.

Mkhize, N. (2004) Psychology: an African perspective, in D. Hook, N. Mkhise, P. Kiguwa and A. Collins (eds) *Critical Psychology***. Cape Town: UCT Press.**
Mkhize, N. (2004) Sociocultural approaches to psychology: dialogism and African conceptions of the self, in D. Hook, N. Mkhise, P. Kiguwa and A. Collins (eds) *Critical Psychology***. Cape Town: UCT Press.**
These two chapters from the South African *Critical Psychology* textbook read and look different from any other textbook chapters in the mainstream catalogue. Their African roots are evident in what is said and the images used. Apart from being excellent chapters in their own right, tackling complex ideas with great clarity, they offer a way into seeing the world differently from the way Western academia sees it.

Questions

1 What can the early work of James, Mead and Goffman offer to our understanding of the self today?

2 To what extent does a person's sense of who they are depend upon the culture in which they were brought up? What problems does this pose for social psychology?

3 What contribution has social learning theory made to our understanding of the self?

4 Explain the difference between social identity theory and social categorization theory and outline the ways this overall approach opens up the concept of identity.

5 What is meant by the term 'intersubjective self'? Does it imply that people can simply choose who they want to be?

6 What contribution has social psychoanalytic psychology made to our understanding of the self?

7 Chose one of the approaches in this chapter as the one you find most credible, and explain why you think it is best.

Chapter 11

The social psychology of relationships

LEARNING OUTCOMES

When you have finished studying this chapter, you should be able to:

1 Outline two different explanations for pro-social behaviour and altruism.

2 Describe in some detail experimental social psychology's research on the bystander effect and its findings, and summarize the main criticisms of this work made by critical social psychologists.

3 Explain what is meant by the 'relationship imperative' and its impact on people's perceptions of being single, and outline at least one approach in social psychology that views singlehood as a dysfunctional state.

4 Describe how interpretative repertoires, ideological dilemmas and subject positions can be used as analytics to gain insight into alternative understandings of what it means to be single.

5 Describe how a narrative approach can help us to understand relationships in terms of three key frames – life cycle, life events and life as progress.

6 Summarize research into 'love styles' as done by Lee and Hendrick and Hendrick.

7 List at least three different kinds of coupled love identified by Watts and Stenner, and explain how Q methodology helped them to identify and explicate them.

> **8** Make a case for the claim that family relationships are constructed within different worldviews that differ from one culture to another.
>
> **9** Explain why relationships within and between communities matter, illustrating your argument with examples from Wike and Cohen Silver's study of the townspeople of Jasper.

Introduction

This chapter is about the ways in which individuals' thoughts, feelings and actions are influenced by being in relationships with others. This includes family relationships and kinship including (but more than) parent–child relationships and being part of a couple, but also social relationships in groups. Woven throughout social psychology's research and theorizing in this field you will find this tension played out – between groups as forces for good and groups as forces for evil – reflecting the political and ideological assumptions to the psychologists concerned. Bear this in mind as you read, and be sensitive to the positions being taken and the stories being told.

In this chapter I have not tried to provide a thinly spread comprehensive coverage of the social psychological work in this field. There is an awful lot of it, from both experimental and critical perspectives. Rather it is a more selective approach, looking in each section at just one or two key examples of the kind of relationship involved, in order to be able to go into rather more depth. These also serve a further purpose, since I have deliberately covered in the chapter a chance to look in some detail at a spread of research methods, giving you opportunities to gain a better understanding of how they work in practice when applied to particular topics and research questions.

The chapter begins with an in-depth look at relationships between strangers, looking at each pole on the helping/not helping dimension. It completes your work on the 'bystander effect' but also includes some more recent stories intended to make you think about situatedness, helping and heroism. The next section is on singlehood, looking at two studies – one of single gay men and the other of single women. This moves us on to attraction and love, focusing here on a Q methodological study of different forms that couple love can take – from the romantic to the pragmatic, virtuous to the raunchy. Family relationships are tackled next, with a study on sisterhood as the main example, The chapter ends with a novel section on relationships in communities, opening up ideas about social capital in a study about how a community – the townspeople of Jasper, Texas, USA – were able to draw upon their strong community resources to manage the social trauma of a horrific racist killing. This, I believe, is an under-theorized and under-researched area that social psychology should bring into its sphere, as a counter to its enduring preoccupation with relationships studied at the individual level.

Sociality and strangers

It may seem a bit strange to start a chapter on social relationships by looking at how we behave socially towards strangers! But in a way, it does drive home that humans (and, indeed, many animals) are almost always social in what they do, even if they are not aware of it.

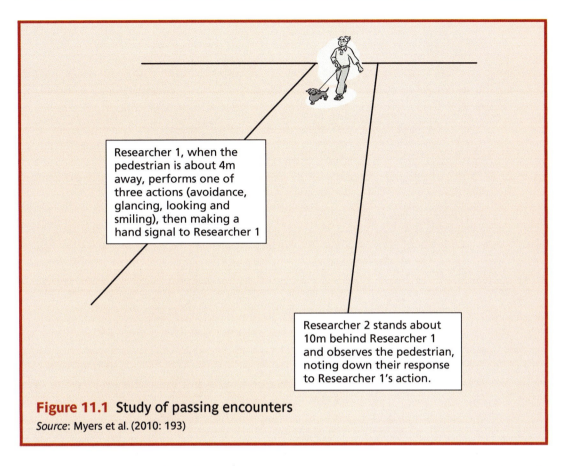

Researcher 1, when the pedestrian is about 4m away, performs one of three actions (avoidance, glancing, looking and smiling), then making a hand signal to Researcher 1

Researcher 2 stands about 10m behind Researcher 1 and observes the pedestrian, noting down their response to Researcher 1's action.

Figure 11.1 Study of passing encounters
Source: Myers et al. (2010: 193)

This is brought home by a field study (Patterson et al. 2007) examining how people in different cultural settings respond to signals of varying intensity of sociality: avoiding eye contact, glancing or directly looking and smiling. The researchers went to places where there were steady streams of people walking past. They worked in teams of two, one researcher at the front initiating the social interaction (or lack of it) with a passer-by while the other researcher observed from 4 metres further on (so could not see which of the three signals had been made) recording the pedestrian's response. This set-up is shown in Figure 11.1.

In this way the research team gathered data from more than 1000 pedestrians in the USA and in Japan. The aim was to compare the two, to test the hypothesis that, because of different cultural conventions, Japanese people would respond far less than Americans.

Not surprisingly, the degree of sociality affected the responses in both cultures – the walkers were more responsive after being smiled at than they were if no social signal had been given. But it was culture that dramatically made a difference. Japanese pedestrians responded least of all to a glance, and only a little more to a smile. In a culture that has strong social rules about respecting privacy, this was to be expected. Equally expected were the responses among Americans, where there are strong social rules about being open and friendly. The American pedestrians reacted very much more to a glance than to averted eyes, and very much more to a direct look and a smile (especially if the smile was from a woman!).

Pro-social behaviour and altruism

Social psychologists have been particularly interested in studying **pro-social behaviour**. This is about people taking action towards strangers in order to be kind and helpful, in settings where such helping and caregiving are not part of their professional role. Examples include the stereotype 'helping an old lady across the road', giving up your seat on a crowded train, as a passenger lifting someone's suitcase onto a luggage rack, letting a driver in from a side road in heavy traffic, and so on. More broadly this includes giving money to charities or doing voluntary work for 'good causes'. **Altruism** tends to be defined as acting for the benefit of others as an end-in-itself, with no expectation of reward and, indeed, sometimes an active avoidance it, such as when a person donates money anonymously.

Both kinds of behaviour (to the extent that they are actually different) are profoundly social. They are encouraged, even required, by many religions and moral codes. If you accept that much behaviour is about staking a claim to a particular identity (Chapter 10), then acts of chivalry, generosity, kindness, compassion and so on are powerful ways to 'do' the identity of a benevolent and authentic person. It means you can feel good about yourself, if your values and beliefs define 'being good' in terms of 'do gooding'. There are other more egotistical rewards too of course – including the pleasure gained from gratitude and social approval, the potential for reciprocation and the sense of contributing to your community.

Sociologists use the term **social capital** to describe the benefits that certain communities and collectives gain through having high levels of mutual support, willingness to help each other out at times of trouble, trust towards and respect for each other and, especially, a sense of common goals and values (Bourdieu 1972; Coleman 1988). You will come to examine this concept more thoroughly towards the end of the chapter when we come to look at relationships within communities. For now, it is worth making the point that there are very real benefits to living among people where pro-social behaviour is common and expected, rather than a rare occurrence in a hostile world of people out to further their own interests and willing to trample over others to achieve their goals. I say this because many psychologists, especially those who take an evolutionary stance, struggle to explain altruism, since it makes no sense if what is at stake is 'survival of the fittest'.

Evolutionary explanations of pro-social behaviour

But explain it they do, suggesting three main processes:

- *Kin selection* where you gain an advantage by being helpful to those who share some of your genetic heritage. This is an aspect of the '**selfish-gene' hypothesis**, where behaviour is seen as motivated by an innate drive to pass on as much of your replicated genetic material as possible to the next generation.

- *Inclusive fitness* is a more complex version of this, where what matters is not an individual's genetic heritage alone, but as part of a whole cohort of reproductive success among related people.

- *Reciprocal altruism* where helping others creates expectations that they will help you in return if you are in trouble, thus improving your chances of survival in such situations.

You can see in these formulations a very individualistic stance being taken, all about individual benefits in a competition for survival between group members. This 'survival of the fittest' element in evolutionary theory – the 'shark-filled-pool' analogy has traditionally been the dominant one. Once a shift is made to theories of co-operation and nurturance (Haraway 1984) – the 'all in it together' analogy – then it becomes easier to make sense of more general altruism in evolutionary terms, as in reciprocal altruism. With 'inclusive fitness' this moves into an explanation that expands to include the joint reproductive success of a whole tribe or other collective. If mutual co-operation and support increase the overall number of children born and reared to reproductive maturity in the tribe as a whole, then each individual member gains an advantage over those in less mutually supportive tribes.

This is just what social identity theory would predict, and it would be quite easy to reformulate it in evolutionary terms. The trouble is that we simply have no way of knowing whether the benefits of mutual support and strong social capital are mediated by our genes or not. Just showing a reproductive advantage of belonging to a well-functioning group does not mean that evolution is the cause.

Experimental social psychological explanations of pro-social behaviour

Once again social learning theory was the traditional approach taken to pro-social behaviour, where children learn to be 'sociable' by being rewarded for such behaviour and punished for being 'unkind' or 'naughty' towards others. Other ideas include the possibility of an altruistic personality type (locating the cause in individual temperament or character) and being situation based, where a person's mood is found to relate to their likelihood of being helpful. Other explanations include the impact of guilt, belief in a just world, and empathy.

More recent theorization within the experimental social psychology tradition focuses on exchange theory, where people are seen to act rather like accountants. In situations that provide opportunities to help, people are seen to explicitly or subconsciously conduct a cost–benefit analysis of benefits to be gained by helping, and costs to be paid. This 'what's in it for me' approach tends to be used more with strangers. Clarke and Grote (2003) distinguish between **exchange relationships** commonly found in cases where people have little or no prior relationship with each other, and **communal relationships** between family, friends and romantic partners.

> Myers et al. (2010: 184–93) provide more detail.

Finally, within the mainstream there are theories that have been incorporated into psychology around norms of social responsibility, fairness and compassion.

Why people do not help

If you recall, this book started with a short account of the rape and murder of Kitty Genovese that took place even though there were people who could see and hear what was going on, many of whom did nothing to help at her time of need. The report of this incident in the *New York Times*, that wrote in disgust about the 'apathy' of these bystanders, was the stimulus for a whole programme of experimental research into what was originally called 'bystander apathy' and has now come to be called the '**bystander effect**'. For many years after that, social psychology textbooks churned out the story, raised questions about what on earth was going on, and then introduced the psychological research. Here is how one of those textbook authors described it: 'What caused the estimated thirty-eight witnesses looking out of their windows to remain totally inactive? The most general answer, according to Latané and Darley, lies in the powerful effect bystanders have on one another in discouraging assistance to another stranger' (Hollander 1976: 239).

We now know (Manning et al. 2007) that the actual events were different from the newspaper version – there were far fewer witnesses, some of them did respond, and Kitty was not murdered or raped in front of the building but later, once she was in a stairwell out of sight. The fact remains, however, that Bibb Latané and John Darley had lunch together soon after the incident and decided to work together on social psychological experiments to investigate the reasons why people may fail to intervene in situations like this. You should have already read in detail about their two initial experiments (Darley and Latané 1968; Latané and Darley 1968) in Chapters 1, 2 and 4. I put them there as great examples of the way that standard, experimental work in social psychology often contains, hidden away in a report of 'debriefing the subjects' section in the paper, accounts of what the subjects said about their experiences and observations of their state of mind (that is, *qualitative* data). Go back and have a look at this (or look at it for the first time if you have not yet studied that chapter) as the qualitative data really are fascinating.

Latané and Darley's studies of the bystander effect

In 1968, soon after the Kitty Genovese incident, two parallel studies were conducted by Bibb Latané and John Darley to investigate the effects of having other people around, when facing an emergency of some kind. They compared what happens when a person thinks they are the only one involved, and when there are others (or they think there are).

In the first experiment (Darley and Latané 1968) the emergency was another participant in the study apparently having a serious fit. The researchers described their procedure like this:

> A college student arrived in the laboratory and was ushered into an individual room from which a communication system would enable him to talk to the other participants. It was explained to him that he was to take part in a discussion about personal problems associated with college life and that the discussion would be held over the intercom system, rather than face-to-face, in order to avoid embarrassment by preserving the anonymity of the subjects. During the course of the discussion, one of the other subjects underwent what appeared to be a very serious nervous seizure similar to epilepsy. During the fit it was impossible for the subject to talk to the other discussants or to find out what, if anything, they were doing about the emergency. The dependent variable was the speed with which the subjects reported the emergency to the experimenter. The major independent variable was the number of people the subject thought to be in the discussion group.
>
> (Darley and Latané 1968: 378)

Note that subjects are referred to as 'he' even though there were 59 female but only 14 male subjects (who only took part in one small part of the overall study)! Anyway, each of them on arriving to take part was led by an experimental assistant to a small room, presented with earphones and a microphone, and told to listen for instructions once they had filled out an initial background information form. Over this system a tape recording of the experimenter explained how he was investigating the kinds of personal problems experienced by students in the high-pressure urban environment of the college. To avoid possible embarrassment when strangers have to talk about their personal problems, he said, each participant in the discussion would take part in a room of their own so they could remain totally anonymous from each other and from the experimenter. He would not listen in on the discussion when it was taking place, but get the information later by questionnaire. And, as the experimenter would not be there, an automatic switching device would be used. This would be set so participants could only give their account in a predetermined order, in turn, and only one could talk at a time. They were told there would be time for open discussion at the end, but this never materialized.

This is what happened in the experimental conditions:

[T]he future victim spoke first, saying that he found it difficult to get adjusted to New York City and to his studies. Very hesitantly, and with obvious embarrassment, he mentioned that he was prone to seizures, particularly when studying hard or taking exams. The other people, including the real subject, took their turns and discussed similar problems (minus, of course, the proneness to seizures). The naive subject talked last in the series, after the last prerecorded voice was played.

When it was again the victim's turn to talk, he made a few relatively calm comments, and then, growing increasingly louder and incoherent, he continued:

I-er-um-I think I-I need-er-if-if could-er-er-somebody er-er-er-er-er-er-er give me a liltle-er-give me a little help here because-er-I-er-I'm-er-erh-h-having a-a-a real problem-er-right now and I-er-if somebody could help me out it would-it would-er-er s-s-sure be-sure be good . . . becausecr-there-er-cr-a cause I-er-I-uh-I've got a-a one of the-er-sei er-cr-things coming on and-and-and I could really-er-use some help so if somebody would-er-give me a little h-help-uh-er-er-er-er-er c-could somebody-er-er-help-er-uh-uh-uh (choking sounds). . . . I'm gonna die-er-er-I'm . . . gonna die-er-help-er-er-seizure-er-[chokes, then quiet].

(Darley and Latané 1968: 379)

This recording was abruptly turned off after the silence. The experimenter began timing the subject's seeking help (or lack of it) from the point the 'victim' started talking. The experiment was run in a variety of different ways, but here let us keep it simple. The main experimental variable was the number of other people that the experimental subject thought were part of the group discussion. This is shown in Table 11.1.

The results Darley and Latané obtained are set out in Table 11.2, though I have concentrated on whether or not the fit was reported at all. All of the subjects who thought that they, alone, could hear what was going on reported the fit, the vast majority (85 per cent) by the time it ended. But only 62 per cent reported it when they thought one other person could hear, and

Table 11.1 Darley and Latané's 1968 study of the factors influencing helping behaviour

Condition	What the experimental subject thinks is happening
The subject just hears the 'victim of the fit' talking	She thinks there are just two people taking part in the discussion, herself and the 'victim of the fit', and nobody else is listening in
The subject hears one other person talking, then the 'victim of the fit'	She thinks that when she hears the 'victim' having the fit, there is another subject listening in
The subject hears four other people talking, then the 'victim of the fit'	She thinks that when she hears the 'victim' having the fit, there are four other subjects listening in

Table 11.2 Effects of group size on reporting the fit and speed of response

Group size	N	% reporting the fit	Average time taken to report it in seconds, from the start of the 'victim' speaking
2 (S + 'victim')	13	100	52
3 (S + 'victim' + 1)	26	62	93
6 (S + 'victim' + 4)	13	31	166

Source: Darley and Latané (1968: 380)

only 31 per cent who thought there were four others. The researchers concluded: '"Diffusion of responsibility" seems the most likely explanation for this result. If an individual is alone when he notices an emergency, he is solely responsible for coping with it. If he believes others are also present, he may feel that his own responsibility for taking action is lessened, making him less likely to help' (Darley and Latané 1968: 215).

In their second study (Latané and Darley 1968) made some changes to explore what happens when people responding to an emergency are able to interact with each other, in a way deliberately made impossible in the first study. The emergency was changed to smoke coming into the room, and experimental subjects encountered this either alone or in the company of others. This time all the subjects were male students who were recruited for a study in which they were told they would discuss 'some of the problems involved in life at an urban university'. When they arrived they were sent to fill in a preliminary questionnaire in a 'waiting room'. Soon after smoke started appearing from a vent in the wall, gradually getting thicker and thicker, so the room got more and more smoke-filled. The dependent variable was how long it took participants to report the smoke.

There were three conditions – subjects acting alone, in a group of three, all of whom were naïve subjects, and in a group of three where the other two were experimental stooges who acted dumb, and, if approached by the subject, muttered things like 'I dunno'. The experimental results were again clear-cut, as shown in Table 11.3.

Participants on their own were much more likely to report the smoke than those in groups of three naïve participants. With others around who were patently not responding, then just one person did. Latané and Darley (1976) worked for many years seeking to understand the

Table 11.3 Effects of group size on reporting the smoke

Group size	condition	N subjects	Total number of subjects reporting the smoke	% reporting the smoke
1	subject alone	24	18 out of 24	75
3	subject + 2 passive stooges	10 (+ 20 stooges)	1 out of 10	10
3	All naïve subjects	24 (8 groups of 3)	3 out of 24	38

Source: Latané and Darley (1968: 217–18)

social processes going on. They identified three forms of 'social inhibition' that can explain whether 'bystander intervention' happens or not:

- *Diffusion of responsibility* – where someone feels less responsible as there are others there who could take action.
- *Audience inhibition* – where someone is less likely to intervene in public situations than in private ones through embarrassment and not wanting to make a fool of themself.
- *Social influence* – where someone is persuaded by another person's lack of response that intervention is not justified or wrong.

In this chapter they describe an ingenious and sophisticated three-in-one experiment, where all three of these potential influences are varied independently. In it subjects were placed in a small booth on their own, containing two closed-circuit video screens and a camera. Except in the 'alone' condition, each subject was taken to the booth accompanied by another 'subject' (that is, an experimental stooge) who was taken on to another booth. This time the incident concerned was seeing, on one of the screens, the experimenter apparently giving himself a severe electric shock by fiddling with some obsolete apparatus. He reacts by screaming, jumping in the air, throwing himself against the wall, and finally falling onto the floor out of camera range (possibly demonstrating that acting ability is a necessary skill for conducting research in social psychology!).

Latané and Darley (1976) thus had five different conditions in which the amount of communication varied, and recorded data on the percentage of subjects intervening. The data they obtained are shown in Table 11.4.

Table 11.4 Data from Latané and Darley's three-in-one experiment on the influence of diffusion of responsibility, social influence and audience inhibition on help giving in emergencies

Condition	Set-up	Cumulative % subjects intervening
Alone	S is totally alone with nobody else present	95
Diffusion	S knows there is somebody else but they cannot see them or be seen by them	84
Diffusion + social influence	S can see the other 'subject' just working on the questionnaire, but cannot be seen by them	73
Diffusion + audience inhibition	S cannot see the other 'subject' but knows they can see them	73
Diffusion + social influence + audience inhibition	S can see the other person and knows they can be seen by them	50

Source: Latané and Darley (1976: 328)

It takes a bit of time and thought to work your way through these data, but the main result is that the more visible the other person to you, and the more you think they are visible to them, the less likely (according to these research findings) you are to respond to the incident. You may like to compare these data to those from the Milgram experiments in Chapter 4. Subjects in those experiments were also less likely to give (apparent) shocks to others, the higher the level of proximity to them.

Is that all there is to it?

A great deal of work has been done since the 1960s and 1970s on different aspects of whether people respond to somebody needing help (see Chapter 11 in Myers et al. 2010 for a very readable account). The bystander effect is strongest when the bystanders are anonymous strangers whom you never expect to meet again. If you know the bystander or the victim, even if only superficially, or if the victim is a child, then their plight is seldom ignored. Being in a positive mood makes you more likely to help, and people help others because it makes them feel good.

Criticisms of experimental approaches to the study of the influence of bystanders

In the 1970s Susan Brownmiller, famous in the USA as a feminist critic, saw the Kitty Genovese incident from a completely different perspective from that of the experimental social psychologists Latané and Darley. She pointed out that: 'Winston Moseley, Genovese's 29-year-old killer, later made an extraordinary confession: "I just set to find any girl that was unattended and I was going to kill her", he calmly announced in court' (Brownmiller 1975: 199). In her detailed treatment of the incident, Brownmiller drew attention to the 'stubborn particulars' of gender in a case such as this – that it was not just a matter of 'bystander apathy', but powerfully influenced by the assumptions and prejudices in the way men's violence towards women is understood. This was a time when 'domestic violence' was little acknowledged or understood, by the public and the police, usually treated as 'private' and hence not something into which an onlooker would be wise to intervene.

Twenty years later a social psychologist, Frances Cherry (1995), in a powerful essay on this incident, draws attention to quite another reading of what was going on and why. Taking her lead from Brownmiller, Cherry rejected the 'group inhibition' and 'diffusion of responsibility' explanations that she had been taught when she was a student of psychology. Once she began reviewing the social psychology literature about rape (Cherry 1983) she changed her mind: 'I found myself returning to view Genovese's murder first within the framework of sex/gender relationships and then within an even larger framework of multiple structures of powerlessness (sex, race, age and class) that play themselves out in our daily lives' (Cherry 2007: 179).

The point here, according to Cherry, is that 1960s was a time in which 'nice' people did not interfere in disputes between men and women – and neither did the police. In popular opinion there was no real acknowledgement that 'domestic violence' was a social problem, far less that anyone should do anything about it. I was a teenager in the 1960s and remember that in those days it was assumed that any woman stupid or brazen enough to be out on the streets at 3 o'clock in the morning was to be regarded as 'fair game'. I agree with Cherry that it is impossible to even begin to work out what the witnesses to the attack were thinking without taking into account the many prejudices and assumptions surrounding this case – which, by the way, included race as well as gender (Kitty was white, her attacker black).

Cherry is highly critical of the whole body of work done by experimental social psychologists on the 'bystander effect'.

> [A]ll were excellent examples of how research can strip meaning from events at the creative phase of theorizing about the world. Sex/gender violence was excluded at that phase of abstracting hypotheses about social reality. The link to the Kitty Genovese incident was stripped of its original gendered particulars, that is, an attack on a woman was no longer an essential component in the laboratory exploration of what the event meant.
>
> (Cherry 2007: 178)

Helping understood as a situated social, cultural and political practice

I am going to end this section with two stories – taken from a British newspaper (the *Guardian*) about two sets of events. They are here to bring together all the stuff you have read about the 'bystander effect' throughout this book. It has been a bit of a theme, as I have been able to use it to raise all sorts of interesting issues raised by social psychological research. These stories take all that, and present actions taken and responses given very much within 'helping' as a *politically* situated social practice as well as a social and cultural one. My point is that 'helping behaviour' is immensely varied, can only be understood within local and contingent contexts, and is 'storied into being' through the place and time of its telling and the standpoint from which it is told.

The costs of trying to help

Jimmy Mubenga died on an aeroplane at Heathrow Airport in October 2010, in the final row of seats of British Airways flight 77 to Luanda. People on the aeroplane reported later that he shouted that he could not breathe, as three large security guards forced his head down into his lap. No one helped him. He was a failed asylum seeker being deported. Later that week, in an article in the *Guardian*, Melanie McFadyean, raised familiar questions about our willingness (or not) to help a stranger in distress:

> 'You could hear the guy screaming at the back of the plane. He was saying "they were going to kill me". He just kept repeating that all the way through.' So said a witness to the horror story that emerged from BA Fight 77 to Angola last week. Jimmy Mubenga begged passengers to help him moments before he died beneath three security guards. And yet none of the passengers went to his aid. Was it because he was a big strong man being held down by three big blokes?
>
> Maybe it was because even as we witness such incidents, we are programmed to think there must be a reason for 'restraining' the person; the people in uniform surely know what they are doing, that it's none of our business. Understandably, when getting involved at all might be dangerous – say in a street fight – we tell ourselves we'd be asking for trouble if we intervened. But that wasn't the case with this flight. At worst one might have been kicked off the flight: tedious, trying, even frightening – but certainly not life-threatening.

And I suspect another element is at work here. A passenger told the Guardian that when Mubenga said 'they are going to kill me' it wasn't clear if he was referring to the guards or his political adversaries in Angola, 'and most of the passengers were not concerned. No one was that alarmed by what he was saying'. The assumption, it seems, was that Mubenga was a failed asylum seeker. This somehow made it reasonable not to help him, because he feared death only on his return. As if that exonerates us from doing or saying anything. This links into an increasing tendency to regard immigrants, and in particular asylum seekers, at best as scrounging gatecrashers and at worst as *untermensch*. Ever tougher government policies militate against compassion, aided and abetted by public and private agencies' contempt for due process. We get the message.

(McFadyean 2010)

Previously, on 5 January 2010, two students, Matt Taylor and Andrew Bowman, did intervene in a similar incident. Taylor tried to approach one of the flight attendants but one of the security guards stopped him. One guard pushed him in the back and told him to sit down and keep quiet. The two demanded to see the captain but staff initially refused, then the captain did come, but dismissed their concerns. They were told they could move seats so they would not be able to hear the man's cries. As the two continued to complain, the aeroplane was turned around and returned to the terminal, where it was met by armed police. Taylor and Bowman agreed to leave the aeroplane, and were questioned for several hours before being escorted to the underground station (Taylor and Lewis 2010: 6).

How to be a hero

In late November 2010 the inquest took place of the deaths of those killed by the terrorist bombings on the London underground and bus on the 7 July 2005. Throughout the proceedings, tales were told of incredible acts of bravery and compassion by people who risked their own lives to save those of strangers, and stayed to comfort those who were dying.

You can download an article from 25 November by Alexander Topping asking the question: what is it that makes people behave so courageously amid devastation? Here is a short extract to give you a flavour of what is an incredibly emotional account:

When PC Dave Hill heard on his radio about an explosion at Edgware Road tube station, he and a colleague changed course and went straight to the scene without stopping to think. At the mouth of the underground tunnel, the thought that there could be a second device occurred him, but he carried on into the dark. Asked why, during the inquest into the deaths of the 52 people that died in the 7/7 bombings, the policeman simply replied: 'Because I was there.'

It was a refrain that was heard, in varying forms, throughout the three-week long evidence of the Edgware Road bombing, which came to a close yesterday. Ordinary men and women who had performed extraordinary feats, who had, in some cases, literally taken a leap into the dark to help maimed and injured passengers in desperate need of help, repeatedly down-played their heroism.

(Topping 2010)

A number of explanations were given by two psychologists. These included having training for and/or experience of similar situations in the armed forces, as well as being self-confident and physically strong. But also there were situations where what mattered was encouragement from another.

Teacher Timothy Coulson, who was part of a group of people who climbed into the bombed carriage after breaking the window of an adjacent train, recalled a young female paramedic arriving on the scene and being overwhelmed by the situation. 'She was quite distressed and in fact broke down upon arrival saying she couldn't do this,' he said. But 'the teacher in him' made him take control of the situation. 'I said, "Yes you can do this. You've got a bag, we have nothing. Let's have a look and see what you've got inside it".'

(Topping 2010)

Try it for yourself

If you can, download both articles in full and read them carefully. Alternatively get together with other students and discuss your reactions – the more varied the group, the livelier the discussion is likely to be. Consider similarities and differences between these two stories and between them and the various versions of the Kitty Genovese story too. Talk about what you think social psychologists can learn from interrogating events and incidents like these – and how can we make sense of them?

Sociality and strangers

Altruism and pro-social behaviour
- Evolutionary psychologists explain pro-social behaviour and altruism in terms of theories of kin selection; inclusive fitness and reciprocal altruism.
- Experimental social psychologists explain them in different ways – in terms of personality, mood, exchange theory, social norms and mixed models that include both cognitive elements (like attention) and more social processes such as self-presentation.

Why people do not help
- Broadly, people are least likely to respond when someone needs help if they are absolute strangers and when there are others around who ignore what is happening. They are most likely to respond if they think they are the only one who knows what is going on, and think nobody can see them.
- Critiques of studies that have identified these effects argue that they mean very little, as they are so de-contextualized that they have removed most of the influences that operate in real life, such as prejudice.
- In real-life situations there can be costs to trying to help in situations, especially where officials are involved. Despite this, human history is full of heroic deeds, where people try to help others, even at serious risk to themselves.

Singlehood

In the UK (as elsewhere in other Westernized societies) a growing proportion of the population are living on their own (single-person households is the official term), most of whom would call themselves 'single'. Singlehood also, of course, includes being a single parent, but here we will concentrate on the kind of singleness of not being part of a couple and living independently from a family.

The **heteronormative** view is that this state of being single is not a choice but a failure. This is especially true for a single woman. She is seen as being unable to get a man in the first place, or to have failed to get him to commit, or to be rubbish at making a relationship work. Even affectionately portrayed as Bridget Jones, single women are popularly depicted as figures of fun, as desperate for a man and obsessed with the dream of an impressive wedding and living happily ever after.

Being single – according to dominant popular wisdom – is a default position, in which women, in particular, gain 'a deficit identity, defined by lack and by the shared conception of women as outside normal family life and intimate relationships' (Reynolds and Taylor 2004: 199). For all the emancipation of women gained over history, this attitude is not so far removed from the pity held towards 'spinsters' in days when it was virtually impossible for women to be self-sufficient economically. Dismissed as 'on the shelf', 'unclaimed treasure' and 'old maids' their identity was (and still is, in many ways) defined by what they are not (that is, properly married).

Singlehood as deficit

Mainstream psychological approaches to being single tend to go along with the 'deficit identity' concept. They treat it as an abnormality that needs to be explained. One approach is to draw on Bowlby's **attachment theory** (Bowlby 1969, 1980), that views the kinds of adult close relationships that people have in adulthood as arising from the problematic quality of their experiences of attachment in early childhood (Mikulincer and Shaver 2007 provide an extensive review).

To get an overall impression of this approach, we will look at a specific study by Schachner et al. (2008) that investigated the impact of attachment on whether or not people adopt a single lifestyle. To do this they administered questionnaires to and interviewed 142 people, with about equal numbers of men and women, and including about 18 per cent of people who said they were bisexual or homosexual. There was also a reasonably representative range of people from minority ethnic groups. They analysed both sets of data through hypothesis testing.

You can soon see their purpose. At the beginning of their paper Schachner et al. note that most research into attachment has been done on couples, where secure attachment (as opposed to anxious or avoidant attachment) is found to be the foundation of a good and satisfying relationship: 'Relatively *secure* individuals, for example, tend to have long, stable, and satisfying relationships characterized by high investment, trust, and friendship. . . . They find it easy to provide responsive care to their relationship partners . . . and are relatively comfortable with intimacy, including sexual intimacy' (Schachner et al. 2008: 480, emphasis in the original). They identify three potential ways that may lead people to live a single life:

1 They may have a more avoidant attachments style, as 'avoidant individuals favor independence and self-reliance' (Schachner et al. 2008: 480).

2 They may have more attachment-anxiety as a result of having faced rejection, this is caused by their 'anxiety, clinginess and intrusiveness' (Schachner et al. 2008: 480).

3 They may have come to prefer other attachment figures, such as parents, siblings or close friends.

Notice what is going on here. All three explanations work from the assumption that singlehood is 'a problem' rather than, say, a lifestyle choice. The word 'avoidant' in the first explanation implies dysfunction (as opposed to a positive choice) even though it is linked with values – independence and self-reliance – that are generally seen as positive virtues in mainstream US society.

This **problematizing** of singlehood clearly informed the hypotheses they tested:

> we predicted that attachment-related issues would be experienced and handled by single adults (compared with roughly matched married adults) in one or both of the following ways: (a) Single adults might exhibit less secure patterns of attachment than partnered adults. (b) Single adults might rely on attachment figures in more or less the same way adults do, but their attachment figures might be people other than a romantic or marital partner (e.g., parents, close friends, siblings). In addition, we explored the possibility that adults who remain single might have had more troubled childhoods or troubled relationships with one or both parents, which resulted in an insecure attachment style and a negative view of long-term romantic relationships.
>
> (Schachner et al. 2008: 480–1)

Single men showed higher levels of attachment anxiety compared with men in couple relationships. Single and coupled women had, on average, much lower and virtually equal scores on attachment anxiety. Men, both single and couple, were found to be significantly more anxious, more avoidant, more depressed and more lonely than the women in the sample. Even so, content-analysis coded interview data did show links to being single: 'Overall, the single participants seem to have had worse relationships with parents during childhood or at least seem to look back on them in that way, with the major issue being neglect, indifference, and lack of parental warmth and affection' (Schachner et al. 2008: 485).

This may well explain the slight association found between being single and depression and general anxiety. Their conclusions accepted, though, that being single is not a sorry state in itself, certainly not for women. However, they did reject DePaulo's (2006) claims that the 'problem' (to the extent that there is one) lies not in individuals but the prejudices about and discrimination towards single people in American society.

Being gay and single

Writing about 'voluntary long-term singlehood' among gay men – or, rather, the lack of it, Andrew Hostetler (2009) adopts the term **relationship imperative** to make sense of why being single as a lifestyle rather than a temporary status is regarded as a *deficit* identity, even among gay men.

In the introduction to his report Hostetler asks the questions: 'Does anyone *choose* to be permanently single? And what does "choice" even mean in this context?' (Hostetler 2009: 500, emphasis in the original). Throughout the paper he is very wary of the idea of 'choice' and whether it is possible to investigate whether people have it or not. Choice is a 'hurrah-word' (seen as intrinsically good and desirable) in mainstream American culture, dominated as it is by neo-liberal ideas of freedom and individual autonomy. It is, he argues, so socially desirable that to agree that you *chose* something rather than having it imposed upon you is virtually meaningless – who *is not* going to say it is their own choice when asked by a researcher?

Despite this, he did attempt to answer questions about being single among the gay community. As he predicted, the great majority of the single gay men who responded to questionnaires agreed to statements about being 'single by choice'.

However, he also conducted biographical interviews with the men in his study, and the accounts given by them indicate more subtle and ambiguous responses. The interviews were devoid of talk about choice and 'voluntary singlehood'. Eighty per cent of the men said they would prefer to be in a relationship and over 60 per cent said they were currently looking for a partner. Being single was not seen as the ideal, but as a better choice than an unsatisfying or unhappy relationship with someone not worthy of you. Indeed, many men talked in terms very similar to the supposedly female search for 'The One':

> I think I went from being afraid of learning about the lifestyle, to being afraid while I was learning about it, to wanting to be in a relationship. I don't think there was a time where I was just out there, happy to be gay and single and not caring about meeting anybody. That came after my first relationship. . . . Yes, I want to have a life-long partnership, but I won't do it just for the sake of doing it. I'll only do it if a person comes into my life that's worth doing it with.
>
> ('Mike', a white, 38-year-old flight attendant, cited in Hostetler 2009: 517)

For those, generally older, men who saw themselves as probably being lifelong single, they reported it as not so much a principled, elective, proactive choice as the product of lots of unsignificant choices: 'I've come to the realization that I'm single because that's what I wanted. . . . Over the years there were a lot of choices I made that sort of insured that I wound up single. Lots of choices' ('Martin', a 46-year-old white male, cited in Hostetler 2009: 518).

Hostetler's analysis of his findings is highly articulate and theoretically driven. He locates what his respondents are saying within an American culture that primarily values relationships because of what people get out of them. In this context, talk of taking a break for some 'me time' or to 'figure out what I want', is, he argues: 'ultimately more about enhancing future intimacy than about advancing singlehood as a viable "alternative lifestyle". For, as conventional wisdom tells us, we cannot love without first knowing and loving ourselves, and a relationship is only worthwhile to the extent that it promotes our further growth and development' (Hostetler 2009: 519).

We can see the 'psy complex' popping up again here – creating a worldview where decisions are taken about relationships by reference to psychological assumptions about what it means to be an authentic, healthy, rational person. Within mainstream, American, psychologized culture, the ideal character is someone who is independent, self-reliant, deserving of the best 'because we're worth it!' Contrast this with the way a Bangladeshi young woman views such a relationship: 'My second sister's got a very good proposal, the guy's a doctor, you know, very religious, well mannered, everything and they will research the background and see whether the elder sister has got married, did she marry into a good family? And all this will be taken into account' (Edwards et al. 2006, as quoted in Lucey 2007: 86).

You will find out more about this young woman and her relationship with her sister in the section on sisterhood.

Being single viewed as a social practice

Jill Reynolds (2008) conducted interviews with thirty single women. Her approach is based on viewing discourse as a social practice that situates what people say within the specific context in which it is being said. Her study is woven around three key concepts in discursive psychology:

- interpretative repertoires
- subject positions
- ideological dilemmas.

Interpretative repertoires

Reynolds takes the term **interpretative repertoires** from Wetherell and Potter (1992). They devised it to describe elements of discourse – at the level of a storyline – that offers an account of or explanation for an issue or topic or phenomenon. Reynolds identified four of them as woven through her interviews on being a single woman:

- singleness as a personal deficit
- singleness as being socially excluded
- singleness as allowing independence and choice
- singleness as a means to self-development and achievement.

These are common and recognized discursive resources that people occupying the lifeworld of the women she recruited can use to talk about the state of being single. They can be customized to answer a question or to make a point or to tell a story. They can be juxtaposed against each other in arguments, or expanded and specified with examples to press home a case for action or inaction.

Subject positions

Subject positions are a different kind of widely shared and understood discursive resource, this time around alternative 'selves' a single woman can be, ones like 'lonely spinster' or 'dangerous divorcee' as opposed to a 'loyal and loving wife' or a 'merry widow'. Reynolds comments that 'different identities are made available through discursive practices and conjured up in conversational interactions' (2008: 50).

Ideological dilemmas

In this context **ideological dilemmas** are the ordinary, everyday lived dilemmas we all face in navigating our way through life (not big-time abstract intellectual ones). They are the choices we face within the bitty, muddled and contrary pushes and pulls involved in making sense of 'what is what' and what to do and not to do. As people try to reconcile contradictory arguments, they draw on both kinds of discursive resources – interpretative repertoires and subject positions – to fathom resolutions and possible solutions.

The dilemmas of singlehood

Examples of these dilemmas include the 'delicate footwork' one woman engaged in to exclude herself from the category of 'single as deficit'. She did this by positioning herself as financially independent, not a loner or alone, having a boyfriend but not one she wants to live with and having lots of friends. Hence she is not a 'loner' but (financially) 'independent'. Another one readily accepts the positioning of herself as 'single' but rejects that of 'spinster'. She defines that position by talking of a friend who falls into that category – with a trundle basket, a cat, who has been in the same job for 30 years and has not moved on. She, by contrast, has a diverse group of eccentric fiends who, like her, do not conform to the norm (the stereotype she has just drawn).

Reynolds explores in fine detail the enormous amounts of rhetorical, discursive work going on in these conversations. Some women spoke explicitly of the contradictions they faced – for example, between the pleasures of being independent against the loneliness of being without a partner.

Relationships

Reynolds's study also applied narrative analysis to her interviews, and she identified three 'frames': life cycle, life events and life as progress. Using these as an analytic allowed her to take a 'bigger picture' approach, through which novel insights could be gained about a different kind of discursive work being done by the women she interviewed:

> The life cycle frame naturalizes the account in a way that has an apparent logic to it. It provides some distance and perspective for the speaker so the emotional experiences can be presented relatively dispassionately in the retelling. It draws on a dominant cultural storyline which participants may want to position themselves against; this also provides a resource that participants can shape to their own ends.
>
> (Reynolds 2008: 95)

What is impressive here is the way her analysis reveals a different aspect of singlehood that is lost in the specificity of discourse analysis, how singleness can be understood as a sequence of events and transitions – you can see similarities here with the Hostetler's (2009) study of single-hood among gay men. Reynolds too explores issues of agency – the 'single by choice' question, and adds a fascinating analysis of the politics of singleness. I end this section with an account from a newspaper article that puts all the 'spinster stuff' into language I recognize. Do you?

> I'm the most self-sufficient, misanthropic person I know and even I was found sobbing in the kitchen on my 27th birthday because another sodding wedding invitation had come through the door which, if you held it up to the light, actually had the words 'There will be a special chair for you at the Desiccated Hags table' engraved on it.
>
> (Mangan 2010)

Singlehood

- Even today when in Western societies there are growing numbers of single people, singlehood is still often seen as a deficit identity.
- Attachment theory explains singlehood as a dysfunctional state, arising from failure to form secure attachments in childhood.
- The gay single men interviewed by Hostetler mainly understood singlehood within the context of a society where the 'relationship imperative' sets coupledom as the norm.
- The single women interviewed by Reynolds certainly recognize the 'singlehood as deficit' interpretative repertoire, but alongside others that include seeing singleness as being socially excluded, as allowing independence and choice, and as a means to self-development and achievement.

Attraction and love

Attraction

A cursory glance at the women featured in popular men's magazines, such as Maxim or Playboy, suggests that men are attracted to young women with smooth skin, long soft hair, large eyes, slender bodies, long legs, curved hips, large pronounced breasts, rounded buttocks, and flat stomachs. . . . In contrast, a reader glancing through Cosmopolitan would conclude that women are attracted to tall athletic men with moderately muscular arms and legs, broad shoulders, little body fat, square and powerful-looking jaws, and toned abdominal muscles. Notably, however, some body types are rarely represented. Women's magazines almost never feature men who are very short, elderly, and fat, with wrinkly skin, open sores and wounds, and mouths with stained and missing teeth.

(Gallup and Fredrick 2010: 240)

This extract is from a paper promoting an evolutionary approach to sexual attraction. Certainly there is evidence from social psychology experiments to show that 'attractive' people are more likely to find friends and get dates, at least in cultures where dating is the norm. The best known social psychologist to take this view is Buss (2005).

How far this is attributable to 'selfish genes' exerting their influence is an open question, given the impact of socialization where, even in fairy stories, the Princesses are both good and beautiful and the witches are wicked and ugly. A plethora of US-based studies show that attractive teachers get ranked as better than less attractive ones, attractive people get better jobs and make more money (Myers et al. 2010: Ch. 10, provides a good review of all this work).

There are some very obvious observations from survey data, including that relationships were more common among people who live close to each other than those who live at a distance – not really meaningful in today's world. It is hardly surprising that people are generally attracted to others who are like them and share their values. This has now been looked at across cultures. Wheeler and Kim (1997), for example, found that people from the USA and South Korea, both found traits like being happy, friendly, popular and sexually warm attractive. But North

Americans alone found being assertive, dominant and strong attractive, whereas North Koreans favoured traits of generosity, sensitivity and trustworthiness. If you go back and look at the values maps in Chapter 9, you will see how these observations fit very well.

As elsewhere, experimental social psychology's social learning theories have been applied here, as have social exchange theory (that you met earlier in the chapter). Attachment theory and other social psychoanalytic formulations have also been applied.

Love

Early social psychological conceptions of love sought to define it as a singular thing. Freud (1922) defined love as striving for an ego ideal, and Reik (1944) as a search for salvation. Maslow (1962), a humanistic psychologist best known for his work on self-actualization, went a bit further and argued for two kinds of love – Deficiency love (D-love) and Being love (B-love).

John Alan Lee's (1977, 1988) research into 'love styles' was the first attempt by a psychologist to construct a detailed typology of alternative ways of making sense of what love is (he called them ideologies). He used a mixture of intensive interviews and getting people to select from a set of around 500 written brief descriptions of what love means by selecting the ones that described their own 'love story'. The end result was Lee's typology of love-styles, as shown in Table 11.5.

Lee drew upon ancient Greek ideas and language to label the different kinds of love people feel and express towards each other. He was quite clear – these are not different kinds of people; they do not represent characters or personalities. Rather they depict whole sets of ideas, ideals, beliefs, expectations and assumptions (what we would now call discourses).

Eros and *Storge* are familiar, often in Western popular imagination seen as the two main stages of a love story – hot, passionate romance at the beginning, turning into a gentler but much deeper companionship as the love matures: the 'hurly-burly of the chaise longue . . . giving way to the deep, deep peace of the marriage bed' (Beatrice Campbell, usually known as 'Mrs Patrick Campbell', quoted in Woollcott 1934).

Table 11.5 Lee's typology of love styles

Lee's definition	Hendrick and Hendrick's definition	
Eros	Romantic, passionate love	The traditional form of 'big romance', 's/he's the One', all-consuming, passionate love
Ludus	Love as a game	Love as a game to be played mainly for a bit of fun
Storge	Companionate love	A love based on friendship and slowly developing affection and companionship
Mania	Jealous love	A dependent love characterized by obsession, jealousy and great emotional intensity
Agape	Selfless love	Altruistic love, all-giving and selfless, where the lover willingly loves without any expectation of love in return
Pragma	Shopping-list love	Shopping-list love, based on a conscious consideration of what one wants in a partner

Source: Based on Lee (1988); Hendrick and Hendrick (1986)

Hendrick and Hendrick (1986) offer us more contemporary language. From their ideas about, for example, *Pragma* as 'shopping-list' love, it is easy to relate this to what people do on dating sites as well as how families and matchmakers operate in cultures where arranged marriages are the norm. Equally, as Hendrick and Hendrick observe, we can see a lot of teenage angst in *Mania*, and such jealous, obsessive love is a recurrent problem tackled in agony-aunt columns. *Ludus* we can connect to characters ranging from Don Juan to 'Jack the lad', today in the West relentlessly portrayed in 'kiss and tell' stories about media icons. *Agape* is redolent of mother-love, and also romantic stories about heroines who martyr themselves for apparently undeserving, cruel and exploitative men who do not deserve them – until, that is, they are revealed as decent and honest husband-material after all. In other words, these are all recognizable forms of love, recognizable, that is, if you live in a culture that provides narratives and representations of this range of love stories.

From a critical psychology perspective this recognizability provides persuasive evidence that love among humankind is less to do with 'natural laws' of human nature, and more to do with deeply sedimented, iconic narratives of social action and representations of identity. Our under-standings of these different meanings of love are constructed for us (as well as by us) through both the commonsense 'what everybody knows' kind of knowledge that permeates our everyday lives and through the constantly retelling of the narratives and re-presentation of the characters, in everything from our childhood 'fairy stories' to the more adult Twilight genre, Facebook and YouTube as well as in 'girlie movies' and classic romances, opera to soap opera, and whole shelf-fulls of self-improvement and 'how to get it right' manuals, listed under psychology!

Watts's study of coupled love

Evidence of the ubiquity of this has been provided by a Q methodological study conducted by Simon Watts for his doctorate, published as Watts and Stenner (2005a). He deliberately included participants from a representative range of minority ethnic groups in the UK. Like Lee, Watts provided participants with cards, on which were written statements describing what love is like. These were sorted in the usual way for a Q study (see Chapter 5), following a grid pattern as shown in Figure 11.2.

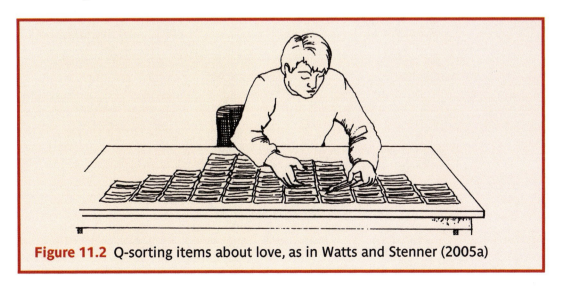

Figure 11.2 Q-sorting items about love, as in Watts and Stenner (2005a)

The items were sorted in this study from −6 (most strongly disagree) to +6 (most strong agree) (two more columns than in the picture) with just a few at each extreme, and more around the middle column, used for items not seen as important, or as ambiguous or vague.

The responses of each participant were factor analysed in a different way from usual, so as to identify alternative, different sorting patterns. In this study each pattern described an alternative point of view about what love means or is like. I would call these alternative discourses on love. Watts and Stenner identified a fair number, but here I concentrate on just six, each of which, I think describes a quite distinctive form of love. In several cases I have given them labels of my own. These are set out in Table 11.6.

Table 11.6 Watts and Stenner's alternative discourses on love

Cupid's arrow	This is the old, familiar romantic story of what happens when a person 'falls head over heels in love'. This love is incredible, overwhelming and irrational. It is like being struck by a passion so intense that you lose sight of your goals, your responsibilities and even any sense of who you are. You are consumed by it and unable to resist. It does not last
Instrumental love	The opposite of Cupid's arrow. This love is not in the least spontaneous but strategic and instrumental, in some cases almost cynical. Love like this is where two people effectively make a bargain to support each other's pursuit of their individual goals and achievements. It is a calculated commitment that you will help each other to each get the most you can out of life. It needs a certain kind of honesty, with each person accepting and loving the other for who they really are. Love in this sense is not defined by closeness but by giving each other space, being tolerant and flexible and willing to compromise and even make sacrifices for each other
Raunchy love	This love is based on self-interest, all about the pleasure and satisfaction you can get out of it, the excitement and the thrill. Rooted in physical attraction and where having lots of great sex is what you are after rather than intimacy, it is great for your ego, your self-esteem and quite possibly your reputation. This love is raunchy and has no illusions. You don't have to even like the other person very much, and there is certainly no long-term commitment
Grown-up love	This love recognizes that being in a committed relationship is far more difficult, messy and problematic than the 'romantic myths' about love that lead people to have unrealistically high expectations about what it can deliver or how sustainable it can be. It also rejects the notion of being 'swept away' by love. Love like this is based on real and hard-won mutual trust, a mature and determined commitment to communicating openly and effectively, on virtues like patience, tolerance and the ability to compromise. This is love has to be 'worked at' and will always involve continuous negotiation and change
Transcendent love	This is an extreme idealization of love, seeing being 'in love' as the deepest, most intense and most significant experience it is possible to have. This love is the essential core of your being. It is what makes you feel alive, contented and fulfilled. Nothing else comes close to matching it. It is a love of deep and mutual commitment to each other and the ultimate way in which two people can relate to each other
Communitarian love	This kind of love is based on strong principles of equity, complete honesty, respect for each other and a commitment to communicating with each other fully. At its core are two people who care for each other equally, are mutually supportive, and share their problems with each other and find solutions together as a team. This is a love that gradually grows stronger and stronger, and can survive all manner of hardship and troubled times

Read these through and see what you think. Do you find them plausible – can you identify couples you know whose relationships fall into these different categories? Which best describes your own opinion of what love is – or should be?

Attraction and love

- Evolutionary theorists explain attraction as a means by which men and women choose as sexual partners those visibly showing qualities that make them reproductively fertile and healthy. This, they argue, is why attractive people get more dates and are more likely to marry.

- Social influences can equally explain associations like these, including the impact of socialization, child-rearing and cultural sanctioning of particular qualities in a partner.

- Love is understood in many different ways, in different contexts, life stages and stages in the relationship.

Family relationships

The very notion of family holds some of the tensions with which the discipline of social psychology struggles – tensions between how to conceptualise self and other, individual and society, private and public. . . . This is why families afford fascinating possibilities for an emerging social psychology in which the individual is isolated from social, cultural and structural processes.

(Lucey 2007: 68)

In her innovative chapter on the social psychology of families, Helen Lucey (2007) points out that although our earliest relationships – and, indeed, some of our most important ones – are in families, social psychology has rather ignored them, delegating their study to developmental psychology. Yet, for almost everyone the first group to which we belong is our family. Families are incredibly powerful social settings and social institutions. Families of different kinds are where children learn about who they are and their place in the world. It is where they become socialized, getting to know about themselves as individuals and as members of group and other collectives. It is through our upbringing in families that we internalize the very complex and diffuse social and cultural rules – rules about how children are supposed to relate to grown-ups, how females are supposed to relate to males (boys to girls, women to men). These rules, of course, differs very widely from one family to another, reflecting differences in culture, class, religion, and social and economic circumstances. It is these differences in socialization that, to a very great extent, account for the ways in which adults vary, for example, in terms of their identities (Chapter 10) and the values that guide their lives (Chapter 9).

Without the care of a family, children fail to thrive, physically as well as emotionally and psychologically. This is what happens to children who grow up in institutions with only extremely limited and uninvolved contact with other people, such as the large number of orphans in Romania under the Ceauşescu regime. Being part of a family is included in the human rights of the child (United Nations Convention on the Rights of the Child). This is because family relationships are viewed as essential for a child's health and development.

Extended families

However, although developmental psychology tends to focus on the centrality of the family for children's development, in terms of social psychology we need to look much more widely at the social relationships that go on within families, across generations and broader kinship groups. In terms of contemporary Western culture, more so among the middle class, many families now function in relative isolation, with, at most, the occasional get-together with extended families at weddings and funerals. This is one of the products of greater social mobility. One route common in the UK is where young people use the opportunity of going to university to move out from the family home. Those economically less advantaged move away to find work, for example, through joining the army or going where jobs are easier to find. Outcomes include increasing distances between family members, families where one or more parents are absent and, in some cases, people losing contact with not just their families but their communities. In Aotearoa/New Zealand, for instance, many of the most socially excluded and deprived Maori are those who have moved away from the lands of their *iwi* to urban areas which results in them being isolated. Mobility has a much broader context, of course, in relation to migration, for reasons ranging from seeking asylum from oppression to seeking employment opportunities or following one's heart.

All of these disrupt traditions where families, historically, have mostly tended to stay in the same locality, with daughters, especially, setting up home as close as possible to Mum and Dad or moving in with their husband's family on marriage. Having grandparents, cousins, aunties and uncles close to hand creates the circumstances favourable to sharing childcare, and to the next generation being able to care for their parents once they get more frail and dependent. At the same time, mobility is often a price willingly paid for opportunity – including, for some, the opportunity to escape from the influence of the family!

Across the world we can see a diversification of family forms, ranging from single-parent families operating in virtual isolation right through to large extended families made up of dense networks of kin, almost whole communities in their own right. In between are all sorts of larger and smaller family units, their composition having real impact on how people can and do live their lives. Fiona Williams (2004) talks of modern, Western families as being 'networks of affection', recognizing that for some people it is family bonds that remain the strongest, whereas for others their most important relationships are with a group of friends who have come to take the place of family – who are kept at arm's length.

Children's accounts of who constitutes their family are instructive. They frequently include not just their parents and siblings but their own friends, neighbours and even teachers they like among what they see as their 'family' (Edwards et al. 2006). In African Caribbean families in the UK, for example, children tend to include a wide range of biologically related and unrelated people (Chamberlain 1999). This makes sense when, for many children, 'being family' is defined by the *quality* of the relationships and the roles people play in their lives, rather than strictly legal/biological definitions (Morrow 1998).

In terms of not just definitions but practicalities, families are legal entities, with law specifying rights and responsibilities as well as entitlements to family members. Legal changes in growing numbers of countries in the world have transformed the constitution of families. For example, lesbian and gay couples have gained the right in some countries to marriage or civil partnerships, and to adopt and foster children. In the UK the 1989 Children Act changed the rules around parenthood, so that parents continue to have parental responsibility for their children even if they are 'in care' (taken away for their own safety and well-being). In some countries grandparents have recently gained rights to maintain contact, even when families split up.

Close-family relationships

This section explores family relationships beyond those of parent and child – with brothers and sisters and grandparents mainly, though in some families cousins, aunts and uncles can be just as close. Here we will concentrate on sibling relationships.

Relationships with brothers and/or sisters

Technically these are called **sibling relationships**. Probably you know the word 'sibling' from a term often used about brothers and sisters – **sibling rivalry**. It is an idea that comes from psychoanalytic theory, where a child's relationships with his or her parents are seem to be the most important, but also very much about jealousy. Boys are seen as being in competition with their fathers for their mother's love and attention, whereas girls are seen in competition with their mothers. Prophecy Coles puts it neatly – siblings are no more than 'bit part' actors in the Oedipal theatre. In other words, sibling rivalry is just an extension of the competition that children feel towards any rival for parental attention and approval, full of 'primal hatred' and 'unfathomably deep hostility' (Coles 2003: 29).

Juliet Mitchell (2000), a feminist psychoanalyst, acknowledges this aspect of sibling relationships, but looks in more detail as the roles that siblings can play as role models ('ego-ideals' in psychoanalytic terminology) or the voices of our consciences that nag us to be good. Classical Freudian theory claims that our fathers are our most important ego-ideals, whose approval and praise we long for.

> But isn't it also likely that the original model may be another child, a heroic or critical older (or other) sibling? For most of us when our conscience is putting us down, making us feel inferior, the voice we hear is reminiscent of the taunting not of adults but of other children.
>
> (Mitchell 2003: 12)

In a study of sibling relationships in different kinds of families Ros Edwards and her colleagues provide an illustration of this aspect of sibling relationships (Edwards et al. 2006). Have a look it – it comes from an interview with two sisters, Habiba and Shabnur, two of five sisters in a Bangladeshi-heritage, Muslim family living in an inner-city neighbourhood of a British town. Habiba is 21 and Shabnur is 15. The other sisters are Azra, 24, Sabina, 20, and Misha, 11. In this extract Habiba and Shabnur are talking about their eldest sister Azra:

Habiba:	I would go out of my way to do something for Azra. And I would not say no. I would not refuse.
Shabnur:	I don't think that's just you with Azra. That's for any of us.
Habiba:	Any of us.
Shabnur:	Any of us.
Habiba:	Because she's the eldest.

Shabnur: I think because we have respect for her and in our eyes she's never done any-thing bad, and so she's so pure and good inside that we all respect her so much. Any of us would be willing to do anything, but she rarely, very rarely, asks us to do anything, does she?

Interviewer: What's special about her, that you all feel like that?

Shabnur: There's something special about her, that's so warm, that all of us really admire her.

Habiba: She's a very genuine person. And if you went to her for advice, you'd know that it's from the heart and it's never meant to be bad. Because some people will hold back and never tell the truth, or be honest. Even when she . . . even when she pressures you to just, say, study, or do something that you can slack in, you don't think. . . . I was so scared of, like, getting a 2.2,[1] I was, like, how am I going to face her? It was very much that I didn't want to let her down, I didn't want her to think that Habiba only got a 2.2. . . .

Shabnur: And the thing is, if somebody shouts at you it's over and done with. But because you see her, like when you have done something bad, she doesn't shout at you, but her expression makes you feel guilty. So that keeps me out of trouble.

Habiba: Because she's so nice to us, you feel bad for letting her down, because she's never let us down.

Shabnur: Yeah.

(Edwards et al. 2006, as cited in Lucey 2007: 84–5)

It is worth reading through the conversation a couple of times, as there is a lot being said here. Think about how it relates to your own experience if you have sisters and/or brothers. It really is a very powerful demonstration of a sibling as a parental figure, certainly in the way conventional psychologists would look at it. To what extent do you think this has to do with the particular character of the sister, Azra, who is being spoken about? To what extent is it a reflection of the family's Bangladeshi heritage?

Relationships with grandparents

The point here, I think, is that the roles of family members vary enormously across cultures, class and historical periods and are better seen as local and specific than universal. Go back and reread (or go and read if you have not so far done so) the section in Chapter 9 about the interplay of Chinese cultural values and grandmothering. This too brings home that instead of their being a simple set of common rules about 'how to do granny', there is an immense diversity of different expectations, mores, conventions and concerns that mould and shape relationships in families.

In both cases ethical and moral values underpin the codes of conduct. Contrast this with the 'companionate' grandparenting style identified by Cherlin and Furstenberg (1986) as the more common in the mainstream culture of the USA, where grandparents are seen more as supplementing parental roles. Cherlin and Furstenberg attributed this in particular to a 'norm of non interference' that requires grandparents to respect the parents' rights to bring up their own

---

[1] This is how we grade degree qualifications in the UK – 1st, 2.1, 2.2, 3rd.

children the way they see fit. They can do this by acting as playmates and treat-providers, who do not get into any serious stuff to do with discipline or managing behaviour. We can also see the influence here of the way that in mainstream society in the West children, childhood and childrearing are all made sense of through the '**psy complex**' (Rose 1979; see Chapter 3). What this means is that psychological theories of child development have become incorporated into everyday common sense – 'what everybody knows', including grandparents. Hence they regard their relationships with their grandchildren as about meeting their emotional needs (to have a secure and happy childhood) and psychological needs (for attachment, approval and a sense of self-worth). From this perspective grandparents are expected to play a special role, offering their grandchildren opportunities to be 'spoiled' and have 'fun', thus complementing parental care that needs to be more practical and regulatory. I can speak from experience when I say there are strong pressures on grandmothers, in particular, to treat this role as extremely important as well as being a source of immense joy and pleasure! (Please note this book is dedicated to my grandchildren.)

However, Nagata and her colleagues (Nagata et al. 2010) added another dimension to their study of differences between European and Chinese grandmothering styles (as described in Chapter 9). They also asked their participants about their own early experiences back in their homelands before they moved to be with their families in the USA. More than a third of them talked about experiences unimaginable to women of the same generation in the USA – Second World War bombings, the Nanking Massacre, the Cultural Revolution, living under Japanese rule, the 228 incident in Taiwan when tens of thousands of Taiwanese citizens were killed. The women denied these experiences had affected their relationships with their grandchildren, but did talk about the enormous contrasts between their own childhoods and those of their grandchildren. One, for example, talked of how she was forbidden to go to school, and so talked to her grandson about how lucky he was to be able to. Another spoke of telling her grandchildren how they should appreciate having so many good things to eat, when she had been deprived of food as a child.

Thus while Nagata and her colleagues acknowledge the powerful impact of cultural values on the way women approach the tasks and role of grandmothering, their study also reminds us that intergenerational factors (that is, different experiences at different life-stages) also influence social relationships in families.

Family relationships

- Families vary enormously and family composition is changing as a consequence of broader social changes like migration and commercial globalization.
- Social psychoanalytic approaches explain phenomena like sibling rivalry in terms of psychic forces such as anxiety and competition for parental attention and approval.
- Other approaches locate the nature of family relationships firmly within social and cultural settings, which differ widely from one social class to another, one cultural heritage to another. This is illustrated by differences in the ways sisters view each other, and the sources that grandparents call upon to inform how they 'do grandma'. In the West family relationships are understood through the 'psy complex', but in other settings obligations to and expectations of other family members are more products of tradition and/or religion.

Community relationships

Relationships within and between communities is not something social psychologists have paid much attention to. It can, however be found in community psychology and there relationships between neighbours and within community groups are seen as extremely important forms of mutual support. Supportive community relationships both help communities to cope with adversity from day to day, and to deal with natural traumas like floods and volcanic eruptions (Paton and Johnston 2004) and the impact of war (Kimhi and Shama 2004).

Sociology provides the most helpful term, I believe, to help us to bring a consideration of community relationships into social psychology. We will start with that, look briefly at ideas around community resilience and then focus in on one particular study – about the way that community relationships helped a small, racially mixed town in Texas to deal with a horrific, racially motivated murder.

Social capital

Social capital is a theoretical concept which entails trust, norms of reciprocity and voluntarism, social networks, associational participation and other social connections. Since social capital incorporates many fundamental social phenomena, it has been possible to use it to explain such diverse outcomes as economic development, political involvement, intergroup relations, educational attainment, social mobility, lifestyles, social control and crime. There is growing evidence that living in such communities makes people not only happier but healthier (Kawachi et al. 2008, provide a review).

According to Borgonovi (2010), social capital can benefit individuals in a number of ways, Communities with high social capital will often provide a resource for knowledge about how to live a healthy life, approval of such a lifestyle and support for it. It is much easier to avoid smoking among people where it is not 'cool' to smoke. Social groups where people help each other out and are supportive at times of trouble can do a great deal to reduce anxiety and distress that can undermine health, both directly and by reducing the temptation to turn to alcohol or drugs for solace. And, simply, it is a lot easier to fight cuts to services and lobby for a safer environment as a community than alone.

In a controversial book called *The Spirit Level: Why More Equal Societies Almost Always Do Better*, Richard Wilkinson and Kate Pickett (2009) use statistical data at population levels to argue that where there is a small difference between rich and poor in a country, the features of social capital are much easier to achieve compared with countries where the gap is huge.

Community resilience

The concept of resilience is normally applied (in psychology at least) to individuals. It is the capacity a person has or can learn that enables them to survive adversity and to flourish, to take the 'hard knocks' of life, cope with them and succeed in their life's goals despite the troubles they have had to deal with. However, in many ways it works best and is most useful in terms of groups of people – family resilience, community resilience and resilience located in other meaningful collectives such as *iwi*. In these contexts it is about the way collectivities can offer each other not just mutual support through their relationships with each other, but also simply make life happier and more fulfilling. In this sense it is linked with the ways communities can build social capital in their relationships – feelings of mutual trust and respect, where each member of the community has a role and is able to contribute to the common good.

Resilience here also links with the Latin American concept of *calidad de vida* (quality of life) that somewhat loses in translation into English, as it is not a way of measuring a person's evaluation of their bodily comfort and ability (as is usually the case in the English-speaking world).

> You have met this use of quality of life already in the community psychology section of Chapter 3.

Quality of life, in this meaning of the words, is much more about life quality as well-being and belonging, linked to cultural and community values. I have argued elsewhere (Stainton Rogers 2004) that this approach, designed to foster resilience in children, their families and their communities, is a better framework for planning and delivering support and services for children than either a children's-needs-based or a children's-rights-based approach.

If you want to follow up the idea of community resilience, Norris et al. (2008) provide a comprehensive review of definitions and its use as metaphor, plus its practical application.

A community responds to a collective trauma

On 6 June 1998 in Jasper, a small town in Texas in the USA, 49-year-old African American, Hames Byrd Jr, was brutally murdered by three White men who offered him a lift. They savagely beat him, chained him to their pick-up truck, and eventually dragged him to his death.

The media called it a lynching, resonating with all those other times when Black Americans had been strung up in crimes of racial hatred. The town was rapidly inundated by national and international crews of journalists, but also a range of political groups including the Black Panthers, armed and in combat fatigues, and the Ku Klux Klan. Jesse Jackson arrived too, with his own agenda, as did other celebrities looking to capitalize on the publicity. The town effectively stopped working normally, virtually under siege. Most residents, however, avoided the public events organized by the outsiders. Instead, they hung yellow ribbons on their houses and over a thousand of them attended a prayer vigil of reconciliation.

An ecological analysis study

Actually, they did a lot more than that. Thomas Wicke, a student at the University of California Irvine and his supervisor Roxane Cohen Silver (2009) conducted a detailed **ecological analysis** of how the townspeople of Jasper did not passively accept what others wanted to make out of their trouble. Rather they actively managed the aftermath, drawing on a number of different forms of community resilience.

By the term 'ecological analysis' Wicke and Cohen Silver position their study within a **transdisciplinary** frame (that is, one that breaks down barriers between disciplines rather than just building bridges). They gathered and brought together a range of different kinds of data – from crime statistics to transcripts from interviews with key players, such as the town's mayor and sheriff. This, they argue, is an approach 'particularly suited to understanding the complex and multifaceted nature of community and disaster' (Wicke and Cohen Silver 2009: 234).

Disasters, especially social disasters like this, usually bring about an initial coming together of the affected community (Kaniasty and Norris 1999) with strong cooperation, high levels of mutual helping and old conflicts ignored or buried in what has been called 'post-disaster utopia'. However, soon after it is typical for there to be a 'second disaster' once the immediate threat recedes and life begins to get back to normal: 'This may include the re-emergence of pre-crisis psychosocial tensions and fissures that had been hidden in the immediate post-disaster phase, as well as longer-term effects on the mental health of individuals . . . that would play out in changes to the community over time' (Wicke and Cohen Silver 2009: 234).

The study was a complex one, bringing together large amounts of quantitative data, comparing measures of crime, economics, education, health and social capital *within* the community five and seven years after the incident; and *against* a comparison, control community (another similar town in Texas) that had suffered no such trauma. Qualitative data was collected in the form of in-depth interviews carried out some years after the event, between March 2005 and 2007. There were 15 interviews, including with Jasper's mayor, sheriff and chief of police, religious and minority group leaders, businessmen, relatives and neighbours of the victim.

A hurt community

The findings were also complex, but showed the expected initial dip in crime rates immediately after the murder, but then a greater rise both in crime and imprisonment compared with the control community. Jasper's divorce rate also increased (though its rates of domestic violence did not). Other indices – like house sales and commercial profit – took a knocking too, providing evidence of a community hurt by its trouble and its aftermath, and the media exposure of its racial tensions for all to see and be horrified by. Doctors who had taken jobs in Jasper changed their minds. Tourists stopped coming. So, too, did commercial enterprise: 'It hurt us economically too. No one wants to locate a company in a racist state', one businessman said. 'The community was hurt because we had a mark, a mark of hate. It hurt us for a whicle. We lost some business that was going to move here. At that time we were on up the rise bringing business in. It did hurt' (Jasper's mayor, as cited in Wicke and Cohen Silver 2009: 243).

More immediately after the murder, the town was ripe for exploitation in the pursuit of grizzly stories and people to blame (much like what happened after the murder of Kitty Genovese, when it was the '38 witnesses' – rather than the murderer – who were publicly vilified for their callous indifference). In Jasper the immediate reaction in the press was to find the town itself guilty. One headline screamed, in massive print across two pages 'The town that shamed America'.

The townspeople were well aware of this, as these extracts from the interviews make plain: 'When the national media got here they were making us to be pot bellied, snuff dippin', beer drinking red necks, east-Texas bigoted police. Ignorant, uneducated . . . Typical stereotypes' (White police officer, as cited in Wicke and Cohen Silver 2009: 242); 'They came here looking for a . . . prejudiced community. A community that was vilifying each other. A community that was for racism. A community that was not together. This whole thing was going to be their example, I guess, of what the whole South was like, of what east-Texas was like' (Black minister, as cited in Wicke and Cohen Silver 2009: 242).

Community resilience

Despite these consequences, Jasper's townspeople showed enormous levels of community resilience. Wicke and Cohen's study set out to discover how this worked.

First, they found that the town had a history of effective institutional organization within its local government (the mayor's and sheriff's offices and the police force), its religious communities (in the form of a ministerial alliance between all the different faiths, Black and White) and in other community-based groups and activities, both singly and working together. When the crisis struck, they mobilized together:

> There was so much misinformation in our community that the Mayor and law enforcement came to our meeting and told us everything they knew – and it was amazing what they told us. And they wanted us to get out into the community (and communicate) the truth as they knew it at the time. . . . We were welcome to go to the Mayor's and the Sheriff's office whenever we wanted. He shared with us everything he knew. He trusted us and, in return, we trusted him.
>
> (Member of the Ministers Alliance, as cited in Wicke and Cohen Silver 2009: 241)

Similar openness with the media gradually had an effect. It was decided to actively pursue direct communication with them, in a strategy to make sure their voice was clearly heard rather than that of others who would misrepresent the town's interests. The sheriff's office took a similar stance. They made allies of the media by immediately passing over to them documents that they had a right to see, but usually had to apply for formally. The aim was to counter the way the mass media stereotyped interracial violence in small towns in places like Texas. The Ministers Alliance, in particular, was mobilized to challenge these stereotypes, and it slowly began to work: 'We found that the longer the people stayed in the town the more honest they became in their reporting because they really saw who we were. . . . They really expected to find a town that was filled with hatred and we weren't' (Member of the Ministers Alliance, as cited in Wicke and Cohen Silver 2009: 248).

What is particularly impressive is the way these groups, between them, dealt with the influx of not just the media but the personalities and the political groups who had arrived, out to make trouble and/or political capital out of their misfortune. So this is what they did. As each group arrived in Jasper, the ministers, the sheriff and the mayor worked out between them which person or group was best placed to confront the incomer. It was the Black community leaders who went to see the Black Panthers, the Black ministers who fronted up to Jesse Jackson and the leader of the white ministers who tackled the Ku Klux Klan. The sheriff took on groups from his own circle of influence, and his summing up of the overall effort was 'It was a non issue. They didn't stay very long.'

Wicke and Cohen Silver conclude that the Ministers Alliance was an invaluable source of social capital – locally based, locally led and able to share responsibility at times of trouble. It was also a driver to produce and sustain social capital in the communities they served, through its own direct links with community members and its alliance with many of the other community-based groups, and with what we would call here in the UK 'local government' officials. These had been built up a long time before the events of 1998, and its crossing of Black–White divisions in a town where the population split almost 50/50 had been particularly important in damping down hostility following interracial crime: 'the strength of the Ministerial Alliance networks between black and white ministers was stronger than racial affinity' (Wicke and Cohen Silver 2009: 244).

> Strong social ties were especially important with regard to the immediate families of the victims. The relationship between the community and immediate relatives of the primary victim developed into a relatively amiable and mutually supportive manner. This was not simply a matter of chance but began with appropriate – in message, messenger, and timeliness – efforts by the community. The Byrds developed strong friendships and trust with the larger community.
>
> (Wicke and Cohen Silver 2009: 244)

As a consequence of this the Byrds exerted a calming influence and refused to take a position demanding retribution. The Byrds supported the community, and the community supported them.

Community relationships

It was reading this paper that convinced me to include this section in this chapter – and, indeed, in the book. For all critical social psychologists' insistence on treating people's thoughts and actions as only meaningful within 'situated practices', so very much of what they do is so incredibly focused on the individual, phenomenological and social psychoanalytic approaches in particular.

Work of the kind carried out by Wike and Cohen Silver brings home, almost like a sledgehammer, how much of what we say, do, feel and think is profoundly situated in our communities and other collectives. The townspeople of Jasper – the Byrd relatives, the sheriff, the mayor, the ministers, the business people and police officers – were all enmeshed within the complex relationship networks operating in their community, profoundly influenced by it and profoundly engaged in influencing it. And we can speculate, perhaps, that maybe part of the problem of the three men who committed the murder was that they were not, but, rather, were isolated within a small and extreme group of virulent racists very much on the 'outside'.

Communitarianism – a contemporary form of humanistic liberalism (see Chapter 2) – is an ideology that views the building of strong and supportive communities as the best way to a 'good society' – one strong in social capital, resilient and able to deal with adversity, fair and unprejudiced, that values all its members and looks after them. Yes, it is all a bit utopian, with resonances with the hippie movement and idealism, as well as a number of religions. It all sounds too good to be true – and probably is.

However, it does offer a counter to equally impractical utopias that are built on the imperative of individual freedom at all costs, and a view that 'survival of the fittest' is the best way to ensure efficiency and progress. In social psychological terms it encourages us to venture into a broader range of 'interpersonal' relationships, to explore and learn from the benefits (and drawbacks) to be gained through relationships within communities and between the groups and organizations that operate within them. In other words, I suggest that social psychologists have a real and expert role to play in answering questions like 'What makes for a good society?' and 'How can we build them?' as much as it concerns itself with individual human happiness and fulfilment.

Community relationships

- Studying relationships in community settings is quite a new thing for social psychology, but is worth doing to open up our discipline beyond its preoccupation with relationships between individuals.

- Communities differ in their degree of social capital – the strengths of their community ties, trust among and between their constitutive groups, and the support they can offer to their members, particularly at times of adversity and trouble. Community resilience is a measure of how able a community is to manage social disasters, especially in the longer term.

- An example of a resilient community, the townspeople of Jasper, shows that when community groups are well established, and able to work in a mutually supportive way with local government and services, then such a community can actively manage the impact of disasters, protect their community from suffering too much harm, and help its people, as individuals and groups, to survive the trauma and to recover.

- Communitarianism is a utopian vision of a 'good society', that may be impossible to achieve but can inspire – including social psychologists.

Resources

The paper on the murder of James Byrd and how the community in Jasper in Texas dealt with its aftermath is available freely at: http://www.ncbi.nlm.nih.gov/pmc/articles/PMC2788142/

Further reading

Hogg, M.A. and Vaughan, G.M. (2008) *Social Psychology*, **5th edn. Harlow: Pearson/ Prentice Hall.**
This provides, in Chapter 13, the best standard, highly detailed and conventional account of experimental social psychology's research and theorizing in this field, with plenty of pretty pictures but also a systematic and comprehensive coverage of all you need to know.

Lucey, H. (2007) Families, in W. Hollway, H. Lucey and A. Phoenix (eds) *Social Psychology Matters.* **Maidenhead: Open University Press.**
This chapter (Chapter 3 in the book) is a great starting point to look in more detail at a range of ways in which social psychologists have studied family relationships. It looks across a much broader range of topics and theories than has been possible here.

Reynolds, J. (2008) *The Single Woman: A Discursive Investigation.* **Hove: Routledge.**
Interesting in itself, this is a good place to learn a lot more about the two methods Reynolds used – discourse and narrative analyses.

Questions

1 Why do people help each other? And why, sometimes, do people 'walk by on the other side' when someone is in trouble? Describe two different kinds of social psychological explanation for each of these, and then say which you think is most useful and why.

2 In what ways do the studies by Hostetler on singlehood among gay men and Reynolds on singlehood in women tell similar stories – and in what ways are they different? Illustrate your answer with examples.

3 'Love is not a rush of hormones or neurological fireworks. It is a complex web of social and cultural expectations and social and cultural practices.' Discuss this claim, illustrating your answer by reference to research evidence.

  Download and read Watts and Stenner's Q methodological study of different 'love styles'. Use your broader reading of this chapter, together with close reading of this paper, to help you answer the question.

4 What is sibling rivalry? Is it a universal within all families where there are siblings, or are there better ways to understand how brothers and sisters relate towards each other?

5 Download the paper (see link above) about community relationships in Jasper from the Internet. Use it to answer the following question: 'What lessons can be learned from a social psychological study of community relationships?'

6 Compare and contrast the narrative approach and the discourse analytic approach to studying relationships. Illustrate your answer with examples.

Communities, groups and intergroup processes

Chapter 12

The social psychology of groups

LEARNING OUTCOMES

When you have finished studying this chapter, you should be able to:

1 Define the differences between incidental, membership and identity reference groups, illustrating each with an example of the level and kind of group commitment involved.

2 Define 'conformity' in relation to group influence, and describe the main processes involved in this phenomenon and the influences upon it.

3 Define 'majority influence' and 'minority influence' in this context, and outline the theories and models that have been devised to explain when and how they each work.

4 Define 'group polarization' and 'Groupthink'. For each, explain why they are thought to happen and the theories to explain why they occur.

5 Outline the main reasons for intergroup conflict, and the steps that can be taken to reduce it.

6 Describe what social psychologists mean by the term 'leadership' and two different approaches to studying this topic.

Introduction

Europe is made up of many different nations, and has long, complicated and often bitter histories of conflict between them. Intergroup relations in Europe are further complicated by a colonial past and the increasingly diverse populations that are a consequence of that. Moreover, all of this is in flux, most notable in terms of the Velvet revolutions and much bloodier 'ethnic' conflicts of the 1980s and 1990s. Since then there has been the gradual 'democratization' of previously communist states into the twenty-first century. European social psychology has been at the very centre of all this (in some cases quite literally). My own memories are of a 'small group meeting' of the European Association of Social Psychology, sited in the Negev dessert (yes, Israel is a member) in the winter of 1990. Its topic was 'Psychology and Politics', so all of us had been invited because of our interest in that aspect of social psychology. About half of the delegates were from the countries in Eastern Europe that were still in the throes of change. Soon after the meeting started we effectively ditched the official programme. We spent our time instead talking about what was happening – and speculating why none of us, despite our knowledge of psychology, had foreseen what would happen. We agreed, though, that for the next few years we would all be taking part in a 'great natural experiment' in which our lives would change, and we, as people, would be changing too. With hindsight I think we got that wrong too – it was not politics that changed us, but technology, but that is another story.

The point I am making here is that because of our geographies and our histories, European social psychologists have been at the forefront of research and theory on and about groups,

> *Völkerpsychologie* and crowd psychology are covered in Chapter 1

and especially conflict between groups (called *intergroup conflict*). From the early *Völkerpsychologie* and crowd psychology of the late nineteenth and early twentieth centuries, Europeans have led the way in this field – social psychologists like Serge Moscovici, Steve Reicher, Mustafer Sharif, Henri Tajfel and John Turner are the 'big names' here.

Times are changing, and social psychologists from an ever-growing list of other countries with their own experiences of conflict are bringing new ideas to our understanding. This adds rather than detracts from the case I am making that the social psychology of groups as studied in the USA is different. Its treatment of intergroup conflict tends to have a rather parochial and narrower definition and scope, mostly centred around race. So, I make no apologies that I have written this chapter from a European perspective, though I do acknowledge that it is, therefore, one story among many that would be possible.

In the chapter I have brought together both general theory and research about groups of different kinds, coverage of what goes on within groups, group polarization and relationships between groups. At the end there is a short section on leadership, since it is an important topic in relation to both how groups are created, inspired and persuaded to act, and how leaders are produced through group processes.

What is a group?

Social psychology takes a very broad sweep when it comes to groups – from collections of, say, four or five people brought together to do an experiment, to viewing, say, 'the Welsh' as a group to which people belong, have allegiance to and from which they derive their social identity. It has studied groups ranging from boys at summer camp to nurses in hospitals, from young joyriders to high-level executives, and from Girl Guides to terrorists. Hardly surprising, then, that Hogg and Vaughan (1998) wryly commented that there are almost as many definitions of a 'group' as there are social psychologists! The trouble is, the term is used very differently in different contexts.

For simplicity (drawing on Kelley 1952) in this chapter I distinguish between three main meanings:

- **Incidental groups** are simply where some people are brought together for a relatively short period of time (a matter of hours at most) with minimal involvement in and commitment to each other. Examples are the kinds of 'small groups' set up to do an exercise in a training session or a workshop at a conference, an audience of mostly strangers at a concert, and a tour group taken to 'see the sights' on a day-trip. What marks out these kinds of groups is that they are made up of people who do not know each other.

> These are the 'minimal groups' Tajfel worked on, which you looked at in Chapter 10 in relation to social identity.

- **Membership groups** are those defined by having members, who, though being members, get to know each other. Members may join and leave the group, but membership typically lasts some time (weeks, months or years) and members have a commitment to the group's common goals and values. Examples include work-based groups (such as a group of nurses or social workers working together as a team), sporting teams and hobby clubs and associations, and committees.

- **Identity-reference groups** are where belonging to the group involves identification with the group, and where affiliation acts as a **reference frame** for a person to know 'who' they are – their social identity (Chapter 10). Generally this is a long-term situation (often for many years or even permanently) and those who belong to the group will tend to know each other well and find each other familiar because they share common experiences, values and norms. Examples include ethnic identity groups (for example, being pakeha or Chinese), religious communities (for example, being a Muslim or a Catholic), political affiliations (for example, being a Christian Democrat or a communist), nationalities and communities (for example, being a Slovak or an Amish), and subcultures (for example, being a 'boy racer' or a football fan).

These three different kinds of groups vary, very broadly, in terms of their durability and the commitment of their membership, as shown in Figure 12.1.

But – you have guessed it – it is nowhere near as simple as this. For example, membership groups are often identity-reference groups too. The distinction between being a member of a political party or pressure group and this being a person's identity-reference group is seldom clear-cut. Equally, social psychologists have studied identity-reference aspects of incidental groups. However, I think you will find the categorization helpful in that social psychologists have studied these groups in broadly different ways and, to some degree, the social psychological processes that are seen to go on within them are different.

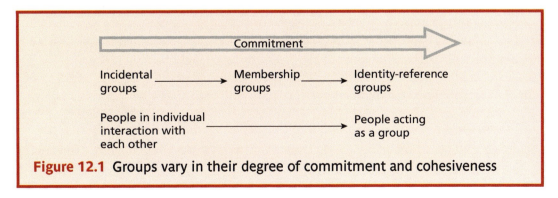

Figure 12.1 Groups vary in their degree of commitment and cohesiveness

I am going to use this section to give you a flavour of the differences between these three kinds of groups by illustrating each one with a key area of research into group processes.

Incidental groups

In social psychology the most common form of incidental group is a group convened for the purposes of an experiment! What distinguishes such groups is their low level of involvement or commitment, and generally this means that there is little, if any, group behaviour going on. A group like this is in many ways more of a collection of individuals interacting together.

The minimal group paradigm

In reality, it appears that commitment is seldom completely absent. Studies in what is called the **minimal group paradigm** (Chapter 10) have shown that almost any element of common fate is sufficient to persuade people to begin to see themselves as part of a group – by, for example, favouring members of 'their' group over members of another group in competitive situations.

Rabbie and Horowitz (1969) demonstrated this by allocating children to groups of four by giving them badges (green or blue). In the control condition the two groups just sat together on different sides of a screen dividing greens from blues. In the experimental condition one group was given a radio and the other was not. Subsequently, in both conditions the screen was removed and the children in turn read out statements about themselves, after which all the other children in both groups rated them on a number of evaluative scales. Children in the control condition showed no significant differences in their evaluations. But children in the experimental condition consistently evaluated children from their own group more favourably.

However, a later study (Tajfel et al. 1971) showed that mere categorization as a member of a group can be enough to engender commitment, and this finding has proved extremely robust in more than 20 replications. However, it gets a lot more complicated, if, for example, group members allocate unpleasant things rather than rewards. There is considerable controversy about whether experimental effects arise from commitment to the group or some other reason. Brown (2001) provides a clear account of this dispute.

Membership groups

In real life, membership groups entail a fair degree of engagement with (and hence commitment to) the group. But experimentally created groups can be induced to behave more like membership groups, for example, when subjects are required to interact with each other and carry out a task together, as shown in Figure 12.2.

Examples of experimentally observable effects of group membership are studies of social influence that either demonstrate social idling (usually called social loafing) or social energizing. These are, in other words, studies of social inhibition and facilitation applied to settings where subjects work together on a common task.

Social loafing

Most early studies in this situation found that overall task performance went down when people work together. The total output for the group was less than the sum of individual outputs that

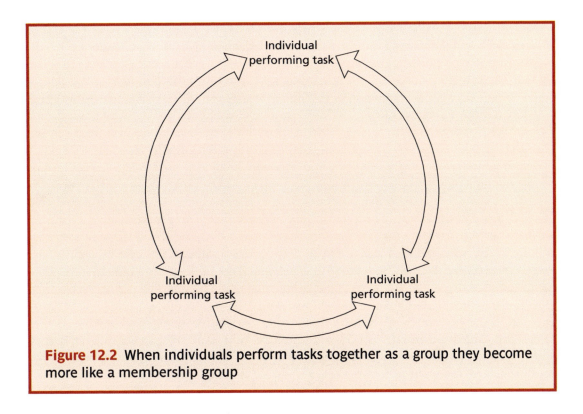

Figure 12.2 When individuals perform tasks together as a group they become more like a membership group

people achieve when working alone. Some of this decrement has been attributed to coordination loss – due, for example, to when people jostle or distract each other. But over and above this, a substantial number of studies have found decrements due to what is called **social loafing** – the tendency for individuals to expend less effort on a task when they do it with others (or think they are doing so). Latané et al. (1979), for example, found that when people are asked to shout together as loud as they could, the amount of noise each person makes is reduced by 29 per cent in two-person groups, 49 per cent in four-person groups and 60 per cent in six-person groups. This effect has been found in almost 80 studies that have been published (see Williams et al. 1993 for a review). These include laboratory and field studies, with physical, cognitive, perceptual and evaluative tasks.

However, the effect is most marked when the task is pretty trivial and meaningless. Where the task is important and meaningful, and/or the group members have a personal stake in the outcome, there is much less drop-off in performance. Notice that this is a parallel finding to research into the 'bystander effect' you first found out about in Chapters 1 and especially 11 in relation to the ways strangers behave towards each other.

Social energizing – or perhaps better defined as organizational citizenship behaviour?

It is now becoming recognized that social loafing is a consequence of working in groups with low commitment to each other and where the group members are required to do trivial and meaningless tasks. In other situations working as a member of a group can energize people into action rather than persuade them to loaf or to idle. We can call this opposite effect **social energizing**, where people work *harder* as a member of a group than alone. This is what happens when the task is important or interesting or fun – and especially when it is all three (Zaccaro 1984)! It also tends to occur when group members think they are competing against another group, and/or where there is strong commitment to achieving a common goal (Guzzo and Dickenson 1996).

More recently researchers from collectivist cultures have adopted the title **Organizational Citizenship Behaviour** to describe the kind of social facilitation that operates in such cultures (Tan and Tan 2008). It would be interesting to see what would happen if we took this up as our preferred term from now on, since, from a collectivist standpoint, it better depicts features that are relevant to its operation.

It is worth noting that the vast majority of studies that found a social loafing effect were carried out in individualistic cultures. Smith et al. (2006) suggest that people from collectivist cultures are more likely to perform best when working together, especially when they think performance will be judged on the group's achievements. Here culturally normative collective values may encourage even members of incidental groups to act as if they belong to an identity-referent or membership group, at least where the task they have to do together is meaningful and important.

In collectivist cultures Organizational Citizenship Behaviour is thus more likely, and Smith et al. (2006) cite a number of cross-cultural studies as evidence for this. For instance, Earley (1989) compared managers in the USA and China working on an 'in basket' simulation task in which they had to deal with a rapid succession of tasks (such as rating job application forms, prioritizing interviews, and so on). Managers were told either that they were working alone and set individual targets, or that they were working as a group with group targets. The US managers completed more tasks in the 'working alone' condition; Chinese managers completed more in the 'working together' condition. Similar energizing effects have been demonstrated with Taiwanese children (Gabrenya et al. 1985) and Japanese subjects (Matsui et al. 1987).

Idling or energizing?

What these differences tell us is that social loafing is not a universal quality of task performance in a group but, again, something of an artefact of experimentally creating incidental groups. Where people are required to do trivial and meaningless tasks, then they are more likely to idle when working in a group than alone. This is particularly so when performing in a group where there is little or no involvement in or commitment to the group, nor any cultural norms to encourage group effort. Without any real stake in the outcome and where any individual's poor performance is less likely to be noticed, people tend to idle. By contrast, with groups that have (culturally) – or are motivated to develop (experimentally) – some degree of cohesiveness and common commitment (that is, they are or become, in effect, a membership group) and where the task is intrinsically interesting or worthwhile, then working together as a group is likely to be energizing.

Identity-reference groups

Identity-reference groups are where people's commitment to the group is so strong that affiliation to it is part of their identity: 'People take on the group characteristics and make these their own, at any rate for the time being, to a greater or lesser extent' (Turner 1991: 35).

A classic experimental study of an identity-reference group is a series of field experiments carried out at summer camps (often called the **Summer Camp experiments**) by Sherif and his colleagues (Sherif et al. 1961; Sherif 1966; Sherif and Sherif 1969). There were three of these carried out in 1949, 1953 and 1954, with slight variations in conditions and measures, but all conformed to the same general plan. Here I describe just one.

Sherif's Summer Camp experiments

The experiment was conducted with white, middle-class 11- and 12-year-old boys who did not know each other. The boys attended a summer camp – in the USA this is a common practice, providing opportunities for an activity holiday in the countryside for children (and a break for their parents!).

However, unbeknown to the boys, the camp was staffed by researchers who observed the boys' behaviour in a situation deliberately structured to examine group behaviour. Sherif himself, for example, was the camp caretaker and handyman as well as leader of the experimental project team. The experiment consisted of four phases: spontaneous friendship formation, group formation, intergroup competition and intergroup cooperation.

Spontaneous friendship formation

On arrival at the camp the boys all spent a short time together. They were free to mix with each other as they liked, and to freely choose partners for games and activities and as room-mates.

Ingroup formation

After a few days the boys were then divided into two groups. They were lodged in cabins some distance from each other and the groups were kept entirely separate. The researchers engaged the boys in activities to develop cohesiveness in the groups, getting them involved in cooperative projects like setting up a camp and cleaning a beach. Rapidly both groups became established. Leaders emerged and names were agreed for the groups – 'Bulldogs' and 'Red Devils' in the first experiment, 'Eagles' and 'Rattlers' in another. Soon in each group there were 'in jokes', secret codes, rules about behaviour, and sanctions agreed and imposed for those who got 'out of line'. Sound friendships were formed, and strong bonds of mutual liking and cooperation developed between group members.

Intergroup competition

Then the researchers brought the two groups together in deliberately competitive situations. A tournament was organized in which the groups competed against each other in a number of different activities for points that were manipulated so the groups were constantly neck and neck. Initial norms of good sportsmanship soon broke down and rapidly the groups became almost fanatical about winning out against each other. As the tension grew, they became more and more hostile towards each other. They began to call each other derogatory names, pick fights and raid each other's camps. 'Bulldogs' put down 'Red Devils' at every opportunity and vice versa. At the same time ingroup cohesion and loyalty became stronger.

Intergroup cooperation

It would be impossible to conduct a study like the Summer Camp experiments today, given the ethical issues it raised. Even at the time, in the first study the researchers were shocked by what happened. They tried a number of strategies to tackle the incredible antagonism that had built up. They got the boys to attend religious services that preached love and cooperation, introduced a third group as a 'common enemy' and engaged the boys in joint ventures that were pleasurable, such as setting off fireworks together. None of these worked – the boys simply turned each event into a new opportunity to attack each other.

In the end the researchers found one that did – creating collective goals that could be achieved only through cooperation between the groups. First, the researchers arranged for the water supply line to break down, in a situation where both groups had to work together to fix it. The boys did cooperate – but as soon as the water supply was returned, they went back on the warpath. However, after a series of several such cooperative ventures, the antipathy between the two groups was eventually reduced enough for most of them to choose to go home on the same bus. In subsequent studies the researchers systematically introduced an intergroup cooperation phase to reduce the hostility created.

Lessons learned

Sherif and Sherif (1969) themselves acknowledged that the Summer Camp experiments were only partially true to life, in that real conflicts between groups are much more complex, containing elements of historical feuds, power and dominance differentials, and structural, material and political inequalities. However, this research is seen as important, since it demonstrated very clearly that antagonistic and hostile behaviour can be generated by group situations. Crucially, these studies have been seen to demonstrate that human aggression is seldom simply a matter of individual pathology or dysfunction. It can be – and usually is – affected by the social influence of group processes.

What is a group?

- *Incidental groups* are characterized by people having little or no involvement in or commitment to the group, individualistic cultural norms and no real stake in what happens. Generally in such situations the impact of the group on individual behaviour is negative – social loafing – or minimal.

- *Membership groups* are where there is only moderate involvement and commitment but individuals see themselves as having some stake in the group's fortunes. The impact of the group is generally positive – encouraging group members to work harder for the group, and to treat other members of the group more favourably than outsiders.

- *Identity-reference groups* provide members with a locus for identification. Individuals shift from a personal to a social identity. It becomes their ingroup. In such ingroups involvement and commitment are high. Members have a strong investment in the ingroup's fortunes. Its successes and failures become their successes and failures. Group membership encourages cooperation within the ingroup and conflict with outgroups.

Social influence in groups

We now move on to explore some of the group processes that experimental social psychologists have studied. We start with research into social influence, beginning with its ability to induce conformity.

Conformity

Conformity is one of the most extensively studied forms of social influence since Allport (1924) observed that groups tend to give more conservative judgements than individuals. Sherif (1936) explained this as the effect of group norms – where people tend to refer to each other and find a 'middle ground' on which to base a decision. He carried out a series of studies using the **auto-kinetic effect**. This is where a small bright light is shone in otherwise complete darkness, and it appears to move even though it is stationary. With no reference point to locate it, people's eye movements give the impression that it is moving. When people are asked how far it is moving, they find it very difficult to tell. When observing the effect in groups of three or four, taking it in turns to call out their estimate, Sherif observed that individuals' estimates tended to converge to the group mean after a few trials.

Norms

Norms are defined as the shared standards of conduct expected of group members. They can either be explicit (for example, norms of confidentiality in juries) or implicit – the kinds of every-day, taken-for-granted conventions that oil the machinery of social interaction. Transgressing social norms can be very disruptive. In a classic study Garfinkel (1967) got students to behave at home with their families as if they were lodgers. For a period of 15 minutes they were very polite, spoke formally and then only when spoken to. Their families were puzzled and got quite angry, accusing them of being selfish, nasty and rude.

The concept of norms was used by Festinger to develop **social comparison theory** (Festinger 1954). Based on social learning theory, it sees norms as operating through people's propensity to want social approval and dislike social censure. For the individual, norms provide a reference frame for social comparison, and hence for guiding behaviour.

Different reference groups have different norms. Which one is followed will depend on which one is relevant to the person at the time. For instance, Tom lives in a student house, his reference group is 'students' and its norm is that only total nerds stay in on a Friday night. Tom will find it hard to resist the group pressure to go out, even if he has an urgent essay to finish. By contrast Dan lives at home with his family whose group norm is that studying is more important than going out. Dan will find it difficult to resist his family's pressure to stay home and study.

Asch's studies of conformity

In Asch's (1951) first classic experiment on conformity, male students were told they were taking part in a study of visual discrimination. They were shown a line, and three other lines to compare it with (see Figure 12.3), and then asked to say which of the comparison lines matched it.

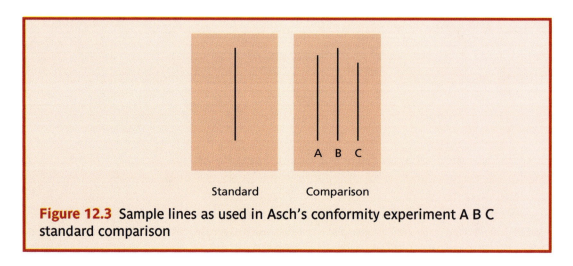

Figure 12.3 Sample lines as used in Asch's conformity experiment A B C standard comparison

This experiment was run with groups of seven or eight; each student had to call out their judgement in a predetermined order. In fact, all but one of the students were stooges who called out the same wrong judgement. Only one was a real subject, who had to answer second to last. Performance was compared between this experimental condition and a control condition in which subjects made their judgements alone. In the control condition the error rate was about 1 per cent. But in the experimental condition Asch found an error rate of about 33 per cent (that is, where the subjects' responses conformed to the group's erroneous response).

It is important to recognize that there were wide individual differences. About 25 per cent of the subjects in the experiment steadfastly continued to give their own independent judgement, despite the repeated pressure of six or seven other people all giving the same (wrong) response. About 5 per cent, on the other hand, conformed to the (wrong) group response every single time. The remaining 70 per cent of subjects conformed some or most of the time.

So did they change their minds about what they saw?

Just like the Latané and Darley (1968a) experiments you found out about in Chapters 5 and 11, it is the insight gained from debriefing interviews that reveals what was actually going on. When the subjects who had conformed with the group decision were asked about how they were feeling after the experiment, they all reported feeling very uncomfortable. The majority said they knew perfectly well that they were seeing things differently from the other members of the group, but felt increasingly uncertain about their own judgement. Others said they were certain they were right but went along with the group so as not to stand out. These conforming subjects reported feeling self-conscious, anxious and even lonely, and feared disapproval. Even some of the independent subjects said they were emotionally affected, but felt it more important to 'stick to their guns' and do as they had been instructed (that is, give accurate estimates). These results suggest that even among those who 'conformed', this is not because they saw things that way. They had not actually been swayed by the majority judgement, but were responding 'politely' to an awkward social situation.

Asch (1956) went on to look at these concerns about social disapproval directly by doing further experiments that changed the conditions so that 16 real subjects took part in the study with just one error-giving stooge. Now the stooge was in a minority, the subjects saw his behaviour as ludicrous, and soon started to chuckle and ridicule him. Even the experimenter found it impossible not to burst out laughing! So it seemed to Asch that social disapproval was a major factor in the conformity. He tested this by another experiment like the first with just one subject and a majority of stooges giving wrong answers. But in this case he allowed the subject to give his responses privately and, sure enough, the error rate dropped to 12.5 per cent.

A large number of replications of Asch's original experiment have been carried out in order to tease out the causes of conformity, each varying different aspects of the experimental conditions. These have shown that there are a large number of influences in play. Deutsch and Gerrard (1955), for instance, in a sophisticated study varying uncertainty and group pressure, found that group pressure had the most impact. But even in their condition where the subject could directly compare the lines (low uncertainty) and had no direct contact with the group, merely observing their responses, an average of 23 per cent of responses conformed with the group's wrong answers. Other studies have varied things like the number of stooges, the confidence with which people spoke, the kind of judgement made and the extent to which the group response was unanimous. All of these affected the result, but showed evidence of some degree of conformity all the same. The most important factor, however, seems to be the isolation of being the only person in the group giving a dissenting response. Where the subject has a supporter, the tendency to conform to the group is virtually extinguished.

Who conforms?

People tend to conform when the situation demands it (Vaughan 1964; McGuire 1968) or when there are other pressures to be compliant. Historically, women have tended to act in a more conforming way than men (see Eagly and Wood 1991 for a meta-analytic study). However, Sistrunk and McDavid (1971) showed this was less of a gender effect than one of expertise and confidence. They got women and men to make judgements that varied in terms of gender-linked knowledge (for example, about mechanical tools or types of needlework), and found that women conformed less than men when making judgements about needlework, whereas men conformed less than women when making judgements about mechanical tools.

Cultural values

Not surprisingly cultural values have an influence, and can create social pressure. There have been at least 24 published replications carried out in 13 countries outside the USA and these show considerable variation in rates of conformity and independence (Smith et al. 2006). The lowest rate of conformity (14 per cent) was found with Belgian students (Doms 1983) and the highest (58 per cent) with Indian teachers in Fiji (Chandra 1973). Conforming behaviour is usually high where cultural values stress deference to authority and, more broadly, cultures where collectivist values dominate tend to be more conforming than individualist cultures.

Berry (1967) found intriguing evidence for this in a study comparing the Temne people of Sierra Leone with Inuit in Canada. Using a variant of Asch's experiment, Berry showed that the Temne were much more conforming. The Temne people make their livelihood from the collective production of a single crop. This involves close cooperation and coordination between them, and so, as one of the subjects in this study said, 'when Temne people choose a thing, we must all agree with the decision' (as reported in Berry 1967: 417). Canadian Inuit, by contrast, gain their livelihood by hunting and gathering on a much more individual basis, and so, Berry argued, group consensus is less salient and valued in their culture.

Smith and Harris Bond (1993) argue that what matters, however, are not so much cultural values in general as those held by a particular group of people at a particular time and in a particular place. They illustrate this by a study that found high levels of independence, despite the participants being Japanese where the expectation is of behaviour highly deferential to authority (Frager 1970). Smith and Harris Bond suggest that this independence may have arisen because the participants in the study were students, taking part at the time when there was a lot of student unrest and rebellion at the university where the study was conducted. These students, they argued, responded by reference to group resistance rather than cultural values.

Equally in a study of the impact of computer-mediated settings, while greater culturally linked conformity was found in face-to-face settings, it was not found when participants performed through electronic means (Cinnirella and Green 2007). One explanation for this offered by the authors is that the fear of rejection is much less in this setting, an important factor in the expression of conformity of people from collectivist cultures (Yamaguchi 1994).

Another way of interpreting data such as these is by considering the behaviour as being enacted within situated social practices – such as taking part in a psychological experiment (quite possibly under strong social pressure to do so) in the context of student unrest, or communicating in 'virtual' rather than 'actual' space.

Minority influence

As noted already, it is very much easier to resist conforming if you are not the only 'odd one out'. Two people can resist much better together than either one could alone. But can you go further – can you persuade the others to move to your position? Your own experience is likely to tell you that you can – sometimes, at least. And, indeed, a number of studies based on Asch's experimental paradigm have found evidence for **minority influence**, where a small minority is able to sway the judgements of the majority (see Wood et al. 1994 for a review).

One of the first of such demonstrations was carried out by Moscovici et al. (1969). They had students participate in a study of, ostensibly, colour perception. The students began by taking a colour blindness test. Then those who passed were put into groups of six and shown 36 slides, all clearly blue, varying only in intensity. The task was to call out in turn the colour shown on the slide. Two of the six were stooges. In one condition (consistent) these stooges always called out that the slide was green. In a second condition (inconsistent) they called out 'green' for 24 slides and 'blue' for 12 of them. There was also a control condition in which all the subjects were 'real'; there were no dissenting stooges. The results obtained are shown in Table 12.1.

Table 12.1 Majority error rates in relation to minority influence

	Conditions – the responses made by two stooges		
	Control – no stooges	Inconsistent – stooges called 'green' only sometimes	Consistent – stooges consistently called 'green'
Error rate	0.25	1.25	8.42

Source: Moscovici et al. (1969)

These results showed that some members of the majority in a group can be persuaded round to the judgements made by a small minority, so long as their judgements are consistent. Further studies followed, again varying the conditions that allowed the specific elements of minority influence to be pinned down. Consistency is identified as a necessary condition, but also it matters how people interpret the behaviour of the minority group.

Models of social influence in groups

There has been a great deal of debate about the psychological processes that are involved in how social influence affects the judgements that people make in group settings. Generally there is agreement among experimental social psychologists that social influence operaties through two main processes: **information influence** and **normative influence** (Kelley, 1952; Deutsch and Gerrard, 1955):

- *Information influence* is where people use the group as an information source. This influence arises from people's desire to feel confident about the judgements that they make. In group settings they use the judgements of others in the group as a source of reliable information.
- *Normative influence* is where people follow group norms. This influence arises from people's desire for approval and acceptance, and their anxiety and discomfort about the possibility of being ostracized or ridiculed, or simply being seen as impolite.

However, there is strong disagreement about whether these processes are the same or different for majority and minority influence.

Same process models

In same process models, social influence (sometimes called social impact) is seen as working in the same way, irrespective of whether it is a majority influencing a minority, or a minority influencing the majority. One version (see, for example, Latané and Wolf 1981) proposes that social influence works according to a kind of cognitive algebra (rather like such models applied to reasoned action and planned behaviour, as described in Chapter 8) where different elements contribute to an overall effect. In this model the difference between minority and majority influence is seen as nothing more than a shift in balance. For example, minority effects will not be found when the minority is heavily outnumbered, because the majority's greater numbers will strengthen the impact of normative influence. But minority influence may arise when the disparity between the majority and minority is relatively small (as was the case in the 4:2 balance in the Moscovici et al. 1969 study) as this will attenuate the majority's normative influence.

In another version of the single process model, information and normative influences are seen as contributing differentially in different situations. Turner and his colleagues, for example, have suggested a model that they (somewhat confusingly) call a **dual process dependency model** (Turner et al. 1987). This model proposes that in situations where people are confident about their own judgement and expertise, they will not be much affected by any informational influence from a minority. Equally, when people perceive the majority in the group in which they are participating as powerful – whether instrumentally (able to give rewards and punishments) or through sheer numbers – then normative influence will predominate. These are seen as operating in an additive manner. Both will generally act as levers for **majority influence** because the balance of influence is usually heavily weighted to the majority.

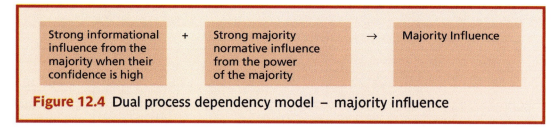

Figure 12.4 Dual process dependency model – majority influence

In minority influence situations the balance gets shifted. This happens when the majority lack confidence in their own judgement, and so conflicting information from the minority can have a relatively greater impact; and when the majority is less powerful and so its normative influence is reduced.

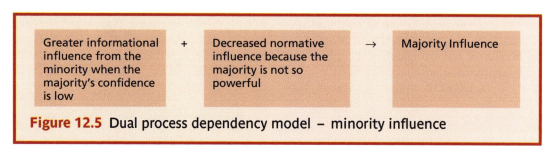

Figure 12.5 Dual process dependency model – minority influence

Different process models

In different process models, majority and minority influence are seen to operate through distinctly different processes. These have mainly been framed within two different approaches: Moscovici's innovation model, based on his concept of social representations (see Chapter 3) and Turner's referent information influence model, based on his concept of social categorization (see Chapter 10).

Moscovici's innovation model

As you saw in Chapter 5, Moscovici developed the concept of social representations to explain how the new ideas of original thinkers come to influence the images, thinking, vocabulary and beliefs of ordinary people. Social representations, in this analysis, are shared understandings and belief structures through which people make sense of the social world. As part of this project, Moscovici ([1961] 1976) developed a specific interest in how novel ideas are transmitted and hence in the ways in which a minority can influence a majority. He saw this as a discrete process of innovation. Not surprisingly, then, Moscovici (see Moscovici and Personnaz 1980; Moscovici 1985) has contested the view that majority and minority influence operate via the same process, and proposed instead a general theory of social influence in which three processes can potentially play a part:

- conformity – where the views of the majority induce the minority to comply
- normalization – where a mutual compromise is reached leading to convergence
- innovation – where a minority persuades the majority to adopt their viewpoint.

Moscovici's model is an early version of what, in the context of attitude change, would now be called the depth-processing model (see Chapter 8) that focuses on the impact of depth of processing. Indeed, in the mid-1990s De Vries et al. (1996) made a specific connection between Moscovici's theorization and this model of persuasion (see Chapter 8). If you recall, the model assumes that in much of our everyday life we do not process incoming information very deeply, but depend on heuristics to respond in a rather mindless, automatic way.

Majority influence, Moscovici claimed, works like this most of the time. It operates through the processes of conformity and normalization. Both of them are passive processes undertaken without much thought. Moscovici said they are when a person pays little attention to the perception or issue itself and instead 'concentrates all his attention on what others say, so as to fit in with their opinions and judgments' (Moscovici and Personnaz 1980: 214). By contrast minority influence, he claimed, works through a different process that he called innovation, where a minority directly challenges preconceived ideas. This sets up a conflict between people's rather mindless, taken-for-granted assumptions and a sustained, principled and coherent alternative viewpoint – that forces people to abandon heuristics (like 'the majority is generally right'), attend to the issue or perception in question, and direct processing effort to it. As we shall see a bit later, the ability to 'change hearts and minds' is seen as the marker of a leader – someone whose charisma and rhetoric can inspire others and convince them not only to see things differently, but to act upon this new insight.

Whether minority influence works or not, Moscovici claimed, depends crucially upon the **behavioural style** adopted by the minority. It has to be strong enough to get the attention of those in the majority and persuasive enough to make them think. The most effective element, he argued, is consistency, where the members of the minority group strongly and consistently give the same message. This disrupts the majority norm and raises doubts about it, drawing attention to a sustained, clear and coherent alternative viewpoint.

Moscovici drew on experimental evidence (for example, Mugny 1982) to define further elements by which the effectiveness of consistency can be further increased. He suggested this can happen by investment (where the minority is seen to have made serious personal or material sacrifices to their cause) and autonomy (where it is seen to be acting out of principle rather than self-serving motives). At the same time he proposed that effectiveness can be undermined both by rigidity (where the minority are seen as too dogmatic) or over-flexibility (where it is seen as too willing to compromise). There is a fine line to tread, Moscovici argued, between being seen as obstinate and unyielding, and being seen as over-accommodating. If they want to change hearts and minds, a minority must stick firmly to their principles but adopt an open-minded and reasonable negotiating style (Moscovici and Mugny 1983). Moscovici's model is shown in Figure 12.6.

In usual situations, majority influence will predominate, since both the information and normative influences will be the fall-back standards governing the judgements made by most members of the group. But where the minority is vocal, coherent and convincing in giving its response or making its argument, the other participants in the group will be pressed to actively process the information it supplies, overriding normative influence and potentially leading them to change their minds. Innovation, in this context, is where a sustained attempt is made to exert information influence. Real-life examples are pressure groups (such as Amnesty International and Greenpeace) that set out to sway public opinion.

Nemeth (1986) has taken this theorization further. She proposed that the effect of having a minority who express different views is it that it gets people to shift from position-relevant processing to issue-relevant information processing. In so doing, the frame of reference is, she

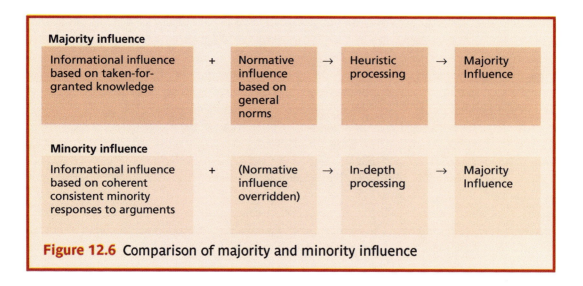

Figure 12.6 Comparison of majority and minority influence

suggested, widened up, getting people to examine a variety of alternatives. She demonstrated this effect in a study in which groups of six carried out a rather difficult discrimination task together (Nemeth and Wachtler 1983). There were two conditions: a majority influence condition (where four members of the group were stooges and called out predetermined responses) and a minority influence condition (where only two members of the group were stooges). The effect of the minority influence was that subjects were induced to consider a wider range of possible answers and came up with more correct solutions.

Turner's referent information influence model

Turner and his colleagues have proposed an alternative model. It also argues for a third form of social influence – **referent information influence** (Turner 1991). In Turner's formulation, however, this is based on social identity theory. Referent information influence is seen to operate through people's self-categorization (see Chapter 10). When they identify themselves as belonging to a particular group they then use that group's norms as standards for their own decision making. Referent information influence comes into play, then, in identity referent groups, either those set up experimentally (as in the Summer Camp experiments) or those occurring 'naturally'.

For instance, take the resistance to group pressure shown by the Japanese students in the study by Frager (1970). This can be explained by assuming that the students categorized themselves as belonging to an ingroup of 'dissatisfied students' in a context where student protest against authority was ongoing at the university at that time. This could have made them more likely to sustain independent (or perhaps better thought of as 'rebellious') judgements than if they had seen themselves as belonging to their more broadly culturally defined social group of 'students of low status who must defer to authority'. In Japanese culture there is a norm where the person who speaks first is viewed as having authority and therefore should be deferred to. A referent normative model suggests that in situations like this, referent group (rebellious students) norm takes over from cultural group (deferential students) norm.

Conformity, in this theoretical context, is a feature of groups where there are no reference group norms in play, only the general norms of the broad culture in which the study is set. Where (as in Japan) these tend to be collectivist – stressing deference, interpersonal harmony and consensus – then, all other things being equal, people will tend to conform. Or, to put it in a less pejorative way, they tend to place their trust in cultural norms (Brown 2001). But if other norms come into play because group members have allegiance to a particular referent group (rebellious students), then they are more likely to act in ways that reflect the referent group norms – in this case, rebelliously.

Social influence in groups

Conformity
- In all of the studies of conformity some people could be induced to conform to a group judgement some of the time.
- Conformity is mainly a product of being 'the odd one out'. Conditions that make this worse (for example, where there are more people in the majority) lead to greater levels of conformity and conditions that alleviate it (for example, having a supporter) reduce conformity.
- However, while they are billed as 'studies of conformity', in all of them there are some people who do not conform at least some of the time, despite social pressure to do so, and in most studies these people are in a majority.
- The processes at work that do persuade people to conform are anything but simple. They depend upon context and, in particular, on the value, salience and meaning of conformity and independence to the people concerned.

Minority influence
- Majorities induce minorities to conform through information and/or normative influences, both of which tend to operate at an automatic level of processing.
- However, minorities can induce majorities to shift their judgement by providing consistent alternative sets of responses or counter-arguments that require active processing.

Group polarization

From the previous analysis of conformity, you might expect that when groups make a decision together they are likely to come up with a compromise – a decision that reflects the average of individuals' independent views. Interestingly, this is not generally the case. Rather, the group decision can be more extreme – this is called **group polarization**.

The original study that identified this phenomenon was carried out for a Master's thesis (Stoner 1961). In it people were presented with a personal dilemma facing a (fictional) person and asked to advise them how to deal with it. They could make one of two recommendations to the person faced with the dilemma. One recommendation was a more appealing course of action, but risky. The other was much less appealing but carried a lot less risk. Stoner got participants in his study to first choose privately which recommendation they would make. Then they joined in a group discussion and told that the group must reach a unanimous decision about which recommendation they would offer. To Stoner's surprise, the group discussions tended to offer the risky course of action more often than individuals did privately. He called this phenomenon the risky shift.

The result also surprised other social psychologists – it went against their assumption that groups would be more conservative in their decisions than individuals. There followed a flurry of experiments investigating the **risky shift**, as it was called. These showed that this move to greater risk was not universal. Further studies found that in some situations groups do make conservative decisions, but, interestingly, when they do so, these also tend to be *more* conservative than the private decisions made by the individuals in the group. The phenomenon was thus renamed group polarization.

Group polarization (Isenberg 1986; Wetherell 1987) is defined as the tendency of group decisions to be more extreme than the mean of the individual decisions made by the members of the group. An example might be a discussion about genetically modified (GM) foods, where the group's decision is that all research and production of GM foods should be banned by law, when only two members of the group privately took this position before the discussion, and some were actually quite in favour in investing in research into GM foods. Van Avermaet defines it more precisely as where there is 'an enhancement of initially dominant position through group discussion' (2001: 427). The phenomenon has been observed in many different situations: in mock juries, negotiations, group counselling, and management teams as well as in experimental settings (see Lamm and Myers 1978 for a review).

Three main theories have been offered to explain the group polarization effect: social comparison, persuasive arguments and self-categorization theories.

Social comparison theory

Based on Festinger's original social comparison theory (Festinger 1954), this focuses on people's propensity to want social approval and dislike social censure. It is also sometimes called **cultural values theory** (Sanders and Baron 1977), recognizing that groups and cultures vary in the actions and behaviours that they endorse.

According to this explanation, talk in the group rapidly shows which views are valued and which ones are rebuffed by the majority. Desire for social approval will then motivate group members to shift the views they express in the direction of the socially sanctioned viewpoint, and this will soon appear to be the group's viewpoint. Indeed, group members may want to be seen as 'better' than the others and will therefore tend to express even more zealous views than the norm. Support is given for this by a finding that people tend to admire views that are more extreme than their own (Jellison and Davis 1973). This process can become a positive feedback loop, with speakers successively seeking to outdo each other in their endorsement for the initial group viewpoint, leading to greater and greater polarization. In this theory it is the position taken rather than the arguments expressed that brings about polarization. Polarization is seen as a process of successive 'upping the stakes', where group members vie with each other to express the **group norm** more emphatically.

An example here is 'flaming' on Internet forums and chat rooms, defined as sending offensive and aggressive messages. When people get stirred up, these messages can rapidly become more and more aggressive. A UK example is what happened to a woman who was caught on CCTV putting a pet cat into a wheelie (garbage) bin outside its owners' house. Posted on Facebook, the images soon aroused mounting hostility ending in death threats towards the woman. Facebook removed the site when this happened. The woman was prosecuted and fined.

Persuasive arguments theory

Persuasive arguments theory (also called informational influence theory) highlights the capacity for novel arguments to change people's opinions (Burnstein and Vinokur 1977). This theory assumes that at the beginning of the discussion, a range of individual viewpoints will be expressed. As this happens, people will hear new arguments that lend support to their own viewpoint and these will be perceived as further evidence to endorse it (Gigone and Hastie 1993). This will encourage them to take an even stronger position, leading, overall, to a polarization. In this theory it is the argument presented rather than the position taken that brings about polarization. Polarization is seen to be a process of mutual persuasion, where the group acts as a resource for marshalling a convincing justification for a specific decision or viewpoint.

Self-categorization theory

There is empirical evidence to support both social comparison and persuasive argument as processes involved in group polarization (see Van Avermaet 2001 for a review). However, neither can fully explain why the effect is sensitive to social context (Wetherell 1987). To address this aspect, there has recently been a turn to **social categorization theory**.

Self-categorization theory was developed by Turner and his colleagues (Turner et al. 1987; Turner 1991), see Chapter 10. It highlights people's tendency to identify with the group – to see it as an ingroup – and then to endorse the norms that distinguish their ingroup from other outgroups. In such a situation the group's norm is not defined as an average position according to what it has in common with the ingroup's beliefs and values but, crucially, how it differs from those of outgroups. The pressure on group members, in this theory, is not for social approval in and of itself (as social comparison theory would claim). Rather group members are motivated to demonstrate allegiance to the ingroup by distancing themselves from the views of outgroups. Social categorization theory proposes that in the course of the discussion, group members will gradually refine the group's decision or viewpoint by contrasting it with the position they assume is held by one or more outgroups.

In this theory it is the contrast with the assumed outgroup's position that brings about polarization. Polarization is seen to be a process of mutual self-categorization as ingroup members, where identifying with the group involves endorsing a position that marks the ingroup off as distinctive from the outgroup(s). Support for this analysis has been provided by Hogg et al. (1990), who carried out a study in which the reference outgroup was varied and this affected the direction of polarization. When confronted with a riskier outgroup, the group's decision became more cautious; when confronted with a more cautious outgroup, the group decision became more risky.

Implications of group polarization

Given that group decision-making is so much a part of modern life, the potential for groups to arrive at polarized decisions has serious implications. Juries, for instance, are assumed to be a means to gain considered and rational and, above all, just judgements about a defendant's guilt or innocence. Moreover, their judgements have serious consequences for the accused – in some parts of the world, literally life or death.

However, in reviewing polarization research, Brown argues that we need to be cautious about reading too much into experimental demonstrations of polarization:

> I think polarization can often be observed in social groups when a 'discussion runs away with itself'. However, formal decision-making groups do not usually exhibit such tendencies. There are several reasons for this: committees have a chairperson who directs the meeting, influences the discussion, sticks to the agenda, and so on. Also, group members may well be aware of each member's idiosyncrasies ('he always exaggerates' or 'she always brings this issue up') . . . More important in stifling any tendency towards polarization is another factor: if you are a member of, say, a management group who discuss an issue, you will be aware that you and your colleagues will have to implement the decisions taken and you are unlikely to go to unmanageable extremes.

(2001: 39–40)

Groupthink

Janis (1982, for example) has documented a number of cases where high-profile groups have made military and political decisions that even the members of those groups, with hindsight, agreed were appallingly stupid and dangerous. Two often cited examples are the Bay of Pigs invasion of Cuba in 1961 (where all the invaders were killed or captured) and the decision to launch the space shuttle *Challenger* (which exploded, killing all on board) in 1986. Janis has coined the term **groupthink** for the extreme polarization that led to these decisions.

Groupthink is what happens when a small, highly cohesive group of like-minded people becomes so obsessed with reaching consensus and so blinkered by it when they reach it, that they lose touch with reality and make a catastrophic decision. Janis argues that there are number of preconditions required for it to happen. The group has to be excessively cohesive and ideologically 'of one mind'. The decision-making must be under stressful conditions and insulated from outside sources of influence and information. And the group leader must be powerful and partial.

Yet maybe not. In 2009 somebody hacked into the email accounts of academics in the Climate Research Group at the University of East Anglia. What was discovered was that in a series of emails to each other and friends in other universities, a series of conversations were going on about how to 'hide' data that contradicted their case for global warming – that is, how to stop it being published! This, not surprisingly, incensed a lot of people, especially the climate change doubters. It certainly did not help the cause. But this example of groupthink does bring home that academics are not immune to allowing themselves to get embroiled in an 'ends justifies the means' kind of conspiracy. It also demonstrates that, in certain circumstances, groupthink can happen online and over time, where, in real-world terms, at least, people are not cut off, but only in the virtual world.

Janis's formulations were based on a mixture of archival and interview methods, and provide compelling accounts of groupthink in action. Attempts to demonstrate it in laboratory conditions have largely been ineffective, and this may well be a phenomenon that it is simply not possible to study experimentally, for practical and ethical reasons.

Group polarization

- When groups make a joint decision following a discussion, there is a tendency for their joint decision to be polarized – to be more extreme than the average individual judgements of participants. There are three theories used to explain this phenomenon:
  - Social comparison theory, where group members are seen to vie with each other to endorse more and more extremely the normative position of group.
  - Persuasive arguments theory, where group members are influenced by the additional arguments of others, further endorsing their own position.
  - Self-categorization theory, where group members are motivated to demonstrate their allegiance to the group by presenting arguments that distance the decision from that made by an outgroup.
- In real-life situations polarization is moderated by longer-term influences, and the knowledge that group members have to implement the decision.
- Groupthink can happen, however, when a group is isolated from the outside, excessively cohesive and ideologically 'of one mind', the decision is made under stressful conditions and the group leader is powerful and partial. This can lead to the group losing touch with reality and making a catastrophic decision.

Intergroup conflict

> When we deal with each other individually, we can be civilized . . . but when we deal with each other in groups, we are like savage tribes in the Middle Ages.
>
> (Berri 1989)

This is a quotation from Nabith Berri, who was, at the time, a leader of one of the factions fighting in the Lebanon. In this section we explore what social psychology can tell us about whether he is right – are groups where people have invested their identity inevitably doomed to be in conflict with each other? Here we will take up the topic of Sherif's Summer Camp experiments from earlier. We focus on the study of conflict between groups within social identity theory.

Competition and conflict

In the Summer Camp experiments Sherif and his colleagues demonstrated that conflict tends to arise when groups are placed in highly polarized competitive situations.

It looks as though these findings are surprisingly robust, even across cultures. Yet a similar study conducted by Tyerman and Spencer (1983) in the UK, carried out in a Boy Scout camp did not produce intergroup conflict. However, the situation was very different. The Boy Scouts is a long-standing membership organization for adolescent boys. It is run on quasi-military lines in which local groups are called 'patrols' and usually meet every week to engage in activities together, with one or more adult leaders. They usually go away to camp each year, where a number of patrols are brought together but live in separate tents. They engage in many activities in patrols, but also regularly take part in competitions together. Tyerman and Spencer (1983) argued that the lack of hostility was because behaviour in the camp was regulated by strong and long-established social norms, which continued to operate during the camp period.

However, Diab (1970) ran a camp similar to Sherif's in the Lebanon and the antagonism generated in the competitive phase was so extreme it proved impossible to continue the camp into the collective goals phase. The boys taking part were ten Christian and eight Muslim 11-year-olds, and Diab and his colleagues found that while initial friendship patterns did tend to follow religious lines, there was a fair degree of cross-over. The boys were allocated randomly to groups and, like the 'Bulldogs' and 'Red Devils', they too soon chose names for themselves – 'The Friends' and 'Red Genie'. However, the group cultures were very different from each other, as these names suggest. 'The Friends' soon became highly cooperative and affable towards each other and set about 'having fun'. 'Red Genie', by contrast, just as rapidly became aggressive and mean, stealing from each other and 'The Friends'. In the competitive situation, 'Red Genie' 'played dirty' and competed with hostility, and were mostly ahead until, in the final stage, 'The Friends' passed them and won the tournament. 'Red Genie' became so aggressive at this point – stealing knives, threatening others with them and attempting to leave the camp by force – that the experiment was terminated.

Smith et al. (2006) argue that we should not read too much into what was a single study with a small group. They draw a general conclusion that intergroup conflict tends to arise where groups are thrown together in isolated settings for short periods, in situations where social norms mitigating against conflict are largely absent.

Boys will be boys?

Before we end this section, it is worth making a significant point – have you noticed that all the studies mentioned so far were conducted with boys? It is interesting to speculate why girls' groups were not studied, or even mixed gender groups. In part this reflects psychology's sexism in that this is just another example of the way that, historically, psychological studies were restricted to studying male behaviour. But it is worth asking the question – would girls have behaved in the same way? Some feminists would argue that conflict of this kind is an overwhelmingly male propensity – whether experimentally induced or in real life. This opens up an awkward subject that social psychologists seem to have veered away from addressing – which, when you think about it, is surprising, given its implications. Maybe this is a case when, genuinely, 'more research is needed'?

Social identity theory and intergroup conflict

As you have seen, social identity theory claims that ingroups tend to favour ingroup members and discriminate against members of outgroups. This idea has been developed to try to explain intergroup conflict.

The explanation starts from the assumption that once group members identify with the ingroup, they gain a social identity in which esteem is gained through affiliation with it. They are therefore motivated to view the ingroup as having high status in relation to outgroups. One way of doing this is to accentuate intergroup differences – to distance the group from outgroups – and then to denigrate the outgroup.

Most theorization has gone on with regard to ingroup of low status. Hogg and Vaughan (2008) suggest that what happens hinges first of all on whether an individual believes it is possible for them to make a shift from a low-status to a higher-status group. If so, they are not motivated to invest in their low-status ingroup, but rather to concentrate their efforts on social mobility. Where, however, they feel they have no chance of 'jumping ship', the only way to gain a positive social identity is to invest in their current low-status ingroup. In situations of social stability the ways in which they can do this are:

- find alternative ways of demonstrating ingroup competence – even if they are transgressive ones such as 'joyriding'
- seek to change the value accorded to the ingroup
- identify other groups that are of even lower status than themselves and act to distance themselves from them.

Demonstrating ingroup value

Emler and his colleagues (Emler and Hopkins 1990; Emler and Reicher 1995) have looked for evidence of outgroup discrimination by **low-status groups** by studying youths engaged in petty crime. They concluded that one motivation for criminality is that it enables youths to impress their ingroup peers – other underachievers at school. By identifying with others in the same position, showing off to them by criminal activity, and denigrating the 'swots' who do well at school, they can find in their ingroup membership an alternative source of a positive identity. Other examples suggested by Brown (2001) are 'punks' and 'crusties'. Groups like these refuse to engage in the 'rat race', and rather establish their own value by setting different standards as to what should be valued, among the ingroup at least.

Improving social respect for the ingroup

An example given here by Hogg and Vaughan (1998) is the promotion of the slogan 'Black is beautiful'. Brown (2001) points to the demands for social change by feminists.

Denigrating groups even lower in the pecking order

Interestingly, somewhat counter-intuitively, it seems that high-status ingroups tend to show greater ingroup favouritism than low-status ingroups (for example, Crocker and Luhtanen 1990). However, there is some evidence of this with low-status groups. Vanneman and Pettigrew (1972), for example, found that among 'poor white trash' in the USA, racist attitudes and support for right-wing politicians tended to be strongest among those who felt the greatest social deprivation.

The effects of conflict

Intergroup conflict has been extensively studied in laboratory settings as well as the kinds of field experiments we have looked at so far. These studies have shown that when acting in groups, people tend to be more competitive (Insko et al. 1990) and more aggressive (Insko and Schopler

1998) than when they do the same task on their own. The stronger the identification with the group, the more these effects spiral upwards (Rehm et al. 1987), especially so where there is competition for scarce material resources (Taylor and Moriarty 1987). Groups also fight over social resources such as respect and esteem (Tajfel and Turner 1979).

Deutsch (1973) has outlined three characteristic consequences of intergroup conflict:

- Communication between the groups becomes unreliable and impoverished. Either available communication channels are not used or are used in ways that deliberately mislead the other. In consequence, neither group trusts the information they get from the other group.

- Norms of trust and fair play break down. The groups become highly sensitive to any differences between them and treat any similarities as if they do not exist. Differential perceptions build up, each group viewing its own behaviour as benevolent and fair but the behaviour of the other group as malicious, hostile and unfair. This leads to suspicion of the other group's motives, a breakdown of trust and fair play, and hence a refusal to address any attempt by the other group to defuse the situation.

- Conflict becomes a matter of principle. The groups each become convinced that the only resolution to the conflict is for them to impose a solution on the other group, by force if necessary. Each side therefore seeks to increase its own power while undermining the power and legitimacy of the other group. In the process the dispute gets escalated, shifting from a clash over a few specific issues to all-out conflict over moral principles and superiority.

These were all demonstrated in a study by Blake and Mouton (1984), in which corporate executives took part in what they thought was a 'training programme'. They were assigned complex problem-solving tasks and told that as part of the training programme their performance would be evaluated by experts. They were not, however, explicitly told they would be in competition. Team spirit was rapidly established and group members were soon to be found huddled together at breaks and meal times planning strategy. While there was not the level of acted-out antagonism found between the boys in the summer camps, intergroup antagonism between these professional men also soared as time went on. At the end of the programme, representatives from all the groups were brought together to evaluate each other's performance. Almost always these meetings ended in impasse, the representatives unwilling to concede that other groups' solutions were as good as their own. When facilitators intervened to impose a judgement, the losing team angrily accused them of being biased and incompetent. Tempers sometimes got so high, the experiment had to be abandoned.

Looking at the minimal group experiments described at the beginning of the chapter, it appears that ingroup membership tends to lead to the downgrading of outgroups, disliking them and discrimination against them.

Conflict resolution

A study by Worchel (1979) has shown that while working for collective goals can reduce intergroup conflict, this works only if the project is successful. If it fails, antagonism can be multiplied rather than reduced. Other factors that social psychological research has established for conflict reduction include:

- Changing perceptions, through education or by the use of media. A good example was the 1966 television docu-drama, *Cathy Come Home*, which changed attitudes in the UK towards homeless people.
- Redrawing the category boundaries. This can be achieved, for example, by creating conditions where the groups come to perceive themselves as belonging to a common group together. Alternatively arrange for social categories (such as gender) to cut across the group boundaries.
- Increasing contact between the groups, for example, by providing community projects and events that bring warring groups together on neutral ground. Contact needs to be sustained, involving, and officially supported and works best when groups are of roughly equal status.

Intergroup conflict

- Social identity theory claims that conflict between groups arises from situations where group members are motivated to emphasize intergroup differences, to distance their ingroup from the outgroup, and then to denigrate the outgroup. This tends to happen most with high-status groups.
- Members of low-status groups will usually, if they believe they can 'jump ship' to a higher status group, invest in making this shift rather than in the ingroup. If they cannot, they can adopt one of three strategies:
  - Find ways (often transgressive) of demonstrating ingroup competence.
  - Find ways to increase perceptions of ingroup value.
  - Find groups even lower in the 'pecking order' to disparage.
- The effects of conflict are that communication and norms of trust and fair play break down, and conflict becomes a matter of principle.
- Intergroup conflict can be reduced by:
  - Engagement in successfully pursuing superordinate goals.
  - Changing 'hearts and minds' through education and propaganda.
  - Crossing or changing category boundaries.
  - Increasing contact between the groups. Contact needs to be sustained, involving, and officially supported.

Leadership

Leadership has mainly been studied by social psychologists in two key fields: politics and business (although it is also relevant in other fields like sport and, most obviously, religion). All define leadership in terms of the ability to influence others, though the impact of influence varies. A good general, social psychological definition is: 'a process of social influence through which an individual enlists and mobilizes the aid of others in the attainment of a collective goal' (Chemers 2001: 376). In the world of management and business studies Project GLOBE (the Global Leadership and Organizational Behavioural Effectiveness programme), for instance, defines leadership on its website (see Resources section at the end of the chapter) as 'influencing, motivating or enabling others to contribute towards the effectiveness of work units and organisations'.

Leadership as a personal quality

Early theorization focused on the characters and characteristics of good leaders – integrity, decisiveness, competence and vision. It also identified those of incompetent and despotic leaders, who have a grossly enlarged sense of their own importance and entitlement to rule, devalue others and do not care about their suffering, will not tolerate criticism and suppress any dissent (Hogan and Kaiser 2006). Hogg and Vaughan (2008) make a case for two different assessments – good leadership and effective leadership, illustrating this by observing that while people will strongly disagree whether Osama bin Laden is a *good* leader – but most would agree he has been an *effective* one.

There is a long tradition in personality psychology of seeking to identify the common personality characteristics of effective leaders. This rather went out of favour, but is now coming back into fashion among those who study the **'Big Five' personality dimensions**. These are shown in Table 12.2. There is evidence that there is a positive correlation with these personal qualities, with extraversion, openness and conscientiousness most strongly linked (Judge et al. 2002).

Table 12.2 The 'Big Five' personality dimensions

	Positive	Negative
Openness	Curious, inventive, adventurous – sometimes linked with intellect	Cautious, conservative
Conscientiousness	Efficient, self-disciplined, organized, achievement-orientated	Easy-going, careless, spontaneous
Extraversion	Energetic, outgoing, optimistic and sociable	Shy, withdrawn, private
Emotional stability	Secure, confident	Nervous, insecure
Agreeability	Friendly, kind, concerned, compassionate, cooperative	Cold, suspicious and antagonistic

Leaders as 'entrepreneurs of social identity'

This term was coined by Steve Reicher (Reicher and Hopkins, 1996). You have already met his work on groups in Chapter 5 and on social identity in Chapter 10. Reicher is a leading player in the development of critical social psychology. In particular, he has been at the forefront of a challenge to experimental social psychology's preoccupation with the *dangers* posed by groups (in the form of crowds and mobs) and, in particular, concern about de-individuation. His made clear that his engagement with the BBC's reality television programme *The Experiment* (an updated re-enactment of Zimbardo's prison study) was to be able to contest what he saw as a biased position. In a more recent review of social identity theory, he is quite clear about his agenda: 'This challenge to the traditional equation of groups with error and irrationality . . . is part of the more general defence of groups against individualism and anti-collectivism that pervade both our culture and our discipline [psychology]' (Reicher et al. 2010: 53).

In this chapter Reicher described how the social identity approach has reinvigorated the study of leadership. This work stresses the extent to which leaders are the product of group's concerns and priorities, as much as or often more than their own leadership qualities in themselves. Leaders – in this view – need to be 'part of the gang', someone with whom the group can strongly identify as 'like us'. Reicher et al. (2007) have speculated that part of George Bush's surprising appeal to the electorate in the USA was the way he blundered when he spoke and all the gaffes he was caught out in. They made him appear an 'everyday American', warts and all, just like 'regular ol' folks like us'. Much the same may be true of Sarah Palin, also notorious for being 'dumb' over politics.

> The ideal leader is expected to be a quintessential representation of the group identity. . . . the leader's ideas and behaviours are evaluated in terms of how closely match the group prototype. . . . However, being recognized as the prototypical member of a social group, and therefore being accepted as group leader, doesn't just happen. Individuals who aspire to become leaders have to convince the group that they are true group stereotypes.
>
> (Myers et al. 2010: 474)

Try it for yourself

Over the next week, take some time to listen to a political leaders talking on the radio or on television. Make notes of what they say and do to come across as 'part of the gang' for their supporters – and, indeed, for all voters. Alternatively, if you are a member of a group yourself and have the chance, do the same for your own leader. To what extent do your observations fit with a social identity perspective on leadership?

As well as leaders needing to personify the group's norms and values if they are to be effective, van Knippenberg and Hogg (2003) identify three further findings from the social identity approach to leadership. First, leadership is only feasible where group members share a common social identity. If there is no 'buy in' to the norms, values and priorities of the group by the group members, then it will be impossible to lead them effectively. 'Herding cats' is one way of putting it! Second, as contexts change, then so does the salience of the different elements of group values and norms. The group's vision of the 'ideal leader' can change as a result, influencing their loyalties. It is in this sense that leaders are 'entrepreneurs of social identity' – instead of dealing in goods and money, they conduct a profitable business of dealing in identities.

But for all this about the way that groups make leaders in their own image, social identity theorists do recognize that, once recognized by the group, they can then have real influence on the values, norms and aspirations of the group. They can inspire the group to pursue new goals, and redefine the group identity. As Fenton-O'Creevy (2001) puts it, they exert their influence by 'the management of meaning' – by getting group members to see things in a particular way.

Reicher and Hopkins (1996) demonstrated how this is done through an analysis of the speeches of two influential British political leaders – Margaret Thatcher and Neil Kinnock – during the miners' strike in 1984–85. Each of them described what what was going on in relation to two categories – a large and good one for right-minded people ('us') led by them, and a small and nasty and dangerous one for their enemies ('them').

For Neil Kinnock, leader of the Labour Party in opposition to the government, 'us' represented society as a whole, but especially striking miners, the Labour Party and those who supported the strike action. The enemy, 'them', were personified by Thatcher herself, as shown in Figure 12.7.

For Margaret Thatcher, Prime Minister at the time and leader of the Conservative Party, 'us' was composed of anti-strikers, Conservative Party members and the working miners. The enemy, 'them', she constructed as 'terrorists', as shown in Figure 12.8.

The rhetorical strategies of each were very similar, the meanings and significance of the players within each group were constructed totally at odds with each other. Thatcher and Kinnock, in their speeches, offered diametrically opposed 'realities' into which they urged their audiences to locate themselves.

Leadership

- Leadership is about the ability to influence others, in ways relevant to the contexts (such as in politics or management).

- Historically leadership was seen as a capacity that some individuals either have naturally, or acquire. Recent work in this field mostly works around the 'Big Five' approach to personality. Leaders are seen as people who are agreeable, extrovert, conscientious and have qualities of openness and emotional stability.

- However, most contemporary work in social psychology around leadership is within the social identity approach. In it, leaders gain their authority to lead by being seen to epitomize the values, norms and aspirations of their reference group, enabling its members to identify with them.

- Group leaders are thus those who can successfully market themselves as personifying all that is best about the group, and, in so doing, gain the capacity to define who the group are and what they stand for.

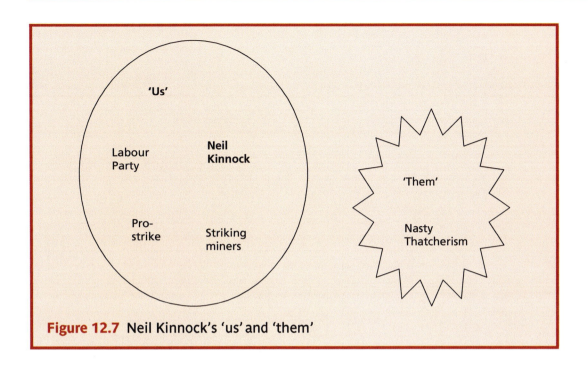

Figure 12.7 Neil Kinnock's 'us' and 'them'

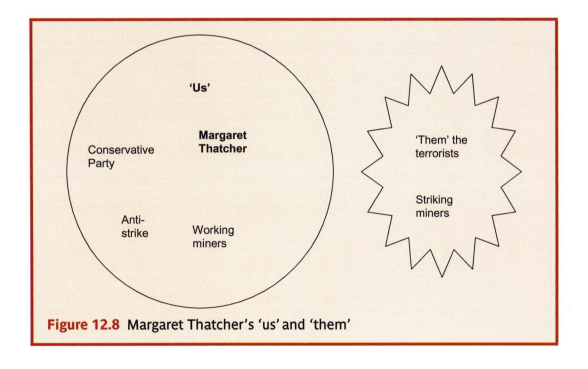

Figure 12.8 Margaret Thatcher's 'us' and 'them'

Resources

Sherif's summer school experiments – a good description is given at: http://www.integratedsociopsychology.net/robbers_cave.html

Asch's conformity experiment: http://www.simplypsychology.pwp.blueyonder.co.uk/asch-conformity.html

Project GLOBE – the Global Leadership and Organizational Behavioural Effectiveness programme: http://www.grovewell.com/pub-GLOBE-intro.html

The official BBC website for The Experiment is http://www.bbcprisonstudy.org/

Further reading

Experimental social psychology

Brown, R.J. (2000) *Group Processes: Dynamics Within and Between Groups,* **2nd edn. Oxford: Blackwell.**
A thoroughly scholarly book that offers a comprehensive review of research and theory in this field.

Hewstone, M., Stroebe, W. and Jonas, K. (eds) (2007) *Introduction to Social Psychology: A European Perspective.* **4th edn. Oxford: Blackwell.**
Given that groups are important in European social psychology, and it is mainly European social psychologists who have led this field, it is not surprising that there are effectively three chapters in this book on groups. Together they provide a thorough, meticulous and up-to-date coverage of the field. Chapter 12 by Van Nijstad and van Knippenberg on basic principles 'does what it says on the tin' very effectively. Chapter 13 by Schulz-Hardt and Brodbeck on group performance and leadership does much the same. Chapter 14 by Kessler and Mummendey on prejudice and intergroup relations brings together work on group conflict and its resolution with an initial section on prejudice. As with the others, the treatment of these topics is thorough and well linked to historical and contemporary illustrations of the issues in question.

Myers, D., Abell, J., Kolstad, A. and Sani, F. (2010*) Social Psychology: European Edition.* **London: McGraw-Hill.**
This is a European version of an American textbook, and so the linkage of European politics and concerns is more superficial. At the same time, critical social psychology is more visible and altogether I think the chapters take a more broadly based approach. There is less precise detail here, and it offers an easier read. Again there are three chapters, but only two relevant here – one on small group influence and another on intergroup relations, conflict and prejudice. The third on social categorization and social identity links more to my Chapter 10, other than its excellent section on leadership.

Leadership

Van Knippenberg, D. and Hogg, M.A. (eds) (2003) *Leadership and Power: Identity Processes in Groups and Organisations.* **London: Sage.**
This takes a social identity approach to the topic, and provides a very readable account of recent social psychological work in this field.

Questions

1 'To be a group, there needs to be more than just a collection of individuals.' Illustrate your answer with examples of research in connection with different kinds of groups.

2 'Many hands make light work.' Is this true? Illustrate your answer with empirical evidence to support the argument you make.

3 To what extent do cultural norms influence what goes on ingroups?

4 What are the explanations given for minority group influence?

5 What is groupthink, and how can it be avoided?

6 Why do groups get into conflict with each other, and how can this conflict be resolved?

7 Define 'leadership'. Outline two different approaches taken by social psychologists to understand how leadership works.

Chapter 13

The social psychology of prejudice

> **9** Justify the statement that much of critical social psychology research is research into prejudice.
>
> **10** Describe three alternative ways in which 'benevolent' sexism can be expressed, and, for each one, identify the linguistic repertoire and subject position associated with each.

Introduction

Prejudice is one of the biggest problems faced by humankind at a time when war and terrorism operate on a global stage, and where conflicts within national boundaries and local communities severely undermine the health and well-being of all, but especially some. It can be argued that prejudice blights the lives and life-opportunities of far more people than pestilence or disease. Yet given social psychology's claim to gain understanding of what and how people think – their attitudes and attributions – it seems it has produced very little to offer in the way of solutions.

Actually this is unfair, and it is easy to lapse into a 'rosy spectacles' view of the past, as this chapter will show. I am old enough to remember the notices put in pubs and bed and breakfasts saying 'no gypsies' or 'no blacks', the laws that made homosexual acts punishable by prison sentences, and the fact that not one of my lecturers when I took my psychology degree were anything other than male, white and upper middle class. Things have (somewhat) changed, though I suspect psychology played a limited role in this, certainly up until recently.

This chapter covers four main aspects of prejudice. It starts with a brief section on defining prejudice, and its different forms. This is followed by a section taking a very salutary look at the prejudice built into social psychology as we still know it and its frankly racist, sexist, heteronormative and class-ridden beginnings. Then there are two sections on the two approaches. One on mainstream, experimental social psychology theory and research into prejudice, and the explanations it has come up with about why it happens. The other is on critical social psychologists' work in this field and what it can add to our knowledge.

This is the last chapter in the book, and there are two ways of looking at that. As a last chapter it does bring together a lot of what went beforehand, and prejudice is a topic that has been – and still is – studied from a wide diversity of perspectives. In this sense it is a good way to round off and review what you have learned. If you have been studiously reading this book through, chapter by chapter in the order presented, you will have already come across the underpinning social psychology theory of and research on what needs to be covered here – behaviourism and social learning theory, intergroup conflict and social identity theory, behaviour seen as situated social practice and the use of discourse and other qualitative analytics to gain insight into 'what is going on' when people think and act in prejudicial ways. If so, it is good news for you. All you will need to do is apply what you already know to put the various approaches to prejudice into context.

But that is not the way most people read textbooks. You dip in and out, don't you? Or follow a route through the chapters your tutor has chosen for you. If this is your situation and you are coming to this chapter early in your study of social psychology, this is what I have done to make it easier. You will find signposts to the chapters where particular theories, topics and issues have been covered in more detail, so you can go back and bring yourself up to date. But, so you do not have to do too much of this, especially if you are pressed for time, I have also done some summarizing for you.

What is prejudice?

Surprisingly enough, this is a field where definition is an issue. Prejudice comes in different forms and with quite different kinds of explanations for why it happens. It is also researched and theorized around different targets – including disablism, homophobia, racism and sexism. It is the forms that make things confusing, though, so let us look at those first. A growing body of those working in this field defines three main categories of prejudice:

- blatant prejudice
- subtle prejudice
- institutional prejudice.

Blatant prejudice

This one is easy to spot, if difficult to stomach. A single example is enough for now, though shocking in its source – a study of police officers' views conducted in 1987. These are extracts from short essays the officers were asked to write on the subject of 'coloured immigration':

> Certain members of the coloured population that I have met are OK but the majority of youths in the W. Indian community are savage ignorant vicious thieving bastards.

> The immigration should be stopped immediately to prevent our towns and cities from being infested with coloureds.

> Over 50% of the trouble caused today either by niggers or because of them. Most of them are just Dirty, Smelly backward people who will never change in a month of Sundays.
>
> (Police officers' accounts, as cited by Colman 1987: 53)

It is this kind of hostility that was the basis of Allport's early definition, as described in his book *The Nature of Prejudice* (1954). Allport was one of the earliest social psychologists to work in this field. He defined prejudice as 'ill-thinking of others without sufficient warrant' (1954: 6) and 'an antipathy based upon a faulty and inflexible generalization' (1954: 9). More generally he saw prejudice as an attitude and divided it into three aspects:

1 *Prejudicial thinking* – prejudiced beliefs about a class or category of people.
2 *Prejudicial feelings* – feelings of disgust about and hostility towards this category of people.
3 *Prejudicial behaviour* – actual or intended actions, ranging from discrimination towards them to extreme violence.

A more recent definition shows how this particular perspective persists in mainstream social psychology today – prejudice defined as: 'the holding of derogatory social attitudes or cognitive beliefs, the expression of negative affect, the display of hostile or discriminatory behaviour towards members of groups on account of their membership of that group' (Brown 1995: 8).

Subtle prejudice

This is a much less obvious expression of prejudice – less to do with outright hostility and more a tendency to assume that your own worldview is the 'norm', and other worldviews are exotic and strange. Seeing things your way feels like it is a 'natural' way for the world to be, but is at the root of the more subtle forms of prejudice. And none of us is immune.

Recently psychologists have begun to theorize about and conduct research into the much more subtle, largely invisible ways in which prejudice is exercised. Given its invisibility it is sometimes seen as more acceptable: 'The critical distinction between blatant and subtle forms of prejudice involves the difference between overt expressions of norm-breaking views against minorities, and covert expressions of socially acceptable anti-minority views' (Meertens and Pettigrew 1997: 55).

Gaertner and Dovido (2000) suggest that what is going on in subtle forms of prejudice is an attempt to reconcile deep-seated negative feelings towards certain others, and a personal self-image of being a fair, tolerant and even-minded kind of person. People who act like this genuinely see prejudice – for example, racism – as wrong. The trouble is, they do not recognize that *they* are being racist.

Deal (2007) makes much the same case for *subtle* **disablism**, forms of prejudice towards disabled people that are not expressed as outright hostility towards them, but in avoidance of them and an unwillingness to engage with disabled people, either directly or in terms of addressing the issues raised by the inequalities that disabled people face.

Try it for yourself

I am not going to ask you to think of an incident when you were prejudiced just now, though I suspect you will be doing so as you read this chapter. Just to get started, think of a time when you were suddenly forced to recognize that your own way of seeing something – something 'obvious', that you just take for granted as being true – is not accepted as so by others with a different worldview from your own.

I remember being a bit puzzled when I was told that oak trees are 'exotic' – what, good old oak trees, exotic? Nah, that is fern-trees and palm trees and firetrees like they have in Africa. Next I felt I was being unfairly criticized in some way by my 'right-on' colleague, forcing me to think again about their 'naturalness'. I got the point fairly fast though, as we were driving through very English-looking rolling pastures with neat little hedges and bungalows (to a psychology conference, as it happens). It took just a little reflection to realize that, of course, none of this was 'natural' at all, but created from the original bush, full of fern-trees and Hui birds, if few obvious kiwis.

This kind of prejudice can be seen as a form of ignorance rather than a malicious intention to be patronizing or unfair. Psychology is full of it still, though things are getting a bit better. Let me give you an example, picked almost at random, from the old books on my bookshelves. It is from a 1981 textbook, *Developmental Social Psychology*: 'We live in a culture that values effort . . . and ability. When these qualities are associated with an outcome, the outcome is considered successful in our culture' (Frieze 1981: 51). At first sight some of you may say, 'What on earth is wrong with that?' Indeed, you may think there is a real attempt here to be specific, and recognize that these things vary by culture. But no, it is all about the 'we' word, the 'our' word. Statements like this may be written with the intention of being sensitive to cultural difference. But they still do not quite get there, in the sense that there is an assumption that the reader, inevitably, belongs to the same culture as the writer.

The assumption is that the book's readers (psychology students and scholars) are obviously going to be part of the 'we' and the 'our' of the writer's own culture. That may well have been largely true in British psychology degrees 1981 (though never entirely), but it is not so now.

It used to be the case that language was much more profoundly sexist than it generally is today (authors are explicitly cautioned about it in the instructions our publishers give us). When I was a psychology student in the 1960s, my textbooks (and most of what I read elsewhere) were written in what felt like to me an irritatingly male kind of way. In those days we did not just have words like 'mankind' and 'chairman' (which still slip into language today) to universally cover both men and women, but the constant use of 'he' and 'his' and 'man', justified by the argument that, in law, the masculine included the feminine, and so the same approach was fine and dandy for academic prose too.

But this is not how people read language like this, and clearly not how people wrote it. Try these two examples from a famous book on humankind's similarities to apes and monkeys to be convinced:

> As for man, he is no different from the rest [of the primates]. His back aches, he ruptures, his women have difficulty in childbirth.

> [M]an can do several things which the animal cannot do . . . Eventually, his vital interests are not only life, food, access to females, etc. but also values, symbols, institutions.

> (Cited in Miller and Swift 1981: 12)

Institutional prejudice

The term most people know is **institutional racism**, and is possibly the most misunderstood concept in relation to racial prejudice in contemporary popular understanding. In Britain it came to public attention through its use in relation to the police, in a government report (the McPherson 2001) following a seriously flawed investigation by the police of the murder of a young black man, Stephen Lawrence. The report concluded that policing in Britain is 'institutionally racist'.

Institutional racism differs profoundly from the kind of overt racism found by Colman and Gorman in 1982 (see also Colman 1987), from which you have already read extracts at the beginning of this section. The second author of this paper, Paul Gorman was Detective Inspector of Police in England at the time, and worked with Andrew Colman on the study that looked at the attitudes, beliefs and rigidity of thinking of recruits to the police force, recently appointed police officers following basic training, and a matched control group. The police recruits were found to be significantly the most conservative, dogmatic and racist in their attitudes. Basic training was found to have a liberalizing effect, but still the newly appointed officers were less open-minded and more dogmatic than the controls – members of the public, not associated with the police. Cole and Gorman concluded that a career in the police tended to attract more prejudiced people than the population at large.

I am not sure whether to feel deeply ashamed of and embarrassed by the statements that you read earlier, or deeply grateful that, some 30 years on, on police officers would not dare write such things knowing that to do so would almost certainly end their career. We no longer tolerate such views in our police force – at least officially.

But it was found in the McPherson Report that the changes in what it is acceptable to say led to complacency – a conviction that this kind of blatant racism had been cut out from the police force, and was no longer a problem. The report was a wake-up call that brought home the fact that in many ways what had happened was a sweeping of the problem under the carpet, and a failure to recognize just how deeply embedded prejudice can be.

Two things were clearly going on. First, the kinds of views expressed in the Colman and Gorman (1982) study had become much less acceptable and there is a real possibility that with education and the gradual recruitment of fellow officers from a broader and more representative minority ethnic mix, hearts and minds were gradually changed; but not across the board. It is clear from the behaviour of the officers investigating the murder of Stephen Lawrence that strong levels of prejudice remained, no longer openly voiced, but in some groups still virulent.

Second, though, more subtle racism was woven through the whole institutional and organizational structure of policing. Institutional racism is a much more subtle form of racism in that it is not intended to be prejudiced – though its impact can be nearly as damaging as out-and-out blatant racism. It is an unconscious racism that permeates the worldview of otherwise well-meaning and well-intentioned people, distorting their thinking and hence their behaviour.

The McPherson Report did not accuse the police in general of being overtly racist, though it did acknowledge that some police officers were. It was saying that a racist, stereotype-distorted mindset was endemic among police officers (as it is within the white community as a whole), and this leads to racist behaviour.

However unintended, institutional racism results in different treatment by the police of white and black suspected criminals, and white and black crime victims alike. This can be seen in the statistics on criminality. In the UK, in proportion to the overall population, more black young men than white are stopped and questioned by the police, of those, proportionately more are charged with a crime, of those, more end up in court, of those, more found guilty and of those, more end up in custody. At every stage of intervention by the police and contact with the judicial system, clear evidence of institutionally racist thinking and decision-making can be found. This is not just a problem in the UK. It is endemic in the USA, as famously demonstrated by the videotaped evidence of police brutality to Rodney King in 1991 (interestingly, recorded by a clearly non-apathetic bystander).

I was shocked to find that in a place like New Zealand, recognized for its institutional commitment to a bicultural society, the situation is, in the twenty-first century, even worse than the UK, though clearly it is recognized as something that urgently needs to be tackled:

Māori are of special interest within the criminal justice system because they are the indigenous people of New Zealand and are also over-represented within the system. Māori represent roughly half of all criminal justice offenders and victims, a proportion far greater than would be expected for the size of the population. There is an urgent need to address this over-representation for the benefit of Māori and New Zealand society as a whole.

(Statistics New Zealand 2009: 22)

Institutional prejudice is not limited to law enforcement. Feminist social psychology scholars like Cherry (1995) have adopted critical approaches in order to examine phenomena like the 'bystander effect' as due to prejudice, not social inhibition. Writing about her re-evaluation of the Kitty Genovese murder, she wrote:

> my own experiences with the women's movement and my own feminist politicization prevented me from seeing this event exclusively within the framework of the unresponsive bystander intervening behaviour. Rather, I found myself returning to view Genovese's murder first within the framework of sex/gender relationships and then within an even larger framework of multiple structures of powerlessness (sex, race, age and class) that play themselves out in our daily lives.
>
> (Cherry 1995, as cited in Langdridge and Taylor 2007: 179)

The Kitty Genovese story has appeared throughout the book, but Chapter 11 has the fullest account of this work.

Looked at like this, much of what critical social psychologists are up to has to do with challenging institutional prejudice. They seek to trouble taken-for-granted understandings of 'what everybody knows' and make visible the prejudice woven into it. Their aim is to undermine the justifications for acting in prejudicial ways, not just as individuals but in what we do collectively, as communities, collectives of all kinds, and within law and other forms of government.

What is prejudice?

Broadly there are three forms of prejudice:

- Blatant prejudice – explicit hostility towards a particular category of people. This includes ageism, disablism, homophobia, racism and sexism.
- Subtle prejudice – often invisible and unrecognized, an assumption of the 'rightness' and 'normality' of one's own group, and hence viewing other groups as not just 'other' but, by implication, inferior.
- Institutional prejudice – based on subtle prejudice, but where it prevails throughout an organization (such as a university) or an institution (such as the police).

Social psychology's prejudice

Mainstream social psychology has been under sustained attack for some time now about its prejudices. These include an almost entire exclusion of women up until about the 1970s, treating them almost as though they were not really people at all and not worth carrying out experiments on (this may, on consideration, have been a benefit). If you do not believe me, go back through the book and make a note of just how many of social psychology's early studies were conducted with only boys or men as subjects.

But if you want a really bizarre example, try this one. So extreme was this tendency to exclude women from the frame that one of the most famous personality tests – the Minnesota Multiphasic Personality Inventory (MMPI) – was developed using only men's responses. This is even more weird, because it had a specific subscale (Mf) designed to test for 'masculinity' and 'femininity'. The two poles were not 'validated' as you would expect, by comparing men's and women's responses. Instead (wait for it – you are not going to believe this) it was done by contrasting responses from a large group of male heterosexual soldiers (to locate the 'male' end) with the responses of 13 homosexual men (to locate the 'female' end)! (See Stainton Rogers and Stainton Rogers 2001 for a more detailed discussion of the sexism involved in the development of scales of masculinity and femininity.) And, believe me, it gets a lot worse when you begin to look at the sexism behind its early theorization.

Another of its prejudices has been its dressing up of social deprivation and inequality as a mere 'variable', and its incredibly patronizing and pejorative treatment of people who do not conform to its liberal, middle-class values. Go back and look at the theories of learned helplessness and locus of control briefly outlined in Chapter 10, and see what you make of them (see Stainton Rogers 1991 for a detailed analysis of this bigotry in relation to locus of control).

However, I am going to focus on social psychology's racism. Historically it was absolutely blatant. Today I think the problem is no longer one of overt racism. While there is still a way to go, except in a few pockets of resistance (some work recently published 'demonstrating' the inferiority of the Rom, for example – I will not lend it credence by citing it), social psychology's explicit and aggressive racist beginnings have largely been consigned to the history books, where one hopes it will remain. No, the problem lies in its institutional racism. I believe this is almost entirely unintended, but it is having a pernicious effect nonetheless.

The racist origins of social psychology

If you go back to Chapter 1 and look at McDougall's theory of social evolution, it is clear that it was profoundly racist. He regarded the behaviour of 'savages' as almost entirely determined by instinct. Only in modern, civilized societies, he concluded, is it possible for individuals to progress to a higher plane of moral conduct, since only there are the social rules sufficiently complex and flexible for individuals to acquire the capacity for self-regulation.

But it is much worse than that. For example, in the 1919 edition of his *Introduction to Social Psychology*, he introduced a new chapter on 'The sex instinct'. In it he contrasted 'civilized' treatment of the female sex with 'primitive' societies, where men regard women as nothing more than an object capable of stimulating their erogenous zones; where a woman is 'merely the chief of many "fetish objects" ' (McDougall [1908] 1919: 419). The consequence, he argues, will be 'an unrestrained and excessive indulgence of the sexual appetite . . . for both sexes'. In a footnote he then goes on to say: 'It has often been maintained, and not improbably with justice, that the backward condition of so many branches of the negro race is in the main determined by the prevalence among them of this state of affairs' (McDougall [1908] 1919: 419).

Scientific racism

According to Richards (1997), McDougall took a more extreme and explicit racist and suprem-acist stance than most of his colleagues in England. This may have been one of the reasons why he moved to work in the USA, where scientific racism was endemic at the time. Richards defines 'scientific racism' as based on evolutionary theory, that took the position that humankind has a common ancestry where:

> [d]ifferent 'racial stocks' could be understood as diverging from a main stem at various times in the long distant past, with some subsequently failing to evolve as far as others. Tree diagrams of this be-came commonplace. The 'biologisation' of human diversity was thus consolidated; not only physical appearance but temperament and culture reflected a people's innate evolutionary status. It was easy to draw up the rankings; White Europeans at the top, Chinese, Indians and perhaps Arabs jostling for silver and bronze medal placings and at the bottom Australian aborigines, Bushmen, Hottentots and Tiera del Fuegans lapped so often it was hardly worth considering them as any longer participating in the event.
>
> (Richards 1997: 13)

Scientific racism was the theory upon which the discipline of **racial psychology** was built, in an explicit quest to document the superiority of the white race. To do so psychologists engaged in some amazing theoretical contortions, in which the better performance of 'black people' on some tasks (such as reaction time) was held up as 'evidence' for their inferior level of develop-ment. This allowed them to argue: 'That the Negro is, in the truest sense, a race inferior to that of the white can be proved by many facts, and among these by the quickness of his automatic movements as compared with those of the white . . . the Negro is, in brief, more of an automaton than the white man is' (Bache 1895: 481).

The history of racism in psychology is highly complex, with subtle twists and turns that were often nudged and sometimes required by local politics. For example, Richards (1997) suggests that one of the greatest inducements for the abandonment of overtly racist theorizing was the horror of Nazi genocide. This shocked the academic community into retrenching from its com-placent acceptance of racist assumptions about the superiority of one 'race' over another. As Richards takes great pains to point out, throughout its history, psychology (along with the other human sciences) was always divided. There were always a brave few who challenged racism, even though they were sometimes in a very small minority.

Nonetheless, an examination of some of the arguments used to support racist theorizing is illuminating. There is not room here to go into this in detail, but I cannot resist giving the fol-lowing example, in part because I think it tells us something about the logic of contemporary psychological theorizing in some quarters, but mostly because it is so breathtakingly ludicrous. Richards calls it 'one of the most hilariously ridiculous pieces of Psychology ever to have appeared' (Richards 1997: 179). Produced in the 1930s in Germany during the rise of Nazism, this is Richards's abbreviated summary from psychological abstracts of a paper by Jaensch (1939), the title of which translates as 'The poultry-yard as a medium for research and clarification in problems of human race differences':

The superiority of Nordic races is reflected in the race differences among chickens. The Nordic chick is better-behaved and more efficient in feeding than the Mediterranean chick, and less apt to over-eat by suggestion. The poultry-yard confutes the liberal-bolshevik claim that race differences are really cultural differences because race differences in chicks cannot be accounted for by culture.

(As cited in Richards 1997: 179)

I am not quite sure what makes this come across as so preposterous, since all Jaensch is doing is inferring principles of human nature from the behaviour of chickens in the poultry-yard. Is this really all that far from inferring universal principles of human learning from the behaviour of rats running through mazes in the laboratory, as behaviourism does? Or inferring universal principles of, say, human gender differences from the behaviour of anything from ants to primates, as does contemporary evolutionary psychology? Maybe it is the elision of human 'races' and chicken breeds that does it, and Jaensch's patently obvious Nazi political agenda writing in Germany in 1939. But this is precisely the kind of 'knowledge' that postmodernism claims is the wolf of politics dressed up in the sheep's clothing of Science. By juxtaposing a patently preposterous claim like this one with the claims made by evolutionary psychology, a postmodern analysis makes its case that Science is a story-telling practice.

The race and intelligence debate

This is probably the best-known field in which racism has been promoted by psychology. Here we can refer not just to preposterous claims made by obscure, politically motivated Nazis, but to much more recent 'star' performers like Hans Eysenck:

The myth of racial equality, while more acceptable in principle to any liberal and well-meaning person than its opposite, is still a myth; there is no scientific evidence to support it. Indeed, as Jensen has pointed out, the *a priori* probability of such a belief is small: '. . . Nearly every anatomical, physiological, and biochemical system investigated shows racial differences. Why should the brain be an exception?'

(Eysenck 1971: 20)

Both Hans Eysenck and Jensen were notorious for their claims that some 'races' had inferior intelligence to others. Jensen published his first paper on this topic in 1969, in which he first argued that intelligence is inherited and therefore not subject to being improved, and second, that since it is genetically determined, measured differences in IQ between different 'races' indicate different levels of intellectual capacity (Jensen 1969). This argument was endorsed by Hans Eysenck's 1971 book, from which the above quotation is taken.

What is fascinating, in a disturbing kind of a way, is that Eysenck and Jensen believed themselves to be in a majority among psychologists in acknowledging the rather embarrassing but nonetheless accurate empirical data demonstrating the intellectual inferiority of certain races: 'I would be prepared to assert that experts (real experts that is) would agree [with] at least 90 per cent of what I am going to say – probably the true figure would be a good deal higher, but there is no point in exaggerating' (Eysenck 1971: 15).

In fact he was very much exaggerating. Thomas Pettigrew (1964), very much an 'expert' in this field reported that he could find only three psychologists among the then 21,000 members of the American Psychological Association (AMA) who would accept the validity of such a claim. Throughout the period in which Hans Eysenck and Jensen (and a small number of others) were proselytizing around this issue, they faced considerable trouble over giving lectures and seminars to state this case, with students and other activists staging demonstrations to try to stop them.

The debate has not gone away. In 1994, Richard Herrenstein and Charles Murray published a book entitled *The Bell Curve: Intelligence and Class Structure in American Life* restating much the same argument. However, this is couched in far less tentative terms and, instead, in highly articulate and outspoken neo-liberal terms. The authors claim that intelligence is not only largely a genetically inherited capacity, but that it largely accounts for differences between rich and poor, and high and low educational achievement and success in life. And, albeit in somewhat muted terms, it claims that there are racial differences in intelligence that go a long way to explaining the social, economic and health inequalities in the USA.

I do not plan to spell out the argument for you. If you are interested – in it and its critiques – then these are easily available with an Internet search. The term 'bell curve' is a good way in.

Psychology's institutional prejudice

Throughout this book I have built up a case that social psychology is institutionally prejudiced. What I mean by this is that social psychology's knowledge – as expressed in its textbooks, the topics it studies and the people it uses as subjects in them – is based on two prejudicial fallacies.

The first is a kind of **head-in-the-sand fallacy**, in which experimental social psychologists simply assume that what they discover from their biased samples (mainly of students, mainly from US campuses) is data that allow them to build and refine universal theories about social psychological processes and phenomena. These, they believe, are psychologically pure – clean and unsullied by any irritating extraneous influences from these students' socialization or enculturation. In particular, they assume that social psychology is immune to the fundamental attribution error, which leads to a prioritization of the importance of individual, a decidedly Western preoccupation.

The second is an **Us and Them fallacy** that is based on the stereotypical view that there are two kinds of people. First there is 'Us', a group of almost exclusively white people, for whom universal laws of human behaviour and experience can be developed to explain social psychological processes and phenomena outside of culture. Then there is 'Them' – exotic and colourful others, for whom these universal laws do not apply because they have 'culture', and it is this 'culture' that determines what they do and how they see the world. This is all so very 'ingroup' and 'outgroup' that you would think social psychologists of all people would be sensitive to their own prejudices. But still there are many who are not.

Social psychology's prejudice

- Early work in social psychology tended to ignore women, or regard them as inferior.

- Some of social psychology's origins were decidedly racist, including a whole strand devoted to the study of 'racial psychology', the purpose of which was to provide evidence of the superiority of the white race and the inferiority of the black race.

- However, there always have been those who have rejected these prejudices, and by the 1970s and 1980s the supporters of there being a link between race and intelligence were already in a small (if vocal) minority.

- Nonetheless, psychology continues to be institutionally prejudiced in some quarters.

Experimental social psychology's work on prejudice

The experimental approach to prejudice has taken several approaches. Some locate the cause of prejudice in the person, either as a distinct personality, or as a particular broad set of values, attitudes and beliefs that, together, add up to a prejudiced worldview, or through social cognitive processes such as categorization and stereotyping. Others locate the cause within conflicts between groups, and the circumstances these create for prejudicial thinking and action. This section runs briefly through all of these, drawing upon research and theory already covered earlier in this book. There are some new approaches here too, showing explicitly some different ways in which prejudice 'works'.

Prejudice sited in the person

You may remember from Chapter 9 that Milton Rokeach did his doctorate on rigidity in thinking and its links to prejudice. His work on values was an attempt to pursue this broad agenda, but in ways that were more comprehensive than a specific focus on deviant and dysfunctional thinking. Rokeach and others like Fisher (1951) saw prejudice as arising from a **dogmatic personality**, in which people suffer from cognitive rigidity – a severe inflexibility of mind, unable to tolerate ambiguity.

The authoritarian personality

You have also met already, in Chapter 10, the work on the **authoritarian personality** usually attributed to Theodor Adorno but mainly carried out by his colleagues, Else Frenkel-Brunswik, Daniel Levinson and Nevitt Sanford. Adorno and Frenkel-Brunswik had fled Nazi Germany's anti-Semitism. The project was profoundly motivated by a desire to understand – and do something about – this kind of blatant prejudice.

These researchers used a variety of techniques to study prejudice. Using questionnaire responses, initially from 2000 adult, white Californians, they found that anti-Semitism (prejudice towards Jews) was associated with hostility towards other 'deviant' minorities such as 'Blacks', homosexuals and 'gypsies' (also exterminated by the Nazis). But this prejudice, they found, was also associated with a broader set of attitudes, values and behaviour:

- strong prejudice towards minority groups and feelings of superiority towards them
- strong deference to authority and a belief in power, dominance and discipline and an obsession with rank and status
- harsh behaviour towards anyone considered inferior, and feeling anger and resentment towards them
- inability to tolerate ambiguity and only comfortable with a regimented and rigidly defined lifeworld
- problems with intimacy in relationships, yet may be preoccupied by sex
- superstitious.

Clinical interviews were conducted on individuals and it was found that people expressing these views and behaviours mostly had a history of brutally harsh upbringings, with cold and rigid parents who showed little affection, had strict rules about how to behave and applied harsh punishments for breaking those rules.

Whereas Rokeach saw prejudice as to do with values, Ardorno and his colleagues were more interested in psychodynamic theories about the impact of child-rearing practices and events in childhood upon adult personality. Hence their conclusion that authoritarianism is about the anger that these children felt towards their parents but could not risk acknowledging. Instead it got 'projected' onto others, such as poorer children or gypsies, that were sanctioned as legitimate targets. Such children often become bullies, and gained relief from acting out their anger. In adult life the targets of their repressed anger may change with circumstances, but prejudice remains. This, Adorno and his fellow researchers concluded, is best understood as an authoritarian personality.

However, both of these – Rokeach's explanation and that of Adorno et al. – incorporate elements of social learning theory, where adult behaviour is learned in childhood via a regime of punishment and reward. These formulations are rather comforting – a 'rotten apple' explanation for prejudice that locates it in the damaged identities of just a few aberrant people.

Values and prejudice

This line of research continues, but in a form that locates the cause of prejudice in people's beliefs, attitudes and, particularly, in their basic value-system. The key psychologist in this field is Norman Feather. You may also recall from Chapter 9, on values, that Feather, working in Australia, conducted research very similar to that of Rokeach. He has sustained this up until the present, certainly up to 2008 in a study he carried out with McKee (Feather and McKee 2008). In particular he sought to develop the expectancy-value theory (that was the basis of Fishbein and Ajzen's theory of reasoned action model).

> You briefly examined this and similar models of how values, beliefs and attitudes determine behaviour in Chapter 8 on attitudes and behaviour.

Feather and McKee's study sought to specify the psychological characteristics linked with racism. They hypothesized that racist attitudes towards Australia's indigenous peoples among white Australians would be linked to values that stress 'tradition' and 'security', mediated by right-wing authoritarian and social dominance variables. They did this by getting completed questionnaires from 148 (42 men, 105 women and one unidentified) students from introductory classes in psychology at Flinders University in Australia.

You can see the parallels here between this more recent work and that done by Adorno and his colleagues in the 1950s. However, Feather and McKee had brought the research more up to date by assessing values using the Schwartz Value Survey, a 57-item, seven-point Likert scale. Right-wing authoritarianism was estimated on a 30-item, 11-point scale and social dominance on a 14-item, seven-point scale. Racist attitudes were measured in a Modern Racism Scale (MRS), seven-item and seven-point, specifically designed for the Australian context. Data were analysed in the usual way using factor analysis.

Among these 'ordinary students' Feather and McKee found a clear gender divide. Male psychology students were found to be significantly more racist, right-wing and socially dominant on average, than the women students. They were also more concerned about power and tradition and less concerned about universalism than the women.

The results of the study are not really surprising. Overall, those expressing the highest levels of racism positively valued power (social status, wealth, authority) and security (safety, harmony and stability), and negatively valued universalism (tolerance, equality, protection of the weak) and benevolence (loyalty, honesty, welfare). However, the authors take pains to point out these are relative measures within only mild levels of expressed racism. There was also some evidence of mediation by authoritarianism and social dominance, but this was in relation to just some of the values. The authors suggest that these are likely to be activated under specific circumstances – such as, say, threats to security.

What this study does add to our understanding of racism is that values clearly are important, although here it is only attitudes that are considered. How far these results can be generalized towards predicting racist behaviour is another matter altogether.

Social cognition models of prejudice

If we take into account the theories recently developed in social cognition, then prejudice is less an attitude or a belief, more the inevitable consequence of particular forms of categorization. If you recall, categorization is where similar things are classified together and treated as an entity. Prejudice arises out of stereotyping in a particular way – one that stigmatizes certain groups. In allowing us to treat particular instances as a single class, stereotypical categorization can lead to inappropriate inferences – that 'feminine talk is a lot of polite talk about silly things; whereas masculine talk is a little blunt talk about important things' (Spender 1979: 41), for example.

Most likely this kind of stereotyping is predominantly 'mindless', and there is evidence to back this up. In Chapter 3 reaction-time experiments were described, in which people were given stimuli such as a pairing of Black–smart compared with White–smart ('smart' meaning 'clever' in the US) (Gaertner and McLaughlin 1983). On average, White subjects responded significantly faster to the White–smart (White–clever) pairing than the Black–smart (Black–clever) one. From this the researchers inferred that these people were exhibiting racial prejudice. Another study by Smith and Miller (1983) at around the same time used this technique to compare stereotypical categorization on the basis of gender, comparing decisions based on attributing a situational cause (that requires much more thought). The stereotypical judgements were much faster.

Depth-processing models may help us to understand an aspect of prejudice that is rather puzzling. In Chapter 8 you were told the story of how, in the 1930s, the sociologist, Richard

LaPiere, took a Chinese couple on a three-month trip across the USA. They stopped at a total of 251 places like hotels, auto camps and restaurants on the trip, and only once did the staff refuse to serve them, even though people in the USA were generally hostile towards Chinese people at the time. Yet when LaPiere later wrote to all the establishments and asked if they would be willing to 'accept members of the Chinese race as guests', of the half who replied, only one said yes, all the rest (92 per cent) said they would not.

The conclusion generally inferred from this account is that attitudes do not predict behaviour. But an alternative interpretation is that responses are different between 'mindless' and 'mindful' thinking. As the Gaertner and McLaughlin (1983) and Smith and Miller (1983) studies show, given a rudimentary stimulus and operating in a setting where responses are trivial, people react mindlessly, with little consideration or attention, based on stereotypical thinking. But when there is more at stake – losing face and looking churlish in a social setting that demands good customer service – thinking (and therefore doing) will be more mindful and less stereotyped.

Prejudice cited in conflict between groups

Overall this process is called **realistic conflict theory**, usually attributed to Sherif et al. (1961). Instead of conflict – and therefore prejudice – being located within individuals' minds, this theory sees it as situated in the circumstances that arise when groups are in competition with each other over scarce resources of different kind, not just in practical terms but also political power and dominance.

The seeds of prejudice can be found in the simple impact of doing tasks in groups. People act in a more competitive way towards each other (Insko et al. 1990) and are more aggressive towards each other (Insko and Schopler 1998) than when they do the same task on their own. However, things really hot up when groups compete against each other. And the more that group members identify with the group, the more these effects spiral upwards (Rehm et al. 1987), especially where there is competition for scarce material resources (Taylor and Moriarty 1987). Groups also fight over social resources such as respect and esteem (Tajfel and Turner 1979). Particularly interesting is the finding that racist attitudes and support for right-wing politicians tended to be strongest among those who felt the greatest social deprivation – 'poor white trash' in the USA (Vanneman and Pettigrew 1972).

Deutsch (1973) has outlined three characteristic consequences of intergroup conflict:

- Communication between the groups becomes unreliable and impoverished.
- Norms of trust and fair play break down. The groups become highly sensitive to any differences between them and treat any similarities as if they do not exist.
- Conflict becomes a matter of principle. The groups each become convinced that the only resolution to the conflict is for them to impose a solution on the other group, by force if necessary.

Alien invasion

With this in mind, consider the following scenario:

Forty-five people were given a coloured scarf, led into a room and to a table, one of six, each with a different colour lamp and tablecloth. Their scarf matched, and in this way they had joined a tribe – yes, this is one of those workshops where you have to dress up a bit and work in teams. The tribes begin by working together on their tribal values and beliefs – about their views on capital punishment, abortion and stuff like that. They are not allowed to vote, they have to argue to consensus. After 50 minutes, the room goes dark and the lamps are dimmed. In walks a wide-eyed, long-clawed alien, who announces:

> *I am a creature from outer space. I have come to destroy Earth. I will give you one opportunity to save the world from utter destruction. You must choose one tribe as the tribe for everyone. You must take on all the attributes of the tribe. You cannot challenge or bargain over any attributes. If you cannot come to full agreement by the end of three rounds of negotiation . . . the world will be destroyed.*

(Shapiro 2010: 634)

Try it for yourself

What happens? Spend some time thinking it through – what would you do in such a situation. If you can, get together a group of students to talk about it together.

Once you have done that, think about the implications for our understanding of prejudice, and what we know about intergroup conflict. If you can, get hold of Shapiro's paper and read it before you do. If you are doing this as a group, then you could have some people read different bits and report back to inform your discussion.

Daniel Shapiro who invented the scenario and has run it as a workshop more than 100 times, says in all but a handful of instances, the world did then explode, figuratively if not actually! It is easy to imagine it happening, and you slightly feel it has the plotline of too many trashy disaster movies and, indeed, stories about attempts to resolve conflicts.

But does this tell us much about prejudice? I am not certain, given how staged the whole thing was. The people taking part knew it was merely an exercise, and certainly would not have believed there was a real alien coming to talk to them with any actual capacity to exterminate everyone in the world.

Sectarian prejudice

I suspect we learn more about 'ingroups' and 'outgroups' by looking at more realistic settings. John Hunter, Maurice Stringer and Robert Watson (1991) did just that in relation to the 'Troubles' in Northern Ireland. That is, they worked with already established identity reference groups there: Catholics and Protestants. If you recall from Chapter 12, identity-reference groups are where belonging to the group involves identification with the group, where affiliation acts as a reference frame for a person to know 'who' they are – their social identity. Whereas to be 'Protestant' or 'Catholic' may mean very little in settings where being or not being a Christian is far more salient, in Northern Ireland, in the 1980s and 1990s, it was absolutely central to the social identity of almost everyone who lived there.

In 1988, a Protestant gunman attacked a Catholic funeral at the Milltown cemetery in West Belfast. He shot and threw grenades, killing three people and injured more than 50 others. He ran away, and his life was saved when he was captured by the Royal Ulster Constabulary, the police force at the time.

A few days later there was another funeral for one of the victims of the attack. Mourners recognized two out-of-uniform soldiers sitting watching in an unmarked car. The soldiers tried to drive off, but were dragged from the car by a large crowd from the funeral and the soldiers were beaten and shot dead. These were not isolated incidents. But what made them different from the many other such killings was both were recorded by television crews, and images of what happened were broadcast internationally.

Three years on from the events, Hunter and his colleagues did an experiment where they showed extracts from the newscast recordings to separate groups of Catholic and Protestant respondents. Using a free-response method, the researchers asked the group members to explain what had happened and why.

The analysis of their responses identified two different attributions of blame:

- Blame the people – the blame for the violence was to do with the evilness of the people involved – their 'bloodlust' or 'psychopathic' tendencies.
- Blame the situation – the blame for the violence was to do with the circumstances of the attack – the need to retaliate for previous attacks.

You will not be at all surprised to know that when explaining violence by their identity group, group members tended to blame the situation; when explaining the violence of their outgroup, they tended to blame the people concerned. These data are shown in Table 13.1.

Commenting on this study, John Dixon wrote: 'It is easy to see how the pattern of attributions ... may sustain a cycle of distrust and recrimination, with each party to a conflict blaming the other for the generation, maintenance and escalation of violence' (2007: 153).

What can be seen here is a version of the **fundamental attribution error** where people tend to overemphasize the personal, and underemphasize the situational causes of actions. Nisbett and Ross (1980) termed this the **actor–observer error** when people assume their own behaviour

Table 13.1 Different attributions of blame for violence for ingroups and outgroups

		Blame people (%)	Blame situation (%)
Catholic group members explain	Catholic violence	17.9	78.1
	Protestant violence	79.2	20.8
Protestant group members explain	Catholic violence	71.5	28.5
	Protestant violence	28.5	71.5

Source: Hunter et al. (1991)

Attribution errors are described in more detail in Chapter 7.

Social identity theory is described in detail in Chapter 10, and its application to intergroup conflict in Chapter 12.

The common cause of football fandom is used in Chapter 6 to illustrate the ways that clothes – such as football scarves and shirts – act as ways of communicating group membership.

Sherif's work on intergroup conflict and Summer Camp experiments are described in detail in Chapter 12.

to be more likely to be situationally determined, and the behaviour of others more likely to be a product of personal intentions or propensities.

What appears to be going on is that, in identity-reference groups (such as Catholics and Protestants in Northern Ireland during the 'Troubles'), members of your ingroup get to be seen as versions of yourself – which is what social identity theory proposes. Data of the kind described in Hunter et al.'s study are not unusual. There have been many such studies that find that people more often blame the situation for negative behaviour among their ingroup, and attribute personal blame more often for negative behaviour among their outgroup (Pettigrew 1979).

Dixon argues that social identity theory and its application to conflict between groups offer a more useful and convincing way of understanding prejudice than either a personality type or social cognition processes like simple categorization and stereotyping. Although he admits that stereotyping may play some part in prejudice, he argues that this is not something that happens in a self-contained kind of way inside individual minds. Rather, stereotyping is something that goes on intersubjectively. Stereotypes 'reflect the broader organisation and ideology of intergroup relations' (Dixon 2007: 154). In other words, stereotypical thinking comes out of the shared conversations between people when they get together in groups. They talk, they egg each other on, they dress in ways that signify their group solidarity and commitment to a common cause, whether this be football fandom, political protest or religious faith.

In this Dixon takes us back to the work on intergroup conflict initiated by Sherif in his Summer Camp experiments. Mustafer Sherif was born Muzaffer Şerif Başoğlu in Ōdemis, Izmir in Turkey, and it was his experiences growing up there that led to his interest in this field:

> It influenced me deeply to see each group with a selfless degree of comradeship within its bounds and a corresponding degree of animosity, descructiveness and vindictiveness towards the detested outgroup – their behaviour characterized by compassion and pre-judice, heights of self-sacrifice and bestial destructiveness.
>
> (Sherif 1967: 154)

It is easy to see how this led Sherif to see prejudice as arising from the politico-economic conditions in which it is situated; as arising through competition for resources, not just material ones, but political and ideological resources too. The Hunter et al. (1991) study is a good example, where a deeply entrenched sectarian conflict is based on a power struggle over nationhood – whether Northern Ireland should be part of the 'island of Ireland' as a political entity, or part of the 'British Isles'. Land, in itself, is not the main issue here, but political control. Dixon observes that this kind of approach is different from that taken by traditional experimental social psychologists. The realistic conflict model locates prejudice within competition between groups, and sees it as 'rational' in the sense that it reflects actual conflict. Both personality and social cognition models, on the other hand, view prejudice as irrational and aberrant.

Tajfel's work on social identity adds to realistic conflict theory a recognition that individuals become prejudiced through their identification with group norms and values, and can become violent when the group justifies this through blaming the situation and absolving the individual from responsibility.

Experimental social psychology's work on prejudice

- Adorno and his colleagues carried our research into prejudicial attitudes and where they come from, using their results to inform a theory of the authoritarian personality.

- Work by Rokeach on 'rigidity in thinking' and, more recently, by Feather on value expectancy, have been used to generate an explanation of prejudice as arising from holding a prejudiced worldview, made up of a coherent set of prejudicial values, beliefs and attitudes.

- Social cognition models explain prejudice as being the consequences of stereotypical and prejudicial categorizations. This form of prejudice is observed particularly when thinking is 'mindless'. More 'mindful' thinking tends to show much less prejudice, such as when responding in a customer service setting.

- Realistic conflict theory was devised by Sherif, based originally on his own experiences of growing up in Turkey when there was a major conflict between sectarian groups. It proposes that groups will be prejudicial to each other when there is conflict between them over resources.

- Tajfel's work on social identity adds to this, explaining individual prejudice in terms of social identification with group norms and values.

Critical social psychology's work on prejudice

Critical social psychologists have produced a massive amount of research and theory about prejudice over the past 30 or so years, though it is seldom billed as that. What I am saying here is that a great deal of work in this field is deconstructive, in that it challenges the taken-for-granted knowledge upon which subtle and institutional prejudice is based. Examples include Kitzinger and Frith's conversational analysis study of 'Just say no' campaigns, and Lavie-Ajayi and Joffe's study of the way the media construct the female orgasm, both of which seek to tease out some of the prejudicial ways in which women's agency is denied or curtailed through the deployment of particular **linguistic repertoires**. As Reynolds's study of singlehood specifically argues, here in relation to the 'dried up spinster' linguistic repertoire, such stereotypes provide resources by which prejudice can be deployed.

> The 'Just say no' study is in Chapter 5 as an example of conversation analysis. The 'female orgasm' study is in Chapter 3, as an example of contemporary social representations research. And the 'dried up spinster' study is in Chapter 11, in the section on singlehood.

In some senses this final section could thus do nothing more than reiterate these studies for you, framing them through a lens that focuses on prejudice. But, if you are keen, you can do this for yourself just by going back and looking at the descriptions of these studies.

Instead you will find two different approaches. The first is a study of 'benevolent' sexism, looking at the way power can be deployed very effectively in what looks, at first sight, like nothing worse than a bit of gentlemanly charm. This is very much about how 'subtle prejudice' works – subtle it may be, but not inconsequential. The second is a very short account of some of the social psychoanalytic theorizing of Franz Fanon, a psychiatrist who has made a massive contribution to our understanding of racism, especially in the context of colonialism.

How to do prejudice with charm

In a number of mainly survey research into sexist attitudes, Glick and Fiske make a distinction between 'benevolent' and 'hostile' sexism as acting in different ways:

> The evidence of the evaluations of female subtypes is consistent with the notion of benevolent sexism as is used to reward women who embrace conventional gender roles and power relations, whereas hostile sexism punishes women who challenge the status quo. This combination of rewards and punishments may be particularly effective in maintaining gender inequality.
>
> (2001: 113)

Their approach and terminology are compliant with the standards required by US academic journals. In many ways their study sits squarely in the experimental social psychology camp. But their analysis – which I have built upon – is much closer to a critical approach, in that it provides an impressive starting point for understanding how prejudice works. In particular, their data offer clues about the way that expressing certain attitudes in a 'benign' manner can lure women into accepting subservient roles and actively colluding in restricting their own agency and authority.

Earlier in the chapter, looking at 'subtle prejudice', it was seen as a less offensive and less oppressive form than 'blatant' prejudice. Glick and Fiske are much less convinced about the 'softer' form of sexism being no more than an attempt to save face, though there may be some of that going on. They are much more suspicious about other motives 'benevolent' sexism may have. It is just as much of a power play as hostile sexism, they conclude, but using reward rather than punishment.

Here I am alluding to Reynolds's study of single women and the approach she used – see Chapter 11. Go back and read the section on her work if these terms are puzzling you.

'Benevolent' sexism is disarming, they say, and intended to be so. It absolves men from being seen as prejudiced, while still enabling them to lay claim to needing greater power, authority and earning capacity. They 'need' these, of course, to be good 'providers'. They are (the darling things, or so the story goes) willing to sacrifice their own needs and wishes in order to properly care for the women in their lives – their wives, their daughters and even their secretaries.

Glick and Fiske (1996) created an Ambivalent Sexism Inventory (ASI) to explore the key differences between the two forms of sexism, and to find out more about the ways that 'benign' sexism works. In critical social psychology's terms, what they are doing with their questionnaire studies is to identify the linguistic repertoires in play when facing the ideological dilemma around how men and women should behave, and the subject positions that men and women can occupy.

Example items from the ASI are given in Table 13.2. Conventional factor analysis on large, international data-sets has allowed Glick and Fiske to identify an interesting factor structure. First, the two kinds of sexism are related – men and women who express one have a tendency to express the other. However, they are separate, indicating that there are two quite different kinds of sexism being expressed. But it gets more complicated, as the benevolent sexism factor splits up into three sub-factors (I have renamed these) each linking to a different linguistic repertoire and subject position. See Table 13.3.

- *Protective paternalism* is the baseline justification for discriminating – 'benignly' – against women. Women need protecting and looking after, and it's men's duty to look after them and keep them safe.

Table 13.2 Glick and Fiske's items in their Ambivalent Sexism Inventory

'Benign' sexism	
3	In a disaster, women ought to be rescued before men
8	Many women have a quality of purity that few men possess
12	Every man should have a woman he adores
Hostile sexism	
4	Most women interpret innocent remarks or acts as being sexist
14	Women exaggerate problems they have at work
21	Feminists are making unreasonable demands on men

Note: The scale is given in full in Glick and Fiske (2001).

Table 13.3 Glick and Fiske's identifying items for the three 'benign' sexism sub-factors

Sub-factors	Example identifying item
Protective paternalism	In a disaster, women ought to be rescued before men.
Women have their own ways of being better	Many women have a quality of purity that few men possess
Men are overwhelmed by love	Every man should have a woman he adores

- *Women have their own ways of being better*, that is, purer, morally superior, more refined. This justification for discriminating – 'benignly' – is to respect women's finer sensibilities and to protect them from getting involved in the smutty, the ethically dubious or the unrefined excesses of a men's world.

- *Men are overwhelmed by love*, so much so that they have an irresistible need to worship, protect and look after their own special, wonderful woman. This is a 'benign' justification for men to idealize and infantilize women.

All of these discursive strategies offer 'disarming' ways to reduce women's autonomy and agency. You can see how attractive the strategies are to men – I could suggest, wryly, they are good ways to 'have your cake and eat it' but that might come over as a bit sexist! But what I do find really insightful about these different sub-factors is that you can see here the lure for women too – especially those who have limited agency and authority, power and resources of their own – to invest in the subject positions created by these linguistic repertoires:

- The 'protective paternalism' linguistic repertoire offers women a position of 'the safe and cared for woman' who will have an easier life with their 'protector' than they would alone. For many women the costs of occupying this position and its consequences may be smaller in comparison than the hardship of 'going it alone'.

- The 'women's superiority' linguistic repertoire offers an attractive position of the 'self-respecting and respectable woman' who can concentrate on being a good wife and mother and does not having to deal with the unpleasant aspects of life, or even acknowledge that they exist.

- The 'men overwhelmed' linguistic repertoire is, perhaps, the most beguiling in the position it offers. What woman can resist the chance to be 'the adored', the centre of her man's world, his destiny? Actually, quite a few, especially those with efficient crap-detectors, but you can (whether you are a man or a woman) see the attraction!

Try it for yourself

It can be thought-provoking to think of how these linguistic repertoires and the subject positions they offer are played out in films and novels and television programmes. It is a useful way to get a better understanding of ideas like these, which helps you remember them (a rather pleasant way of revising, in other words). Do it alone or, if you can, chat with other students. Think of some examples of each of these linguistic repertoires and subject positions.

My musings gave me any number of candidates for the safe and cared for woman protected by her man, including most romantic stories from *Pride and Prejudice* to *Bridget Jones*: images of the women in *The Godfather* for the self-respecting woman, and a perfume advertisement for the 'adored'. What did you find?

Foxes in sheep's clothing

I hope you do not find all this a bit trivializing in relation to a subject as serious as prejudice. There are two important points I am trying to make. The first is that critical approaches stress – and gain evidence for the position – that prejudice of this kind is not a rare occurrence, confined to the actions of a few nasty people. It is commonplace and everywhere, hard to pin down, ephemeral even, but deeply woven into our daily conversations, in all our relationships and interactions, in all the things we watch and hear and read in our entertainment and our working lives. Prejudice is the kind of thing that Foucault was talking about with his idea of 'the micropolitics of power' and his vision of power as a 'dense network'. At first it may be hard to acknowledge that it is a kind of prejudice that ultimately motivates the portrayal of a strikingly beautiful woman, walking sensuously as she takes off her luxuriant, golden dress and throws off her necklace, her husky and seductive voice whispering '*je t'adore*'. But do try it, and in so doing you may find your crap-detector stirring!

My second point is that even the most 'benign' forms of prejudice matter, perhaps, indeed, they matter more because they are so pervasive.

> Benevolent sexism, though a kinder and gentler form of prejudice, is pernicious in that it is more likely to be accepted by women, as well as men, especially in cultures where women experience a high degree of threat from men. . . . [B]enevolent sexism corresponds to other kinds of paternalistic prejudices, directed at groups that are lower in status and viewed as cooperative or nonthreatening.
>
> (Glick and Fiske 2001: 113)

In racism, this can be called Uncle-Tom-ism, alluding back to the justifications used by slavers, and visible in the way members of certain groups in British society still think and talk about 'our Commonwealth cousins'! Such paternalism is also common in the way people with disabilities are infantalized, not just by some of the well-meaning people who look after them but in social policies and service provision that deny them the same kind of participation that others enjoy.

Psychoanalytic work on prejudice

Frantz Fanon is recognized as the leading scholar who took a psychodynamically informed critical psychology approach to prejudice, mainly in the form of racism. Fanon was a psychiatrist and a revolutionary. His book *Black Skin, White Masks* (1952 in French, translated into English in 1986) has been highly influential on psychology, especially in France, South Africa and South America. Also seen as a postcolonial scholar, Fanon's work stands out because it engages specifically with the psychological.

His main focus was on the impact of the juxtaposition of white and black in the context of colonization and, in particular, the psychological harm that racism does to both black and white. First, and controversially, he takes Freud's question 'What does a woman want?' and rephrases it: 'What does the black man want?' and then answers it by saying 'The black man wants to be white'.

> Fanon was writing in French and in 1952, when such linguistic sexism was the norm.

Derek Hook (2004) reminds us that this answer is very specifically located in a context of postcolonialism, where white people had everything and black people had next to nothing. Fanon explores, in depth, the way in which this 'wanting to be white' is woven into the unconscious more than the conscious, in language and dreams and daydreams, in actions that range from the direct (such as hair straightening and skin whitening) to the more obscure (such as choice of consumer goods and entertainment).

Equally he examines the psychic work going on in the **imaginary** of the white colonizers, in their profound guilt which gets projected onto the colonized blacks 'a hatred of one's victims [is] proportionate to the guilt one feels for injustices and violence one has subjected them to' (Hook 2004: 121). Thus Fanon theorizes that in postcolonial settings, racial prejudice is a form of psychic harm that comes as a consequence of being the oppressor – a somewhat tautological conclusion that racism causes racism! What we can get out of this idea, I think, is a recognition that blatant prejudice is not a comfortable thing to live with, it is highly anxiety-provoking both in the perpetrator and in the target.

Racism is seen by Fanon as a form of neurosis, a phobia, indeed, making racists irrationally disgusted with and fearful of the phobic object. He goes further, stating that these anxieties are also manifested in sexual attraction, so the phobic object is desired as well as feared.

In all this the 'black who wants to be white' is not left out, for she or he has to battle with psychic anxiety of their own, inevitable in ambiguously owning and not owning a stigmatized identity: 'As I begin to recognize that the Negro is the symbol of sin, I catch myself hating the Negro. But then I recognise I am the Negro. . . . this is a neurotic situation in which I am compelled to choose an unhealthy, conflictual, situation fed on fantasies [that are] hostile and inhuman' (Fanon [1952] 1986: 197).

These neuroses, black and white, arise from but also contribute to what Fanon calls **Manichean thinking** – a worldview in which everything is divided into opposing poles, like black/white, where one is inevitably negative and the other positive.

The colonial world is divided into compartments . . . The colonial world is cut in two. The dividing line, the frontiers are shown by barracks and police stations. . . . The settler's town is a town of white people and foreigners. The town belonging to the colonized people, or at least the native town, the Negro village, . . . is a place of ill fame, populated by men of evil repute.

(Fanon [1963] 1990: 29–30)

Try it for yourself

Fanon's experience of colonization was in Martinique in the Caribbean. To what extent do you think his ideas are solely about the impact of colonization? Where else can you think of where explanations like these might fit? This is a topic that would be interesting to discuss as a group.

Critical social psychology's work on prejudice

- Much of critical social psychology research and theory is about prejudice – in that it challenges taken-for-granted knowledge used to justify prejudice.
- 'Benign' sexism comes in at least three forms:
  - the argument that men are prepared to sacrifice themselves to look after women
  - that women are 'better' than men in ways that set them aside from the lives of men
  - that men adore women, and want to worship them.

  All three provide subject positions that can lure women in – but at the cost of their agency and autonomy.
- Frantz Fanon has theorized that in postcolonialist settings both the oppressors and the oppressed suffer from neurotic anxiety, harming them both. The oppressors feel guilt and fear but also desire towards the phobic object – the black, in his case. The oppressed experience conflict between their black identities and their desire to gain the benefits of being white. Together these result in a split and divided world.

Resources

An amusing, tongue-in-cheek, analysis of female character, showing all the ways to avoid being a 'strong female character': http://www.overthinkingit.com/wp-content/uploads/2010/10/Overthinking-It-Female-Character-Flowchart.png

You can calculate your own degree of authoritarianism via: http://www.anesi.com/fscale.htm

This is very much a US source and so will only lead you to US-based, mainstream information. But it does offer an easy way to access lots of interesting and vatried material on prejudice and other topics in this book: http://www.socialpsychology.org/social.htm

Further reading

Myers, D., Abell, J., Kolstad, A. and Sani, F. (2010*) Social Psychology: European Edition.* **London: McGraw-Hill.**
Chapter 14, especially pages 506–24, offers a thorough and readable review of experimental social psychology's work on prejudice.

Dixon, J. (2007) Prejudice, conflict and conflict reduction, in W. Hollway, H. Lucey and A. Phoenix (eds) *Social Psychology Matters.* **Maidenhead: Open University Press.**
Part of the Open University's Social Psychology course, this chapter gives a very clear and focused account of personality, social cognition and realistic conflict theories of prejudice and a similarly easy to understand account of discursive work in this field. It is highly selective in its coverage (as is the whole approach in the book) but what is lost in detail is more than made up for in the depth of understanding you can gain from it. I would make this my first choice if I wanted to find out more about this topic.

Hook, D. (2004) Fanon and the psychoanalysis of racism, in D. Hook, A. Collins, P. Kiguwa and N. Mkhize (eds) *Critical Psychology.* **Cape Town: University of Cape Town Press.**
This is a detailed account of Fanon's psychoanalytical work, that, at the same time, examines Fanon's key concepts and theoretical positions and applies them to racism in colonized life worlds, including South Africa.

Questions

1 What is the difference between blatant and institutional prejudice? Illustrate your answer in relationship to racism in the police force, making sure you include some coverage of recent research.

2 Explain what is meant by 'subtle' racism in general, and 'benign sexism' in particular. Why is it something we should worry about?

3 'Social psychology is based upon the work of racist men, and still largely continues to be an instrument of racist prejudice.' Discuss this claim, providing evidence to support your argument.

4 What do you think is the best social psychological theory for explaining prejudice? Illustrate your answer by reference to research in this field.

5 Refer back to Daniel Shapiro's alien-in-the-room scenario used for running workshops on resolving intergroup conflict. Explain why you think most of his workshops ended up in the extermination of the human race.

6 How can social psychology's research and theory help us to understand what is going on in sectarian violence?

7 Either:

    a. Choose any popular advertisement selling perfume for women. Describe the linguistic repertoire that provides its 'script', the image of femininity it is offering to women, and the costs and benefits there may be for a woman positioning herself in this way.

Or:

    b. Choose any popular advertisement selling beer to men. Describe the linguistic repertoire that provides its 'script', the image of masculinity it is offering to men, and the costs and benefits there may be for a man positioning himself in this way.

Glossary

A

Abduction is a 'logic of research' in which hypotheses are generated through identifying and seeking to explain anomalies or data that do not fit the current theory.

Account as used here as a technical term in conversational analysis. It is a culturally sanctioned justification or explanation for behaving in a certain way.

Actor–observer error: in attribution theory, this is when people assume their own behaviour to be more likely to be situationally determined, and the behaviour of others more likely to be a product of personal intentions.

Affiliation is used in social psychology in social identity theory to refer to identification with an ingroup.

Agency is the location of the cause of an effect.

Altruism is defined as acting for the benefit of others as an end in itself, not for gain.

Analytics are strategies and procedures to interpret data – to analyse them.

Associative networks is a term used in social cognition to describe the way connections between categories are organized semantically.

Attachment theory was developed by John Bowlby to describe the way that babies (and some other young animals), from their very first days, instinctually form strong social bonds with the person nurturing and caring for them – usually their mothers to start with and then a wider group of kin and carers. The theory claims that strong attachment in infancy and throughout childhood is essential for attaining a healthy adult identity.

Attitude is any feeling towards or opinion about something or someone that is evaluative.

Attitude object is anything a person can express an attitude towards.

Attractiveness is a term used in group theory that is not to do with physical attractiveness, but is about group members developing bonds of liking for and affiliation with other group members.

Audience is a term used in studies of social influence to describe the people observing the behaviour under study.

Authoritarian personality is one in which the person adopts highly rigid views, which are usually strongly prejudiced.

Autokinetic effect is where a small bright light is shone in otherwise complete darkness, and it appears to move even though it is stationary.

Automatic processing (sometimes called mindlessness) is where people take in information and respond to it with little conscious awareness or cognitive effort.

B

Balance theory claims that people seek balance in their attitudes, so that they are consistent.

Bandwagon books is how Mary Crawford (1995) describes the kinds of books that capitalize upon the latest pop-psychology theme, in her case the idea that men and women speak different languages and are set up to misunderstand each other.

Behavioural style is a term used in Moscovici's theory of minority group influence, and describes whether, for example, the minority are consistent or not.

Behaviourism assumes that *all* behaviours are learned though experience.

Being-in-the-world is a term adopted by Heidegger ([1928] 1962) to describe the way that people are always ever engaged with and in the world. It makes explicit the claim that there can never be a separation between people and situations, that one cannot be present without the other.

'Big Five' personality dimensions are held by personality theorists and researchers to be those that express the key qualities of the human personality. They are openness, conscientiousness, extraversion, emotional stability and agreeability.

Body language is a form of non-verbal communication, in which ideas and messages are signified by stance, gestures, and so on.

Bottom-up processing is processing driven by stimulus input.

Bystander effect describes situations where the more people who observe a situation where there is danger or a person is in trouble, the less likely it is that any one of them will intervene.

C

Capilano Bridge study was a field experiment where subjects' arousal was varied naturally – they were interviewed either on an ordinary bridge or a very scary one.

Categorization is where similar things are classified together and treated as an entity.

Cocktail party phenomenon is where you can, for example, spot your own name in a conversation, even though you are not attending to it. It shows that extraneous noise is being processed, if only superficially.

Cognitive algebra is where all the relevant information is weighed according to its salience and value and then a calculation is made to end up with an overall evaluation (for example, of the attitude object).

Cognitive consistency is where people adjust their attitudes in ways that maintain consistency.

Cognitive miser describes a person processing information in ways that restrict the expenditure of cognitive resources.

Cognitive psychology grew out of disillusionment with information processing models of human thinking. It stresses the active, meaning-making and meaning-interpretation qualities of human communication, thinking, memory, and so on.

Cognitive strategies are those where people direct the way they process information, in order to serve a particular function or optimize their performance.

Collective representations are those that are shared *between* people. It is a term adopted by Durkheim for representations shared among people, as opposed to those unique to individuals.

Communal relationships as defined by Clark and Grote (2003) are those based on kinship, friendship and couples, as opposed to exchange relationships more based on what people get out of them.

Communitarianism is a philosophy informed by John Rawls's 1971 book, *A Theory of Justice*, a contemporary form of liberal humanism. It balances individual freedoms with communal responsibilities, arguing that strong and supportive communities are the most effective basis for 'a good society' and hence human well-being and fulfilment.

Community psychology has developed along two different strands – from communitarian political movements in South America, and from humanistic psychology in the USA. Community psychologists work in ways and locations where they are actively involved in projects to tackle inequalities, prejudice, exclusion, exploitation and oppression.

Concourse is a term adopted by William Stephenson (1953), the inventor of Q methodology. He uses it to describe all the things that can be said or thought about the topic being studied. A Q set is constructed through sampling the concourse – identifying statements that, together, cover the full range of opinion about the topic.

Conditions is a term that, when used in relation to experiment, has to do with the settings in which variables are being manipulated. In the simple case of an experiment to find out if something (X) affects behaviour, there are two conditions: an experimental condition (where X is applied) and a control condition (where it is not).

Conditions of instruction In Q method this is where participants adopt different positions from which to sort – such as 'as I saw things as a teenager', 'how my therapist would see it', 'as I see it when I am happy'.

Conformity where the views of the majority induce the minority to comply.

Confounding variables are ones that the experimenter does not intend or want to vary but may affect the results of an experiment.

Confucian work dynamism is a term used by the Chinese Culture Connection to describe a set of values that stress interpersonal harmony and cooperation among groups who work together and view time as elastic and expendable rather than needing to be 'saved'.

Connected self is a version of the self where it is seen in terms of relationships with others (for example, kinship ties and responsibilities).

Constant comparative analysis is a term used in grounded theory research, where categories are refined by looking for broader, superordinate categories.

Constitutive language as defined by the philosopher, Austin (1962) is language that merely describes 'what is' – the grass is green – as opposed to performative language that makes things happen – 'I pronounce you man and wife'.

Construct is the term used to describe the abstract, theoretical concepts being studied.

Contact cultures are those where body contact (such as touching in various ways) is a common form of communication.

Conversation analysis is a form of discourse analysis that focuses on the units and forms of talk – such as conversational openings and closings, turn-taking and repairs.

Corollaries is a term used in personal construct theory to describe its basic assumptions and principles.

Correspondent inference is from attribution theory and concerns the degree to which the person whose behaviour is being judged is seen as behaving according to a stable and enduring disposition.

Crip theory has commonality with 'queer theory' in that it provides an analytic standpoint from which to identify the ways in which a group – in this case, people with disability – are discriminated against, excluded, subjected to prejudice, and so on.

Critical hermeneutics of suspicion is a term initially adopted by Ricoeur (1971) to describe a form of analysis that systematically 'peels back' the layers of meaning, attending, in turn, to different ways in which meaning can be deployed. It is about digging beneath what is taken-for-granted, and working

out what is going on – who gains, and what do they gain, by assuming the world works in *that* way?

Critical narrative analysis is a term adopted by Langdridge (2007) to distinguish the particular form of phenomenological analysis he uses, in contrast to IPA (Interpretative Phenomenological Analysis).

Critical realism is the foundational philosophy behind the retroductive logic of inquiry, within a postmodern epistemology and ontology. In it, analysis is conducted by reference to an established theory – such as feminism, Marxism or postcolonialism.

Critical relativism is the foundational philosophy behind the abductive logic of inquiry, within a postmodern epistemology and ontology. In it, analysis is conducted through attending to contradictions and dislocations in the data, where everything is open to scrutiny and no prior assumptions are made about the theoretical framework that should be applied.

Critical social psychology is the term I have adopted in this book to describe a collection of approaches that contest experimental social psychology. These include social constructionist, postmodernist, discursive and narrative approaches to social psychology. Its main elements are a rejection of Scientific method as the means to gain knowledge, a claim that social psychology is always an ideological endeavour, and a view of the social world that contends it is constructed through people's meaning-making not something 'out

there' waiting to be discovered.

Crowd psychology is an early branch of psychology developed in France and Italy in the late nineteenth century. It was based on the notion that 'crowds' and 'mobs' appear to act as though they have a single mind – called the 'group mind'. Acting in this way, it was thought, reduces people to the 'lowest common denominator', almost as if, as a mob, they become like a primitive animal.

Cultural values theory recognizes that groups and cultures vary in their values, especially the actions and behaviours that they endorse.

D

Deduction is a logic of inquiry where hypotheses are tested, by manipulating one or a small number of variables and observing their effect. Where this does not conform to the prediction made in the hypothesis, then the hypothesis is rejected. Where the effect does conform, then the hypothesis is given support. Note: it is never possible to prove the hypothesis; there is always a possibility that the effect is due to chance.

Defence mechanism is a concept used in psychoanalytic theory, to describe a strategy for coping with anxiety. An example is where memories of distressing and upsetting events are blocked.

Dependent variable is the variable in an experiment that is used to observe the effect of the independent variable.

Descriptive interviewing is an approach that aims to give participants in a study the opportunity to speak for themselves without interpretation.

Descriptive phenomenology a term adopted by Langdridge (2007) to identify where a phenomenological approach is taken to gain insight into people's experiential accounts with the focus placed on the account itself rather than analysis.

Descriptive research uses an inductive approach, and is intended to provide the basis for an accurate description of the phenomenon in question.

Dialectical is where things are in a reciprocal relationship to or interaction with each other.

Disablism is a term adopted by Deal (2007) to describe the subtle forms of prejudice towards people with disabilities, in parallel with ageism, racism and sexism.

Disclaiming is a term used in discourse analysis, referring to discursive strategies used to deny something (for example, that you are racist).

Discourse is a word with multiple meanings in different contexts and as used by different theorists. In discourse analysis its referents range from the micro (where it can be applied to very specific elements in text) to macro (in terms of 'big' discourses – such as feminist, neo-liberal, Islamist, hetero-normative, and so on). Overall it is a term that highlights the meaning-making qualities of talk and text, and how what is said can be used to play 'language games'.

Discourse analysis is a generic term applied to a range of semiotic methods for scrutinizing text – which can be talk, writing or even visual images – to gain insight into its meanings and what it is being used to signify.

Discursive practices discourse analysis tends to be very specific in its application. It focuses on what a particular text element – such as a short extract of talk – is being used to achieve. More broadly this approach examines the ways in which discourse is used strategically – to do things like persuade, impress or undermine another person.

Discursive psychology is a generic term applied to approaches that assume that social reality is constructed by subjective and intersubjective 'effort after meaning', where discourse is seen as the main means by which people construct, communicate and interpret meaning.

Discursive resources discourse analysis takes a 'broad-brush' approach, looking at discourse in an almost ecological way. It is less concerned with what a particular person says at a specific time and more concerned with the ways different discourses interact with each other, mutate over time, gain dominance in certain settings and cultural locations. For example, this approach traces the ways in which new discourses (such as feminism) have posed a challenge to the dominant discourse of patriarchy.

Dispositional inference is a stage in attribution, where a judgement is made based on a stereotype (for example, 'women are emotional').

Dogmatic personality is a more general term for authoritarian personality, and was used by Milton Rokeach to describe the work he did in his doctoral thesis.

Double-blind experiment is where both subject and experimenter do not know the experimental hypothesis or the condition under test.

Dual process dependency model explains social influence in groups as operating in terms of a person's confidence in their own judgement. When they are confident, they act according to it – but when they lack confidence, they follow group norms.

E

Ecological analysis is where a wide range of measures and methods are used to address a particular research question. Wicke and Cohen Silver (2009) used this approach to explore ways in which effective and supportive community relationships can help communities to be resilient in the face of trouble.

Ego-defence is from psychodynamic theory, and is a strategy to protect the ego from being undermined or harmed.

Emblem is a gesture that stands in for speech, such as a soldier's salute or a police officer's upheld hand signalling 'stop'.

Emotional labour is the hard work involved in presenting a cheery face for hours on end, however obnoxiously the customers are behaving.

Empiricism is the basis of scientific epistemology, where objective data are the sole means to gain valid knowledge.

Emplotment is where a string of incidents are woven together to form a narrative, so that they become a meaningful story.

Epistemological constructivism describes the philosophical basis of personal construct theory, with a modernist ontology (where the social world is seen as 'real' and singular) but a postmodern epistemology (wherein there are multiple knowledges that are socially constructed).

Epistemology is a theory of knowledge.

Equilibrium is a term used by Herzlich (1973) to describe a social representation of health where it is seen as a state of positive well-being, where body and soul are in harmonious balance.

Esteem function is the way an attitude enables individuals and collectives to achieve and maintain status, respect and honour.

Ethnolinguistic groups are groups defined by their ethnic commonality and their use of a common slang or patois.

Ethnomethodology is an approach to research that works in naturalistic settings and is usually informed by critical realist ontology and epistemology.

Ethogenics is a term often attributed to Rom Harré (1997) to describe a broadly postmodern, social constructionist approach to social psychology. Today it is seldom used, as it has become incorporated into critical social psychology.

Eurocentric is a specific form of ethnocentrism, which is the assumption that European culture is 'the norm' and every other culture is 'other' (and a bit exotic and strange). This focuses on the way Europeans tend to see themselves in this way.

Evolutionary psychology is rooted in evolutionary biology and sociobiology, and claims that human behaviour is moulded by evolution and encoded in the genes.

Exchange relationships as defined by Clark and Grote (2003) are those that are formal and based on mutual interest (where resources of different kinds are exchanged), including institutional relationships in the workplace.

Expectancy-value models assume that people decide between alternative courses of action through estimating the probabilities for each possible action and that it will bring about benefits and/or avoid negative consequences to themselves.

Experimental social psychology is the term used in this book to describe the approach taken by those who view it as a Scientific endeavour, based on hypothetico-deductive methods and positivist assumptions about the epistemological and ontological basis on which psychology should be based.

Experimental subjects are the people taking part in an experiment.

Experimenter effects are where researchers act in ways that affect the outcome of the experiment, in unintended ways.

Explain is to 'smooth over' – it is where the causes of effects are identified and complexity is 'ironed out'.

Explicate is to 'unfold' – it is where insight is the goal, not explanation.

Expressive function is where attitudes allow individuals and collectives to communicate their beliefs, opinions and values and, thereby, to identify with those individuals and groups who share them.

Externalization when used in social constructionist theory is about the way that cultures, societies and social groups of different kinds make sense of – and therefore 'make' – their social worlds, including a whole range of social institutions and constructs.

Extreme case formulation is a term used in discourse analysis, where someone is seeking to justify taking or recommending a particular action by expressing the worst case scenario.

F

Face is a term used by Goffman to describe the positive social value a person effectively claims for themselves by the line others assume they have taken during an interaction.

Face work goes on in social interaction, where people have a mutual commitment to keep each other 'in face'.

Factor analysis, in its traditional sense, was invented by Charles Spearman in his early studies of intelligence among schoolchildren. It is a statistical technique for investigating which things 'hang together'. Spearman wanted to find out if intelligence was basically a single, coherent capacity or made up of different components such as where verbal intelligence is independent from mathematical intelligence.

False consensus effect is where people tend to assume that others are more likely to behave like them than they actually do.

Falsification is seeking to disprove a rule or a theory's predictions.

Feminist psychology not surprisingly is psychology that is informed by feminist theory and principles. It adopts an analytic that highlights the role of patriarchy in the construction of a 'man-made world' that disadvantages, silences and undermines women. In terms of principles early feminist psychologists made major contributions by, for example, making research more participatory, respectful and sensitive to the ways power is exercised by researchers. These have informed critical psychology more generally, applied, for example, in contexts around colonialism, disability and other forms of prejudice and oppression.

Field experiments are experiments carried out in naturalistic settings rather than the laboratory.

Field theory is a term used in gestalt theory, where behaviour is seen to be influenced by the 'psychological field' or 'social climate' in the same way that the perceptual field influences what a person sees.

Focus groups are where a group is brought together in order to explore attitudes and opinions; they are often used in market research.

Foucauldian discourse analysis is another term for macro discourse analysis, where the analysis is at the level of discourses that operates intersubjectively.

Fundamental attribution error is where people tend to overemphasize the personal causes, and underemphasize the situational causes of actions.

G

Gaydar is a kind of cultural radar that allows gay people to recognize whether another person is gay or straight.

Gaze has (at least) two meanings. In non-verbal communication it has to do with the way people look at each other. In postmodern theory, it is about the semiotic 'lens' through which people view the world – such as a 'male gaze' or a 'feminist gaze'.

Gestalt appraisal is based on the whole of something, not just its constituent parts.

Gestalt psychology is based on the idea that 'the whole is more than the sum of its parts' and, more broadly, that we can only make sense of phenomena within their contexts. Applied to social psychology, it is about the way that people perceive objects, including social objects, where the 'figure' is viewed in relation to the 'ground'.

Governmentality is a Foucauldian term, refined especially by Nicolas Rose (1998), that highlights the ways in which institutions and societies in general regulate and control individuals – for example, by establishing and promoting ideas about 'the good citizen' to which people are expected to aspire, and which is used to control 'deservingness' for various freedoms, services and levels of autonomy and choice.

Grounded theory is not only a general term to refer to research where theories are developed from interpretation and analysis of the data (rather than the other way around) but also a specific research method (described in detail in Chapter 5).

Group dynamics is a field of study developed by Lewin in the 1940s. It concerns the ways in which individuals act differently when they are part of a group, compared with when they are acting alone. For example, working on a task together as a group can either have the effect of making individuals work harder (social energizing) or less hard (social loafing), according to circumstances.

Group initiation is where in order to join a group the person is expected to participate in an activity or ritual – such as swearing an oath.

Group mind was a concept first used by McDougall ([1908] 1919) that, according to Reicher and Haslam (2006), has haunted psychology throughout its history. It is the idea that once people collectivize together, they lose their individual humanity and begin to act as an inhuman, savage 'mob', lacking in compassion and decency (a bit like the Borg of science fiction).

Group norms are the norms endorsed by the group – as opposed, say, to cultural norms.

Group polarization is where a group decision is more extreme than the average when group members make the decision individually.

Groupthink is what happens when a small, highly cohesive group of like-minded people becomes so obsessed with reaching consensus and so blinkered by it when they reach it, that they lose touch with reality and make a catastrophic decision.

H

Head-in-the-sand fallacy is where social psychologists assume that what they discover from studying samples of US students are universally nomothetic theories about social psychological processes and phenomena.

Health-in-a-vacuum is a social representation of health where it is seen as an absence of illness.

Hedge (sometimes called a preface) is a word or utterance like 'uh' at the start of speech, used to 'hedge around' difficulties to come.

Heteronormativity is where male–female sexual relationships are seen as normal and are taken as being the-way-things-are. Other sexualities and relationships are generally ignored and invisible – for example, in terms of services provided or laws about entitlements. This differs from homophobia (where non-hererosexualities are seen as unnatural or forms of sickness).

Heuristic processing is where information is processed using 'rules of thumb' (such as the majority are usually right).

Historical inquiry (Foucault calls it 'genealogy') is an approach to discourse analysis that looks for the origins of a particular discourse and then traces its 'life history' through different times and locations, to arrive at an overall understanding of its operations in the 'here and now'.

Horizon of understanding is a term devised by Gadamer (1975) to describe the kinds of 'what everybody knows' assumptions that provide the backcloth against which we make sense of the world. Mkhize (2004b) uses it to depict the conditions of apartheid in which Nelson Mandela and Steve Biko constructed their identities

less as 'technologies of the self' and more as ethical subjects.

Human science disciplines are those that study some aspect of people, such as anthropology and economics.

Human-heartedness is a value dimension varying from values of kindness, compassion and emotional nurturance to values of conscientiousness, perseverance and thrift.

Hypothetico-deductive method or **hypothetico-deductivism** is the process of making deductions from the testing of hypotheses.

I

Identity-reference groups are where belonging to the group involves identification with the group, and where affiliation acts as a reference frame for a person to know 'who' they are – their social identity.

Ideological dilemmas was the title of an influential textbook written by Billig, Condor, Edwards, Gane, Middleton and Radley in 1998, *Ideological Dilemmas: Social Psychology of Everyday Thinking*. The term has subsequently been adopted as an analytic device to focus on and explore the kinds of everyday dilemmas that are woven into people's lives: to look for a new job? To stay in a bad relationship or leave? To buy a new car, or washing machine or phone?

Idiographic means specific to particular instances, as opposed to generally lawful.

Illustrator is a posture or gesture that accompanies speech, generally reinforcing its message, such as using your hand to point directions.

Imaginary is a term adopted by Lacan (1977) as part of three

orders – the imaginary order, the symbolic order and the real order. The imaginary concerns a person's 'mirror image' or image of themselves. It plays an important role in the process of identification as a developmental stage or task, where one makes sense of one's self through identification with others.

Immersive virtual environments are places like Second Life where people can, in avatar form, interact with others in virtual terms.

Implicit attitudes are attitudes based on stereotypical thinking, that *can* affect other judgements without the person being aware of their influence.

Implicit measures are measures in an experiment that infer a person's thinking (including their unconscious thinking) rather than test it directly by self-report.

Impression formation is how people form their first impressions of others.

Incidental groups are where two or more people are merely together for a relatively short period of time and have minimal involvement in and commitment to each other.

Independent variable this is the variable in an experiment that is varied by the experimenter.

Individual representations are those that are unique to the person.

Individuo-centred approach focuses on the ways in which social grouping, social institutions and social forces are determined by the behaviour of individuals and the processes going on within individual minds.

Induction is a logic of inquiry based on observing events and phenomena, looking for regularity or patterns, and, based on these, formulating ideas or hypotheses about what is going on. In the case of social psychology these are in the form of 'laws of social behaviour'.

Information influence is where people use the group as an information source.

Ingroup is the group to which a person belongs.

Innovation is a term from Moscovici's theory of minority influence, where a minority persuades the majority to adopt their viewpoint.

Institutional racism differs profoundly from overt racism; it is a much more subtle form of racism in that is not *intended* to be prejudiced – though its impact can be as damaging as out-and-out blatant racism.

Instrumental function is where attitudes direct people to act within the social world in ways that enable them to pursue their goals, both individual and collective.

Integration is the term used by the Chinese Cultural Collective to describe whether the self is seen in individualistic or relational terms.

Internalization when used in social constructionist theory is where the objectified social world becomes known and understood by individuals through processes of socialization and enculturation.

Interpersonal distance is the distance at which two people interact; intimates get up close, friends less so, and strangers prefer to keep their distance.

Interpretative Phenomenological Analysis is usually associated with Jonathan Smith (see Eatough and Smith 2009) and called IPA. It is a specific form of interpretative analysis he developed offering a clear and systematic set of rules and stages for examining phenomenological accounts. IPA's popularity reflects a preference among qualitative researchers for such clarity, but is challenged by some as too inflexible. Langdridge (2007) offers an overview and some alternatives.

Interpretative repertoires is a term devised by Wetherell and Potter (1992) to describe elements of discourse – at the level of a storyline – that offer an account of or explanation for an issue or topic or phenomenon.

Intersubjectivity is subjectivity (experiencing, thinking, perception) that is based upon common impressions, symbols, ideas and understandings shared between people rather than being the products of individual minds.

Introspectionism is the exploration of thought processes by, literally, individuals internally reflecting on their own experiences of remembering, perceiving, and so on.

Issuance is the property of something to 'be an issue' – that is, to be something about which people are concerned and/or have contested views.

K

Knowing of the third kind was a term devised by John Shotter to describe the various kinds of embodied knowledge we use to make sense of our relationships and communication with others – the gestures, touches, glances, and so on that signal warmth or coldness, pleasure or disdain.

L

Laboratory experiments are conducted in controlled settings. In social psychology this is often just an ordinary room.

Langue is that aspect of language that is its abstract system of syntax and semantics, and that is virtual and outside of time.

Leakage is where non-verbal cues indicate a person is being dishonest.

Learned helplessness is a term adopted by Seligman (1975) to describe people whose childhood experiences taught them that they have no control over their destiny. So, he argued, in adulthood they are incapable of helping themselves – they are passive and incapable.

Liberal humanism is an ideology that gives priority to the well-being and well-functioning of a 'good society', in which individuals have a duty to contribute to the good of society through collective effort.

Liberal individualism is an ideology that gives priority to a person's individual autonomy and freedom. In it institutions like the Church or the State are seen to have little or no right to intervene in how an individual chooses to live their life.

Liberation psychology is generally attributed to Ignacio Martín-Baró (1966), a psychologist from El Salvador executed by a government hit squad in 1989. It takes a radical line – that psychology should be a force of liberation to all those who are oppressed and exploited.

Likert scale is a scale consisting of a set of statements, and boxes (or whatever) that people mark to indicate, say, their agreement with the statement – for example, ranging from 'strongly agree' to 'strongly disagree'.

Linguistic repertoires is a term used by Potter and Wetherell (1987) to describe the discursive resources people draw upon to achieve particular ends.

Locus of control is about whether a person sites control in themselves or in chance, luck or fate, seen to be a product of their learning experiences as children.

Logic of inquiry is a rationale for adopting a particular approach to research, based on specific epistemological and ontological assumptions. Induction and deduction are the two best known – abduction and retroduction much less so.

Low-status groups are social groups consisting of marginalized or socially excluded people (for example, 'the underclass') or those regarded by an ingroup as inferior (for example, 'gypsies').

M

Macro-discourse analysis is sometimes called Foucauldian discourse analysis. It is an approach that explores the ways in which different discursive resources are deployed in, for example, responding to the ideological dilemmas in everyday life. It is concerned both with the textuality of discourse (what it is about) and its tectonics (how one discourse moulds and shapes another).

Major histocompatibility complex (MHC) is genetic material that contains information that allows for the recognition of genetic similarity and is the basis of the immune response.

Majority influence – informational influence based on taken-for-granted knowledge.

Manichean thinking a worldview in which everything is divided into opposing poles, like black/white, where one is inevitably negative and the other positive.

Market research is where research is carried out in order to inform commercial decisions – for instance, to find a new brand name for a product or discover what kinds of people are most likely to be interested in a new service.

Marxist psychology draws on Marxist theory as its major analytic framework. Its best known proponent is Ian Parker (Parker 2009 is a good place to start).

Mass media are forms of collective communication such as television and newspapers.

Matched-guise technique is where a series of tape-recorded speech extracts are recorded, all spoken by the same highly skilled actor but each one in a different accent or dialect. Subjects in the study give their impression of the speaker by responding to different evaluative dimensions.

Membership groups are groups that people join and can leave; in such groups people see themselves as having a stake in the group's fortunes and can be strongly committed and involved.

Metaphysics is usually defined as the study of 'knowing and being'; it brings together the philosophical examination of epistemology and ontology.

Micro-discourse analysis is where analysis is specifically directed to particular instances of text, and what is being done in a particular conversation in particular circumstances.

Micropolitics of power is a term devised by Foucault to describe the complex webs of power and resistance that operate in people's relations with one another, whether as individuals or as groups.

Minimal group experiments were originated by Tajfel (Tajfel et al. 1971); these were studies examining the minimal conditions under which people act together as a group rather than just a collection of individuals. They showed that it took very little – loyalty is shown to somebody you are told is a member of your group and nothing more.

Minimal group paradigm is where social effects are studied in incidental groups. Almost any element of common fate seems to be sufficient to persuade people to favour members of 'their' group over members of another group.

Minority influence is where a minority is able to sway the judgements of the majority.

Mixed method research has two meanings, which can be confusing. Quantitative social psychologists often use it specifically to refer to a project that includes some small contribution of qualitative research in a predominantly quantitative study. Among qualitative researchers it is used more broadly to refer to any study that uses a mix of methods, often all of them qualitative.

Modernism is the name given to a set of ethical beliefs and values, practices and endeavours, that were developed in Europe and the USA during the historical period of the Enlightenment in the eighteenth century.

Moral discipline is a set of values relating to respect for superiors and the value of diligence and hard work.

Morphemes are the units of speech composed of phonemes, and are usually words.

Motivated tactician is a term used to describe cognition where different processing strategies are used tactically, to optimize the chances of achieving goals.

N

Narrative psychology explores the ways in which people make sense of the social world and their lives within it through constructing knowledge into a story.

Natural sciences are those that study the natural (as opposed to the human) and include physics, chemistry and biology.

Negative bias is where, once a negative impression is formed about someone, it tends to persist and lead to negative evaluation.

Neo-liberalism is an ideology based on the language of consumerism – of markets, customer choice, targets and outcomes – that seeks to promote human progress by making our endeavours more profitable and more effective and rewarding the fittest and most capable.

Non-contact cultures are those where body contact (such as touching in various ways) is seldom used as a form of communication.

Normalization is a term from Moscovici's theory of minority influence, where the minority and majority members of a group agree on a compromise judgement.

Normative influence is where people in a group follow group norms.

Norms are defined in experimental social psychology as the shared standards of conduct expected of group members.

Null hypothesis is devised in an experiment as that which falsifies the experimental hypothesis.

O

Objectification is one of the 'moments' in the social construction of reality, whereby ideas, concepts, and so on are taken to be 'real things'.

Observational measures are those taken from direct observation of the behaviour of subjects that is relevant to the research question.

Ontology is the branch of philosophy concerned with what things 'are' – their 'being-in-the-world'. A good example is the different ontological positions taken by experimental and critical social psychology over the nature of the social world. Experimental social psychology sees it as something separate from people – an external medium within which individual people operate. Critical social psychology sees the social world as a product of human thought and action.

Operant conditioning is a process whereby people change their behaviour in response to either a regime of rewards

(called reinforcement) or punishments (negative reinforcement).

Operationalization describes the way a construct is 'made operational' (that is, usable) in the form of variables that can be measured in a particular study.

Opinion polls are studies of public attitudes, as used, for example, by political parties to find out about voting intentions in the period before elections.

Organizational citizenship behaviour (OCB) is a term adopted by Tan and Tan (2008) to describe the form of social facilitation that operates in cultures that function collectively.

Organizational function is where, by categorizing objects in the social world along evaluative dimensions, attitudes act as guides to help people – as individuals and collectively – attend to these objects, understand them and feel about them.

Outgroup is any group other than a person's ingroup, but usually refers to the comparison group(s) in a study of social identity.

P

Palliative is a term used in discourse analysis; it is where someone seeks to ameliorate potential rudeness of, say, rejecting the invitation.

Panopticon was a design for a prison invented by Jeremy Bentham in 1785, designed to make all prisoners easily observable at any time by a small number of guards. Foucault used it as a metaphor for self-regulation – the way we behave as though we are constantly under scrutiny, and so conform.

Paradigm shift is where one paradigm is overthrown and replaced by another, in which radically different questions are asked and methods used, and theorization is based on different assumptions.

Paralanguage is the non-linguistic elements of speech, things like 'ums' and 'ahs', grunts and sighs, speed, tone and pitch of voice, and so on.

Parole is that aspect of language that operates in a speech community, such as English or French.

Patois is a developed and inclusive way of talking that has not only a particular accent, but also its own grammar and terminology, such as Rastafarian.

Performative language as defined by the philosopher, Austin (1962) is language that makes things happen – 'I pronounce you man and wife' as opposed to constitutive language that merely describes 'what is' – the grass is green.

Personal construct theory is primarily a theory about how individuals build up and use 'personal constructs' to make sense of and operate within the social world.

Personal self is the self that is self-aware of being 'you' and conscious of your own thoughts and feelings.

Persuasion is where a deliberate attempt is made to change people's attitudes and is concerned with the cognitive processes involved in how that change is brought about.

Persuasive arguments theory proposes that group polarization works through people taking notice of additional arguments that support their own opinion, thus making it stronger.

Phenomenological causality is a term adopted by Heider to describe the ways in which people attribute the causes of events and things that happen to them, including locating agency in people and in nature.

Phenomenological methods are those where people seek to report their subjective experiences.

Pheromones are chemicals exuded (for example, by sweat glands) that communicate through the sense of smell.

Phonemes are the basic, meaningless sounds in spoken language, like the 'th' at the beginning of 'think, or the 'oo' at the end of 'kangaroo'.

Polysemic means a word having a number of different meanings – such as 'madam' that ranges from an expression of disapproval ('she was a little madam') to overblown courtesy ('what would madam like for dessert?).

Positivism is the epistemological position that there can be a straightforward one-to-one relationship between things and events in the outside world and people's knowledge of them.

Postcolonial psychology is where psychology is informed by postcolonial theory, as used by MacLeod and Bhatia (2009).

Postcolonial theory originated from a specific critique of the impact of national forms of colonialism in places like Africa and India, where whole states were made subject to foreign powers including Belgium, Britain, France and Holland. Today it is becoming more general in its scope to examine the impact of colonization of other kinds such as economic and linguistic.

Postmodernism is a reaction and challenge to modernism. It disputes modernism's claim that there is a singular objective knowledge that can be gained through scientific inquiry. Rather, postmodernism regards all knowledge as socially constructed. It contends that there are many knowledges, each one arising from different standpoints (that is, that knowledge is always *positioned* by the person or group promoting it). Postmodernism is fundamentally concerned with the relationship between knowledge and power – what actions, for example, a particular knowledge allows and what it prevents.

Post-structuralism is a form of postmodernism, specifically applicable to language and other sign systems where the focus moves beyond subjectivity to look at intersubjective spaces and processes whereby sign systems are deployed to create particular realities.

Power as a term is used in this book mainly as a framework for analysis of 'what is going on' in social practices of different kinds, and in constituting social phenomena. It focuses, in particular, on issues of dominance and oppression in the way power is exercised – but also other forms of interaction like nurture, care and cooperation.

Power distance is a value dimension relating to the amount of respect and deference expected between superiors and their subordinates, and the formality of social interactions.

Preface see **hedge**.

Presencing function is where some action (such as constructing a story) is carried out in order to make something 'real' – to bring it to our attention as a 'real thing'.

Presencing practices are where some kind of social reality is made and/or made real. For example, a Gay Pride procession presences a particular form of homosexuality – one that is celebratory (as opposed, say, to one which presences homosexuality as an illness).

Primacy effect is where the first information in a list has a greater effect than information later in that list.

Primatology the study of primates and, in particular, primate societies – the relationships and social life of monkeys and apes.

Priming is where prior information or other manipulation of experimental conditions affects subsequent behaviour.

Problematizing is the turning of something into a problem – in the way, for instance, that young people's drinking is commonly treated as 'a problem' even if it is quite mild, whereas the drinking that goes on among adults is not usually.

Processing-depth models of social cognition view it as operating in one of two distinctly and qualitatively different levels of processing. Information processing about something that is mundane and unimportant tends to be 'mindless' and automatic. But information processing that matters or is out of the ordinary tends to be carried out in depth and with careful consideration.

Pro-social behaviour is where people act to benefit strangers in any way or for any reason.

Proxemics is the study of the distance that people adopt when communicating with each other.

Psy complex A term invented by Nikolas Rose (1979), Goodley and Parker (2000: 4) define it as 'that dense network of theories and practices which make up the apparatus of psychology inside and outside colleges and clinics, including its power to define what people think about themselves and their own personal resources for change'.

Psychoanalytic social psychology is, confusingly, sometimes called psychosocial psychology. It is where psychoanalytic theory and its concepts and methods are adopted by social psychology.

Psycholinguistics views language as the main medium for thought, and examines the ways in language affects thinking.

Psychological social psychology studies how social events and phenomena influence the ways in which individual people feel, think and act. It is concerned with the psychological processes (such as social perception and cognition) that go on within individual minds.

Psychosocial psychology is, confusingly, sometimes used to refer to psychoanalytic social psychology. Its other meaning is the bringing together of sociological and psychological approaches to social phenomena and processes.

Q

Q factor analysis is the inverted form of regular factor analysis devised by William Stephenson, where it is whole patterns of Q sorting that are correlated with each other.

Q methodology, invented by William Stephenson, it uses an inverted form of factor analysis as a pattern analytic to identify alternative accounts, viewpoints and opinions on a topic or issue.

Q set, in Q method this is the set of Q items that will be presented to participants.

Q sorting, in Q method this is the process of placing the items of the Q set into the positions on the Q grid.

Qualitative research is where behaviour is observed rather than measured. Little q qualitative research is where it is used experimentally, and is coded according to predetermined categories. Big Q qualitative research makes no attempt to measure or pre-categorize what is being observed.

Quality of life is not a way of measuring a person's evaluation of their bodily comfort and ability (as is usually the case in the English-speaking world). It is much more about life-quality as well-being and belonging, linked to cultural and community values.

Quasi-experiment is another name for field experiment, where researchers capitalize upon situations where relevant factors are being varied naturally.

Queer psychology rejects the idea that people can be classified according to their 'sexuality' – that is, that there is such a thing as a sexual identity. Instead it explores sexuality as it is instantiated through situated social practices.

Queer theory challenges heteronormative assumptions that prioritize heterosexuality as the-way-things-are and, indeed, the classification of people in terms of their sexual practices and desires.

R

Racial psychology was the study of psychological differences between different races in an explicit quest to document the superiority of the white race.

Realistic conflict theory is where group conflict is seen to arise from competition between groups over scarce resources, rather than as the product of group processes and forces (such as prejudice).

Received pronunciation is that pronunciation of a language assumed to be the standard, and is often accorded a higher status than, for example, a regional accent.

Recency effect is where items at the end of a list are remembered or have more effect than items in the middle.

Reference frame is a set of norms that a person uses as a reference point to judge their own.

Referent information influence is seen to operate through people's self-categorization. When they identify themselves as belonging to a particular group they then use that group's norms as standards for their own decision-making.

Reflexive self is the part of a self that is able to observe, plan and respond to one's own behaviour.

Reflexivity is being self-aware, and able to, for example, judge one's own behaviour or thinking and gain insight.

Reification is where an abstract idea or a number of coexisting ideas or events get conceptually turned into a 'thing'. An example is premenstrual tension.

Relational self is the self that comes from interconnected relationships with others, such as family or community.

Relationship imperative is a term used to describe the pressure that people feel to be in a relationship – to be one of a couple.

Representativeness is about making sure that the people taking part in the study are representative of the people the researcher wants to find out.

Reserve of health is a social representation of health based on the idea that health is a resource or an investment.

Resistance is a term adopted by Foucault to describe the strategies that people use to resist power being exercised over them.

Respondents is the name given to the people taking part in a survey.

Retroduction is a logic of inquiry that seeks to identify systematic regularities in social action and social phenomena, in order to speculate about the structures and mechanisms underlying them.

Reversal of agency is a term devised by Vickers to describe the misattribution of agency, where, for example, a 'victim' is blamed for the harm done to them and the perpetrator absolved of responsibility for the harm they did.

Risky shift is where, in group discussions, the group adopts a more risky decision than the individuals did privately.

Role expectations are those that require people to act in accordance to preconceived notions relating to their role.

S

Schema is a cognitive structure that represents knowledge about a concept, including its attributes and the relations among these attributes.

Science, using a capital letter indicates that this is a science that uses a hypothetico-deductive approach to gaining knowledge.

Scientific racism is a theory that assumes that humankind has a common ancestry, but some races are more advanced than others.

Scopophilia is where somebody gains pleasure (often sexual pleasure) through looking at someone or something. Derived from Freudian theory, the idea has been taken up by film theorists like Laura Mulvey (1975).

Script is a well-rehearsed and well-remembered repertoire for action, sometimes viewed as a schema about an event.

Selection task problem was devised by Wason to examine people's tendencies to make induction errors when problem solving.

Selective attention is where someone has to divide their attention between two or more tasks, and prioritizes one of them.

Self-categorization theory is where a person identifies with a social group, and hence categorizes themselves as a member of that group.

Self-esteem refers to the attitudes that people hold about themselves.

Self-monitoring is about the way people monitor their behaviour to tailor it to different situations and circumstances.

Self-perception theory argues that people know who they are by observing their own behaviour.

Self-presentation is about how you portray yourself (to yourself, and to others) in a good light.

Self-report measures are where subjects respond directly to questions – for example, by completing a questionnaire.

Self-schema is another way of saying self-image, in that it is a composite made up of a variety of ways in which we judge and see ourselves.

Self-stereotyping is where a person identifies with a social group, and categorizes themself as a member of that group, and adopts the stereotypical behaviour and persona expected of members of that group.

'Selfish-gene' hypothesis is a form of evolutionary theory claiming that human behaviour is the product of 'survival of the fittest' where acts that lead to survival are favoured over those that do not.

Semantic describes those aspects of language to do with the meanings of words, sentences and utterances.

Semiotics is the study of signs and symbols and how they convey significance and meaning.

Severe initiation is an initiation into a group that involves pain, discomfort and/or embarrassment. It can be a powerful means to establish loyalty to the group.

Sibling relationships are those between brothers and sisters.

Sibling rivalry, according to Freud, is a psychodynamic process in which siblings compete for their parents' love and attention.

Sign systems are systems of signifiers and signifieds, whereby messages about meaning are communicated.

Significant correlation is where the correlation between two values reaches statistical significance – that it, it is highly unlikely to have arisen through chance.

Significant difference is a technical term in statistics. A difference is significant if it is sufficiently large that, statistically, it is very unlikely to be a matter of coincidence or chance.

Signification is the process of using signs to communicate significance and meaning.

Signified is that aspect of something (such as an article of clothing) that refers to what it is intended to mean.

Signifier refers to the physical characteristics of the sign.

Signifying act is when a person expresses a sign or symbol by the articulation of a message. This can be in language, but also by an act (such as marching in a Gay Pride rally).

Situated social practice refers to very specific social actions, as opposed to broad categories like 'condom use'. It is used by critical psychologists to recognize that, say, using a condom or not is a very different issue on a first date compared with using one within a 'marriage-on-the-rocks'.

Situational correction is a stage in attribution where a person corrects their stereotyped view of a disposition, and take into account the influence of the situation or context.

Social capital draws parallels with economic capital, and is about the social support and other resources (such as level of trust) that contribute to individual and collective well-being and resilience.

Social categorization theory highlights people's tendency to identify with the group – to see it as an ingroup – and then to endorse the norms that distinguish their ingroup from other outgroups.

Social cognition comprises the processes involved in perceiving, understanding and responding to the social world. As a concept it is based on the general principles of cognitive psychology.

Social comparison theory argues that people want social approval and dislike social censure, and so comply to group norms.

Social constructionism is the term generally used for approaches to social psychology that are informed by postmodernism. Its main emphasis is upon the way that reality is constructed through social processes – another way of putting this is intersubjectively.

Social desirability effect is where people act in ways that make them look good.

Social energizing is where people work harder as a member of a group than alone.

Social exclusion is a process by which some members of a society or collectivity ('immigrants', 'good-for-nothings') are prevented from full participation and excluded from the provision of services.

Social facilitation is where the effect of doing a task in front of others tends to improve performance.

Social identity is the identity a person gains as a member of an ingroup; it is a sort of sociocultural 'glue' which plays a significant role in sustaining social and cultural groups.

Social identity theory was originated by Tajfel (Tajfel et al. 1971) and has come to be a dominant approach to identity in social psychology, particularly outside the USA.

Social influence is about the ways that other people and social processes between people can affect a person's behaviour.

Social interaction is where people are acting in relation to each other.

Social intervention is a term more frequently used in the Spanish-speaking world to denote actions taken to promote health, well-being and social inclusion. Examples include programmes to help people give up taking drugs, or to educate parents about hygiene in the home.

Social learning theory assumes that people's behaviour is the product of learning – for example, it is determined by the rewards and punishments they receive in their childhood.

Social loafing is where individuals expend less effort on a task when they do it with others (or think they are doing so).

Social perception is concerned with the ways in which people make sense of the social world of other people (in their actions both as individuals and groups).

Social practices is a term increasingly used to replace concepts like 'health behaviour', and a framework which looks at specific social practices in terms of their context and meaning. A good example is condom use seen not as a 'behaviour' but a wide range of different social practices.

Social representations is a concept developed by Moscovici to refer to the shared understandings and belief-structures, through which people make sense of the social world. According to Moscovici's social representations theory, a social group is a group with common, shared, social representations.

Social self is the self that arises and is acted out in a social situation.

Socio-centred approach is one that focuses on the ways in which the behaviour and experiences of individual people are determined by their membership of social groups and social institutions and by social forces.

Sociolinguistics is the study of language in experimental social psychology; it focuses on how language is used in social situations.

Sociological social psychology studies how people act together and interact to produce social phenomena (such as crowd behaviour). It is concerned with how social processes (such as group cohesion and social identity) arise from social forces (such as the influence of group norms).

Sociology of knowledge is the study of how knowledge is made, marketed and contested and the purposes served, such as promoting the interests of a particular group.

Speech is the term in English used to mean *parole*: that which is particular to the use of language in a specific situation.

Speech style is the manner in which people speak in different contexts (for example, talking to children or adults).

Standpoint a position taken, such as postmodern, heteronormative or neo-liberal, from which 'what is going on' is interpreted.

Stereotyping is where something is categorized according to an over-generalized and often negative category, as in sexist stereotyping.

Stooge is a member of the experimental team, briefed to act as if they are a subject in an experiment in ways that establish one of the experimental conditions. For example, in studies of compliance, stooges give wrong answers.

Stream of consciousness in a person's stream of consciousness, James proposed, all manner of thoughts, emotions, states, feelings, images and ideas continually coexist at some level.

Structuralism is the global, all-encompassing study of the architecture of meaning – of what meanings can be constructed, by whom and how and why and from what.

Subject position a term important in Foucauldian theory, indicating potential identities available to be taken up.

Subject positioning is where a person is positioned through strategies of regulation. An example is a person who was abused in childhood, who may be positioned as a 'victim' by the actions and expectations of people like counsellors or psychiatrists – or as a 'survivor' within a self-help group.

Subjectification is, literally, to 'make subject' or 'make subject to' a particular form of power, as in a Queen and her subjects.

Subjective norms are composed of other people's expectations and a person's own motivations to comply with them.

Substantivity is when a transitive state becomes actual – for example, when we notice, we realize, we recognize, we become aware of *something*.

Summer Camp experiments were Sherif's classic experimental studies of group cooperation and conflicts carried out with boys attending US summer camps.

Survey research is where data are gathered by asking people to fill in questionnaires, or they are interviewed – face to face, by telephone or by email.

Symbol is a sign where its meaning is based upon a shared ideology or institution. Examples include flags and religious symbols like the cross in Christianity.

Symbolic interactionism is a sociological theory, focusing on the ways in which people interact with each other through expressing and sharing meaning.

Symbolic order is another Lacanian term, alongside the imaginary and the real. It denotes the ways in which the outside world is constructed – for example, through patriarchy – creating all sorts of constraints upon certain people (in this example, women).

Syntactic rules are the linguistic rules that determine how words are fitted together.

Systematic processing is processing that involves conscious and systematic thought, as opposed to automatic processing; it is demanding but much more strategic and insightful.

T

Talk is a term used by discourse analysts to refer to any sort of speech, usually naturally occurring, such as in meetings or counselling sessions.

Technology of the self is a term adopted by Foucault to convey the ways in which a 'self' is constructed through regulatory control – for example, through strategies for controlling and regulating sexuality (see Chapter 3).

Tectonics is a term adopted by Curt to refer to those aspects of discourse that relate to how it is produced, maintained and promoted, and how discourses vie against and impinge upon one another.

Text when used as a technical term is any human product or action that signifies something. Although it is usually language, it can be, for instance, a painting or a building.

Textuality is a term adopted by Curt to refer to those aspects of discourse that have to do with its semiotic qualities, and hence its potential to wield power.

Theoretical sampling is a term used in grounded theory analysis, designed to increase rigour and refinement by 'standing back' from the data analysis and looking at it in a more global, analytic manner.

Theoretical saturation is a term used in grounded theory analysis, where, after a number of analytic iterations through the different stages, nothing new is being discovered. It is the end point at which analysis is completed.

Theory of reasoned action is where people's behaviour is seen to be a product of their attitudes plus other elements including subjective norms and values.

Thingification is another (uglier but easier to understand) term

for reification, the process whereby ideas get turned into things.

Top-down processing is where information stored in memory (such as schema) is used to enable higher order, more complex thinking processes.

Transdisciplinarity is where disciplinary boundaries (for example, between psychology and geography) are broken down. It is more profound than 'interdisciplinarity' which merely seeks to build bridges between disciplines.

Transitivity is where thoughts are immanent rather than substantive – outside of our awareness and at the 'back of our minds'.

U

Us and Them fallacy is the stereotypical view that studying white people can tell you about social psychological processes and phenomena, whereas the study of black people is the domain of cross-cultural psychology.

V

Value system is where values are organized.

Values are stable and enduring convictions – often moral principles – that people hold about what matters to them and/or what they believe to be good or bad, worthwhile or worthless.

Variable is where a construct is defined in a way that can be measured.

Variance A statistical term indicating how much of the variability in the whole data-set can be 'explained' by the factor.

Visual dominance behaviour is where a person expresses or seeks to impose dominance by the use of eye gaze (such as 'staring someone out').

Völkerpsychologie is an early branch of psychology developed in Germany in the late nineteenth century. Difficult to translate exactly, it is the psychological study of the way the 'folk' or ordinary people in a particular society tend to share a similar worldview – they have similar opinions and beliefs.

W

Western is a term which, when capitalized, does not describe the geographical western area of the world. Rather it refers to the industrialized, rich areas of the world that include Australia and New Zealand. However, it does not just denote relative wealth and the accessibility of advanced technology – this is also true of the richer countries on the Pacific Rim. Crucially 'Western' refers to places where the dominant culture is one that has emerged from Western (as opposed to Eastern) religious beliefs and a more general worldview of individualism.

References

Abelson, R.P. (1981) The psychological status of the script concept, *American Psychologist*, 36: 715–29.

Adorno, T.W., Frenkel-Brunswick, E., Levinson, D.J. and Sandford, R.N. (1950) *The Authoritarian Personality*. New York: Harper.

Aiello, J.R. and Jones, S.E. (1971) Field study of the proxemic behaviour of young children in three subcultural groups, *Journal of Personality and Social Psychology*, 19: 351–6.

Ajzen, I. (1991) The theory of planned behaviour, *Organizational Behaviour and Human Decision Processes*, 50: 199–211.

Ajzen, I. and Fishbein, M. (1972) Attitudes and normative beliefs as factors influencing behavioural intentions, *Journal of Personality and Social Psychology*, 21(1): 1–9.

Ajzen, I. and Madden, T.J. (1986) Prediction of goal-directed behavior: attitudes, intentions and perceived behavioral control, *Journal of Experimental Social Psychology*, 22: 453–74.

Allport, F.H. (1920) The influence of the group upon association and thought, *Journal of Experimental Psychology,* 9: 159–82.

Allport, F.H. (1924) *Social Psychology*. Boston, MA: Houghton Mifflin.

Allport, G.W. (1935) Attitudes, in G. Murchison (ed.) *Handbook of Social Psychology*. Worchester, MA: Clark University Press.

Allport, G.W. (1954) *The Nature of Prejudice*. Reading, MA: Addison-Wesley.

Antaki, C. (1988) *Analysing Everyday Explanations: A Casebook of Methods*. London: Sage.

Argyle, M. (1988) *Bodily Communication*. London: Methuen.

Argyle, M. and Ingham, R. (1972) Gaze, mutual gaze and proximity, *Semiotica*, 6: 32–49.

Aronson, E. and Mills, J. (1959) The effects of severity of initiation on liking for a group, *Journal of Abnormal and Social Psychology*, 59: 177–81.

Arribas-Ayllon, M. and Walkerdine, V. (2009) Foucauldian discourse analysis, in C. Willig and W. Stainton Rogers (eds) *The Sage Handbook of Qualitative Research in Psychology*. London: Sage.

Asch, S.E. (1946) Forming impressions of personality, *Journal of Abnormal and Social Psychology*, 41: 258–90.

Asch, S.E. (1951) Effects of group pressure on the modification and distortion of judgements, in H. Guetzkow (ed.) *Groups, Leadership and Men*. Pittsburgh, PA: Carnegie Press.

Asch, S.E. (1952) *Social Psychology*. Englewood Cliffs, NJ: Prentice Hall.

Asch, S.E. (1956) Studies of independence and conformity: a minority of one against a unanimous majority, *Psychological Monographs: General and Applied*, 70, 170 (whole no. 416).

Ashworth, P. (1997) Breakthrough or bandwagon? Are interventions tailored to stage of change more effective than non-staged nterventions? *Health Education Journal*, 56, 166–74.

Ashworth. P. (2003) An approach to phenomenological psychology: the contingencies of the life-world, *Journal of Phenomenological Psychology*, 34(2): 145–56.

Atkinson, J.M. and Drew, P. (eds) (1979) *Order in Court: The Organization of Verbal Interaction in Judicial Settings*. London: Social Sciences Research Council.

Augostinos, M., Tuffin, K. and Rapley, M. (1999) Genocide or failure to gel? Racism, history and nationalism in Australian talk, *Discourse & Society*, 10: 351–78.

Augostinos, M., Walker, I. and Donaghue, N. (2006) *Social Cognition: An Integrated Introduction*, 2nd edn. New York: Sage.

Austin, J.L. (1962) *How to Do Things with Words*. Oxford: Oxford University Press.

Bache, G.M. (1895) Reaction time with reference to race, *Psychological Review*, 2: 475–86.

Bailenson, J.N., Blascovich, J., Beall, A.C., and Loomis, J.M. (2001) Equilibrium revisited: mutual gaze and personal space in virtual environments, *Presence*, 10: 583–98.

Bailenson, J.N., Blasovich, J., Beall, A.C. and Loomis, J.M. (2003) Interpersonal distance in immersive virtual environments, *Personality and Social Psychology Bulletin*, 29(10): 819–33.

Bakhtin, M.M. (1981) *The Dialogic Imagination*. Trans C. Emerson and M Holquist. Austin, TX: University of Texas Press.

Bales, R.F. and Slater, P.E. (1955) Role differentiation in small decisionmaking groups, in T. Parsons and R.F. Bales (eds) *Family, Socialization and Interaction Process*. Glencoe, IL: Free Press.

Bannister, D. and Fransella, F. (1986) *Inquiring Man: The Psychology of Personal Constructs*. London: Croom Helm.

Bardi, A. and Schwartz, S. (2003) Values and behaviour: strength and structure of relations, *Personality and Social Psychology Bulletin*, 29(10): 1207–20.

Bargdill, M.M. (2000) The study of a life of boredom, *Journal of Phenomenological Psychology*, 31(2): 188–219.

Bargh, J.A., Chaiken, S., Govender, R. and Pratto, F. (1992) The generality of the automatic attitude activation effect, *Journal of Personality and Social Psychology*, 62: 893–912.

Barthes, R. ([1957] 1967) *Elements of Semiology*. New York: Hill and Wang. (Originally published in French.)

Bartlett, F.C. (1932) *Remembering*. Cambridge: Cambridge University Press.

Bauman, Z. (2005) *Liquid Life*. Cambridge: Polity Press.

Baumeister, R. (2005) *The Cultural Animal: Human Nature, Meaning and Social Life*. New York: Oxford University Press.

Baumeister, R.F., Campbell, J.D., Krueger, J.I. and Vohs, K.D. (2003) Does high self-esteem cause better performance, interpersonal success, happiness or healthier lifestyles? *Psychological Science in the Public Interest*, 4(1): 1–44.

Baumeister, R.F. and Covington, M.V. (1985) Self-esteem, persuasion and retrospective distortion of initial attitudes, *Electronic Social Psychology*, 1(1): 1–22.

Beattie, G. (2004) *Visible Thought: The New Psychology of Body Language*. London: Routledge.

Beaulieu, C.J. (2004) Intercultural study of personal space: a case study, *Journal of Applied Social Psychology*, 34(4): 794–805.

Bem, D. (1972) Self-perception theory, in L. Berkowitz (ed.) *Advances in Experimental Social Psychology*, Vol. 6. New York: Academic Press.

Bengry-Howell, A. (2005) Performative motocar [sic] display: the cultural construction of young working class masculine identities. Unpublished PhD thesis, University of Birmingham.

Berger, P.L. and Luckmann, T. (1967) *The Social Construction of Reality*. Harmondsworth: Penguin.

Berri, N. (1989) as quoted in editorial, *Indianapolis Star*, 12 September.

Berry, J.W. (1967) Independence and conformity in subsistence level societies, *Journal of Personality and Social Psychology*, 7: 415–18.

Bilic, B. and Georgaca, E. (2007) Representations of 'mental illness' in Serbian newspapers: a critical discourse analysis. *Qualitative Research in Psychology*, 4: 167–86.

Billig, M. (1997) Rhetorical and discursive analysis: how families talk about the Royal Family, in N. Hayes (ed.) *Doing Qualitative Analysis in Psychology*. Hove: Psychology Press.

Billig, M., Condor, S., Edwards, D., Gane, M., Middleton, D. and Radley, A. (1998) *Ideological Dilemmas*. London: Sage.

Blackman, L. and Walkerdine, V. (2001) *Mass Hysteria: Critical Psychology and Media Studies*. Basingstoke: Palgrave.

Blaikie, N. (2010) *Designing Social Research: The Logic of Anticipation*, 2nd edn. Cambridge: Polity.

Blake, R.R. and Mouton, J.S. (1984) *Solving Costly Organisational Conflicts*. San Francisco, CA: Jossey-Bass.

Bohner, G. (2001) Attitudes, in M. Hewstone and W. Stroebe (eds) *Introduction to Social Psychology*, 3rd edn. Oxford: Blackwell.

Bohner, G., Maskowitz, G. and Chaiken, S. (1995) The interplay of heuristic and semantic processing of social information, *European Review of Social Psychology*, 6: 33–68.

Borgonovi, F. (2010) A life-cycle approach to the analysis of the relationship between social capital and health in Britain. *Social Science & Medicine*, 71(11): 1927–34.

Bornat, J. (2002) Doing life history research, in A. Jamieson and C. Victor (eds) *Researching Ageing and Later Life: The Practice of Social Gerontology*. Buckingham: Open University Press.

Bourdieu, P. (1972) *Outline of a Theory of Practice*. Cambridge: Cambridge University Press.

Bourdieu, P. (1993) *The Field of Cultural Production*. New York: Columbia University Press.

Bowlby, J. (1969) *Attachment and Loss*, Vol. 1: *Attachment*. London: Hogarth Press.

Bowlby, J. (1980) *Attachment and Loss*, Vol. 3: *Loss*. London: Hogarth Press.

Brah, A. (1996) *Cartographies of Diaspora*. London: Taylor and Francis.

Braun, V. and Clarke, V. (2006) Using thematic analysis in psychology, *Qualitative Research in Psychology*, 3: 77–101.

Breckler, S.J. (1984) Empirical validation of affect, behaviour and cognition as distinct components of attitude, *Journal of Personality and Social Psychology*, 47: 1191–205.

Breckler, S.J. and Wiggins, E.C. (1989) Affect versus evaluation in the structure of attitudes, *Journal of Experimental Social Psychology*, 25: 253–71.

Brickman, P. (1980) A social psychology of human concerns, in R. Gilmour and S. Duck (eds) *The Development of Social Psychology*. London: Academic Press.

Brinkmann, S. and Kvale, S. (2009) Ethics in qualitative psychological research, in C. Willig and W. Stainton Rogers (eds) *The Sage Handbook of Qualitative Research in Psychology*. London: Sage.

British Psychological Society (BPS) (2009) BPS ethical guidelines. http://www.bps.org.uk/the-society/code-of-conduct/code-of-conduct_home.cfm

Broadbent, D. (1958) *Perception and Communication*. New York: Pergamon.

Brown, P. and Fraser, C. (1979) Speech as a marker of situation, in K.R. Scherer and H. Giles (eds) *Social Markers in Speech*. Cambridge: Cambridge University Press.

Brown, R.J. (1995) *Prejudice: Its Social Psychology*. Oxford: Blackwell.

Brown, R.J. (2000) *Group Processes: Dynamics Within and Between Groups*, 2nd edn. Oxford: Blackwell.

Brown, R.J. (2001) Intergroup relations, in M. Hewstone and W. Stroebe (eds) *Introduction to Social Psychology*, 3rd edn. Oxford: Blackwell.

Brown, S.D. and Stenner, P. (2009) *Psychology Without Foundations*. London: Sage.

Brown, S.R. (1980) *Political Subjectivity: Applications of Q Methodology in Political Science*. New Haven, CT: Yale University Press.

Brownmiller, S. (1975) *Against Our Will: Men, Women and Rape*. New York: Simon and Schuster.

Bruner, J. (1957) On perceptual readiness, *Psychological Review*, 64: 123–52.

Bulhan, H.A. (1985) *Franz Fanon and the Psychology of Oppression*. New York and London: Plenum Press.

Burgoon, J.K., Buller, D.B. and Woodall, W.G. (1989) *Nonverbal Communication: The Unspoken Dialogue*. New York: Harper and Row.

Burman, E. (1999) Appealing and appalling children, *Psychoanalytic Studies*, 1(3): 285–9.

Burnstein, E. and Vinokur, A. (1977) Persuasive argumentation and social comparison as determinants of attitude polarization, *Journal of Experimental Social Psychology*, 13: 315–32.

Burr, V. (1995) *An Introduction to Social Constructionism*. London: Routledge.

Buss, D.M. (2005) *The Handbook of Evolutionary Pychology*. New York: Wiley.

Butler, J. (1993) *Bodies That Matter: On the Discursive Limits of 'Sex'*. New York: Routledge.

Butler, J. (1990) *Gender Trouble*. London: Routledge.

Butler, J. (2003) Critically queer, in P. du Gay, J. Evans and P. Redman (eds) *Identity: A Reader*. London: Sage.

Butt, T. and Langdridge, D. (2003) The construction of the self: the public reach into the private sphere, *Sociology*, 37(3): 477–94.

Cadinu, M., Maas, A., Rosabianca, A. and Keisner, J. (2005) Why do women underperform under stereotype threat? Evidence for the role of negative thinking. *Psychological Science*, 16(7): 572–8.

Cairns, K. (1993) Sexual entitlement and sexual accommodation: male and female responses to sexual coercion, *Canadian Journal of Human Sexuality*, 2: 203–14.

Campbell, C. and Jovchelovitch, S. (2000) Health/community and development: towards a social psychology of participation, *Journal of Community and Applied Social Psychology*, 10: 255–70.

Caprara, G.V., Schwartz, S.H., Cabaña, C., Vaccine, M. and Barbaranelli, C. (2006) Personality and politics: values, traits, and political choice, *Political Psychology*, 27(1): 1–28.

Cartwright, D. (1979) Contemporary social psychology in historical perspective, *Social Psychology Quarterly*, 42: 82–93.

Cattell, R.B. (1966) *The Scientific Analysis of Personality*. Chicago, IL: Aldine.

Chaiken, S. (1987) The heuristic model of persuasion, in M.P. Zanna, J.M. Olson and C.P. Herman (eds) *Social Influence: The Ontario Symposium*, Vol. 5. Hillsdale, NJ: Erlbaum.

Chalmers, A.F. (1999) *What Is This Thing Called Science?* 3rd edn. Buckingham: Open University Press.

Chamberlain, K. (2000) Methodolatry and qualitative health research, *Journal of Health Psychology*, 5(3): 285–96.

Chamberlain, M. (1999) Brothers and sisters, uncles and aunts: a literal perspective on Caribbean families, in E. Silva and C. Smart (eds) *The New Family?* London: Sage.

Chandra, S. (1973) The effects of group pressure in perception: a crosscultural conformity study, *International Journal of Psychology*, 8: 37–9.

Charmaz, K. and Henwood, K. (2009) Grounded theory, in C. Willig and W. Stainton Rogers (eds) *The Sage Handbook of Qualitative Research in Psychology*. London: Sage.

Chemers, M.M. (2001) Leadership effectiveness: an integrative review, in M.A. Hogg and R.S. Tindale (eds) *Blackwell Handbook of Social Psychology: Group Processes*. Oxford: Blackwell.

Cherlin, A.J. and Furstenberg, F.F. (1986) *The New American Grandparent: A Place in the Family, a Life Apart*. New York: Basic Books.

Cherry, F. (1983) Gender roles in sexual violence, in E.R. Allgeier and N.B. McCormick (eds) *Changing Boundaries: Gender Roles and Sexual Behaviour*. Palo Alto, CA: Mayfield.

Cherry, F. (1995) Kitty Genovese and culturally embedded theorizing, in F. Cherry *The Stubborn Particulars of Social Psychology: Essays on the Research Process*. London: Routledge.

Cherry, F. (2007) Kitty Genovese and culturally embedded theorizing, in D. Langdridge and S. Taylor (eds) *Critical Readings in Social Psychology*. Maidenhead: Open University Press.

Cherry, F. (2009) Social psychology and social change, in D. Fox, I. Prilleltensky and S. Austin (eds) *Critical Psychology: An Introduction*, 2nd edn. London: Sage.

Chiari, G. and Nuzzo, M.L. (1996) Psychological constructivisms: a metatheoretical differentiation, *Journal of Constructivist Psychology*, 9: 163–84.

Chiari, G. and Nuzzo, M.L. (2000) Hermeneutics and constructivist psychotherapy: the psycho-therapeutic process in a hermeneutic constructivist framework, in J.W. Scheer (ed.) *The Person in Society: Challenges to a Constructivist Theory*. Giessen: Psychosozial Verlag.

Chiari, G. and Nuzzo, M.L. (2004) Steering personal construct theory toward hermeneutic constructivism, in J.D. Raskin and S.K. Bridges (eds) *Studies in Meaning 2: Bridging the Personal and Social in Constructivist Psychology*. New York: Pace University Press.

Chinese Culture Connection (1987) Chinese values and the search for culture-free dimensions of culture, *Journal of Cross-Cultural Psychology*, 18: 143–64.

Chinn, S.E. (2010) Performative identities: from identity politics to queer theory, in M. Wetherell and C.T. Mohanty (eds) *The Sage Handbook of Identities*. London: Sage.

Chiou, W. (2007) Customers' attributional judgements towards complaint handling in airline service: a comfirmatory study based on attribution theory, *Psychological Reports*, 100(3): 1141–50.

Chomsky, N. (1957) *Syntactic Structures*. The Hague: Mouton.

Chrz, C., Čermák, I. and Plachá, J. (2006) Cancer, finitude and life configuration, in K. Milnes, C. Horrocks, N. Kelly, B. Roberts and D. Robinson (eds) *Narrative, Memory and Knowledge: Representations, Aesthetics and Contexts*. Huddersfield: University of Huddersfield Press.

Cialdini, R.B., Borden, R.J., Thorne, A., Walker, M.R., Freeman, S. and Sloan, L.R. (1976) Basking in reflected glory: three (football) field studies, *Journal of Personality and Social Psychology*, 34: 366–75.

Cinnirella, M. and Green, B. (2007) Does 'cyber-conformity' vary cross-culturally? Exploring the effect of culture and communication medium on social conformity, *Computers in Human Behavior*, 23: 2011–25.

Clark, M.S. and Grote, N.K. (2003) Close relationships, in T. Milton and M.J. Lerner (eds) *Handbook of Psychology: Personality and Social Psychology*, Vol. 5. New York: Wiley.

Clark-Carter, D. (2009) *Quantitative Psychological Research: The Complete Students Companion*. Hove: Psychology Press.

Clarke, V. and Peel, E. (eds) (2007) *Out in Psychology: Lesbian, Gay, Bisexual, Trans, and Queer Perspectives*. Chichester: Wiley.

Code of Ethics Review Group, NZ Psychological Society, NZ College of Clinical Psychologists and the NZ Psychologists Board (2002) http://www.psychology.org.nz/Code_of_Ethics

Coleman, J. (1988) Social capital in the creation of human capital, *American Journal of Sociology,* Supplement 94: 95–120.

Coles, P. (2003) *The Importance of Sibling Relationships in Psychoanalysis.* London: Karnac Books.

Colman, A.M. (1987) *Facts, Fallacies and Frauds in Psychology.* Winchester: Unwin Hyman.

Colman, A.M. and Gorman, L.P. (1982) Conservatism, dogmatism and authoritarianism in British Police Officers, *Sociology,* 16: 1–11.

Cooley, C.H. ([1902] 1922) *Human Nature and the Social Order,* revd edn. New York: Scribner's Press.

Copper, C., Mullen, B., Adrales, K., Asuncion, A., Gibbons, P., Goethals, G.R., Riordan, V., Schroeder, D., Sibicky, M., Trice, D., Worth, L. and Lippsitt, N. (1993) Bias in the media: the subtle effects of the newscaster's smile, in G. Comstock and F. Fischoff (eds) *Media Behaviour.* Newbury Park, CA: Sage.

Cosmides, L. (1989) The logic of social exchange: has natural selection shaped how humans reason? Studies with the Wason selection task, *Cognition,* 31: 187–276.

Cousins, S.D. (1989) Culture and self-perception in Japan and the United States, *Journal of Personality and Social Psychology,* 56: 124–31.

Crawford, M. (1995) *Talking Difference: On Gender and Language.* London: Sage.

Crocker, J. and Luhtanen, R. (1990) Collective self esteem and in-group bias, *Journal of Personality and Social Psychology,* 58: 60–7.

Croyle, R. and Cooper, J. (1983) Dissonance arousal: physiological evidence, *Journal of Personality and Social Psychology,* 45: 782–91.

Crusco, A.H. and Wetzel, C.G. (1984) The Midas touch: the effects of interpersonal touch on restaurant tipping, *Personality and Social Psychology Bulletin,* 10: 512–17.

Curt, B. (1994) *Textuality and Tectonics: Troubling Social and Psychological Science.* Buckingham: Open University Press.

Daly, M. (1978) *Gyn/Ecology: The Metaethics of Radical Feminism.* London: The Women's Press.

Darwin, C. (1872) *The Expression of Emotions in Man and Animals.* New York: Philosophical Library.

Davidson, J. (1984) Subsequent versions of invitations, offers, requests and proposals dealing with potential or actual rejection, in J.M. Atkinson and J. Heritage (eds) *Structures of Social Action: Studies in Conversational Analysis.* Cambridge: Cambridge University Press.

Day, K. and Keys, T. (2008) Starving in cyberspace: a discourse analysis of pro-eating disorder websites, *Journal of Gender Studies,* 17(1): 1–15.

Deal, M. (2007) Adversive disablism: subtle prejudice towards disabled people, *Disability & Society,* 22(1): 93–107.

Deardorff, J., Tschann, J.M. and Flores, E. (2008) Sexual values among Latino youth: measurement development using a culturally based approach, *Cultural Diversity and Ethnic Minority Psychology,* 14(2): 138–46.

Deaux, K. and Wrightsman, L.S. (1988) A study of normative and informational social influences upon individual judgement, *Journal of Abnormal and Social Psychology,* 51: 629–36.

DePaulo, B. (2006) *Singled Out: How Singles Are Stereotyped, Stigmatized, and Ignored, and Still Live Happily Ever After.* New York: St. Martin's Press.

Deutsch, M. (1973) *The Resolution of Conflict.* New Haven, CT: Yale University Press.

Deutsch, M. and Gerrard, H.B. (1955) A study of normative and informational social influences upon individual judgement, *Journal of Abnormal and Social Psychology,* 51: 629–36.

De Vries, N.K., De Dreu, C.K.W., Gordijn, E. and Schuurman, M. (1996) Majority and minority influence: a dual role interpretation, in W. Stroebe and M. Hewstone (eds) *European Review of Social Psychology*, Vol. 7. Chichester: Wiley.

Diab, L.N. (1970) A study of intragroup and intergroup relations among experimentally produced small groups, *Genetic Psychology Monographs*, 82: 49–82.

Dibiase, R. and Gunnoe, J. (2004) Gender and culture differences in touching behaviour, *Journal of Social Psychology*, 144(1): 49–62.

Di Giacoma, J.-P. (1980) Intergroup alliances and rejections within a protest movement: analysis of social representations, *European Journal of Social Psychology*, 10: 329–44.

Dion, K.K., Bersheid, E. and Walster, E. (1972) What is beautiful is good, *Journal of Personality and Social Psychology*, 24: 285–90.

Dixon, J. (2007) Prejudice, conflict and conflict reduction, in W. Hollway, H. Lucey and A. Phoenix (eds) *Social Psychology Matters*. Maidenhead: Open University Press.

Domenici, D.J. (2008) Implications of hermeneutic constructivism for personal construct theory: imaginally construing the nonhuman world, *Journal of Constructivist Psychology*, 21(1): 25–42.

Doms, M. (1983) The minority influence effect: an alternative approach, in W. Doise and S. Moscovici (eds) *Current Issues in European Social Psychology*, Vol. 1. Cambridge: Cambridge University Press.

Douglas, M. (1966) *Purity and Danger*. London: Routledge and Kegan Paul.

Dunant, S. (ed.) (1994) *The War of the Words: The Political Correctness Debate*. London: Virago.

Dunn, D.S. (2009) *Research Methods for Social Psychology*, Oxford: Blackwell/Wiley.

Durkheim, E. (1898) Representations individuelles et representations collectives. *Revue de Metaphysique et de morale*, 6: 273–302.

Dutton, D.G. and Aron, A.P. (1974) Some evidence for heightened sexual attraction under conditions of high anxiety, *Journal of Personality and Social Psychology*, 30: 510–17.

Eagly, A.H., Ashmore, R.D., Makhijani, M.G. and Longo, L.C. (1991) What is beautiful is good, but . . . : a meta-analytic review of research on the physical attractiveness stereotype, *Psychological Bulletin*, 110: 109–28.

Eagly, A.H. and Chaiken, S. (1984) Cognitive theories of persuasion, in L. Berkovitz (ed.) *Advances in Experimental Social Psychology*, Vol. 17. New York: Academic Press.

Eagly, A.H. and Chaiken, S. (1998) Attitude structure and function, in D.T. Gilbert, S.T. Fiske and G. Lindzey (eds) *The Handbook of Social Psychology*. New York: McGraw-Hill.

Eagly, A.H. and Wood, W. (1991) Explaining sex differences in social behaviour: a meta-analytic perspective, *Personality and Social Psychology Bulletin*, 17: 306–15.

Earley, P.C. (1989) Social loafing and collectivism: a comparison of the United States and the People's Republic of China, *Administrative Science Quarterly*, 34: 563–81.

Eatough, V. and Smith, J.A. (2009) Interpretive phenomenological analysis, in C. Willig and W. Stainton Rogers (eds) *The Sage Handbook of Qualitative Research in Psychology*. London: Sage.

Edwards, D., Ashmore, M. and Potter, J. (1993) Death and furniture: the rhetoric, theology and politics and theory of bottom line arguments against relativism. Mimeograph, Discourse and Rhetoric Group, Loughborough University.

Edwards, D. and Potter, J. (1992) *Discursive Psychology*. London: Sage.

Edwards, D. and Potter, J. (1993) Language and causation: a discursive action model of description and attribution, *Psychological Review*, 100(1): 23–41.

Edwards, R., Hadfield, L., Lucey, L. and M. Mauthner (2006) *Sisters and Brothers: Sibling Identities and Relationships*. London: Routledge.

Ekman, P. (1973) Cross-cultural studies of facial expression, in P. Ekman (ed.) *Darwin and Facial Expression*. New York: Academic Press.

Ekman, P. (2003) *Emotions Revealed*. New York: Times Books.

Ekman, P. and Friesen, W.V. (1974) Detecting deception from the body or the face, *Journal of Personality and Social Psychology*, 29: 188–98.

Ellis, W.D. (1938) *A Source Book of Gestalt Psychology*. New York: Harcourt Brace.

Emerson, P. and Frosh, S. (2004) *Critical Narrative Analysis in Psychology: A Guide to Practice*. London: Palgrave Macmillan.

Emler, N. and Hopkins, N. (1990) Reputation, social identity and the self, in D. Abrams and M. Hogg (eds) *Social Identity Theory: Constructive and Critical Advances*. London: Harvester Wheatsheaf.

Emler, N. and Reicher, S. (1995) *Adolescence and Delinquency: The Collective Management of Reputation*. Oxford: Blackwell.

Erikson, E. (1956) The problem of ego identity, *Journal of the American Psychoanalytic Association*, 4: 56–121.

Evans, G.W., Lepore, S.J. and Allen, K.M. (2000) Cross-cultural differences in tolerance for crowding: fact or fiction? *Journal of Personality and Social Psychology*, 79(2): 204–10.

Exline, R.V., Ellyson, S.L. and Long, B. (1975) Visual behaviour as an aspect of power role relationships, in P. Pliner, L. Krames and T. Alloway (eds) *Nonverbal Communication of Aggression*, Vol. 2. New York: Plenum.

Eysenck, H.J. (1967) *The Biological Basis of Personality*. Springfield, IL: C.C. Thomas.

Eysenck, H.J. (1971) *Race, Intelligence and Education*. London: Temple Smith.

Fanon, F. ([1952] 1986) *Black Skin White Masks*. London: Pluto Press.

Fanon, F. ([1963] 1990) *The Wretched of the Earth*. Harmondsworth: Penguin.

Farr, R. and Moscovici, S. (1984) *Social Representations*. Cambridge: Cambridge University Press.

Farr, R.M. (1996) *The Roots of Modern Social Psychology*. Oxford: Blackwell.

Fazio, R.H. and Zanna, M.P. (1981) Direct experience and attitude-behaviour consistency, in L. Berkowitz (ed.) *Advances in Experimental Social Psychology*, Vol. 14. San Diego, CA: Academic Press.

Feather, N.T. (1970) Educational choice and student attitudes in relation to terminal and instrumental values, *Australian Journal of Psychology*, 22: 127–44.

Feather, N.T. (1971) Value differences in relation to ethnocentrism, intolerance of ambiguity and dogmatism, *Personality*, 2: 349–66.

Feather, N.T. (1982) *Expectations and Actions: Expectancy-Value Models in Psychology*. Hillsdale, NJ: Erlbaum.

Feather, N.T. (1991) Human values, global self-esteem and belief in a just world, *Journal of Personality*, 59: 83–106.

Feather, N.T. and McKee, I.R. (2008) Values and prejudice: predictors of attitudes towards Australian Aborigines, *Australian Journal of Psychology*, 60(2): 80–90.

Fenton-O'Creevy, M. (2001) *Leadership in the New Organisation*, Block 2.

Festinger, L. (1954) A theory of social comparison processes, *Human Relations*, 7: 117–40.

Festinger, L. (1957) *A Theory of Cognitive Dissonance*. Stanford, CA: Stanford University Press.

Festinger, L. (1980) Looking backward, in L. Festinger (ed.) *Retrospections on Social Psychology*, Oxford: Oxford University Press.

Festinger, L. and Carlsmith, J.M. (1959) Cognitive consequences of forced compliance, *Journal of Abnormal and Social Psychology*, 58: 203–10.

Fiedler, K. and Bless, H. (2001) Social cognition, in M. Hewstone and W. Stroebe (eds) *Introduction to Social Psychology*, 3rd edn. Oxford: Blackwell.

Fincham, F. and Hewstone, M. (2001) Attribution theory and research: from basic to applied, in M. Hewstone and W. Stroebe (eds) *Introduction to Social Psychology*, 3rd edn. Oxford: Blackwell.

Fincham, F.D. and Bradbury, T.N. (1988) The impact of attributions in marriage: an experimental analysis, *Journal of Social and Clinical Psychology*, 9: 31–42.

Fishbein, M. (1967) A consideration of beliefs and their role in attitude measurement, in M. Fishbein (ed.) *Readings in Attitude Theory and Measurement*. New York: Wiley.

Fishbein, M. and Ajzen, I. (1975) *Belief, Attitude, Intention and Behaviour: An Introduction to Theory and Research*. Reading, MA: Addison-Wesley.

Fisher, J. (1951) The memory process and certain psychosocial attitudes, with special reference to the Law of Praganz, *Journal of Personality*, 19: 406–20.

Fiske, S.T. (1980) Attention and weight in person perception: the impact of negative and extreme behaviour, *Journal of Personality and Social Psychology*, 38(6): 899–906.

Fiske, S.T. and Taylor, S.E. (1991) *Social Cognition*, 2nd edn. New York: McGraw-Hill.

Flick, U. (ed.) (1998) *The Psychology of the Social*. Cambridge: Cambridge University Press.

Fornäs, J. (1995) *Cultural Theory and Late Modernity*. London: Sage.

Foster, D. (1993) On racism: virulent mythologies and fragile threads, in L.J. Nicholas (ed.) *Psychology and Oppression: Critiques and Proposals*. Braamfontein: Skottaville.

Fösterling, F. (1988) *Attribution Theory in Clinical Psychology*. Chichester: Wiley.

Foucault, M. ([1975] 1977) *Discipline and Punish*. Harmondsworth: Penguin.

Fox, D., Prilleltensky, I. and Austin, S. (eds) (2009) *Critical Psychology: An Introduction*, 2nd edn. London: Sage.

Frager, R. (1970) Conformity and anti-conformity in Japan, *Journal of Personality and Social Psychology*, 15: 203–10.

Freire, P. (1972) *Pedagogy of the Oppressed*. Harmondsworth: Penguin Educational.

Freire, P. (1995) *Pedagogy of Hope: Reliving Pedagogy of the Oppressed*. New York: Continuum.

Freitas, M.F.Q. (2010) Voices from the south: the construction of Brazilian community social psychology, *Journal of Community and Applied Social Psychology*, 10: 318–26.

Frentz, T.S. (2009) Split selves and situated knowledge: the trickster goes titanium, *Qualitative Inquiry*, 15: 820.

Freud, S. (1905) *Three Contributions to the Theory of Sex*. New York: Dutton.

Freud, S. (1917) *Introductory Lectures on Psychoanalysis*. Harmondsworth: Penguin.

Freud, S. (1922) Certain neurotic mechanisms in jealousy, paranoia, and homosexuality, in *Collected Papers*, Vol. 2. London: Hogarth.

Frick, R.W. (1985) Communicating emotions: the role of prosodic features, *Psychological Bulletin*, 97: 412–29.

Frieze, I.H. (1981) Children's attributions for success and failure, in S.S. Brehm, S.M. Kassin and F.X. Gibbons (eds) *Developmental Social Psychology*. Oxford: Oxford University Press.

Frosh, S. (2010) Psychoanalytic perspectives on identity: from ego to ethics, in M. Wetherell and C.T. Mohanty (eds) *The Sage Handbook of Identities*. London: Sage.

Frosh, S. and Young, L.S. (2009) Psychoanalytic approaches to qualitative psychology, in C. Willig and W. Stainton Rogers (eds) *The Sage Handbook of Qualitative Research in Psychology*. London: Sage.

Gabrenya, W.K., Wang, Y.E. and Latané, B. (1985) Social loafing on an optimising task: cross-cultural differences among Chinese and Americans, *Journal of Cross-Cultural Psychology*, 16: 223–42.

Gadamer, H.G. (1975) *Truth and Method*. New York: Continuum.

Gaertner, S.L. and Dovido, J.F. (2000) *Reducing Intergroup Bias: The Common Ingroup Identity Model*. Hove: Psychology Press.

Gaertner, S.L. and McLaughlin, J.P. (1983) Racial stereotypes: associations and ascriptions of positive and negative characteristics, *Social Psychology Quarterly*, 46: 23–30.

Gallup, G.G. and Frederick, D.A. (2010) The science of sex appeal: an evolutionary perspective, *Review of General Psychology*, 14(3): 240–50.

Galzio, M. and Hendrick, C. (1972) Effect of music accompaniment on attitudes, *Journal of Applied Social Psychology*, 2: 350–9.

Game, A. (1991) *Undoing the Social: Towards a Deconstructive Sociology*. Buckingham: Open University Press.

Garfinkel, H. (1967) *Studies in Ethnomethodology*. Englewood Cliffs, NJ: Prentice Hall.

Geertz, C. (1975) On the nature of anthropological understanding. *American Scientist*, 63: 47–53.

Gergen, K. (1973) Social psychology as history, *Journal of Personality and Social Psychology*, 26: 309–20.

Gergen, K.J. and Gergen, M.M. (1981) *Social Psychology*. New York: Harcourt, Brace Jovanovich.

Gergen, K.J. and Gergen, M.M. (eds) (1984) *Historical Social Pyschology*. Hillsdale, NJ: Erlbaum.

Gigone, D. and Hastie, R. (1993) The common knowledge effect: information sharing and group judgement, *Journal of Personality and Social Psychology*, 65: 959–74.

Gilbert, D.T., Pelham, B.W. and Krull, D.S. (1988) On cognitive busyness: when person perceivers meet persons perceived, *Journal of Personality and Social Psychology*, 54: 733–40.

Giles, D.C., Pietrzykowski, S. and Clark, K.E. (2007) The psychological meaning of personal record collections and the impact of changing technological forms, *Journal of Economic Psychology*, 28: 429–43.

Giles, H., Bourhis, R.Y. and Taylor, D.M. (1977) Towards a theory of language in ethnic group relations, in H. Giles (ed.) *Language, Ethnicity and Intergroup Relations*. London: Academic Press.

Giles, H. and Coupland, N. (1991) *Language: Contexts and Consequences*. Buckingham: Open University Press.

Giles, H. and Johnson, P. (1981) The role of language in ethnic group relations, in J.C. Turner and H. Giles (eds), *Intergroup Behaviour*. Oxford: Blackwell.

Giorgi, A. (ed.) (1985) *Phenomenology and Psychological Research*. Pittsburgh, PA: Duquesne University Press.

Giorgi, A.P. and Giorgi, B. (2009) Phenomenological psychology, in C. Willig and W. Stainton Rogers (eds) *The Sage Handbook of Qualitative Research in Psychology*. London: Sage.

Glaser, B.G. and Strauss, A.L. (1967) *The Discovery of Grounded Theory: Strategies for Qualitative Research*. Chicago, IL: Aldine.

Glick, P. and Fiske, S.T. (1996) The ambivalent sexism inventory: differentiating benevolent and hostile sexism, *Journal of Personality and Social Psychology*, 70: 491–512.

Glick, P. and Fiske, S.T. (2001) An ambivalent alliance: hostile and benevolent sexism as complementary justifications for gender inequality, *American Psychologist*, 56: 109–18.

Goffman, E. (1955) On face-work: an analysis of ritual elements in social interaction, *Psychiatry*, 18: 213–31.

Goffman, E. (1959) *The Presentation of Self in Everyday Life*. New York: Doubleday.

Goffman, E. (1963) *Behavior in Public Places*. New York: Free Press.

Goffman, E. (1967) *Interaction Ritual: Essays on Face-to-face Behavior*. Garden City, NY: Anchor.

Goldstein, D.M. and Goldstein, S.E. (2005) Q methodology study of a person in individual therapy, *Clinical Case Studies*, 4(1): 40–56.

Gonzalez-Crussi, M. (1988) *On the Nature of Things Erotic*. London: Picador.

Goodley, G. and Parker, I. (2000) Critical psychology and action research, *Annual Review of Critical Psychology*, 2: 3–18.

Gough, B. and McFadden, M. (2001) *Critical Social Psychology: An Introduction*. Basingstoke: Palgrave.

Granada, H. (1991) Intervention of community social psychology: the case of Colombia, *Applied Psychology: An International Review*, 40(2): 165–80.

Graumann, C.F. (2001) Introducing social psychology historically, in M. Hewstone and W. Stroebe (eds) *Introduction to Social Psychology*, 3rd edn. Oxford: Blackwell.

Gray, J. (1992) *Men Are from Mars, Women Are from Venus*. New York: HarperCollins.

Greenwald, A.G. (1968) Cognitive learning, cognitive response to persuasion, and attitude change, in A. Greenwald, T. Brock and T. Ostrom (eds) *Psychological Foundations of Attitudes*. New York: Academic Press.

Grimshaw, A.D. (1981) Talk and social control, in M. Rosenburg and R.H. Turner (eds) *Social Psychology: Sociological Perspectives*. New York: Basic Books.

Grujic, L. and Libby, W.L. Jr (1978) Nonverbal aspects of verbal behaviour in French Canadian French–English bilinguals. Paper presented at the meeting of the American Psychological Association, Toronto, September.

Gur, R.E., Kohler, C.G., Ragland, J.D., Siegel, S.J., Lesko, K., Bilker, W.B. and Gur, R.C. (2006) Flat affect in schizophrenia: relation to emotion processing and neurocognitive measures, *Schizophrenia Bulletin*, 32(2): 279–87.

Guzzo, R.A. and Dickenson, M.W. (1996) Teams in organizations: recent research on performance and effectiveness, *Annual Review of Psychology*, 47: 307–38.

Haddock, G. and Maio, G.R. (2001) Attitude: content, structure and functions, in M. Hewstone, W. Stroebe and K. Jonas (eds) *Introduction to Social Psychology: A European Perspective*, 4th edn. Oxford: Blackwell.

Haire, M. and Grune, W.E. (1950) Perceptual defenses: processes protecting an organised perception of another personality, *Human Relations*, 3: 403–12.

Hall, E.T. (1966) *The Silent Language*. New York: Doubleday.

Hall, J.A. and Veccia, E.M. (1990) More 'touching' observations: New insights on men, women and interpersonal touch, *Journal of Personality and Social Psychology*, 59(6): 1155–62.

Hamaguchi, T. (1985) Prospects for self-reliance and indigenisation in automobile industry: case of Maruti-Suzuki project, *Economic and Political Weekly*, 20(1): 115–22.

Hamilton, D.L. and Zanna, M.P. (1972) Differential weighting of favourable and unfavourable attributes in impressions of personality, *Journal of Experimental Research into Personality*, 6: 204–12.

Hamilton, D.L. and Zanna, M.P. (1974) Context effects in impression formation: changes in connative meaning, *Journal of Personality and Social Psychology*, 29: 649–54.

Han, S. and Shavitt, S. (1993) Persuasion and culture: advertising appeals in individualistic and collectivistic societies. Unpublished manuscript, Champagne, IL, University of Illinois at Urbana.

Haney, C., Banks, W.C. and Zimbardo, P.G. (1973) Interpersonal dynamics in a simulated prison, *International Journal of Criminology and Penology*, 1: 69–97.

Hanlin, C.E., Bess, K., Conway, P., Ecans, S.D., McCown, D., Prilleltensky, I. and Perkins, D.D. (2009) Community psychology, in C. Willig and W. Stainton Rogers (eds) *The Sage Handbook of Qualitative Research in Psychology*. London: Sage.

Hanson-Easey, S. and Augoustinos, M. (2010) Out of Africa: accounting for refugee policy and the language of causal attribution 2010, *Discourse and Society*, 21: 295–323.

Haraway, D.J. (1984) Primatology is politics by other means, in R. Bleier (ed.) *Feminist Approaches to Science*. London: Pergamon.

Harmon-Jones, E., Brehm, J.W., Greenberg, J., Simon, L. and Nelson, D.E. (1996) Evidence that the production of aversive consequences is not necessary to create cognitive dissonance, *Journal of Personality and Social Psychology*, 70: 5–16.

Harré, R. (1977) The ethogenic approach: theory and practice, in L. Berkowitz (ed.) *Advances in Experimental Social Psychology*, Vol. 10. New York: Academic Press.

Harré, R. (1979) *Social Being: A Theory for Social Psychology*. Oxford: Blackwell.

Harré, R. (1997) Social life as rule-governed patterns of joint action, in C. McGarty and S.A. Haslam (eds) *The Message of Social Psychology: Perspectives on Mind in Society*. Oxford: Blackwell.

Harré, R. and Secord, P.F. (1972) *The Explanation of Social Behaviour*. Oxford: Blackwell.

Hauck, P. (1981) *Jealousy: Why it Happens and How to Overcome It*. Philadelphia, PA: Westminster.

Hayes, N. (1993) *Principles of Social Psychology*. Hove: Psychology Press.

Healey, K.M., Pinkham, A.E., Richard, J.A. and Kohleret, C.G. (2004) Do we recognize facial expressions of emotions from persons with schizophrenia? *Schizophrenia Research*. doi:10.1016/j.schres.2010.04.004.

Heatherton, T.F. and Vohs, K.D. (2000) Interpersonal evaluation following threats to the self: roles of self-esteem, *Journal of Personality and Social Psychology*, 78(4): 725–36.

Heidegger, M. ([1928] 1962) *Being and Time*. Oxford: Blackwell.

Heidegger, M. (1971) *Poetry, Language, Thought*. New York: Harper and Row.

Heider, F. (1946) Attitudes and cognitive organisation, *Journal of Psychology*, 21: 107–12.

Heider, F. (1953) *The Psychology of Interpersonal Relations*. New York: Wiley.

Hendrick, C. and Hendrick, S. (1986) A theory and method of love, *Journal of Personality & Social Psychology*, 50(2): 392–402.

Henley, N.M. (1977) *Body Politics: Power, Sex and Nonverbal Communication*. Englewood Cliffs, NJ: Prentice Hall.

Henriques, J., Hollway, W., Urwin, C., Venn, C. and Walkerdine, V. (1984) *Changing the Subject: Psychology, Social Regulation and Subjectivity*. London: Methuen.

Henwood, K., Griffin, C. and Phoenix, A. (eds) (1998) *Standpoints and Differences: Essays in the Practice of Feminist Psychology*. London: Sage.

Hepburn, A. (2003) *An Introduction to Critical Social Psychology*. London: Sage.

Heritage, J. (1984) *Garfinkel and Ethnomethodology*. Cambridge: Polity.

Herrenstein, R.J. and Murray, C. (1994) *The Bell Curve: Intelligence and Class Structure in American Life*. New York: Free Press.

Herzlich, C. (1973) *Health and Illness*. London: Academic Press.

Herzog, T.A. (2005) When popularity outstrips the evidence: comment on West, *Addiction*, 100: 140–1.

Hewstone, M. (1983) Attribution theory and common-sense explanations: an introductory overview, in M. Hewstone (ed.) *Attribution Theory: Social and Functional Extensions*. Oxford: Blackwell.

Hewstone, M., Stroebe, W. and Jonas, K. (2007) *Introduction to Social Psychology: A European Perspective*, 4th edn. Oxford: Blackwell.

Hildum, D.C. and Brown, R.V. (1956) Verbal reinforcement and interviewer bias, *Journal of Abnormal Psychology*, 53(4): 108–11.

Hiles, D. and Čermák, I. (2009) Narrative psychology, in C. Willig and W. Stainton Rogers (eds) *The Sage Handbook of Qualitative Research in Psychology*. London: Sage.

Hilgard, E.R. (1953) *Introduction to Psychology*. London: Methuen.

Hilton, D.J. (1990) Conversational processes and causal attribution, *Psychological Bulletin*, 107: 65–81.

Hodge, R. and Kress, G. (1988) *Social Semiotics*. Cambridge: Polity.

Hofstede, G. (1980) *Culture's Consequences: International Differences in Work-related Values*. Beverly Hills, CA: Sage.

Hofstede, G. (1983) Dimensions of national cultures in fifty countries and three regions, in J. Deregowski, S. Dzuirawiec and R. Annis (eds) *Explications in Cross-Cultural Psychology*. Lisse: Swets and Zeitlinger.

Hogan, T. and Kaiser, R. (2006) What we know about leadership, *Review of General Psychology*, 9: 169–80.

Hogg, M.A., Turner, J.C. and Davidson, B. (1990) Polarised norms and social frames of reference: a test of the self-categorisation theory of group polarisation, *Basic and Applied Social Psychology*, 11: 77–100.

Hogg, M.A. and Vaughan, G.M. (1998) *Social Psychology*, 2nd edn. Oxford: Oxford University Press.

Hogg, M.A. and Vaughan, G.M. (2008) *Social Psychology*, 5th edn. Hemel Hempstead: Prentice Hall.

Hollander, E.P. (1971) *Principles and Methods of Social Psychology*, 2nd edn. Oxford: Oxford University Press.

Hollander, E.P. (1976) *Principles and Methods of Social Psychology*, 3rd edn. Oxford: Oxford University Press.

Hollway, W. (1989) *Subjectivity and Method in Psychology: Gender, Meaning and Science*. London: Sage.

Hollway, W. (2007) *Social Psychology Matters*. Maidenhead: Open University Press.

Hollway, W. and Jefferson, T. (2005) Panic and perjury: a psychosocial exploration of agency. *British Journal of Social Psychology*, 44: 147–63.

Hollway, W., Lucey, H. and Phoenix, A. (2007) *Social Psychology Matters*. Maidenhead: Open University Press.

Hook, D. (2004) Fanon and the psychoanalysis of racism, in D. Hook, A. Collins, P. Kiguwa and N. Mkhize (eds) *Critical Psychology*. Cape Town: University of Cape Town, Press.

Hook, D., Collins, A., Kiguwa, P. and Mkhize, N. (eds) (2004) *Critical Psychology*. Cape Town: University of Cape Town Press.

Hostetler, A.J. (2009) Single by choice? Assessing and understanding voluntary singlehood among mature gay men, *Journal of Homosexuality*, 56(4): 499–531.

Hovland, C.I., Janis, I.L. and Kelley, H.H. (1953) *Communication and Persuasion*. New Haven, CT: Yale University Press.

Hovland, C.I. and Weiss, W. (1951) The influence of source credibility on communication effectiveness, *Public Opinion Quarterly*, 15: 635–50.

Hunter, J.A., Stringer, M. and Watson, R.P. (1991) Intergroup violence and intergroup attributions, *British Journal of Psychology*, 30: 261–6.

Husserl, E. ([1900] 1970) *Logical Investigations*. Trans. J.N. Findlay. New York; Humanities Press.

Ibáñez, T. and Íñiguez, L. (eds) (1997) *Critical Social Psychology*. London: Sage.

Igarashi, Y. (2006) Role of critical psychology in Japan: protest against positivistic psychology and search for new knowledge of the mind, *Annual Review of Critical Psychology*, 5: 156–66. www.discourseunit.com/arcp/5.

Ingham, R. (1993) Old bodies in older clothes, *Health Psychology Update*, 14: 31–6.

Inglehart, R. (2005) The worldviews of Islamic publics in global perspective, in M. Moaddel (ed.) *Worldviews of Islamic Republics*. New York: Palgrave.

Inglehart, R., Foa, R., Peterson, C. and Welzel, C. (2008) Development, freedom, and rising happiness: a global perspective (1981–2007), *Perspectives on Psychological Science*, 3(4): 264–85.

Insko, C.A. (1981) Balance theory and phenomenology, in R. Petty, T. Ostrom and T. Brock (eds) *Cognitive Responses and Persuasion*. Hillsdale, NJ: Erlbaum.

Insko, C.A., Dardis, G.H., Hoyle, R.H., Scholoper, J. and Graets, K.A. (1990) Individual-group discontinuity as a function of fear and greed. *Journal of Personality and Social Psychology*, 58: 68–79.

Insko, C.A. and Schopler, J. (1967) Triadic consistency: a statement of affective-cognitive-conative consistency, *Psychological Review*, 74: 361–76.

Insko, C.A. and Schopler, J. (1998) Differential distrust of groups and individuals, in C. Sedikedes, J. Schopler and C. Insko (eds) *Intergroup Cognition and Intergroup Behaviour*. Mahwah, NJ: Erlbaum.

Isaacs, S. (1928) *An Introduction to Social Psychology*. London: Methuen. (Published under the name of Susan Brierley.)

Isenberg, D.J. (1986) Group polarisation: a critical review, *Journal of Personality and Social Psychology*, 50: 1141–51.

Jaensch, E.R. (1939) Der Hünerhof als Forschungs- und Aufklärungsmittel in menschlichen Rassenfragen, *Zeitschrift für Tierpsychologie*, 2: 223–58.

James, W. (1890) *The Principles of Psychology*, Vol. 1. New York: Holt.

James, W. (1907) *Psychology*. London: Macmillan.

Janis, I. (1982) *Groupthink*, 2nd edn. Boston, MA: Houghton Mifflin.

Janis, I.L. (1954) Personality correlates of susceptibility to persuasion, *Journal of Personality*, 22: 504–18.

Janoff-Bulman, R. and Frieze, I.H. (1987) The role of gender in reactions to gender victimization, in R.C. Barnett, L. Beiner and G.K. Baruch (eds) *Gender and Stress*. New York: Free Press.

Jellison, J.M. and Davis, D. (1973) Relationships between perceived ability and attitude extremity, *Journal of Personality and Social Psychology*, 27: 430–6.

Jensen, A.R. (1969) How much can we boost IQ and scholastic achievement? *Harvard Educational Review*, 39: 1–123.

Joas, H. (1985) *G.H. Mead: A Contemporary Re-examination of His Thought*. Cambridge: Polity.

Jodolet, D. (2008) Le Mouvement de Retour vers le Sujet et l'approche des Représentations Sociales. *Connexions*, 89: 25–46.

Johnson, R.W., Kelly, R.J. and LeBlanc, B.A. (1995) Motivational basis of dissonance: aversive consequences or inconsistency, *Personality and Social Psychology Bulletin*, 21: 850–5.

Jones, E.E. and Davis, K.E. (1965) A theory of correspondent inferences: from acts to dispositions, in L. Berkovitz (ed.) *Advances in Experimental Social Psychology*, Vol. 2. New York: Academic Press.

Jones, E.E., Davis, K.E. and Gergen, K. (1961) Role playing variations and their informational value for person perception, *Journal of Abnormal and Social Psychology*, 63: 302–10.

Jones, E.E. and Goethals, G.R. (1972) Order effects in impression formation: attribution, context and the nature of the entity, in E.E. Jones, D.E. Kanouse, H.H. Kelley, R.E. Nisbett, S. Valins and B. Weiner (eds) *Attribution: Perceiving the Causes of Behaviour*. Morristown, NJ: General Learning Press.

Jones, S., Guy, A. and Omrod, J.A. (2003) A Q-methodological study of hearing voices: a preliminary exploration of voice hearers' understanding of their experiences, *Psychology and Psychotherapy: Theory, Research and Practice*, 76: 189–209.

Jordan, N. (1953) Behavioural forces that are a function of attitudes and cognitive organisation, *Human Relations*, 6: 273–87.

Jourard, S.M. (1966) An exploratory study of body accessibility, *British Journal of Social and Clinical Psychology*, 5: 221–31.

Jovchelovitch, S. (2002) Social representations and narrative: stories of public life in Brazil, in J. László and W. Stainton Rogers (eds) *Narrative Approaches in Social Psychology*. Budapest: New Mandate.

Judd, C.M. and Kulik, J.A. (1980) Schematic effects of social attitudes on information processing and recall, *Journal of Personality and Social Psychology*, 38: 569–78.

Judge, T.A., Bono, J.E., Iles, R. and Gerhardt, M.W. (2002) Personality and leadership: a qualitative and quantitative review, *Journal of Applied Psychology*, 87: 765–80.

Kaniasty, K. and Norris, F.H. (1999) The experience of disaster – individuals and communities sharing disaster, in R. Gist and B. Lubin (eds) *Responses to Disaster*. Ann Arbor, MI: Braun-Brumfield.

Katz, D. (1960) The functional approach to the study of attitudes, *Public Opinion Quarterly*, 24: 163–204.

Kawachi, I., Subramanian, S.V. and Kim, D. (2008) *Social Capital and Health*. New York: Springer.

Kelley, H.H. (1952) Two functions of reference groups, in G.E. Swanson, T.M. Newcomb and E.L. Hartley (eds) *Readings in Social Psychology*. New York: Holt, Rinehart and Winston.

Kelley, H.H. (1967) Attribution theory in social psychology, in D. Levine (ed.) *Nebraska Symposium on Motivation*, Vol. 15. Lincoln, NB: University of Nebraska Press.

Kelly, C. and Breinlinger, S. (1995) Attitudes, intentions and behavior: a study of women's participation in collective action, *Journal of Applied Social Psychology*, 25: 1430–45.

Kelly, G.A. (1966) A brief introduction to personal construct theory, in D. Bannister (ed.) *Perspectives in Personal Construct Theory*. London: Academic Press.

Kiesler, C.A. and Kiesler, S.B. (1969) *Conformity*. Reading, MA: Addison-Wesley.

Kimhi, S. and Shamai, M. (2004) Community resilience and the impact of stress: adult response to Israel's withdrawal from Lebanon, *Journal of Community Psychology*, 32(4): 439–51.

King, N. (1998) Template analysis, in C. Cassell and G. Symon (eds) *Qualitative Methods and Analysis in Organizational Research*. London: Sage.

King, N., Thomas, K., Bell, D. and Bowes, N. (2002) *Evaluation of the Calderdale and Kirklees Out of Hours Protocol for Palliative Care: Final Report*. Huddersfield: Primary Care Research Group, School of Human and Health Sciences, University of Huddersfield.

Kitzinger, C. and Frith, H. (1999) Just say no? The use of conversational analysis in developing a feminist perspective on sexual refusal, *Discourse and Society*, 10(3): 293–316.

Kleinke, C.L. (1986) Gaze and eye contact: a research review, *Psychological Bulletin*, 100: 78–100.

Knapp, M.L., Hart, R.P. and Dennis, H.S. (1974) An exploration of deception as a communication construct, *Human Communication Research*, 1: 15–29.

Kondo, D. (1990) *Crafting Selves: Power, Gender and Discourses of Identity in a Japanese Workplace*. Chicago, IL: University of Chicago Press.

Kraut, R.E. and Poe, D. (1980) Behavioural roots of person perceptions: the deception judgements of customs officers and laymen, *Journal of Personality and Social Psychology*, 39: 748–98.

Kreifelts, B., Ethofer, T., Huberle, E., Grodd, W. and Wildgruber, D. (2010) Association of trait emotional intelligence and individual fMRI-activation patterns during the perception of social signals from voice and face, *Human Brain Mapping*, 31: 979–91.

Kristeva, J. ([1974] 1984) *Revolution in Poetic Language*. Trans. M. Waller. New York: Columbia University Press.

Kuhn, T.S. (1970) *The Structure of Scientific Revolutions*, Vol. 2, 2nd edn. Chicago, IL: University of Chicago Press.

Lacan, J. (1966) *Écrits*. Paris: Seuil.

Lacan, J. (1977) *Ecrits: A Selection*. Trans. A. Sheridan. London: Tavistock.

LaFrance, M. and Mayo, C. (1976) Racial differences in gaze behaviour during conversations: two systematic observational studies, *Journal of Personality and Social Psychology*, 33: 547–52.

Lakoff, R. (1975) *Language and Woman's Place*. New York: Harper and Row.

Lal, J. (1999) Situating locations: the politics of self, identity and 'Other' in living and writing the text, in S. Hess-Beiber, C. Gilmartin and R. Lyndberg (eds) *Feminist Approaches to Theory and Methodology: An Interdisciplinary Reader*. Oxford: Oxford University Press.

Lalljee, M. (2000) The interpreting self: a social constructionist perspective, in R. Stevens (ed.) *Understanding the Self*. London: Sage.

Lambert, W.E., Hodgson, R.C., Gardner, R.C. and Fillenbaum, S. (1960) Evaluation reactions to spoken language, *Journal of Abnormal and Social Psychology*, 60: 44–51.

Lamm, H. and Myers, D.G. (1978) Group induced polarization of attitudes and behaviour, in L. Berkowitz (ed.) *Advances in Experimental Social Psychology*, Vol. 11. New York: Academic Press.

Langdridge, D. (2007) *Phenomenological Psychology: Theory, Research and Method*. Harlow: Pearson.

Langdridge, D. and Taylor, S. (2007) *Critical Readings in Social Psychology*. Maidenhead: Open University Press.

Langer, E.J. (1978) Rethinking the role of thought in social interaction, in J.H. Harvey, W.I. Ikes and R.F. Kidd (eds) *New Directions in Attribution Research II*. Hillsdale, NJ: Erlbaum.

Langer, E.J., Blank, A. and Chanowitz, B. (1978) The mindlessness of ostensibly thoughtful interaction: the role of 'placebic' information in interpersonal interaction, *Journal of Personality and Social Psychology*, 36: 635–42.

LaPiere, R.T. (1934) Attitudes and actions, *Social Forces*, 13: 230–7.

Latané, B. (1997) Dynamic social impact: the societal consequences of human interaction, in C. McGarty and S. Alexander (eds) *The Message of Social Psychology: Perspectives on Mind in Society*. Oxford: Blackwell.

Latané, B. and Darley, J.M. (1968) Group inhibition of bystander intervention in emergencies: diffusion of responsibility, *Journal of Personality and Social Psychology*, 8(4): 377–83.

Latané, B. and Darley, J.M. (1976) Help in crisis: bystander response to an emergency, in J.W. Thibout and J.T. Spence (eds) *Contemporary Topics in Social Psychology*. Morristown, NJ: General Learning Press.

Latané, B., Williams, K.D. and Harkins, S.G. (1979) Many hands make light work: the causes and consequences of social loafing. *Journal of Personality and Social Psychology*, 37: 822–32.

Latané, B. and Wolf, S. (1981) The social impact of majorities and minorities, *Psychological Review*, 88: 438–53.

Lavie-Ajayi, M. and Joffe, H. (2009) Social representations of female orgasm, *Journal of Health Psychology*, 14: 98–107.

Lazarus, R.S. (1991) *Emotion and Adaptation*. Oxford: Oxford University Press.

Le Bon, G. (1896) *The Crowd: A Study of the Popular Mind*. London: Ernest Benn.

Le Bon, G. ([1896] 1908) *The Crowd: A Study of the Popular Mind*. London: Unwin. http://cupid. ecom.unimelb.edu.au/het/lebon/crowds.pdf.

Lee, J.A. (1977) A topology of styles of loving, *Personality and Social Psychology Bulletin*, 3: 173–82.

Lee, J.A. (1988) Love styles, in R.J. Sternberg and M.L. Barnes (eds) *The Psychology of Love*. New Haven, CT: Yale University Press.

Lenoble, R. (1943) *Essai sur la notion de l'expérience* (*Essay on the Concept of Experience*). Paris.

Leventhal, H. and Hirshman, R.S. (1982) Social psychology and prevention, in G.S. Sanders and J. Suls (eds) *Social Psychology of Health and Illness*. Hillsdale, NJ: Erlbaum.

Lewin, K. (1947a) Frontiers in group dynamics, *Human Relations*, 1: 5–42.

Lewin, K. (1947b) Group decisions and social change, in T.M. Newcomb and E.L. Hartley (eds) *Readings in Social Psychology*. New York: Henry Holt.

Lewin, K. (1951) *Field Theory in Social Science*. New York: Harper and Row.

Lewin, K., Lippitt, R. and White, R.K. (1939) Patterns of aggressive behaviour in experimentally created 'social climates', *Journal of Social Psychology*, 10: 271–99.

Li, L.M.W. and Harris Bond, M. (2010) Analyzing national change in citizen secularism across four time periods in the World Values Survey. *World Values Research*, 3(2): 1–13.

Lindesmith, A.R., Strauss, A.L. and Denzin, N.K. (1999) *Social Psychology*, 8th edn. London: Sage.

Lindner, G.A. (1871) *Ideen zur Psychologie der Gesellschaft als Grundlage der Sozialwissenschaft*. Vienna: Gerold.

Lorber, J. (1994) *Paradoxes of Gender*. New Haven, CT: Yale University Press.

Lucey, H. (2007) Families, in W. Hollway, H. Lucey and A. Phoenix (eds) *Social Psychology Matters*. Maidenhead: Open University Press.

Maas, A. and Cadinu, M. (2003) Stereotype threat: when minority members underperform, *European Review of Social Psychology*, 14: 243–75.

MacLeod, C. (2004) Writing into action, in D. Hook, A. Collins, P. Kiguwa, P. and N. Mkhize (eds) *Critical Psychology*. Cape Town: University of Cape Town Press.

MacLeod, C. and Bhatia, S. (2009) Postcolonialism and psychology, in C. Willig and W. Stainton Rogers (eds) *The Sage Handbook of Qualitative Research in Psychology*. London: Sage.

Mahood, L. and Littlewood, B. (1997) Daughters in danger: the case of 'campus sex crimes', in A.M. Thomas and C. Kitzinger (eds) *Sexual Harassment: Contemporary Feminist Perspectives*. Buckingham: Open University Press.

Mangan, L. (2010) There's nowt so queer as love, *Guardian Magazine*, 11 September.

Manning, R., Levine, M. and Collins, A. (2007) The Kitty Genovese murder and the social psychology of helping: the parable of the 38 witnesses, *American Psychologist*, 62: 555–62.

Manstead, A.S.R. (2008) Research methods in social psychology, in M. Hewstone, W. Stroebe and K. Jonas (eds) *Introduction to Social Psychology: A European Perspective*, 4th edn. Oxford: Blackwell.

Manstead, A.S.R. and Semin, G. (1980) Social facilitation effects: more enhancement of dominant responses? *British Journal of Social and Clinical Psychology*, 19: 119–36.

Manstead, A.S.R. and Semin, G. (2001) Methods in social psychology: tools to test theories, in M. Hewstone and W. Stroebe (eds) *Introduction to Social Psychology*, 3rd edn. Oxford: Blackwell.

Marková, I. (1987) *Human Awareness*. London: Hutchinson.

Marková, I. (2008) The epistemological significance of the theory of social representations, *Journal for the Theory of Social Behaviour*, 38(4): 461–87.

Markus, H. and Wurf, E. (1987) The dynamic of self-concept: a social psychological perspective, *Annual Review of Psychology*, 38: 299–337.

Marsh, P., Rosser, E. and Harré, R. (1974) *The Rules of Disorder*. London: Routledge and Kegan Paul.

Martin, C.L. and Halverson, C.F. (1981) A schematic processing model of sex stereotyping in children, *Child Development*, 52(4): 1119–34.

Martín-Baró, I. (1966) *Memory of a Commitment: Ignacio Martín-Baró's Psychology*. Bilbao: Desclée de Brouwer.

Martín-Baró, I. (1996) *Writings for a Liberation Psychology: Ignacio Martín-Baró*, eds A. Aron and S. Corne, 2nd edn. Cambridge, MA and London: Harvard University Press.

Maslow, A.H. (1962) *Toward a Psychology of Being*. Princeton, NJ: Van Nostrand.

Matsui, T., Kakuyama, T. and Onglatco, M.L. (1987) Effects of goals and feedback on performance in groups, *Journal of Applied Psychology*, 72: 407–15.

McDougall, W. ([1908] 1919) *An Introduction to Social Psychology*. London: Methuen.

McFadyean, M. (2010) Death on flight 77: would you look away? *Guardian*, 20 October. http://www.guardian.co.uk/ comment is free/2010/Oct/20/jimmy-mubenga-death-asylum.

McGuire, W.J. (1968) Personality and susceptibility to social influence, in E.F. Borgatta and W.W. Lambert (eds) *Handbook of Personality: Theory and Research*. Chicago, IL: Rand-McNally.

McGuire, W.J. (1986) The vicissitudes of attitudes and similar representational constructs in twentieth century psychology, *European Journal of Social Psychology*, 16: 89–130.

McKeown, B. and Thomas, D. (1988) *Q Methodology*. Beverly Hills, CA: Sage.

McKeown, M., Hinks, M., Stowell-Smith, M., Mercer, D. and Forster, J. (1999) Q methodology, risk training and quality management, *International Journal of Health Care Quality Assurance*, 6(12): 254–66.

McKinlay, A. and McVittie, C. (2008) *Social Psychology and Discourse*. Chichester: Wiley-Blackwell.

McPherson, W. (2001) *The Stephen Lawrence Inquiry*. London: HMSO.

Mead, G.H. ([1934a] 1977a) *Mind, Self and Society: From the Standpoint of a Social Behaviourist*, ed. C.W. Morris. Chicago, IL: University of Chicago Press.

Mead, G.H. ([1934b] 1977b) *On Social Psychology*, ed. A. Strauss. Chicago, IL: University of Chicago Press.

Meertens, R.W. and Pettigrew, T.F. (1997) Is subtle prejudice really prejudice? *Public Opinion Quarterly*, 61(1): 54–71.

Mehrabian, A. (1972) Nonverbal communication, in J. Cole (ed.) *Nebraska Symposium on Motivation*, Vol. 19. Lincoln, NB: University of Nebraska Press.

Middlemist, R.D., Knowles, E.S. and Mutter, C.F. (1976) Personal space invasions in the lavatory: suggestive evidence for arousal, *Journal of Personality and Social Psychology*, 33: 541–6.

Mielewczyk, M. and Willig, C. (2007) Old clothes and an older look: the case for a radical makeover in health, *Theory Psychology*, 17: 811–37.

Mikulincer, M. and Shaver, P.R. (2007) *Attachment in Adulthood: Structure, Dynamics, and Change*. New York: Guilford Press.

Milgram, S. (1963) Behavioural study of obedience, *Journal of Abnormal and Social Psychology*, 67: 371–8.

Milgram, S. (1965) Some conditions of obedience and disobedience to authority, *Human Relations*, 18: 57–76.

Millar, M.G. and Millar, K.U. (1996) The effects of direct and indirect experience on affective and cognitive responses and the attitude–behaviour relation, *Journal of Experimental Social Psychology*, 32: 561–79.

Miller, C. and Swift, K. (1976) *Words and Women: New Languages in New Times*. Garden City, NY: Doubleday Anchor.

Miller, C. and Swift, K. (1981) *The Handbook of Non-Sexist Writing*. London: Women's Press.

Miller, G.A. (1953) What is information measurement?, *American Psychologist*, 8: 3–11.

Miller, G.A., Galanter, E. and Pribram, K. (1960) *Plans and the Structure of Behavior*. New York: Holt, Rinehart and Winston.

Mishler, E.G. (1995) Models of narrative analysis: a typology, *Journal of Narrative and Life History*, 5: 87–123.

Mishler, E.G. (1999) *Storylines: Craftartist's Narratives of Identity*. Cambridge, MA: Harvard University Press.

Mitchell, J. (2000) *Mad Men and Medusas: Reclaiming Hysteria and the Effects of Sibling Relationships on the Human Condition*. Harmondsworth: Penguin.

Mitchell, J. (2003) *Siblings, Sex and Violence*. Cambridge: Polity Press.

Mkhize, N. (2004a) Psychology: an African perspective, in D. Hook, A. Collins, P. Kiguwa and N. Mkhize (eds) *Critical Psychology*. Cape Town: UCT Press.

Mkhize, N. (2004b) Sociocultural approaches to psychology: dialogism and African conceptions of the self, in D. Hook, A. Collins, P. Kiguwa and N. Mkhize (eds) *Critical Psychology*. Cape Town: UCT Press.

Mol, A. (2008) *The Logic of Care: Health and the Problem of Patient Choice*. London: Routledge.

Montero. M. (2009) Community action and research as citizenship construction, *American Journal of Community Psychology*, 43: 149–61.

Moradi, B., van den Berg, J.J. and Epting, F.R. (2009) Threat and guilt aspects of internalized anti-lesbian and gay prejudice: an application of personal construct theory, *Journal of Counseling Psychology*, 56(1): 119–31.

Morrow, V. (1998) *Understanding Families: Children's Perspectives*. London: National Children's Bureau.

Moscovici, S. ([1961] 1976) *La Psychoanalyse: son image et son public*. Paris: Presses Universitaires de France.

Moscovici, S. (1985) Society and theory in social psychology, in J. Israel and H. Tajfel (eds) *The Context of Social Psychology: A Critical Assessment*. New York: Academic Press.

Moscovici, S. (2003) Le Premier Article, *Le Journal des Psychologues*, Numéro hors série: 10–13.

Moscovici, S. (2008) *Psychoanalysis: Its Image and its Public*. Cambridge: Polity Press.

Moscovici, S. and Hewstone, M. (1983) Social representations and social explanations: from the 'naïve' to the 'amateur' scientist, in M. Hewstone (ed.) *Attribution Theory: Social and Functional Explanations*. Oxford: Blackwell.

Moscovici, S., Lage, E. and Naffrechoux, M. (1969) Influence of a consistent minority on the responses of a majority in a colour perception task, *Sociometry*, 32: 365–80.

Moscovici, S. and Marková, I. (2006) *The Making of Modern Social Psychology: The Hidden Story of How an International Social Science Was Created*. Cambridge: Polity.

Moscovici, S. and Mugny, G. (1983) Minority influence, in P.B. Paulus (ed.) *Basic Group Processes*. New York: Springer-Verlag.

Moscovici, S. and Personnaz, B. (1980) Studies in social influence: minority influence and conversion behaviour in a perceptual task, *Journal of Experimental Social Psychology*, 16: 270–82.

Mugny, G. (1982) *The Power of Minorities*. New York: Academic Press.

Mulvey, L. (1975) Visual pleasure and narrative cinema, *Screen*, 16(3): 6–18.

Mulvey, L. (1992) Visual pleasure and narrative cinema, in M. Merck (ed.) *The Sexual Subject: A Screen Reader in Sexuality*. London: Routledge.

Murphy, G. (1929) *A Historical Introduction to Modern Psychology*. London: Kegan Paul, Trench, Trubner.

Murphy, G. and Murphy, L.B. (1931) *Experimental Social Psychology*. New York: Harper.

Myers, D., Abell, J., Kolstad, A. and Sani, F. (2010) *Social Psychology: European Edition*. London: McGraw-Hill.

Nagata, D.K., Cheng, W.J.Y. and Tsai-Chae, A.H. (2010) Chinese American grandmothering: a qualitative exploration, *Asian American Journal of Psychology*, 1(2): 151–61.

Neisser, U. (1966) *Cognitive Psychology*. New York: Appleton-Century-Crofts.

Nemeth, C. (1986) Differential contributions to majority and minority influence, *Psychological Review*, 93: 1–10.

Nemeth, C. and Wachtler, J. (1983) Creative problem solving as a result of minority versus majority influence, *European Journal of Social Psychology*, 13: 45–55.

Newcomb, T.M. (1961) *The Acquaintance Process*. New York: Holt, Rinehart and Winston.

Nigbur, D., Lyons, E. and Uzzell, D. (2010) Attitudes, norms, identity and environmental behaviour: using an expanded theory of planned behaviour to predict participation in a kerbside recycling programme. *British Journal of Social Psychology*, 49: 259–84.

Nightingale, D.J. and Cromby, J. (1999) *Social Constructionist Psychology: A Critical Analysis of Theory and Practice*. Buckingham: Open University Press.

Nisbett, R.E. and Ross, L. (1980) *Human Inference: Strategies and Shortcomings of Social Judgement*. Englewood Cliffs, NJ: Prentice Hall.

Norris, F.H., Stevens, S.P., Pfefferbaum, B., Wyche, K.F. and Pfefferbaum, R.L. (2008) Community resilience as metaphor, theory, set of capacities and strategies for disaster readiness. *American Journal of Community Psychology*, 41: 127–50.

Nuttin, J.M. (1985) Narcissism beyond gestalt and awareness: the name letter effect, *European Journal of Social Psychology*, 15: 353–61.

O'Dell, L. (1997) Child sexual abuse and the academic construction of symptomologies, *Feminism and Psychology*, 7(3): 334–9.

Ogden, J. (2003) Some problems with social cognition models: a pragmatic and conceptual analysis, *Health Psychology*, 22(4): 424–8.

Oppenheim, N. (1992) *Questionnaire Design, Interviewing and Attitude Measurement*. London: Pinter.

Ozdemir, A. (2008) Shopping malls: measuring interpersonal distance under changing conditions and across cultures, *Field Methods*, 20: 226.

Parker, I. (1989) *The Crisis in Modern Social Psychology – and How to End It*. London: Routledge.

Parker, I. (1997a) *Psychoanalytic Culture: Psychoanalytic Discourse in Western Society*. London: Sage.

Parker, I. (1997b) Discursive psychology, in D. Fox and I. Prilleltensky (eds) *Critical Psychology: An Introduction*. London: Sage.

Parker, I. (2005) *Qualitative Psychology: Introducing Radical Research*. Maidenhead: Open University Press.

Parker, I. (2009) Critical psychology and revolutionary Marxism, *Theory & Psychology*, 19(1): 71–92.

Parker, I. and Spears, R. (eds) (1996) *Psychology and Society: Radical Theory and Practice*. London: Pluto Press.

Parkinson, B. (2008) Social perception and attribution, in M. Hewstone, W. Stroebe and K. Jonas (eds) *Introduction to Social Psychology: A European Perspective*, 4th edn. Oxford: Blackwell.

Paton, D. and Johnston, D. (2004) Disasters and communities: vulnerability, resilience and preparedness, *Disaster Prevention and Management*, 10(4): 270–7.

Patterson, M., Iizuka, Y., Tubbs, M., Ansel, J. Tsutsumi, M. and Anson, J. (2007) Passing encounters East and West: comparing Japanese and American pedestrian interactions, *Journal of Nonverbal Behaviour*, 31(3): 155–66.

Peirce, C.S. ([1940] 1955) Abduction and induction, in J. Buchler (ed.) *The Philosophy of Peirce: Selected Writings*. London: Routledge and Kegan Paul. (Republished in 1955 as *Philosophical Writings of Peirce*. New York: Dover.)

Pelphrey, K.A. and Carter, E.J. (2008) Charting the typical and atypical development of the social brain, *Developmental Psychopathology*, 20: 1081–102.

Perinbanayagam, R.S. (1985) *Signifying Acts*. New York: Aldine de Gruyter.

Pettigrew, T.F. (1964) *A Profile of the Negro American*. Princeton, NJ: Van Nostrand.

Pettigrew, T.F. (1979) The ultimate attribution error: extending Allport's cognitive analysis of prejudice, *Personality and Social Psychology Bulletin*, 5: 461–76.

Petty, R.E. and Cacioppo, J.T. (1981) *Attitudes and Persuasion: Classic and Contemporary Approaches*. Dubuque, IA: Brown.

Petty, R.E. and Cacioppo, J.T. (1986) *Communication and Persuasion: Central and Peripheral Routes to Attitude Change*. New York: Springer.

Pittman, T.S. (1975) Attribution of arousal as a mediator of dissonance reduction, *Journal of Experimental Social Psychology*, 11: 53–63.

Popp, D., Donovan, R.A., Crawford, M., Marsh, K.L. and Peele, M. (2003) Gender, race, and speech style stereotypes, *Sex Roles*, 48(7/8): 317–25.

Popper, K. (1959) *The Logic of Scientific Discovery*. New York: Basic Books.

Posner, M.I. (1966) Components of skill performance, *Science*, 152: 1712–18.

Potter, J. (1996) Attitudes, social representations and discursive psychology, in M. Wetherell (ed.) *Identities, Groups and Social Issues*. London: Sage.

Potter, J. and Wetherell, M. (1987) *Discourse and Social Psychology: Beyond Attitudes and Behaviour*. London: Sage.

Potter, J. and Wetherell, M. (1995) Discourse analysis, in J.A. Smith, R. Harré and L. Van Langenhove (eds) *Rethinking Methods in Psychology*. London: Sage.

Prochaska, J.O. and DiClemente, C.C. (1982) Transtheoretical therapy: toward a more integrative model of change, *Psychotherapy: Theory, Research and Practice*, 19(3): 276–88.

Prochaska, J.O. and DiClemente, C.C. (1983) Stages and processes of self-change in smoking: toward an integrative model of change, *Journal of Consulting and Clinical Psychology*, 51: 390–5.

Prochaska, J.O. and DiClemente, C.C. (1986) Toward a comprehensive model of change, in W.R. Miller and N. Heather (eds) *Treating Addictive Behaviors: Processes of Change*. New York: Plenum.

Prochaska, J.O. and DiClemente, C.C. (1992) Stages of change in the modification of problem behaviour, *Progress in Behaviour Change*, 28: 184–218.

Prochaska, J.O., DiClemente, C.C. and Norcross, J.C. (1992). In search of how people change, *American Psychologist*, 47: 1102–14.

Psathas, G. (1995) *Conversational Analysis: The Study of Talk-in-action*. Thousand Oaks, CA: Sage.

Rabbie, J.M. and Horowitz, M. (1969) Arousal and ingroup–outgroup bias by a chance win or loss, *Journal of Personality and Social Psychology*, 13: 269–77.

Radley, A., Hodgetts, D. and Cullen, A. (2005) Visualising homelessness: a study in photography and estrangement, *Journal of Community and Applied Social Psychology*, 15: 273–95.

Ratele, K. and Duncan, N. (2003) *Social Psychology: Identities and Relationships*. Cape Town: Cape Town University Press.

Rawls, J. (1972) *A Theory of Justice*. Oxford: Clarendon Press.

Reason, P. and Rowan, J. (1981) *Human Inquiry: A Sourcebook for New Paradigm Research*. Chichester: Wiley.

Rehm, J., Steinleitner, J. and Lilli, W. (1987) Wearing uniforms and aggression: a field experiment, *European Journal of Social Psychology*, 17: 357–60.

Reicher, S. and Haslam, S.A. (2006) Rethinking the psychology of tyranny: the BBC prison study, *British Journal of Social Psychology*, 45: 1–40.

Reicher, S., Haslam, S.A., Alexander, S. and Platow, J. (2007) The new psychology of leadership, *Scientific American Mind*, 18(4): 22–9.

Reicher, S. and Hopkins, N. (1996) Self-category constructions in political rhetoric, *European Journal of Social Psychology*, 26: 353–71.

Reicher, S., Spears, R. and Haslam, S.A. (2010) The social identity approach to social psychology, in *The Sage Handbook of Identities*. London: Sage.

Reik, T. (1944) *A Psychologist Looks at Love*. New York: Farrar and Rinehart.

Reynolds, J. (2008) *The Single Woman: A Discursive Investigation*. London and New York: Routledge.

Reynolds, J. and Taylor, S. (2004) Narrating singleness: life stories and defecit identities, *Narrative Inquiry*, 15(2): 197–215.

Rhodewalt, F. and Augustsdottir, S. (1986) Effects of self-presentation on the phenomenological self, *Journal of Personality and Social Psychology*, 50: 47–55.

Rice, S. (1986) *It was a Dark and Stormy Night: The Best(?) from the Bullwer-Lytton Contest*. London: Abacus.

Richards, G. (1997) '*Race', Racism and Psychology: Towards a Reflexive History*. London: Routledge.

Rickett, B. (2010) Working without sacrifice: acceptance and resistance to dominant discourses around women's occupational risk, *Feminism and Psychology*, 20(2): 260–6.

Ricoeur, P. (1955) The model of the text: meaningful actions considered as texts, *Social Research*, 38: 530–47.

Ricoeur, P. (1970) *Freud and Philosophy: An Essay on Interpretation*. Trans. D. Savage. New Haven, CT: Yale University Press.

Ricoeur, P. (1971) The model of the text: meaningful action considered as text, *Social Research*, 38: 529–62.

Ricoeur, P. (1981) *Hermeneutics and the Human Sciences*. Cambridge: Cambridge University Press.

Riley, S., Frith, H., Archer, L. and Veseley, L. (2006) Institutional sexism in academia, *Psychologist*, 19(2): 94–7.

Rim, Y. (1970) Values and attitudes, *Personality*, 1: 243–50.

Ringleman, M. (1913) Recherches sur les moteurs animés: travail de l'homme, *Annales de l'Institut National Agronomique*, 2nd series, 12: 1–40.

Rokeach, M. (1968) *Beliefs, Attitudes and Values: A Theory of Organisation and Change*. San Francisco, CA: Jossey-Bass.

Rokeach, M. (1973) *The Nature of Human Values*. New York: Free Press.

Rokeach, M. (1976) The nature of human values and value systems, in E.P. Hollander and R.G. Hunt (eds) *Current Perspectives in Social Psychology*, 4th edn. New York: Oxford University Press.

Rommetveit, R. (1980) On 'meanings' of acts and what is meant and made known by what is said in a pluralistic world, in M. Brenner (ed.) *The Structure of Action*. New York: St. Martin's Press.

Rorty, R. (1980) *Philosophy and the Mirror of Nature*. Oxford: Blackwell.

Rose, N. (1979) The psychological complex: mental measurement and social administration, *Ideology and Consciousness*, 5: 5–68.

Rose, N. (1998) *Inventing Ourselves: Psychology, Power and Personhood*. Cambridge: Cambridge University Press.

Rosenberg, S., Nelson, C. and Vivekanathan, P.S. (1968) A multidimensional approach to the structure of personality impressions, *Journal of Personality and Social Psychology*, 39: 283–94.

Rosenburg, M. (1969) The conditions and consequences of evaluation apprehension, in R. Rosenthal and R.L. Rosnow (eds) *Artefact in Behavioural Research*. New York: Academic Press.

Ross, E.A. (1908) *Social Psychology*. New York: Macmillan.

Rotter, J.B. (1966) Generalised expectancies for internal versus external control of reinforcement, *Psychological Monographs*, 80(1): 1–28.

Ruckmick, C.A. (1912) The history and status of psychology in the United States, *American Journal of Psychology*, 23: 517–31.

Sacks, H. (1995) *Lectures on Conversation*: Volumes I and II, ed. G. Jefferson. Oxford: Blackwell.

Salancik, G.R. and Conway, M. (1975) Attitude inference from salient and relevant cognitive content about behaviour, *Journal of Personality and Social Psychology*, 32: 829–40.

Sanders, G.S. and Baron, R.S. (1977) Is social comparison relevant for producing choice shifts? *Journal of Experimental Social Psychology*, 13: 303–14.

Sarbin, J. (ed.) (1986) *Narrative Psychology: The Storied Nature of Human Conduct*. New York: Praeger.

Saussure, F. de (1959) *A Course in General Linguistics*. New York: McGraw-Hill.

Saussure, F. de (1974) *Course in General Linguistics*, ed. J. Culler. Trans. W. Baskin. London: Fontana.

Saville Young, L. and Frosh, S. (2009) Psychoanalytic approaches to qualitative psychology, in C. Willig and W. Stainton Rogers (eds) *The Sage Handbook of Qualitative Research in Psychology*. London: Sage.

Sawiki, J. (1991) *Disciplining Foucault: Feminism, Power and the Body*. London: Routledge.

Sayer, A. (1992) *Method in Social Science: A Realist Approach*, 2nd edn London: Routledge.

Schachner, S.A., Shaver, P.A. and Gillath, O. (2008) Attachment style and long-term singlehood, *Personal Relationships*, 15: 479–491.

Scher, S. and Cooper, J. (1989) Motivational basis of dissonance: the singular role of behavioural consequences, *Journal of Personality and Social Psychology*, 56: 899–906.

Schwartz, S. (1999) A theory of cultural values and some implications for work, *Applied Psychology: An International Review*, 48(1): 23–47.

Schwartz, S. and Boehnke, K. (2004) Evaluating the structure of human values with confirmatory factor analysis, *Journal of Research in Personality*, 38: 230–55.

Schwartz, S.H. (1992) Universals in the content and structure of values: theory and empirical tests in 20 countries, in M. Zanna (ed.) *Advances in Experimental Social Psychology*, Vol. 25. New York: Academic Press.

Schwartz, S.H. (1994) Cultural dimensions of values: towards an understanding of national differences, in U. Kim, H.C. Triandis and G. Yoon (eds) *Individualism and Collectivism: Theoretical and Methodological Issues*. Newbury Park, CA: Sage.

Schwartz, S.H., Bardi, A. and Bianchi, G. (2000) Value adaptation to the imposition and collapse of communist regimes in East-Central Europe, in S.A. Renshon and J. Duckitt (eds) *Political Psychology: Cultural and Crosscultural Foundations*. London: Macmillan.

Sears, D.O. (1983) The person–positivity bias, *Journal of Personality and Social Psychology*, 44: 233–50.

Sears, D.O., Peplau, L.A. and Taylor, S.E. (1991) *Social Psychology*, 7th edn. Englewood Cliffs, NJ: Prentice Hall.

Segal, H.A. (1954) Initial psychiatric findings of recently repatriated prisoners of war, *American Journal of Psychiatry*, 61: 358–63.

Segall, M.H., Dasen, P.R., Berry, J.W. and Poortinga, Y.H. (1990) *Human Behavior in Global Perspective: An Introduction to Cross-Cultural Psychology*. New York: Pergamon.

Seligman, M.E.P. (1975) *Helplessness: On Depression, Development and Death*. San Francisco, CA: Freeman.

Seligman, M.E.P., Abramson, L.Y., Semmel, A. and von Baeyer, C. (1979) Depressive attributional style, *Journal of Abnormal Psychology*, 88: 242–7.

Semin, G. and Rubini, M. (1990) Unfolding the concept of person by verbal abuse, *European Journal of Social Psychology*, 20: 463–74.

Semin, G.R. (1997) The relevance of language to social psychology, in C. McGarty and S.A. Haslam (eds) *The Message of Social Psychology*. Oxford: Blackwell.

Semin, G.R. and Fiedler, K. (1988) The cognitive functions of linguistic categories in describing persons: social cognition and language, *Journal of Personality and Social Psychology*, 54: 558–68.

Semin, G.R. and Manstead, A.S.R. (1983) *The Accountability of Conduct: A Social Psychological Analysis*. London: Academic Press.

Shank, G. (1994) Shaping qualitative research in educational psychology, *Contemporary Educational Psychology*, 19: 340–59.

Shank, G. (1998) The extraordinary ordinary powers of abductive reasoning, *Theory and Psychology*, 8(6): 841–60.

Shannon, C. and Weaver, W. (1949) *The Mathematical Theory of Communication*. Urbana, IL: University of Illinois Press.

Shannon, C.E. (1948) A mathematical theory of communication, *Bell Systems Technology Journal*, 27: 379–423, 623–56.

Shapiro, D.L. (2010) Relational identity theory: a systematic approach for transforming the emotional dimensions of conflict, *American Psychologist*, 65(7): 634–45.

Shavitt, S. (1989) Operationalizing functional theories of attitude, in A.R. Pratkanis, S.J. Breckler and A.G. Greenwald (eds) *Attitude Structure and Function*. Hillsdale, NJ: Erlbaum.

Shavitt, S. and Fazio, R.H. (1991) Effects of attribute salience on the constancy between attitudes and behaviour predictions, *Personality and Social Psychology Bulletin*, 17: 507–16.

Sheridan, J., Chamberlain, K. and Dupuis, A. (in press) Timelining: visualising experience, *Qualitative Research in Psychology.*

Sherif, M. (1936) *The Psychology of Social Norms.* New York: Harper and Row.

Sherif, M. (1966) *In Common Predicament: Social Psychology of Intergroup Conflict and Cooperation.* Boston, MA: Houghton Mifflin.

Sherif, M. (1967) If basic research is to have bearing on actualities, *Journal of General Education*, 19(2): 99–111.

Sherif, M., Harvey, O.J., White, B.J., Hood, W. and Sherif, C. (1961) *Intergroup Conflict and Cooperation: The Robbers' Cave Experiment.* Norman, OK: University of Oklahoma Institute of Intergroup Relations.

Sherif, M. and Hovland, C.I. (1961) *Social Judgement.* New Haven, CT: Yale University Press.

Sherif, M. and Sherif, C. (1969) *Social Psychology.* New York: Harper and Row.

Shotter, J. (1981) Telling and reporting: prospective and retrospective uses of self-ascriptions, in C. Antaki (ed.) *The Psychology of Ordinary Explanations of Behaviour.* London: Academic Press.

Shotter, J. (1984) *Social Accountability and Selfhood.* Oxford: Blackwell.

Shotter, J. (1993a) Vygotsky: the social negotiation of semiotic mediation, *New Ideas in Psychology*, 11(1): 61–75.

Shotter, J. (1993b) *Conversational Realities: Constructing Life Through Language.* London: Sage.

Showers, C. and Cantor, N. (1985) Social cognition: a look at motivated strategies, *Annual Review of Psychology*, 36: 275–305.

Silverman, D. (2001) *Interpreting Qualitative Data: Methods for Analysing Talk, Text and Interaction*, 2nd edn. London: Sage.

Simon, B. and Trötschel, D. (2008) Self and social identity, in M. Hewstone, W. Stroebe and K. Jonas (eds) *Social Psychology: A European Perspective*, Oxford: BPS Books.

Singh, D. (1993) Adaptive significance of female physical attractiveness: role of waist-to-hip ratio, *Journal of Personality and Social Psychology*, 65: 293–307.

Sistrunk, F. and McDavid, J.W. (1971) Sex variables in conforming behaviour, *Journal of Personality and Social Psychology*, 2: 200–7.

Smith, B. and Harris Bond, M. (1993) *Social Psychology across Cultures.* Hemel Hempstead: Harvester Wheatsheaf.

Smith, B.H. (1988) *Contingencies of Value: Alternative Perspectives for Critical Theory.* Cambridge, MA: Harvard University Press.

Smith, E.R. and Mackie, D.M. (2000) *Social Psychology.* Philadelphia, PA: Taylor and Francis.

Smith, E.R. and Miller, F.D. (1983) Mediation among attributional inferences and comprehension processes: initial findings and a general method, *Journal of Personality and Social Psychology*, 44: 492–505.

Smith, J., Harré, R. and Van Langengrove, L. (eds) (1995) *Rethinking Methods in Psychology.* London: Sage.

Smith, L.T. (1999) *Decolonizing Methodologies: Research and Indigenous Peoples.* London and New York: Zed Books.

Smith, M.B., Bruner, J. and White, R.W. (1956) *Opinions and Personality.* New York: Wiley.

Smith, P.B., Harris Bond, M. and Kağitçibaşi, C. (2006) *Understanding Social Psychology across Cultures: Living and Working in a Changing World.* London: Sage.

Smyth, M.M. (2001) Fact making in psychology. *Theory and Psychology*, 11: 609–36.

Smythe, D. (1994) *Counterclockwise: Perspectives on Communication from Dallas Smythe*, ed. T. Gubacl. Boulder, CO: Westview.

Snyder, M. and DeBono, K.G. (1987) A functional approach to attitudes and persuasion, in M.P. Zanna, J.M. Olson and C.P. Herman (eds) *Social Influence: The Ontario Symposium*, Vol. 5. Hillsdale, NJ: Erlbaum.

Spender, D. (1979) Language and sex differences, in H. Andresen (ed.) *Osnabrücker Beiträge zur Sprachtheorie: Sprache und Geschlecht II.* Oldenburg: Red.

Spivak, G.C. (1988) Can the subaltern speak? in N. Carey and L. Grossberg (eds) *Marxism and the Interpretation of Culture.* Urbana, IL: University of Illinois Press.

Stainton Rogers, R. (1995) Q methodology, in J.A. Smith, R. Harré and L. Van Langenhove (eds) *Rethinking Methods in Psychology.* London: Sage.

Stainton Rogers, R. and Stainton Rogers, W. (1992) *Stories of Childhood: Shifting Agendas of Child Concern.* Hemel Hempstead: Harvester Wheatsheaf.

Stainton Rogers, R., Stenner, P., Gleeson, K. and Stainton Rogers, W. (1995) *Social Psychology: A Critical Agenda.* Cambridge: Polity.

Stainton Rogers, W. (1991) *Explaining Health and Illness: An Exploration of Diversity.* Hemel Hempstead: Harvester Wheatsheaf.

Stainton Rogers, W. (2004) 'Promoting better childhoods: constructions of child concern', in M.J. Kehily (ed.) *An Introduction to Childhood Studies.* Maidenhead: Open University Press.

Stainton Rogers, W. (2006) Authenticity, agency and action, *Psychology of Women Section Review, 2004*, 6(1): 29–42.

Stainton Rogers, W. (2009) Research methodology, in D. Fox, I. Prilleltensky and S. Austin (eds.) *Critical Psychology: An Introduction*, 2nd edn. London: Sage.

Stainton Rogers, W. (2011) Changing behaviour: can critical psychology influence policy and practice? in C. Horrocks and S. Johnson (eds) *Advances in Health Psychology: Critical Approaches.* Basingstoke: Palgrave Macmillan.

Stainton Rogers, W. and Stainton Rogers, R. (1997) Does critical social psychology mean the end of the world? in L. Ibañez and L. Iniguez (eds) *Critical Social Psychology.* London: Sage.

Stainton Rogers, W. and Stainton Rogers, R. (2001) *The Psychology of Gender and Sexuality.* Buckingham: Open University Press.

Stainton Rogers, W. and Willig, C. (2009) Review and prospect, in C. Willig and W. Stainton Rogers (eds) *The Sage Handbook of Qualitative Research in Psychology.* London: Sage.

Statistics New Zealand (2009) *Review of Crime and Criminal Justice Statistics Report 2009.* Wellington: Statistics New Zealand.

Steele, C.M. (1988) The psychology of self-affirmation: sustaining the integrity of the self, in L. Berkowitz (ed.) *Advances in Experimental Social Psychology*, Vol. 21. San Diego, CA: Academic Press.

Stenner, P., Watts, S. and Worrell, M. (2009) Q. Methodology, in C. Willig and W. Stainton Rogers (eds) *The Sage Handbook of Qualitative Research in Psychology.* London: Sage.

Stenner, P.H.D. (1992) Feeling deconstructed? With particular reference to jealousy. Unpublished doctoral dissertation, University of Reading.

Stenner, P.H.D. (1993) Discoursing jealousy, in E. Burman and I. Parker (eds) *Discourse Analytic Research: Repertoires and Readings of Texts in Action.* London: Routledge.

Stephan, C.W. and Stephan, W.G. (1990) *Two Social Psychologies*, 2nd edn. Belmont, CA: Wadsworth.

Stephenson, W. (1953) *The Study of Behavior: Q-technique and Its Methodology*. Chicago, IL: Chicago University Press.

Stevens, R. (1996) The reflexive self: an experiential perspective, in R. Stevens (ed.) *Understanding the Self*. London: Sage.

Stoddart, D.M. (1990) *The Scented Ape: The Biology and Culture of Human Odour*. Cambridge: Cambridge University Press.

Stoner, J.A. (1961) A comparison of individual and group decisions involving risk, unpublished Master's thesis, Massachusetts Institute of Technology, Cambridge, MA.

Stroebe, W. (2001) Strategies of attitude and behaviour change, in M. Hewstone, W. Stroebe and K. Jonas (eds) *Introduction to Social Psychology: A European Perspective*, 4th edn. Oxford: Blackwell.

Sutton, S. (2001) Back to the drawing board? A review of applications of the transtheoretical model to substance use, *Addiction*, 96: 175–86.

Sutton S.R. (2005) Another nail in the coffin of the transtheoretical model? A comment on West, *Addiction*, 100: 1043–5.

Swift, D.J., Watts, D.M. and Pope, M.L. (1983) Methodological pluralism and personal construct psychology: a case for pictorial methods in eliciting personal constructions. Paper presented to the Fifth International Conference on Personal Construct Psychology, Boston, MA.

Tajfel, H. (1972) La catégorization sociale, in S. Moscovici (ed.) *Introduction à la Psychologie Sociale*, Vol. 1. Paris: Larousse.

Tajfel, H. (ed.) (1978) *Differentiation between Social Groups: Studies in the Social Psychology of Intergroup Relations*. London: Academic Press.

Tajfel, H., Billig, M.G., Bundy, R.P. and Flament, C. (1971) Social categorization and intergroup behaviour, *European Journal of Social Psychology*, 1: 149–78.

Tajfel, H. and Turner, J.C. (1979) An integrative theory of intergroup conflict, in W.G. Austin and S. Worchel (eds) *The Social Psychology of Intergroup Relations*. Monterey, CA: Brooks/Cole.

Tajfel, H. and Turner, J. (1986) The social identity theory of intergroup behaviour, in S. Worchel and W.G. Austin (eds) *Psychology of Intergroup Relations*. Chicago, IL: Nelson.

Tak, J., Kaid, L.L. and Lee, S. (1997) A cross-cultural study of political advertising in the United States and Korea, *Communication Research*, 24: 413–30.

Tan, H.W. and Tan, M.L. (2008) Organizational citizenship behavior and social loafing: the role of personality, motives, and contextual factors. *The Journal of Psychology*, 42(1): 89–108.

Tannen, D. (1990) *You Just Don't Understand*. New York: Ballantine.

Tarde, G. (1903) *The Laws of Imitation*. Trans. from the French 2nd edn by E.C. Parsons. New York: Holt.

Taylor, D.A. and Moriarty, B.F. (1987) In-group bias as a function of competition and race, *Journal of Conflict Resolution*, 31: 192–9.

Taylor, M. and Lewis, P. (2010) Men 'thrown off flight' for raising concerns about deportation, *Guardian*, 1 November.

Tesser, A. (1993) The importance of heritability in psychological research: the case of attitudes, *Psychological Review*, 100: 129–42.

Thompson, K.R. (2006) Axiomatic theories of intentional systems: methodology of theory construction, *Scientific Inquiry*, 7(1): 13–24.

Tiffin, J., Knight, F.B. and Josey, C.C. (1940) *The Psychology of Normal People*. Boston, MA: Heath.

Topping, A. (2010) http://www.guardian.co.uk/uk/2010/nov/25/edgeware-road-inquest-ordinary-heroes/print

Tourangeau, R. and Rasinski, K.A. (1988) Cognitive processes underlying context effects in attitude measurement, *Psychological Bulletin*, 103: 299–314.

Triplett, N.D. (1898) The dynamogenic factor in pacemaking and competition, *American Journal of Psychology*, 9: 507–33.

Tuffin, K. (2005) *Understanding Critical Social Psychology*. London: Sage.

Turner, J.C. (1982) Towards a cognitive redefinition of the social group, in H. Tajfel (ed.) *Social Identity and Intergroup Relations*. Cambridge: Cambridge University Press.

Turner, J.C. (1991) *Social Influence*. Pacific Grove, CA: Brooks/Cole.

Turner, J.C., Hogg, M.A., Oakes, P.J., Reicher, S.D. and Wetherell, M.S. (1987) *Rediscovering the Social Group: A Self-categorization Theory*. Oxford: Blackwell.

Turner, J.S. and Rubinson, L. (1993) *Contemporary Human Sexuality*. Englewood Cliffs, NJ: Prentice Hall.

Tyerman, A. and Spencer, C. (1983) A critical test of the Sherifs' robbers' cave experiments: inter-group competition and cooperation between groups of well acquainted individuals, *Small Group Behaviour*, 14: 515–31.

Uleman, J.S., Newman, L.S. and Moskowitz, G.B. (1996) People as flexible interpreters: Evidence and issues from spontaneous trait inference, in M.P. Zanna (ed.) *Advances in Experimental Social Psychology*, Vol. 29. San Diego, CA: Academic Press.

Van Avermaet, E. (2001) Social influence in small groups, in M. Hewstone and W. Stroebe (eds) *Introduction to Social Psychology*, 3rd edn. Oxford: Blackwell.

Van Hooff, J.A. (1972) A comparative approach to the phylogeny of laughter and smiling, in R. Hinde (ed.) *Non-verbal Communication*. Cambridge: Cambridge University Press.

Van Knippenberg, D. and Hogg, M.A. (eds) (2003) *Leadership and Power: Identity Processes in Groups and Organisations*. London: Sage.

Vanneman, R.D. and Pettigrew, T.F. (1972) Race and relative deprivation in the urban United States, *Race*, 13: 461–86.

Vaughan, G.M. (1964) The trans-situational aspect of conforming behaviour, *Journal of Personality*, 32: 335–54.

Vickers, J.M. (1982) Memoirs of an ontological exile: the methodological rebellions of feminist research, in A. Miles and G. Finn (eds) *Feminism in Canada: From Pressure to Politics*. Montreal: Black Rose.

Vygotsky, L.S. (1962) *Thought and Language*, eds and trans E. Haufmann and C. Vakar. Cambridge, MA: MIT Press.

Wason, P.C. (1966) Reasoning, in B. Foss (ed.) *New Horizons in Psychology*. Harmondsworth: Penguin.

Wason, P.C. (1968) Reasoning about a rule, *Quarterly Journal of Experimental Psychology*, 20: 273–81.

Watts, S. and Stenner, P. (2005a) The subjective experience of partnership love: a Q methodological study, *British Journal of Social Psychology*, 44: 85–107.

Watts, S. and Stenner, P. (2005b) Doing Q methodology: theory, method and interpretation, *Qualitative Research in Psychology*, 2: 67–91.

Wedekind, C., Seebeck, J., Bettens, F. and Paepke, A. (1995) MHC dependent mate preferences in humans, *Proceedings of the Royal Society of London*, B 260: 245–9.

Weigel, R.H. and Newman, L.S. (1976) Increasing attitude–behaviour correspondence by broadening the scope of the behavioural measure, *Journal of Personality and Social Psychology*, 33: 793–802.

Weigel, R.H., Vernon, D.T.A. and Tognacci, L.N. (1976) Specificity of the attitude as a determinant of attitude–behaviour congruence, *Journal of Personality and Social Psychology*, 30: 724–8.

West, C. (1984) *Routine Complications: Troubles with Talk between Doctors and Patients*. Bloomington, IN: Indiana University Press.

Wetherell, M. (1987) Social identity and group polarization, in J.C. Turner, M.A. Hogg, P.J. Oakes, S.D. Reicher and M.S. Wetherell (eds) *Rediscovering the Social Group: A Self-Categorization Theory*. Oxford: Blackwell.

Wetherell, M. (1998) Positioning and interpretative repertoires: conversational analysis and post-structuralism in dialogue, *Discourse and Society*, 9(3): 387–413.

Wetherell, M. (2010) The field of identity studies, in M. Wetherell and C.T. Mohanty (eds) *The Sage Handbook of Identities*. London: Sage.

Wetherell, M. and Maybin, J. (2000) The distributed self: a social constructionist perspective, in R. Stevens (ed.) *Understanding the Self*. London: Sage.

Wetherell, M. and Mohanty, C.T. (2010) *The Sage Handbook of Identities*. London: Sage.

Wetherell, M. and Potter, J. (1992) *Mapping the Language of Racism: Discourse and the Legitimation of Exploitation*. Brighton: Harvester Wheatsheaf.

Wheeler, L. and Kim, Y. (1997) What is beautiful is culturally good: the physical attractiveness stereotype has different content in collectivist cultures, *Personality and Social Psychology Bulletin*, 23: 795–800.

Whitcher, S.J. and Fisher, J.D. (1979) Multidimensional reaction to therapeutic touch in a hospital setting, *Journal of Personality and Social Psychology*, 37: 87–96.

Whorf, B.L. (1956) *Language, Thought and Reality*. Cambridge, MA: MIT Press.

Wicke, T. and Cohen Silver, R. (2009) A community responds to collective trauma: an ecological analysis of the James Byrd murder in Jasper, Texas, *American Journal of Community Psychology*, 44: 233–48.

Wicker, A.W. (1969) Attitudes versus actions: the relationship of verbal and overt behavioural responses to attitude objects, *Journal of Social Issues*, 25(4): 41–78.

Wiggins, J.S., Renner, K.E., Clore, G.L. and Rose, R.J. (1971) *The Psychology of Personality*. Reading, MA: Addison-Wesley.

Wiggins, S. and Potter, J. (2009) Discursive psychology, in C. Willig and W. Stainton Rogers (eds) *The Sage Handbook of Qualitative Research in Psychology*. London: Sage.

Wilbraham, L. (2004) Discursive practice: analysing a lovelines text on sex communications for parents, in D. Hook, A. Collins, P. Kiguwa and N. Mkhize (eds) *Critical Psychology*. Cape Town: University of Cape Town Press.

Wilkinson, R.G. and Pickett, K. (2009) *The Spirit Level: Why More Equal Societies Almost Always Do Better*. Harmondsworth: Penguin.

Wilkinson, S. and Kitzinger, C. (2009) Conversation analysis, in C. Willig and W. Stainton Rogers (eds) *The Sage Handbook of Qualitative Research in Psychology*. London: Sage.

Williams, F. (2004) *Rethinking Families*. London: Calouste Gulbenkian Foundation.

Williams, K.D., Karau, S.J. and Bourgeois, M. (1993) Working on collective tasks: social loafing and social compensation, in M.A. Hogg and D. Abrams (eds) *Group Motivation: Social Psychological Perspectives*. London: Harvester Wheatsheaf.

Williamson, L.M., Buston, K. and Sweeting, H. (2009) Young women and limits to the normalisation of condom use: a qualitative study, *AIDS Care*, 21(5): 561–6.

Willig, C. (1995) 'I wouldn't have married the guy if I'd have to do that': heterosexual adults' constructions of condom use and their implications for sexual practice, *Journal of Community and Applied Social Psychology*, 5: 75–87.

Willig, C. (2001) *Introducing Qualitative Research in Psychology: Adventures in Theory and Method*. Buckingham: Open University Press.

Willig, C. (2007) Reflections on the use of a phenomenological method, *Qualitative Research in Psychology*, 4: 209–25.

Willig, C. (2008) *Introducing Qualitative Research in Psychology: Adventures in Theory and Method*, 2nd edn. Buckingham: Open University Press.

Willig, C. and Stainton Rogers, W. (2009) *The Sage Handbook of Qualitative Research in Psychology*. London: Sage.

Willis, F.N. and Dodds, R.A. (1998) Age, relationship and touch initiation, *Journal of Social Psychology*, 138(1): 115–23.

Wilson, T.D. and Hodges, S.D. (1992) Attitudes as temporary constructions, in L.L. Martin and A. Tesser (eds) *The Construction of Social Judgements*. Hillsdale, NJ: Erlbaum.

Wood, W., Lundgren, S., Ouellette, J.A., Busceme, S. and Blackstone, K. (1994) Minority influence: a meta-analytic review of social influence processes, *Psychological Bulletin*, 115: 323–45.

Woollcott, A. (1934) *While Rome Burns*. London: Arthur Barker.

Worchel, S. (1979) Co-operation and the reduction of intergroup conflict: some determining factors, in W.G. Austin and S. Worchel (eds) *The Social Psychology of Intergroup Conflict*, Monterey, CA: Brooks/Cole.

Worrell, M. (2001) The discursive production of child sexual abuse. PhD thesis, The Open University.

Wundt, W. (1897) *Outlines of Psychology*. New York: Stechert.

Wundt, W. (1900–20) *Völkerpsychologie: eine Untersuchung der Entwicklungsgesetze von Sprache, Mythus und Sitte*, 10 vols. Leipzig: Winter.

Yamaguchi, S. (1994). Collectivism among the Japanese: a perspective from the self, in U. Kim, H.C. Triandis, C. Kağitçibaşi, S. Choi and G. Yoon (eds), *Individualism and Collectivism: Theory, Method, and Applications*. Thousand Oaks, CA: Sage.

Yardley, L. and Bishop, F. (2009) Mixing qualitative and quantitative methods, in C. Willig and W. Stainton Rogers (eds) *The Sage Handbook of Qualitative Research in Psychology*. London: Sage.

Zaccaro, S.J. (1984) Social loafing: the role of task attractiveness, *Personality and Social Psychology Bulletin*, 10: 99–106.

Zajonc, R.B. (1968a) Cognitive theories in social psychology, in G. Lindzey and E. Aronson (eds) *The Handbook of Social Psychology*, 2nd edn, Vol. 1. Reading, MA: Addison-Wesley.

Zajonc, R.B. (1968b) Attitudinal effects of mere exposure, *Journal of Personality and Social Psychology*, 9 (monograph supplement 2, part 2).

Zajonc, R.B. and Burnstein, E. (1965) The learning of balanced and unbalanced social structures, *Journal of Personality*, 33: 153–63.

Zanna, M.P. and Fazio, R.H. (1982) The attitude–behaviour relation: moving toward a third generation of research, in M.P. Zanna, E.T. Higgins and C.P. Herman (eds) *Consistency in Social Behaviour: The Ontario Symposium*, Vol. 2. Hillside, NJ: Erlbaum.

Zimbardo, P.G., Banks, W.C., Haney, C. and Jaffe, D. (1973) The mind is a formidable jailer: a Pirandellian prison, *The New York Times Magazine*, 8 April: 38–60.

Zuckerman, M., DePaulo, B.M. and Rosenthal, R. (1981) Verbal and nonverbal communication of deception, in L. Berkowitz (ed.) *Advances in Experimental Social Psychology*, Vol. 14. New York: Academic Press.

Author Index

Subject Index

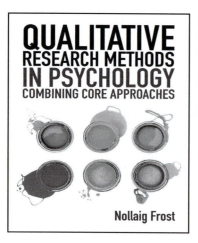

QUALITATIVE RESEARCH METHODS IN PSYCHOLOGY
Combining Core Approaches

Nollaig Frost

9780335241514 (Paperback)
June 2011

eBook also available

Qualitative Research Methods in Psychology: From Core to Combined Approaches provides research students with practical guidance and thoughtful debate on carrying out qualitative research in psychology. The book is written in a clear and accessible manner designed to support students from the beginning of their research experience at undergraduate level through to postgraduate research and beyond.

Key features:

- Includes case studies and group projects
- Provides problem-based questions
- Incorporates reference lists

www.openup.co.uk

OPEN UNIVERSITY PRESS
McGraw - Hill Education

POSITIVE PSYCHOLOGY
Theory, Research and Applications

Kate Hefferon and Ilona Boniwell

9780335241958 (Paperback)
June 2011

eBook also available

"Kate Hefferon and Ilona Boniwell have done an excellent job on this introduction to Positive Psychology! I encourage educators, students and everyone else interested in an updated, well-written and culturally balanced approach to the scientific study of human flourishing, to read this highly accessible, yet rigorously crafted text; and to get it under your skin by ways of carefully chosen tests and exercises."
Hans Henrik Knoop, Aarhus University, Denmark and President, European Network for Positive Psychology

This new textbook combines a breadth of information about positive psychology with reflective questions, critical commentary and up to date research.

Key features:

- Contains personal development exercises to help meld together research and application
- Experiments boxes detail the most influential positive psychology experiments to date
- Measurement tools presenting popular positive psychology tools

www.openup.co.uk

CONSUMER PSYCHOLOGY

Cathrine V. Jansson-Boyd

9780335229284 (Paperback)
2010

eBook also available

Informed by psychological theory and supported by research, this book provides an overall understanding of consumer behaviour and underlying thought processes. Psychology is central to an effective understanding of consumer behaviour and this book shows how it can be used to explain why people choose certain products and services, and how this affects their behaviour and psychological well-being.

Key features:

- Incorporates chapters with an introduction, key terms and a summary
- Includes study questions or class exercises
- Comprises topics illustrated with real-life examples, including adverts and case studies

www.openup.co.uk

OPEN UNIVERSITY PRESS
McGraw - Hill Education